# THE AFRICAN REVOLUTION

# The African Revolution

## A HISTORY OF THE LONG NINETEENTH CENTURY

RICHARD REID

PRINCETON UNIVERSITY PRESS

PRINCETON & OXFORD

Published by Princeton University Press
41 William Street, Princeton, New Jersey 08540
99 Banbury Road, Oxford OX2 6JX

press.princeton.edu

All Rights Reserved

ISBN 978-0-691-18709-9
ISBN (e-book) 978-0-691-26695-4

British Library Cataloging-in-Publication Data is available

Editorial: Ben Tate and Josh Drake
Production Editorial: Jenny Wolkowicki
Jacket design: Chris Ferrante
Production: Danielle Amatucci
Publicity: Alyssa Sanford and Carmen Jimenez
Copyeditor: Francis Eaves

Jacket image: Sirintra Pumsopa / Shutterstock

This book has been composed in Minion 3

Printed in the United States of America

10 9 8 7 6 5 4 3 2 1

FOR ANNA ZIMENA HERZBERG

# CONTENTS

# ILLUSTRATIONS

MAP 1. East African roads in the nineteenth century. The book is structured around the southernmost road, running through Tabora (Unyanyembe). *Source*: Richard Reid, *Political Power in Pre-Colonial Buganda* (Oxford: James Currey, 2002)

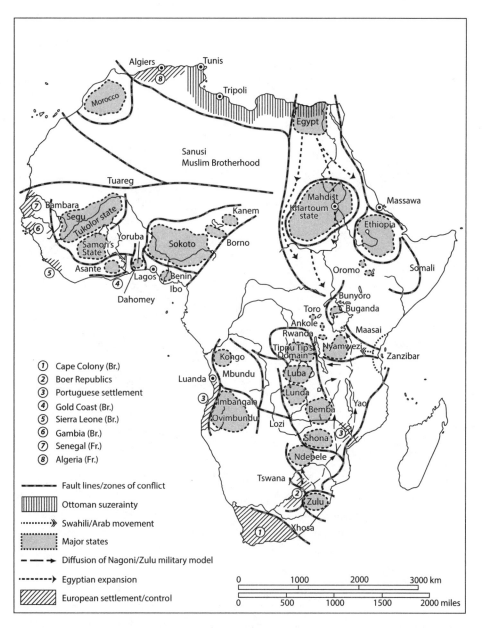

MAP 2. Revolutionary Africa in the nineteenth century
*Source*: Richard Reid, *Warfare in African History* (Cambridge: Cambridge University Press, 2012)

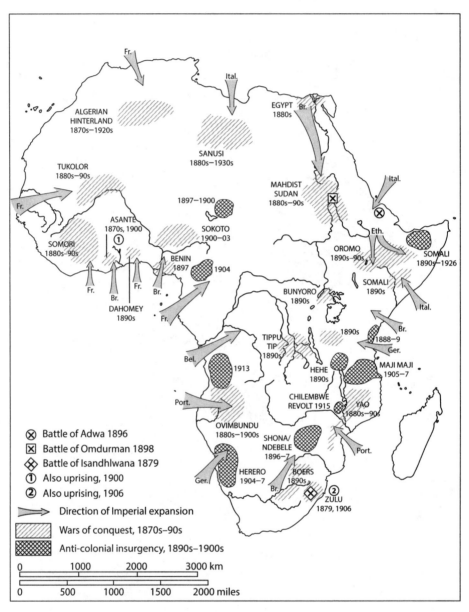

Map legend:

- ⊗ Battle of Adwa 1896
- ⊠ Battle of Omdurman 1898
- ◈ Battle of Isandhlwana 1879
- ① Also uprising, 1900
- ② Also uprising, 1906
- → Direction of Imperial expansion
- Wars of conquest, 1870s–90s
- Anti-colonial insurgency, 1890s–1900s

Map labels:

ALGERIAN HINTERLAND 1870s–1920s
SANUSI 1880s–1930s
EGYPT 1880s
Br.
Ital.
Fr.
TUKOLOR 1880s–90s
MAHDIST SUDAN 1880s–90s
Ital.
Fr.
ASANTE 1870s, 1900 ①
1897–1900
SOKOTO 1900–03
Eth.
OROMO 1890s–90s
SOMALI 1890s–1926
SOMORI 1880s–90s
BENIN 1897
1904
SOMALI 1890s
Fr. Br. Br.
DAHOMEY 1890s
Fr.
BUNYORO 1890s
1890s
Ital.
TIPPU TIP 1890s
1890s
1888–9
Ger.
MAJI MAJI 1905–7
Bel.
1913
HEHE 1890s
Port.
CHILEMBWE REVOLT 1915
YAO 1880s–90s
OVIMBUNDU 1880s–1900s
SHONA/ NDEBELE 1896–7
Port.
HERERO 1904–7
BOERS 1890s
Ger. Br.
② ZULU 1879, 1906

Scale:
0 1000 2000 3000 km
0 500 1000 1500 2000 miles

MAP 3. The "Scramble" for Africa and its aftershocks
Source: Richard Reid, *Warfare in African History* (Cambridge: Cambridge University Press, 2012)

# PROLOGUE

THE CENTRAL THREAD in the account which follows is a stretch of road in what is now Tanzania. In the nineteenth century, it ran from the Indian Ocean coast, ascending into the lightly wooded, elevated plateau land of central-east Africa, through the small but perfectly positioned chiefdom of Unyanyembe, and then onward to the west until it reached Lake Tanganyika.[1] This road—and the myriad characters and communities along it—represents my hook, my framework, and in some ways my method, with all it implies about change, mobility and liminality. And so the analysis is interspersed with a series of vignettes which hopefully illustrate the core themes with which the book is concerned: political instability and reinvention, economic transformation, social aspiration, violence, historical memory. The vignettes themselves are also built around particular *dramatis personae* who seem to me to embody those themes. Thus we encounter Msabila and Mkasiwa, locked in bitter political contest; Mirambo, leader of an insurgent polity; Hamed bin Muhammed—a.k.a Tippu Tip—merchant and warlord; Henry Morton Stanley and Tom von Prince, itinerant Europeans in the global age; Edward Hore, missionary and amateur ethnologist. And we begin with Isike, ruler of Unyanyembe, whose life—as well as his death at the hands of the Germans and their local allies—encapsulates much of Africa's global nineteenth century, and is representative of normative understandings of 'The Scramble'. Crucially, the dynamics discernible along the road and the personalities who both exemplify those dynamics and drive them forward offer a way into reconstructing Africa's transformative nineteenth century, and a means by which we can understand 'The Scramble' as the culmination of multiple processes working in parallel and in intersection with one another. The road allows us to do so over a much longer timeframe than conventional histories of 'partition' permit. It provides us with insights into political contestation, insurgency, socioeconomic innovation; illustrates the creative power of volatility and liminality; demonstrates the impact of outside intrusion, and allows us a closer look at the intruders themselves and Africans' interactions with them; and ultimately gives us a sense of how we might rethink 'The Scramble' itself, and how the events comprising it have been interpreted subsequently.

––––––

I FIRST ENCOUNTERED THE ROAD—from a distance of several thousand miles and a hundred years—as an undergraduate student of African history. It has stayed with me ever since, in various ways, though it has evolved as an idea. And so, the narrative thread running through what follows represents something of a return to a 'first love'; a desire to recapture, maybe, that time of (relatively) uncomplicated fascination, the innocent passion that I associate with early discovery. For me, the journey begins quite a long way from Africa: in central Scotland, to be precise, where in the spring semester of 1991 I encounter African history as an undergraduate for the first time. It is during that season in the northern parts of our unstable union—when the gloomy winter begins to recede and the bright sunshine suddenly begins to light up the fiery oranges and vivid greens of the Ochil Hills—that I am introduced to the drama of Africa's nineteenth century. I do not want to take that particular course: there is a first-come, first-serve system in operation, in the days before student choice became a thing, and I rank the Africa course sixth out of six in terms of preferences. Everyone is desperate to do US history, which sounds cool. I don't get on that one, or even on the next four. Instead, I am assigned to get to grips with 'The Making of Modern Africa, Part 1: The Nineteenth Century'—at least I *think* that was what it was called—and I am a bit disappointed, frankly.[2] By the end of the semester, life has changed. And here I am.

This anecdote has less to do with the potential pitfalls of untrammelled student choice—though that's worth pursuing another time, perhaps—than with the incongruous and often unglamorous contexts within which journeys sometimes begin. Of course, my journey doesn't start there at all, in reality; things are happening further upstream. I am male, white, working class—I'm not sure if that is the correct order—from a Belfast suburb, brought up in a Protestant and Unionist community. I grow up in the 1970s and 1980s amidst the violence of the conflict curiously and quaintly known as 'The Troubles' (old ladies in Ulster would refer to young wives' pregnancies in much the same way). I can't say there is no connection whatsoever to Africa, growing up. There is a handful of family links, but all of a distinctly neocolonial hue, and none of them particularly auspicious for anyone seeking a decolonised genealogy. There is an uncle who lived in Sierra Leone in the 1960s, working in insurance. He had servants and everything, and brought home sundry wooden ornaments. His mother, my grandmother—a tough wee Belfast woman who started smoking (I worked out) when the Japanese invaded Manchuria, though there is no proven link between the two events—had an African sculpture of a naked woman (noticeable to a ten-year-old kid) in her front room, which had come all the way from Freetown, and it stood incongruously beside the pewter Ulster Defence Regiment figurine. My uncle is given to offering alarming guidance about what we can euphemistically term 'native inclinations'. There is a distant cousin in Zimbabwe, part of a wave of white settlement to what was then Rhodesia, whose views of Africans would be recognisable to his late nineteenth-century forebears. Mostly I remember his extraordinarily bushy sideburns, which had colonised much of his face—seizing the best land between the ears and the middle of the face where hair doesn't generally thrive—and which I fondly imagine were cultivated in the good old times before ZANU's revolution, and retained thereafter, because colonists needed to stand their ground. On excessive facial hair as on other things. Some other even more distant relative lives in what was then Swaziland, and seems to regularly send my mother little glass animals; a peculiarly dainty and fragile wildlife.

In the early 1980s, as Thatcher's reforms decimated what was left of Belfast's manufacturing sector in which my father worked as a 'spark' (electrician), I recall him coming home one day muttering that it might be an idea to move us all to South Africa. I have no clue where this came from; though it was a popular notion that South Africa—even in the early 1980s—was a place where a working-class immigrant with a trade could do very well. Certainly better than in Belfast, where the violence was escalating, the hunger strikes had begun and my dad was on a one-day week. It was a thrilling prospect. But it quickly vanished, and South Africa was in any case going up in smoke itself. He wouldn't have been the last Unionist to find himself on the wrong side of history, but relocating the family to sunny Johannesburg in c. 1982 would have taken some beating.

All of which is to say—there *were* connections to this 'Africa' place, but they were of a tenuous nature; and dubious, too, though we all have our furrows to plough and are the products of our moments. It would be several years before I set foot in the place myself. A few months after my undergraduate eyes were opened, my first proper girlfriend and I managed to get the funds together for a trip to Crete. While we were there, the news was all about the coup against Gorbachev, threatening to destroy at birth the brave new post–Cold War order into which we in Generation X were just feeling our way. But I was more fixated with the fact that, if you struck out from the southern Cretan coast, the next land mass you'd hit would be Africa. And I confess that, after recovering from a nasty bout of sunstroke, I did indeed stand on that shore like a blistered Pliny the Elder, and gazed longingly across the sparkling blue—actually more or less directly at Qaddafi's Libya—wondering what novelty would emanate from the place, and more prosaically, when or if I'd ever manage to get there myself.

But in the meantime, new obsessions were in train, and Africa's past offered a form of escape, and possibly, I have to confess, a way of organising and perhaps projecting inchoate feelings about my own homeland. Studying Africa's nineteenth century opened up a whole wonderful past to me: a world of upheaval and opportunity, subjugation and resistance, conflict and transformation. It was an era of remarkable characters and their remarkable communities. Of external challenges, above all from the direction of an aggressive Europe with its increasingly racialised view of the globe. In truth I have never left that world, for in most of my own work—bar some adventures in the more recent past—I have been fixated with the drama of that epoch. I became engrossed by Mirambo, who was for me a figure of heroic proportions, his evident flaws only adding to his charisma. I confess, too, that I was drawn to another traveller on the road, Henry Morton Stanley, a screwed-up, complicated individual who was not only a fascinating product of global upheaval, but who seemed, in some disquieting ways, to be a kind of distant prototype of all white people who write about Africa. All in all, the road was one of extraordinary drama, of personalities and processes which presented in bold, vivid colours. With new-convert zeal I had written my final-year undergraduate thesis on the Nyamwezi people of the area: how they transformed the societies within which they lived, and grasped the opportunities on offer from an advancing, violent, external frontier. But Andrew Roberts, my eventual doctoral supervisor—who had himself written quite a bit on the topic before I was even born—didn't think there was enough in all this for a PhD thesis (after all, he had had it covered!); and so, reflecting that tendency for life-changes to happen in the quietist of corners, I shifted a loosely defined project north, to Uganda.

Still, I have episodically returned to the memory, time and again, of that glorious first awakening; the discovery of new things, and the creation of new passions. We age, become a little grumpier, more cynical, less nimble, weary sometimes of the larger professional workload that—if we are lucky—comes firmly attached to the innocent enthusiasm. Above all, I have returned time and again to the idea of Africa's transformative, indeed revolutionary, nineteenth century; the remarkable, multicoloured, dynamic, entrepreneurial, violent nineteenth century. I've sought to frame that seminal era in the way that I had immediately understood it when I first encountered it as a student—as absolutely fundamental to an understanding of modern Africa; not as warm-up act to what came later, the colonial and postcolonial twentieth century, but rather as foundational in terms of political creativity and volatility, in economic dynamism and social and cultural behaviours. Everything that followed needed to be understood in that light. In subtle and sometimes not-so-subtle ways, I came to believe, carts had been put before horses; standard periodisation— placing the colonial era and its immediate aftermath as front and centre of the modern narrative—obscured what truly mattered in Africa's modern trajectory. This, indeed, was the blinding brilliance of the present, as the sinologist Maurice Freedman put it.[3]

———

THESE RUMINATIONS AND OBSESSIONS, and any contribution I've been able to make to the field, have been facilitated by a host of personal and professional relationships. Many people are responsible for the hubris, limited self-awareness and levels of vigorous anxiety which underpin this book and have made it possible. But this is not the moment for an unseemly blame-game. Let me instead record my thanks to a handful of those who have taught, inspired or otherwise shoved me in one direction or another. For some years I had been contemplating a big comprehensive history of Africa's nineteenth century, one of those projects which sits in a list of possible future projects gathering dust. Along came Princeton University Press, in the form of commissioning editor Ben Tate. Princeton was interested in a history of 'The Scramble'. I thought I would try to marry the two projects. But in truth this is neither a big comprehensive history of Africa's nineteenth century, nor a history of 'The Scramble' in the conventional sense. Those endeavours I leave to better historians with greater energy and vision than I currently possess. And so, I both apologise to, and thank, Ben for offering me the opportunity to produce what follows. An anonymous reviewer of the original proposal, submitted several years ago—to whom I am also profoundly grateful for their helpful comments and pointers—suggested that I would "need to take [my] time over this". Well, I believe I have taken my time; and in fact the project has changed quite a bit since that original proposal. And so I offer my thanks to Princeton University Press for their patience.

A little further back, Ken Armstrong (or 'Mr Armstrong', as I should always think of him) was the most inspirational of history teachers, at Friends' School Lisburn, and someone to whom I owe an enormous debt. I didn't do quite as well in my A-Levels as I'd hoped, but the articulacy and delicacy with which he approached the study of the past—a deft meld of the passionate and the clinical—has had more of an enduring influence than I understood at the time as a discombobulated teenager. Later foundations were laid by Robin Law, the late John McCracken and Andrew Roberts, each of whom I have thanked in books gone by, but I have no qualms about saying it again: at various times and contexts, they showed me by example what it was to be a historian. Numerous other friends and colleagues over the years have provided, inadvertently or otherwise, inspiration, support and counsel: in particular I'd like to mention Eyob Abraha, Dave Anderson, Godfrey Asiimwe, Gareth Austin, Shiferaw Bekele, Jamie Belich, Erica Charters, Uoldelul Chelati, Christopher Clapham, the late Jan-Georg Deutsch, Shane Doyle, Frank Edward, the late Richard Greenfield, Tony Hopkins, Rob Iliffe, Dixon Kamukama, Abraham Keleta, Pamela Khanakwa, Martin Klein, Miles Larmer, Murray Last, Cherry Leonardi, John Lonsdale, Christopher Muhoozi, Izabela Orlowska, Hannah Petros, Alan Strathern, Lynn Thomas, Andy Thompson, Justin Willis and the late Amanuel Yohannes. I'm deeply grateful to the anonymous readers of an earlier draft of the book. I thank the History Faculty at Oxford for granting me sabbatical leave over much of the 2022–23 academic year, and the colleagues who picked up the slack; and I'm grateful to the Beit Fund for financial support. None of these folks are responsible for my own intellectual failings, of course.

My daughters, May and Thea, I thank for simply existing in the world, and above all in mine, and I apologise for sometimes being less than I ought to be. The excuse that 'dad is writing a book' has steadily diminishing power, I've discovered, and perhaps was always a cover for deeper inadequacies. I have dedicated this book to their mother, who has made me *think* more than anyone else in my life; and though the nature of our relationship has changed, she has enriched my life immeasurably.

Truth be told, I have wondered, as time goes on, what I'm doing on this road at all; pondered the prejudices and inclinations which I bring to the study of it, especially as someone male, pale and increasingly stale pronouncing on the histories of Africans. I'm not entirely certain I have a coherent set of thoughts on that yet. What I do know—drawing on anthropological work in particular—is that a road is a useful concept in this respect, a metaphor which allows us to think about time and motion and perspective, and the relationship between the author and the thing they're observing.[4] It is a continually unfolding frontier, an inherently liminal space, on which—provided we aren't stationary—time and space are always in motion. The other thing I know, relatedly, is that this book is the product of a traumatic period across the globe, politically, socially, and now economically: a period of the pandemic and of inept and/or sinister government, of 'post-truth', of helpless anger. This has made me think about instability, and liminality, a little differently. No doubt it reflects my own sense of what is, or has become, 'normal'. Everything we write is the outcome of the times in which we write it. At its best this can be an exercise in constructive self-awareness.[5] But at the very least—and I hope this offering meets this bar—it begins as do most journeys of self-discovery with a view to healing: with a weary, slightly fearful acknowledgment that there is an issue to be addressed.

# PART I

# Parameters and Contexts

# Act I

## Isike at the Crossroads

### I

IT IS THE EARLY HOURS OF 12 JANUARY 1893, and Isike, ruler of Unyanyembe in central-east Africa, has withdrawn to the inner enclosure of his fort. He is trapped and running out of options. A short distance away, a hostile force is closing in: an assorted army under the command of Lieutenant Tom von Prince comprising a contingent of German troops and bolstered by an array of local allies. Just a few hours earlier, these forces had succeeded—after months of failure—in gaining the upper hand against Isike's own soldiers, and had destroyed his outer fortifications. Now, Isike has taken refuge in his inner sanctum, where he keeps his remaining supplies of gunpowder.[1] Perhaps he contemplates the only choices left to him: surrender or death. Whatever the nature of those deliberations, he chooses death. A little before dawn on the 12th, the German-led force scales the walls and despite the courage of Isike's men, they are unable to match the German breech-loaders' rate of fire. Now the enemy is just metres away. Isike carefully lights a fuse, and touches it against his stores of ammunition. The whole magazine goes up in a terrifying explosion.

Alas, Isike isn't *quite* dead—or at least, not dead enough for the Germans. They drag him, badly injured and barely conscious, to a nearby tree and hang him. They then shoot dead one of his children, his young son, who happens to be in the vicinity.[2] Von Prince will recall, years later and with no apparent self-awareness, that Isike died "a hero's death", and will

3

muse that "[i]f his timing had been a little more exact, a great deal of his conqueror would also have gone up in the air".[3] He will write this in a memoir published in 1914, with the Second Reich in its pomp. A few months after this, he will meet his own end, killed fighting the British at the Battle of Tanga in German East Africa.[4]

What renders this scene especially powerful is the apparent clarity with which lines are drawn. Isike takes on, in this telling, a heroic hue; he is a resister, a warrior, confronting the onslaught of European invasion. It is the end of the road, however, and a brutal new order beckons; he has done his best, but now there is only rupture, and destruction. The Germans, on the other hand, reveal the moral vacuum at the heart of whatever enterprise they believed they were involved in. Here, in all its ugly simplicity, is the awful violence of imperialism, often forgotten by the very people who accuse those seeking to remember it of trying to change the past.[5] Isike might have laid claim to a certain heroism, his own violent past as a slave-dealer notwithstanding; but his son—a defenceless child, killed on the spot—had no such agency at his disposal. The Germans don't even appear to have fought particularly valiantly. They had guns, lots of them, and used them to deadly effect—eventually, that is, for they had been bested frequently by Isike's own army over the preceding months. But it is hardly the stuff of Teutonic legend. They hadn't even really done it on their own—far from it, in fact, having relied on a host of local allies to get close to Isike's enclosure and to ultimately lay claim to this patch of East Africa. Easy, then, for the conceited von Prince to reminisce two decades after the fact about Isike's "heroic death". There is—apparently—no remorse about how he placed Isike's semiconscious body in a noose, or how he had his son killed.[6] These were the irrelevant minutiae of civilisation-building among savages, the quotidian particles of dust thrown up as Africa is dragged into some semblance of 'modernity', or quasi-modernity, or some sort of liminal state which would prepare them for it. In any case the circumstances of von Prince's own death remind us that these were Great Empires, destined to fight amongst themselves, while African subjects looked on bewildered, or died of typhoid, or famine, or were killed in service as *askari* (colonial soldiers); but the Great Empires, crucially, are front and centre of the picture, the global entities within which Africans adapt, and mediate, and mitigate, and live their lives.

Above all, the manner of Isike's death, and the destruction of his enclosure, suggests *conquest*, and thus *rupture*. A rapid end to something, and the beginning of something else. 'The Scramble' involves many terrible traumas, and African suffering on a shocking scale; but its supposedly blinding speed and intensity throws everything else—including, most importantly, what led to it—into shade. We are reminded of Okonkwo at the end of Chinua Achebe's great novel. Faced with colonial invasion, and the evaporation of everything that he had known—and that had made him such a towering figure in his own community—the complicated, energetic, anxious Okonkwo takes matters (or the only matter he could) into his own hands:

> Then they came to the tree from which Okonkwo's body was dangling, and they stopped dead. [...] The Commissioner went away, taking three or four of the soldiers with him. In the many years in which he had toiled to bring civilisation to different parts of Africa he had learned a number of things. [...] Every day brought him some new material. The story of this man who had killed a messenger and hanged himself would make interesting reading. [...] He had already chosen the title of the book, after much thought: The Pacification of the Primitive Tribes of the Lower Niger.[7]

Achebe wrote *Things Fall Apart* on the eve of Nigerian independence; a new era was upon Nigerians and all Africans, it was supposed. And yet Achebe's gaze—and that of many others, including scholars and producers of culture—was drawn backward to the moment of putative 'conquest'. It cemented the notion that 'The Scramble' for Africa had been a traumatic juncture, a seismic remaking of the landscape in which Africans must operate. It reinforced the idea of the enduring significance of the partition, and the 'conquest' it seemingly involved—for both Africa and Europe, and ultimately the world at large. Okonkwo was a fictional character, of course. But Achebe's genius was to distil the anguish of the age in Okonkwo; to drive home with such lucidity the idea of catastrophe. For Achebe, presumably, the only logical conclusion to the story was

Okonkwo's self-destruction, in the face of European aggression; self-murder as the old world was swept away by a new order, represented in the novel by a dispassionate colonial official who, even as he looked on Okonkwo's cadaver swaying from the branch of a tree, was mulling over the book he would write about his civilising adventures. Achebe knew his colonial ethnography, and the context within which much of it was produced.

Isike is not a fictional character, however. His attempted self-destruction, and his subsequent murder, were very real, as was the intense emotional turmoil he must have experienced in his final moments as he contemplated the strange and entangled journeys which had led him to this point. And it is those journeys with which we are concerned here, in particular what they tell us about a tumultuous, revolutionary and ultimately global epoch, and, as we will see, the ways in which they find their echoes elsewhere across the continent during that era.

Isike had become *mtemi*, or paramount ruler, of Unyanyembe in 1876 upon the death of his father, Mkasiwa. He evidently had ambition and ability, but this was a febrile, turbulent time, and the capture of the chiefship of Unyanyembe had become a serious prize, sought by many. At first, he was vulnerable. He was challenged by a relative, Nyungu-ya-Mawe, already a successful, energetic warlord among the Kimbu to the south. Nyungu, moreover, had the support of the Nyamwezi leader Mirambo, another regional hegemon, who dominated the road to the west and who had spent the last few years at war with Unyanyembe—or, at least, with the powerful community of coastal merchants who resided there. But Isike enlisted the help of that community—little could happen in Unyanyembe without them—and saw off Nyungu's challenge.[8] Over the next few years, Isike not only survived—no mean feat in this neighbourhood at this time—but prospered. He outlived his adversaries Nyungu and Mirambo, both of whom died in 1884, and manipulated the multiple risks and threats by which he was surrounded on a daily basis. He had to manage carefully the influential and well-armed Swahili merchants, whose interests were primarily pecuniary. For above all, Isike's status, and the significance of Unyanyembe, rested on its commercial value. Unyanyembe itself was not a major producer of the kinds of commodities in demand across the

region—in fact, in many ways it was pretty inconsequential from that perspective. Its importance lay, rather, in its position as a transit handler of
goods coming from a wide area. The great advantage to being the *mtemi*
of Unyanyembe was that the polity sat on a vital crossroads. Roads flowed
into Unyanyembe from all directions: from the south, and the rich commercial frontiers opening up across the grasslands there; from the lacustrine north, where a string of bustling states competed for control over
lucrative trade routes; from the west, where Isike's road became someone
else's, running through the violent hunting grounds of the eastern Congo
basin and through the entrepot of Ujiji; and of course from the east, from
Bagamoyo on the coast, and beyond that from Zanzibar and the Indian
Ocean world.[9] Isike's domain sat astride a network which linked that great
ocean with the central Congo basin, and beyond that the Atlantic world.
Trade flowed through Unyanyembe, and in many ways was its lifeblood.
It was what connected Unyanyembe to the world. Isike himself had done
very well out of it, taxing commerce in his domain and acting as a trader
in his own right, and lived in some style as a result. He had an impressive
house, dressed in the finest garments from the coast and owned pillows
and "a thick soft carpet", according to a Swedish traveller who passed
through in 1886.[10] He also owned a large number of guns and plenty of
ammunition, of course, imported from the coast, enabling him to exert
some political and military influence over a wider area. The chiefs of Unyanyembe dealt in elephant tusks and people. Like thousands of others,
this was a matter of aspiration, and innovation. But then again . . . the great
*dis*advantage to being the *mtemi* of Unyanyembe was also, precisely, that
the polity sat on such a vital crossroads. In many ways it was a geopolitical
reality which destabilised politics, and made rulership a lonely and vulnerable business, opening up opportunity and presenting peril in equal
measure. The *mtemi* profited mightily from his position as the main transit
handler of slaves and ivory in the area; but as a consequence he also dealt
in violence, and understood all too well the existential dangers of being a
dealer in violence. The commerce which flowed through his realm attracted thieves and bandits, but while he publicly decried robbery and
corruption, he quietly ensured that he received his share, and had his arrangements with those who operated in the political and commercial

gloaming of his polity. He had to face down ambitious relatives who would seize his position in a heartbeat; some of them even worked for hostile neighbours who feared and resented Unyanyembe's geopolitical position and Isike's role in it. Isike, in short, lived a dangerous, interesting life at the heart of a revolution which had been shaping the region for decades.[11]

Still, one increasingly existential hazard with which he hadn't reckoned was Germany. Unyanyembe, so tiny compared to the global powers whose representatives now pressed in on him from the east, seemed to have become disproportionately significant. It was evidently at the centre of dramatic global shifts; apparently in the eye of the storm. When Europeans had first shown up, they were—with one or two exceptions—rather an unthreatening, even fearful lot; they spent much of their time ill, and often appeared to be lost, though definitely in search of something. Later, however, they took on an altogether more brutal, determined aspect, inserting themselves into the gaps created by the region's transformation, and bringing ever better weapons to the pursuit of influence and leverage. After over a decade as ruler of Unyanyembe, Isike had proven himself to be a pragmatic man, certainly not someone who was ineluctably unreconciled to dealing with foreigners. He had been doing so his whole life. But his problems with this particular group of intruders began in the late 1880s. In 1886 a German trader, Giesecke, was killed following a commercial dispute, and Isike confiscated his property—as he believed was his right— and from that point a momentum of antagonism built up between Isike and the Europeans. In 1889, weary of their machinations and intrigues, Isike forced a group of missionaries belonging to the White Fathers out of their base at Kipalapala. The Germans began to build a coalition against him. In 1890 an Ottoman scientist named Emin Pasha, formerly governor of the Egyptian province of Equatoria, arrived at Tabora, the main town in Unyanyembe and the centre of a transregional network.[12] He came with a thousand soldiers and two explorer-diplomats in the late nineteenth-century mould, Franz Stulmann and Wilhelm Langheld. Isike watched on anxiously as Emin Pasha forged a treaty with the ever-opportunistic coastal community at Tabora, the latter agreeing to recognise German suzerainty in exchange for the ability to choose their own *wali*, or head of community. Bruised by this coalescence of increasingly hostile interests, but cognisant of his own vulnerability, Isike agreed to surrender two of his cannons and make a payment of ivory to demonstrate his faith in the new arrangement; but antagonism only increased through the early 1890s. In April 1892 Isike's son led an attack on a passing German column, in response to which the Germans successfully attacked his base at Ipuli. A few weeks after this defeat, in June, the Germans turned their attention to Isike himself. He could still hold his own, though: he managed to repel a German assault, and closed down all the caravan routes through his territory.[13]

There was still, in theory, an opportunity for peaceful resolution. Isike had in fact attempted to agree an armistice with a Commander Sigl; but the problem was now in Tabora itself, for two sovereign authorities in the town placed Isike in an impossible position. The anthropologist Otto Raum—himself born in German East Africa a mere decade after these events—put it best, perhaps: Isike needed power "over life and death of subjects; in maintaining public order by the suppression of robberies, slave-abduction, and interference with caravans; in levying tolls; and in controlling contacts between Africans and whites".[14] In other words, Isike had a right to the sovereign supremacy due to him as ruler of Unyanyembe. Any 'armistice' with the representatives of the Second Reich was going to make that impracticable. And so they mustered their forces, and made their advance on his enclosure—the confrontation seemingly inevitable, supposedly as inevitable as the outcome itself.

## II

ISIKE DIED, IT SEEMS, IN THE FACE OF GLOBAL MODERNITY. And modernity came armed to the teeth. His passing, and the seeming destruction of Unyanyembe's sovereignty, marks what is conventionally posited as the most fundamental temporal boundary in African history: the partition of the continent at the end of the nineteenth century, and its morphing from *precolonial* to *colonial*; or, perhaps—for it sometimes seems that this is what is *really* meant—from premodern to modern. With death, and the violent encounter, comes fracture. Here, we have endings, and we have beginnings. It is a scene which is being replicated across the African landmass at precisely the moment that Isike is strung up from a tree: a casual survey will reveal myriad other communities fighting 'suicidally', resisting the new era with their supposedly archaic weapons and arcane fetishes. In much of this, we see the enduring valorisation of the idea of conquest and resistance and heroism—for many good and understandable reasons. The idea of rupture also undergirds, if in often spectral ways, the fixation with the colonial moment. Moreover, Isike seems to perish in strange temporal isolation, for his and a multitude of other stories are frequently told as part of a singular and hermetically sealed moment of time: the 'Partition', 'The Scramble'. This has allowed the focus of attention, whether of a negative or positive bent, to be firmly on external, primarily European, dynamics; it has also allowed for the casting of a revolutionary epoch in Africa into some serious shade, at least in terms of its long-term implications and legacies.

In reality, the moment of Isike's murder represents the culmination of a remarkable era of African transformation, revolution, reformation. What follows is a modest attempt to reposition that remarkable era in Africa's modern trajectory. Isike's stretch of road captures in microcosm the experience of millions of Africans in the course of the long nineteenth century: the role of insurgency, of political volatility and instability, of fractured and contested succession; but also of creativity, and innovation, and aspiration. The road enables us, too, to explore the contexts within which Europeans moved in the late nineteenth century. For above all, Isike's road was a global one—representatives from across the world travelled on it, and the people living along it became part of that world. Isike's road thus leads us to a contemplation of the very nature of Africa's place in modern global history. In the course of the nineteenth century, and in concentrated form, we see the convergence of a number of the salient vectors involved in reciprocal global change—both in Unyanyembe itself, and along one of the most important roads in African history: namely, that stretching from Bagamoyo on the coast to Ujiji on the shore of Lake Tanganyika. The world comes to Unyanyembe; but Unyanyembe also comes to the world, and shapes that world in its own way. This is an African story, and an Afro-global one, as much as a European or an imperial one. Unyanyembe illustrates Africa's nineteenth-century experience of goods, gods and guns; the example of Unyanyembe demonstrates the potential of micro-global history to elucidate the impact of macro-global forces.[15] It also presents us with an opportunity to try to understand the role of individual communities in what can feel like a tsunami of global forces, threatening to submerge such communities and reduce them to footnote, at best. Again, Unyanyembe presents us with an entry into an exploration of Africa's place in global history—and not just Africans' experience of and engagement with the world, but also Europeans' own experience and conceptualisation of the area, and the road, and its characters. This is a story of motion, and energy, and direction of travel: it is Isike's road, as much as his polity, which justifies our opening gambit, and which enables us to link the era of partition with the processes unfolding *within* Africa—and in Europe, and in the Indian Ocean world—over the course of the preceding decades.

As for Isike himself, he is not one of the most famous, or noted, protagonists of Africa's nineteenth century. Few if any people beyond Africa and outside of the realm of Tanzanian history will ever have heard of him. Likewise his political realm, Unyanyembe, doesn't figure in global histories, or even, prominently at least, in histories of the partition. But there are very good reasons for selecting the area as our recurring point of reference in exploring Africa's nineteenth century and the ways in which that transformative, indeed revolutionary, era culminated in the partition of the continent. What follows is concerned with that larger set of processes and events; and Unyanyembe, and the road which runs to it and through it, exemplifies the story and underpins the narrative. This was Isike's road; and it was Africa's.

# 1

# Complicating Conquest

## The Inescapable Partition

WHAT WAS THE RELATIONSHIP between the remarkable and turbulent transformation in evidence across much of Africa in the course of the nineteenth century, and the European partition of the continent—the so-called 'Scramble for Africa'—at the end of it? What role had African dynamics and agencies of change played in the facilitation, even actualisation, of European imperialism, culminating in 'conquest'? These questions are far from simple, at least in terms of their implications; more on which at a later juncture. What seem clear enough are the remarkable transformations wrought by Africans' capacity for innovation and aspiration and reform during this extraordinary era, as well as by the violence which frequently attended these dynamics. But it is worth asking questions about the lasting significance of the period, particularly in relation to 'The Scramble', which appears to have its own distinctive, weighty import in the historiographical canon. The idea of it has also had a profound influence on periodisation: specifically, the long-standing division of Africa's past into three broad phases—'precolonial', 'colonial', 'postcolonial'—each of which, obviously enough, places enormous and in my view wholly undue weight on what was once termed 'the colonial moment'.[1] In the interests of full disclosure: I use the terms myself; I know that they are widely and tacitly understood; and I haven't yet come up with anything that looks like a decent substitute. But I have become deeply hostile to the idea of some*thing*, or some*one*, being 'precolonial', and sustained exploration of the long nineteenth century has doubtless fostered that hostility. 'The Scramble', in other words—however messy and incomplete—supposedly involved the distinctive passage from one very clearly demarcated epoch to another. Explicitly, it ushered in the era of colonial rule; implicitly, at least, it marked the beginnings of Africans' entry into global modernity—although plenty of contemporary or near-contemporary commentators (and participants) were pretty overt in their assertion that the great task of 'civilising' (then a proxy for 'modernis-ing') Africa had begun in earnest.[2] Relatedly, there was the question of 'The Scramble' itself as denoting a more or less quarantined passage of play, one which might involve a fair amount of African agency—and many have certainly thought so—but which more commonly has come to be dominated by historians of European empire and imperialism, and which has been largely associated with the potency of phenomena emanating from the Global North. I have many close colleagues in this field—some of my best friends, as they say, are historians of empire—and I respect their work very much. But the shift toward Big Imperial Histo-ries invariably, if inadvertently, has meant keeping Africanist scholarship firmly in the Area Studies box; all very interesting, in other words, but not the stuff of discipline-defining, endowed-chair-acquiring scholarship.[3] It is also true that more or less contemporaneously with the rejuvenation of imperial history, beginning in the 1990s, historians of Africa were losing interest in 'The Scramble', and were either concerning themselves with 'precolonial' topics or—altogether more commonly—fixing their sights firmly on the twentieth century and the 'colonial moment'.[4] A few others, of course, were also seeking to position Africa within the global histories which were arising at the same time.[5]

What I have tried to do, however, is identify certain phenomena and dynamics in the course of Africa's long, global, and revolutionary nine-teenth century, and see if these help in any way explain the partition, the 'conquest', of the continent between the 1870s and 1900s. In so doing, I am not seeking to fundamentally overturn too many received wisdoms, or alienate my imperial-historian friends and colleagues. In fact, it seems to me that quite a few fellow-travellers have shown the way over the last half-century or more, even if their work has never truly coalesced to form a distinctive revisionist position: it has been too disparate and piecemeal to gain the traction that is the outcome of critical mass.[6] It has been crowded out by the very decisive shift in the Africanist academy into the twentieth century, which represents—implicitly or otherwise—a perception that 'The Scramble' marked a clear conceptual, temporal and epistemic boundary. It has been marginalised, too, by the consolidation of Imperial History, and also—ironically, in some ways—by postcolonial scholarship which, in its wholly laudable determination to reconstruct the impact of empire and colonialism on millions of Asians and Africans, is almost by definition more concerned with 'decoloniality' than with what we exasperatingly term the 'precolonial'. I am, however, seeking to complicate the narrative: to place Africans front and centre of the story; to assert the fundamental significance of the continent's nineteenth century in understanding what comes after—not as prologue, but as dominant component in the story; and to make a little messier the histories of how empires get built and, more specifically, what 'The Scramble for Africa' meant and what it actually involved.

'The Scramble' is a mainstay in the historiographical canon, a venerable notion, an inescapable feature in the temporal landscape. As monuments go, it attracts fewer visitors than it once did. But there it stands, nevertheless, gathering a little wear and tear, splattered by pigeon-droppings, but imposing and unmistakable for all that. Since the contemporary treatises of John Scott Keltie, J. A. Hobson and Frederick Lugard,[7] 'The Scramble' has been posited as a distinct passage of time, a seminal moment, a period of conquest which is understood and examined largely on its own terms. It rapidly became a foundational marker, a boundary post, in the great temporal plain encompassing Africa, Europe, and swathes of the wider world. It clearly demarcates something which comes to be called *the precolonial* from something called *the colonial*. Books—this author's included—and university courses, and of course epistemological, methodological, conceptual approaches, and public discourse, have generally adhered to the boundary (with some exceptions) ever since. On the face of it, there are some very good reasons for this. At the beginning of the 1870s, much of the African continent was in African hands; in little more than a generation, almost the entire landmass was, in various forms, under foreign control. The period has been understood as a remarkable and transformative 'moment' for Africa in social, economic, political, cultural and intellectual terms, one which was made possible by the putative economic and technological surge enjoyed by Europe over the preceding century or more, and which enabled Europe— or its leading players—to impose itself on vast swathes of the globe, Africa included. It was a period which witnessed European empire at its zenith, and which—according to one preeminent narrative—ushered in the 'modern' era for millions of Africans. By the time of the First World War, Africa, with the exception of Ethiopia and Liberia, was under French, British, German, Italian, Portuguese and Belgian rule. There are certain 'facts' about 'The Scramble' which are firmly established, and well documented: the sheer scale of cartographic rearrangement of the African continent; the mighty effort of will—political and military—involved on the part of several European nations, at their imperial apexes; the violence inflicted on millions of Africans which characterised the exercise. There are European diplomatic machinations which lead to the large-scale partition of an entire continental landmass, laying the groundwork for future sovereign nation-states. There are violent confrontations between European or (more commonly) European-led armies and Africans which lead to decisive and often devastating victories; and conquest is frequently attended by extraordinary, at times genocidal, levels of violence which engulf populations beyond battlefield clashes, shattering communities and setting them on a spiral of underdevelopment which would last for decades, and which continues to blight many such communities at the time of writing. There is a rich body of scholarship on the violence which routinely attended European imperialism, based on irrefutable bodies of evidence.[8] This is the case despite the efforts on the part of successive governments in the 'postcolonial' Global North to whitewash such histories, and to distract from lived experiences with self-soothing narratives about the supposed beneficence of empire.[9] What follows is not an attempt to reread those histories critically, but rather to place the events and processes of the late nineteenth century in a rather longer-range timeframe than is usual; to problematise certain aspects of 'The Scramble', situating these in the context of African historical development; and to reflect in a (hopefully) more nuanced way on certain aspects of the 'conquest' narrative.

The enormous body of literature on the events of the late nineteenth century renders anything approaching a comprehensive survey impossible.[10] In some cases, there is, frankly, little to improve upon: witness, for example, John Lonsdale's superlative essay in the sixth volume of the *Cambridge History of Africa* which remains an essential read, and which manages to be both comprehensive exploration and characteristically eloquent overview.[11] At the other end of the publishing cosmos, professional academic historians might feel a little sniffy about Thomas Pakenham's blockbuster, but it is, in its way, a terrific read, rendered in compelling technicolour detail—at least when it comes to the European angle, for Africans themselves habitually appear as rather more one-dimensional characters than their white counterparts.[12] In any case, in between the erudite monumentalism of Cambridge University Press and pacey narratives for the lay reader is an array of scholarship handling 'The Scramble' in a variety of ways and with varying levels of detail, but all of it approaching the topic as a singular 'episode', and all of it essentially describing the abrupt intrusion of foreign powers into Africa and the subjugation of pretty much the entire continent between the 1870s and the First World War.[13] The topic obviously occupies a central place, too, in the larger-sweep textbooks and surveys of African history.[14] Meanwhile Africa and its conquest are central to work on the 'new imperialism' of the late nineteenth century (alongside Southeast Asia), and so figures prominently in the writings of historians of European empire.[15] This body of scholarship is increasingly complemented by—indeed, some might say, intimately intertwined with—work on the global nineteenth century.[16]

And so, specialist textbook coverage aside, Africa and the moment of its great partition now draws rather more attention from global and imperial historians than it does, in general, from among historians of Africa who have rather lost interest in 'The Scramble'—at least in terms of new explanations rooted in *African* as opposed to metropolitan dynamics.[17] It remains the case, moreover, that colleagues in the two fields are somewhat distinct species, only rarely conversing with one another. There are, of course, exceptions: Tony Hopkins and Frederick Cooper were well-

established historians of modern Africa before turning their attention—
graduating, perhaps?—to rather larger canvases concerned with empire
and imperialism.[18] Selected essays in the *Oxford History of the British Empire* likewise demonstrate the potential for commissioning Africanist
scholars to write about imperialism, for the results can be interesting.[19]
But the failure to integrate two largely discrete fields of historical enquiry
has been a characteristic of approaches to the Afro-European century in
general, and to 'The Scramble' in particular.[20] From an 'Africanist' perspective, some of the best work dealing with the period has focused on
how conquest and partition were experienced, and navigated, rather than
on whether anything which happens locally can help *explain* the whole
thing.[21] There are no doubt all sorts of very good reasons for this. Research
agendas move on apace, of course; fashionable new foci invariably mean
the placing of dull old topics in storage. The gradual shift, over several
decades, of the centre of scholarly gravity into the colonial (and indeed
postcolonial) period is indicative of the fact that there is now rather more
interest in what came after partition rather than in what led up to it. For
sure this reflects in large part the relative abundance (and diversity) of
particular types of primary source material for the period after 1900; the
colonial archive has reigned supreme methodologically for several decades
now, ruthlessly exploited and ferociously critiqued in equal measure. And
things have moved on to reflect intellectual and cultural concerns, themselves shadowing deeper social shifts (and political debates) in the Global
North in particular, with ever greater interest in coloniality and the de-
colonial: concepts which are often framed in Manichean terms. The field
is now considerably more excited about decolonisation, for example, than
about what led to the 'colonial moment' in the first place.

The project at hand, then, is an attempt to consider the longer-term
confluence of African as well as European and global dynamics and how
these might offer some explanation—or, at least, context—for 'The Scramble'. In fact, a great many clues have already been left by a formidable but
disparate body of work stretching over several decades. Right from the
beginnings of 'African History' as part of the mainstream scholarly canon
in the 1950s and 1960s, some of the most pioneering and exciting work
was done on the transformations of the nineteenth century: the social,

political and economic revolutions driven by millions of Africans during this extraordinary, and in many ways extraordinarily traumatic, era. The dynamism and energy of that era are evident in the foundational work of the Africanist academy—so much so, indeed, that it is impracticable to cite even a sample here.[22] That work did not often explicitly point toward an Africa-facing 'explanation' of 'The Scramble'; and there was a tendency, in that early scholarship, to end the narrative in the 1890s, or around 1900, reinforcing the notion of the rupture involved in the period 'c. 1880–c. 1900'.[23] This is what we might term 'despite-ism': in other words, *despite* the remarkable political and economic changes wrought by Africans, and of course wrought upon them, in the course of the nineteenth century, *despite* all the progress made in terms of creative engagement with global modernity, 'The Scramble' was visited upon them nonetheless, from beyond their shores, the outcome of dynamics over which they had little or no control. This was an interpretation which solidified in the years that followed, and variations of it—essentially highlighting the vibrancy and the revolutionary nature of Africa's nineteenth century, possibly even involving Africans' own path to 'modernisation', all of which is subverted by colonial invasion—continue to appear.[24] Be that as it may, the raw material for a slightly different interpretation is there for the taking, and a sizeable chunk of that raw material forms the basis for what follows.

Over several decades, others have looked for alternative explanations, or at least more nuanced interrogations of the roles played by local context and local dynamics.[25] Saadia Touval identified a greater role than might be supposed for Africans in the creation of boundaries and the implementation of treaties on the ground, while Ronald Robinson critiqued a prevailing Eurocentrism in arguing that European power, frequently little more than an illusion, only translated into 'empire-building' owing to the agency of local actors and dynamics.[26] (More recently, a similar argument has been made for the early modern period in relation to supposed European armed supremacy.)[27] David Fieldhouse likewise encouraged us to look less at metropolitan impulses and more at the 'periphery', where empire was actually *made*.[28] Indeed some fine area-specific work on East and South Africa has explicitly demonstrated how this was the case, and how local, not metropolitan, interactions actually led to the 'fabrication', the 'making', of empire.[29] John Darwin, meanwhile, has highlighted the importance of local 'bridgeheads' in influencing the form of imperial expansion.[30] Over several decades, scholars have drawn attention to instances of 'sub-imperialism' on the part of African actors who facilitated, to borrow Moses Ochonu's phrase, 'colonialism by proxy'.[31] In a West African context, a number of scholars pointed toward the critical importance of local responses to a changing commercial context—chiefly the transition from slave trade to so-called 'legitimate' commerce—and argued that *African* dynamics, whether reflecting resilience or disintegration, drew reluctant and vexed Europeans into 'empire-building'.[32]

## A Prospectus

IN THE COURSE OF THE NINETEENTH CENTURY, but especially in the last twenty years or so, a number of groups, foremost among them Europeans, were able to take advantage of a period of sustained instability within Africa stretching back over several decades. They achieved leverage within and between polities and communities thanks to that instability, taking advantage of fissures and factionalism within and between states and societies, and making use of liminal and displaced people—themselves the outcome of an era of prolonged instability—in staking their claims. At the same time, however, intruding foreigners were themselves co-opted into a range of conflicts in complex ways, with local actors also capable of taking advantage of instability to bolster their own positions, win new allies and pursue ongoing and deep-rooted reformist and entrepreneurial projects. From that perspective, what we normatively comprehend as 'The Scramble' was *both* symptomatic of Europe's expansionist urges (which were of course also the manifestation of tumult and instability within Europe itself), *and* the culmination of African reformist dynamics. Our aim, fundamentally, is to revisit the idea of 'The Scramble' as a period of rupture, reframing it as part of a deep-rooted, culminative process of change and co-option; and to re-centre Africa's temporal landscape, placing emphasis on the enduring significance of the long nineteenth century in comprehending the continent's 'modern' historical trajectory.

To begin with, Africa's long, unstable nineteenth century was the age of insurgency and innovation.[33] It was an era characterised by multiple, overlapping 'partitions', as it were, each underpinned by a turbulent reformism. We can debate when this begins, assuming it does indeed have a beginning; I identify the late eighteenth century—the period between the 1770s and 1790s—as a convenient narrative starting point. In some cases, notably on the Atlantic side of the continent, insurgency was at least in part the outcome of intensifying global interaction, which placed new pressures on existing political orders and raised the material stakes involved in reformist challenges to those orders. But global cultural, intellectual and economic exchange was not always involved, at least not initially, even if these factors invariably come into the story eventually. In other scenarios, existing cultures of internal challenge, reformism and contestation—characteristic of Africans' centuries-long quest to settle land, maximise resources and build enduring polities and communities—were at least as important, if not more so. These contests deepened in the course of the global nineteenth century.

I would argue that these various insurgencies, which come in all shapes and sizes, must be understood as a fundamental part of the story of the 'partition' of Africa; in a variety of ways, Africans' *own* partition of their *own* continent. Ultimately, the 'lines on the map' which create the territorial parameters for future African nation-states may be 'arbitrary' in many cases (though by no means all), but the colonial order they purportedly represent is also the outcome of a century or more of essentially local political thought and military development, and of the ways in which those local dynamics intersected with exogenous impulses. While some insurgencies were primarily about political power—sometimes incorporating novel or rejuvenated ideological and theocratic elements—others were essentially economic, or commercial, in nature, and were the result of material aspiration into which political (and, again, sometimes ideological) considerations were incorporated.[34] In some cases, violent contestation and long-established patterns of fission and fusion led to the creation of new states; in others, the reformation of older ones, as a result of contested succession and the absence of what we can broadly term the 'peaceful transfer of power'. Everywhere, there emerged new forms of political leadership, often based on merit rather than mere inheritance, in which especial value was placed on political vision, military skill, material ambition and the organisational prowess to realise it.

The decades preceding the era of partition were characterised by creative, often violent, volatility across the continent. An understanding of the 'moment' of partition between the 1870s and the 1910s simply isn't possible without an appreciation of this—and nor is a comprehension of the continent's long twentieth century. In fact, it is possible to discern a deeper pattern of ongoing, restless political reform and contestation in African history, creative as well as destructive, always energetic, always entrepreneurial, rooted in political ideas and intellectual reformism as well as material opportunism. This is a dynamic—or multiple dynamics acting in tandem—which renders societies 'unstable' while also being expansive, adaptable, open to change and characterised by internal contestation; it defines long-established states and societies and facilitates the emergence of new ones.[35] The central point here is that nineteenth-century processes and dynamics—which, I propose, go a long way to explaining and contextualising 'The Scramble'—have deep roots and precedents, and don't suddenly 'happen'. It's important to outline this *longue durée* dimension. Crucially, the escalation of global forces in the nineteenth century and various European ethnicities' armed, nationalist expansionism intersects with the transformation of a multitude of communities across the African landmass. In many areas, we can trace these patterns back over several preceding centuries. But it is important to emphasise the intensity of such transformation, and the context—the intrusion of global imperialism and the emergence of new forms of capitalism—within which it happens in the nineteenth century. This was an epoch of revolutionary politics in both continents: in Europe, the aftermath of the Enlightenment and the rise of the nation-state; in Africa, the new military and political forms forged as a result of demographic and economic change. We can identify 'warlords' and entrepreneurs of violence in both Africa and Europe as the outcome of an expansion in political scale, and the intersection of political dynamics emanating from both continents. In both Africa and Europe, a military revolution underpins wider societal and political change, and fundamentally alters the scale and aims of warfare as well as the culture and practice of other forms of violence.

In Africa, our primary focus, this level of instability created flux between polities and communities, leading to creative and unstable frontiers. These, it can be argued, had long been a feature in a historically underpopulated landmass; in the course of the long nineteenth century, they become sites of new communities, reformist projects and violence, especially as states wax and wane, creating shifting transitional zones which are politically fertile and materially insecure in equal measure. The appearance of large numbers of what we might term 'people in between' needs to be understood in conjunction with two other overlapping phenomena. The first is the increasing prominence of intermediary groups, the product of intensifying global commercial and cultural and religious exchange: communities which often occupy a liminal space between endogenous and exogenous entities, and which are critical to the relationships unfolding between the two. Second, internal contestation and fissure arising from insurgency leads to communities of the disaffected and the displaced, which are often equally critical as bridges between African society and external actors. In other words, we need to consider African communities' foreign relations in an encroaching world; how states and societies dealt with 'the external' in political, military, diplomatic, cultural and economic terms. Dealings with 'the external', the mediation and refraction of the exogenous—as well as the capacity to influence it—are at the centre of our story.

'Empire' is messy, and its construction is a messy business. One of the core myths generated around the imperialism of the late nineteenth century at the time was that it involved the imposition of order and stability on the savage, violent corners of the world. The irony is that European empires in Africa were the *products* of the very instability across the continent—the creative volatility—which they claimed to have subdued under an imposed *pax*. European travellers, missionaries, political and commercial representatives and a diverse array of chancers, themselves the outcome of profound social, economic and political turbulence in Europe itself, thrust themselves through both guile and brute force, and frequently relying on blind luck, into the crevices and zones of flux created by African reformist dynamism. They often followed the paths forged by maritime and coastal entrepreneurs, in some ways the sharpest manifestation of transitional, liminal, transformational communities: by Mediterranean mercantile elites, Afro-Brazilian investors and cultural innovators, Ottoman adventurers and soldiers, Indian Ocean business communities, Swahili commercial pioneers. Analyses which focus on European technology, organisational and logistical genius, a thrusting, pioneering spirit, and indeed armed, vicious racialism have their place, and an important one. But they only take us so far, and they tend, whether knowingly or otherwise, to accentuate fundamental difference: in terms of economic capacity, levels of 'development', political capacity, relative significance in global history. They also tend to position Europe as the sole locus of change, eclipsing the impulses emanating from the western Indian Ocean, the eastern Mediterranean Sea, the Red Sea and the Persian Gulf. A more nuanced interpretation—one which recognises the intrinsic messiness of human endeavour, and which seeks to reposition both African and European agency and responsibility—is in order.

There might always need to be a debate around the degree to which transformations in Africa in the nineteenth century were the product of purely endogenous dynamics, and the extent to which we can place an analytical premium on African agency and on local drivers of change. But there can be little question that indigenous dynamics at least intersected with, and were in many areas the outcome of, external dynamics; of the rapidly escalating global dimension, on all sides of the continent. The African global presence expanded in the course of the long nineteenth century, and in turn invited global interventions and intrusions. It has long been clear that long-distance commerce was critically important in driving what we might broadly characterise as an African revolution; and that firearms, for example—one of the continent's most significant imports—often shaped military and political change in important ways. Yet we need to balance the exogenous alongside undoubted endogenous processes of change, some of them in train since, or with their roots in, the sixteenth century. The African 'genius' is clear enough, marked by an extraordinary and constantly evolving creativity. But this is fuelled by increased global connectivity in the course of the nineteenth century. It seems irrefutable that there is a spectacular confluence of the local and the global. Meanwhile, it *might* be worth considering whether the continent's century of globalisation constitutes its embrace of that thing we call 'modernity'; or we might question whether the notion is even of much use to us. This isn't a question which I find particularly compelling, as may become clear in what follows. Either way, in the end, it is Africa's nineteenth-century culture of reformist insurgency, its dynamic culture of innovation, and the creative interstices which are the distinctive outcomes of change, which compel us to rethink the nature of 'The Scramble'.

I'm not naïve about this. It isn't an approach without its challenges. For some, this might look like a kind of thinly disguised colonial apologia, a revisionist position which somehow lets Europeans off the hook and places the 'blame' on Africans for their own conquest. The extension of a thesis which emphasises African agency, and often pretty violent agency at that, might be that one is almost 'absolving', or at least mitigating the blame for, Europeans and their own violent conduct. But this is really only controversial if we continue to frame the partition itself in old-fashioned *conquest* terms—a process in which Africans are either 'resisters' or 'collaborators'—rather than partition being part of an ongoing exercise in political, economic, social and cultural *reformation* across the continent, an exercise driven in large part, if not exclusively, by global interaction; the consequences of which continue to be felt, as well as misunderstood. With the recognition of 'co-option'—and thus agency—comes an element of responsibility, naturally. European aggression and violence and co-option of Africans is clear enough. Europe's violent brutality is everywhere in evidence, underpinned by extraordinarily (and enduringly) virulent racism. However, the partition of Africa by Africans was already under way long before Europeans intervened in pursuit of their own imperial projects. Ideas about European exceptionalism alongside African victimhood narratives contribute to the temporal partition which blights an understanding of African history—and, in fact, that of Europe—over the longer term. It obscures the dynamism and entrepreneurialism, frequently manifest in a violent instability, of Africa during this era, consigning the long nineteenth century to the status of a murky prelude, while privileging the twentieth century—rather than understanding the 'late

precolonial' period as in itself crucial to outsiders' empire-building projects, and framing 'colonial' and 'postcolonial' episodes as aftermath and
legacy. Taken together, volatility and liminality lead to new forms of
entrepreneurialism—most visibly but by no means exclusively manifest,
perhaps, in terms of recruitment into foreign militias and armies[36]—as
well as offering opportunities for leverage and exploitation on the part of
external actors. These various elements are not simply supplementals in
the story of 'European conquest'; they are vital to understanding rolling
processes of reformation and contestation and aspiration within the continent, and to an appreciation of the reciprocal co-option of agencies
from outside it. It is this story of Africa's nineteenth century that I have
tried to tell here.

# PART II

# Instability and Creativity

# Act II

## Msabila Ousted, Mbula Mtelya Transformed

### I

AT SOME POINT IN THE COURSE OF 1860, Msabila, *mtemi* of Unyany-embe, found himself expelled from office. He was thrown out into the bush with a handful of followers, deprived (as he saw it) of his rightful inheritance.[1] He had little chance of challenging the coup d'état, given the strength of the enemies arrayed against him. Msabila—known as 'Mnwa Sele' in some accounts—isn't a towering figure in the historical record, even by the relatively meagre standards of that record for mid-nineteenth-century central-eastern Africa. He appears in a handful of sources for a short time before disappearing into the epistemological darkness, his death methodological as much as biological, never to be heard from, or of, again. But he is a compelling character on our road, in terms of both his own story, and what he embodies: the exemplary and portentous nature of his experience as well as of the circumstances of his ouster.

Msabila had succeeded his uncle Fundikira upon the latter's death in 1858. His succession, crucially, was not uncontested: indeed, a culture of challenge and contestation was now the hallmark of Unyanyembe political life, given how lucrative the position of *mtemi* had become.[2] There was much to be gained by becoming paramount chief, and much to be lost by being ousted. On this occasion, Msabila's challenger was a cousin,

Mkasiwa Kiyungi, described in one contemporary account as "one of Chief Fundi Kira's kinsmen".[3] Mkasiwa was not happy at Msabila's accession; so unhappy was he, in fact, that he launched a war against the new *mtemi*. Msabila, it seems, didn't have much military capacity on his own; he needed help. And so, he turned to an increasingly powerful group in Unyanyembe: the community of coastal traders, mostly from Zanzibar but some from further afield, whose presence had so transformed the polity and who had thus far, tacitly at least, supported Msabila's accession. The great adventurer-merchant Tippu Tip later recalled in his autobiography that his father, Muhammed bin Juma, a pioneering member of the coastal trader community, had actually "installed" Msabila.[4] This might have been a retroactive case of self-aggrandisement, but the power of the group is clear enough from Msabila's need to woo them: according to Tippu Tip, he "gave my father [. . .] many tusks from his stocks, and more besides, to give to the Arabs to enlist their support". It worked. The 'Arabs'—the shorthand term for these agents of Indian Ocean commerce—joined the fray, and Mkasiwa was forced to flee.[5]

Msabila was apparently secure. The coastal merchants were invested in the security which Unyanyembe provided them. Above all, they were keen to keep their costs low—after all, trade was a risky business in this part of the world. Imagine their chagrin, then, when the newly anointed Msabila began to question the arrangement according to which resident merchants were exempt from taxation. This didn't seem quite right to him, and so he imposed a 'property tax' on all merchandise passing through his domains.[6] It was not the first—nor of course the last—time an African ruler would overestimate his sovereign authority in the age of global economy. But quite why he believed that Muhammed bin Juma and his colleagues had no particular interest in local politics, and would not be moved to intervene when their interests were threatened, is in some ways difficult to comprehend. Tippu Tip felt moved, years later, to judge Msabila "a worthless creature, really". Muhammed bin Juma rallied the coastal community, announced the need to remove Msabila by force if necessary, and moreover launched a search for the exiled Mkasiwa, who would be brought back and installed as *mtemi*. The final straw, Tippu Tip alleges, was when, as skirmishing escalated, Msabila killed Muhammed bin Juma's mother-in-law. A war duly ensued, and "[i]n the fourth month we re-moved the chief and made Mkasiwa chief in his place".[7]

And so, the young Msabila found himself in the bush, perhaps reflect-ing on the wisdom of inviting the coastal merchants—a ruthless bunch, as it turned out—into his political affairs at all; as we will see a little later, he certainly expressed such bitter regrets in the account provided by John Hanning Speke, who got himself involved in the conflict. But then maybe some blame can be laid upon his uncle and predecessor, Fundikira, who might have educated his nephew on the precedents which had already been established in the vicinity.

For it was Fundikira, himself not long installed as *mtemi*, who had en-ticed the coastmen to Unyanyembe in the first place, in 1852, when he set aside a discrete settlement, Kazeh, near his capital for their use. He in-vited them to relocate from their base at nearby Puge, in Sukuma terri-tory, where they had been since around 1845, but events there offered a portent of what was to come.[8] A local chief, Mpagama, had secured the merchants' support against a rival, Msimbira. They had guns, which was presumably part of their appeal, and for their part, there may well have been material inducements on offer. Or at the very least, the outsiders espied an opportunity to secure influence in the event—no doubt keenly anticipated—of an Mpagama victory. Whatever the case, they eschewed what might have been the more prudent philosophy—*stay out of local conflicts*—and got involved; and it didn't work. In the account told to the explorer Richard Burton, the Mpagama faction had the upper hand for several days, but were undone by the sudden desertion of the coastmen's 'slaves'. Msimbira hesitated instead of immediately counterattacking, al-lowing his opponents to withdraw to safety—at which point, despite the escape, Mpagama abruptly announced that he could no longer guarantee the merchants' safety. Things unravelled at speed, and the coastal community—including the prominent Swahili trader Snay bin Amir and the Khoja Indian merchant Musa Mzuri—considered it prudent to aban-don Puge altogether. At this point, Fundikira stepped in deftly, and the merchants accepted his offer of sanctuary at Kazeh.[9] The fate of Mpagama—who appears in the great sweep of our narrative all too fleet-ingly, but with a critical role in shaping it—is unknown.

There was much for Msabila to ponder in his abrupt exile. A genera-tion earlier, becoming the paramount chief of Unyanyembe would scarcely have had much significance beyond the polity itself: now, however, it had considerable global importance, such was the transformation experienced by the region since the 1820s and 1830s. At that time, Unyanyembe was in relative terms a largely insignificant microstate some way off the beaten track. By the time Msabila came of age, Unyanyembe sat on a global com-mercial crossroads, its capital—a series of interconnected settlements which formed the nuclei of what would become Tabora—straddling a junction at which several roads met. Unyanyembe was a hub around which exciting, lucrative new commercial frontiers, involving the export of enslaved labour and elephant tusks, were expanding. This was the con-temporary commercial equivalent of discovering a massive deposit of oil or gas or gold beneath fields which had for centuries sustained modest agro-pastoralism. The community was now destined for transformation—whether for good or ill, and it was usually skewed in the direction of the latter. This was no mere matter of geological serendipity, however, but rather had required considerable effort and forward planning on the part of Msabila's forebears.

In the 1830s, Unyanyembe was a small, relatively unimportant chief-dom, nestling in the lightly wooded plateau land stretching south of Lake Victoria. It was some way off the emerging, preeminent trade route con-necting the interior with the coast which ran through Kimbu territory further south. But then, around 1840, *Mtemi* Swetu annexed the area of Tabora. We cannot know for certain what prompted the move, but it was very likely connected to the fact that by the late 1830s, the more southerly artery was becoming problematic for coastal merchants owing to the in-creasingly hostile activities of the Sangu. The latter had recently accumu-lated firearms as a result of the very same commerce which they now threatened to undermine, adopting an aggressive stance toward the mer-chant caravans moving tentatively but inexorably into the interior, and waging a series of wars amongst themselves. The southerly route may also have been threatened by the irruption of another new dynamic, originat-ing more than a thousand miles to the south: this was the appearance of the Ngoni, in provenance refugees from the ground zero of the *Mfecane*—

the political and military revolution in south-east Africa—a few years earlier, and now pioneers, entrepreneurs and settlers in their own right. The arrival of the Ngoni and the bellicosity of the Sangu provided Swetu with his opportunity. It led to the creation of Isike's road, for coastal traders now looked for a safer route to the north, one which ran toward Tabora and Unyanyembe itself.[10] For Swetu, apparently observing these developments closely, Tabora was a serious investment. At some point over the next few years—and certainly by the time Richard Burton and John Hanning Speke arrived in the area in the mid-1850s[11]—Swetu was succeeded by his son Fundikira, who built on his father's initial investment, transforming his chiefdom into the most important commercial hub in the region, and who accumulated serious wealth on the back of it.

Swetu and Fundikira calculated that it was a net gain to have the coastal community permanently resident within Unyanyembe. Whether they anticipated the more deleterious impacts is unknown: those consequences included widening divisions within the enlarged chiefdom and introducing novel forms of instability within the political order. But then the opening up of territory to foreign investors—a scenario with which we are so familiar in the early twenty-first century—was in its first flush in mid-nineteenth century Nyamwezi country. Who knew where it would lead?

Either way, Msabila wasn't quite done yet—not by some distance. What followed was an intense and bloody conflict, with wider repercussions. Msabila did not go quietly; he challenged the situation with which he was confronted, with considerable force. He was able to do so because, Speke tells us, he was a wealthy man with "vast resources", even after his ouster: Fundikira had been "a very rich man, and had buried vast stores of property, which no one knew of but [Msabila], his heir".[12] We have various sources for the ensuing conflict—including that, again, of Tippu Tip, as well as some accounts which made reference to the importance of the war a few years later, in the 1870s—but the most important is that provided by Speke, the exploring British army officer who became involved in events, if peripherally; and a little less detailed is the account provided by his companion and second-in-command, James Augustus Grant. If Muhammed bin Juma, Snay bin Amir and Musa Mzuri were representative of an expanding, dynamic Indian Ocean world, encompassing western India and the Persian Gulf as well as East Africa, then Speke and Grant were pioneers from a different direction: namely, restless, expansionist, turbulent Europe, whence people came seeking to understand, impose themselves on, and certainly self-realise in, a world hitherto unknown to them. A concatenation of push and pull meant that agents of change from both European and Indian Ocean worlds descended on Unyanyembe and its surrounds.

Oddly enough, given the burgeoning culture of racism of which Speke was a product, Msabila comes out rather better in the European's account than the "worthless creature" in Tippu Tip's assessment. He was, wrote Speke, "as fine a young man as ever I looked upon. He was very handsome, and looked as I now saw him the very picture of a captain of the banditti of the romances." Here, he is the wronged hero, and the brave leader of men in exile. When he first arrives to meet Speke, in January 1861, he is accompanied by thirty men armed with muskets.

> He began the conversation by telling me he had heard of my distress from want of porters, and then offered to assist me with some, provided I would take him to Kazé, and mediate between him and the Arabs; for, through their unjustifiable interference in his government affairs, a war had ensued, which terminated with the Arabs driving him from his possessions a vagabond.[13]

Msabila related his version of events to Speke earnestly and in detail, describing how he was generous in his provision of gifts to the coastmen upon his accession:

> Then after this I established a property tax on all merchandise that entered my country. Fundi Kira [sic] had never done so, but I did not think [of] any reason why I should not, especially as the Arabs were the only people who lived in my county exempt from taxation.[14]

Speke listened closely to Msabila's account, and was sympathetic. He was all too aware, however, that the 'Arabs' wanted only his interlocutor's destruction, and that Msabila's prospects—despite having a sizeable army at his disposal—were dim. Msabila seemed to be aware of it himself. He was now desperate to end the war—hence his request that Speke mediate on his behalf—but, "though I wish to make friends, they will not allow it, but do all they can to hunt me to death".[15] He was regretful, too, of his actions, telling the Englishman that "he had never taken a single tax from the Arabs, and would gladly relinquish his intention to do so". All he wanted, now, was to "get his crown back".[16] But the 'Arabs' were in no mood to reconcile, at this point at least. Some days later, Speke met with some of the coastmen, who expressed the hope that Speke, rather than acting as mediator, would either kill or capture Msabila the next time he saw him, "for the scoundrel had destroyed all their trade by cutting off caravans [...] and then preventing his subjects selling them grain". He had broken trust, reneging on "treaties" agreed with Fundikira, and there was no going back.[17]

Even allowing for the fact that the bulk of our sources for these events are European, with an inbuilt tendency toward disparaging and gloomy reportage, the war appears to have been devastating across a wide area, through which cut the road linking Unyanyembe to the world. Both sides routinely attacked the small settlements characteristic of the region, destroying villages and the crops which sustained them. Hunger, perhaps even outright famine, was widespread.[18] The area became dangerous, and depopulated, with surrounding villages having "no inhabitants but the sick, aged, dying, and starving, or idiots", and Speke and Grant were warned not to venture out without an armed guard.[19] The army mustered by Mkasiwa and his allies waged a particularly brutal form of economic war, seizing livestock as a means of smoking Msabila out from his various hiding places.[20] But Msabila kept coming back. One particularly ferocious battle, related by Grant, resulted in a "severe defeat" for the Mkasiwa coalition, including the death of Snay bin Amir. Grant was seemingly as sympathetic as his companion Speke to Msabila's plight, observing that "the people of [Unyanyembe] had been fighting against the real heir to uphold the puppet appointed by them in his stead".[21] Mkasiwa would doubtless have objected to the notion that he was anyone's puppet; but the idea that Msabila had been wronged would spread, in time, and his ousting was destined to become a *cause célèbre*, with far-reaching consequences. Speke, indeed, went so far as to claim that Msabila "was so much liked by the Wanyamwezi, they would, had they been able, have done anything to restore him".[22] On another occasion, we are told that the Nyamwezi "all inwardly loved him for his great generosity, and all alike thought him protected by a halo of charm-power so effective against the arms of the Arabs that he could play with them just as he liked".[23] We don't know what evidence, if any, Speke had for making this extraordinary claim; but given the duration of Msabila's own struggle, and its longer-term implications, there may be something in it.

The war continued to escalate even during the short time in which Speke and Grant were observers. Msabila intercepted a supply of ammunition and seized it for himself.[24] Mkasiwa may have been focused on consolidating his position as *mtemi* of Unyanyembe—this was *his* particular war—but the coastmen had larger ambitions. For them, this conflict was part of a much wider struggle. They intended, according to Speke, to move into Gogo territory to the east, where "they would fight all the Wagogo who persisted in taking taxes and in harassing their caravans".[25] But beneath the bellicose bluster, the war was taking a terrible toll across a wide area. "[T]he native villages", Speke reported, "were all in ruins [. . .]. The Wanyamuezi, I was assured, were dying of starvation in all directions." In addition to the direct impact of the war, the rains had been light, and the harvest had failed. Thus was the precariousness, the fragility, of life in the region exposed by the violence. The 'Arabs', meanwhile, sought to diversify in economic terms in order to protect themselves. "Instead of the Arab appearing merchants, as they did formerly, they looked more like great farmers, with huge stalls of cattle attached to their houses," observed Speke.[26] But they also needed political resolution. Now, the coastmen, apparently wearied by the bloodiness and material cost of the conflict, initiated a new bid for peace—and once again (according to Speke himself, at least) called on the mediating services of the *mzungu*.[27] This time, they offered Msabila a sizeable tract of land to govern—the same, or thereabouts, as that which Fundikira had governed—just not in the exact same place as the latter, for the merchants wished to keep Mkasiwa in post. All of this, they told Speke, "can be easily managed". But not as easily as they imagined, for Msabila himself (having previously treated with "disdain" the idea that he might be offered an alternative place to rule) could not be found. He had been "driven from 'pillar to post' by the different native chiefs, as, wherever he went, his army ate up their stores, and brought nothing but calamities with them". Moreover Msabila now had a profound distrust of the merchant community, "as they had broken faith so often before, even after exchanging blood by cutting incisions in one another's legs—the most sacred bond or oath the natives know of".[28]

As for Mkasiwa, he appears to have been busy bolstering his own military capacity, and there can be little doubt that one of the other consequences of the ousting of his rival was an increasing militarisation of the polity. He ordered a number of his "officers"—whether army commanders or political office-holders, or both, is unclear—to organise a contingent of soldiers to assist the coastmen, in what can be read as an attempt to both wage war with Msabila and consolidate his own position.[29] Within a few years, it was reported that Mkasiwa's army consisted of some three thousand soldiers—a sizeable force in a total population (according to Stanley's estimate for Unyanyembe) of twenty thousand.[30]

The war rumbled on. There was another attempt by the coastal community at resolution, and another attempted mediation. Msabila, though suspicious, agreed to meet the mediators. At this point it seems that Msabila had no particular issue with being offered other territory to govern: it wasn't "absolutely necessary" to have Unyanyembe returned to him, "as the lands of Unyanyembe had once before been divided". The real stumbling block, rather, was the issue of Mkasiwa himself, whom Msabila wanted deposed and executed. "Could the Arabs [. . .] suppose for a moment that [Msabila] would voluntarily divide his dominions with one whom he regarded as his slave! Death would be preferable." Shortly after, negotiations collapsed and Msabila swore that he would not rest until Mkasiwa was dead.[31]

That isn't quite how it panned out. The last Speke heard of Msabila was a few weeks later, when he was holed up in a *boma* (stockade) surrounded by an array of hostile forces—"the Arabs had allied themselves with the surrounding chiefs"—and running out of both men and water. "[T]here was no hope for him now," Speke concluded.[32] But he somehow managed to escape this tight spot, and kept up the campaign to reclaim his inheritance for several more years—the resources at his disposal ever more depleted, one imagines. Msabila met his end in around 1865—a later European account claimed that the war had lasted for five years—when he was captured and beheaded by the prominent veteran of the Unyany-embe coastal community, Khamis bin Abdullah.[33] His own energetic struggle, with all its devastating consequences for ordinary communi-ties caught up in the violence, was over. But for the region—Unyanyembe, the Nyamwezi, the road and a multitude of communities adjacent to it and further beyond it—this was only the beginning.

Msabila's is a poignant tale, rich in those perennials of human tragedy, hubris, loss, exile. But more specifically, it captures the story of contested succession in Africa, and the violent struggle for legitimacy. Succession was now hotly contested, not least because of the opportunities on offer to incumbents and foreign residents alike. Ever greater global engagement had at length fuelled insurgency in Unyanyembe, and created the condi-tions for violent entrepreneurialism, presenting the ambitious and ex-panding chiefdom with an existential crisis and one which would have far-reaching consequences for this stretch of the road, as well as for a great deal of adjacent territory. Above all, what transpired in Unyanyembe pre-sents us with a blueprint for what was happening across much of Africa in the course of the global, revolutionary nineteenth century.

Msabila's war needs to be understood as sitting at the intersection of several dynamics: political unsettlement, the fracturing and remaking of polities and the recourse to violence to address contested succession; the escalation of the lucrative long-distance commerce which was itself a driver of violence in the region, in this case the slave trade, as well as ivory; the wider opportunism which characterised a swell of young people linking themselves to particular causes, or simply in pursuit of material gain; the increasing interjection of foreigners into the affairs of indigenous polities. It raises questions about the impact of displacement, and exile; contests around legitimacy and succession in an age of intensifying globality and exogeneity. It is emblematic of instability, but such instability was also cre-ative, reformist, inquisitive. The story of Msabila's ousting involves people exploring and probing ideas about how to govern, and be governed, about how to manage ever intrusive external dynamics; and people navigating the consequences of earlier manifestations of those dynamics. In the course of the nineteenth century, such succession contests grew in scale and intensity. The material and social stakes involved increased markedly, as did the levels of armed force brought to bear in such conflicts; and all this was happening at a time of creeping outside interest in the continent's affairs, with such exogenous forces able to exploit the fissures thus opened up within the polity. From this perspective, the events of the 'The Scramble' in the final years of the nineteenth century were several decades in the making. And so, we will see Msabila's experiences—and not forgetting those of his arch-rival, Mkasiwa—replicated elsewhere, suggestive of a creative volatility which characterised African political culture during an increasingly global age. These internal conflicts appeared especially intense in those polities with substantial external commercial connections, and/or those with particularly powerful military complexes which sat at the very heart of the political establishment.

## II

PERHAPS IT WAS HIS FIRST SIGHT OF THE OCEAN, stretching flat and blue and glistening in the distance, glimpsed on a journey as a young porter to the coast. To see the water had become a landmark on the young Nyamwezi male's passage to manhood, and would surely have infused in him a trembling passion, as it did so many others who made the trek from the East African interior to the Indian Ocean shoreline in search of lucre. Or perhaps it was his first encounter with the Ngoni, long-term refugees and migrants from a southern African revolution several decades earlier, who settled near his village when he was a mere boy. They would have been a fearsome, fascinating vision: these inward migrants from a long way off, with their new ways of war and self-organisation and dress, exuded an uncompromising, exotic appeal. Maybe it was the death of his father, a minor chief of Uyowa, followed by the passing of another male relative, both of whose territories he inherited, and then amalgamated, giving him a modest but workable base from which to do things, to seize his chances in a changing world which offered less security but more opportunity than that of his elders. Perhaps it was all these things which led to the transformation of the young Nyamwezi man named Mbula Mtelya

Kasanda. But above all it was certainly his exposure to the new commercial currents coming from the east, to the merchants following the road into the interior in search of their own transformations; and his understanding of what had happened to Msabila, the legitimate ruler of the famed entrepôt of Unyanyembe, expelled into the bush by foreigners and conspirators, and hunted down until his undignified murder; a salutary lesson in what might happen if rulers didn't strengthen themselves, and impose themselves on a rapidly shifting landscape. Mbula Mtelya—who would become better known to the world as 'Mirambo'[34]—would seek to do precisely that.

Mirambo's life, his times, and the manner of his insurgency along the western stretch of our road encapsulate so much about the era under examination.[35] His revolution is all the more remarkable when we consider the deeper political, environmental and demographic landscape of which he and his forebears were a product. Historically, the region was one of low population density, with small-scale communities scattered across a wide area. Predominantly subsistence farmers who kept some cattle, they would move episodically in order to turn land over to fallow, and work arable land and pasture until it was time to move on again. This was a challenging environment, characterised by thin soils in which people grew crops dependent on rain.[36] The need to carefully manage land combined with intermittent political disputes to create a self-perpetuating pattern of fission, fusion and migration, and this is the world in which Mirambo's immediate ancestors lived in the late eighteenth and early nineteenth centuries.

Things had begun to change—one imagines quite rapidly—by the time Mirambo was born, in around 1840. The trade routes which now snaked through the region fundamentally altered the political and economic landscape, as we have already observed in discussing the recent past of Unyanyembe itself: indeed, by the time Mirambo was a small child, the area was already transforming. The details of his early ascent remain a little sketchy. But the most likely scenario is that he inherited the leadership of a small chiefdom, Uyowa, a few miles to the north-west of Unyanyembe, following the death of his father.[37] This was possibly around 1860—just as Unyanyembe's own crisis was getting under way. In Kabeya's account, he also laid claim, legitimately, to the throne of nearby Ulyankulu, though it is certainly possible that force was involved against a brother who also asserted his right to the inheritance. Either way, having acquired the chief-ship of both Uyowa and Ulyankulu, Mirambo amalgamated them into a single unit, which at some point would become known as 'Urambo' (lit-erally, 'the country of Mirambo'). He used this core as the basis for a re-markable exercise in territorial expansion, creating a much larger entity which sat squarely across the road linking Unyanyembe with Ujiji on Lake Tanganyika. Control of the road, indeed, seems to have been one of his primary objectives, if not *the* primary objective. Naturally, given that level of ambition, relations with Unyanyembe, and, particularly, with the coastal community there, were antagonistic. Indeed the first reports on him—notably that of Stanley in 1871—were largely regurgitated Arab propa-ganda. Stanley repeated the account told to him that Mirambo wasn't of royal descent at all, but was rather the head of a gang of mere bandits when the rightful ruler of Uyowa died. Mirambo took advantage of the political vacuum by seizing the chiefdom by force, instigating a nasty conflict in the area; and then, shockingly, "conceived a grievance against Mkasiwa, and against the Arabs, because they would not sustain him in his ambi-tious projects against their ally and friend, with whom they were living in peace".[38] Before the upstart became a serious nuisance, he was merely "a pagazi [porter] for an Arab", moreover.[39] No doubt Stanley's source meant this as an insult, but it was commonplace for young Nyamwezi men to serve as porters in coastal caravans by the 1840s and 1850s, and Mi-rambo almost certainly had done so.[40]

His transformation began quietly. Neither Speke nor Grant have any-thing to say about him, nor do they even hint that anything was happen-ing in the vicinity of Uyowa. Tippu Tip explicitly states, in reference to the Msabila crisis, that "at this time no one knew about Mirambo".[41] He may have begun to assert himself in the second half of the 1860s. Stanley recorded in 1871 that Mirambo "had for the last few years been in a state of chronic discontent with the policies of the neighbouring chiefs"; Verney Lovett Cameron, passing through in 1873, was told by the leader of a coastal caravan that Mirambo "had been fighting the Arabs for some three or four years".[42] Still, there may have been periods in which the insurgency was becalmed, or at least the hostility between Urambo and Unyanyembe less acute than it was to become: Cameron suggests that "for a number of years [Mirambo] evinced a strong friendship towards the Arabs and even yet maintained friendly relations with many of them".[43] The British consul at Zanzibar, John Kirk, commented in 1869 that "[t]he road between the coast and Ujiji is at present open, and safe even to small bodies of men".[44] But once insurgency was under way, it was ferocious. For Cameron, it all started because "some unprincipled fellow took advantage of [Mirambo's] good nature to obtain a large quantity of ivory on credit, and when payment became due laughed at Mirambo for having trusted him".[45] Stanley relayed what he claimed were Mirambo's own words regarding the cause of his war with Unyanyembe: "'The Arabs got the big head [...] and there was no talking with them. Mkasiwa of Unyanyembe lost his head too, and thought I was his vassal, whereas I was not. My father was King of Uyoweh, and I was his son. What right had Mkasiwa or the Arabs to say what I ought to do?'"[46] There were no doubt incidents and accidents; there always are. But a confluence of dynamics produced the Nyamwezi revolution: the ousting of Msabila and the overweening power of the coastal community in Unyanyembe; the revolutionary ideas about the nature of kingship and expanding cultures of belonging which resulted; the seemingly endless possibilities offered by guns and commerce in inspiring new visions of what an enlarged, empowered polity might achieve. Mirambo had no problem with coastal merchants per se: he relied on them, somewhat perilously at times, for the access to global trade they offered, and his later friendship with Tippu Tip suggests that he recognised and respected the power of Zanzibar. But the transformation he led, and represented, was remarkable indeed.

The substance of Mirambo's revolutionary insurgency is well documented, but worth summarising here. He harnessed the turbulence engulfing the area to create a restless, bristling, energetic 'empire' of sorts, larger than any polity in living memory, which encompassed an approximate triangle between Unyanyembe and the shores of lakes Victoria and Tanganyika. The foundation of the state was an army of opportunistic, violent young men, often themselves simultaneously displaced and inspired by socioeconomic pressures and by the wider war created by the

Unyanyembe crisis; they were known as *ruga ruga*, the vernacular phras-
ing indicating a youthful unmarried soldier, although the term came to
be applied to a rather broader, more loosely defined category of armed
entrepreneurs who were coming into adulthood in the 1850s and 1860s.
Undergirding the Urambo state was a novel approach to military tactics
and strategy, in large part associated specifically with Mirambo, who was
unquestionably an innovative and inspirational leader, at the head of a
highly mobile group of armies; but almost certainly also the outcome of
a conceptual reimagining of the utility and objectives of war on the part
of a group of Nyamwezi military reformers. They and Mirambo himself,
moreover, would surely have drawn at least some inspiration from the
Ngoni who had arrived in the area in the 1840s and 1850s—offshoots of
(or, perhaps, refugees from) the Zulu revolution and resultant 'Mfecane'
in south-east Africa some years earlier, which had involved some major
innovations in warcraft: speed of manoeuvre and deployment, the element of surprise, ferocious close-order combat, professional levels of discipline and structure. A contingent attacked Ujiji on the shore of Lake
Tanganyika in the 1850s,[47] and other groups settled across a swathe of
present-day northern-central Tanzania, where other aspirational and disturbed communities sought to emulate their ethos and practice of war.
Mirambo and his circle used similar tactics in overwhelming numerous
chiefdoms across an ever wider area. Stanley no doubt reflected a popular
notion when commenting that Mirambo seemed to be "possessed of ubiquitous powers".[48] In the course of these wars, more young men were incorporated into the ranks of the army, and tributary relationships were
enforced, with local leaders. Conquered chiefs were often removed from
power, but ruling dynasties were co-opted rather than eliminated, presumably in an attempt to reduce the chances of provincial rebellion, and
members of the deposed ruler's family were appointed to run "the interior government" of subdued polities.[49] In outlying provinces and settlements, a limited form of direct rule was practised, in which governors
were selected from among a caste of "armed slaves" who seem to have
constituted something of a political and martial elite.[50] Mirambo himself
practised royal polygyny on a large scale, marrying selected women from
conquered districts.[51]

The scope and scale of war increased dramatically, and it was used to pursue larger political, economic and social goals—a spectacular shift away from the kinds of limited objectives associated with the low-level organised violence of the preceding era. Above all, Mirambo was possessed of a remarkably enhanced political vision, one which is indicative of the philosophy behind the insurgency. In 1882, in a conversation with Jerome Becker, a representative of the International African Association (IAA), he said,

> Here, there are too many chiefs. There should be no more than two or three, allied with each other [. . .]. If the Arabs had thought to come to some understanding with myself, Mutesa [*kabaka* of Buganda] and Isike, the country would be at peace, and we wouldn't be fighting each other all the time. [. . .] I hate the Arabs, but I'm not so mad as to prefer perpetual war when we have a clearly defined common interest.[52]

A prescient and perceptive observation; but Mirambo was also a violent individual, ruthless in pursuit of military and political power, and unrestrained in his willingness to sacrifice others in the course of doing so. "Iron has broken heads," went a popular victory song sung by his soldiers; "the bullets have broken heads".[53] He was, moreover, a trader in people, a dealer in the enslaved. People were merchandise; it was one of the few options open to him—that and the collection and export of ivory—in pursuit of control over his own life, and that of his community. This wasn't a question of morality, or humanity. This was a question of survival. Yet contemporary reportage invariably describes his grace, his charisma, his *stillness*. An almost mesmerising capacity for quiet reflection comes across in his reported conversations with Europeans. When one missionary put it to him that "war was so bad that we ought to do all in our power to avert it", Mirambo replied that "he was of the same opinion": no bombast, no eulogising the martial prowess on which he had based his own revolution. Rather, as he told his somewhat awed interlocutor,

> he was trying now to accomplish his object without war. He hoped he should succeed and would only resort to war as a last resource. [. . .] He said he would never go to war any more if [the Arabs] would let him

live in peace; for he had been fighting ever since he was a little boy, and now the only fighting he wanted to do was [. . .] with elephants in the forest.[54]

This points to a degree of self-awareness on the part of a man who knew what he had done, and who rather wished it wasn't so, or hadn't been necessary. But, given the nature of the our road in the mid-nineteenth century, it had been. Of course, he hadn't quite succeeded in building something permanent; he had the capacity to acknowledge that, too, once commenting gloomily, "My headmen obey me only out of fear [. . . and] as for my captains, they are good for nothing but fighting."[55] The military revolution, and in fact the social transformation on which it was based, had outpaced the political reform, the time and diligence, required to consolidate those remarkable innovations. He died in 1884, and there wasn't much of a Urambo state left by the time the Germans showed up at Isike's compound; nor was there any attempt to resurrect it at any point. But even this reflects something of his strange genius, and his energy, for he was everywhere—commanding and cajoling and threatening, so much so that the state relied too much on him alone—and yet, curiously, nowhere. Still, as he indicated to Becker of the IAA, it hadn't been for a lack of ambition: naïve, perhaps, but visionary.

The Nyamwezi greenfield revolution was spectacular; but it was not unique. Just to the south of Unyanyembe, a Kimbu relative of Msabila had perhaps even more reason to be enraged at the treatment of his kinsman. Nyungu-ya-Mawe—'the pot of stone which will not break'—harnessed the same regional forces as his episodic adversary and occasional ally Mirambo had, and fostered a similar kind of insurgent politics with a view to creating to a larger, more assertive and fundamentally transformative entity. A little less is known about Nyungu than about Mirambo, in large part because his state lay south of our road, and so he is discussed in fewer contemporary sources, and in less detail. But there can be no doubt that the creative as well as the destructive processes under way in Kimbu country were every bit as innovative and revolutionary as those among the Nyamwezi.[56] Together, along with a host of smaller, more localised insurrections based on armed reformism, these new polities transformed the road, in ways that could scarcely have been imagined when the coastal community of Tabora thrust Msabila into the bush.

The greenfield insurgencies of Mirambo and Nyungu were at least in part, if not wholly, a response to the political situation in Unyanyembe under Mkasiwa and his coastal backers, and these were Mirambo's main antagonists for much of the 1870s and early 1880s, some periods of armistice, if not 'peace', notwithstanding. The conflict was deadlocked until some time in 1875; early the following year, Mirambo told Stanley that "'the war is over now—the Arabs know what I can do, and Mkasiwa knows it. We will not fight any more'".[57] In fact Mkasiwa had held his ground in a period of remarkable tumult; he drew much of his power from his association with a particular contingent of the coastal community, and was all too aware that he was a member of but one branch of Unyanyembe's ruling elite, with simmering resentment and potential opposition located in other lineages: Msabila's, most obviously, but also Fundikira's.[58] At any rate, in late 1876, Mkasiwa succumbed to illness. His successor was Isike, under whom conflict would soon resume, and who would outlive Mirambo, and Nyungu. By that time, however, the communities involved along the road were ineradicably entangled—paradoxically—in a volatile, fractious, but ultimately creative and revolutionary politics, of which these various figures were both products and practitioners.

# 2

# Flux and Frontier

ONE OF THE LONGEST-STANDING, and still in many respects compelling, interpretations of the events of the late nineteenth century focused on the collapse of 'collaborative' regimes on the edges of European imperial expansion, inducing the rapid transition from the preferred 'informal' type of empire to more formal control.[1] Robinson and Gallagher, the scholars most closely associated with this framework, were concerned with a kind of instability. But what happens if we reconsider that analysis from both a more localised, Africa-facing perspective, and a longer-term one? A great deal of evidence points toward a more nuanced, dynamic form of instability, infused with political and material creativity, which is critical in contextualising both African societies' turbulent, transformative nineteenth century and 'The Scramble' in which it culminates. Inspiration is provided by work on frontiers, both as concepts and as physical places, and what it indicates about the nature of African political culture—both state- and empire-building, and the responses to those exercises. In John Iliffe's survey history, the author memorably characterises Africans as among the world's most remarkable "frontiersmen", moving across, adapting to, and "colonizing" some of the most challenging environments—physical, climatic, and epidemiological—on the planet, and seeking to build sustainable political orders as they did so.[2] They had to navigate variable rainfall, and areas in which the soil was thin, and develop ways of cultivating and keeping animals accordingly. Livestock were also vulnerable to the predations of the tsetse fly, which caused trypanosomiasis ('sleeping sickness') in thickly wooded areas, and which fundamentally

shaped the kinds of communities humans could create, and their location. People themselves, meanwhile, had to reckon with the human variant of sleeping sickness, and with malaria, the deadly perennial in Africa's
epidemiological landscape. The achievements of these people were manifold, and all the more remarkable given that much of the continent, for
much of its history, was underpopulated. Thus the builders of those
political orders had to contend with the fact that, according to the well-
established formulation, the African architects of war and political power
aimed at the control of people rather than of land per se. The process was
characterised by instability, and by incessant insecurity. This would become a matter of moral judgment on the part of intruding foreigners, as
we shall see; but more importantly it was a historical reality, and reflects
a distinctive African genius rather than the flaws it was later supposed to
represent. Instability is central to the story of Africans' colonisation of their
own landmass. Here it is important to draw attention to some of the key
work undertaken on the 'frontier' in history in understanding the evolution of political culture in Africa. Interpretations of frontiers in a range
of contexts around the world have evolved over the past century or so.[3]
Frederick Jackson Turner, famously, attributed transformative power to
the frontier in US history;[4] in the African context, others have associated
the frontier with continuity, replication and conservatism.[5] The perspective adopted in my own work is much inspired by Igor Kopytoff's conceptualisation of the 'internal' African frontier as a core dynamic in the
continual and continuing evolution of community and identity, a place
in which groups migrating from nearby societies characteristically constructed social and political orders using the various bits of intellectual
and historical and cultural equipment that they brought with them.[6]

Yet it is important to comprehend the process as being shaped, too, by
the politics of insurgency, and by an energetic reimagining—reform, not
simply reiteration—which is key to comprehending both instability and
creativity in Africa's past.[7] The history of volatility and violent contestation long pre-dates the nineteenth century, of course; armed insurgency,
political contest and reformist challenge were perennials in African
political history. Africa, it is worth reminding ourselves, presents two of
the most spectacular insurgencies in human history, both occurring in the

thirteenth century. In the 1230s, in the West African savannah, as the authority of the Ghana empire was disintegrating, a young warrior named
Sunjata led a revolt among the Mande to overthrow the Susu ruler Suman-
guru. He went on to found the Mali empire. In the 1260s, on the other
side of the continent, the Amhara soldier Yekuno Amlak overturned the
administration of the Zagwe dynasty to establish a new Christian state in
the Ethiopian highlands. Mali and Ethiopia were two of the continent's
most remarkable political projects, each founded through armed insurrection. It is no coincidence that in each case, insurgency gave rise to extraordinary exercises in celebration and commemoration: in Mali, the
'Epic of Sunjata', transmitted orally for countless generations by *jeli*, or
bards, telling a story of courage, honour and the overcoming of seemingly
insuperable odds by this brilliant leader; and in Ethiopia, the *Kebra Negast*, a chronicle relating 'The Glory of the Kings', assembled in the late
thirteenth and early fourteenth centuries by Tigrayan monks, which
assigned to the new regime a holy provenance and bloodline, and a ferocious righteousness underwritten by a direct relationship with the Al-
mighty.[8] That insurgency should produce some of the continent's greatest
oral and written literature reflects the importance of reformist challenge
in the African political and historical landscape. And while Sunjata's 'Epic'
and Solomonic ideology may be regarded as singular achievements, they
are not unique. In sum, these dynamics constituted an ongoing effort
by Africans themselves to demarcate, to 'partition', to impose themselves
on often challenging landscapes through the creation of new societies
and cultures. A glance at a standard textbook political map depicting
Africa in, say, the middle of the second millennium CE will reveal the
continent's 'precolonial' past in Pollock-esque fashion, the landmass
splattered with blobs of various sizes and shapes, representing states and
empires both big and small. But it is also clear that there were perennial
constraints—political, economic, social, technological, environmental—
on the exercise of power in a territorial sense,[9] and those constraints were
both the cause and the outcome of the continual re-creation of politically
fallow interstices. Territorial liminality was an integral part of evolving
political cultures, which allowed for some remarkable exercises in ingenuity and reform. It also involved the positing of frontier zones as places

of episodic exploitation; they were frequently necessary, too, in the articulation of cultural myths emphasising the distinctiveness and vitality of civilisation in juxtaposition with dark, ungoverned spaces beyond. Communities relied upon the flickering shadows on their edges, which formed an essential part of the equipment at the disposal of the builders of those communities. Assuming that not all people could be controlled, and that some would always break away and seek to build new orders just out of reach, at least in terms of direct administration, these would come to be regarded as inhabiting dark, ungoverned spaces beyond, simultaneously bolstering ideologies aimed at internal cohesion and unity, and offering opportunities for periodic military endeavour into those borderlands which were the *sine qua non* of civilised community.[10]

In a landscape characterised by flux, insurgent reformism and political contestation, then, fecund frontier zones were emblematic of opportunity and constraint. Constraint, because they demonstrated the limitation on the administrative and extractive power of African states and societies; opportunity, because it was in the interstices thus created that entrepreneurial communities, accepting (indeed, integrating) the insecurity associated with such spaces, could take advantage of the absence or weakness of 'statehood' and suzerainty, and create new or amended forms of economic initiative, cultural identity and social organisation. In some cases, state-builders or their proxies found it impossible to impose themselves on outlying regions far from metropolitan centres for long; centrifugal forces invariably reasserted themselves. In other cases, there was scarcely any need to impose control on scattered populations inhabiting difficult or unproductive terrain; in fact, there was an interest in not doing so, and rather maintaining unstable frontier zones as pools of coerced labour and as justification for military establishments and cultures. Elites sought to build social and political systems which bound people to particular groups, but existential threats were constant. Sometimes the pursuit of violence, and the growth of deep-rooted, intricate militarisms, were inimical to longer-term economic and political development.[11] But across the board, the very nature of the process meant continual contestation and the need for reinvention. Instability meant restless reformism in pursuit of cohesive identities, continual fission and fusion, the quest for

control over people and access to resources, openness to external opportunities, and these were constants in African history. They can be identified in dramatic if often elongated processes of migration and diffusion:
in the expansion of Arab colonisers along the Mediterranean littoral and
its hinterland, and along the Nile valley and into Sahel;[12] in the rolling
diffusion of Bantu-speaking communities across the subcontinent;[13] in
the centrifugalism of the great state-building projects of relative antiquity, in the West African savannah and in the Ethiopian highlands.
Nineteenth-century developments, up to and including 'The Scramble',
can only be properly understood against this vivid backdrop.

Long-term, creative volatility in Africa can be considered in two broad
strands. The first, as outlined above, concerns a deeper history of a political
culture in Africa which is inherently mobile, the result of the struggle for
control over people and resources, and to master, or at least adapt to, challenging physical and demographic circumstances, and involves continual fission and fusion, reinvention, contest and challenge. This is in
the very fabric of African social and political history. Insurgency has a
long history, from this perspective; instability is hardwired into Africa's
historical development. The second category of analysis concerns those
societies involved in global trade and various forms of political and cultural interaction, especially from the sixteenth century onward, leading
to entrepreneurial insurrections which develop remarkably responsive
and successful political cultures that are highly militarised and thus inherently volatile. These two strands ultimately converge, and spectacu-
larly so in the nineteenth century.

There is no doubting the significance in this context of external intrusions: most dramatically in the form of an Atlantic economy driven by
early modern Europe based on the forced migration of people. On a purely
human level, of course, the tragedy of the Atlantic slave trade is clear, and
the deleterious effects over several centuries on African economic development and demography—as well as the structural racism which steadily
intensified during its operation, and endured long after its ending—are
well documented.[14] Over several decades there has been a range of efforts
to understand not only the impact of the slave trade on African societies
themselves, but also the contribution made by African enslaved labour

to the development of 'Western' economies.[15] The traumas and pressures of this era have a direct bearing on our comprehension and our framing of a long, global nineteenth century, and of course it is important to remember that those traumas and pressures continued deep into the nineteenth century itself, on both sides of the continent. But so too does the degree of African agency, including that of enslaved people themselves, which has been demonstrated in terms of the shaping of an Atlantic world.[16] This work has sought, overtly or otherwise, to understand victimhood and agency as subtly but profoundly intertwined elements of the human experience.

The slave trade facilitated, and in its turn was facilitated by, a remarkable level of dynamic reformism—entrepreneurialism in both political and economic terms—across a host of African societies and cultures. That reformism, that entrepreneurialism, was resourceful and creative; it is the often-brilliant manifestation of African agency amidst some very global, certainly transoceanic, forces for change. It was also brutal, and violent, and engendered or exacerbated existing patterns of volatility and instability. New forms of military organisation led to the militarisation of society more broadly, and the production of cultures which celebrated violence in its various forms. Polities were increasingly organised around the practice of violence against nearby populations, creating interstitial zones and volatile frontier spaces as well as displaced communities which were compelled continually to adapt and reform. In some areas, the export of people exacerbated existing long-term patterns of underpopulation and uneven demographic distribution, placing an ever greater importance on the need to control people within polities, often through expanded systems of slavery. Armies, meanwhile, became central to political authority, or complementary centres of power, which might in turn foment political challenge and insurgency. Groups of gifted, charismatic soldiers with evolving visions of political and economic power could rapidly attract followers and either overthrow existing orders or migrate to create new ones. Such volatility was characterised by remarkable ingenuity and energy; it also, by necessity and indeed design, tended to perpetuate instability, in that rules of succession were often fragile at best, or even—in a number of scenarios in the nineteenth century—non-existent.

A deeper historical trawl of instability and contestation reveals the importance of the Atlantic slave trade in at least partially explaining the rise of a particular form of insurgent creativity across a wide area. We can debate, of course, how much specific states and societies are the direct result of those commercial interactions: in some cases, the latter may have constituted but one of a number of dynamics, intersecting with more localised issues. The rise of Oyo, to take but one relatively well-known example, in the first half of the seventeenth century is concurrent with the expansion of slave trading in the Bight of Benin, which was itself driven by the expansion of the plantation economy in the French, British and Dutch Caribbean. The polity of Oyo certainly pre-dated Atlantic commerce, and forms part of a rich tradition of kingship and political organisation in the area dating back hundreds of years.[17] But what we know as *imperial* Oyo, which used cavalry to expand across and dominate the woodlands north of the coastal forest, establishing itself as a key supplier of captives to the coast, is closely associated with the export trade of the seventeenth and eighteenth centuries. Such a successful operation required a degree of militarisation which in turn both energised and, in the long run, destabilised Oyo. These early modern manifestations of African volatility and creativity involved an enlargement of scale and vision and a binding of economic and political interests, and echoes one interpretation of similar developments in Europe, which suggests that states were at root about the mobilisation and organisation of violence and the power of coercion.[18] War certainly transformed these West African entities, which in turn accumulated the ability to transform their environments in far-reaching ways.[19] We see a similar situation with respect to Dahomey, a ferociously well-organised insurgency whose advent in the early seventeenth century likewise coincided with the intensification of the slave trade along the adjacent stretch of coast. The Fon, the dominant linguistic and cultural group in Dahomey, turned a commercial opportunity—the seizure and sale of people—into a political and military one, creating a centralised system of command and control and a culture of militarism in a dangerously insecure environment. They forged the kingdom of Dahomey in the process. But as with Oyo, Dahomey's very foundations were infirm, and its multifaceted elites never resolved the paradox that the successful insurgency-cum-state was built on violence and that violence could divide and consume internally as much as it could unite and be harnessed for external domination.[20] In much the same period, external commercial stimuli were at least in part responsible for the federation of several Akan chiefdoms in the course of the seventeenth century, under the leadership of the first paramount ruler, the Asantehene, Osei Tutu. The military component of effective governance was deeply embedded in Asante institutions from the outset.[21] A military culture built around ideas of honour, courage and loyalty was central to the new Wolof states which appeared in the seventeenth century in the area of modern Senegal, again largely in response to the demand for slaves at the coast. The Wolof polities were the product of war, in the waging of which they made use of armies of *ceddo*, or royal slaves; this made for a process of political formation and reformation which was both dynamic and unstable.[22] In many respects we can see these political innovations as the result of opportunistic insurgencies, conducted by rebels, outlaws and the marginalised, who in time, and often very swiftly, become military aristocracies.

Instability in the Atlantic zone of Africa took a particular form. But there are cases of a similar pattern in the deeper past of fusion followed by fission from elsewhere in the continent. As the Akan and the Fon were constructing new political and cultural systems, so too was the Kalonga dynasty, which was reforming—with considerable vigour—the long-established Maravi state on the southern shores of Lake Malawi. This remarkable military power was revitalised by a leader named Masula in the first half of the seventeenth century, and he established profitable commercial relationships with the Portuguese in the Zambezi valley. After Masula's death in around 1650, however, the Maravi 'empire' broke apart, with a number of constituent chiefdoms pursuing their own political and economic paths: but this was precedented. The Maravi themselves had come about after the founders of the Kalonga dynasty had migrated to the south-east from their Luba homeland: again, fission, fusion, and at length fission.[23] It is the perfect exemplar of the fluid, dynamic, ingenious but volatile pattern of government-making and belonging which characterised much of African history in this era and beyond.

The role of exogenous forces is clearly critical at particular junctures in explaining, or at least contextualising, internal rupture up to and including what we can broadly define as 'civil war'. In particular, the question of dependency on the slave trade, and the disruptive power of that commerce, is key in western and central Africa, sometimes with devastating consequences for individual states. The model case study is perhaps Kongo, a relatively strong, unified entity at the start of the sixteenth century, with a rich agricultural base and drawing on a range of resources via tribute across a wide area. With the appearance of the Portuguese, members of the Kongolese political elite espied an opportunity: for teachers, craftsmen, soldiers. Portugal itself wanted slaves. It seemed a straightforwardly symbiotic relationship, but divisions swiftly arose in Kongo between those who were willing to link their political and material fortunes to engagement with the foreigners, and those who were increasingly of the view that they were dangerous and should be expelled. Specifically, particular groupings clashed over whether the slave trade was becoming overly intrusive, destroying the political fabric of the kingdom as well as the social capital on which it rested, and whether the king—usually a baptised Roman Catholic—was in fact under excessive Portuguese influence. The kingship was bolstered by regular contingents of Portuguese musketeers, and by the reframing of Christianity as a celebration of royal authority. But armed factionalism destroyed Kongo in the course of the seventeenth century.[24] In Kongo, fractures were formed between those for and against foreign intrusion—although the question might reasonably be asked whether, or to what extent, those lines of division reflected longer-standing political, cultural or provincial fissures within the kingdom. Even so, external forces, especially those as intrinsically destructive as those associated with the transatlantic traffic in human beings, created, or at the very least exacerbated, fissures within previously more or less stable, cohesive entities, leading to the formation of camps with specific views on the very nature of global engagement. Such forces instigated long-running points of contest and conflict within the body politic, which might in the most extreme scenario culminate in the destruction of the state itself, or its dissolution into a host of new ones claiming the inheritance of the defunct polity. More broadly, the length and breadth of the vast Atlantic zone in the era of the slave trade witnessed the rise of a host of armed enterprises, opportunist commercial rackets which evolved rapidly into complex states built around sophisticated but potentially explosive military cultures.

Ethiopia, between the early sixteenth and early seventeenth centuries, exhibits similar experiences of internal fissiparity intersecting with external intrusions. Under the influence of the great matriarch Eleni, Emperor Lebna Dengel (reigned c. 1507–1540) saw the Portuguese as natural allies in the escalating struggle with the nearby Sultanate of Adal, especially after the latter's invasion under the banner of jihad in 1529.[25] But the Portuguese, when they arrived in 1541 under the leadership of Vasco da Gama's son Christopher, came with an agenda: there were suggestions of concessions in terms of coastal territory, and of a role for the Roman Catholic Church in Ethiopia, in exchange for their alliance. By the time da Gama's force turned up, Lebna Dengel had been killed in the fighting, but his son Galawdewos allied himself with the Portuguese contingent and in 1543 the remnants of the Portuguese forces combined with those of Galawdewos and inflicted a major defeat on the Muslim forces. However, this military struggle, and the seemingly straightforward alliance it involved, was only the beginning of the story. Portuguese Jesuits now established a more or less permanent presence at the Ethiopian court, where they became increasingly influential, and would remain for several generations. For most of Galawdewos's reign the Jesuits tried to bring about his conversion to Catholicism. While Galawdewos never did become Catholic—indeed he went on to publish a famous document, his *Confession of Faith*, in which he confirmed his confidence in the teachings of the Orthodox Church— he was nonetheless remarkably tolerant of the Catholic presence in Ethiopia. The presence of the Catholic alternative at the royal court in the late sixteenth century made the court politically unstable; and when Galawdewos was killed in battle in 1559, the Portuguese themselves became involved in the customary succession battle immediately afterwards. They backed the wrong side, and were 'exiled' to Tigray. But they slowly recovered political influence, and in the early 1600s the insecure emperor Za Dengel apparently converted to Catholicism in search of allies. He was killed in a swift rebellion provoked by his heresy, but soon after, in 1607,

Susenyos seized the throne, again using the external support provided by the Portuguese, and apparently under the influence of the talented and charismatic Jesuit leader Pedro Paez. Susenyos's brother, Ras Sela Kristos, converted to Catholicism, followed shortly afterwards by the emperor himself, in 1612. Notably, however, Susenyos did not make his conversion public until ten years later, in 1622. But by the time he did so, there had already been a series of anti-Catholic uprisings, as a wider perception grew that the Jesuits had an egregious hold on the imperial court. An increasingly aggressive approach to the Ethiopian Orthodox Church, moreover, provoked a violent backlash, and open revolt against the now-Catholic king. Rebellion was widespread; Catholic converts were seized and summarily executed. In 1632, there was a major battle in Lasta province between Susenyos and the forces amassed against him by his own brother, Malka Kristos; although Susenyos won, the cost was some eight thousand dead.[26] Only after this serious civil strife did Susenyos revert to the Orthodox faith—or at least issued a public edict declaring freedom of worship, which was in effect a restoration of the Orthodox faith—and then abdicated. An ill and broken man, he died very shortly afterwards. His son and successor Fasilidas (reigned 1632–1667), who had witnessed the bloodletting, expelled the Jesuits, executed the diehard Catholic converts and closed down communications between Ethiopia and Europe. He made agreements with the rulers of Massawa and Suakin, the key Red Sea ports, to prohibit the entry of Europeans into the Christian highlands. Suspicion of, and the struggle against, Catholicism continued deep into the seventeenth and eighteenth centuries.[27]

In west-central Africa and in the Horn, external drivers were clearly seminal, and civil wars and insurgencies were fought between groups over who could secure the best access to external resources, be those earthly or divine. In yet other scenarios, these drivers were less prominent, or even non-existent, until much later. With the decline of the Mutapa kingdom in the area of modern Zimbabwe in the seventeenth century, largely the result of contested succession, there emerged a new military force which sought to both take advantage of, and impose itself on, the violent disorder. This was the famously disciplined fighting force known as the Rozvi, the destroyers, under the command of the *changamire*. The Rozvi polity had external commercial relationships with the Portuguese—the Zimbabwe plateau had long been connected to the Indian Ocean coast—but in some respects these were less significant than the diligent governance of local resources: farmland, livestock, wildlife. In the eighteenth century, the Rozvi expanded across the plateau, in part making good use of the firearms they were able to import, but the occupant of the office of *changamire* was above all concerned to use his relatively small, well-armed and trained, and rapidly mobilised regiments to maintain order in a region given to internal strife.[28] As elsewhere, reformist insurgency was accompanied by military professionalisation.

Local socioeconomic struggles and ideology were often critical. Across the board, political genius was much in evidence: the marshalling and inspiration of insurrection, the realisation of reformism, the power of reinvention, the pursuit of political order and material wealth and the transformation of these rebellious movements into something larger-scale, brimming with ideas and culture. And yet, at the heart of many of these situations was instability: the same drivers which had sparked the original insurgency were still present, while the militarisation of the polity created a fundamental tension at the centre: armed factionalism, competition, simmering conflict. The violence inherent in state-building projects produced reactions, too, on peripheries which were themselves sources of insurgency and resistance.

# 3

# The Age of Insurgency

## A Tale of Two Coups

IN THE LATE EIGHTEENTH CENTURY, two coups d'état fundamentally reshaped the political and cultural landscape in their respective regions, and were portents of what was to come more broadly. These were internal contestation within the Oyo empire, and the disintegration of the Solomonic state of Ethiopia. Distinct characteristics are discernible in each case, but there are also some important commonalities. The long nineteenth century was characterised by coups and contested succession, aiming at the transformation, relaunching or reformation of existing polities, or the seizure of opportunities presented by control of the polity itself. Turbulent and invariably violent contestations over succession were emblematic of deep-rooted processes of political reform and rejuvenation and reconstitution. African polities both wrestled with and actively embraced instability. This was both the cause and the consequence of a military revolution across the continent in the course of the nineteenth century.[1] At the same time, the shifting external commercial environment—increasingly intrusive and transformative patterns of global trade—placed considerable pressure on particular polities, most obviously across Atlantic Africa and the thick hinterland, driving rupture and crisis within polities in the late 'precolonial' period.

Oyo offers an early example within our timeframe of what we might term a 'brownfield' revolution, involving a coup d'état, internal revolt, or contested succession which happen *within* an existing polity, and which are aimed at transforming, reforming or reviving it—although this could also lead, as in the case of Oyo, to the polity's collapse and obliteration. In the case of Oyo, none of this can be comprehended without first acknowledging the power of the military at the centre of the polity, a position of authority and indeed autonomy which had become steadily more entrenched in the course of the seventeenth and eighteenth centuries. In the late seventeenth century, the brutal authoritarianism of Alafin Karan led to his rejection by the Oyo Mesi, the central council of state, and provoked an army mutiny whose intervention led to his overthrow and death (he was burnt to death in a palace fire started by his own soldiers). From this point onward, military leaders nurtured a degree of autonomy from royal authority for the army, and although the *alafin* still had the power to initiate wars and dispatch the army, royal control over the army command was in reality limited.[2] An officer corps was under the control of the Oyo Mesi, but the top commanders wielded considerable political influence: in particular, the *basorun*, the commander of the metropolitan army and the leading military figure for much of the eighteenth century with serious political heft; and the *kakamfo*, commander of the provincial army.[3] Political rivalry centred on the relative independence of the army escalated in the course of the eighteenth century, and in particular in the 1770s, when Alafin Abiodun attempted to weaken the incumbent *basorun* by allying himself with the *kakamfo*, who swung the contest in the king's favour by bringing in soldiers from the provinces against the metropolitan army. The *kakamfo*'s star was thus in the ascendant, but the problem of an overmighty military commander remained for the imperial centre. In the 1790s, Alafin Awole found himself confronted by a dangerously ambitious *kakamfo* named Afonja, and the former's decision to dispatch soldiers against the latter provoked a constitutional crisis.

By the 1790s, the Oyo state—a key transit-handler of slave exports and high-value imports for much of the eighteenth century—was under strain, and exhibiting a serious decline in power. Initially this stemmed from a series of revolts on its northern frontier, among the Nupe and the Bariba, but it was greatly exacerbated by the internal political crisis which engulfed Alafin Awole. The latter is described in the Rev. Samuel Johnson's

monumental history of the Yorubas as "a tall and handsome Prince"—
although his physical attributes were of little consequence, for

> his reign was a very unhappy one; it marked the commencement of
> the decline of the nation until it terminated in the tragic end of the
> fifth King after him. The cup of iniquity of the nation was full; cruelty,
> usurpation, and treachery were rife, especially in the capital; and the
> provinces were groaning under the yoke of oppression.[4]

At the centre of the mounting crisis—ironically, in many ways, given
its centrality to Oyo's imperial success over the previous two centuries—
was the army. In 1796, Awole sent units against Kakamfo Afonja, but
it was Afonja who mobilised more efficiently, sending troops to the capital where, in time-honoured Oyo fashion, the *alafin* was compelled to
commit suicide. It was a coup d'état with far-reaching consequences, for
it cemented the position of a faction-riven army at the centre of politics,
and further weakened the imperial centre in a period of incipient collapse. Oyo's decline was compounded by a steady decline in revenue from
slave exports, long the mainstay of the state's strength. The reduction in
the slave trade deprived the state of critical imports, resources which
were essential to the maintenance of the empire. This was a particularly
disastrous blow for a polity with a powerful military complex embedded
in government, one which could only be maintained through external
sources of revenue and (in the form of guns) military hardware.[5] Like
Hemingway's character in *The Sun Also Rises*, who describes how he went
bankrupt, Oyo collapsed in two ways—gradually, then suddenly—and
wrestled with these burgeoning internal crises through the 1800s and
1810s. In 1817, a revolt in Ilorin precipitated a civil war which ravaged what
remained of the state through the 1820s, while at the same time Fulani
forces pressed in from the north. By the middle of the 1830s, the old capital
had been abandoned to the bush,[6] and the surviving guardians of the
ancien regime fled south to the forest, creating New Oyo, where the ceremony, if little of the actual authority, of the old order was maintained.
The process of maintaining the rituals and symbols of an ancient political
order was an immensely important one, of course, and the site sought to

recreate stability and constancy in a ferociously turbulent era. But that version of Oyo had, to all intents and purposes, ceased to exist.

If the cup of iniquity was full in Oyo, something similar could be said—and in effect was, by contemporary chroniclers—of Ethiopia. Here, a few years earlier, at the end of the 1760s and beginning of the 1770s, the position of emperor, *negus negast* (king of kings), with a bloodline to Solomon and a Covenant with God himself, was reduced to titular status owing in large part to a coup d'état carried out ostensibly for the very protection of the Solomonic state. But Ethiopia in fact quickly ceased to exist in any practical sense, as a range of provincial insurgencies erupted, representing the assertion of regional identities and the triumph of the centrifugal forces which had long rendered the governance of Ethiopia such a challenging project. This was the beginning of the period known as the Zemene Mesafint—'the Age of the Princes', a deliberate Old Testament allusion[7]—which endured into the middle of the nineteenth century, and in some ways beyond, involving violent conflict between autonomous kingdoms over territory, the Solomonic inheritance and the burgeoning long-distance trade along the Red Sea.[8] The Zemene Mesafint would later be framed as a tragic interregnum, a brutal but temporary hiatus in a history defined by the continuity of an entity called 'Ethiopia'; but the reality was rather more complicated, involving deep and ongoing cultural and political fissures running through the Ethiopian highlands, and its consequences endured far beyond the supposed later 'reunification' of the state by a sequence of reinvigorated emperors between the 1850s and the 1890s.

In Solomonic Ethiopia, where the distinction between 'brownfield' and 'greenfield' insurgency is hazy, we can discern a deep history of contestation: any regime that sought to claim supreme authority in the name of the empire—either side of the Zemene Mesafint—was confronted with those who rejected the idea virulently, and contested its legitimacy. In large part that was because Ethiopia's very history was steeped in insurgency, and in the nineteenth century this was particularly clear in the case of Tewodros, to which we will return later. In the course of the eighteenth century, the armed nobility in the provinces regularly demonstrated a capacity to raise ever larger and better-equipped armies in defiance of the imperial centre; often these rebellions were concerned with access to and control over land known as *gult*, which were the large estates underpinning both economic and military power, and distributed as rewards to loyal allies. In the 1770s and 1780s, following what was in effect a coup d'état on the part of the powerful Tigrayan warlord Ras Michael, the emperor—*negus negast*, or 'king of kings'—was reduced to titular head of an entity which existed largely in name only, and in chronicles. 'Ethiopia' was contested to the point of destruction. It persisted as an *idea*, however, and through the first half of the nineteenth century a cycle of conflict endured, at least in part with a view to the capture of that idea by numerous groups, usually ethnically or regionally defined. The contest was particularly intense between the kingdoms of Shewa, Gojjam, Wollo and Tigray, to all intents and purposes independent entities, each seeking to represent and lay claim to an ancient imperium.[9] They could field professional armies of up to fifty thousand men, many equipped with firearms. Solomonic Ethiopia had long been characterised by a violent centrifugalism, a persistent struggle between ideological centre—rooted in a militant biblical vision, shaped by cultural and ethnic exceptionalism—and muscular regionalism. For all of Ethiopia's state-centred royal and imperial history, with its projection of an intrinsic stability over time, the polity itself was, and in many ways remains, profoundly and creatively *un*stable. It was the peculiar outcome of a simmering, endemic culture of insurgency—captured in the Amharic term *shiftanet* (banditry, broadly translated)[10]—and the wars of the period between the 1770s and the 1850s represented the undiluted reality of Ethiopia's history. The tumult rendered leadership a perilous business indeed, and in an age of rolling warfare and inherited grievances, rulers were given to gloom about the state of the world should they happen to depart from it. "When I am dead", Ras Welde Selassie of Tigray remarked to a visiting European emissary in 1810, "all will come again to confusion."[11] Ethiopia demonstrates the institutionalisation of civil war, of episodic challenge and counter-challenge as a necessary means to the revitalisation and reinvention of the state itself. Still, the devastations of the Zemene Mesafint presented a particular challenge to contemporary chroniclers, who could find no comfort, no purifying outcome, in the violence. Instead, they despaired.[12]

Still, in the course of the nineteenth century, the *idea* of Ethiopia as an armed imperium gathered momentum and involved the mobilisation of military culture and refashioned ideas about the past: in this network of conflict, in the reinvention of the *habesha* polity, lay the roots of modern Ethiopia. The solution to violent centrifugalism eroding the very fabric of the state seemed to be ... particularly *successful* violent centrifugalism, in which one particular group under a charismatic leader might impose order on the pandemonium. For a time, Tewodros presented such a solution: after leading a remarkable insurgency over a number of years, he had himself crowned *negus negast* in 1855. The greenfield insurgency captured the brownfield site—both physical and conceptual—and Tewodros's regime involved efforts to restrict the power of the Orthodox Church, which he saw as flaccid and grasping (ironic, given the emperor's own early monastic ambitions and lifelong proclivities); and to professionalise the army, thus creating the backbone of a more effective state. This has been framed, inevitably perhaps, in terms of a somewhat inchoate lunge for 'modernity'.[13]

And yet Tewodros himself was shortly to encounter the insurrectionist centrifugalism with which a long line of his predecessors had had to contend, and was soon embroiled in an astonishingly bloody civil war which escalated in the course of the 1860s. In this period, a series of provinces rose in revolt against his rule, which was seen as lacking legitimacy, in large part because of the emperor's own brutal methods of keeping provinces in check. The Church kicked back, to a great extent in response to his violent treatment of their sacred sites and status. His army was predatory, and largely self-serving, provoking virulent counter-resistance wherever they roamed; critically, in terms of his material ambition, he lost control of the north, including the Tigrinya highlands.[14] He spent much of his reign at war with his own people, about whom he was as despairing as the chroniclers who recorded the brutalities inflicted by him were aghast at what they were witnessing.[15] Ultimately, for all his visions of a cohesive, righteous and unchallengeable state, Tewodros was unable to secure the monopoly on the means of violence which might have made that possible. His turbulent reign, which ended with his suicide in the face of a British invasion in 1868, may have presented the Solomonic state *in extremis*;

but armed contestation, including various forms of *shiftanet*, continued to be an intrinsic part of *habesha* political culture and practice. Much of the myth-making around imperial unity and permanence was the product of the regimes which followed Tewodros: that of Yohannes IV in the 1870s and 1880s, whose neo-Solomonic project drew heavily on ideas about continuity of ceremony, place and ritual;[16] and that of Menelik II, under whom the idea of Ethiopia as a unified, ancient empire took on a new vigour, especially after his famous victory over the Italians at the Battle of Adwa in 1896.[17] The Zemene Mesafint—to some extent even the reign of Tewodros himself—was seen as an aberration from the natural order; but violent contest was never very far from the surface of Ethiopian politics, neither under Yohannes nor under Menelik.

## Greenfield Rebels

INSURGENCIES OFTEN SOUGHT A MORE or less complete break from extant polities—though for sure there was never a tabula rasa for entrepreneurial and adventuring insurrectionists who sought greenfield sites for their new societies. They carried with them political traditions and ideas and experience, and frequently iconography and repurposed institutions and symbolism. But they sought novelty and freedom from prior constraints. They sought to reimagine political, military and, as we will see, commercial work. As with internal contestations, to which many greenfield insurgencies were intimately linked, the latter were representative of deeper patterns of reformation and reinvention which only intensify in the course of the nineteenth century and which crucially coincide with, and ultimately draw in, ever more aggressive external adventures. In numerous cases, too, insurgencies were directly spurred by external commercial interactions, by global exchange. And so we return to the late eighteenth century, where we discern two major insurrections, seismic on their own terms but also illustrative of wider patterns during the long nineteenth century: Islamic reformism among the Fulani in the West African savannah; and the growing pressures on Ngoni society which would ultimately give rise to the Zulu revolution. These insurgencies, and the others which we will survey in what follows, were transformative in their respective regions, and encapsulated the vitality as well as the volatility of the age. The age of creative volatility was manifest in a number of ways. But certain core themes are discernible across time and space. In some cases, armed insurgencies arose during periods of wider conflict during which extant political orders were already disintegrating. We can discern internal rupture and armed conflict, driven by succession disputes within polities within established polities, including states which pre-date the nineteenth century itself. Other insurgencies led to the creation of wholly new polities. Sometimes, insurgency led inadvertently to socioeconomic innovation; in other cases, insurgents already had innovation front and centre of their reformist programmes. Virtually all putschists and rebels proclaimed the need for political and cultural reform, and pursued rupture as a means to renewal. In that sense many were future-focused, even if the notion of 'modernisation'—a label retrospectively attached to many of them by a later generation of historians—would not have made much sense to most insurgents themselves. But many also drew consciously, and often simultaneously, on the past, laying claim to precedent. Insurgencies frequently involved political and ideological re-invention, and historical reimagining; they were characterised by an attempt at political reordering and an invention of tradition—in a way, again, usually associated with the big bang of colonial modernity.[18] Some saw themselves as restorative, and perceived no contradiction in the co-alescence of past and future.

If Oyo and Ethiopia represented what we might term 'brownfield' contestations, at least initially, the Fulani and the Ngoni, separated by a couple of thousand miles, were involved in the creation of largely new sites of political and economic power. Notably, both groups were predominantly pastoralist, and there may be something in the idea that at certain historical junctures—whether as a result of an eruption of ideological or theological energy, or because of material pressures on the broader community—pastoralists are the more effective instigators (and exporters) of explosive revolution than sedentary states in modern African history. Their inherent mobility and adaptability, combined with histories of marginalisation and persecution in certain areas, render many pastoralist societies natural reformers and insurgents.[19] Fulani activists were inspired by the models of resistance and action offered by early Islam, but perhaps even more importantly, by several centuries of Islamic reform-ism across the Sahel belt and the Saharan world itself, and were able to draw on a deeper history of reformist theocratic insurgency.[20] Over the long term, many Fulani had converted to Islam as a result of their encoun-ters with other Muslim communities, for example the Tuareg; many were drawn to Islam, moreover, following their experiences of margin-alisation at the hands of the sedentary agricultural states in which they settled in search of pasture, and which often treated them with suspicion and contempt (as well as imposing taxes and restrictions on them as cattle-keepers). Fulani harnessed these experiences in constructing a more structured sense of grievance, and were drawn to the models of righteous resistance and reform offered by Islam. They could point to the incom-petence and illegitimacy of Hausa government across the region, wherein the Hausa urban elites in charge of a string of city-states identified as Mus-lim yet failed to properly apply *shari'a* law, tolerated polytheism and spent much of their time engaged in war with one another. Above all, as the Hausa became more deeply enmeshed in the slave trade during the seventeenth century, the people their armies captured as slaves to be ex-ported were often themselves Muslim—which was illegal under Islamic law.[21] From the early eighteenth century, as a result, some of the most prominent religious leaders in the area were Fulani.[22]

It is thus no coincidence that in the course of the eighteenth century there were two major instances of jihadist uprisings involving Fulani ac-tivists and soldiers. The theocratic polities which resulted from jihadist wars in Futa Jalon (1725–c. 1750) and Futa Toro (1769–1776) provided models of successful insurgency and a structure for others to follow.[23] The Fulani cleric Uthman dan Fodio (1754–1817) began to preach against cor-rupt and (he alleged) apostate Hausa elites in the state of Gobir in the 1770s. He faced down persecution and harassment as his reputation grew in the course of the 1780s and 1790s, establishing a sizeable following among the disaffected and the marginalised. Compelled at length to leave Gobir—in effect the performance of *hijra*, or withdrawal, in emulation of the Prophet—he launched a jihad in 1804. Within a few years, a highly effective blend of insurgent fervour and military innovation (using infantry squares in combination with rapidly deployed cavalry units) meant that several states had fallen to the Muslim forces, including Gobir, Katsina and Kano. Jihadist zeal reached as far as Lake Chad to the east, and the edges of Yoruba territory, the northern frontier of troubled Oyo, to the south.[24] Indeed, it was Muslim pressure which arguably caused the final collapse of Oyo, after Uthman's successors invaded the northern Oyo province of Ilorin.[25]

The official narrative within this highly literary, intellectual culture was that this was indeed a jihad, a movement of the Faithful, which led to the creation of a theocracy representing the restoration and purification of Islam following a period of sustained neglect and backsliding on the part of Hausa rulers. Yet other factors were clearly at work: Fulani pastoralists' sense of grievance against Hausa farmers, indicative of a powerful socio-economic motive; or the language and culture which bound together many of the insurgents, suggesting a sense of ethnic solidarity which may well have strengthened in the course of the fighting. This was a hetero-geneous movement, and there were no doubt many reasons to join it—as was the case in almost all insurgencies across the period. Whatever the individual motives for those willing to invest in the collective effort, by 1810 Uthman had created a novel polity: a sprawling caliphate compris-ing several largely autonomous emirates,[26] which fundamentally reshaped the political landscape across a swathe of West Africa, remaining the domi-nant force in the region for the rest of the nineteenth century, and which provided a model for Islamic insurrection elsewhere. It was by any stan-dards a remarkable achievement, and one of the most successful insurgen-cies anywhere in Africa during the period under examination. Arguably one of the most striking features of this case was the retirement of the insurgent leader himself into a life of monastic contemplation, with ac-tive leadership passing to Uthman's brother Abdullahi and his son Mu-hammad Bello. They perpetuated the revolution, encouraging insur-gency across the region in a way that would further revitalise Islam but in the longer term destabilise their own political creation, for the Caliphate could not remain in control of the forces it had unleashed. The insurgent revolution involved the proliferation of fracture, in this case ongoing competition over claims to righteousness.

In terms of energy, impact and endurance, the Fulani revolution was matched by events in the South African lowveld. The Ngoni, in contrast to the Fulani, had no history of identity rooted in religious faith, nor is there any evidence for some form of ideological struggle in the area's deeper past. But their own struggles were no less urgent for all that. What became the Zulu state began as one of the most spectacular insurgencies in Africa's nineteenth century, emerging following several decades of escalating conflict between Ngoni groups and borne aloft by a combination of military reform, brilliant if brutal political leadership and a remarkable expansion in political and economic ambition. Until the first half of the eighteenth century, the Ngoni—like the Fulani, again, a primarily pastoral people—were organised into compact, autonomous chiefdoms, which were usually associations of homesteads built around kinship links, whose central material raison d'être was securing and protecting access to grazing and arable land. A series of novel pressures and dynamics, including a period of higher than average rainfall, which coincided with the introduction of maize to the area by the Portuguese, and the expansion of overseas trade through Delagoa Bay, coalesced in the second half of the eighteenth century to create larger, more centralised polities among the Ngoni, as they did among the Tswana further west. An increase in human population as well as in the size of cattle herds appears to have given rise to heightened levels of conflict between these polities by the 1790s and 1800s—violence which only further increased when rainfall dropped below average levels, as it appears to have done at this point. In the process, the age-sets which had been the core structural block of Ngoni society became repurposed for warfare, and developed much more explicitly military functions as well as a regimental ethos. Violence heightened over claims to pasture, but the demand for ivory in particular at Delagoa Bay also drove conflict over the elephant populations along the Indian Ocean hinterland.[27]

As a result of ongoing processes of expansion and absorption, three major confederations emerged: the Ngwane under Sobhuza, the Ndwandwe under Zwide and the Mthethwa under Dingiswayo. In the course of intensifying warfare in the 1800s and 1810s, the Ngwane were expelled northward, leaving the Ndwandwe and Mthethwa groupings to struggle over land and resources, and, increasingly, over control of commerce. During one encounter, following Dingiswayo's death, a young commander from the Zulu—a relatively insignificant chiefdom which was part of the Mthethwa confederation—known as Shaka stepped in and exhibited, at this early stage, the military prowess for which he was to be famed. Under his leadership, the Mthethwa inflicted a series of defeats on the Ndwandwe, eventually compelling them, and a number of other Ngoni groups, to flee the area. 'Shaka's wars' were known locally as the Mfecane, derived from a Xhosa term indicating great hardship, or, in the Sotho language, Difaqane, meaning a 'scattering'. In both cases, the suggestion of extraordinary tumult is clear. Shaka oversaw the refinement of military innovations which were already, in all likelihood, under way, including the use of standing regiments (*amabutho*), the arming of soldiers with short stabbing spears (assegais) rather than throwing spears for hand-to-hand combat, and the development of speed and surprise in assault, overwhelming opponents with discipline and controlled aggression.[28] Just as significant was the loyalty to this new form of kingship which was absolutely core to the regimental ethos. The outcome was the creation of a Zulu state—and, with it, something of an evolving mythology around Shaka himself—which was the dominant force in the region by the 1820s.[29] A Zulu identity expanded almost exponentially, with the incorporation of conquered districts into the state and the conscription of the young men of those districts into the regimental system. The Zulu had begun the nineteenth century small and relatively insignificant; within a couple of decades, to be 'Zulu' was to be part of a region-wide corporate identity, on the back of a remarkable insurgency. The Zulu state was a singular achievement: its prosecution of war renowned, its discipline admired as well as feared. But of course its rise was attended by deep internal fractures and instabilities, as well as introducing a new level of instability into the region, and beyond.

One major consequence of the Mfecane was one of the most remarkable outward migrations in modern African history, that of a multitude of Ngoni groups moving away from the Zulu-dominated lowveld and across a huge swathe of central and eastern Africa.[30] Many of the communities they came into contact with sought to emulate their systems and cultures of military organisation and leadership. These various groups moved into the frontier zones between established polities and created or recreated new political orders, or took advantage of regional flux to settle in new areas and absorb people. They crossed the Limpopo, and the Zambezi, and moved among the chain of lakes which dominated the eastern side of the continent: Malawi, Tanganyika and Victoria; and in so doing, they were, in their way, shaping the political landscape across a huge area. One of the most dramatic instances of armed mobility is that of Mzilikazi, renowned military leader and formerly close advisor to Shaka, who seceded from the Zulu state in the early 1820s, probably as the result of a power-struggle with Shaka, and struck north with his army and camp followers. Over the next few years the community based themselves in Mozambique, then in Transvaal, before settling in the area of present-day Zimbabwe in 1840, where they became known as 'Matebele'— the term was used locally to describe anyone coming from the coast— though they referred to themselves as 'Ndebele'. There was a great deal of violent conflict along the way, but also absorption of people into the community, including through enslavement, and emulation of Ndebele military organisation and culture. The state which Mzilikazi carved out around modern Bulawayo in south-west Zimbabwe proved to be an enduring one, and remade the political and cultural landscape in the area—though as with the Zulu state itself, its very success, based on a vigorous militarism and a hierarchy rooted in distinctive form of heroism through arms, was also a source of internal instability.[31] Other Ngoni groups moved even further afield, reaching the areas of present-day Zambia, Malawi and ultimately, at some point in the 1850s, Tanzania, where a young Nyamwezi who would later come to be known as Mirambo encountered them. As we have seen, they may well have made a lasting impression on him, in terms of military tactics and the potentially transformative power of insurgency. They certainly did so elsewhere, and the Chewa, Bemba, Hehe, Bena and Sangu, for example, were inspired to imitate Ngoni regimental structures and their disciplined, aggressive methods of fighting (if often repurposed for defence rather than aggressive expansion), with implications for the perception and function of kingship itself.[32]

The Ngoni were simultaneously refugees from, and the exporters and disseminators of, new political and military visions. Yet other exiles from the violent remapping with the Zulu revolution at its epicentre coalesced and consolidated for the purposes of self-protection, and in the process created equally novel entities. The most celebrated example of this is the Sotho kingdom, under the leadership of Moshoeshoe. The latter took the decision to move his original chiefdom to the Maseru plateau, in present-day Lesotho, which could be more easily defended against Zulu marauders. The core settlement was later renamed Thaba Bosiu (mountain at night), apparently as a consequence of its tendency to grow in size during the hours of darkness, for this was the period when large numbers of refugees from warfare in the area would arrive. From the 1830s onward, Moshoeshoe's singular achievement was to create a community out of refugees and strangers who were welcomed and integrated into the kingdom, and the new state survived through a combination of defensive skill and Moshoeshoe's own renowned diplomatic acumen.[33]

A West African jihad, and the Mfecane: what meanings can we attach to them? The fact that they date to the closing decades of the eighteenth century is in part a matter of chance—but not entirely; for in their various ways these events were the products of shifting and intensifying global interaction. The Ngoni were directly involved with global trade; and the Fulani and Hausa jihadists, while they were drawing on a different kind of global network of considerable antiquity—that related to the Faith itself—were also at least in part inspired to act by the fact that Hausa political and commercial elites were in the habit of enslaving other Muslims (illegal under *shari' a* law), some of whom were dispatched for sale southward into the nefarious Atlantic system, or north across the Sahara toward the Mediterranean. Those global interactions were thus the cause of heightened instability. But they also fuelled a desire for reform and rejuvenation, or the building anew of decrepit social and political orders; they inspired economic innovation and, in some cases, led to economic desperation. The greenfield revolutions among the Fulani and the Ngoni had in common a marked tendency to inspire extraordinary zeal among those caught up in the transformative violence: in south-east Africa, many more people came to self-identify as 'Zulu' than had originally belonged to that modestly sized community, seeing clear economic and political advantages in so doing; and at least a proportion of the Shehu's army were pastoralists enraged by the imposition of the *jangali*, a tax on cattle thought up by agricultural Hausa rulers. Above all, each of these processes represented a vigorous form of territorial and conceptual partitioning and reimagining, of the kind that would typify Africa's nineteenth century.

The sequence of events leading to the Fulani jihad, and ultimately the creation of the Sokoto Caliphate, and those among the Ngoni driving centralised and militarised state formation, belong to the same 'moment': a period of fomentation followed by the explosion of new political energy— as well as potentially destructive forces—suggestive of a subcontinent on the cusp, between the 1760s and the 1800s. The Fulani and Ngoni in many respects capture some of the dynamics at the heart of our story. But there are many other examples which represent other typologies of political creativity and volatility.

## Volatility and Ingenuity (1): Contesting the Polity

PATTERNS OF CREATIVE VOLATILITY are discernible across time and space. In a number of cases, the creation of new entities or the reinvigoration of old ones involved a degree of intrinsic instability, stemming from the fact that almost all of these polities were highly militarised, with the army or at least entrepreneurs and specialists in violence occupying central roles in the body politic. This frequently had deleterious consequences for the internal stability of the polity itself: soldiers were ambitious for themselves, or occupied the role of king-makers; war was episodically required to manage expectations, never mind to bolster economic systems. And so succession was commonly disputed, and political orders periodically contested. The Zulu state, for example, may have represented a potentially troublesome, apparently unmovable obstacle to Boer settler and British administrator alike for much of the nineteenth century; but in reality it was a profoundly unstable entity, riven with factionalism and beset by dynastic and familial rivalries. In large part these internal fissures were the result of the early kingdom's very success, and the revolutionary militarism which evolved rapidly as a result. Its founding father, Shaka, famously, was assassinated in 1828, ostensibly in response to his brutal excesses and growing toward omnipotence. One of his assassins, Dingane, succeeded him;

but, by all accounts lacking the military skill and political acumen of his half-brother, Dingane found it impossible to retain loyalty within the military establishment, and a number of chiefs deserted him in the course of the 1830s. He met the same fate as his predecessor when he was overthrown by Mpande in 1840, assisted by a contingent of Boers under the command of Andries Pretorius in vengeance for Dingane's massacre of Piet Retief and a group of Voortrekkers in 1837. Dingane himself was eventually murdered while seeking to escape the clutches of the rebels.[34] And Mpande in his turn discovered the difficulties involved in balancing the needs of various factions and of the army, not to mention the encroachment of Boers and the growing British political presence in Natal. Mpande largely withdrew from active leadership from the mid-1850s, from which point the de facto ruler was Cetshwayo, who was confronted with a series of existential threats during the 1860s: recurrent drought which meant, among other things, the deterioration of crucial pastureland; overpopulation, a particular crisis in the context of water and food shortage; encroaching European threats in the form of both British and Boers. He formally succeeded Mpande in 1872. Cetshwayo's own succession had only been possible through the shrewd killing of potential rivals and the careful management of rival factions within the political elite, as well as the support of key figures such as the trader John Dunn, who settled in the kingdom, observed Zulu custom and became one of the wealthiest and most influential characters in the kingdom.[35] At the same time, any man, whether incumbent or pretender, hoping for political longevity was heavily dependent upon female allies and relatives. Women increasingly occupied pivotal roles in the competition over the kingship between lineages, and exercised influence over political contestations at the heart of the kingdom.[36] Cetshwayo was no exception. He also sought external diplomatic legitimacy (as he saw it) by requesting that Sir Theophilus Shepstone, British secretary for native affairs in Natal, crown him in 1873. It was a method of governance which sustained him for a few years; but the limitations of the approach were brutally exposed in the wake of Cetshwayo's defeat at the hands of the British in 1879, when the Zulu kingdom descended into a devastating civil war during the early 1880s which left it exhausted and broken.[37] The creation of the Zulu state had been an act of political and military genius; but the nervous, restive energy and extraordinary dynamism—and advanced level of militarisation—which characterised Zulu politics in and around Ulundi were also its greatest weaknesses, especially in the face of foreign machinations and intrusions.

Dahomey had a rather longer history of honing war and military culture in pursuit of political and economic goals, owing to its association with (some would say existential debt to) the Atlantic slave trade. The Fon of Dahomey were exceptionally successful in their own terms. At the same time, however, a political establishment so intimately bound up in warfare, and infused in the celebration of violence, lent the state a certain unstable energy. The state functioned in a highly militarised environment, with militarism—created, in essence, for the capture of people, whether for domestic usage or export—intrinsic to the operation of the state itself. Challenges to incumbent rulers were episodic; Dahomean kings understood the power of the army all too well, and an unerring vigilance was required when it came to armed factionalism at the capital Abomey. The importance of the military is evident from the burgeoning European sources for the eighteenth century, although the motivation for waging war and gathering captives was a matter of fierce argument between those defending the slave trade and those seeking its abolition. In the slave trader and administrator Archibald Dalzel's vivid if problematic account, King Kpengla is apparently adamant:

> In the name of my ancestors and myself I aver, that no Dahoman man ever embarked in war merely for the sake of procuring wherewithal to purchase your commodities. I, who have not been long master of this country, have, without thinking of the market, killed many thousands, and I shall kill many thousands more. [. . .] Besides, if white men [choose] to remain at home, and no longer visit this country for the same purpose that has usually brought them hither, will black men cease to make war? I answer, by no means. And if there be no ships to receive their captives, what will become of them? I answer for you, they will be put to death. Perhaps you may ask, how will the blacks be furnished with guns and powder? I reply by another question; had we not clubs, and bows, and arrows, before we knew white men?[38]

Either way, the centrality of militarism to the state is clear enough; and, even if Kpengla had ever actually uttered these words (supposedly to Lionel Abson, governor of Ouidah, not to Dalzel himself), his assessment was somewhat shallow, rather skimming over the simmering tensions which such an obvious fixation with war had produced over time. By the late eighteenth century, Dahomean success rested on an extensive programme of military recruitment and training, in which young apprentices were attached to regular soldiers. A regimental culture celebrated courage and killing, and inculcated a deep sense of loyalty to individual units. At some point in the nineteenth century, women were also incorporated into the military system, suggesting an increasingly socially comprehensive approach to mobilisation, and were organised into female regiments.[39] As elsewhere in this period, senior military commanders were individuals—and represented offices—with substantial political influence: in Dahomey's case, the *agau*, overall head of the army; and the *zohenu* and *fosupo*, his deputies. The centrality of the army in the political order was increasingly evident, although it formed only one part, albeit an especially significant part, in a fluid, competitive and schismatic political landscape in the late eighteenth and early nineteenth centuries. Kpengla himself died of smallpox, but his death sparked a bitter struggle for succession involving several rival claimants to the vacant throne. The two senior chiefs, the *migan* and the *mehu*—who were also apparently responsible for the 'right-hand' and 'left-hand' wings of the army[40]—selected Kpengla's eldest son Agonglo, but opposition persisted and at length Agonglo was compelled to offer a range of concessions (including lowering taxes and easing restrictions on participation in the slave trade) in order to shore up his position. But an increasingly precarious commercial position—including dwindling European demand for slaves—led to Agonglo accepting Catholic missionaries from Portugal in a desperate attempt to entice the Portuguese back. This prompted a violent backlash which led to his assassination in 1797. His successor, Adandozan, lasted rather longer, but faced an increasingly restive army and accusations that he was militarily unsuccessful. He was deposed, in his turn, in 1818.[41] For our purposes, this is not about the various doings of kings, compellingly dramatic though those may be; rather, it is about the very real forces for change, the swirl of factional interests posing reformist challenges, across Dahomean society. Moreover, as at the heart of the Zulu state, so in Dahomey, elite women used their power over lineages and their positions at the centre of kinship networks to exercise considerable political power at the royal capital, most obviously in the person of the queen mother, a dynamic which can be dated to, and which certainly intensified from, the mid-eighteenth century, when King Tegbesu relied heavily on his queen mother Hwanjile in consolidating his power. The royal palace itself was in many ways both a hierarchical and a predominantly female institution, where a cohort of the king's wives and dependents—*ahosi*—was augmented by an extensive community of female slaves captured in war.[42] This gendered arrangement of political power had its parallels in Oyo, where the *alafin* was advised by a stratum of elite women, including the queen mother (the *iyalode*), who were resident at the royal palace;[43] and, as we see below, in Asante.

Factional contest in Dahomey was increasingly evident in the first half of the nineteenth century, a period in which King Gezo was perched somewhat precariously at the apex of a highly militarised, and inherently restless, political system. Gezo was all too aware of the occupational hazards of a man in his position: he himself had come to power on the back of the coup d'état which had removed Adandozan, and owed his success to various parties, including the prominent wealthy Brazilian slave trader Francisco Felix de Souza, as well as key contingents of the Dahomean army. In some respects, Dahomeans were wrestling with some very distinctive issues—not the least of which was the especial significance of the export trade. But the coup which removed Adandozan and propelled Gezo to power is illustrative of the broader theme: internal challenges and struggles over strategy and policy, and the riven nature of the polity. These fault lines shaped Dahomean politics, and at the capital in particular the atmosphere could be febrile. By the middle of the nineteenth century, a vigorous debate had emerged within Dahomey over the direction of foreign policy and the nature of the state's external engagement. Key positions crystallised into the 'Elephant' and 'Fly' parties. The 'Elephant' party—comprising the king, military commanders, and wealthy Creole traders—argued for continued involvement in the slave trade, a hostile stance toward the British and the maintenance of the military establishment with a view to doing what it had always done best: destroying nearby rivals and capturing and selling people at the coast. In the course of the 1840s, notably, this faction pushed for the escalation of war with the Egba state over control of commercial highways. Meanwhile the 'Fly' party—a loose affiliation of female soldiers (the so-called 'Amazons'), shrine priests and traders who saw the potential of 'legitimate' commerce—emerged to challenge some of the assumptions underpinning the 'Elephant' position, proposing moving away from the slave trade and toward commercial agriculture, restoring friendly relations with Britain, and reorienting toward peaceful co-existence with neighbouring states (such as Egba, with its capital at Abeokuta).[44] In particular, Gezo was wary of arousing the ire of the army in the event of him attempting to put a stop to the slave trade, the army's raison d'être, telling a British diplomatic mission in the late 1840s that any such move would "deprive him of his throne".[45] To another European emissary, he declared that "my people are a military people, male and female; my revenue is the proceeds of the sale of prisoners of war".[46] He was also all too aware of what he owed to merchants like de Souza. In contrast to his predecessor Kpengla several decades earlier, Gezo was explicitly acknowledging the importance of the slave trade to Dahomey, and the instability of his polity in military and political terms owing to the nature of the kingdom's long-term external relationships. In time, the 'Fly' party achieved ascendancy—not least because of the severe economic pressures confronting the wealthier Creole traders—but deep divisions remained within the Dahomean political (and military) establishment. Rampant factionalism was evident within the Dahomean ruling elite in the final years of Gezo's reign, and when he died in 1858 the succession of the man who had long been his heir apparent, Badahun, was the subject of bitter contestation. Badahun did indeed succeed his father, taking the name Glele, but deep divisions remained over the nature of, and access to, Dahomey's external trade as the kingdom transitioned from the slave trade to the export of palm oil.[47]

Asante, interestingly, seems to offer a very similar scenario to that of Dahomey: a centralised and militarised political entity which owed much, in terms of provenance and development, to the Atlantic slave trade. Military reforms in the late eighteenth century led to greater royal control over

the army. By the 1820s, Asante certainly had its own internal fissures opening up around the issue of the nature of external economic engagement.
Asante also looks very like Oyo, given the number of rebellions in the
northern provinces which might threaten to fatally damage the state. Yet
Asante navigated these challenges a little more successfully than Oyo,
avoiding the civil violence of the latter through a more judicious transition
to an economy oriented toward commercial agriculture, while bolstering
the importance (and the prestige) of economic entrepreneurship alongside
older, ostensibly more venerable military offices. Like Dahomey, Asante
too had its robust factionalism: the 'peace' and 'imperialist' parties which
corresponded very approximately to Dahomey's 'Fly' and 'Elephant'
groupings respectively. The 'peace' faction advocated the further development and diversification of overseas trade as the basis of Asante's future
wealth and security; the 'imperialist' grouping argued instead for military
aggression as the only guarantee of both. Again, however, it was the 'peace'
coalition which gained ascendancy in the latter decades of the nineteenth
century, although this must not be misunderstood as some kind of 'retreat'
on the part of the military, or anything like a 'total victory' of one group
over another. This was more of a rebalancing, a finessing of priorities and
agendas.[48] The military remained crucial to the very survival of the state,
as conceived by the nineteenth century, for provincial uprisings on the
edges of the polity were commonplace, symptomatic of an endemic
resistance to the Asantehene, and emblematic of an 'empire' which had
only limited capacity, periodically, at least, on its outer reaches.[49] The importance of an expanding diplomatic corps, alongside the military establishment, is testament to a process of recalibration;[50] but in fact by the late
nineteenth century, the state's capacity to coerce subjects into military
service—previously a critical function of the 'social contract' in the absence of a standing army—had become severely impaired, in large part
because of the state's neglect of the 'contract' itself. Thus would Asante's
military capacity become weakened, owing primarily to internal sociopolitical dynamics rather than external pressures, at a crucial juncture: specifically, the British invasion in 1896.[51] Still, it is important to note a certain
paradox around gender roles at the core of the state throughout this period.
The militarisation of state and society in Asante by the eighteenth century

arguably involved the marginalisation of women from politics because, in a culture shaped and dominated by armed men, they were unable to exercise much leverage. Nonetheless, as in other monarchical, centralised states, elite women had influential roles in government, most dramatically manifest—as in Dahomey—in the person of the *asantehemaa*, or queen mother, even though there were cultural and constitutional constraints on menopausal women. Despite these constraints, the fractured, crisis-laden Asante royal court in the 1880s offered an opportunity for a particularly shrewd *asantehemaa*, Yaa Akyaa, who bribed, schemed and threatened her way to becoming the de facto ruler of the kingdom, placing her young son, Prempeh I, on the golden stool. The measure of her influence is reflected in the fact that, following their defeat of Asante in 1896, Yaa Akyaa was exiled (with her son) to the Seychelles.[52]

In Asante and Dahomey, internal contestation can be seen to be in large part the outcome of long-term external interactions. But in other scenarios, similar levels of volatility within the polity can be identified, in somewhat different circumstances. The deep past of the Great Lakes region is one characterised by attempts to build robust local communities, to settle land, to maximise both human and material resources, to create networks of loyalty and reciprocal obligation which would endure. In many cases they did.[53] Among a chain of compact but intricate polities strung out along a corridor west of Lake Victoria, there were origin-stories involving rebellion: the very provenance of the entity was rooted in uprising and resistance, perhaps involving branches of older dynastic and cultural systems eschewing hegemons, as in Karagwe or Nkore.[54] But with the expansion of state-formation projects between the sixteenth and the eighteenth centuries came heightened levels of violent competition, not only between polities in a relatively densely populated area, but within them, in pursuit of stability and cohesion as well as the useful 'otherisation' of neighbouring rivals. Ironically, these polities had sought to mitigate the threat of internal challenge through various constitutional mechanisms and socio-cultural processes: the creation of networks of belonging and reciprocity; the murder of royal kinsmen; the attempt to secure loyalty through personal appointments to provincial governorships, and to place all land—or all valuable land, at any rate—in the gift of the monarchical centre. But the enlarged political and military remits of such appointments made them more powerful, and thus the very system had built into it the potential for insurgent defiance, and potential sources of alternative authority.[55] Rebellion was enmeshed in the fabric of political culture.

In Buganda, all bristling militarism and territorial as well as economic ambition, domestic politics in the eighteenth and nineteenth centuries was characterised by reformist challenge and counterchallenge. Successive Ganda elites honed a public culture of militarism in pursuit of dominance of, or at least greater influence over, an ever wider region. In so doing, internal reform involved new practices and systems of warfare. During the first half of the eighteenth century, Kabaka (king) Mawanda pushed forward reforms which saw the centre acquire greater control over political appointments and over the land which came with such chieftaincies, and this in turn had military implications; for these chiefs were also army commanders, and were expected to contribute contingents of soldiers to expansionist campaigns.[56] The result was a more pronounced hierarchy, but also greater propensity for armed factionalism and challenge within that hierarchy—especially as the Ganda culture of militarism honoured individual heroism and pointed to the ways in which individuals might raise themselves up to positions of great status, even (or, perhaps, especially) those from humble beginnings, as a consequence of their deeds on the battlefield.[57] Meanwhile, paralleling the expansion of a military culture, succession was a recurrent problem: new rulers and their entourages frequently came to power as the result of an armed struggle, and thereafter felt obliged to emphasise the rupture involved in the new regnal cycle in order to distinguish themselves from their predecessors. One common and relatively pacific way of doing this was the construction of a new royal capital;[58] but only after the execution of members of rival lineages, a purging of potential dissent. Rupture might be good for the state, and by implication for society at large. The recorded oral history of the kingdom describes cyclical (one might say biblical) familial contests and kabakas needing to be ever vigilant against those who desired a stake in the system, and who sometimes achieved the overthrow of hubris and overambition.[59]

There were meaningful efforts to regularise royal succession in the course of the nineteenth century, and to prevent, or at least diminish, the levels of violence which had frequently attended the death of rulers and the emergence of new ones in the seventeenth and eighteenth centuries.[60] This might involve prolonged negotiation and horse-trading (an inapt metaphor in the lacustrine context) on the part of senior chiefs who championed particular favourites in advance of the actual succession. In Kagwa's account, civil wars more broadly reflected poorly on particular kings' leadership abilities, and were (obviously enough) an indictment of the efficacy of the institutions and offices of state. But Kagwa was writing from a specific vantage point—seeking to cement a new political order in the late 1890s and early 1900s, and in so doing highlighting the evils of unchecked monarchical tyranny—when in reality he was all too aware how in his own lifetime factionalism and at times a ferocious competitiveness continued to define politics at the centre. Nor were these contests the preserve of male claimants and insurgents, but rather frequently involved powerful women as the anointed guardians and champions of specific lineages and kinship communities. Elite women, despite often coming under attack by their male counterparts fearful of alternative sources of authority, were able to exercise considerable autonomy and influence on their own accounts in the upper echelons of a turbulent, fractious, competitive society.[61]

In the second half of the nineteenth century, the glorification of military culture, and specifically the prestige attached to the ownership of guns, created fissures within the political establishment. A younger generation of military chiefs was increasingly rewarded with rank and, by implication, political status by Kabaka Mutesa (reigned c. 1857–1884) in order to shore up his position; but they often seemed more interested in court intrigue than proving themselves on the battlefield, much to the chagrin of some older chiefs who came to despise the firearm as the weapon of the coward and the dilettante. Such insularism, and the political factionalism which attended it, in some ways most publicly visible in the adherence to imported foreign faiths, coincided with a decided downturn in Ganda military fortunes from the late 1870s and through the 1880s.[62] Internal crises, meanwhile, had long prompted the interventions of close neighbours: nearby wars of succession always represented opportunities. But one such crisis, beginning in the late 1880s and involving a relatively callow and apparently somewhat troubled *kabaka*, Mwanga, coincided with a more aggressive British commercial and political presence in the region. This coalescence of dynamics may have had an unusual outcome—the creation of an imperial protectorate under white administrators—but the Ganda chiefly oligarchy which had seized power by the end of the 1890s, defining itself according to allegiance to imported religions, was the product of a political contest a long time in the making.[63]

Buganda may have only been first visited by long-range merchants and travellers as recently as the 1840s, but external engagement intensified in the half-century that followed, raising the stakes involved in internal contestation—and no doubt complicating it. Still, interaction with foreigners was no prerequisite for cycles of contested succession and ferocious factionalism. Witness Rwanda in precisely the same period. Mwami Kigeri Rwabugiri, widely framed as Rwanda's greatest warrior-king (reigned 1865–1895), had dealings with German agents in order to acquire firearms;[64] but otherwise this comparatively secluded state experienced markedly intense, convoluted succession crises and dynastic factionalism, in keeping with the pattern of internal insurgency characteristic of other, better-connected polities in the area.[65] To a very considerable extent, those internal contestations had their roots in the formation of chiefdoms across Burundi and Rwanda in the seventeenth and eighteenth centuries, characterised as they were by coalitions of armed entrepreneurs offering protection against surrounding marauders. These were highly militarised, dynamic, territorial kingships, rooted in the proposition that they would impose order within a defined area—which they frequently did—but at the same time thriving on disorder, or the threat of it, and particular groupings drew authority from episodic factional conflict.[66]

This was especially stark in Bunyoro, Buganda's near neighbour and, episodically, bitter rival, where it was seen as vital to fight for the throne, in order to secure the best person to sit on it.[67] By the nineteenth century, Bunyoro had practically institutionalised 'civil war', reflecting deeper political traditions in the region of organic internal political contestation which in some ways embraced the notion of episodic instability, of crisis and even catastrophe, as a necessary component of ongoing renewal. Indeed, it was Bunyoro's increasingly bitter internal wrangles and contestations that had contributed to the state losing ground to the Ganda in the course of the eighteenth century. Nonetheless, it was regarded as natural and entirely appropriate that following the death of an incumbent *mukama*, contenders for the kingship would marshal armies and take to the field of battle. The leading chiefs, according to one account, remained aloof from the conflict while the contending princes gathered armies of 'peasants' together and did the best they could. It was, in effect, a constitutional mechanism.[68] These conflicts also served to underpin, paradoxically, the importance of good government, and certainly the *ideal* of it: during these periods of violent interregnum, chaos and plunder were sanctioned, so that people learned the value of loyalty to the king who eventually won. A similar process is evident in Karagwe, and in the chiefdom of Bukumbi when attempts at consensus failed.[69] This was presumably rooted, as it was in Buganda, in the region's antiquity, when the need for protection from powerful political and military elites in the forging of new communities was paramount.

In Bunyoro, however, the presumed necessity of restorative violence didn't prevent a sense of calamity at the awful loss of life involved. In the account compiled by the great early twentieth-century Nyoro author John Nyakatura, the sense is conveyed that 'internal wars' were understood differently from wars of external expansion or from those fought for commercial gain. Internal wars were more bitter, the protagonists more conflicted, and more keenly aware of the tragedy involved. Nyakatura tells us that Prince Omudaya felt despair at the deaths caused by his solders during a civil war over succession in the 1850s; the loss caused him "great depression", so much so that he forbade the customary triumphalist beating of the drum on the way back from the battlefield.[70] Mukama Kabalega, having come to power following another civil war in 1869, would have witnessed such devastation at first hand. Indeed the desire for greater internal security may have been one of the factors in his far-reaching military reforms in the 1870s, the chief result of which were the new regiments of riflemen, the *barusura*. If the imposition of an internal *pax* was one of his goals, however, it hardly succeeded: the *barusura* were notoriously rapacious, ill-disciplined soldiers, and their main purpose was the extension of Nyoro power across the region, chiefly at Buganda's expense. In that respect, Kabalega was rather more successful, as Bunyoro enjoyed a resurgence in the 1870s and 1880s as arguably the most dynamic military power in the northern lacustrine region.[71] But Bunyoro's most successful *mukama* in modern times did little to address the issue of internal instability, which mattered somewhat less to him than did the project of imposing Nyoro power on the interstitial zones crisscrossing the region.

From a certain perspective, putschists and rebels in Oyo and Ethiopia respectively might be seen as representing essentially conservative interests, seeking to protect privilege and an existing order; yet in other ways they were seeking to reform that order, even if in so doing they came to destroy it. They were also increasingly globally connected, conscious of the significance of long-distance commerce, whether via the Atlantic Ocean or the Red Sea. The question of whether these contestations constitute 'civil war', in the broadly understood sense of that term, may be merely an issue of semantics; but perhaps it is more important than that. In fact, of course, as David Armitage explains, the meaning of the concept itself has changed over time, and is differently understood according to circumstances.[72] A number of the intellectual definitions tackled in the course of Armitage's analysis reflect the European, and above all classical Mediterranean, roots of the concept, and don't always hold for African states and societies in the nineteenth century. Still, it is worth experimenting with the concept, if momentarily. Not much in the way of sustained attention has been given to the notion of 'civil' conflict—that is, war between citizens—in Africa's deeper past. It is a phenomenon predominantly associated with postcolonial dysfunction, and indeed the literature on the contestation of the state in modern Africa is voluminous.[73] This is perhaps because the phenomenon is seen as a peculiarly *modern* one, involving (on the whole) clearly defined sovereign entities populated by citizens; and these conflicts are all the more tragic and poignant given the dashed hopes for independent statehood that such conflicts seem to embody. There may be, as Christopher Cramer has demonstrated, a robust logic to them;[74] but they are, again, mostly framed in a postcolonial context. In Africa's deeper past, ideas about citizenship and shared sovereignty are altogether murkier, and harder to demonstrate definitively, certainly at the critical moments of rupture. The idea of conflicts representing 'civil' wars would often not have been recognisable to the protagonists themselves, especially within polities which were themselves in such flux. Frequently, opposing groups were not 'simply' fighting over the future of an agreed, defined political space. Often, they fought because the political space (which might itself be comparatively novel) was not a stable entity. Insurgent armies drew on networks which transcended frontier zones and interstices, and were less concerned with the territorial integrity of nations and communities than they were with opportunities for reform and reinvention. As Armitage suggests in reference to the American civil war, the term 'civil war' implied unity as much as division, and "recognition of commonality amid rupture";[75] and this is clearly problematic in a nineteenth-century African context. In other words, just as often, 'civil wars' in Africa did not take the form of those in Rome, or the Greek polis, or within the parameters established by a shared view of 'citizenship'. They involved insurgencies which eschewed the existing order altogether and which sought greenfield rejuvenation, leading to novel cycles of creative volatility and the creation of new fault lines of between difference and belonging. These were among the most potent expressions of the nineteenth-century African reformation.

Nonetheless, at least some of the basic elements with which one might associate 'civil war' are present in a number of our brownfield contestations: in Bunyoro, Buganda, Ethiopia, the Zulu state. It is perhaps less clear that the term can be applied in cases of provincial rebellion when the province in question seeks autonomy, regarding itself as ruled by an illegitimate, distant imperium. But the key point is that these long-running internal contests created the environments in which intruders could seek leverage. At the same time, even those external intrusions were seized upon by various groups as an opportunity to remake and reform the polity itself, representing the latest stage in a long-term pattern of reformation.

## Volatility and Ingenuity (2): Insurgency and Mobility

INSURGENCIES CAME IN ALL SHAPES AND SIZES. But they had in common the tendency toward centralisation and domination: the rise of particular groups, with new cultures of command and control, with a view

to dominating others in the vicinity in areas where there was sometimes—
at least in the relatively recent past—little tradition of consolidated authority. Still, the shift did not necessarily mean the emergence of 'states',
which is often a rather lazy term conveniently deployed to describe
anything that resembles territorial and hierarchical control. In reality,
'state' is frequently a somewhat prescriptive label, which fails to capture
the fluidity and mobility of these entities. Greenfield insurgencies were
markedly common across swathes of eastern and central Africa, where
armed adventurers created new polities, new armies and new ways of
using them. They emerged in the transitional spaces, the flux and flow,
created by the expansion of global commerce; they were the outcome of
heightened opportunity as well as instability, and the breakdown of older
social orders. The story of the Sumbwa entrepreneur and military leader
Msiri illustrates the pattern. He was born with the name Ngelengwa, in
Bulebe, a little to the north of the Unyanyembe road, and it seems his
father, himself a trader, may have visited the area of Katanga far to the
south-west at some point in the 1840s and made blood-brotherhood with
a number of chiefs there. Initially involved in the slave and ivory trades of
the area, and caught up in the turbulence of the period, Ngelengwa spot-
ted opportunities to do greater things, but these required getting out of
the neighbourhood of Unyanyembe and Urambo. So around 1856, he
took the route his father had taken—the route used by the copper
traders—and travelled south-west, setting himself up in Katanga, to the
south-west of Lake Tanganyika. There he reinvented himself as 'Msiri',
gained permission to establish himself in the western dominions of the
Kazembe state (more on which later), and created a hugely important
new commercial and military entity dealing in slaves and ivory: the Yeke
kingdom or 'Garenganze'. From the late 1860s until his death in 1891,
Msiri's was the dominant force in a vast region linking two oceans as well
as commercial highways running across central and eastern Africa.[76]
With its private security forces (absolutely necessary given the attacks on
him from various directions), recruited among the youthful displaced
and ambitious, its creative blend of novel and established political practice, its thriving new urban centre of Bunkeya and adroit deployment of
violence for commercial ends, the story of Garenganze, and of Msiri, is

one that brilliantly captures the spirit of the age. The fact that Garenganze itself scarcely endured beyond Msiri's death is of course indicative of the volatility of the era; but it was the sheer energy involved that produced the fission and fusion and, again, fission. It was a violent, golden age, involving the opportunistic and entrepreneurial carving up of territory and resources in ways so inventive, so profoundly pioneering, that it makes later European efforts in 'The Scramble' (and in some ways afterwards) seem flimsy and insubstantial by comparison.

Across the Atlantic zone, greenfield insurgencies had long been intimately linked to the opportunities offered by the slave trade, as we have seen, and the outcome was invariably some of the most remarkable experimentation in political organisation and control of people and their labour. This was the 'slaving state' model, the product of seventeenth- and eighteenth-century processes of cumulative militarisation. In the seventeenth century, the Imbangala represent an early form of the violent, insurgent entrepreneurialism which both fed, and was fed by, global commerce. These highly mobile, militarised communities emerged in the wake of the collapse of the Kongo kingdom, and came to embody the raid-and-trade culture which defined a vast area.[77] Closer to the period under examination, the Bambara kingdom of Segu along the upper Niger River illustrates the pattern of fission and fusion, of vitality as well as volatility, very effectively. At the beginning of the eighteenth century, a young man named Biton Kulibali took control of the age-set in which he was serving and used it as the nucleus of a rapidly expanding professional army, making use of slave soldiers known as *tonjon*. There was precedent in the region, further west, for the use of slave soldiers: witness the *ceddo* (royal slave) armies in Senegal; and like the earlier Wolof states, Kulibali now mobilised his army in pursuit of a political project. Around 1712 he founded Segu, although to some extent the state was the reinvigorated version of a long-defunct entity in the area which had itself been an entrepreneurial project emerging in the wake of the decline of Songhay. In other words, Kulibali had precedents and inspirations on which to draw in imagining what the military state might do and how it might operate. Segu was closely bound to the slave trade, and by the end of the eighteenth century was one of the most vigorous producers of captive people in West Africa.[78]

Notably, the Bambara rivals whom Kulibali had defeated in (re)creating his state fled north-west out of reach, where they emulated his entrepreneurial spirit and founded the Kaarta kingdom.[79] In central Africa too, the pattern of migration, cultural borrowing and political reformation is exemplified by the Kazembe state, an offshoot of the Lunda network of polities—sometimes mischaracterised as an 'empire'—which were themselves experiments in insurrection and political reinvention organised to take advantage of the global commerce which was reaching across the southern Congo basin in the second half of the seventeenth century.[80] Kazembe was the outcome of a Lunda faction's migration east toward the Luapula River, carrying with it key aspects of Lunda military and political culture and philosophy, and reconstituting itself around the leader designated 'Mwata Kazembe', itself the repurposing of the older Lunda title, Mwata Yamvo. Kazembe was a globally connected insurgency, positioned to take advantage of the trade routes which ran both westward to the Atlantic coast and eastward to the Indian Ocean.[81]

Elsewhere across central and eastern Africa, there emerged new, bustling polities creating ever more professional militaries with a view to tapping into, and further developing, transcontinental trade. These were movements which, under a new class of charismatic reformers who were invariably skilled and even visionary practitioners of violence, consciously or otherwise challenged and eschewed extant sociopolitical orders and explored novel ways of capturing and exploiting human, animal and other resources as well as governing and organising society. They were invariably dependent on a generation of newly restless youth willing and able to challenge existing social and political conventions. As elsewhere across the continent, they reimagined and consequently redesigned the political and cultural landscapes within which they arose; they were producers of new political art forms, and were responsible for the creative flux onto which colonialism would later be superimposed. The Yao exemplify the phenomenon: dominant across the trans-Zambezi zone, and the model of effectual predation, Yao war leaders created novel armed communities of soldiers and their camp followers to take advantage of the burgeoning slave trade around Lake Malawi.[82] As in other cases—for example, the Imbangala and the Yoruba—these groups emerged in the wake of state collapse, taking advantage of the fission and the interstices and the material opportunities to forge new ways of governing and belonging. In the case of the Yao, the fillip was the collapse of the Maravi complex. In the course of the nineteenth century, a similar pattern of local militarisation, and to some extent centralisation, in a somewhat different setting, can be identified among predominantly pastoral communities such as the Maasai and Turkana, where new, innovative forms of leadership, often charismatic and spiritual, sought to arm youth in pursuit of larger economic and political goals than would have been envisaged previously. The emergence of these novel entities in the dry scrubland of the central Rift Valley was accompanied by more centralised forms of leadership and the institution of new forms of military organisation under specialist command. As among the Ngoni of southern Africa, age regimentation was weaponised among the Turkana and Maasai and ever larger groupings sought to secure access to pastureland. In the process of political expansion, of course, new elements of conflict and insecurity were introduced into the Rift Valley.[83] In Angola, among the Ovimbundu, who had a longer history of commercial interaction with the Portuguese, and the Chokwe, who were relative newcomers from the mid-nineteenth century onward, there was new entrepreneurial vigour and the targeted use of violence in pursuit of profit.[84] In the Zambezi valley, the *prazeiros*, the plantation owners descended from early Portuguese settlers, had by the nineteenth century largely shaken off any semblance of metropolitan control from Lisbon and developed into an Afro-European community which organised 'Chikunda' armies, private forces comprised of slave-soldiers aimed at imposing the *prazeiros'* influence over a wide commercial catchment area.[85] Each of these exemplifies the tendency toward armed entrepreneurialism, military adventurism, in the middle decades of the nineteenth century; frequently, if not exclusively, driven by global commerce.

In other cases, communities sought to rejuvenate themselves in the shadows of moribund states and empires, occupying those same spaces once governed by hegemonic potentates but doing so in such a way as suggests genuine reformism and innovation. The city-states of the Yoruba, asserting themselves in the wake of Oyo's collapse and in many ways seeking to reclaim and refashion the political iconography and symbolism of that empire, did so between the 1810s and the 1830s. Initially the main axis of conflict was between the old Oyo core and the insurrectionist Ilorin province, the latter's rebellion assisted by Fulani holy warriors and thus a combination of centrifugal discontent and the influence of the new power-bloc in the region, Sokoto. This was soon compounded by a new war between Owu on one side and Ife and Ijebu on the other. With the abandonment of the old imperial capital in the early 1830s, the Yoruba wars reached a new level of intensity. Many of these city-states had innovation thrust upon them, borne of necessity, for in some cases new settlements were the outcome of destitution and migration and wider unsettlement. As a contemporary report observed of Abeokuta, the Egba capital, in 1861,

> Abbeokuta is the name applied to a collection of Towns each of them the nucleus, or rather residue of a tribe which depopulated and expelled in former times by internecine or general war from its ancient farms and hereditaments was compelled to fly and ultimately settling down in a rocky district founded a new town and colony called after the former one.[86]

Dynamism and insecurity went hand-in-hand, typically—the story of so much of Africans' nineteenth century. These insurgents were well-armed revolutionaries, in many respects epitomising a wider military revolution across the continent.[87] Ijaye and the Egba were mainly engaged in warfare with Dahomey, which, having overthrown its former subordinate position to Oyo, was resurgent to the west and keen to take advantage of what it saw as Yoruba disarray. Indeed Dahomean aggression almost certainly drove the kinds of military and political innovation which came to characterise the Yoruba microstates of the area. The Ijebu, just to the north of Lagos and commercially well positioned, sought to soak up the displaced and the enslaved resulting from this violence, and were assiduous exporters of people in exchange for firearms, among other commodities. But it was Ibadan, like Abeokuta a nineteenth-century creation, which emerged as the most powerful city-state from the 1830s and 1840s, waging successful wars with the Fulani, Egba and Ijaye, the last being effectively demolished as an independent presence at the beginning of the 1860s. From the late 1870s, several remaining Yoruba polities formed an alliance in an attempt to curb Ibadan's power. The key point here is that Ijaye, the Egba, the Ijebu and Ibadan represented an energetic new form of militarised urbanism, competing with one another over access to vital gun imports. They were governed by specialists in war who commanded armies comprising young professionals—'war boys'—adept at the use of imported weaponry, including both matchlocks and, increasingly, flintlocks. But these were no *ingénus*. They belonged to communities which carried forward a wealth of experience of intensive globalism, and of political leadership—increasingly organised around urban sites, as in the case of Oyo-ile itself[88]—which was perhaps a millennium in the making, but which espied opportunities for new ways of being independent agents. These micro-polities remade themselves in the turbulent nineteenth century, and in the process remade the political landscape of present-day south-west Nigeria, fighting a series of wars amongst themselves until the 1890s, aimed at both political dominance and control of burgeoning and lucrative commerce along the Atlantic seaboard.[89]

In the Ethiopian highlands and, crucially, the adjacent escarpments and lowlands, a similar process unfolded. We have discussed Solomonic Ethiopia in the context of internal contest; but the story of Kassa—later Emperor Tewodros II—exhibits many of the characteristics of the greenfield insurgency, albeit one which comes to co-opt a much older political imaginary. The story of the early part of Kassa's life is one of family drama, with the young man, born around 1818, of minor nobility, robbed of his rightful inheritance following familial machinations and, after a period of religious training, compelled to fall back on *shiftanet* (banditry) to make his way in an uncertain world. But he was also (and perhaps more importantly) a product of the frontier, which had long shaped the very essence of Ethiopian political culture. In his case, he and his followers were the outcomes of a very particular stretch of frontier, Qwara in the northwest highlands, abutting the hot lowlands of the Nile basin in modern Sudan, and it is in this rugged but creative environment that his insurgency fomented. In this borderland, part of a network of contested frontiers that made up the geopolitical fabric of the Zemene Mesafint, he encountered well-organised men with flintlocks coming from the north: by the 1840s, the Egyptians' advance up the Nile was well under way. Kassa knew them as 'Turks', based on his understanding that Egypt was at least nominally part of the Ottoman Empire; whoever they were, they offered a glimpse of a possible military future, and Kassa wanted to be part of it. Kassa's insurgent army became better equipped and trained, and began to win decisive engagements. As momentum gathered during the 1840s and into the early 1850s, Kassa and his enlarged army came to dominate an ever wider swathe of the highlands, enabling him to lay claim to—and win—the imperial throne, as Tewodros II, as he was crowned in 1855. This was an insurgency which would culminate in the reformation of the state itself, and lead to the emergence of an Ethiopian polity which would draw heavily on antiquity but which was in many respects a wholly new, even revolutionary, entity.[90]

Still, to focus solely on those conventionally *habesha*—that is to say, central and northern highland—processes would be to neglect other political and cultural creatives who were equally, indeed if not more, significant in the making of modern Ethiopia. In the course of the seventeenth and eighteenth centuries, and still evolving in the early nineteenth, Oromo migrations were remapping the southern and central massif. Many Oromo became acculturated into *habesha* society and politics, converting to Christianity—a defining feature of semitic highland identity—and contributing to the armies so important to the exercise of territorial influence. But others, often Muslim, created their own polities, evolving and reforming pre-existing ideas about social, administrative and military organisation for the purpose, and by the middle decades of the nineteenth century these entities abutted the southern rim of the *habesha* kingdoms, mostly obviously Shewa.[91] These creations were as innovative in their form and as important in their impact in the moulding of the nineteenth-century entity known as Ethiopia—and arguably, over the longer term, even more important. In fact, their very presence, as significant as his interaction with the 'Turks' to the north, fired Tewodros's own mission to preserve and expand what he (and other highlanders) perceived as the Solomonic essence of the imperial state.

Faith and ideology were also at play in West Africa in the same period, notably among Islamic rebels inspired by the model provided by Sokoto. Fulani insurgents were instrumental in the revitalisation of Islam in Bornu in the early years of the nineteenth century, for example.[92] Later on, the Tukolor state was also the outcome of a jihadist uprising in 1852 led by al-Hajj Umar Tal, an eminent Muslim scholar who had undertaken the *hajj* and visited Sokoto, and who preached with increasing vigour against infidel influences and unworthy irreligious Muslims. One of his most significant achievements was to hold together a somewhat disparate army comprising an elite cavalry corps of dedicated Muslims, the *talaba*; later enslaved converts serving as soldiers, the *sofas*; and a large conscript contingent, the *tuburru*, who were not generally known for their religious devotion. Yet under the banner of rejuvenated Islam, Umar Tal appealed to, and won the support of, a range of groups who had been marginalised by existing political orders and displaced by seemingly cyclical violence across the region. Umar Tal captured a swathe of Bambara territory, and in a short space of time Tukolor encompassed land stretching from present-day southern Mali to Guinea. Its rise had been brilliant, and rapid; but the state itself was comparatively rickety, and was never quite able to consolidate, nor to fully address the socioeconomic, ethnic and cultural fractures encompassed within it. The army, moreover, remained riven by the internal tensions that Umar Tal had managed temporarily to overcome in pursuit of revolutionary theocracy. That theocracy, moreover, overreached itself in attacking a neighbouring Muslim state, Masina, with its capital at Hamdalahi, in 1862. Umar Tal's capture of Hamdalahi provoked a furious response, and he was soon confronted, as was so often the case, with a fresh insurgency fuelled by a sense of outrage and the perception of Tukolor illegitimacy. Umar Tal was killed in 1864, and it was once again the issue of contested succession which undermined the cohesion of the state: in this case, conflict erupted between his nephew, Tijani, and his son, Ahmadu Seku, and within a few years Tukolor had largely ceased to exist.[93] In the vortex created by its implosion, a new wave of jihadist violence swept through the Wolof of the Senegambia region, leading to widespread destruction, but also the conversion of large numbers of Wolof.[94]

The pattern of transformative insurgency was well established across the region; indeed, in some respects it might be viewed as a West African Sahelian speciality. Over a few creative, turbulent decades in the nineteenth century, jihadist uprisings inspired others, intersecting with one another and causing ripples of fracture and driving fusion, often short-lived, across a vast region. In the 1870s another insurrectionist state-building exercise was under way between the upper Niger and the area of present-day Liberia, this time under the charismatic leadership of the Mandinke Samori Ture, whose family came from the transregional West African commercial class known as *wangara*. He himself had been a slave-soldier—apparently offering his service in that capacity to liberate his mother, who had been seized in a slave raid—before climbing the ranks of military command in the service of various warlords. His schooling in the art of politics and war took place amidst the jihadist violence in the area of Toron and Konyan (Samori's birthplace) under Mori-Ule Sise, whose death in 1845 left a vacuum which was in time filled by Samori himself. Commanding ever larger armies, he began to assert his own political authority over tracts of land, and conquest—the result of innovative military tactics, and a well-organised system of provincial recruitment—emboldened him to fashion his own polity using a network of subjugated local leaders who had pledged allegiance. Not unlike Tewodros in the Ethiopian highlands, he tapped into the power of historical vision: in this case, Sunjata's great insurgency to found the Mali empire six centuries earlier. He also used Islam—later in his career he took the title *imam*—but much less so than Tukolor, or Sokoto before it. Much more important was the cohesiveness engendered by commerce (he was enthusiastically supported by other *wangara*), by sheer military might and by the judicious use of violence against wayward 'subjects.'[95]

The term 'empire' is often used (and often in scare quotes) to describe the achievements of Umar Tal and Samori. But if we are to consider their creations as such, they exhibited very particular West African characteristics, and the term must be understood as meaning something quite different from its classical or European application. They were rapidly realised, brilliantly and violently executed explosions of political, and at various points religious, energy; but they were riddled with fissures and tensions, and were as unstable as they were spectacular. To consider them 'failed states', in that context, is to miss their point: their point was not to build enduring political orders, or at least, this was in no way a priority. Their purpose, rather, was to seize opportunities, tap into the energy of various constituencies, create change through armed power: to be entrepreneurial. Their entire point was their restlessness; their consequences included the generation of further opportunities—as well as risk, of course, as Samori would later discover. The French advance into the Sahel would soon constitute Samori's greatest existential threat, and French officers came to see his state as the single largest obstacle to their imperial ambitions in the region. Other insurgencies, much more Islamic in their identities and motivations, arose at least partly through the need to organise against foreign incursion: Abd al-Qadir in Algeria; Sidi Muhammad ibn Ali al-Sanusi in Libya; Muhammad Ahmad ibn Abdallah in Sudan. Al-Qadir organised men on horseback from the desert edge, asserted the need to rejuvenate the Muslim faith—recognising the motivational power such a call could have—and mobilised Sufi ideas about deference in order to create a broad front against the French in Algiers after 1830. Qadiriyya resistance continued for decades even after al-Qadir's capture and exile at the hands of the French in 1847.[96] Al-Sanusi founded the Sanusiyya in the same decade, likewise creating or reviving networks of belonging which linked the communities dispersed across the Fezzan, Cyrenaica and the central Sahara. The movement was at least ostensibly concerned to resist the Ottoman authorities in the coastal provinces, whom its members regarded as not true to Islam—though Sanusi merchants became the chief suppliers of slaves to Tripoli. Decades later, the Sanusiyya would lead resistance to the Italian presence in Tripolitania and Cyrenaica, with considerable success.[97] Between the 1820s and the 1870s, in the face of the Egyptian penetration of the upper Nile valley, reformist Sufi brotherhoods proliferated and became ever more popular, especially as the Egyptians brought with them their own clerics and holy orders. While an energetic Sufism in some areas dated to the late eighteenth century, it became one of the most important manifestations of anti-Egyptian sentiment. Some, such as the Khatmiyya, chose to work with the Egyptians, and became politically important in other ways as a result; but many encouraged militant resistance: the Majdhubiyya, for example, the reformist movement introduced into the region by Muhammad al-Majdhub, and the Sammaniyya, who only started working in the area around the beginning of the nineteenth century under Ahmad al-Tayyib ibn al-Bashir, but who were increasingly rooted in local communities and disengaged from the political elites hovering above them.[98] It was a member of the Sammaniyya, Muhammad Ahmad ibn Abdallah, who in 1881 proclaimed himself the Mahdi—the messianic figure in Shi'a doctrine—and launched an insurgency against the Turkish-speaking elite prominent in the modernising Egyptian administration, with the aim of creating a new theocracy which drew on long-standing ideas about the restoration of 'true' or 'pure' Islam. The epicentre of the uprising was among the Baqqara, the Arabic-speaking pastoralists of Kordofan and the Nuba mountains, who conquered much of the region to the west of Khartoum in 1882–83. Their success inspired others, notably the Arab groups on the banks of the Nile itself, to join in.[99] As in many other cases in the preceding decades, the result was an expansive but unsteady new entity, a coalescence of communities and concerns, and after the Mahdi's death in 1885 his successor Khalifa Abdallahi was more secularly concerned with effective administration in the face of external threats than with the perpetuation and export of Islamic revolution.

In many of these scenarios, novel dynamics—the infidel threat, as well as (paradoxically) the commercial opportunities the infidel represented—were at work. But in each case, too, the insurgency adhered to a deep-rooted pattern across Sahelian and Sudanic Africa: the mobilisation of Islam and the promise of its renewal, and the direct appeal to the marginalised and persecuted on contested, shifting peripheries. Muhammad Ali in Egypt was aiming at something more secular, perhaps, even, something more permanent, in what we might term a hybrid insurgency. An army officer in Ottoman service, born in Macedonia to an Albanian family, Muhammad Ali took advantage of the turmoil in Egypt in the wake of the Anglo–French conflict over the Nile Delta to seize control of the nominally Ottoman province in 1805. In the years that followed, he and a circle of ambitious, visionary reformers created a new military and political order which involved a sophisticated bureaucracy borrowing heavily from the European model (and using European advisors). It led to the creation of an army of some two hundred thousand men, equipped with vast numbers of imported firearms, which was deployed in pursuit of territorial expansion: Egypt under Muhammad Ali effectively seized control of the Red Sea, including wresting control of the

Holy Places of Islam, Mecca and Medina, from the Wahhabis who were pushed out of western Arabia. Indeed Egyptian imperialism was at least in part rooted in a hostility to revivalist Islam, viewed in Cairo as an obstacle to the kind of military-commercial state envisaged by Muhammad Ali (and his successors). Cairo controlled the vibrant Red Sea ports of Suakin and Massawa from 1846, when they were leased to the Egyptian administration by the Ottomans. There was also a landward surge to the south, up the Nile Valley into Sudan, in the process defeating the Funj sultanate and overcoming Mamluk resistance in the early 1820s. This remarkable project involved the carving out of a vast 'empire' which resembled the exercises in military and commercial partition taking place further south among the Nyamwezi, the Lunda, the Yao. This was even more territorially ambitious, and following the founding of Khartoum, at the confluence of the Blue and White Niles, in 1824, Egyptian armed entrepreneurialism pressed southward to nudge the edges of embattled Ethiopia and the northern lacustrine states. Muhammad Ali's grand project also involved some remarkable economic reform, to which we turn in greater detail later, as he sought an expanded export economy based on cotton, an autochthonous industrial base, and extended taxation to pay for his distinctive brand of revolutionary imperialism. When his forces invaded Palestine and Syria in the early 1830s, however, the British and French governments decided they had seen enough, and in the decade that followed inflicted a series of defeats on the Egyptian army designed to clip Muhammad Ali's wings. He had been effectively pegged back by the early 1840s, his army reduced to eighteen thousand under the terms of a punitive treaty, and his plans for a modern economy thwarted. Muhammad Ali himself died in 1849.[100] It was a portent of how certain European powers might be prepared to act if they perceived a threat in the ambitions of new, emerging African elites—especially in areas, such as the Levant, deemed to be within their spheres of interest, for whatever reason; but, leaving aside for the moment its somewhat bathetic ending, Muhammad Ali's Egyptian experiment was emblematic of the transformative energy erupting across the continent, an energy which was involved in partitioning and reconfiguring the political and social landscape.

———

THE DISTINCTION BETWEEN brownfield contests (which took place within more or less well-established entities) and greenfield insurrections (aimed at the creation of substantially novel political and cultural and economic entities) is nonetheless rarely a firm one, in the African context: they are not mutually exclusive, and it is exceedingly rare to identify one which doesn't have at least an element of the other. But the cardinal point is that insurgencies which were aimed at the creation of novel communities, or which eschewed existing political orders and aspired to secede from them, and those which posed a direct challenge to extant political systems with a view to capturing and reforming those systems, represented patterns of creative volatility. It is creative volatility which characterises much of Africa's transformative nineteenth century, and which helps contextualise the partition of the continent just as much as—if not even more than—the possession of superior technology on the part of ambitious foreigners.

In these turbulent decades, violent insurgency served multiple purposes. It was aimed at the creation, consolidation, redistribution of wealth. By the same token, it was concerned with the management of people, the real wealth of every community. Above all, this was about people exploring ideas about how to govern, and be governed, at the same time as managing intensifying external dynamics. This was instability as experimentation, the probing of boundaries, and the making of new ones, both physical and conceptual. Insurgency was also aimed—paradoxically, perhaps, given the outcome—at cohesion, unity and in at least some cases (if by no means all), the establishment of stronger, more permanent, more stable polities. In this, it can be safely argued, success was limited: the very nature of insurgent projects, as well as of much African political culture in the eighteenth and nineteenth centuries, rendered enduring cohesion difficult if not downright impossible. But the outcome was invariably spectacular: embodied in the breathtaking mobility and innovation of Msiri or Mzilikazi, *this* was the true 'partition' of Africa, the reconfiguration of space and form and belonging—on which later European territorial and political demarcations were overlaid. Nor is it the case that violent insurgency, chronic instability, precluded anything that can be described as a higher human achievement: art, or thought. Far from it. Men and women working in craft, and sculpture, as well as those inhabiting worlds of public memory and historical ceremony, realised great cultural achievements throughout this era. Sometimes they did so at the very heart of political culture, seeking to create work which could assist in stabilisation through memorialisation, depicting founding figures in bronze or clay, or constructing the chronicles around heroes. But sometimes they did so in liminal, turbulent, transitional spaces, at the edges of things, perhaps transgressive, seeking the reform or representation which many insurgents themselves sought.

Because of the high level of militarisation involved in these new political projects, the increasing significance of military establishments and the widening cultural and practical application of violence, the political entities involved were intrinsically volatile, and the nature of the leadership involved, inspiring intense personal loyalty for relatively short periods of time, meant that rules of succession were neglected in favour of dynamic individualism. Indeed, it can be safely proposed that military reformism and economic ambition invariably outran administrative and institutional reform: not that the latter were completely absent—the evidence is clear on that point—but that efforts in that direction were slower to develop, and were less of a priority, than those made with a view to developing effective methods of force and immediate material opportunism. Moreover, instability was not simply an unfortunate corollary of reformist, insurgent impulses; it was often the entire *point*, the purpose, the essence of the entrepreneurialism which led to the creation of new entities or novel versions of extant ones.

The question of technology more broadly is worth dwelling on for a moment. This was clearly an era—the eighteenth and nineteenth centuries—in which firearms were being imported into Africa in ever greater quantities. The operational impact of guns is variable across the continent, of course, but we do know that many states and societies were altering their military tactics and structures in order to accommodate them and make their deployment more effective. With regard to the foregoing discussion, this is true, for example, of a number of coastal West

African polities, including Dahomey and the Yoruba microstates; it is also the case for the Ethiopian highlands, where armies made ever more effective use of imported technology. There is now a substantial body of work on the subject more broadly, interest in which has been periodic over the last few decades.[101] The question of where imported technology sits in our analysis calls for a certain amount of nuance. In short, guns were not in themselves the cause of coups or insurgencies; deeper, more substantive underlying factors were at play, clearly. There is no question that they did sometimes embolden rebels and entrepreneurs, however, heightening levels of insecurity as a result, while also driving innovation in organisation as well as, in some cases, expanding the scale and reach of political, economic and military projects. The significance of guns for the sustenance of those projects is demonstrated by the degree to which access to firearms was the prime objective of much commercial conflict in the course of the nineteenth century. This reminds us, too, of course, of the reliance of most African military establishments— notwithstanding some local capacity for repair and maintenance, and the manufacture of bullets—on external suppliers for both arms and ammunition. The gun, in other words, was both a cause and an effect of violence for much of the era, in a curious cycle of reformist experimentation, even as we acknowledge that the real-world impact of firearms in the practice of war varied across the continent.

Finally, the outcomes of insurgent movements did not always reflect the progressive (or even innovative) intentions that may have existed at their outset. But the focus on outcomes rather than drivers and forms is an inherently teleological exercise, and frequently draws us to misleading conclusions about the origins and aims of insurgency itself. In fact, as we will see, the idea of nineteenth-century instability has been distorted by more recent interpretation, and by persistent tropes around a savage barbarity which was supposedly uniquely African, and a manifestation of the African character. In many ways it *was* the era of trial and error on the part of variously developmentally focused, visionary or just plain opportunistic political elites, both old and new. Mistakes were made, but all endeavour was characterised by remarkable energy, creativity and purpose.

The long nineteenth century was Africa's age of insurgency: an era of contestation and coup d'état, of reformist rebellion, of what we might broadly term 'creative volatility'. This is the context within which we need to understand the European 'conquest' at the end of the nineteenth century. An array of foreign adventurers and opportunists sought to take advantage of local fission and cleavage, and were themselves frequently co-opted into local contests and conflicts. Ultimately, a focus on instability helps explain the manifold ways in which European imperialism was realised, and at the same time it was often the case that African protagonists regarded foreign intrusion as an opportunity for furthering reform or combating nearby insurgencies and marginalising dissidents and opponents. Europeans, in other words, were often simply the latest manifestation of volatility, and represented the same concoction of threat and opportunity with which millions of Africans across the continent had lived for decades.

# PART III

# Aspiration and Innovation

# Act III

## Hamed bin Muhammed Goes West

### I

THE AMBITIOUS YOUNG ZANZIBARI HAMED bin Muhammed el-Murjebi, who first made his way to Tabora and beyond in the 1850s, was no pioneer, exactly. He was following what was by then a well-trodden path,[1] and was the scion of a prominent commercial family based at the coast but with a lineage which stretched to the Gulf of Oman. Born around 1832, of predominantly Zanzibari Arab heritage but also with some Nyamwezi blood on his mother's side, he followed his grandfather Juma bin Rajab el-Murjebi, and his father Muhammed bin Juma westward into the interior in search of wealth and status. His grandfather may have been instrumental in getting a chief named Moura (or Mtula) appointed ruler of Uyowa—this man was Mirambo's own grandfather—suggesting that coastal merchants were already exercising some considerable influence in the 1830s.[2] As for Muhammed bin Juma, he was already a prominent figure in the Zanzibari commercial community in Unyanyembe by the 1850s, and had played a leading role in the political machinations of 1859–60, leading to Msabila's expulsion from office. But his son, who became better known as Tippu Tip, was certainly to become one of that community's most famous and successful members—so much so, indeed, that he came to regard himself as a class apart, in many respects, and would remain largely aloof from the affairs, and the wrangles, of the Unyanyembe

'Arabs'.[3] In the 1860s and 1870s, following initial financial backing from the wealthy Zanzibari businessman Taria Topan,[4] he was based mostly in the Manyema region of eastern Congo, including the area of Tetela which was particularly rich in ivory, where he created one of the most dynamic of the raid-and-trade 'empires' which characterised the era. His presence was felt across a vast area around Lake Tanganyika.[5] His business was mostly ivory and slaves, each requiring the organisation of violence over a wide area, using armed slaves who were themselves the products of dislocation and violence in recent years, and he became extremely rich in the process. This was a remarkable exercise in interstitial econom-ics, with Tippu Tip and his lieutenants slicing through and demarcating mobile spheres of influence within which brutal extraction of human and animal resources was organised by ruthlessly efficacious armed mer-chants. They preyed upon, and generated, displaced and traumatised communities in the eastern Congo basin. They took advantage of extant volatility, and created new forms of instability with a view to spawning further opportunities for leverage and exploitation.

Tippu Tip was himself the creation of what amounted to a 'golden age' for Zanzibar, for it was that sultanate's remarkable expansion in the course of the nineteenth century which was central to the region's socio-economic transformation. And Zanzibar's revolution was both cause and consequence of a resurgent Indian Ocean world of commerce and con-nectivity, beginning in the late eighteenth century, which bound together in vibrant triangularity the Arabian Peninsula and the Persian Gulf, In-dia's western littoral and the Swahili city-states of the East African coast,[6] of which Zanzibar swiftly emerged as one of the most significant, becom-ing the gateway into the eastern African interior.[7] This singular status was achieved through the investment of time and energy on the part of the Sultanate of Oman, which had ruled the island since the end of the sev-enteenth century. In the early decades of the nineteenth century, Omani rulers paid more and more attention to their East African principality. At first, their commercial agents hovered by the ocean, reliant on the African middlemen further upcountry to deliver the commodities intrin-sic to the materiality of the Indian Ocean world. But soon they were funding the caravans which snaked their way toward, and beyond,

Unyanyembe, and investing heavily in the ivory and slave trades. Zanzibar itself became the site of a thriving slave-based plantation economy, which attracted further investment from Indian entrepreneurs, based around spices, especially cloves. In 1840, Sultan Sayyid Said of Oman moved his capital permanently from Muscat to Zanzibar's Stone Town to oversee more directly the veritable commercial revolution unfolding across the region. A period of dispute between his sons followed Sayyid's death in 1856, resolved only in 1861 when Oman and Zanzibar effectively became separate entities, with Sultan Sayyid Majid bin Said becoming ruler of the latter.[8] Throughout this period, Zanzibar established an informal empire latitudinally, reaching to Lake Tanganyika and the eastern Congo basin, and longitudinally, stretching along the coast of present-day Tanzania and Kenya to take control of or wield influence over numerous Swahili entrepôts.[9] It was a process of regional partition which, like many other similar exercises across the continent supposedly inimical in terms of sustained economic and political development, was more influential over the long term than anything later foreign demarcations could muster. A swathe of East Africa was, and continues to be, profoundly shaped by the Swahili- and Arabic-speaking Zanzibari project in commercial and cultural transformation—and of course by the manner in which that project was shaped by the peoples of the mainland interior.

Tippu Tip was one of the most notable, and certainly visible, representatives of the *wangwana*, a class of Swahili-speaking, Afro-Arabian merchant-adventurers along the coast who formed the core of the trading caravans shuttling between Zanzibar and Ujiji (and who were also critical to many a European expedition as armed protection and translators).[10] They were both entrepreneurs and intermediaries. In the middle and later decades of the nineteenth century, they were crucial in the development and consolidation of our road, in the creation of commercial leverage and opportunities across central-east Africa, and in the diffusion of Islam and Swahili culture (and language) as far west as the Congo forest. In the numerous communities who were both engulfed in, and contributed to, the commercial revolution, Swahili dress and architecture were adopted. Many converted to Islam, which—quite apart from the spiritual succour offered by the faith at the level of the individual—offered tangible advantages, notably in the form of association with a transregional commercial and cultural as well as cosmological network. The medical and technical knowledge of the newcomers was greatly in demand. The latter often married into local political elites with a view to cementing alliances and wielding influence. Swahili itself became the lingua franca of a vast interconnected region.[11] Above all, Tippu Tip and the *wangwana* embodied a new and vibrant globality, for they were products of the networks traversing the Indian Ocean; they stood on the shore, part of the great sea, and spoke its languages; but they were linked through kinship and ambition and cultures of aspiration to the continent unfolding before them to the western, landward side. The *wangwana* epitomised the energetic, pioneering liminality of the age, and did more than almost any other group, bar the Nyamwezi themselves, to globalise and transform the region.

Tippu Tip personified the innovation and aspiration of the era. But there were many others, more or less visible in the historical record. For example, Muhammed bin Khalfan, known as Rumaliza, also moved along our road in search of profit and power. Supported financially, like Tippu Tip, by Taria Topan, Rumaliza operated west of Lake Tanganyika from the 1860s. He emulated Tippu Tip's methods of domination and extraction, shifting his focus somewhat to the area around Lake Tanganyika from the early 1880s, and in the process becoming one of the most powerful figures in Ujiji.[12] Rumaliza represented the open, fluctuating, violently competitive nature of the region in the middle and later decades of the nineteenth century, embodying both brutal opportunism and brilliant entrepreneurialism. Moreover, while he enjoyed Zanzibari financial backing, he was insurgent and he occupied—and created—liminal spaces. He himself was a liminal person, and his actual physical commercial and political domain proved ephemeral. But the very force of his creation and the enduring culture which it represented profoundly shaped the colonial statehood which would claim to have conquered him and his ilk, and which would essentially seek to replicate what he had done.

Ujiji itself, moreover, located at the de facto terminus of our road, offers a good example of the incipient urbanisation which symbolised cultures of aspiration and innovation in the form of the entrepreneurial clusters which made up the built environment. The coastmen had established a permanent settlement in this quiet fishing village at some point during the 1840s. It was quickly transformed, as a result of both the consolidation of the coastal community and also the entrepreneurialism of nearby communities, including the Jiji themselves. The vulnerability of the settlement was evident early on, when an attack by some Ngoni, possibly in the 1850s, forced the entire coastal community to evacuate and take refuge on Bangwe Island on Lake Tanganyika.[13] Perhaps for this reason, the coastmen sought to keep firearms out of the hands of the locals, and appear to have largely succeeded in doing so, save for the armed slaves they employed to attack communities to the north.[14] By the 1870s, Ujiji was a thriving market town, attracting traders from across a wide area around the northern shores of Lake Tanganyika, with an 'Arab' quarter, complete with resident 'governor', at its commercial and political centre. In 1876 Henry Morton Stanley was impressed, noting that "[t]he hum and bustle of the market-place, filled with a miscellaneous concourse of representatives from many tribes, woke me up at early dawn". At Ujiji, "we behold all the wealth of the Tanganika [sic] shores"; the 'Wajiji' themselves were "sharp, clever traders"; "a brave tribe, and of very independent spirit, but not quarrelsome"—praise indeed; "the most expert canoemen of all the tribes around the Tanganika". There was evidently much wealth to be derived from the steady stream of coastal merchants heading both west and east.[15] Beyond the bustle, there were tensions, clearly: between 'Arabs' and locals, and within the coastal community itself, to the point where rival factions vied for political as well as commercial control of the town. Tippu Tip was sometimes waging war in the neighbourhood, for example in the early 1880s; Mirambo posed a continual threat. Contemporary accounts suggest an often febrile atmosphere, a nervy, liminal environment, defined by a frontier mentality, far from Zanzibar—and indeed that was normally how many coastal merchants wanted it. Sometimes conflict closed the road east altogether.[16] Yet, for all that, this was a lively, industrious, cosmopolitan place which reflected the ambition and the innovation of the age: a product of the road itself and all it represented.

# II

COASTAL MERCHANTS were part of a long-range network of culture and commerce, encompassing continents and oceans; but at the much more local level, the presence of these entrepreneurs transformed Tabora and Unyanyembe. There had been a permanent settlement of people from the coast and their camp followers in Unyanyembe since the early 1850s, as we have seen. Unyanyembe was a critical commercial hub, where hundreds of miles of road converged, and where political and economic elites transformed what was otherwise a rather unremarkable polity into a transit handler of exports and imports. By the early 1870s, merchants from the coast were spread across two residential clusters at the very heart of the polity, mostly in Tabora itself and, to the south-west, Kwihara. Each of these clusters was situated less than a couple of miles from the royal enclosure, which was at Kwikuru to the east.[17] Within this compact triangle, modestly populated though it was, was situated the great fusion of material and political power in the region. The local economy was transformed as a result. The newcomers had brought—or, perhaps more accurately, stimulated—violent predation; but they also facilitated a new kind of vibrant diversity and stratification within the local economy, and an energetic culture of exchange and reciprocity. The size and strength of the 'Arab' community varied according to circumstances, but it clearly grew over time. Richard Burton noted in 1857 that the coastal merchants "rarely [...] exceed twenty-five in number; and during the travelling season, or when a campaign is necessary, they are sometimes reduced to three or four".[18] A similar dynamic was observed in 1873, when Verney Lovatt Cameron was told that the entire coastal community, with the exception of a "cripple", had left Tabora to fight Mirambo.[19] Yet these were clearly exceptional circumstances. As David Livingstone observed in 1872, "the eighty so-called Arabs here have twenty dependents each, [and therefore] 1500 or 1600 is the outside population of Unyanyembe in connection with the Arabs"[20]—a sizeable community indeed. Within that community, whose members "live comfortably, and even splendidly", thanks in no small measure to "regular supplies of merchandise, comforts, and luxuries from the coast", Burton drew attention to the presence of "itinerant fundi, or slave artisans—blacksmiths, tinkers, masons, carpenters, tailors, potters, and rope-makers". The "exorbitant wages" which Burton suggests they demanded indicates perhaps a marketplace that valued their specialist skills highly.[21] The coastal merchants and their extensive entourages introduced new crops to Unyanyembe, engendering a greatly enlivened local agronomy. Stanley followed Burton in noting the comfort of the merchants' lives at Unyanyembe, but went further in pointing to the flourishing agriculture which had been introduced: rice, sweet potatoes, maize and millet.[22] Livingstone later described the abundance of "[p]omegranates, guavas, lemons and oranges [. . . ;] mangoes flourish, and grape vines are beginning to be cultivated; papaws grow everywhere. Onions, radishes, pumpkins and watermelons prosper."[23] Although some contemporary reports imply a colonist economy which was largely self-sufficient and isolated from an African one,[24] this was almost certainly a misreading of what was in fact a thriving and integrated local economy. Notably, Burton asserted that "[t]he price of provisions in Unyamwezi has increased inordinately since the Arabs have settled in the land", suggesting a direct impact on the local market.[25] The porters who were hired for coastal caravans were frequently paid in imported commodities which thus made their way into the local economy. It is clear, moreover, that the coastal community remained heavily reliant on the supply of basic foodstuffs, including grain, from local producers: we have seen how this dependency was exposed during the war against Msabila in the early 1860s, when the destruction of local crops as a result of the violence had an immediate impact on the coastal merchants themselves.[26] Above all, of course, there was the long-distance commerce itself which fundamentally and permanently altered the material basis of power in Unyanyembe.

Mirambo's state was itself a socioeconomic phenomenon. At the heart of the project was the drive to dominate the road and the global trade which streamed along it: his insurgent polity was a commercial enterprise as much as a political one, drawing its internal potency from a complex web of tributary relationships which yielded livestock and ivory, and directing a revolutionised military system toward the seizure and export of slaves as well as elephant tusks.[27] Of course, Mirambo was all too aware that the wars he waged in order to establish control of trade roads frequently disrupted the very trade which he was seeking to dominate, and on which he relied heavily, especially in terms of a regular supply of guns and ammunition. His opponents, moreover, were frequently also his suppliers.[28] Neither he nor his peers ever successfully resolved this dilemma, which in some ways encapsulates a central problem confronting millions of Africans in the nineteenth century: that global commerce, with all the opportunities it presented, invariably fuelled violence which in time brought Africans into conflict with foreign commercial interests. Nonetheless, the Nyamwezi themselves were clearly active agents of socioeconomic change.[29] The people who would come to be identified under that ethnonym inhabited an area which on the face of it exemplified the idea of the enclosed, unreachable, materially inhibited heart of Africa, hidden away from the world for centuries. In fact, there is some evidence, across the wider region, of a deeper history of engagement with global trade, if likely indirect: the cowrie shells found in tenth-century graves west of Lake Tanganyika, for example, and the glass and sea-shell beads in the northern lacustrine region, both of which are suggestive of links with the Indian Ocean coast.[30] But certainly in the nineteenth century the Nyamwezi were involved in a veritable socioeconomic revolution. When the first *wangwana* caravans appeared, Nyamwezi volunteered their services as porters; and as we have already noted, to travel to the fleshpots of the coast, to behold the ocean, quickly became a vital rite of passage among young men. As Burton explained it,

> From time immemorial the Wanyamwezi have visited the road to the coast, and though wars and blood-feuds may have temporarily closed one line, another necessarily opened itself. Amongst a race so dependent for comfort and pleasure upon trade, commerce, like steam, cannot be compressed beyond a certain point [. . .]. Porterage, on the long and toilsome journey, is now considered by the Wanyamwezi a test of manliness [. . .]. The children imbibe the desire with their milk, and six or seven years old they carry a little tusk on their shoulders.[31]

But for many, it wasn't enough simply to lend their labour to the global economy. Many began to trade on their own accounts, seeking their own share of the commodities—the cloth, the guns, the sundry manufactured and prestige goods—which they had previously only carried for others.[32] They didn't only travel to the coast, moreover: they became involved in a range of transregional commercial activities converging on Unyanyembe, including the lucrative copper trade coming from Katanga to the south.[33] Many others took to the bush to become the *ruga ruga*: young, unmarried, professional soldiers whose energy was harnessed by large-scale entrepreneurs such as Mirambo and Nyungu-ya-Mawe in pursuit of their state-building projects; but above all, the *ruga ruga* were privateers, mercenaries and armed adventurers, simultaneously tapping into and shaping global trade, whether as soldiers or merchants or both. They hunted elephants for their tusks or captured ivory from adversaries; they seized people and sold them eastward. In so doing, they represented a wholesale rejection of the social and economic order of their ancestors: no mere subsistence farming or herding of livestock for them, nor the smallness of the world which their mothers and fathers had inhabited.[34] Now, material aspiration and social ambition drove them toward exciting new horizons. It was a risky business; but the potential rewards evidently made the danger, and the investment of life and limb, worthwhile. The outcome was a highly volatile economic landscape characterised by adventure and creativity, as well as by death and destruction; new social and political orders were shaped by intergenerational conflict, or at least divergence.[35] It may be that the chief exports involved were unsustainable over the long term: ivory represented a diminishing resource, with elephant herds disappearing from ever wider areas;[36] anti-slave trade forces were gathering on the horizon.[37] But we must take care to avoid teleology. In the moment, the socioeconomic revolution under way was underpinned by rationality, and, though brutally violent, was defined by the investment of both energy and imagination. Along the way, the Nyamwezi created a sense of themselves as a more or less coherent group, defined by language, custom and shared experience. They had begun the nineteenth century as dispersed communities of grain farmers sharing only a nebulous linguistic and cultural association. As the century progressed, they became 'Nyamwezi': in the coastal idiom, 'people of the new moon', those who came from the west.[38] In other words, a key element of the dynamic process of aspiration and innovation was not simply material acquisition: it was about the creation of a larger community, of networks of belonging, an ontological revolution which overran earlier, more localised publics.

Yet amid the volatility, new urban centres characterised by economic diversity and vibrancy arose. We have already noted the cases of Tabora and Ujiji. Urambo, Mirambo's capital, might have exhibited a particular level of dynamism given its geopolitical significance, but it nevertheless seems to exemplify broader trends. Urambo was a thriving economic centre by the late 1870s and early 1880s, albeit an itinerant one. It was a busy, cosmopolitan, stratified environment, exhibiting the nervous socioeconomic energy of which the wider state was a product. Contemporary reports describe an urban sprawl of numerous interconnected hubs— Mirambo's own settlement at the heart of it may have had upwards of 15,000 inhabitants in 1880—characterised by its "smart, business-like proceedings" and by much more than the militarism which outwardly defined the state. It was interspersed with plots of land on which farmers cultivated for town and army, and was populated by blacksmiths, potters and the ever-present "enterprising" porters.[39] Given that a generation earlier nothing on this scale had existed in the area (with the partial exception of Tabora in Unyanyembe itself) the scale of the socioeconomic transformation is indeed remarkable. Numerous other settlements, if less extensive than Urambo, were enhanced and fortified in the same period.[40] At the same time, of course, this process of population movement, of urbanisation or proto-urbanisation, produced some deleterious environmental side-effects. Socioeconomic and political insecurity along our road seriously disrupted communities' ability to carefully manage a fragile ecosystem, which had previously been achieved through dispersed patterns of settlement: this kept bush, and trypanosomiasis or sleeping sickness, under control. More concentrated human settlement invariably meant the abandonment of formerly cultivated land around villages to bush,[41] which resulted in the advance of the tsetse fly, and thus of sleeping sickness.[42] It was a process which also generated depopulated interstitial and frontier zones which offered points of entry to aggressive foreign intruders in search of opportunities for leverage.

# III

HAMED BIN MUHAMMED EL-MURJEBI was unquestionably a singular character, a dominant figure across a wide area who travelled along, and cast a lengthy shadow upon, our nineteenth-century road. But he was also more broadly emblematic of a remarkable age of socioeconomic transformation, indeed revolution: the spirit of the age was one of creativity, ambition, accumulation. Older patterns of living and working did indeed endure, but they were increasingly eschewed by a new generation of innovators and seekers of wealth and adventure. It was an age of uncertainty, of violence, of coercion; but it was also one of risk-taking and self-realisation and new forms of belonging and being, in which endogenous initiatives toward economic reform were increasingly linked to the possibilities presented through global engagement. Tippu Tip no doubt represented the proactive—and frequently violently aggressive—advance of a commercial frontier with its centre of gravity in a transoceanic economy; but this was no one-way traffic. The road was quickly crowded with those moving in the other direction, toward the shore; and the peoples along it fundamentally altered the global economy in the process of changing themselves to meet its challenges and its opportunities.

# 4

# Material Worlds

## Enterprise, Entrepôts, Entrepreneurs

INNOVATION AND ECONOMIC REFORM, driven by a culture of aspiration, were manifest in different ways at various levels: from the level of the individual and the small-group community, to the larger collective, including state-level enterprise. It was evident both within reformist polities, and in between them, in the interstitial and frontier spaces which offered opportunities for new forms of material organisation, or variations of old ones.[1] In some cases, we espy elite-led projects in relatively enduring polities, instigating economic reforms and seeking to adapt to shifting circumstances. In other scenarios, we see insurgencies directed at the fundamental reconceptualisation and reorganisation of resources and prospects, usually if not always in response to external engagement. And then there are ordinary women and men operating below or beyond the level of centralised statehood, producing and gathering for export, from beeswax to palm oil. Africans, whether extant elites or entrepreneurial upstarts, sought to grasp the opportunities presented by intensifying global interaction.[2] The expansion of global trade was increasingly critical to political and military ambition, and in many respects the tangible outcomes of commerce, or the prospect of them, drove innovation on multiple levels, and along with it new or expanded forms of coercion. A great many of the insurgencies and internal contestations surveyed earlier were motivated by ideas about material wellbeing and personal or collective transformation: even those which were most visibly and publicly about 'politics', or ideology, or theology, rarely if ever lacked some set of notions about material improvement. They both reflected and facilitated forceful currents of social change, and were manifestations of social aspiration. Political insurrectionists were also economic reformers and innovators. Much violence in nineteenth-century Africa was essentially economic in provenance and objective. To some extent it was an enclosed circle of cause and effect, not least in the heightening demand for guns, which was the key aim for many societies and states. Guns were thus used to make war more effectively, in an attempt to control trade even more tightly. In West Africa, foreign imports, including cloth and guns, were used by states and societies on or near the coast to buy horses from traders to the north, as in Oyo before its collapse, and among the competing Yoruba microstates subsequently. Access to and control over trade was vital to the actualisation of political power, and in the context of military hardware had very real and tangible implications. External commerce also presented opportunities for enrichment on the part of state-level political elites and their entourages and followers. The categorisation of certain commodities as being of a luxury or prestige nature was critical to gatekeeping elites who were drawn to the magnetic power of such imports, which could be used to secure political support. In centralised polities such as Dahomey and Buganda, ruling groups in the nineteenth century used the commodities to which they had access as elite traders for distribution among supporters: systems of patronage and distribution which were designed to channel newfound materiality into political support. In Dahomey, for example, the 'annual customs' involved, in part, the performance of the redistributive power of the monarchical centre.[3] In Asante, the accumulation of wealth, including through trade with commercial agents at the coast to the south, was an existential and philosophical matter as much as one of crude materialism, central to the very notion of 'being Asante'—and when in the middle decades of the nineteenth century the state began to intrude more aggressively (and, it was perceived, illegitimately) on the lives of those private citizens able to accumulate wealth in this way, it produced severe, even irresolvable, tensions within state and society.[4] In West Africa broadly, the objects acquired through trade worked their way into representations of, and negotiations around, political authority, and were integrated into material life at the local level.[5] The significance of the exogenous grew as the nineteenth century progressed: these were elites (and their associates) reaching out to the world, and publicly demonstrating their ability to do so, in order to consolidate internal power bases.

The gravitational pull of transregional and global commerce bent many polities into a particular shape at various points in the course of the nineteenth century. Ethiopia's turbulent era is, for all sorts of reasons, frequently framed in terms of a distinctive ideology, rooted in Solomonic mythology. But the highland polity was as much as anything the product of material forces of a rather more temporal nature. State-builders (actual and would-be) in the northern highlands were particularly advantageously positioned along trade routes linking the Sudanese borderlands and the central massif to the Red Sea and the Gulf of Aden. The expansion of the slave trade through Massawa, for example—by mid-nineteenth century the port was under Egyptian administration, ostensibly on behalf of the Ottoman empire—empowered Tigray in the course of the Zemene Mesafint, which was as much as anything a prolonged struggle over commerce. It drew political rulers northward toward the Red Sea shore in search of more robust commercial relationships with Europe, Arabia and southern Asia. Tigray's increasing commercial prominence is demonstrated in the role played by the province's ruler, Ras Michael, in seizing control of the imperial centre of Gondar at the end of the 1760s. Upwards of ten thousand slaves were being sold annually through Massawa alone by the late eighteenth century, and were destined for the Arabian Peninsula and the Persian Gulf in particular. The capture of people for export, frequently along the escarpment and lowland peripheries of the *habesha* state, became a central engine of political and social as well as of commercial change.[6] The traffic in human beings was an essential component of material power in nineteenth-century Ethiopia, but it also had cultural and indeed racial dimensions. A professional class of merchants emerged, many of whom were Muslim, in some ways accentuating a cultural gulf between Christian highlanders—whose aristocratic elite ostensibly eschewed direct involvement in the grubby operational side of commerce as unmanly and unchivalrous, even if the distance they supposedly maintained was always more myth than reality—and Islamic communities. Moreover, the Orthodox Christian core defined itself against the putative savages, often darker-skinned, lurking on its frontiers. A violent cultural as well as material entrepreneurialism justified the enslavement of the supposed barbarians on the state's peripheries. This was reflected in a pejorative vocabulary used to describe various groups: the derogatory term *shanqalla*, notably, denoted captives from the western escarpment and Sudanese lowlands, and *baria*, indicating 'black slaves', was used to describe communities (in particular the Nara) in present-day Eritrea's western lowlands.[7] Material aspiration as well as ideological identity led to violence taking on a particularly racial character, which in turn produced a form of statehood whose elites developed an ever sharper sense of their biological and cultural superiority.

Slaves were important; but Ethiopia exported a range of other commodities, including ivory, skins, gold and various spices, which merchant caravans, generally enjoying the armed protection of political authorities as far as their jurisdictions reached (beyond which they could be vulnerable), carried to the shores of the Red Sea and the Gulf of Aden. In exchange, imported guns, in particular, were increasingly seen as critical to the exercise of political and military power across the highlands. Provincial elites, especially in the central and northern highlands, sought to establish monopolies on particular trade routes through which guns and a range of other imports could be acquired.[8] This had already been evident under Tewodros, of course, whose own insurgency had involved ideas about economic reform and reconstruction; he, too, had been increasingly concerned with access to the Red Sea coast in what would become Eritrea.[9] It is no coincidence that the resurgent Tigrayan-led neo-Solomonic state of Yohannes IV flourished in the 1870s and 1880s as Red Sea commerce likewise thrived in the wake of the opening of the Suez Canal. Late nineteenth-century Ethiopia was as much a large-scale exercise in economic innovation as it was a project of the political imagination: Menelik's state represented a geopolitical finessing of Yohannes's Tigrayan vision, with more southerly Shewa—at the heart of the imperium from 1889 onwards—better placed to access the burgeoning trade through Zeila and Djibouti in the Gulf of Aden. This geopolitical positioning in many ways had its roots much earlier in the century, when during Sahle Selassie's reign Amhara merchants and political leaders began to reimagine the Shewan kingdom as sitting astride both northbound and eastbound commercial highways. But Menelik proved especially adept at building up one of the most impressive arsenals of modern firearms in Africa by means of these routes.[10] He also recognised the need to create an economy capable of supporting Ethiopia's extensive and burdensome military establishment. The empire which fanned out across the south in the 1880s and 1890s, into the adjacent lowlands inhabited by peoples, such as the Oromo and Somali, long seen as inferior (and, simultaneously, threatening) by highland state-builders, involved colonial settlement and resource extraction which were linked to Ethiopia's commercial position. Those conquests would be dressed in the language of *habesha* cultural and ethnic exceptionalism, but in a very real sense they were driven by economic innovation and a newly energised sense of material aspiration on the part of the Amhara.[11] The empire which resulted was as much the product of a socioeconomic revolution as it was a political one.

States and their agents could evidently accomplish remarkable things, when motivated to do so by emerging external opportunities. As we have seen, this was by no means unprecedented: in the era of the slave trade at its height, in the seventeenth and eighteenth centuries, the Atlantic region had seen the rise of some of the most innovative economic enterprises anywhere on the planet during this period, involving centralised polities whose efficacious deployment of violence was at least partly aimed at the maximisation of external opportunities.[12] The enormous operation organised by the Dahomean state to conquer a stretch of the coast, including the critical entrepôts of Allada and Ouidah, in the 1720s exemplifies the point.[13] Asante's eighteenth-century conquests were also, to an extent, large-scale economic enterprises; this is even truer of the slaving campaigns of Segu, or Oyo.[14] War and commerce were inextricably linked in these energetic exercises in state-led entrepreneurialism which used armed force to access external trade, and then to maintain themselves as regionally dominant commercial centres. What looks, on the face of it, like a terrifying illogic—Africans selling off the continent's most precious resource, namely people—in fact was imbued with a very clear rationality at the local level: exporting undesirables, whether criminals from within, or foreigners from without, in order to elevate and maintain economic status in order to attract followers. To see this process in any other way is intrinsically teleological.

One of the most spectacular operations of this magnitude during the transformative nineteenth century involved Buganda. This was a polity whose capacity to expand, innovate and govern according to material strategy had already been demonstrated in the eighteenth century through its acquisition of arable land, pasture and some of the best resources in the area for weaponry: namely, wood and iron. Between the 1730s and the 1790s, reform of the state had involved greater control on the part of the kingship over land and the political appointments attached to it; and, closely linked to that, the development of an economy based on the acquisition of livestock and the control of people, including through capture and enslavement. There was a clearly gendered element to this process, encapsulating the paradox inherent in the stratification of women across the continent in the eighteenth and nineteenth centuries. While, as we have noted, elite women were in a position to carve out significant spheres of political influence, the expansion of centralised administrative power over people as well as land meant, in general, the subordination of women in socioeconomic terms, and the accumulation of enslaved women as emblematic of political status.[15] In the realm of exogeneity, the kingdom's indirect links to a global market can be traced to at least the second half of the eighteenth century,[16] but the Ganda were confronted with a rapidly shifting commercial environment by the 1830s and 1840s, when the demand for ivory and slaves escalated dramatically. The response of its political class in the 1840s, under the leadership of Kabaka Suna, was to harness the ancient resources and skills of the shoreline communities in the attempt to take control of Lake Victoria. It was no coincidence that the first coastal merchants had arrived in the kingdom in 1844, and within a few years had a permanent presence at the royal capital.[17] The outcome, the result of a display of the state's power to coerce and mobilise labour in pursuit of commercial gain, was a fleet of canoes capable of traversing the lake between its northern and southern shores. An array of vessels of various shapes and sizes had both military and commercial utility, with the larger boats up to twenty-five or thirty metres (eighty or one hundred feet) long and capable of carrying people and commodities in unprecedented volumes. With respect to the original objective of achieving mastery over the lake, the project fell a little short; but the endeavour, and the vision underpinning it, was magnificent.[18] Under Suna, and his successor Mutesa, a coalescence of political, military and commercial interests seized with alacrity the opportunities presented by the demand for enslaved people. This was a globalised form of the long-standing practice of controlling people as wealth, stretching back over several centuries in the Great Lakes region. In so doing, the Ganda contributed substantially to the creation of a network of trans-lacustrine interconnectivity, a veritable system of trade and transport and capital, which would fundamentally reshape the material landscape of the region. The slave trade, fed by wars with the Soga, the Nyoro and various societies to the west of the kingdom, profoundly altered the kingdom and its social composition, and injected a new level of energy into its economic performance. So much so, that it was no exaggeration for Kabaka Mutesa to declare in 1882 that "[t]he power of my chiefs and my people depends on this traffic, and I have no right to hinder it".[19] He was effectively powerless, he declared a few months later, in the face of such seismic material transformation: "Those cursed slave dealers really rule my people. This I myself formerly encouraged, but it has assumed such dimensions that it cannot I fear be stopped."[20] Assuming he was not being disingenuous to his European audience, this was a striking statement from the head of a state whose apparatus had been substantially reorganised to engage with such commerce over the preceding four decades. In fact the Ganda court had done a reasonable job of controlling the coastal community: in the early 1860s, for example, the latter was described as being confined to a particular area of the royal capital and as being routinely kept waiting by the *kabaka*, their subordinate status apparently deliberately emphasised.[21] But Mutesa was also aware of the situation in Karagwe, further south, where 'Arab' merchants had been able to achieve a position of considerable influence at the heart of the polity, much as they had in Unyanyembe.[22] Be that as it may, and despite the risks in terms of intrusive outside influence, the spirit of Ganda entrepreneurialism was ever present, and within two decades of Mutesa's death, the adaptable and attentive chiefly class had turned to the production of cotton as the surest path to profitable global engagement—both commercial and political.

States and societies innovated in a range of ways. In some cases, new communities rooted in insurgency were essentially predatory, heavily reliant on the 'harvesting' of people through widespread slave-raiding campaigns. In the case of the trans-Zambezi zone, a range of peoples were able to tap into both Atlantic and Indian Ocean commercial complexes, which met in the middle decades of the nineteenth century, and forged entrepreneurial identities as a result. Men were advantageously positioned, overwhelmingly so, to take advantage of these opportunities, given the cultures of armed adventurism which privileged their social and supposed biological positionality. But as elsewhere, much depended on socioeconomic provenance and context, reflecting heightened gender-based stratification. Among the Shona, for example, women from the lowest socioeconomic backgrounds were increasingly vulnerable to commodification and objectification, but others could see their sociopolitical significance increase in the course of an average life-cycle, from the bearing of children, and the influence which motherhood, as well as marriage, bestowed; to the postmenopausal stage in life, when women were considered senior members of the sociopolitical establishment, more like men than women in fact, and were accorded respect and were able to exercise natural authority. From these positions women, though exposed to the same vagaries as men, could effect change or influence the transformations already under way in an age of turmoil.[23] Nevertheless, these were commonly environments in which there were evidently more opportunities for men than for women, even while the majority of both men and women alike lived with the quotidian threat of violent coercion. In the western Sahel, Umar Tal's Tukolor state exported captives through the 1850s, and this was its main resource to secure crucial imports, including firearms; likewise Samori Ture, whose militarised polity was largely sustained through slaving wars, the 'products' of which were sold across the region in exchange for horses and guns, including the breech-loading rifles which he favoured over the older flintlock muskets. For a time, while he had access to the

Buré goldfields, he also exported gold to fund his wars and his political order. Samori did oversee the expansion of a coterie of trusted professional merchants to do his business for him: in fact the Dyula, as the commercial class of predominantly Soninke and Malinke were known, were key to the Samorian state's expansion, and sought to develop agricultural exports in addition to lucrative human traffic.[24] Even so, predation focused on the capture of people was to a large extent the raison d'être of such energetic, even frenetic, entities. The Sultanate of Darfur, a more gradual project which by the late eighteenth century had emerged as a significant presence at the eastern end of the Sudanic zone, skilfully established itself as a key commercial hub: roads linking desert, savannah and Nile Valley converged on Darfur in the course of the nineteenth century, and caravans moving across vast distances to take advantage of emerging transregional opportunities were protected by successive sultans.[25]

Others developed vibrant new systems of economic production. The roots of the insurrection leading to the establishment of the Sokoto Caliphate at least partly lay in socioeconomic grievance, and Uthman dan Fodio's jihad succeeded on the back of widespread anger on the part of pastoralists—as the Fulani were—around the imposition of a specific tax on cattle, the *jangali*, by mainly agricultural elites. This was 'culture war' territory, of course: to Hausa landowners, the Fulani with their livestock and their itinerant tendencies were an intrusive, untrustworthy, potentially subversive lot; to the Fulani, those Hausa put up a façade of being Muslim, but in reality behaved like infidels, or worse, apostates. Not only did they tax cattle-owners, an un-Islamic act in itself; they also owned slaves who were at least as Muslim as they themselves claimed to be, and of course under *shari'a* it was illegal to enslave another Muslim. And so it was a deep sense of socioeconomic rage which acted in parallel with the loftier theological goals of Uthman dan Fodio and his circle in driving forward the revolution. Once the Caliphate was established, though, whatever short-term insurrectionist economics might have been in play were largely supplanted by a slave-based plantation economy which was honed during the first half of the nineteenth century. Women were key to the economic functioning of the new order. Female slaves, the number of whom increased dramatically in the early decades of the nineteenth century, worked on smallholder farms and larger plantations. They also worked increasingly in salt production.[26] The enforcement of seclusion according to Islamic custom certainly inhibited the roles that free and elite women could perform in the public sphere, but they developed local trade networks that enabled them to generate considerable personal wealth.[27] Across the Sahel region, the work of enslaved women freed up elite women to work in the production of cloth, and they used both female and male slaves themselves.[28] Moreover, Sokoto comprised an economic system— as revolutionary in its way as the insurgency which had made it possible— which was geared toward local production and consumption as well as toward export.[29]

The Zulu also embarked on a substantive reorganisation of society around cattle and war, with the soldier class also responsible, when not on active military campaign, for careful management of the kingdom's extensive animal resources. The origins of the insurgent state, after all, lay in an earlier struggle over pasture and water: ownership of livestock had for centuries formed the material basis of political authority across the wider region, with specialist agricultural labour being undertaken pre-dominantly by women. Women themselves were in general subordinated within a militarised social system which was built around patriarchal power, but their labour was crucial to the economic operation of the state.[30] The state itself now sought more efficient ways of combining the management of cattle, farming and military service, a holistic system of violence and production rooted in a version of the age-regimentation which had long been practised by the Ngoni of the area. Concentrated settlements which were essentially economic units were organised around individual *amabutho*—military regiments—involved men tending to cattle and women engaged in cultivation. It was a system which also fostered a deepening sense of 'Zulu' identity across the expanding kingdom. These settlements were dispersed once the soldiers of the particular age-set reached marriageable age and were in effect demobilised, indicating the degree to which the state meticulously sought to combine demographic as well as economic management.[31] This, of course, was the bedrock of an economy which was also increasingly global-facing, as long-distance commerce escalated in the course of the nineteenth century: young Zulu men were also tasked with elephant hunting, with ivory becoming one of the kingdom's most valuable exports.[32]

At the other end of the continent, Egypt under Muhammad Ali offers a remarkable instance of far-reaching economic reform, including efforts toward industrialisation. The Egyptian military revolution was infused with commercial ambition from the outset, and involved growing hegemony in the Red Sea, culminating (from a trading point of view) in the lease of the ports of Suakin and Massawa by the Ottoman authorities to Cairo in 1846. But the military and political project needed funds to sustain it, and Muhammad Ali (and his successors) recognised that nothing short of an economic revolution would be required to consolidate any military and territorial expansion. Tax reform was initiated to increase the flow of revenue to the treasury. But much more was envisioned. Ambitious irrigation schemes were inaugurated with a view to expanding the production of cotton, Egypt's primary commercial asset and earner of foreign exchange. Cotton production did indeed increase dramatically in the first few decades of the nineteenth century. Cairo sought to capitalise on this by importing European technology aimed at kickstarting industrialisation, particularly involving textile and arms manufacturing.[33] In time, it would attract the envy, and arouse the anxiety, of western European states.

Further south, however, across the upper Nile region—far from the sophisticated visions of urban industrialism nurtured in the Nile Delta—the Egyptian presence was rather more predatory. Here, a new breed of armed adventurers and merchants used their base at Khartoum, established in 1824, to connect with their compatriots operating along the Red Sea coast to engage in the regional ivory and slave trades. They practised a similar form of interstitial, entrepreneurial violence among the communities of southern Sudan as that seen in the eastern Congo basin, the Zambezi valley or the western Sahel. They collected ivory and captured people and dispatched their cargoes eastward, both to Suakin and into the Ethiopian highlands, in the process carving out an informal empire of violent commercialism.[34] Upon these rough-hewn partitions, which reached the northern lake region by the 1860s, Europeans would later superimpose territorial imperialisms of their own.

Meanwhile, in the years following Muhammad Ali's death in 1849, Egyptian reformist elites would seek new ways of pursuing the ideas which had driven the revolution. Khedive Ismail envisioned industrial and urban development on a grand scale. Under his close supervision, Cairo was redesigned as the showcase for the dynamic, 'modernising' state, with Paris as the inspiration. Ismail oversaw the construction of the Suez Canal, begun under his predecessor Muhammad Said in 1859 and completed in 1869, which transformed the Red Sea—and the much of the world beyond it, in truth—in commercial terms. His government sponsored the building of transport and communications infrastructure, including railways and telegraphs. Arguably the most dramatic aspect of this great national enterprise was Ismail's aspiration to move Egypt to an entirely different continent. "My country is no longer in Africa," he is supposed to have declared. "We are now a part of Europe."[35] But if these achievements stood out against some of the putatively more ephemeral innovations of Ismail's sub-Saharan contemporaries, they came at a considerable price. While Muhammad Ali had aimed at the creation of new sources of income from *within* Egypt, Ismail relied on European loans to realise his particular vision of the modernising, developmental state. The debts mounted, and the vultures of high finance quickly circled. By the end of the 1870s Egypt was bankrupt, Ismail was removed from power, and the nation's business was increasingly under the supervision of European creditors and advisors.[36] Egypt in the 1870s would come to be emblematic of the story of failed modernisation in the face of Europe's ruthlessly effective imperial aggression and the insuperable power of financial capital: while Ismail was designing Cairo, the British and the French had designs on Egypt itself. No doubt there is a valid strand of interpretation here. But for our purposes, nineteenth-century Egypt is an exemplar of the kind of socioeconomic revolution—of the patterns of aspiration and innovation—which are in fact in evidence across much of the continent during this remarkable era; and into which, it can be argued, Europeans were co-opted, at least as much as they imposed themselves, whether in Cairo or Kordofan. It is also worth noting the striking irony that at least some of the money used to fund Egyptian economic and urban renewal, and which later ostensibly caused the temporary abeyance of Egyptian sovereign autonomy, represented wealth which was itself the result of African innovation on the other side of the continent over the previous two or three centuries, during the era of the Atlantic slave trade.[37]

In Atlantic Africa, the international context for the shifting forms of economic reform and material aspiration was the abolition of the slave trade by most western European governments between the 1800s and the 1830s, and the growing demand for agricultural produce and raw materials, later known generically as 'legitimate commerce'.[38] Of course, the impact was variable through the first few decades of the nineteenth century. Oyo in the 1790s and 1800s, as we have seen, experienced a marked dip in demand for the human exports on which the empire relied so heavily, and was an early victim of global economic vicissitudes—notwithstanding the fact that commercial pressure was only one of a number of factors contributing the state's mounting crises. But others continued to thrive as slaving states; notably Dahomey, which tapped into Brazilian demand and where, for a time, the political establishment linked its fortunes to its Brazilian connections.[39] For several of the Yoruba microstates, too, the 'illegal' slave trade was their commercial mainstay through much of the first half of the nineteenth century.[40] Much of the insurrectionist and reformist violence among the Yoruba, including the conflict between Owu and the Ife-Ijebu coalition which instigated several decades of war, was aimed at control of particularly critical commercial highways. The Yoruba exemplify the explicit and deliberate interlinking of commercial and military power which defined Africa's transformative nineteenth century. The Ijebu, inhabiting the Lagos hinterland, took advantage of their geographical position to become the dominant importers and sellers of firearms through that increasingly critical port. Others relied heavily on this commerce: the Egba, centred on Abeokuta, were under continual pressure from Dahomey to the west and desperately sought access to the coast through various commercial agents to acquire the guns (and, of course, the ammunition) vital to their self-defence.[41] Violent insecurity drove commercial innovation, even as war itself invariably disrupted the flow of trades—a perpetual dilemma for states and societies in this region and indeed across the continent through the nineteenth century. At the same time, a gender hierarchy involved the control of women's labour by men and the exclusion of most women from more profitable, high-end commerce. Nonetheless the work of women in internal trade had been critical to Oyo's urban economy, as was their role in agricultural production.[42] That positionality continued to evolve in the course of the wars of the nineteenth century, in which women were crucial in the provisioning of armies and the establishment of food markets close to the military action. Some achieved prominence and influence as a result.[43] Dahomey itself, of course, was another state whose wars, including those with the Egba from the early 1840s onward, were in large part frequently economic in objective: uninterrupted access to coastal commerce was needed to acquire the guns with which the Dahomean army fought the wars for the slaves needed to exchange for firearms in the first place. We must avoid reducing multi-layered violence to a neat circularity with its own internal (il)logic, but there does indeed appear to be a melding of cause and effect in purely operational terms—although of course this interpretation overlooks the importance of domestic slavery as well as the deeper cultural and political significance of warfare and militarism for the Dahomean state. The latter certainly sought to pursue a form of 'total war', by most conventional appreciations of that admittedly contested term, aiming at the capture of Abeokuta itself, which was attempted in 1851 and again in 1864, though both times unsuccessfully.[44]

Nonetheless, across the Atlantic region, the gradual transition from the export of human beings to 'legitimate commerce' presented a challenge for a number of states. Classically, this was supposed to constitute a calamity for the highly militarised, politically centralised states which had thrived on the slave trade—an economic activity which could only be effectively and profitably organised at the level of the state itself. In other words, for much of the previous two centuries or more, particular kinds of politico-military elites had enjoyed a monopoly on overseas trade and its supposed benefits—which often weren't, it must be said, distributed particularly widely, or equitably, within the communities involved. Declining demand for slaves and increasing external demand for commodities such as palm oil, beeswax or groundnuts which didn't require large-scale political structures to organise, or the maintenance of extensive military organisations to operate, supposedly presented an existential challenge to seventeenth- and eighteenth-century political economies: a 'crisis of adaptation', as one prominent historian famously had it. Tony Hopkins had in mind, specifically, the Yoruba states' turbulent transition from slave trade to palm oil production in the 1870s and 1880s, which, he argued, led political elites to wage war in order to maintain both status and revenue.[45] Earlier in our period, the collapse of Oyo perhaps exemplifies the phenomenon, albeit *in extremis*; Senegambian societies experienced violent transitions similar to those described for the Yoruba.[46] It has been argued that not all societies underwent such traumatic shifts, largely because the role of the export trade itself was not so important, in fact, and has sometimes been exaggerated.[47] But it is clear that other polities did indeed seek to alleviate the impact of changing commercial patterns by diversifying their exports, or by shifting their focus to the supply of slaves for more local, 'domestic' markets—'legitimate commerce', after all, depended on slave labour across the continent—or a combination of export and local trade. Economic futures, and the very character of the state, were the subject of heated debate within Asante, as we have seen in a different context: here, there was the shift toward a more diversified economy, which had long rested on farming and gold-mining as much as on the export of people, and the evolution of sociopolitical esteem and status is indicated in the increasing honour bestowed on particularly successful merchants by the Asante state by the middle of the nineteenth century.[48] Asante also benefited from the strength of its commercial links to the savannah region to the north and to the trans-Saharan network.[49] Even Dahomey, long resistant to the new commercial pressures (and another case study for the 'crisis of adaptation' thesis) at length had to reckon with the sharp fall in demand for slaves in the 1850s and 1860s, and moved into the production of palm oil. This did not render the army obsolete, by any means: wars were fought to acquire slaves now to sustain and expand domestic production. Moreover, the political centre imposed a tax on the export of palm oil in the 1850s—the period of the kingdom's own transition away from the slave trade and toward agricultural exports—in an attempt to exclude small-scale merchants from muscling in on overseas trade.[50] This was, of course, an indication of the enormous significance of overseas commerce itself, reflected, too, in the political factionalism at the centre of the state as various groups wrestled over access to and control over trade, especially as the state's hegemonic role was increasingly robustly contested.[51]

Shifts in the nature of global trade generated conflict at the very heart of polities, but there could be no denying the reality that this was increasingly the era of new forms of production and entrepreneurialism, as external demand for certain commodities—vegetable oils, especially palm oil; groundnuts; rubber; beeswax; cotton—grew steadily. Farmers and merchants in communities along the Atlantic littoral, often operating on a smaller scale than had previously been possible, turned to production for export: palm oil across much of the coastal forest zone between the Niger Delta and the province of Sierra Leone; cotton in the coastal areas of present-day Nigeria, Ghana and Senegal, where groundnuts were also embraced by eager cultivators, as they also were in Gambia; rubber across a swathe of central Africa. In many cases, such production could involve anyone with access to relatively modest (in contrast to the business of capturing and exporting large numbers of human beings) amounts of land and labour—often family labour supplemented by slaves, and these were often women. Women themselves, meanwhile, were central to the emergence of a comprador class in Sierra Leone, and became active and highly competitive in a commercial network across the territory, linking European firms at Freetown with the communities of the interior. They came to dominate the kola nut trade in the course of the nineteenth century.[52] A particular group of Yoruba women constituted a similar comprador class: mostly returnee former slaves from Sierra Leone, they became known as the Saro, and mobilised their connections to British agents and exposure to Christianity to forge a vibrant commercial community in Lagos and Abeokuta.[53] In central Africa, some women also moved into cash crop production, although the sector was dominated by men, and those female traders who were prominently successful were outliers rather than typical.[54] More broadly, the widening of access also meant the acquisition of imports—including firearms, which enabled communities to hold their own against hostile neighbours—by ever larger numbers of people, further quickening the pace of socioeconomic change.

African peasant production drove economic change across much of the continent in the course of the long nineteenth century, and the responsiveness, adaptability and entrepreneurialism of these economic agents continued to do so deep into the twentieth century, by which time African endeavours formed the bedrock of what became known as the 'cash crop revolution' of the colonial era. In the early years of the twentieth century, peasant production was both encouraged by colonial administrations and further stimulated by heightened global demand, new tax regimes—requiring African farmers to pay their taxes in officially recognised currencies, which could only be acquired by marketising their labour—and of course through the construction of transport infrastructure: railways and, increasingly, roads. Mechanised transport, moreover, facilitated production deeper in the interior than previously, whereas most cash crop farming in the nineteenth century had only really been possible on or near the coast, from where low-value, bulky items could be more easily carried to market. Thus, for example, railway expansion in British Nigeria drew the Yoruba into cocoa production, and in time allowed Hausa farmers to cultivate groundnuts further north.[55] In French Senegal, where groundnuts had long been an export staple for communities near the shoreline, the expansion of the railway into the interior in the years prior to the First World War led to a remarkable increase in production for export: from 50,000 tons in 1897 to 240,000 tons in 1913, with similar developments across the western Sahel once the railway reached Bamako from Dakar in 1923, and in the palm oil-producing territories of Dahomey and Côte d'Ivoire.[56] In Côte d'Ivoire, too, the French colonial administration facilitated an export economy based on cotton.[57] It is worth noting that railways weren't *always* critical to the putative economic achievements of the early colonial state: the remarkable success of the cocoa-farming communities in the British Gold Coast territory between the early 1890s and 1914 was the outcome very largely of their own initiative and planning, not of the local railway line which only began to have an impact in the early 1920s.[58] Still, in general, this was indeed an economic expansion remarkable in its scale, and made possible through the creation of industrial infrastructure by foreigners. The scale of the shift was perhaps most stark across eastern and central Africa, regions with comparatively little history of commercial agriculture, but from the late nineteenth and early twentieth centuries onward suddenly and vigorously engaged in it: coffee among the Chagga around Kilimanjaro;[59] or cotton in southern Uganda, introduced by the energetic British Cotton Growing Association, but embraced with extraordinary success by a class of Ganda entrepreneurs.[60] German and French administrators employed a combination of coercion and enticement in developing commercial cotton production in their territories in eastern and central Africa respectively. Initially, at least, rather more emphasis was placed on coercion, with sometimes catastrophic results.[61] The British built on Muhammad Ali's early nineteenth-century innovative visions in Egypt in developing irrigation systems, constructing dams and deepening canals, in order greatly to expand cotton cultivation, while at the same time, ironically, laying the foundations of the kind of industrial base Muhammad Ali had had in mind by investing in processing plants for sugar and tobacco as well as cotton.[62] Further south, one of the great success stories, at least in the short term, in British Sudan was the Gezira Scheme, run by the Sudan Plantations Syndicate, which also involved the large-scale expansion of irrigation which facilitated cotton production.[63]

In reality, however, the commercial revolution had begun in the middle decades of the nineteenth century, and the most important component was not the application of 'superior' technology to Africa, stimulating though that frequently was in certain places in a later period, but rather the cultures of innovation which characterised millions of Africans' engagement with the global economy throughout the previous century.[64] Cash crops had a much longer history in the Atlantic world than across eastern (with the exception of Zanzibar), central and southern Africa, where European economic and technological stimuli had a much more abrupt and, ostensibly, transformative effect; but across the entire continent, the decades preceding this had been characterised by verve and vision on the part of African entrepreneurs and producers and workers (and of course consumers) of many hues, both female and male. The entrepreneurial class itself was dominated by men, but in certain contexts women were pioneers. The cash crop revolution was a deeply gendered phenomenon, in that while commercial agriculture opened up opportunities for some elite women, more broadly the burden of subsistence farming fell on women. There were highly successful women traders, and in the Niger Delta women were among the most effective producers and sellers of palm oil.[65] Across the board, this was the energy into which later European colonial states tapped, harnessing it, and attempting to manage it, in novel ways. Colonial economies, while often introducing new levels of commercial, bureaucratic and infrastructural intricacy, were ultimately rooted in the era of African creativity and liminality.

## Striving, Moving, Belonging

YET THIS WAS NOT SIMPLY a matter of factors of endowment and marketing. It was also about multi-layered social and material aspiration, a desire to remake and reimagine status and wellbeing, a drive for self-improvement. No doubt straightforward avarice had its place. But wealth was never simply about materiality.[66] Particular forms of tangible commodity implied a form of personal self-realisation and social transformation which was as much about the abstract, the ideological, the spiritual, as it was about the lurid demonstration of brute force or grasping materialism. Heightened levels of social stratification and the emergence of new socioeconomic groupings reflected novel forms of cultural and ontological as well as material ambition. At the Ganda royal court, proximity to imports such as guns, cloth and a range of other manufactured goods generated competition among factions (and individuals) for ever closer association with the source of such access—although ultimately it didn't guarantee loyalty to the extant regime, as factions increasingly believed they should and could have their own access to such exterior linkages.[67] By the same token, various groups sought access to the external in pursuit of personal social and material advancement. Again, there was relatively recent precedent for this in the context of the eighteenth-century slave trade: witness the various commercial interests vying for influence within Dahomey, or, in a less centralised but no less competitive environment, among the Imbangala. The latter, indeed, illustrate very effectively the emerging significance of professional violence, increasingly organised around extraterritorial commercial roads and entrepôts, as a means to material and social advancement and wellbeing.[68] War offered a way in, and a way up.

Heightened levels of social and economic mobility resulted from access to global trade, including the greenfield innovations which led to distinctive forms of entrepreneurship and which in many ways represented the most dramatic manifestations of social upheaval. Social flux meant social mobility, both upwards and downwards, with new groups of people, both women and men, albeit principally the latter, claiming positions of economic and political power through access to firearms, imported cloth and sundry manufactured and 'luxury' goods. In essence, again, while access to global trade was often controlled by long-standing elites with access to military hardware, it could also increasingly be achieved by people historically further down the social hierarchy. Lives and fortunes rested on the ability to compete successfully for access to the export trades, pushing further the frontiers of competition and the kind of creative volatility that characterised local politics. Social mobility and insurgent politics were often two parts of the same phenomenon, and thus in many cases involved a direct challenge to existing sociopolitical orders. In the Niger Delta, a region which would come be known as the 'Oil Rivers', a series of ferociously competitive commercial city-states such as Bonny and Calabar saw the emergence of trading 'houses' in response to demand for palm oil, which lubricated the British industrial revolution, just as profits from the transport of the enslaved had funded European economic transformation in the first place. Across the myriad Niger mangrove riverways, commercial institutions asserted influence over more or less defined areas to secure access to European trading companies keen to purchase palm oil, and hereditary political authority became vested in successful merchants in what amounted to a dramatic reconfiguring of social status as well as political power. It was a situation of creative flux which led to some of the most remarkable manifestations of social mobility and new political power, for in these circumstances those of modest provenance—most obviously, slaves—could purchase and manoeuvre their way to elevated status.[69] The case of Jaja stands out: born in the early 1820s, this young slave in Bonny succeeded in buying his own freedom, whereupon he worked to take control of the Anna Pepple trading house, one of the

most prominent commercial enterprises in the area. Following a dispute
with the rival Manilla Pepple house in 1869, he left Bonny, taking a community of devoted followers with him to establish the new settlement of
Opobo. Jaja turned Opobo into one of the most important commercial
entities in the Delta in the 1870s, dominating the palm oil business and
having himself recognised as a 'king' as a result. Jaja's is a noteworthy story,
encapsulating the societal fluidity and entrepreneurialism, and of course
the courage required to realise ambitions, of the age.[70] In the early
twentieth-century Niger Delta, the story of Omu Okwei of Ossamari is
as illustrative as that of Jaja. From a relatively lowly background, she was
famed for her business acumen, building up a veritable commercial empire in the early decades of the twentieth century based on her control of
local import and export, though it is important to note that she did so in
large part through carefully cultivated connections with prominent men
in the area, including those involved in the Royal Niger Company and in
banking at Onitsha. Omu Okwei became a prominent social and political figure in later life, but of course other women weren't so fortunate.[71]
Similar patterns of social mobility were in evidence through the long
nineteenth century: among the Tio along the central stretch of the Congo
River, for example, older, more established forms of kingship became
increasingly ceremonial and performative, while real power drained
away toward the merchant-chiefs who dominated the riverine export
trade.[72] Of course these new elites were as keen as any other to protect
their privileged positions. Even within the Niger Delta micro-polities,
predominantly but not exclusively Igbo-speaking, rulers sought to maintain control of the trade itself: in Old Calabar, in 1862, the senior chiefs
outlawed the sale of palm oil below a certain amount, to prevent the kind
of commercially fuelled insurgency and the social mobility of which
they themselves had been a product in the first place.[73]

Comparable waves of socioeconomic transformation unfolded across
eastern and central Africa. The global context for this commercial and
social revolution was the reinvigoration of the eastern African slave trade
from the late eighteenth century onward, which would see (as a conservative estimate) between twenty thousand and thirty thousand people per
year forcibly removed from the continent in the 1820s, and seventy thou-

sand per year at the height of the trade in the 1860s, not to mention the hundreds of thousands of enslaved people moved by force *within* a vast area between the Red Sea coast and Mozambique in the course of the nineteenth century. The drivers of this commercial expansion are numerous, but they include greater demand from across the Muslim world after the expansion of the Russian Empire had shut down older central Asian sources of unfree labour; the expansion of coffee and sugar plantations on French-owned islands in the Indian Ocean; Brazilian traders moving beyond the Atlantic in search of business along the coast of Mozambique and the Zambezi valley; and the rise, as we have seen, of the Zanzibar Sultanate as a dominant commercial force.[74] More broadly, a swathe of eastern Africa was ever more connected to the global economy, and shaped by the growing demand for African ivory, after the opening of the Suez Canal in 1869.

In Buganda, access to foreign imports indicated a level of cosmopolitan sophistication which denoted elevated social as well as political status. In an increasingly febrile, competitive environment, higher-end cotton cloth, notably, had a profound impact on local fashion, and on how people with the access to such goods dressed publicly. It was an outward demonstration of aspiration and upward mobility.[75] This wasn't a question of associating all things exogenous with inherent 'superiority', or consciously imbuing those commodities with a value which by default involved the denigration of the 'local'. It *did* mean the co-option of the external, the global, with a view to achieving internal power; the translation of new forms of materiality into heightened local authority and influence. In more greenfield scenarios, this dynamic manifested itself differently, but with broadly comparable implications. The Sumbwa entrepreneur Msiri, who came from a community a little north of our road, was a pioneer; a busy, brave, brutal investor in people and space, who took those investments far to the south, and created a business empire built on both violent extraction and extraordinary personal courage. As we have also seen in the context of armed insurgency, the Yao, stretching across a swathe of present-day southern Tanzania, Malawi and Mozambique, rivalled the Nyamwezi in exercising authority over their own labour, even, arguably, those who were enslaved people in the service of larger insurgencies. They did so in various capacities, whether as individual entrepreneurs, or as traders and porters and soldiers, whether in small groups or as part of larger projects under charismatic leadership. They were critical to the kind of commercial expansion which involved an influx of guns and other imports, and the export of people. They embodied aspiration and flux; they transformed their social and political landscapes; and they created economic networks within which new forms of material acquisition as well as identity and belonging were possible.[76] In the area of present-day south-central Kenya, the Kamba grasped the opportunities on offer to form a vibrant commercial community, positioning themselves as vital middlemen along a trade highway of growing significance.[77]

Crucially, participation in violence was key to social advancement and self-realisation. The societal and material and fundamentally existential significance of violence for groups like the Imbangala in the eighteenth century was replicated across the continent in the nineteenth century: among the Nyamwezi, Yao, Yoruba, Wolof, Tigrinya, Amhara, Zulu, Fulani. Among the Ganda, armed heroism became central to the very notion of being a member of the extended community known as Buganda; and war, increasingly inextricably linked to the external world, was a passage— albeit a risky one, with no guarantees for success whether individual or collective—to heightened social status and material gain.[78] The practice as well as the culture of violence was a matter of social aspiration among the Chikunda armies commanded by the Afro-Portuguese *prazeiros* or plantation owners along the Zambezi valley, and representing the kind of privatisation of violence which was also common among the Yao.[79] No group embodied these dynamics more dramatically than communities across central Africa, including the Chokwe and the Ovimbundu. These remarkable networks of endeavour and identity, pragmatically materialistic as well as ontological enterprises, imposed themselves on the trades in ivory, beeswax and, later, rubber, especially with the decrease in the volume of overseas slave exports from the 1830s and 1840s onward. The Ovimbundu, organised into a network of kingdoms in the central plateau inland from Benguela, became increasingly engaged in the export business, especially as the number of Portuguese traders in their vicinity receded with the abolition of the slave trade, presenting opportunities for the Ovimbundu themselves. Historically less important polities, including Huambo, Bié and Bailundo, asserted themselves at the expense of previously more important ones, such as Caconda.[80] The Ovimbundu had long been engaged in overseas commerce;[81] the Chokwe further east were relative newcomers by comparison, but their commercial expansion in the middle decades of the nineteenth century was remarkable. Swiftly positioning themselves as the chief competitors of the Ovimbundu, they dominated the ivory and wax trades, accumulating significant numbers of firearms and expanding their numbers by absorbing people, especially women, into their communities. When the elephant population decreased in the areas to which they had access, Chokwe swiftly transitioned into middlemen, and became among the most prodigious and energetic of transporters and sellers of ivory at the coast.[82] Both Ovimbundu and Chokwe were well positioned when the rubber boom arrived in the later nineteenth century.

The intersection between social and material status on the one hand and positionality based on violence or the threat of it on the other was not confined to state-based scenarios, nor to communities inherently outward looking, of course. In East Africa, Maasai and Turkana communities were increasingly rooted in the idea of armed endeavour in the course of the nineteenth century, and under new forms of charismatic, often prophetic leadership, revised long-standing pastoral cultures to incorporate ideas about status based on martial prowess. Among the Maasai, for example, a gerontocratic system was honed to harness, and simultaneously carefully to manage, youthful aggression. These more aggressive, acquisitive cultures were both cause and consequence of heightened conflicts over pastureland and herds, to some extent driven by environmental and climatic factors. In the first instance, they reflect broader indigenous patterns of economic innovation and the social valorisation of violence, but in time these conflicts would mesh with external intrusions.[83]

These developments had socioeconomic and demographic consequences, mostly dramatically manifest in West Africa. This was an era of economic pressure as well as of opportunity. Notably, for example, the range of commodities now in demand was really only economically viable to produce on or near the coast: groundnuts or palm oil were bulky, low-value goods, and the cost as well as the logistical challenges involved in long-distance transportation meant that production boomed close to the ocean, where the best profits were to be had. As a result, over several decades, people migrated from the interior to the coast and began to cluster around those sites of production where their labour would be most valuable.[84] At the same time, prolonged slaving violence, most visibly among the Yoruba, resulted in mass displacement. People moved in search of security, notably southward from the open savannah, where they were vulnerable to attack, toward the relative protection of the forest, and as they did so they fuelled further interstitial violence, often living by predation in the desperate search for material advantage amidst the turmoil. One major outcome of these migratory movements was increasing urbanisation, the result of 'clustering' around existing towns and the creation of new urban sites.[85] Moreover, this insurgent form of urbanisation often involved the rise of relatively new centres, such as Abeokuta, Lagos and Ibadan, at the expense of formerly important urban sites, such as Ouidah.[86] Fortification, meanwhile, whether in the form of stockades, moats, or a combination of mounds and ditches, was one of the most visible manifestations of a veritable military revolution across the region, but it was also emblematic of profound social and demographic change.[87] The growing prevalence of the urban or at least the proto-urban in the context of socioeconomic insecurity and military ambition can be discerned in eastern Africa, too.[88]

Demographic change and population movement defined the era elsewhere, too. Across swathes of eastern, central and southern Africa, migration and mobility are key to understanding Africa's transformative nineteenth century, and to grasping both the scale and the significance of its myriad experiences, and expressions, of both innovation and liminality. Labour, in its various guises, both free and unfree, and involving a spectrum of agency, moved vast distances. Migration was often coerced—the enslaved don't generally have much input into where they end up—but it was also opportunistic, searching, acquisitive, aspirational. Porters, merchants, soldiers, camp-followers and concubines migrated continually across the areas of modern-day Tanzania, Mozambique, Angola, Malawi, Zambia and South Africa, and in so doing forged new ways of identifying, producing, living. In the late nineteenth century and in the early decades of the twentieth, much of this subcontinental pattern of labour migrancy would be replicated as part of a brutal transregional mining economy, which involved a new level of violent magnitude; but people had been moving across this area for work and opportunity, or through no choice of their own, for much of the long nineteenth century. The tendency to reduce all African agency in this context to the category of 'resistance' is perhaps to submit to a 'colonial-centric' teleology.[89] That said, there were often devastating environmental consequences, as we have noted in the context of our road: the movement of people often meant the abandonment of land, the rejuvenation of bush and the advance of new disease environments, especially with respect to sleeping sickness. Dislocation across large areas created new 'internal' diasporas within the continent and led to seismic shifts in population distribution, and in some areas disrupted the age-old African capacity to manage the landscape. The outbreak of trypanosomiasis in a number of areas in the late nineteenth and early twentieth centuries—an outcome of the African revolution and of the culture of innovation—represented an opportunity for leverage to intruding foreigners, and was utilised by colonial states to impose control over populations. This is clear across German East Africa, along the Ugandan shore of Lake Victoria, in the lower Congo and then in the northern area of the Belgian Congo, in Northern Rhodesia.[90]

In Egypt, the corollary of state-led economic endeavours—in what amounted to one of the most dramatic manifestations of social transformation anywhere in the continent, though certainly one with echoes elsewhere—was the creation of a new middle class, engaged in administration, land-ownership and a range of professions (legal, pedagogical, literary) which were predominantly urban and, by many accounts, 'modern.'[91] Life may not have changed much for the farmers who cultivated the cotton, of course; and they comprised the vast bulk of the population. But Muhammad Ali's state instigated new forms of social stratification, and opened up opportunities for many, driven by a programme of material renewal and economic expansion. Socioeconomic transformation was therefore also about belonging and identity. As with the Nyamwezi in the middle decades of the nineteenth century, so, too, with a newly assertive Egyptian middle class: the two are distinct, no doubt, in the particularities and contexts, and in vernacular articulation, but there is clear common ground in terms of how social change and material aspiration gave rise to an ever sharper sense of community, defined in relation to work, language, lived experience.[92] It was as carefully constructed as it was 'organic', as identification always is, but no less authentic and quotidian for that—especially in times of extraordinary turbulence. Widespread enslavement often led to coerced collectivism, as well as, conversely, to the otherising of communities from whom the enslaved were habitually drawn; but bonds of ideological fealty, affective connection, faith, and of course, rather more contingently, opportunism and the provisional alignment of interests were also at play during this tempestuous era. Shared notions of the collective were the product of cultural behaviours over the *longue durée*; of systems of domination; of martial or commercial prowess; of physical environment. The term 'ethnicity' is so often unfit for purpose, utilised as an umbrella for all manner of behaviours loosely connected with 'the human condition', and certainly the human desire to be included, and to rationalise exclusion. We do not, I think, have to subscribe to either 'primordialist' or 'instrumentalist' camps to recognise the vitality and inventiveness underpinning such publics.[93] However we categorise these communities, many of them emerge, and are consolidated, in the course of the global, transformative nineteenth century: Yoruba, Zulu and Ganda, for example, become, in different ways and contexts, collective as well as individual articulations of aspiration. In many respects, these are doubtless strengthened in an era of insecurity and, from both near and far, external challenge. But they were never monolithic blocs, simplistically demarcated as they were on later colonial-era maps. Cultural and linguistic identifications were a matter of fission as well as fusion: witness the dispersal of signs and symbols following Lunda migrations, and their adaptation to insurgent environments; or the re-creation of certain elements of Nyamwezi identity, above all Nyamwezi entrepreneurialism, in the establishment of Msiri's Garenganze state—named after the community near Unyanyembe from which Msiri and many of his circle originally hailed. 'Ethnicity', from that perspective, wasn't a matter of immutable and impermeable solidity: it was rolling and evolving, often over long distances, at times simultaneously inclusive as much as exclusive. It was, paradoxically, one of the most dynamic manifestations of liminality, rather than the timeless certainty with which it is often wrongly associated. Certain elements might become more or less fixed for periods of time—language, aesthetic production and performance, shared memory, sense of place, cosmology—but even these were subject to periodic amendment, as was the group of people in a position to do the amending. These networks of belonging were conditional, and they were contextual.[94] There seems little question, for example, that a sense of 'Fulani' belonging was not only a provenance of the insurgencies which remade West African geopolitics in the eighteenth and nineteenth centuries; it was actively enhanced, even in some areas actively created, in the course of those insurgencies. To be Fulani became a matter of aspiration, and an expression of belonging which was itself an act of innovative self-realisation, and indeed resistance, with a growing awareness of pan-regionality which transcended locale, even if the latter remained significant in the lives of most people. Relevant here, too, is the degree to which a number of early fighters in jihadist uprisings were not Muslim to begin with, but converted to the faith as the insurrection gained momentum. This is evident in the very roots of the insurgency which led to Sokoto—and as we have seen, this was closely related to socioeconomic consciousness; and it is present, too, in the other Islamic reformist movements which arose in the years subsequent. Aspiration and innovation, in other words, also meant the creation of networks of belonging defined by a sense of place and time, and by sociocultural behaviour in both. Such communities were not always wholly coherent, or consistent; they were volatile, and shifting. But they could also be adhesive enough over the long term. This, too, was a core component of Africa's nineteenth-century revolution. In the late nineteenth and early twentieth centuries, these dynamics, unfolding still, intersected with the exigencies of the 'colonial' moment. Colonial administrations both tapped into, and in some cases no doubt altered, the course or process of collective belonging in various ways. Missionaries had a significant role to play in terms of translation of text into vernaculars, and in the groupwork involved in worship itself.[95] But to attribute transformative power to European discourse and bureaucracy at this particular juncture is to ignore the energetic forms of self- and collective identification which were under way throughout the nineteenth century, and in some cases rather earlier than that.[96]

At the same time, materiality and the creation of new networks of social capital was frequently attended by new forms of spirituality and self-awareness, and in fact the embrace of imported systems of belief and thought was part of the same process by which people sought access to tangible things. This, too, was a matter of aspiration and reimagining the self as well as the collective—intellectually, theologically, ontologically. Among the Ganda, by the late 1860s, Islam was winning converts at the royal court a generation after the first coastal merchants arrived at the north end of Lake Victoria. Many converted, no doubt, for reasons of private spiritual conviction. But Islam also represented a global network of connection and exchange, of goods as well as beliefs, membership of which became a matter of self-realisation. Kabaka Mutesa, who professed to be Muslim by the early 1870s, espied a rather more pragmatic use for Islam: namely, as a means to centralising royal power and restricting the influence of the mediums representing the kingdom's powerful deities. But many also embraced Islam, conversely, as a means to resisting royal prerogative—a number of young converts were executed by Mutesa in the mid-1870s after they defied him, and accused him to failing to properly observe the faith—and self-improvement. From the late 1870s and through the 1880s, many more Ganda would convert to Christianity for many of the same reasons. Factionalism, coalescing around adherence to either Islam, Protestantism or Catholicism, would map onto deep-rooted fissiparity at the centre of the kingdom;[97] but for our purposes here, conversion to foreign religion was part of a much larger set of dynamics by which the exogenous was co-opted and mobilised for a range of purposes. In a similar vein, many Yao entrepreneurs converted to Islam, and conversion was common around Lake Malawi among a number of communities. These were people on the frontiers of both commercial and theological exchange, and the experience made them receptive to new forms of aspiration and expression. Just as receptive to imported faiths were the people displaced by violence and by the uncertainty and traumas of the age, and in this context conversion was usually an assertion of self and an expression of both hope and aspiration, as well as resistance, in the face of seemingly insurmountable challenges.[98] This was demonstrably the case in southern Africa, for example among the Tswana: here, women of the Tshidi subgroup were among the first converts to Christianity, arguably as a result of both their socioeconomic subordination and their liminality, in search of new ways of achieving autonomy and of asserting themselves.[99] The Christian converts whom the Zulu called *amakholwa* would become crucial intermediaries in the intensifying encounter between Africans and Europeans.[100]

## Coercion

VIRTUALLY ALL OF THESE SCENARIOS share one element: cultures and processes of coercion, which invariably involved otherisation in various forms, including the practice of enslavement and participation in the slave trades. Aspiration and innovation were frequently expressed in terms of violence; opportunism almost always required it, for ultimately social, economic and political power was rooted in, and expressed through, the number of people 'owned' or over whose lives control was exercised. In the course of the nineteenth century, levels of enslavement increased dramatically; for every ambitious innovator, keen to tap into the opportunities on offer, there were many more people whose personal freedom was severely curtailed, with the burden falling disproportionately on women. The violent insecurity of what we might term the oceanic economies, both Indian and Atlantic, represented an opportunity for many, and a catastrophe for many more, for servitude and suffering were the corollaries of ambition and accumulation. Material transformations were attended by heightened and often novel levels of interpersonal as well as collective violence. Inevitably, there is a moral issue to be grappled with here, one which isn't perhaps best addressed by the ongoing and sometimes simplistic discussion around 'decoloniality'. In this specific context, it is important to recognise the distinction between a celebration, if that is the correct term, of the innovators—the entrepreneurs, such as Mirambo, or Tippu Tip, who are above all the quintessence of forceful agency in the nineteenth-century Global South—and the enslaved, the oppressed, the marginalised: those upon whom violence is inflicted and who are the victims of others' ambition and aspiration. In the African context, as elsewhere, the latter tend to be voiceless; the vast majority have disappeared into the shadows.[101] But the key point is that African agency generated victims. As is well documented, the slave trade died a slow death in Atlantic Africa: millions of Africans were taken out of the continent down to the 1860s.[102] Until that point, entire economic and political systems were organised around the capture and export of people; and after that point, the ownership of people *within* communities was critical to economic and political success. Similar patterns are discernible across eastern and central Africa, too, even as the flow of people diminished across the Atlantic: in fact, across regions linked to the Indian Ocean, the forced migration of the enslaved escalated in the 1840s and 1850s, just as the volume of enslaved people crossing the Atlantic was tailing off. The economies of many insurgencies and reformist movements were organised precisely for the purpose, and involved a level of social flux of the form and scale which had enabled those movements in the first place. Across the period, moreover, the trans-Saharan slave trade continued to thrive, as it had for several centuries.[103]

Material and political aspiration relied heavily on various forms of enslavement and control. The success of the Chokwe, the Ovimbundu, the Lunda or the Yao was built on the back of unfree labour, but they were hardly alone. Zanzibar's plantation economy was based on an uninterrupted supply of enslaved people. Dahomey had long made extensive use of slaves in various ways within its domestic economy, and continued to do so through the nineteenth century, indeed expanding the use of unfree labour with the reorientation toward commercial agriculture from mid-century onward. Moreover, the enslaved—not least those to be sacrificed to honour the royal ancestors—played a critical role in the political and cultural life of the kingdom. The slave population of Buganda increased dramatically in the course of the eighteenth and nineteenth centuries, and was critical to the functioning of society and economy.[104] Millions of enslaved people were either exported beyond the continent, contributing to extant diasporas in the Americas, in particular, but also across the Indian Ocean, Gulf and central Asian worlds; or were forcibly moved within the continent, often over substantial distances, especially in eastern and central Africa. Enslaved people, generated through warfare, were used in agriculture, and as porters; they were mobilised to produce commodities for export after the decline of the slave trade in the Atlantic world, a paradox which to disappointed European abolitionists came to emblematise the supposedly benighted state of the continent. Arguably the treatment of chattel slaves worsened in the course of the century, as they were relatively cheap and needed to be worked hard in a competitive, insecure environment. Slaves were soldiers in the new armies which transformed political landscapes. Sometimes they were merchants operating on behalf of wealthy owners and, as noted earlier, worked themselves into positions where they could acquire their freedom and trade on their own accounts, even achieving considerable political power. In that sense enslavement was not a monolithic, unchanging status. But the central point here is that the nineteenth-century African revolution was to a very substantial degree based on the expansion of an enslaved population, and the often violent control of labour. These were economies of coercion; the social mobility evident for many was only possible through the lack of freedom of many more. The ability to accumulate wealth through external links, direct or indirect, invariably meant the ability to control and coerce people informally or overtly. It certainly meant the ability to expand retinues of 'domestic' slaves who could be made to work on commercial agricultural projects, with labour increasingly harnessed to production for export and ultimately to sustain aspirational communities and classes of people created by the flux of the global nineteenth century.

The gendered dimensions to these developments were deep, and wide. In the context of the slave trade, men were more likely to be sold overseas; women were more often retained for the domestic trade and for domestic slavery, for which they were preferred because they lacked kin and could be more easily incorporated into the host society. Enslaved women were also increasingly used for agricultural labour, especially in coastal societies, in some areas enabling free and higher status women to engage in other activities, notably trade. Within new economies in which men were increasingly engaged in external commerce, women assumed a critical new role as producers of food for local consumption, thus facilitating the political and military revolutions which changed the nineteenth-century landscape.[105] For men, material wealth meant the ability to expand domestic enclosures and households. Male elites purchased female slaves to expand domestic compounds, and aspiration was frequently sexual in its provenance and practice: women were vital, in that sense, to the operation of material power, and the usage of female slaves increased substantially across the continent in the course of the century. Likewise, the eastern African slave trade in the nineteenth century disproportionately affected women, as well as children, and in general involved the reduction of hundreds of thousands of women to the status of commodity, marketised on the basis of their reproductive capacity and their potential labour, and in some contexts their perceived aesthetic qualities.[106] In many scenarios, womanhood was reduced to motherhood, which was associated with helplessness and justified masculinised cultures of security and protection but also enabled greater control over women's lives, in the context of both productive and reproductive labour.[107] In some cases, as among the Kikuyu and Nandi in Kenya, ideologies were developed which explicitly articulated ideas about the intrinsic inferiority of women vis-à-vis men; and so we can identify the nineteenth-century revolution as leading to some very particular divisions of social, economic and political labour within communities, based explicitly on ideas about gender.[108]

In sum, the rise of new economies, especially those geared toward agricultural production, involved a much wider and more intensive use of slaves within the continent.[109] Commercial agriculture involved bringing more land under cultivation in order to maximise profits, which meant using more labour. In fact some commodities, such as palm oil, required more labour than others in terms of both production and transportation, and so demand for labour surged. Yet this was not only about production for export. In those areas which had been particularly badly affected by the slave trade—notably across the vast region of present-day Angola and Congo—a gender imbalance had resulted, the result of the loss of large numbers of younger men. The decline of the slave trade and gradual demographic recovery brought new strains on domestic food production, which needed to be expanded to meet local demand; and again, this led to the increased use of slave labour. Later on, European colonial administrations contributed substantively to the hardening and deepening of cultures of compulsion, designing and ruthlessly utilising systems of forced labour in pushing forward production for export in those areas not well served by existing systems of cash crop farming: the Belgians in Congo, the French in Côte d'Ivoire and Cameroon, the Portuguese in Mozambique, the Germans in Tanganyika. They introduced their own form of violent economics, bolstered by increasingly entrenched cultures of racism, and these were invariably shockingly brutal—for all the anti-slavery rhetoric by then so core to most European imperial projects.[110] In some respects, however, this can be regarded as the latest stage in an era of economic change which had been substantially based on coercion.

———

THESE VARIOUS AND MULTI-LAYERED EXERCISES in material aspiration, reformation and renovation were diverse. But taking a wide view, they can be seen to have involved the long-term creation of overlapping networks of entrepreneurialism and extraction; systems of infrastructure and connection; and pools of capital—human, animal, mineral and agronomic—which Africans then sought to manage in the most effective ways they knew how.[111] Insurgent and reformist economies also generated violence, and clearly much warfare during Africa's long nineteenth century was concerned with control of resources, including both land and people. Violence was a means to the acquisition of wealth. In some scenarios these were, at least initially, largely local, relatively self-contained conflicts, emblematic of deeper, long-standing efforts to innovate with a view to maximising and managing resources. But as the century drew on, violence escalated in parallel with the growing significance of the external commercial frontier, and most conflicts involved the intersection of the local and the global, as Africans sought to harness external opportunities in order to enhance local authority and status or even create it from scratch. Certainly, the overwhelming evidence from Africa's long, global nineteenth century suggests an enthusiasm, even a ferocious zealotry, for engagement with new economic opportunities, and a capacity for risk-assessment and frequently risk-taking which reflected the social flux of the decades preceding formal European interest in the continent. The courageous itinerancy and armed innovation exhibited by Msiri, or Jaja, or indeed Tippu Tip himself—African in lived experience, if not wholly in biological ancestry—are genuinely breathtaking, once we remove anachronistic moral evaluation, and represent a material partition of the continent involving an African agency which long precedes, and in fact creates the structure for and facilitates, later European efforts. These individuals are emblematic of the frontier spirit of a new cohort of entrepreneurs who moved within, and pushed outward, commercial as well as political interstices. They took advantage of volatility and created new forms of it, and the communities which resulted demonstrated a remarkable capacity to organise violence in order to seize the opportunities on offer. The force of African entrepreneurialism during this era is critical to understanding the continent's economic experience in the twentieth century, and beyond.

In the course of the long nineteenth century, Africans produced the social and material infrastructure which not only maximised the opportunities presented through global engagement, but which also, ironically, facilitated global intrusion. Europeans, initially at least, rarely represented anything other than the latest opportunity for social and economic improvement and advancement; for some, at least. From a certain perspective, those later exercises in foreign economic intervention represented simply the latest wave of material and social reformation in a long century of innovation. But of course, Africans' variegated long-term exercises in innovation and aspiration also created, or exacerbated, liminality and generated frontiers of exploitation and marginalisation. Innovation happened on the back of coercion and exploitation; aspiration and upward social mobility for some also meant dispossession and impoverishment for others. A host of African political systems and socioeconomies were primarily, in the final analysis, organised around predation rather than production, although some successfully balanced both. Such rapacity depended, increasingly, on imported military technology—an array of firearms, and in some cases heavier ordnance—which, in a somewhat circular pattern, much commercial endeavour was focused on acquiring. Guns were deployed, and serviced, in an ever more sophisticated fashion, and were at the centre of a gradually escalating arms race in nineteenth-century Africa, utilised in pursuit of the acquisition and control of people and other resources. Predation undoubtedly allowed the unlocking of some remarkable, and remarkably violent, entrepreneurial energy; it facilitated the rapid mobilisation of new orders and speedy responses to external opportunities. But it also meant that that same energy often outran efforts at socioeconomic consolidation and diversification, and created further patterns of volatility, of fissure and interstice. Of these, intrusive forces were also able to take brutal, if at first inchoate, advantage.

An emphasis on the dynamism of African agency is not incompatible with recognising the long-term, deleterious effects of what has been broadly characterised as underdevelopment in terms of Africa's socioeconomic relationship with the Global North, encompassing the long epoch of the trans-Atlantic slave trade.[112] The essential power of the underdevelopment thesis, broadly understood, is undeniable, and its central tenets are well attested—not only for Africans, but for North and South Americans, Asians, Europeans themselves. Millions of Africans in the nineteenth century were in various ways struggling to reform and compete in an increasingly inequitable world, in which the balance of commercial power was ever more unfavourable to them. Again, ironically in some ways, African entrepreneurship and reformist initiatives rendered Africans themselves susceptible to outside interference, not least through indebtedness to foreign commercial concerns. Africa's material revolution was fraught with risk, intersecting with, and indeed energising, the intrusions of equally innovative and avaricious foreigners with ever expanding global leverage and technological potency. And yet we must be careful not to flatten the narrative into one of victors and victims. Many Africans did indeed thrive in these circumstances, and successfully imposed themselves on and, through their individual and collective labours, and the creation of socioeconomic architecture and capital, shaped the global economic order in more nuanced ways than are allowed for by normative narratives of underdevelopment. There may have been no 'Great Divergence' between Africa and western Europe with the drama and significance described by those highlighting the difference between Britain and China in seeking to explain the rise of Western hegemony and the modern global economic order.[113] According to those narratives, it is a given that the world of the industrial factory blows away that of the wattle hut. But the focus, whether overt or covert, on apparent material difference has long seemed to me a red herring. Of greater interest, over the long term, are the myriad ways in which Africans sought to refashion the material bases of political power with a view to engaging with, and co-opting, the exogenous. In some ways, it is more a matter of convergence than divergence, for Europeans and Africans alike deployed various forms of violence in pursuit of resource extraction and socioeconomic improvement. Above all, the networks of communication and the pools of socioeconomic capital are critical to understanding the later 'colonial' (and indeed 'postcolonial') economy, which was rooted in the *African* enterprise, entrepôts and entrepreneurs of the long nineteenth century. Despite the culturally and racially motivated eschewal of anything like an African 'achievement', and the mantle of 'civilising' mythology with which European actors draped themselves, Africans' proven ability to innovate and to organise critical resources rendered commercial adventures in the continent an attractive project; Africans had created the socioeconomic framework and embodied the aspirational culture without which the European imperial project would have been neither possible nor desirable.

The very force of African armed economic endeavour—the power of social aspiration and the drive to innovate—brought Africans into conflict with Europeans, in time. In that sense, nineteenth-century Africans were victims of their own, albeit mixed, successes. Later foreign intruders would come either to co-opt African networks of endeavour, and the conflicts they invariably engendered, or to impose themselves on them and pull them in new directions. The great rivers, for example, on which Europeans were fixated—the Niger, the Senegal, the Congo, the Zambezi, the Nile—were precisely the sites of much African insurgency and innovation. Europeans harnessed dynamic entrepreneurial cultures and patterns of mobility. There has been debate over whether we regard the 'problem' in the late nineteenth century as being one of African resilience (they were too robust and therefore needed to be crushed); or, conversely, African weakness (they buckled under growing outside commercial pressure) in economic and institutional terms.[114] But it is certainly evident that the dynamism and success of African enterprise in a large number of cases apparently necessitated its erasure by European-led imperial projects. Dynamic upstarts needed to be demolished precisely because of the energy they exhibited, which would have diminished both European control and ability to extract profit. Even then, the project to crush African agency was only possible thanks to the existence of the very zones of unstable interstice, liminality and creativity which had facilitated Africa's energetic engagement with exogenous forces in the long nineteenth century in the first place. The framework within which 'The Scramble' would happen had long been established. That framework also relied upon the emergence of an array of social and economic intermediaries, groups and communities which were part of networks which straddled the endogenous and the exogenous.

All the more remarkable, then, that Europeans would also come to impose certain narratives about modernity, development and materiality on the processes which had been led by Africans themselves; and deep into the twentieth century, Africans were in effect held responsible for their own 'falling behind' almost everyone else owing to their own deplorably violent behaviour and woeful incapacity. African aspiration and innovation were wilfully or otherwise misunderstood; representatives of the Global North imposed ideas about standards of material wellbeing (which, ironically, ignored most people's experience of impoverishment and marginalisation within Europe itself ), and ultimately wove narratives about how armed, divinely sanctioned intervention was justified in the name of some higher civilising mission. Of course, that very process of intervention was itself a somewhat deranged manifestation of Europe's own socioeconomic volatility and entrepreneurialism—and indeed of the liminality being experienced, in the very same period, by many of its own people.

# PART IV

# Liminality and Leverage

# Act IV

## The Progress of John Rowlands

### I

HENRY MORTON STANLEY and his lavishly funded expedition had a singular purpose as they moved along the road—to Unyanyembe, and then beyond it, toward Ujiji on the shore of Lake Tanganyika—in the course of 1871. It wasn't his first mission to Africa. That had been several years earlier, when he reported on the Napier expedition against Emperor Tewodros in 1868 for the *New York Herald*.[1] But it was arguably the defining journey of his life, for he had been charged, famously, by the wealthy proprietor of the *Herald* with locating the celebrated missionary David Livingstone, from whom no one in Europe had heard for some time.[2] Stanley was determined that he would do so, and envisioned the task handed to him with something approaching a sense of Destiny. Imagine his frustration, then, that as he reached Unyanyembe, where he was warmly welcomed by the coastal merchant community, he discovered that a war was raging to the west, blocking the road. This, of course, was the conflict which had erupted between the insurgent Mirambo and Unyanyembe; or, more precisely, between Mirambo and the Mkasiwa regime which had allied itself with the 'Arabs'. In a striking echo of the situation confronting his fellow traveller Speke, who ten years earlier had run head-on into the original crisis following the ousting of Msabila, Stanley was temporarily stuck at Tabora. As with Speke, Stanley found himself navigating the danger and the debris of the revolution which had been unfolding along the road for much of the previous half-century. After three months' hiatus, he managed to break out, and headed westward, taking a slightly more southerly route to avoid Mirambo and the war. And, famously, he did indeed 'find' Livingstone a few weeks after that, at Ujiji, in November 1871. It was the crowning achievement of the young man's career to date—one which, tragically in many ways, he never really surpassed—and he had come a long way.

He had come a long way, but not just in terms of the approximately eight hundred miles he had covered from Bagamoyo on the Indian Ocean coast to Ujiji. He had begun life in 1841, when Unyanyembe was establishing itself as a global hub, as John Rowlands, in Denbigh, north Wales. He was born out of wedlock—his birth certificate, to his permanent shame, listed him as 'John Rowlands, bastard'—and was quickly abandoned by his mother, while his supposed father (though the paternity is disputed) died soon after he was born. After a period living with other members of the wider family, the child Rowlands was placed in a workhouse. His young life was defined by social change in an industrial age, the product of an impoverished Celtic fringe, and of a family broken by economic stress and oppressive cultural sanction. He was shaped by crushing poverty, of a kind common across mid-century Britain, and in his impoverished circumstances in north Wales, as socioeconomic change ravaged places on the peripheries of the great Victorian transformation, Rowlands should have had little chance in life. And yet, he was also to be the product of European globalism, and was borne aloft by transatlantic currents and thrust outward into the world in search of adventure, status, and perhaps analgesia. He emigrated to the United States in 1859, where he reinvented himself. The story of how he came to call himself by his new name, apparently that of a benefactor who took him under his wing for a time, is difficult to unravel;[3] but what is clear is that in the course of the early 1860s, Henry Morton Stanley was created: a smart, hard, ambitious young man, motivated by the stigma of his birth and the deprivation of his youth. He fought, briefly, in the American Civil War—on both sides, in fact—and later became a journalist, seizing the opportunities on offer as a result of the boom in print media, growing literacy rates, increasing popular interest in global events among a global public, travel made easier by technological advances, and imperialism. Stanley may have been, in many ways, an idiosyncratic, singular character; an oddity even in a Victorian age characterised by its panoply of eccentrics. But his life exemplifies the violence and the miscomprehension and the entrepreneurialism of the age of empire, globalisation and intensifying cultural interaction. He found himself, long before he was famous for finding someone else, via the expanding networks of trade, travel and adventure. Just as Africa's long nineteenth century was one of creative volatility and dynamic liminality, so too was Europe's: one of restless social change, episodic political turmoil, economic transformation, violent outward expansion. Just as it represents the trauma of rapid socioeconomic change, Stanley's story, too, encapsulates the global age of aspiration and innovation.[4] In some striking ways, Stanley embodied Europe's own anxious desire to understand and impose itself on the world, his reckless journeying and breathless reportage reflecting in microcosm the violence, prejudice and insecurity of European humanitarian, civilising, imperial missions. Beneath the bluster and the breech-loaders, he was desperate to assert his uncertain manhood in an uncertain world. At the same time, the search to make sense of his own place in that world was attended—inevitably, it seems—by a process of otherisation and vilification. It was not enough for Stanley to be elevated, to adapt the famous aphorism; others must be denigrated. His story is the story of Europe in Africa.

As with Mbula Mtelya, so had Stanley been transformed; and by the time the latter was on the march toward Unyanyembe, his mission was as much about making his own name and escaping his illegitimacy and his brutal past as it was about plucking Livingstone from his fever-ridden concealment. He returned to the road in 1874–76, this time financed by both the *New York Herald* and the *Daily Telegraph*. His assignment was now to chart the Great Lakes and identify the source of the Nile.[5] In the process of these journeys and, perhaps more importantly, publishing hefty books about them, he did a great deal—arguably more than anyone else—to characterise our road and its environs in particular ways, and in shaping a wider public imagining of 'Africa' as a uniquely tragic and barbaric place, desperately in need of European intervention in order to effect its salvation. This also seemed to justify Stanley's own liberal deployment of violence as he did his exploring, something which drew censure even at the time—although we can see his violence, the outcome of a brutal paternalism underpinned by an entrenched set of racial ideas, as a portent of things to come rather than an anomaly. He wasn't immune to the power and charm of particular characters, of course: having characterised him as a scoundrel and a bandit when trying to get past Unyanyembe to Ujiji in 1871, Stanley lauded Mirambo's Napoleonic genius in 1875, even becoming his blood-brother. Perhaps, somewhere unfathomably deep, he recognised a kindred spirit in self-conscious rebirth. He also demonstrated an interest in Africa's history, with the foreshortening, the framing of an essentially ahistorical culture, only hardening later on.[6] But above all it was the Hobbesian vision of primitive violence which lay at the core of the narrative. Others had already conceptualised the continent in these terms, including Thomas Fowell Buxton and Livingstone himself.[7] Stanley, moreover, was the latest in a line of Europeans stumbling along the road, the living, breathing corollaries of upheaval and transition at home and global opportunity and exchange abroad. We might consider the dark eccentricity of Richard Francis Burton, or the imperial professionalism of his erstwhile companion and later rival John Hanning Speke, the two of them having bickered their way to Lake Tanganyika in the mid-1850s; or, again, David Livingstone himself, representing the moral conscience in the age of empire, whose exhausted march to Tabora from Ujiji was undertaken in the last few months of his life before illness claimed him for enduring martyrdom.[8] But Stanley, capable of telling a compelling story, was possessed of a particular talent, for both prose and the identification of an audience ever more eager for tales relating derring-do in the midst of the exotic and the bloodthirsty.[9] Classic projection, perhaps, given the suppressed horrors of his childhood. But there was a ready market for it, nonetheless, and a large canvas on which to paint.

Stanley did much, then, to invent the road, in terms of the dissemination of particular imagery to an eager European and North American public; but the road also invented him, drawing out his own liminality, shaping him through the communities he encountered, communities which had been undergoing dramatic, and traumatic, change for several decades— just as in Denbighshire and a thousand places like it in the turbulent Global North. As he moved through East Africa, he was the continually evolving product, whether he knew it or not, of events and processes over which he had little or no influence. He was co-opted, buffeted, altered. The myth-making that quickly developed around these men, and a handful of women, obscured their more nuanced, complex interaction with Africans and African societies, disguised their vulnerabilities and concealed the extent to which they were the products of African dynamics and not simply the conquerors of landscapes and creators of enduring frames of reference. Stanley and his men inhabited the liminality, the interstices, of the road opened up by many before them. The vast majority of the people in his expeditions were themselves the direct outcome of those very dynamics.[10] The road on which Stanley travelled was a punctuated one, illustrating the energy and uncertainty which were the outcome of the very limits of power on the part of the entrepreneurial polities which had arisen in recent decades. Indeed, those vibrant spaces—the spaces in between—were in some senses critical to the creation of nascent identities, forged in contradistinction to the dark ungoverned places supposedly surrounding energetically luminous new polities, and essential to the spirit of entrepreneurialism which now defined the region. To travel on this road was to move continually through zones of ambiguous or contested control, through shade and shadow. Stanley's progress along the highway was only possible because of those liminal spaces, the absence of neat lines and precisely demarcated points of entry to and exit from zones of authority. Those were inimical to the African revolution. But their absence also presented opportunities for interfering foreigners and their agents: people like Stanley himself, in fact.

# II

AND PEOPLE LIKE KARL PETERS. The first trained historian on our road, Peters was an ardent nationalist, an advocate of the *Völkisch* movement, and in his formative years had sat at the feet of Heinrich von Treitschke, the ultra-nationalist historian and passionate champion of German imperialism.[11] Peters endeavoured to be the man to singlehandedly realise German colonial ambitions, carving a bloody trail across eastern Africa, and desperately collecting 'treaties' with African rulers who might then be presented as having submitted to German rule. He did so at first in a private capacity: a founding member of the Gesellschaft für Deutsche Kolonisation (GfdK: Society for German Colonisation), he travelled in 1884 to East Africa as a representative of the newly formed Deutsch-Ostafrikanische Gesellschaft (DOAG: German East Africa Company). Bismarck was initially sceptical, and refused funding. But the prospect— aggressively played up by the energetic Peters—of losing ground to Britain, or indeed to Leopold II of the Belgians, persuaded Bismarck (whose National Liberal allies in the Reichstag were in any case fervently pro-empire) to step in. Peters's efforts had in some senses pulled the German Reich into the imperial project in the region. But while a hero to many, he was also, to critics, a problematic ambassador for Germany, chiefly on account of his being notoriously violent toward Africans: in fact he was dismissed from his position as Reichskommissar in 1897 when it came to light that he had had his African concubine and her lover (who also happened to be his servant) put to death and their villages destroyed. This was a distinctly sordid racism, not untypical among a certain kind of man, whereby sex with local women was perfectly compatible with generally brutal treatment of the 'native' population. Above all, Peters believed in his, and Germany's, right to blunder violently through the liminal spaces, exploiting the weak points in African polities through threat, bluster, persuasion and outright force. The Africans he encountered on his journeys were to him little better than apes, or perhaps simple-minded children; in Africa, the notion of a Germanic 'Master Race' could be demonstrably validated. No wonder he was so admired on the far right in Germany, or that he was later pardoned by Wilhelm II, or that later still he was regarded as a national hero by the Nazis. A man for the era, indeed: imperial bombast incarnate, yet emblematic of the deep anxieties and fears that infused the ethnonationalist racial underpinnings of the newly unified Germany.[12]

Karl Peters's freneticism made it possible for people like Lieutenant Tom von Prince to come and make their own mark. When von Prince and his contingent of the Kaiserliche Schutztruppe für Deutsch-Ostafrika (Imperial Protectorate Force for German East Africa) advanced toward Unyanyembe in 1892, they presented themselves—unlike Stanley—as a conquering force. Much violence was committed by von Prince and his men as they proceeded, for they were there to assert control over the vast province, still largely a bureaucratic and administrative fiction, of German East Africa, as it had been designated just a few years earlier.[13] But they were following a road older than Germany itself—the version built by Bismarck, at any rate—and which had been forged by Nyamwezi and Swahili merchants and adventurers since at least the 1820s and 1830s. Many of the narratives describing this particular subplot of the German conquest of the region tell a singular story, of von Prince's inexorable march through tribes simultaneously startled and recalcitrant, the occasional setback notwithstanding, and of the irresistible manifestation of German imperial ambition, itself the product of pressure and machination in faraway Europe.[14] That aspect of the history before us has its place, of course. But at the local level, we see the importance of the road itself, and the dynamics which shaped it, from which von Prince's Schutztruppe was hardly immune. Once more, though this time armed with greater territorial and military intent than at any point previously, a European force was reaching uncertainly for footholds among the interstices, trying to cross socioeconomic and political landscapes being remade in front of them. Once more, those landscapes shaped and pulled the travelling party, buffeting and co-opting it, and producing the raw material, the actual people, on which its success depended.

And, of course, von Prince himself was a liminal, global being, not some ironclad national entity—despite appearances—whose ineluctable Prussian destiny was to be in East Africa in the final years of the nineteenth century and the early years of the twentieth. He was the creation of a global and imperial age, a time of mutability and vicissitude, born in 1866 to a British father, Thomas Henry Prince, who had been the head of police on the British-administered island of Mauritius, and a German mother. His father died when he was a child, at which point he returned with his mother to Germany. After spending some time in England for his education, his mother's family brought him back to Germany, where he joined the Imperial German Army following his graduation from the Kassel Military Academy. One of his classmates there had been Paul von Lettow-Vorbeck, later his superior and the legendary military commander of German colonial forces in East Africa during the First World War.[15] This was a youth forged during the Second Reich at its militaristic and nationalistic height, and coinciding with the eruption, following Bismarck's earlier eschewal of the idea that Germany had any need for far-flung colonies at all, of imperial and colonising zeal.[16] The nation was new, and its place in the world undetermined; von Prince's life, and that of his classmate von Lettow-Vorbeck, needs to be understood in the context of that frenzied transition.[17] Above all, this was a life formed in a nineteenth-century European globality, a world of flux and transnationality, and he was as much a product of instability and the liminality which was its corollary as was a Tippu Tip or a Mirambo, in whose footsteps he now trod.

But von Prince also understood how to do some co-opting of his own; and if, like Stanley, his progress was facilitated by liminality and entrepreneurialism, he appreciated—also like Stanley, and other *wazungu* before him—that those same dynamics could be harnessed in pursuit of larger goals. In the most practical of terms, von Prince drew critical support from various groups and communities who were also the products of liminality and globality. German success against Isike was dependent upon years of political fission and fusion, the resentful rivals and disaffected relatives which the transformation of Unyanyembe had produced, reaching all the way back to the succession crisis following the death of Fundikira in 1858. Von Prince needed the support of 'Arabs' and a range of coastal agents who had become the key operators at the intersection between the local and the global, and who had emerged from a culture of flexibility and adaptability. From that perspective, Isike was not undone by German military might, or at least not by that alone; but rather, by the political schisms and rivalries which defined local politics, and by the social and commercial revolutions, driven in no small way by globalising forces, which had fundamentally transformed the region. The challenges facing Isike were hardly unique. A little further west, and also in the Germans' gunsights, was the great insurgent-state of Urambo. Its rise had been spectacular, its achievements manifold; it represented in dramatic fashion the disgorgement of new socioeconomic and political impulses. But at the heart of its success was the person of Mirambo himself, and after he died in 1884 the transience of the polity, and the conditionality of loyalty to him, was exposed. Mbula Mtelya had named himself 'Mirambo', or 'corpses', in keep-

ing with the *Zeitgeist*. The name of his brother and successor, Mpand-
oshalo, meant 'cultivator of fields'. Whether or not this indicated a shift in
the ethos and purpose of the state is unclear; but in any case, it was too
late. By the beginning of the 1890s, numerous districts were in revolt, or
had otherwise pulled away, and Urambo—which was by now under German rule, at least in a formal sense—was reduced to a rump.[18] Across the
surrounding area there appeared the latest manifestation of fissiparity,
contest and opportunism, offering tumultuous corridors along which determined foreigners like von Prince might advance.

Above all, von Prince needed his *askari*, those locally recruited soldiers
who did not merely materialise at German will: they were the very stuff
of the revolution, the consequence of prolonged violence and political
experimentation, of expansion and contraction, of the opportunism and
entrepreneurialism which had been the defining characteristic of Africa's
nineteenth century. In the late 1880s, with a view to creating an armed
force which would bring German East Africa violently into being, Her-
man Wissmann had recruited six hundred 'Sudanese' men while in Cairo.
In Mozambique, he enticed three hundred and fifty 'Zulu' to join up. And
in Aden, some fifty Somali were similarly induced to form part of the
conquering force.[19] With the probable exception of 'Somali', the terms used
to describe these recruits are a little misleading, and certainly imprecise.
Most 'Sudanese' were in fact from southern Sudan, probably quite far
south, and were also known as 'Nubi', as they were too by the British in
Uganda.[20] The 'Zulu' were in fact Shangaan, or Tsonga, from the area of
the Gaza kingdom established in the 1820s by Soshangane, a Zulu military
commander, and in time absorbing a number of communities from the
Limpopo valley and southern Portuguese Mozambique.[21] In each case,
recruitment would give rise to particular forms of racial categorisation on
the part of German officers, based on supposed martial characteristics:
the 'Nubi' were regarded as making the finest soldiers; the Shangaan rather
less so.[22] However the Germans characterised their soldiers, recruitment
was made possible by the local but widely shared experience of military
and/or commercial revolution and the creation of new frontiers of possibility, out of which flowed willing and able labour. In these three cases,
we see transregional migration arising from rapid political and economic
change: Somali had been driven to the coast in the face of the expansion

of Menelik's Ethiopia, as well as by drought and resultant famine, and were doubtless eager for work and sustenance; likewise the 'Nubi', displaced by decades of violent Egyptian expansion across the upper Nile region, and evidently migrating to Cairo in search of opportunity. Shangaan were themselves the product of a revolution and a subsequently unstable political and socioeconomic environment, beginning with the Mfecane, and later the growing incursions of white power in South Africa and Mozambique.

The fact that Berlin was able even to imagine building a place called 'German East Africa' was due to the transformation of African state, society and economy by Africans themselves over several preceding decades. In time, the focus shifted toward recruitment of men from within the German colony itself—especially as, by 1892, most Shangaan had returned to Portuguese East Africa upon completion of their contracts, and the British had placed restrictions on recruitment out of Sudan.[23] The preference, now, was for Sukuma, the 'people of the north', inhabiting the vibrant corridor between Unyanyembe and Lake Victoria; the Manyema to the west of Lake Tanganyika, presumably on account of their ferocious reputation; and, of course, the Nyamwezi themselves, the product, as we have seen, of war and revolution spanning several decades, and thus possessed of the combination of entrepreneurial spirit and military expertise which made them desirable to colonial recruiters.[24] In many respects, indeed, in terms of methods and personnel, the new territory was built on the Germans' co-option of pre-existing forms of military predation and control, and a continuation of long-standing local conflicts.[25]

# III

ISIKE AND HIS PREDECESSORS had done very well out of the globality emanating from Zanzibar, harnessing it and, notwithstanding the fact that it was a perilous, volatile business, using it to generate wealth and status at the local level. But European globality was something different, certainly in its altering state in the course of the 1880s, and Isike soon struggled with it. In this period, there were increasing numbers of *wazungu* in the area, and they were increasingly troublesome. These weren't the scientists of the International African Association, or the men of God, representing the

White Fathers or the London Missionary Society. Isike hadn't minded those; in fact he saw some benefit in the connections they offered. But now there were Europeans coming who were interested in the ivory trade, and who were beginning to force their way into the commerce on which Isike, and so many other Nyamwezi, depended. They exhibited a new level of aggression in their interest in the area. That was when the trouble began, in the second half of the 1880s;[26] and, from Isike's perspective, that was what had led the Germans to him, their weapons pointed at his enclosure. More broadly, an array of Europeans were arriving—exploring, proselytising, prospecting—who were the harbingers of a new manifestation of globalisation, driven by industrial, scientific and cultural revolutions in Europe itself.

In the 1899 edition of *Through the Dark Continent*, Stanley included a preface in which his salvationist vision for the continent had evidently become even more robust. The European 'Scramble' was already proceeding apace. Von Prince, meanwhile, had established a plantation for himself in the territory he helped create, embodying the idea of developmental interventionism undergirded by a distinctive Prussian masculinity transposed onto a colonial canvas. The narratives these men awarded themselves, and were awarded by others, suggested an enduring stability and unquestionable rectitude in the mission and the actions undertaken to accomplish it. But they were liminal products of an unstable environment in Europe, which was projected into the wider world; and ultimately Africa's revolution had made them both.

# 5

# Being and Becoming *mzungu*

## A Short History of Mission Creep

THE HISTORY OF EUROPE IN AFRICA IS A LONG ONE—depending, of course, on how we define our terms. The relative proximity of the two landmasses meant that contact and movement, in both directions, was inevitable. A western European probing of the coastal edges of and, in time, intrusion into the continent became even more inexorable with the development of naval technology in the fifteenth and sixteenth centuries. Ever greater attention is being paid to the role of Africans in European society from the medieval period onward.[1] Our purpose here, however, is to sketch out the notion of a European presence, influence, intention, territorial traction and ultimately 'empire', in Africa itself. Much of this has been exhaustively narrated. It seems important, however, to lay down a certain framework before we turn to the context within which it might best be understood. In the broadest of terms—and even that exercise is open to a critical biopsy—the European presence in Africa might be understood in three broad phases. The first is the era of early modernity, including the Atlantic slave trade, characterised by the existence of Dutch, Portuguese, French, British, Danish and German forts along stretches of the West African coast; by Portuguese incursions, and sometimes attempts at settlement, in the kingdom of Kongo, on the Angolan coast, along the Zambezi valley and in the Ethiopian highlands; and by the Dutch at the Cape of Good Hope. The second, in the era of shifting economic and moral orthodoxy, is the period from the late eighteenth century to the

middle decades of the nineteenth, when coastal holdings expanded somewhat (and occasionally changed hands), and when there was a greater
will and capacity to seek indirect leverage or direct control at the local level
in very specific circumstances. The third is the era of seemingly unleashed
imperial potential in the last third of the nineteenth century, when continental Africa apparently becomes subsumed in a wave of European
empire-making. Our primary focus is on the latter two phases, and especially the third. It is worth noting at this point the historiographical
convention that for much of the first two phases, European states and/or
commercial concerns, in their various iterations, were decidedly diffident
about *any* kind of significant territorial possession in Africa; a reluctance
apparently evidenced by the lack of meaningful territorial acquisition
over the three centuries prior to the late nineteenth century.[2] It is this,
fundamentally, which gives rise to the idea of a 'scramble' for Africa between the 1870s and 1900s. Leaving aside, for the moment, the fact that
this tends to marginalise the African dynamics which are the heart of this
analysis, it is certainly true that there is a marked expansion in
Europeans' willingness to commit resources to their various adventures
in those decades, although my argument here is that this is very much
enmeshed with the processes unfolding within the continent.

Our purpose here, however, is to step back, and survey the European
context. At the end of the eighteenth century, the European presence in
Africa was limited, and included a handful of trading posts on the West
African coast, the British territory of Sierra Leone, the Dutch settlement
in Cape Town and the long-since altered Portuguese entrepôts on the
lower Zambezi. But intra-European conflict spilled over into the continent in the form of the Anglo–French struggle over Egypt—entwined
within a larger European struggle around revolutionary ideology and national identity: the Napoleonic Wars, which were unfolding just as the
Fulani and the Ngoni and the Yoruba were undergoing their own transformations further south. Napoleon's invasion and brief occupation of
the Nile Delta between 1798 and 1801, when he was expelled by an
Anglo-Ottoman force, constitute a richly symbolic moment. The forces
of supposed political and technological modernity had seized not only a
major centre in the Islamic world, Cairo, and in so doing reduced a hub

of Muslim and African civilisation to mere prize; they also appeared to be competing over the glories of antiquity themselves, thus laying claim to their ownership, and their legacy. Napoleon was of course interested in the rather more temporal matter of control of the eastern Mediterranean; but his zeal for co-opting archaeology in pursuit of legitimacy had already been demonstrated in Europe itself, most obviously in Italy.[3] Short-lived it may have been, but the Napoleonic conquest of Egypt in many ways laid the intellectual and cultural foundations, and presaged much of the literary and moral discourse, of modern European imperial ambition.[4] Its ending, of course, would also lead to the emergence of Muhammad Ali, Egypt's great reformer and empire-builder. At the opposite end of the continent, at the same moment, Europe's wars engulfed Cape Colony, captured by the British from the Dutch East India Company in 1795. Britain, recognising the strategic significance of controlling the Cape of Good Hope, made its occupation permanent in 1806. The contrast, in the European mind, could hardly have been greater: between the land of the pyramids and pharaohs, the co-opted power of ancient civilisation, and that of the 'Bushmen' of the Cape, eking out a miserable existence from the soil, with only the small but growing urban centre of Cape Town providing any light in the darkness. And then there were the Boers, the rough-hewn Dutch pioneer farmers of Cape society, at best quietly resentful of British administration, at worst actively unreconciled and hostile to it. Be that as it may, in this way were diverse pieces of the continent made part of Europe's own narratives, and travails, at the outset of the period under examination. And after all, they each, in their way, bore out Pliny the Elder's celebrated first-century remark that there was always something new coming out of Africa (though he was referring, in fact, to fauna).

   In the decades that followed, there were important shifts, in large part connected with several European states' abolition of the slave trade. The factors behind these various legislative acts, strung out between the 1790s and the 1830s, have been elucidated by a number of others and require only summary here. There had been a gradual swing in economic thinking, a reflection of changing economic realities, through the second half of the eighteenth century, toward a new orthodoxy which held that systems based on wage labour were ultimately more profitable and had much greater potential for growth than those based on chattel slavery.[5] Owners of sugar plantations in the Caribbean, for example, had seen their profits steadily diminish through the second half of the eighteenth century.[6] Industrialisation—much of it fuelled by profits originally derived from the slave trade itself, of course—was under way. The economic logic seemingly worked in happy parallel with the humanitarian argument, which held, simply put, that it was an affront to all civilised nations to persist in the enslavement of fellow human beings. This particular factor has long drawn much more attention than anything to do with hard-headed economics in the public remembrance of abolition in Britain, for example, for it supposedly highlighted the benevolent essence of the British themselves.[7] At the same time, African activism was critical in drawing attention to the awful iniquity of the traffic, while spectacular acts of resistance— for example, the Haitian revolution of 1791 under the leadership of Toussaint Louverture—both chimed with the humanitarian and revolutionary sentiments of the age and reinforced emerging economic orthodoxy: for slave rebellion drove down profits.[8] It would take a few years for most Africans to be aware of the implications, but it was a seismic period for Europe, and the world—obviously in terms of stopping European involvement in the largest forced migration in human history, but also in terms of the role Europeans now awarded themselves as global arbiters of moral and economic progress with the power, and the right, to judge others, and if necessary to intrude corporeally into their lives. Abolition reflected rapid socioeconomic change in Europe itself, and the resultant quest for moral rectitude in anxious times.

Increasingly, these restless dynamics found expression in various forms of armed, political incursions. European governments could find themselves drawn into, or in various ways motivated to intervene in, a range of local scenarios for an array of reasons. If turn-of-century clashes over Egypt or South Africa were the product of convulsions within Europe, geopolitical wrangling and the self-conscious assimilation of antiquity, in other contexts interventions were at least in part the consequence of novel forms of moral energy. In the 1820s the British, invigorated by their newfound abolitionist zeal, considered it necessary to send troops against Asante, the slave-dealing affront to civilisation threatening British commercial interests (and pride) on the Gold Coast. It didn't go well: the British forces were crushed by the Asante army in 1824, and the governor, Sir Charles McCarthy, was killed and decapitated.[9] That particular war was drawn out for several more years, eventually ending in a stalemate and a treaty;[10] but conflicts would recur in the decades ahead, the British often caught between the political machinations of the coastal communities and the territorial and commercial ambition of the Asante state. But the moral conviction episodically stirring the British to armed action, reluctant though such action often was, grew stronger as the century wore on. Elsewhere, moral mission was presented for domestic consumption, and it aligned with the exigencies of domestic politics. When Charles X of France found himself in need of a dose of glory to bolster his flagging post-revolutionary regime, his attention turned to the Mediterranean, and specifically the 'Barbary Coast', where the troublesome *bey* of Algiers, Hussein, represented relatively low-hanging fruit. Algiers, after all, had long been engaged in piracy, slave-raiding and slave-trading.[11] African economic activity and the promise of a worthy (and relatively straightforward) victory—and the fact that Ottoman authority was by now weak in the western Mediterranean—enticed the French to intervene, and the attack on and seizure of Algiers and Oran in 1830 was duly carried out efficiently enough. A coastal strip had been consolidated within the next couple of years.[12] But from these vainglorious incursions there followed decades of extreme violence, and from it sprang a process by which French national identity was ultimately dragged into an existential crisis from which it has in many ways yet to recover. And as Paris discovered, colonialism was complicated: by the frontier spaces in which military strength operated, and from which the necessary manpower was often drawn; by the ways in metropolitan power might be co-opted by actors on the 'periphery'; by colonists themselves, who in Algeria were a motley population with competing and often contradictory demands and needs. Responsibility for subjugating the new province was handed to General Thomas Bugeaud, veteran of Napoleon's wars and vehement opponent of democracy, with a proven track record of brutally suppressing disorder in France in the 1830s.[13] Bugeaud transformed the French military presence in Algeria, waging innovative and ruthless and to a considerable extent successful irregular warfare, and ultimately making a seminal contribution to later thinking about colonial warfare in both France and further afield.[14] Violence soon defined the territory, both that inherent in settler culture, and at the outer edges of the colony, where the French and their coastal allies were drawn into the mountains from the early 1840s to confront Abd al-Qadir's jihadist resistance. They got rid of him, in 1847, but the armed insurgency persisted.[15] In any case Charles X was gone long before that, for adventures in Algeria weren't enough to save him from ousting and exile.

The tentacular spasms of European curiosity were appearing elsewhere in the region, too: in Egypt, to be precise, where Muhammad Ali's programme of rejuvenation was under way in the wake of the Napoleonic drama. The Egyptian context also provides a useful demonstration of how contradictory European impulses could be. Muhammad Ali was keen to make use of European skills and hardware as he developed his vision of a Red Sea empire and pulled away from Istanbul in the process. He employed European advisors in building an extraordinary army. Other European consultants were brought in to talk to the Egyptian authorities about technical education and irrigation. Others still advised on the use of the machinery being imported to kickstart an industrial revolution, beginning with textiles and armaments. They were all very happy to be there, and did well out of this particular gig. Muhammad Ali also sent the brightest and the best, or the best connected, at least, directly to Europe for training of various kinds. But then, in the late 1830s, when the results began to appear—rapid growth in cotton production, aggressive expansion into the Red Sea and the Levant—Britain and France, and of course the Ottoman Empire, were suddenly deeply concerned, and moved to peg the upstart Muhammad Ali back. It had all become a bit too much, and so there was an armed intervention in Palestine and Syria, resulting in an Egyptian defeat; enforced and humiliating demilitarisation; and the breaking open of Egyptian markets (similar to what was being imposed on China through the treaty ports) to European competitors.[16] It was supposed to be a limited operation, but European interests remained.

While successive French regimes committed themselves to a settler empire in North Africa, the British sought to consolidate their new holdings in South Africa, facilitating the dispatch of a wave of settlers in the 1820s. At the same time, however, they remained diffident about the cost and trouble involved in securing the eastern frontier militarily against the Xhosa—much to the annoyance of those Boer settlers who were now squeezed up against the Xhosa and suffering land shortage as a result. The British only reluctantly agreed to the periodic deployment of troops against them (including in the mid-1830s), and even then, with only specific and limited objectives.[17] The British authorities were rather more enthusiastic about the application of a particular form of enlightened, liberal empire for which the Cape was a laboratory, much as Sierra Leone had been in creating a new kind of 'native' society. They granted rights to African workers in the form of legally binding contracts and judicial protection in the event of employers breaching contracts; introduced the private ownership of land; replaced Boer officials with British ones; made English the language of education and the law. Arguably the most important intervention was the abolition of slavery in 1834.[18] Mistrust of British motives, and a lack of faith in their methods of governance, were major factors in the departure of large numbers of Boers from Cape Colony into the 'interior' with a view to setting up their own micro-colonies. In the course of the 1840s, the gaze of the British followed the Voortrekkers as they crept through the crevices created by the Mfecane and its aftermath, unsure how to respond. They annexed the Natal territory in 1843, and the Orange River community in 1848. But by the mid-1850s, again gripped by ambivalence and confronted by political opposition closer to home, they withdrew, temporarily at least, and in the main let the Boers get on with it.[19] A more aggressive attitude was being developed toward the Xhosa, some of whom were resettled in reserves following the annexation of a swathe of their territory, and who were increasingly pulled into a migrant labour system sustaining settler farms across the Cape.[20] But for the time being, the British were largely uninterested in extending any more formal political control in South Africa than was strictly necessary.

By then, in any case, events elsewhere were distracting a swift succession of governments in London: Peel's second administration (Conservative), 1841–46; Russell's first (Whig), 1846–52; Derby's first (Conservative), which was created in February 1852 but was gone by December; Aberdeen (a Peelite-Whig coalition), 1852–55; Palmerston's first (Whig), 1855–58; Derby's second (Conservative), 1858–59; Palmerston's second (Liberal), 1859–65. The issue facing this unstable circus of mid-century statesmen was the stubborn persistence of the slave trade in parts of West Africa. How to coax, to civilise, to persuade—to demonstrate and effect Britain's moral supremacy? Palmerston might well believe that "trade begets kindly feelings" but, if that failed, or if it was the wrong kind of trade, then a few artillery shells might do the trick.[21] Missions were dispatched to Dahomey in the late 1840s and early 1850s imbued with at least some of the spirit of Thomas Fowell Buxton's recent book on to how to improve the African 'condition',[22] in an attempt to lure its leaders away from the export of human beings—something the British had until relatively recently engaged in themselves, at quite a considerable profit; but they had since changed their minds, and rather reinvented themselves in the process. Efforts were made to establish whether the mighty Niger might be navigated, and, more importantly, whether Europeans might survive in the area long enough to uncover commercial opportunities and persuade refractory Africans by their very presence. The British government backed an expedition to the Niger Delta in 1841 with precisely these aims in mind, but malaria decimated the party and the whole thing had to be abandoned. Another government-supported attempt in 1854, under the command of the Scottish explorer and naturalist William Balfour Baikie, was more successful.[23] But it was in Lagos, situated on the frontier of global economic change, that London decided to assert itself. British ships were anchored just beyond the rolling surf around the sandbars opposite the great port. The violent entrepreneurialism of the Yoruba contradicted British ideas (at that moment) about what commerce should involve; specifically, the ruler of Lagos persisted in the slave trade itself, and the British bombarded the town from the sea in 1851 as punishment, practising the euphemistically termed 'gunboat diplomacy' which simultaneously exhibited Britain's technological power and betrayed its political naivety. At length, and having singularly failed to manipulate the regime at a distance, the British annexed Lagos in 1861.[24] Their presence fundamentally altered the balance of power in the area (as well as notionally laying the territorial foundation stone for what would become Nigeria). But they were also co-opted into Yoruba dynamics, and their presence was as much the product of a distinctive Yoruba energy (in Britain's view, misdirected) as of any grand metropolitan design.

Meanwhile, on a different part of the West African coast, an embryonic French presence was establishing itself. Along a stretch of the littoral linking the rivers Saloum, Senegal and Casamance, General Louis Faidherbe sought to transform what had been a modest trading post into a major centre of French control, in keeping with the ambitions of the Second Empire under Napoleon III. Senegal was, in truth, a rather modest part of the grand imperial design envisioned by the Emperor of the French, who was eager to reassert France on a global stage following the turmoil of the Second Republic, and who oversaw particularly dramatic expansion in South-East Asia and the Pacific. Nonetheless, from the mid-1850s to the mid-1860s, Faidherbe—who had served under Bugeaud in Algeria but who developed his own approach to campaigning and administration—founded the port of Dakar and extended French control into the interior, effectively stymying the ambitions of Umar Tal to the east.[25] That he was able to do so owed much to his establishment of the Tirailleurs sénégalais, an infantry corps made necessary by the lack of French troops.[26] The new territory also represented something of an experiment in colonial culture, for Faidherbe, a keen student of African culture and history, and something of an Islamophile, developed in practice the idea, reflecting the spirit of the 1848 revolution, that 'assimilation' of Africans was possible, and that accordingly they should be fully enfranchised. From this period, Senegalese Africans were sent as representatives to Paris, embodying the particular Gallic interpretation of a 'civilising mission' as well as reflecting ongoing political debates (and sociopolitical upheaval) in France itself.[27] Still, if the growth of Senegal reflected the ambition of the Second Empire, Napoleon III's deposition in 1870 during the Franco–Prussian War led to the suspension of any further expansion. French imperial ambitions were, for now, on hold.

At the same time, Britain had demonstrated its ability to launch sophisticated, short-term campaigns in challenging environments through a much-publicised expedition against Tewodros of Ethiopia in 1867–68. While not conventionally included in examinations of European empire-building in Africa, and for good reasons—the British mission was limited in its objectives and the army quickly withdrew once those had been achieved—it was in many ways portentous, demonstrating a deft combination of hardy resolve (as the British themselves saw it), tactical skill and technological superiority. A breakdown in communications between the Ethiopians and the British, whom Tewodros had long courted as potential allies, led to the emperor imprisoning a large number of Europeans in revenge. The British government launched a remarkable campaign, involving infantry, elephants as transport, and modern ordnance, to free them and destroy Tewodros's regime. They advanced from the Eritrean coast at Zula into the highlands and did what they came to do, Tewodros committing suicide in the face of advancing British troops.[28] But it was portentous in other ways, too. The framing of Tewodros as an insane potentate whose removal was a moral imperative marked a shift toward the racialisation of violence against Africans, even if this had appeared in various forms some decades earlier: for example, in British attitudes toward Asante, or in Bugeaud's campaigning in Algeria.[29] It was also the case that, for all the logistical and military capacity exhibited by the British, the passage of their army from coastal lowlands to the mountains had been made possible in large part because of widespread hostility to Tewodros himself, and the turmoil across the massif as a result. The British had modern guns and impressive organisation; but they moved through the vacuums and interstices created by an imploding state, and a *habesha* revolution.

## Scrambles

THERE IS A SHIFT, IT SEEMS, DURING THE 1870S. This is certainly the decade which is conventionally posited as the chronological marker between the era of limited European intrusion and that of 'The Scramble'. It's clear enough that there are a number of examples of commitment on the part of a number of European states to some form of overseas territorial domination in Africa before about 1870; not to mention, in the long-established paradigm, 'informal' spheres of influence.[30] France, Portugal and Britain were all involved in significant investment in territorial imperialism, whether on a 'small' scale—the control of ports such as Lagos—or comparatively larger, notably Algeria or Cape Colony. But things do indeed change in the course of the 1870s from the European perspective, certainly in terms of the enlarged scale of the imperial project and heightened volatility within Europe itself. When the British invaded Asante in 1873–74, their capacity to fight a war in such an environment had improved significantly. They were armed with Snider breech-loaders and seven-pounder guns. They had potable water, and their sappers created the infrastructure required for a steady advance, while locally recruited porters carried the equipment. And this time, the military victory was followed by the declaration of crown protectorate status over the adjacent Gold Coast, a signal to Kumasi that the British were here to stay. Still, sometimes this happened despite, and not because of, the stances of metropolitan governments. The fact that some of Britain's most dramatic imperial entanglements, for example, happened under the watch of the second Liberal, ostensibly anti-imperialist, administration of William Gladstone between 1880 and 1885 is suggestive of the power of dynamics within Africa itself.[31]

Right at the same moment that the British were attacking Asante, much of Europe and North America—according to some scholars at least—was entering a period of economic depression which would only end in the mid-1890s. The characterisation of the late nineteenth century in this manner is contested, of course; others have argued that there was no 'depression', certainly as the term would be understood in the next century, and that the data are either unreliable or unsupportive of the depression thesis.[32] What is clear, though, is that the period between the 1870s and 1890s was one of heightened competition between industrial nations, characterised not by economic stagnation but by intense commercial rivalry and, in some sectors, diminishing returns. This fundamentally altered the context in which existing territorial holdings, and projects of further territorial expansion, in Africa were understood. We don't, in fact, have to adhere to a Eurocentric interpretation of events to appreciate that Africa's economic *potential* was increasingly what mattered to warlords and capitalists in Paris, London, Lisbon, Brussels or Berlin: such optimism seemed justified by the West African palm oil which had long lubricated

British industry, or the wild rubber which was of increasing importance in Europe. And so the pace of intrusion increased. An intensifying set of impulses found an outlet in grand schemes and military interventions, carried out by an assortment of entrepreneurs, adventurers and soldiers, agents of an increasingly aggressive capitalism directed outward toward supposedly untapped and even as yet undiscovered markets, and of a culture of intrusion and aspiration which was simultaneously anxiously restive and baldly self-righteous. European empire in Africa may be considered in many ways the outgrowth of Africa's nineteenth-century reformation; but Europeans still succeeded in achieving considerable leverage amidst the turbulence, utilising the organisational, logistical and technological sophistication at their disposal. Governments did so, in the first instance, through chartered commercial companies tasked with prising open markets and, where appropriate, administering enclaves and spheres of influence with more or less official backing. This risky but potentially lucrative system of outsourcing empire saw the proliferation of business concerns with African interests: in the French sphere, for example, the Compagnie française de l'Afrique occidentale, the Société colonial de la côte de Guinée and the Compagnie française de commerce africain; and representing British interests, the Royal Niger Company, the British South Africa Company and the Imperial British East Africa Company. Alongside the Bremen- and Hamburg-based German firms, these were the *wazungu* who were (literally as well as metaphorically) at the business end of imperial expansion.[33]

The International African Association (IAA) was among the most ambitious of these business enterprises, and one of the first in the era of the European so-called 'new imperialism'. It was created by King Leopold II of the Belgians in the mid-1870s—and employed Henry Morton Stanley for a time—with a view to carving out a sphere of influence in the Congo basin for economic extraction. Much of the language developed around the IAA was humanitarian in tone, but this was a cover for the cardinal aim behind the exercise: namely, commercial exploitation and rapid profit. It was also a project infused with Leopold's own extraordinary vanity, reflecting his conviction, not an uncommon one across Europe by the middle of the 1880s, that Belgium should have a colony of some kind or other, preferably at minimal cost. In fact, what became the Congo Free State was Leopold II's personal domain, which he acquired (having failed to get hold of the Philippines, an earlier notion) with the agreement of the other major European powers.[34] What followed were some of the worst atrocities of the era—shocking to contemporary observers, even by the standards of that era—in which private companies were handed licenses to operate in the Congo basin with minimal regulation. Their primary objective was the collection of wild rubber, which they did by employing brutal and brutalised armies to terrorise communities into providing it. Extreme violence, up to and including executions and massacres, was common. It took the establishment by a group of social and humanitarian activists of the Congo Reform Association in 1904, in order to scrutinise and publicise these widespread abuses (a report by the diplomat Roger Casement, later executed by the British for his role in the Irish 'Easter Rising' of 1916, was especially influential) to make the Belgian government force Leopold to hand over responsibility for the territory to the government itself in 1908.[35] The situation in the Congo was extreme in many respects, and the scandal around it may be regarded as a major milestone in the development of the concept of global human rights.[36] But it represented, if *in extremis*, the fundamental problem with chartered companies and the privatisation of empire. They were often woefully inefficient, short-termist, uninterested in the nuance and delicacy required for efficient administration and frequently engaged in violence against Africans themselves. By the 1920s they would for the most part be superseded by ostensibly more 'professional' colonial bureaucracies.

The activities of the IAA from the mid-1870s coincided with, and in some respects reinvigorated, French, British and German intrusions elsewhere, fuelling a curious panic about relative international standing. Largely unconscious of the fact that Africa's own revolution was reaching something of a culmination, and that in many respects they were being drawn into and shaped by that revolution, European governments made new efforts to consolidate existing holdings and acquire new ones. Both British and French agents in West Africa, afforded greater protection from malaria through the development of quinine prophylaxis, adopted an increasingly aggressive stance toward their African counterparts in the 1870s and 1880s. Justifications included the continued presence of such monstrous obstacles to both trade and progress as Asante and Dahomey, and the persistence of the regional slave trade—for example among the Wolof in Senegal, which successive French governments used as an excuse to push into the interior.[37] The concern to protect commercial investments meant escalating conflict with African merchants. The latter were the outcome of the extraordinary socioeconomic transformation across the region in recent decades; but to Europeans, they were increasingly troublesome impediments to commercial traffic, demanding either credit or higher prices for their merchandise, and this led French and British traders either to use violence against them or to attempt to bypass them altogether. The British did so, notably, by using steamships to move up the Niger, seeking to render irrelevant the entrepreneurs crowded across the Delta: in such a way did exploration, which had long been focused on the continent's major river systems, intersect with overtly commercial interests.[38] For some, and from a purely *mzungu*-centric perspective, these endeavours can be seen to have involved the foundations of what would become African nation-states, at least in a broad territorial sense; the conception of the modern African political order. But often this was less a matter of planned impregnation than of premature diplomatic and cartographic ejaculation, as a range of European agents splattered maps with imagined territories which were as much about the disgorgement of social, political and economic anxieties at home, and of course their co-option by Africans, as about the deliberate and careful construction of empires. Governments, meanwhile, were often drawn in grudgingly, simultaneously anxious about, and yet dependent upon, the activities of merchants and consuls in Africa itself.[39] Through these various characters, territorial entities, or spheres of influence at least, began to take shape in ways that are well known, but worth outlining in broad strokes here.

In France, the governments of the Third Republic, seeking the restoration of pride in the wake of their humiliation at the hands of the Prussians, revived an imperial vision for West Africa by the end of the 1870s. This involved a grand pincer movement, linking up the French settlement in Senegal with its holdings further around the coast. The French began to extend their railway from Senegal in the direction of the upper Niger valley, and now flung themselves, and their African soldiers, across the vast spaces of the Sahel and southern Sahara.[40] Much further south, along the Congo River in the early 1880s, Pierre Savorgnan de Brazza—product of an eclectic, noble, artistic Franco-Italian background, and committed to non-violence in his exploring—wound his way through numerous communities collecting apparent concessions and treaties of 'friendship', seeking to establish tangible French influence, which he apparently did most clearly in the treaty he signed with the Makoko, the Tio ruler, who accepted his offer of French protection.[41] De Brazza was fêted at home for eschewing the violence associated with Stanley elsewhere in the central African forest, and later with his German counterpart Karl Peters, but even so his endeavours, including the development of armed force in the late 1880s in the form of Senegalese troops, laid the basis of French colonial hegemony in the region: the area of the present-day Republic of the Congo.[42] Still, despite the enthusiasm for imperialism of prominent figures such as prime minister Jules Ferry, vacillation and uncertainty back in Paris was the bane of empire-builders across the region throughout the period: while the strike against Dahomey in 1892 was swift and decisive, the drawn-out conflict through the 1890s with Samori further north—involving as it did significant French casualties at the hands of Samori's hardened troops—induced anxiety among those in France worried about both finances and outcomes.[43] Fortunately for the latter, many of the new territories were the stuff of phantasmic geography, notably the equatorial projections of Ubangi-Shari, Middle Congo and Gabon, for it would be some years before there was a meaningful French presence across those regions. Still, in their way, the French were making their contribution to the rolling new frontiers characteristic of the long nineteenth century. Unlike the Msiris or the Tippu Tips of the era, however, the French intervention was rather more illusory, and certainly tenuous.

Britain moved to extend its long-standing presence along the West African coast from Gold Coast and Lagos eastward, establishing a de facto commercial monopoly in the Niger Delta under the control of a private company chartered by the British government, the Royal Niger Company (formerly the United African Company and then the National African

Company).[44] To the RNC fell the responsibility of getting rid of all those overmighty African entrepreneurs who had made the socioeconomic transformation of the region possible in the first place. Later, it was a logical extension of control at Lagos to assert authority over the Yoruba, in the early 1890s, and to attack Benin, in 1897.[45] At the same time, forward momentum and anxiety about French manoeuvres in the Sahel pushed British-led forces north of the Gold Coast to attack Asante, and propelled British agents north of the forest into the savannah, where the Sokoto Caliphate was invaded in 1900, and subdued, militarily at least, in 1903.[46] In the meantime, the empire-sceptic Otto von Bismarck had finally resolved, in 1884, to establish protectorates over Cameroon and Togo in West Africa, if for no other reason than to put a brake on the Anglo-French frenzy of claim and counterclaim. As with the British in the Niger Delta, in Cameroon the Germans sought to break the power of the great Douala middlemen who had long thrived in the era of global commerce—many of them, indeed, had sought British protection—and they did so via the tried and tested method of levering themselves into local rivalries and deepening fissures between competing groups.[47] Having wedged himself into West Africa, Bismarck would quickly do the same in East Africa.

In the 1870s, meanwhile, the British had new ambitions in South Africa, largely fired by the existence of precious material under the earth. First were the diamonds discovered north of Cape Colony in the late 1860s. Environmental happenstance—not the self-awarded 'civilising mission', nor visions of global development, nor concern for the spiritual poverty of the natives—provided the impetus for imperial expansion in the territory. This was a question of geology rather than ideology. The British initially envisaged a Federation which would take advantage of geopolitical location and emerging mineral wealth. The area where enormous diamond fields were discovered in the late 1860s and early 1870s was annexed as 'Griqualand West' (even though the Griqua leader had actually requested Boer protection), and was swiftly awash with British capital. A single company with political connections to the government in the Cape, De Beers, came to control the extraction of diamonds, and the resultant economic ecosystem was defined by a dynamic if brutal migrant labour system and heightened competition over farmland to produce food for the burgeoning urban centre of Kimberley.[48] But the proposed grand federation didn't quite go to plan, not least because of the resilience of African polities, including the Xhosa, whose resistance compelled the British authorities to abandon the idea of further land expropriation. And then there were the Zulu—a largely unknown quantity at this point, as they hadn't fought any major wars for quite a few years, but still worrisome. They inflicted a heavy defeat on an ill-prepared British force at Isandlwana in 1879, which was inevitably transformed into a heroic last stand;[49] and although a few months later the British returned to crush the Zulu army, and a much-diminished Zululand would become a crown colony in 1887, it was another indication that hegemony over South Africa wouldn't be quite as straightforward as had been thought.[50] Yet another such signal came when in 1880 Transvaal, which had accepted annexation three years earlier on account of its need for protection from the Zulu, rebelled and inflicted a series of defeats on British forces, forcing a British withdrawal in 1881.[51] But when gold was discovered in Transvaal in 1886, it fundamentally transformed regional power dynamics. Over the next few years, British interests and those allied with them agitated for greater control of mining and influence over Transvaal politics, including Cecil Rhodes's failed attempt to overthrow the government of Paul Kruger; and in 1899, faced with intolerable political pressure and a British military build-up on his borders, Kruger declared war. It was a ferocious conflict, the culmination of long-term pressures and competing interests,[52] in which British military weaknesses were initially exposed, in part explaining Britain's brutal mistreatment of civilians; but sheer military might wore down Boer resistance.[53] The peace agreement of 1902 was one of the foundation stones of the Union of South Africa, created in 1910, and in which considerable efforts were made to reintegrate and placate the Afrikaner community.[54] The upshot of these complex political machinations was the creation of a mining economy built on a brutal system of labour exploitation and migration: one of the most oppressive such systems on the continent during the 'colonial' era.[55] Even the operation of that economic order, however, was shaped by the African political dynamics of the long nineteenth century, and, as we have noted earlier, was in fact—whether knowingly or not—tapping into a long-extant pattern of labour migration across the region developed over the preceding decades. The very nature of African political culture, insurgent statehood, and economic innovation in the nineteenth century created the landscape, the defiles and ridges, through which European capital had to move, and within which it had to operate. Industrial-era, colonial South Africa seems, from a certain angle, a monstrously exogenous imposition indeed. But it was also the product of a very distinct local environment. Relations between Europeans and Africans, meanwhile, especially in the context of escalating violence, sharpened each community's sense of its own moral and political authority, and shaped ideas about race and gender.[56] These were the dynamics which, much more that De Beers's machines, created the South Africa of the late nineteenth and early twentieth centuries.

At the same time, a dangerous level of intra-*wazungu* jostling was unfolding along the Mediterranean coast. Much of it was centred on Egypt, where European influence intensified, or was co-opted, if we prefer, during the reigns of khedives Muhammad Said and Ismail; as too was European settlement, with thousands of economic migrants and opportunists making Cairo their home between the 1850s and 1870s. French and British finance was needed to realise Ismail's dreams of 'modernity' in particular: the grand cities, an industrial base, modern technology in the spheres of war and communications and print. Opened in 1869, the Suez Canal—a project long resisted, it might be noted, by Muhammad Ali, for reasons that would become painfully clear to his political descendants— was built using European money and expertise. The debt became a mountain, and the creditors grew increasingly twitchy. This was a co-option with severe blowback. At last came national bankruptcy, and in 1879 Ismail was removed. The rivalrous French and British, and especially the latter, were increasingly in control of anything in Cairo that really mattered, including the banks and the ports; and it was a French company that owned the Suez Canal.[57] Within a few years, the situation provoked a nationalist backlash, led by the army officer Ahmed Urabi, and the formalisation of British control following a bloody military confrontation. Britain was concerned to secure the Canal—the artery to India— and to protect its financial interests, and had been particularly anxious that Urabi, should he have succeeded in overthrowing the khedival regime, would default on Egypt's voluminous debts.[58] In the midst of the Egyptian bankruptcy crisis, France was experiencing political crisis at home—in general, episodic domestic crises had an enormous bearing on *wazungu* endeavours during this period—and so was incapable of decisive action as events in Egypt unfolded. Still, a little earlier, there had been opportunities further west. The relative diminution of British interest in Tunisia in the 1860s and 1870s (Britain having formerly been the provider of 'protection' to Tunis) opened the way for Paris, seeking, again, to recalibrate in the wake of the drubbing inflicted by Prussia, and nervous about growing Italian interest in the region. That was one of the factors behind the French decision to seize Tunis in 1881; the others being British aggression in Egypt, extensive French commercial investment in Tunisia itself and the appearance of more or less organised hostility within the territory to both European interests and the incumbent regime.[59] Tunisia, in other words, might spiral out of control, leaving investors bereft, opening the way to the predations of unscrupulous intruders (the Italians), and destabilising the wider region.

An important geopolitical corollary of the Egyptian crisis was the foisting on the Sudan as its new governor one General Charles Gordon, religious zealot, veteran of the Taiping Rebellion in China and patriot-at-arms, tasked with the suppression of the slave trade there.[60] His death in 1885 at the hands of the Mahdists at the fall of Khartoum delivered to the British another righteous martyr, and an illustration of doughty, unflinching masculinity. It was to be more than a decade before the full logistical and military force of British imperialism was unleashed on the Sudanese. In 1898, the British and their allies crushed the Mahdists at the battle of Omdurman, in what was a formidable demonstration of modern technological and industrial warfare. The high death toll inflicted on the Sudanese was justified on account of their blood-curdling fanaticism—which was of a different magnitude, apparently, from that of Gordon, now suitably avenged.[61] In the meantime, Anglo–French enmity spilled over into Sudan, and when armed expeditionary forces from each side encountered one another at Fashoda, a small settlement on the banks of the White Nile, in 1898, a general war briefly threatened.[62] It was averted—neither Paris nor London could quite imagine, in the final analysis, actually *going to war* over this—but it was nonetheless an interesting, micro-cosmic insight into intra-European unease, exported to and consequently conditioned by Africa itself.[63]

'Securing' Sudan formed part of a larger picture from London's per-spective: namely, control of the Nile from delta to headwaters, which meant in broad terms the linking up of British interests on the Indian Ocean coast, and indeed British India itself, with those in Cairo and Khar-toum. In East Africa, the same nervous, moralising energy that Britain had long directed at West Africa was brought to bear on Zanzibar and the Indian Ocean world. In fact, this dated back to the Moresby Treaty in 1822, under the terms of which Oman prohibited the import of slaves from East Africa; but, for all Britain's lofty intent, the slave trade, and the practice of slavery, thrived for much of the nineteenth century. It did so because there was a basic rationality to it, regardless of the public despair of Liv-ingstone and others. Nonetheless, Zanzibar, under British pressure, agreed to end the slave trade from the mainland in 1873.[64] This did not make a British East African empire inevitable. But it was an indication of the moral and material parameters within which Britain believed it had the right, the duty, indeed, to operate. Later, having agreed their portion of East Africa—present-day Kenya and Uganda—with Berlin, the British pro-ceeded to demarcate with some remarkably straight lines a vast region of east and north-east Africa, creating Sudan (and, indirectly, South Sudan) in the process. These lines skirted around the Ethiopian empire; left the Italians a little space to operate in Eritrea and Somalia; ran neatly to the shores of the Red Sea and the Indian Ocean; and squared up Egypt, a neat box of desert and river at the top of the map. On paper, it was the *mzungu* power to chart and map writ large. But the British went further, demon-strating their ability to thrust metal through rock and fundamentally alter the landscape. Arguably the most spectacular investment on the part of the British government outside South Africa was the construction between 1896 and 1901 of a railway running through Kenya, from the coast at Mom-basa, via the embryonic settlement at Nairobi, to Kisumu on the shore of Lake Victoria. The 'Uganda Railway', as it became known, built using imported South Asian labour, was a remarkable demonstration of the tech-nological and infrastructural power of the *mzungu*, and it opened up a range of possibilities for both white settlement in the Kenyan highlands and African commercial agriculture in Uganda itself.[65] Yet, in subtle ways across this region, processes of co-option and territorial overlay were at work. In the Lake Victoria region, what became 'Uganda' was not quite as artificial and externally imposed as might be assumed: it was formed in a more or less discrete arena of inter-community cooperation and conflict over several centuries, and the British were knowingly or otherwise guided in their 'carving up' by a multiplicity of local actors and local dynamics.[66] On a larger canvas, in terms of the sprawling entity known as Sudan, the colonial territory was in many ways superimposed, in terms of reach and scale, upon the Egyptians' own vast project of the nineteenth century.

It was the need for international agreement by the middle of the 1880s that prompted Bismarck to host a conference in Berlin, held over several weeks in December 1884 and January 1885, and involving representatives from all the European states with interests in Africa. In the minds of some, not least Bismarck himself, it was all getting a little out of hand, and needed some careful management. The Berlin Conference has taken on something of an iconic, landmark status in the history (and the historiography) of modern Africa: not quite its Westphalian moment, perhaps, but something approaching it; seminal, defining, cartographically tectonic.[67] How much actual importance can be attributed to a single diplomatic event in an entirely different continent is a matter of serious debate; and, in any case, Berlin only really involved agreement on a handful of quite specific things, and one very large thing: that, implicitly or otherwise, the European partition of this vast landmass could and probably should proceed, but that everyone must behave like gentlemen (Europeans to one another, that is), and no one should risk starting a war (between Europeans, that is) for the sake of some distant protectorate. More particularly, there was a general agreement that free trade should be protected, especially on the rivers—the Congo and the Niger—which had of late been the focus of much rivalry. Accordingly, there was recognition of Leopold's authority across an enormous swathe of territory in the Congo basin in return for the freedom of international commerce there.[68] But there was also concern to tighten up the protocol involved in actually laying claim to particular territories, and so the principle of 'effective occupation' was established, largely the brainchild of Bismarck who was keen to override the 'spheres of influence' concept hitherto favoured by the British. This meant that claims over particular territories would only receive international recognition if the claimant nation could demonstrate that it was already in effective occupation of that territory.[69] In this way were the unscrupulous and frequently unrecognised activities of thrusting entrepreneurs such as Karl Peters and Pierre Savorgnan de Brazza—and indeed of missionaries—abruptly elevated to the level of statecraft. Of course, the lines drawn up were still often more in the imagination than pertaining to any empirical reality; the lines thrusting through peoples and landscapes about which the esteemed delegates knew next to nothing were expressions of crude aspiration and naked national (and some personal) ambition. Still, as conferences go, it has huge symbolic meaning: anyone in doubt about that might try imagining a congress of various African leaders circa 1885 arguing about who should get what in front of a vast map of Europe.

The entry of Belgium, or at least a Belgian presence, was a relatively novel development in the African landscape; and there was another new arrival, too. Italy, itself a recent creation following several years of internal conflict, was one of those seeking international stature and apparently espying in Africa an opportunity to achieve it. An Italian presence increased in the southern Red Sea in the course of the 1880s, encouraged by Britain, which saw it as a useful foil to the French. By the early 1890s, despite the occasional drawback, the Italians had crept into the Benaadir (southern Somalia), and onto the Eritrean plateau opposite Ethiopia. It was in the latter setting that Italy's dreams of imperial grandeur unravelled. With an army encamped for weeks facing Menelik, and domestic political instability piling pressure on General Baratieri, the Italian commander moved his forces forward on 1 March 1896 only to find the Ethiopians ready and waiting. At Adwa, the Italian army was routed, and in Rome Francesco Crispi's government fell; anti-government protestors chanted the name 'Menelik'—a figure which Italian political and military elites had framed as little more than a pumped-up savage—in the streets.[70] Italy, the product of political turmoil, and of a bombastic but apprehensive search for national identity in a volatile and combative age, exported those anxieties to north-east Africa, and in time to the Libyan coast, and in both places it found new angsts with which to grapple. At the other end of the temporal scale was Portugal, by now much diminished in the European context, but with the oldest presence in Africa of any European power. For Lisbon, its African holdings were critical to any pretensions to 'great power' status; not for the first time, nor the last, Africans were inadvertently implicated in European political or economic machinations; and so, in the 1880s and 1890s, Portuguese army officers and colonial officials sought to extend coastal territory into the interior, especially in Mozambique and Angola, elbowing their way among the British, or Germans, or Belgians.[71]

The final acts of the European 'Scramble', as conventionally defined, were in North Africa—curiously enough, given that this was the region which had witnessed some of the earliest European intrusions. Morocco became a French protectorate, with a slice going to Spain, in 1912. At the same moment, in 1911–12, the Italians were claiming, with a very large dollop of exaggeration, that the conquest of Libya was complete, thanks to one of the earliest deployments of air power by a European imperial power. There was to be no repeat of Adwa in Cyrenaica, and so the continued presence of the defiant Sanusiyya beyond the Mediterranean littoral was conveniently ignored. The point was, Libya looked like a big territory on the map, as befitted a great nation such as Italy. But of course, to conceptualise the 'Scramble' in these temporal and spatial terms is to adhere to the notion of 'beginning', 'middle', 'end', rather than complex processes of continuity and legacy, liminality and interstitiality. The paradox, but nonetheless the reality, of 'partition' was that beyond the urban centres of the Mediterranean coast, toward the desert, the oxygen of European authority grew steadily thinner, and Africa's creative volatility went on.

## Exporting Energy

EUROPE WAS A CONTINENT in turbulent flux in this period, experiencing a multitude of transformations in terms of economic organisation, politics, society and culture.[72] These would increasingly intersect with those of Africa; developments across the two landmasses were symbiotically connected, as indeed they had been for several centuries in the context of an Atlantic world. There was no monolithic 'Europe', of course, no un-differentiated community of 'Europeans', any more than this was the case with respect to 'Africa' or 'Africans'. Our concern, however, is to identify themes which are germane to our understanding of how Europeans in various capacities and contexts engaged with Africa, how the former in-fluenced the latter, and how Europe was itself co-opted into processes of transformation led by Africans themselves.

To begin with, modern imperialism had its roots in nationalism, or (some would argue) new forms of it. To a degree this seems counterintui-tive, given that, according to a particular branch of scholarship, modern nationalism is the *response* to empire, a hostile reaction to it rather than its cause.[73] But the modern nation, as defined in terms of its ideological and economic construction in the decades following the French and American revolutions,[74] ultimately gave rise to the extension of national interests into extraterritorial or overseas contexts.[75] Empire-building might also generate nationalist fervour—'imperial ethnicities'—and help to re-solve ethnic tensions at the metropolitan centre.[76] The transition from nation to empire wasn't a linear one, of course: additional overseas com-mitments were seen as burdensome and unnecessary in Paris and Lon-don, for example, for much of the nineteenth century. The story of Europe in Africa in the nineteenth century is also infused with episodic changes of government in European states, with elections being won on anti-imperialist platforms, with vacillation and hesitation, with uncertainty about the value of global adventures. But with the escalation of national-ist competition within Europe—notably between France and Germany after the latter's defeat of the former in 1870–71 during the Franco–Prussian war—the idea of outmanoeuvring rivals in settings beyond Europe itself became an issue of national self-interest, even if still not a politically un-problematic one.[77] As in Africa, so in Europe, if in a different format and context: the rise of new kinds of polities, even if some located their roots in a more ancient past,[78] bristling with ambition, innovation, curiosity, greed, insecurity, and led by political elites who used episodic constitu-tional reform (and crisis) to instil in communities of citizens an ever sharpening sense of patriotic duty and responsibility. They had at their disposal, too, the increasingly effective and professionalised use of armed force, alongside innovations in weaponry which accelerated as the century wore on. The reorganisation of violence, the reimagining of what it could achieve, and the reconceptualisation of war as a national endeavour were critical to Europe's new states, especially as intra-European enmity intensified. To a considerable extent, this could be dated to the revolutionary wars of the late eighteenth century, when the appearance of 'mass' war in the name of *la patrie* involved the symbiosis of political, social and military change. The decades that followed witnessed a veritable revolution in communications, transport and infrastructure, increasingly efficient military bureaucracy, and technological advances.[79] Europe's warlords often appeared in more subtle guises than their African counterparts in the same period, but warlords they were; and a particular strand of scholarship has identified certain core elements (use of technology, discipline, an aggressive military tradition, responsiveness to challenge, the primacy of capital rather than manpower) as comprising a 'Western way of war'.[80] Not everyone accepts that there is such a thing. But there is little question that Europe's new military energy was unleashed on the back of industrialisation and rapid economic, scientific and technological change.[81]

Industrialisation was in many ways made possible by both earlier colonial expansion (in the Americas) and enthusiastic participation in the Atlantic slave trade; and so once again it is worth reminding ourselves how much these developments, for some the manifestation of a singular European genius, were as much the outcome of African ingenuity, and African trauma, as anything else.[82] In the nineteenth century, industrial transformation generated turmoil within European societies—ironically, perhaps, it was one of the drivers behind increased European emigration overseas—and ultimately fuelled interest in opportunities overseas for commercial expansion.[83] The hegemony of industry and science, moreover, generated a belief in the inherent superiority of European economic endeavour, regardless of the evident distress, dislocation and marginalisation that were its corollaries across Europe itself in both urban and rural settings, which fed into ideas about the need to 'develop' others less fortunate. Ideas about material progress and 'development' were in large part externalised; such redistributive, uplifting power was not directed to places like Blantyre, David Livingstone's impoverished hometown, or Denbigh, which was Stanley's, but pushed outward, taking many men and women with it. Such 'development' could best be effected through trade, it was believed, at least in the first two thirds of the nineteenth century, after a series of European governments had abolished the slave trade. When trade failed, it was often because those with whom European merchants were trying to do business were, it was supposed, in the grip of a primitive savagery. The contrast, moreover, between such primitivity and the mechanised extraction of precious minerals was stark indeed. Economic arguments thus intersected with ideas about race (evolving in parallel with those about 'the nation'), which dated to the era of the slave trade and the late Enlightenment and which foregrounded notions of material and cultural dissimilarity between peoples at different stages of mental and social acuity.[84] We'll return to this in due course: suffice to say here that the racialisation of the European worldview was in part the outcome of pseudoscience, and in part the consequence of Europeans' own unsettling experience of rapid economic, social and political change, and their resultant attempt to compare and rationalise the behaviours of Others whom they encountered in the age of globality.

Christian missionaries were frequently at the forefront of that endeavour, representative of an evangelical surge, a fightback on behalf of God against the secularising direction of travel associated with the Enlightenment. It was the externalisation of similar endeavours in a domestic setting, in an age of impoverishment and dislocation and (as they saw it) increasing godlessness, especially in the context of depravation in burgeoning and brutal industrial centres.[85] Religion became a core component in the self-appointed civilising mission, and evangelists saw it as their sacred duty to go forth into the world, to the places where Satan reigned, in search of souls to salvage. They were closely involved in the abolitionist movement: indeed, the overlap between the two groups was pronounced, and represented a powerful new socially reformist lobby in western Europe, embodying the alliance of the spiritual and the humanitarian. The interconnection between evangelical work and exploration was also powerful, and organic: for how could missionaries meaningfully engage with the spiritual and moral health of African communities if not by moving among them directly, and finding physical as well as scriptural pathways to their salvation? In time, too, religion would be mobilised in pursuit of imperial legitimacy, although in truth the relationship was never a straightforward one.[86] Missionaries might come to lobby for political intervention, and the presence of communities of African acolytes might ease the passage of such intrusion, to some extent. But missionaries could also be critics of imperial government and champions of the communities within which they worked. The goal of bringing God to the 'heathen' was not necessarily compatible with the aims and desires underpinning imperial intrusion.

In the meantime, however, missionary societies went forth and certainly multiplied in the course of the long nineteenth century. The London Missionary Society (1795), Church Missionary Society (1799) and the Wesleyan Methodist Missionary Society (1813, although Wesleyan missions' work had begun in the 1780s) were at the forefront of the British Protestant effort. Later, in the 1860s, the efforts and exhortations of David Livingstone, Victorian Britain's most celebrated campaigner and proselytiser, would lead to the creation of the Universities' Mission to Central Africa. From their base in Algiers from 1868, the Missionaries of Africa, more commonly known as the 'Pères Blancs' (White Fathers), was the most prominent of the French Catholic organisations, alongside the Societas Mariæ (Society of Mary, or Marists; 1817) and the Lyon-based Societé des missions africains (Society of African Missions, or SMA Fathers; 1868).[87] Many more appeared along the way: the American Board of Commissioners for Foreign Missions in the United States (1810–12); the Società dell'apostolato cattolico, or 'Padri pallottini' (Pallottine Fathers) in Italy (1835); the Mill Hill Fathers (1866), Anglo-Dutch but founded in London; the Sheut Fathers in Belgium (1860); the Societas verbi divini (Society of the Divine Word) in the Netherlands, composed largely of German exiles (1875). The goals of these movements, if not their doctrines, were broadly similar: the suppression of the slave trade and the promotion of productive commerce; and the pushing back of the frontiers of heathenism and darkness and salvation of as many souls as could be persuaded to leave the path toward damnation. These aims covered, quite literally, a multitude of sins—including, of course, much that was central to African society, culture, politics and economy. An early territorial manifestation of the Christian project was Sierra Leone, the Georgian 'Province of Freedom' set up in the 1780s to resettle liberated slaves who would then become the frontier-folk of a new society, Christianised, educated and industrious, and in various ways and through various connections 'assimilated' into Anglo culture.[88] Most mission activity before the late nineteenth century was rather less dramatic in scope and scale, though. Missionaries often found themselves working among the displaced and the traumatised, in communities caught up in political conflagration and social upheaval; indeed, these often constituted their most fertile ground: witness conversion rates among the Khoisan, or the Yoruba, or the Ganda. Missionaries themselves came from a diverse range of backgrounds, moreover.[89] But those various provenances and contexts reveal socioeconomic change at home, and doubtless these formative experiences they brought with them to their endeavours among the heathen. Livingstone's penurious early life in Blantyre illustrates the point: just as Stanley can never truly be separated from his childhood of deprivation and indignity, so too Livingstone, likewise the product of the cold, hard Celtic frontier. He famously studied by candlelight in the single room in which his family lived and slept, in a tough Lanarkshire mill village which was a few stones' throw from the filthy, slum-generating, and yet pulsating, empire-fuelling industrial centre that was Glasgow.[90]

In time, the voices of those championing direct political intervention grew louder, and in certain circumstances they had some influence. In Buganda, in the late 1880s and early 1890s, the increasingly vigorous missionary lobby could point to the remarkable rates of conversion among the Ganda elite as indicative of how this special but beleaguered community was deserving of some kind of formal protection. Many Ganda had already died for their faith, put to death by Kabaka Mwanga in 1886.[91] To this could be added the martyrdom of Bishop James Hannington, killed—again, on the orders of Mwanga—attempting (rather foolishly, it must be said) to enter the kingdom via a forbidden route.[92] Missionaries in coastal West Africa and on the north bank of the Congo River wielded increasing influence over popular and political opinion in the French Third Republic, their endeavours creating the moral framework within which protectorates might be declared and recalcitrant Africans attacked. This was the case despite the fact that the Third Republic itself was infused with anticlericalism; a dilemma resolved by emphatically distinguishing the Church in France from the activities of missionaries overseas, whose work was both noble and patriotic.[93] Even the alpha-imperialist Karl Peters sought religious balm to soften his habitually callous empire-building on behalf of the Reich, setting up the Evangelische Missionsgesellschaft für Ostafrika (Evangelical Missionary Society for German East Africa)—even if missionaries themselves found Peters's character and behaviour not quite to their taste.[94] Much would be done in the name of 'Christian conscience', although in Britain the principle was established whereby religious devotion was not in itself justification for the extension of formal control; there needed to be something a little more tangible, a clear economic or strategic interest, in the first instance. Thus in Uganda, Britain, represented initially by the Imperial British East Africa Company, was rather more concerned about securing the headwaters of the Nile than the supposed piety of some Ganda chiefs. When the company hit financial problems, the Liberal government of Rosebery finally agreed to step in and declare a protectorate, though with some reluctance. The Nile was the key issue; but unquestionably missionary work lubricated what was, for the Liberal administration, a self-chafing manoeuvre.[95] In Nigeria, the core concern was the stabilisation of commerce and the realisation of the Niger's potential; but it helped that missionaries in Abeokuta were able to portray the Yoruba as a people deserving of salvation and protection, especially vis-à-vis the savage evil that was Dahomey to the west. Moreover, the efforts of an emergent local class of converts—manifest in the Egba United Board of Management—were suggestive of a progressive, enlightened community which warranted special attention.[96] That same ability to depict certain characters as mired irredeemably in sin was used to powerful and egregious effect in Rhodesia, where Cecil Rhodes's claim to Ndebele territory was supported by missionaries who loathed the Ndebele king, Lobengula. So one of them mistranslated the relevant treaty to Lobengula—helping Rhodes to get his hands on a lot of land, but setting in motion a tragic sequence of events.[97] Missionaries laid the groundwork, too, for colonial administration among the Tswana:

significant rates of conversion and missionary discourse persuaded many Tswana to request and/or accept British protection from the marauding Boers. Still, missionaries had no control over how the Tswana integrated the Gospel into their own philosophy and worldview and asserted owner-ship over the messages contained therein, reflecting a wider phenomenon to which we'll shortly return .[98] In Nyasaland (Malawi), and in Northern Rhodesia (Zambia), British protectorates, again outsourced to Rhodes's British South Africa Company, were mainly aimed at warding off the Portuguese, and involved a great deal of violence against a range of Afri-can communities: Swahili, Chewa, Ngoni, Yao, Bemba. But the brutal methods of subjugation and the committing of resources to the new ter-ritory were justified in the name of the anti-slave trade campaign—the Yao and Swahili were often identified as the chief culprits—in which mission-aries had been prominent, representing Livingstone's legacy. And so, what was a nakedly political and violent act also, fortuitously, looked like *the right thing to do.*[99]

And then there was technology.[100] The global agitation—moral, com-mercial, civilisational, military—of Europeans was facilitated by nautical technology, especially the introduction of steam in the 1830s and 1840s, which enabled faster travel over greater distances, linking zones of conflict and commerce ever more efficiently.[101] Constantly improving firearm tech-nology provided a degree of protection (as well as, obviously, commercial status) when in situ. From the 1860s, notably, breech-loader rifles were in common use by European forces, increasing both rate of fire and mobility compared with the laborious job of muzzle-loading. Muzzle-loaders re-maining predominant in African armies, and although breech-loaders were acquired by Africans in the 1870s and 1880s (for example, by the Yoruba and the Ethiopians), they were still at a disadvantage in terms of both quan-tity and the skills required to repair them and use them to maximum effect. Later, European-led forces also had machine guns, including the first fully automatic machine gun developed by Hiram Maxim: while these weren't universally used by colonial armies, even at the height of European military operations in the 1890s and 1900s, they were clearly hugely destructive when they were, especially in open country. As the writer and polymath Hilaire Belloc famously (or notoriously) put it, "Whatever happens we have got / The Maxim gun, and they have not."[102] Heavier ordnance was often impractical, certainly in challenging physical environments beyond the coast, not least purely in terms of transportation. But light artillery was increasingly deployed, and enabled the rapid storming of fortified political centres. The French made effective use of them in the western savannah, for example—which often led to swift capitulation.[103] Meanwhile, the telegraph enabled more rapid communications, and thus decisions to be made and resources to be redirected more efficiently. But there was no greater protection than that afforded by advances in medical science. The increasing use of quinine against malaria from the 1850s onward meant that, usefully enough, Europeans didn't die at quite the rate they had previously in the 'White Man's Grave', as a swathe of West Africa had been known, and in fact could actually now stay in malarial regions for relatively long periods of time.[104] They were propelled to do so by a desire to represent newly embraced nationhood; to evangelise and to explore, often simultaneously, and increasingly to lay claim to the places they imagined they had discovered; to achieve fame and status and perhaps wealth in a turbulent, uncertain, anxious age; and above all, to grasp economic opportunities, for there was much business to be done in capital-heavy Europe, and a great deal of appetite to do it.

The exploratory instinct, meanwhile, was not distinctive to Europe's nineteenth century, clearly. But its scale and intensity, as well as the scientific and ultimately the political and economic purposes behind it, were particular characteristics of the era. So, too, was the level of cultural judgment which increasingly attended it, or at least followed from it. Geographical expeditions were undertaken for a whole range of reasons, including very private ones.[105] But central to the idea of 'exploring', at least in the first instance, was the rise of Science: the belief in the ability, indeed the need, to impose on the 'unknown' swathes of the world, and on the world of nature; to comprehend it and chart it, to measure and quantify it.[106] The impetus, in the late eighteenth and early nineteenth centuries, was both commercial and scientific: namely, the unprecedented desire to identify the continent's economic potential in terms of resources, markets, terrain, climate. This was directly linked to industrialisation in Europe itself, buttressed by the presumed moral authority arising from the Enlightenment, which required levels of knowledge about Africa which had not been particularly important during an era in which the primary economic goal of Europeans in Africa was the extraction of human beings—and this had largely been undertaken by Africans themselves. Exploration, in other words, reflected the corporeal need for men, and a few women, to assess the navigability of rivers, to move among the major centres of population, to measure the fertility of the soil, in order to both realise Europeans' own economic ambitions in the age of industry and capital, and to assist Africans in their own material and civilisational development. It was a compelling narrative which *wazungu* developed for themselves; and, it would seem, a remarkably enduring one.

In institutional and organisational terms, the spirit of the enlightened, curious, industrious *mzungu* was distilled in the proliferation across western Europe of intellectual societies dedicated to the discovery of the darker reaches of the world—in some ways for its own sake, as befitted the men of inherited wealth often in charge of them, but increasingly with scientific and commercial purpose. These societies arose from the Enlightenment, and were, in their way, the product of the revolutionary ferment of the age; they would gain momentum through the creation of new social classes of high-minded adventurers and determined evangelists, and as a result of the technological advances which propelled them into the world.[107] In London in 1788, a cluster of learned gentlemen and wealthy patrons had established the Association for Promoting the Discovery of the Interior Parts of Africa, commonly and unsurprisingly abbreviated to 'the African Association'—with a particular concern to realise African's commercial potential and, more specifically, to reach Timbuktu, the great West African seat of Islamic learning which in the European mind was associated with gold.[108] In the early nineteenth century, a number of similarly-minded professional organisations appeared: in Paris in 1821, the Société de géographie; in Berlin in 1828, the Gesellschaft für Erdkunde zu Berlin; in London in 1830, the Royal Geographical Society.[109] In the decades that followed, they sponsored numerous quests which rested upon the presumption of the right to intrude, and this, in turn, grew in parallel with the idea that it was necessary to 'discover' rivers, mountains, lakes and so forth because the people inhabiting these regions were markedly inferior, and were little more than part of the landscape itself.[110] This, then, was discovery rendered both practical—the tapping into Africa's natural resources and commercial arteries—and moral, or humanitarian, because it would inevitably lift Africans from the sinful, depraved despond which Europeans had imagined for them. The focus, again, was often on the continent's great rivers: the Nile, Niger, Congo, Zambezi.[111] But others increasingly struck out across the landmass. Death or injury often awaited, although again quinine prophylaxis helped after the 1850s. Above all, they were carried along by, and frequently caught up in, the tempests of change raging around them; sometimes they dimly grasped what was happening as they hauled themselves through war and revolution, and certainly many left accounts of events which are simultaneously among the richest and most problematic for historians. James Bruce, for example, was present at the moment the Ethiopian empire imploded and the region embarked on several decades of inter-state conflict. Mungo Park witnessed the convulsions resulting from slaving violence in the western Sahel at the end of the eighteenth and beginning of the nineteenth centuries. Hugh Clapperton and the Lander brothers, Richard and John, travelled through Hausa and Yoruba territory in the 1820s as the Oyo state was collapsing and as the recently-founded Sokoto Caliphate asserted itself. Between the 1840s and the 1870s, David Livingstone observed the effects of political insurgency and commercial violence across a vast region from the trans-Zambezi zone to the eastern Congo basin. And, likewise, John Hanning Speke, Richard Burton, Verney Lovatt Cameron and Henry Morton Stanley, as we have seen, bore witness to—though didn't always comprehend—innumerable manifestations of creative volatility between the Indian and Atlantic Ocean shorelines. Battered and frequently confused, they imposed, as is often the wont of foreign analysts, their own interpretations and narratives on what was unfolding around them.[112]

By the 1870s and 1880s, intrepid expeditions had crossed over more or less explicitly into exercises in proto-imperialism, as in the case of Stanley in the Congo. Along the way, this was activity which generated an idiosyncratic form of masculinity: it mostly, if not quite exclusively, involved men, and moreover middle-class men from professional, often military, backgrounds. A Freudian or some other form of psychoanalytical interpretation of exploration is no doubt possible, if somewhat beyond the competence of this author. But clearly it was at least partly motivated by some form of desperate desire for heroism, or super-heroism, perhaps combined with frustrated sexual desire. At some subconscious level it was also perhaps driven by the desire to mitigate the impact of the massive socioeconomic dislocation of the nineteenth century, of cloying urbanism, a search for primitive idylls in an epoch of toxic machinery, or for savagery, a way of projecting the brutality of modern life onto those truly barbarian places on the earth, or perhaps to self-persuade that modernity was vastly superior.[113]

———

WHAT IS CLEAR ENOUGH IS THAT AN UNSTABLE COCKTAIL of nation, industry, guns, racism and God had given rise to political systems, elites and cultures which celebrated particular forms of mammon, militarism and morality, underwritten by notions about national and racial superiority—and in some places, a rampant exceptionalism—and made practicable by technical innovation. Buoyed by the rise of nation-states and an increasingly global reach, Europeans' experience of Africa was shaped by evangelists, explorers and assorted entrepreneurs. On the ground, Europeans stimulated much change in those societies within which, or on the edges of which, they operated. In time their impact would escalate, and they would inflict a great deal of violence on Africans, compounding a century of upheaval, exacerbating its deleterious outcomes and stymying some of Africans' own more creative initiatives. But, as exemplified by Stanley himself, this was a groping, blundering imperialism, as no doubt much empire-building was (and is), disjointed for the most part, its reasons incoherently articulated, or at best its justifications a jumbled bag of half-developed notions about the state of the world and Europe's place in it. In time, again, it became a brutal one, too. Yet this was a nervous, anxious probing of Africa, a reflection of enormous social and political ruptures in Europe itself, and of emerging patterns of gendered behaviour and in particular a drive for masculine self-realisation; an imperialism well armed, and increasingly well resourced, but inchoate

in aim and meaning. Above all, and to a remarkable degree, it was characterised—in some ways even ultimately motivated—by profound ignorance.
The technological innovation which facilitated Europe's intensifying interaction with Africa was remarkable in itself, and that same technology,
broadly defined, would enable Europeans to insert themselves with greater
or lesser efficacy into a range of scenarios across the continent. But the
technology, though it contributed mightily to the growing sense of global
superiority, and in Britain an entirely unjustified and enduring sense of
exceptionalism, in many ways outran the political planning, or emotional
intelligence, or any real sense of purpose, and certainly the moral justification for intrusion in the first place. That would be developed some time
after the fact. For Europe too was in a liminal condition in the course of
the long nineteenth century: thanks to their logistical and technological
potency, Europeans were able to export that liminality, and their own
anxieties, over some extraordinary distances. There is a certain irony
involved in the European exploitation of 'civil war' in Africa, given that
for a handful of European nations imperialism was in some ways an
outlet for pressure within Europe itself, and the fact that Germany and
Italy, for example, had recently undergone intense and prolonged civil
violence—'wars of unification'—of their own.

Agents and representatives of those places no doubt carried those anxieties and perspectives with them; perhaps even saw in Africa things
which they knew were their own, but dared not admit as much. Instead,
they projected. And so, too, shifting African contexts and dynamics and,
of course, live informants fundamentally shaped Europeans' approaches
to the continent as they tumbled across it, buffeted and co-opted.[114] African political forms and economic dynamism, in many ways mirroring
what was happening in Europe itself, stimulated much transformation in
the latter. This was the case even in those scenarios where imperialism
seems so dominant, with such an unambiguous monopoly on 'agency'.
Economic power and the capacity to use it on the part of European business interests, for example, was most visibly demonstrated at either end
of Africa, in Egypt and in South Africa, between the 1870s and 1900s. For
this reason, no doubt, these regions have hogged much of the limelight

in Eurocentric analyses of 'The Scramble'. In many ways they are actually fairly anomalous, however, and have a curiously distorting effect on our understanding of events elsewhere. Still, there is no doubting the acquisitive, organisational power of European capital following the discovery of diamonds at Kimberley and gold in the Transvaal. Here was restive socioeconomic ambition writ large. And in khedival Egypt, too, French and British financial and strategic interests drove competition over control of the Nile Delta and the adjacent Suez Canal. In both cases, too, wider geopolitics played a critical role, one over which local actors apparently had little or no direct influence. Both regions were enmeshed in national-imperial dramas which increasingly characterised intra-European relations, be in Anglo–French enmity over Egypt and the Nile, or Anglo–Portuguese–German rivalry across southern Africa. And yet, in both cases, African dynamics were in fact critical in the long-term definition of these political, economic and cultural environments. In Cairo, successive regimes pursued programmes of reform and expansion which drew in European interests, tapped into European models and utilised European personnel. The outcomes were unpredictable; but Egyptian actors were always at the centre of the process. South Africa's political and social landscape fundamentally shaped the manner in which European capital flowed into the region, and industrialism was inescapably and profoundly altered by ongoing African dynamics, whether in terms of population movement, political mobility, or social relationships, notwithstanding the brutality of the economic and racial order which would arise in the decades after the 1880s.

This, then, was the great convergence: the interaction of two continents, each spurring change in the other, each in many respects mirroring the other in terms of the broad shape of those changes, if not always in the particulars. Convergence was there in the cultures of aspiration and reform and in the pursuit of profit; in the increase in social mobility, both upward and downward; in the cultures of violence and large-scale projects in political rejuvenation and expansion; in the globality of outlooks; in the exercises in ideological and religious reformation. Europeans encountered African insurgencies and reformist polities and their turbulent aftermaths; Africans encountered the European nation-state and its imperial appendages. Each influenced the other in sometimes subtle but always intense ways. The nature of the interaction varied from context to context, and played out in myriad forms, whether on the sandbars opposite Lagos, or on the highveld in the southern African interior, or on the approaches to Isike's enclosure.

# 6

# Interstice and Intermediacy

## Liminal Spaces

FRONTIERS AND INTERSTICES were of seminal importance in the deeper African past, something we explored in an earlier section.[1] A number of political and commercial entities, underpinned by a restless, potent, innovative militarism, were markedly successful in terms of a rolling demarcation, pushing forward territorially and extending armed reach; but usually, beyond a certain point, that process morphed into one of indirect influence or indirect rule, rather than formalised administrative control. Expansion was inevitably attended by contraction. Warcraft was honed to extraordinary effect, often becoming the most visible manifestation of political and economic ambition, which was increasingly aimed at the destruction of the enemy's ability to resist and their material resources. But both war and the ambition it served also rendered many states and societies inherently unstable, prone to internal fissures and tensions. Creative volatility by definition involved the incessant generation and regeneration of liminal spaces and communities, interstitial zones and groupings defined by cultural, political and economic creativity, by construction as well as by destruction. African statehood had historically used turbulent frontier zones both as buffers and as areas from which human and animal resources could episodically be drawn. These spaces had vibrant, symbiotic relationships with the centre, and the latter itself could be transitional, and host to the same liminal, creative forces of reform and contestation. In the ebb and flow of volatile frontier spaces, and in the context of internal contestation, communities and cultures, factions and offshoots, were created which were simultaneously vulnerable and opportunistically poised: the people in between, who would form the essential material for imperial expansion and the creation of new identities and communities, as had been the case throughout the nineteenth century. The surge in particular forms of economic enterprise, often rooted in violent coercion, led to the proliferation of marginalised, transitional, migrant and refugee communities, which often relocated to areas harder to attack but with fewer resources, and which were critical, directly or indirectly, to the colonial project. These are the circumstances which complicate our understanding of how European empires were actually built, with a sharper focus on the primacy of local exigency, liminality and opportunism: local agency was either borne of socioeconomic pressure and vulnerability, or was the product of relative political advantage.

In the course of the long nineteenth century, millions of Africans inhabited liminal space, the zones between fluctuating states and cultural cores, in the clefts within contested polities, in the febrile commercial corridors in which violence and enterprise thrived. The creation of economies organised around war in the two centuries prior to our period, most dramatically, but not exclusively, in the Atlantic zone, had intensified the long-standing pattern in African political culture of drawing sustenance from contested interstitial spaces and borderlands, both physical and conceptual. By the beginning of the nineteenth century, patterns of such contest and consequent displacement were common, leading to the rolling re-creation of contested, liminal spaces. These were environments shaped by opportunity, coercion, exploitation and resistance; characterised by the gloamings of authority, episodically being made and remade. In the context of the later nineteenth century, the relevance of liminal spaces, in both their physical and their social manifestations, is twofold. Firstly, they were breeding grounds for new forms of community and identity which in various ways and contexts interceded between the endogenous and exogenous, taking advantage of, even weaponising, their liminal positionality. Intermediacy doubtless carried risks, and had long been associated with vulnerability as much as with the pioneering spirit that came to define African political and economic culture. But intermediacy also involved opportunities for co-option and harnessing. Intermediaries of various kinds, who were the direct consequence of Africa's revolutionary century, formed the critical mass necessary to the creation of the 'colonial order'. The entrepreneurial, violent flux characteristic of nineteenth-century African political culture, the liminal spaces which it produced, were the building blocks of European empire in Africa. Secondly, and conversely, these communities and spaces presented opportunities for leverage on the part of well-organised, and well-armed, interlopers and adventurers—by the late nineteenth century largely, if not quite exclusively, European—with economic and political designs. The capacity for co-option was reciprocal. Permeable places brought together interfering foreigners and resourceful communities for whom such intrusions were nothing new, even if some of the weaponry and logistical apparatus might have been, for this is how things had been for much of the nineteenth century. White trespassers were the latest, if perhaps the most unusual, in a sequence of armed entrepreneurs and innovators. While the great, mobile reformist and entrepreneurial projects and movements of the nineteenth century constituted the essence of the African revolution, and count among the continent's most spectacular achievements of the era, they also opened up a vast network of fissures and apertures which were just as likely to offer attractive prospects and usable points of entry to grasping foreigners and their proxies. The latter were able to tap into and exploit long-standing cultures of aspiration and innovation, of the kind which had produced such dramatic socioeconomic change across the continent during the long nineteenth century; and likewise, they sought to exploit the lithe political entrepreneurialism which had produced cultures of reform and challenge and some of the most remarkable entities anywhere in the world in that period, but which were perpetually vulnerable to internal fissure and thus external leverage. Political enterprise and nimble conceptualisations of suzerainty meant that African elites often thought in terms of advantageous partnership with useful incomers. African political and economic projects had been partitioning the continent for several decades before Europeans arrived with breechloading rifles and machine guns; but the African reformation also offered multiple openings to foreign adventurers bent on intrigue and the exercise of influence. They were able to overcome numerical weakness—and indeed cultural ignorance—through shrewd exploitation of the insecurities and instabilities in many African polities.

## Contest and Contingency

PROLONGED CONFLICT CAUSED the displacement of people, militarised and traumatised communities and created zones of instability around centralised states. This is especially evident during the external slave trade. Dahomean armies had long reached beyond the kingdom's cosmological and administrative core in search of captives, preying especially on comparatively decentralised communities adjacent to it, and creating a turbulent interstice among the Mahi, for example.[2] In other scenarios, given the logistical limitations on the reach of armies, slaving states actively relied on circles of interstitiality wherein slaving wars were in effect outsourced to client and tributary societies who supplied captives to the major centres. Often this was a matter of self-protection: smaller-scale, decentralised communities found that offering a regular supply of captives to larger neighbours was reasonable insurance against predation aimed in their direction. Asante was in receipt of large numbers of slaves in this manner by the late eighteenth century, and tributary zones enabled Asante to extend its reach much further to the north than would otherwise have been possible.[3] Yet these arrangements were subject to episodic challenge, and Asante was confronted with rebellions on its outer reaches throughout the nineteenth century, insurrections which constituted an arc of instability across present-day central and northern Ghana.[4] By the middle decades of the nineteenth century, Dahomey had also turned its attention to the Yoruba polities to the east, previously off limits while the Oyo empire, to which Dahomey was tributary, was in its pomp. In all likelihood, too, it was a strategy necessitated by steady depopulation to the north and west of Dahomey as a result of decades of marauding. Ferocious attacks on Abeokuta, the Egba capital, in 1851 and 1864 opened up a volatile frontier zone in what would become western Nigeria.[5] The intra-Yoruba wars—the outcome of Oyo's implosion and the resultant flux across the Bight hinterland—likewise created fluidity and instability in the region, a grid of conflict which created channels of the displaced and the transitory, constituting fertile ground for the labours of Christian missionaries, who were active in the area by the middle decades of the nineteenth century. They were crucial in the portrayal of the Yoruba as a benighted people consumed by violence and in need of salvation, and offered sanctuary to increasing numbers of willing souls. Those resident at Abeokuta reserved their most vociferous condemnation for Dahomey, for they had witnessed at first hand Dahomean aggression and savagery, they said.[6] Such reportage, and the political lobbying which attended it, opened the possibility, in the minds of some Yoruba leaders, notably in Ibadan, that Europeans, and the British in particular, might be useful partners and facilitators. This dated in a tangible political sense to the establishment of a permanent British presence, and of course an exhibition of British power, at Lagos in 1861, but the potential for external leverage increased markedly during the 1870s and 1880s. Ibadan was identified by the British as a potential point of entry into the region, its relative reach and strength offering the hope of political and economic development. Ibadan received, and willingly accepted, British support. But when an array of other Yoruba polities forged an alliance in opposition to Ibadan's power, British agents found that they were compelled, and were able, to reposition themselves as counsellors and mediators; and, at the end of lengthy negotiations in 1892–93, administrators.[7] Missionaries, again, had been critical in easing the entry of officialdom at the local level, and in pushing for government intervention in the first place.[8]

The political reach of even some of the most significant polities on the continent was limited, and in many respects they created, through their very success, new fault lines both within and beyond the polity itself, which were sources of vulnerability and challenge. This is not to suggest that such entities did not exhibit remarkable endurance and adaptability: many did, and survived deep into the twentieth century, and in a number of cases endure still. In many cases, moreover, African states over a long period of time had themselves had been adept at co-opting groups which potentially posed a threat, drawing to the centre from social or physical peripheries communities with economic or military skills to

offer. Buganda absorbed those with economic specialisms in metalwork-
ing, for example, in the course of its expansion, and their integration
spurred further economic growth and social stratification.[9] In some ways
this mitigated the threat from ominous frontiers, although it never eliminated it, and it also meant that the incoming community itself was able
to shape the polity into which it had entered. This was the case in Ethiopia, where Oromo kingdoms developed in the southern and central highlands and Oromo became military and political leaders at the very heart
of the Solomonic state in the course of the eighteenth and nineteenth
centuries.[10] More broadly, however, polities had to learn to live with inherent instability, and with the dangerous vitality which came with evolving political and material creativity. Take, for example, the Zulu state—an
insurgent polity which had long emitted something like pure energy, but
one which was in many respects essentially parasitic, suffused with the
factionalism which is inescapably part of revolutionary insurrection. Increasingly, adjacent communities either moved out of Zulu military
range, or emulated their military structure and ethos. The Mfecane created a band of interstices and unstable frontier zones across the lowveld.
Perhaps, in some existential way, that had been its entire point. This
pattern was replicated across a swathe of eastern and central Africa, as
Ngoni or their eager emulators dispersed beyond the epicentre of the Zulu
revolution into the lacustrine region and the east African plateau. With the
creation of new polities—Mzilikazi's Ndebele, or Moshoeshoe's Sotho—
came volatile borderlands and violent zones of transition; and similarly
concentric patterns of instability were created with the transformation of
societies across present-day Zambia, Malawi and Tanzania which imi-
tated Ngoni methods and structures.[11] In the crowded political space to
the west and south-west of Lake Victoria, escalating conflict between a
range of polities, most obviously the axis of competition between Buganda and Bunyoro, created a network of interstice and contestation. Yet
often those unstable and shifting borderlands were in fact critical to the
very functioning of the polity. Militarised states in Rwanda and Burundi—
akin to Nkore, Buganda, Bunyoro, Toro—in many ways drew their legitimacy in the existence of the perennially insecure frontier, rooting it in the
protection elites could provide to loyal subjects.[12]

The far-flung insurgent states of the West African savannah, those of Umar Tal and Samori, wrestled with the same centrifugal forces with which their medieval and early modern predecessors had been confronted. They struggled to impose themselves over long distances for long periods of time. So, too, did the sprawling polity with its nominal 'centre', Sokoto—actually positioned in the far north-west of the Caliphate—whose rulers lacked the capacity, perhaps even the will, to impose themselves on its far-flung constituent parts. The rivalrous emirates retained a considerable degree of autonomy through the nineteenth century, though the rambling theocratic coalition was bound together by a fear of the very Islamic radicalism on or within its borders which had been its own taproot. Specifically, popular anticipation of the coming of the Mahdi, the messianic figure associated in particular with Shi'a Islam, in the late nineteenth and early twentieth centuries understandably made Sokoto's relatively parvenu clerical elites anxious about challenges to their credentials as legitimate Muslim rulers; and thus, paradoxically, eager to co-opt an infidel power, the British, after the latter had defeated them militarily, into consolidating their rule.[13]

Ethiopian state-builders often laid claim, in rhetoric at least, to the Red Sea coast.[14] But the reality was that the area of the Eritrean highlands, the *kebessa*, constituted a volatile frontier zone into which they might episodically make incursions, but over which they had no enduring control. At times it constituted a useful buffer; at others, an existential threat.[15] Moreover, Tigrayan revolt was especially problematic for political elites further south, as it blocked their access to increasingly vital commercial highways. And as Tewodros discovered, Tigrayan hostility allowed an intrepid but otherwise vulnerable British force to move into a position of attack relatively unimpeded. Under Yohannes, Tigray comprised the centre of the neo-Solomonic state, but he was also confronted with the problem of volatile northern frontiers. In Eritrea, the Egyptians launched military assaults in the mid-1870s, which Ethiopian forces warded off; in the mid-1880s, under British tutelage, Egypt withdrew, only to be replaced by the Italians. Meanwhile to the north and north-west, a new set of volatile and often hostile borderlands evolved as a result of the Egyptian expansion into Sudan, leading to the creation of outposts in the western and northern parts of Eritrea in the middle decades of the nineteenth century. With the overthrow of the Egyptian administration by the Mahdist movement, a new threat appeared; and indeed, Yohannes himself was killed in an engagement with the Mahdist army in 1889.[16] As the outcome of a series of insurgencies and state-level convulsions over several decades, late nineteenth-century Ethiopia was built on a network of fault lines and frontier zones, both internal and external, which empowered an exceptionalist culture and ideology— Ethiopian leaders portrayed the Christian kingdom as encircled by Muslims bent on its destruction—but which could be exploited both by external enemies and by those within the territory seeking to contest and remake the state itself.[17] This remained the case even, and perhaps indeed especially, after Menelik's triumph against the Italians at Adwa. Similar dynamics were at work in Morocco, in at least certain respects analogous to Ethiopia in terms of terrain, territorial reach and political form. Beyond the reach of even nominal Ottoman control in the Maghreb, Morocco had proven impervious to European petitions during the early nineteenth century, and in fact its support for Abd al-Qadir's struggle against the French in Algeria had provoked a French attack in 1845. Crucially, however, peripheries and fissures—reflecting the limitations on the Sultan's power—provided much more exploitable points of entry to foreign interests. Unable to prevent outlying groups in the north from attacking the Spanish enclaves of Melilla and Ceuta, the Moroccan government found itself on the receiving end of a series of punitive Spanish assaults, and sued for peace, agreeing to pay Madrid considerable financial compensation. Morocco had to raise the money in London, and it came with strings attached, including control over certain areas of Moroccan trade. In the 1870s and 1880s the dynamic Sultan Mawlai al-Hasan set about the systematic and brutal extension of state control over various dissident and recalcitrant groups, and established the kingdom as the dominant force in north-west Africa even as the 'partition' was unfolding across the region. It was eventually, in 1912, divided up between France and Spain, and the former in particular used dynastic and political fissiparity and contest to great effect.[18] It was ironic that in the 1920s the energetic anticolonial resistance which was carried out by Abd al-Krim in the Rif mountains represented precisely the kind of precipitous insurgency which al-Hasan had sought to crush half a century earlier.[19]

In each of these scenarios, foreigners with some skill, local support and a fair amount of good fortune could insert themselves into these interstices, manoeuvring and co-opting in pursuit of leverage. The French took advantage of the ongoing violent rivalry between Samori's Mandinke state and Ahmadu Seku's Tukolor. The latter believed they were safe from French attack following a series of agreements, leaving them to concentrate on the more important business of local hegemony, only to find themselves assaulted by Senegalese troops in 1889 and largely defeated by 1893.[20] Samori had internal insurgents as well as Ahmadu and the French to contend with, and so understandably he periodically pursued agreement with the French in order to buy time. But following the French-led invasion in 1891, the combination of external pressure and internal fissure proved insurmountable, and Samori was compelled to sue for peace in 1898.[21] The British likewise harnessed the geopolitical unsettlement and armed competition that were the result of decades of political and military reformation, in seeking to isolate and weaken the Zulu. This did not preclude the need for direct assaults, as is clear enough from the evidence. But the capacity for political manoeuvre and positioning, and, crucially, the ability to recruit soldiers and mobilise key factional support, was as vital as battlefield showdowns, if not more so.

In other scenarios, notably in coastal West Africa, growing commercial influence and, increasingly, overt aggression were more significant. As we have seen, one major upshot of the region's socioeconomic transformation in the course of the nineteenth century had been the emergence of an array of entrepreneurs and self-made rulers, inhabiting new material as well as political spaces in an era of rapid change. They were the very essence of vibrant liminality. But their positionality with respect to a global economy shifted over time. In broad terms, down to the 1850s, many prospered as a result of the high prices offered by European merchants for their produce, while managing to keep their own costs low through the use of slave labour and that of extended kinship networks. Prices plateaued somewhat in the middle decades of the nineteenth century and then, in the 1870s, they began to fall—including for palm oil, the long-standing West African economic staple for which cheaper substitutes had been found elsewhere. Inevitably, tensions escalated sharply between African producer or middleman on the one hand and European buyer on the other. Debt became a widespread issue, as African merchants, seeing their profit margins falling, relied on the credit extended to them by their European counterparts. It was unsustainable. Creditors increasingly resorted to violence to retrieve debt.[22] At the frontiers of commercial interaction, African entrepreneurs found themselves financially beholden to, and regarded as a political nuisance by, long-term external trading partners.[23] The story of Nana Olomu is illustrative. The Itsekiri chief, the long-serving 'governor' of Benin River under an arrangement with the British consul for the bights of Benin and Biafra, had occupied a prime middleman status down to the mid-1880s, and his community had thrived as a result. But the British, better able to navigate the myriad waterways of the Delta, and inclined to push their influence beyond the coast, began to bypass the Itsekiri, prompting Nana Olomu to attack nearby rivals (the Urhobo) in the early 1890s. The British moved against him, and so did several rival Itsekiri chiefs who swiftly came their own agreement with the British, and Nana Olomu, isolated and weakened, was captured and exiled.[24] His position, and his fate, was comparable to that of Jaja of Opobo in terms of the riverine entrepreneurialism of the age, even if operating in a somewhat different context. Jaja had also fallen foul of the British authorities when in 1887 he was seized and deported for refusing to cease taxing British traders, apparently unaware of—or wilfully ignoring—the 'fact' that as a result of the Berlin conference Opobo had been designated British territory.[25] It was a stark indication of how circumstances could swiftly turn against successful African traders, including those who had grasped commercial opportunities, as Olomu's predecessors had since the 1850s, when vicissitudes were favourable. We have noted how this has involved, for some scholars, a debate about whether African economic weakness or resilience is at issue here. Clearly there is variation from place to place. But in general this might be seen as a somewhat simplistic rendering of a more nuanced set of dynamics. Above all, the very same energetic agility which had driven African enterprise in the first place had become a source of vulnerability, or at least exposure, for at this moment foreign intruders were able to take advantage of Africans' dependence on, and vigorous engagement with, global dynamics, and to achieve leverage in the social flux and intermediacy which African enterprise had generated.

## Communities and Cultures of Intermediacy

AN ASSORTMENT of intermediaries, exiles, expatriates, mixed race communities, creole cultures and various so-called 'sub-imperialists' not only facilitated colonialism, but were proactive in its actual creation.[26] At the same time, a narrow focus on the notion of formal externally imposed 'colonialism' neglects scenarios involving more subtle and complex forms of global engagement, leading to the emergence of new communities, whether defined by lived experience, language, locale, or in time culture and ethnicity, on the very frontiers of the inventive liminality which made 'empire' a conceivable project. Some of the earliest examples appeared in western Africa, such as the polyglot, transnational African settler community in the British 'Province of Freedom', or Sierra Leone (lion mountains: derived from the Portuguese description of the land as it appeared from offshore). This remarkable Atlantic society was comprised of African-Americans loyal to the British during the American War of Independence and various freed slaves, settled in the area around Freetown from the 1780s onward. The creole community which developed in the early decades of the nineteenth century was an illustration of the dynamic hybridity which would proliferate, in different forms and circumstances, across the continent. In time Sierra Leone, in addition to its liberated and resettled population, attracted ambitious people from across the region owing to the educational prospects offered by Freetown, and then produced a vigorous diaspora which spread back out across West Africa.[27] As part of a transatlantic world—encompassing an anticolonial war, and moral and economic debates around abolition, on opposite sides of the ocean—Africans and African-Americans in Sierra Leone were not merely passive vessels of global currents, nor victims salved by shifts in external opinion, but creators of vibrant cultures and active agents in the forging of communities fundamental to the European intervention in Africa.[28] So, too, in Liberia, the site of another vivacious community closely tied to the African-American diaspora in the United States; Liberia was created under the auspices of the American Colonization Society and involved the settlement of people of colour, both free and recently emancipated.[29] In both Liberia and Sierra Leone, it is worth noting, relations between littoral creole communities and those in the hinterlands were perennially tense and episodically violent, even as commercial connections were increasingly vital to both.[30] Hybridity of the kind emerging in Monrovia or Freetown was a strange and threatening thing, and no less likely to provoke armed confrontation than anything overtly 'imperial' in the white-skinned sense. In those territories, it also represented, microcosmically, hierarchy and inequality, rooted in access—to goods and God and governance, above all—which was global in its provenance, but local in its praxis.

Less overtly exogenous in provenance, perhaps, but borne of a very similar coalescence of outside enticements and internal dynamics, was Fante society on the Gold Coast. This was a commercially dynamic, cosmopolitan community with close links to European traders, especially British, and also comprised a growing number of émigrés from Asante who were active critics of the state lurking to the north. Indeed their anti-Asante propaganda was instrumental in the hardening British interpretation of Kumasi as a barbarous obstacle to progress in the region.[31] When Asante forces attacked the coastal strip, the Fante looked to the British for support, and although London was often reluctant to commit itself to their protection, British forces were indeed dispatched there in 1873–74 to launch a punitive invasion of Asante which ended with London declaring a protectorate over the Fante coast.[32] Britain had thus acquired another slice of territory, just down the coast from Lagos, albeit one for which there was not huge enthusiasm at home; but more importantly, Fante agency in the creation of this lively zone of cultural and political exchange and innovation was critical. Here was a community increasingly shaped by its embrace of Christianity, but as importantly by its energetic, 'modernising' programme of social and political reform, arguing for the creation of a self-governing confederacy of states in the territory. Ultimately, it was a programme which British administrators eyed suspiciously, and Fante modernising, progressive ambitions were thwarted in the face of metropolitan hostility infused with racial judgment; but, in the middle decades of the nineteenth century, the Fante offer a superb example, even if the circumstances were quite exceptional, of nineteenth-century African reformers inhabiting a liminal space and seeking to carve out of that space a pioneering sociopolitical enterprise, defined, indeed strengthened, by its hybridity and the intellectual exchange which was the corollary of its intermediacy.[33] Crucially, too, the Fante demonstrate the ways in which 'empire' contained the seeds of its own destruction: the very nature of the global encounter produced new forms of intermediate community and new forms of interaction which in some ways facilitated the extension of external influence, but which at the same time would come to involve the challenge and contestation, and ultimately the eschewal, of that external power's own political culture and cosmology. In the meantime, Gold Coast society would go on to generate recruits for the British colonial army in the area, while an emerging middle class of translators and clerks and functionaries of various kinds would come to constitute the gel of the British Empire in the region, and in so doing exercise their own leverage over that empire and how it operated.[34] Something similar can be said of those reformist-minded regimes which selected aspects of supposed 'modernity' and sought to revitalise polity and society while simultaneously seizing the opportunities presented by external engagement. This was the case in Tunisia, for example, where efforts were made toward social, political and economic reform in the middle decades of the nineteenth century, an endeavour which rendered Tunis a profitable and cosmopolitan place for both European commercial agents and a growing Tunisian middle class alike. The authorities even requested British protection in the 1830s against both France (rampant in Algeria) and the Ottomans.[35] In time, that would prove an unwise invitation to European political interests which—vampirically—would thereafter feel able to enter at will. Still, while both the Fante and the Tunisians experienced colonial rule, they actively shaped the environments within which that later transpired.

Elsewhere, those who embraced Christianity, or a syncretic interpretation of it—that is, the integration of certain Christian concepts and principles into extant cosmologies, traditions and prophetic cultures[36]—were likewise interstitial communities, and formed a critical part of the overall African reformation, serving as intermediaries between the local and the global. Spiritual conversion, or cosmological adaptation, as is well attested, occurred for myriad reasons: distress, displacement, opportunism, profound theological reimagining.[37] Foremost among those drivers was the belief that certain elements in Christian theology could be absorbed and repurposed in the context of long-standing, deep-rooted patterns of insurgent reformism. These processes of adaptation and co-option came in many forms. The impact of African converts coming from outside to work in African communities had a long history. Philip Quaque was born in the Gold Coast in 1741 and was sent to England to be trained in the ministry, becoming the first African to be ordained by the Church of England. In the late 1760s he returned to Africa to evangelise among 'his own'.[38] He was a pioneer; many others would follow, especially those alumni of Sierra Leone who would move across the region in the nineteenth century, apparently liberated and transformed, to teach the gospel. Many of these were Yoruba, enslaved (often as children) as Oyo was collapsing, and were headed westward in chains before being rescued and resettled in Freetown and its environs. Doubtless the most celebrated instance of this was the great clergyman Samuel Ajayi Crowther, who embodied a transatlantic, migratory world as well as that liminal, reformist space between the local and the global. Enslaved as a child, whose ship was intersected by a British anti-slavery vessel, he was settled in Sierra Leone where he attended Fourah Bay College, converted to Christianity, and after many years as a missionary among the Yoruba was made bishop of the Niger Mission in 1864.[39] The pioneering Yoruba (and Nigerian) historian Samuel Johnson, likewise, was a product of these turbulent dynamics: enslaved, liberated, resettled in Sierra Leone, and following conversion and training eventually dispatched to preach at Oyo in the 1880s and 1890s.[40] He often found a willing audience, and certainly one which was open to his message: in the middle decades of the nineteenth century, in the midst of warfare and displacement, many Yoruba found sanctuary, both physical and spiritual, in the mission stations proliferating across the area. In the later nineteenth century these people would often become eager exponents of the essential tenets of the 'civilising mission', not because they constituted some form of imperial lackey, but because they had co-opted the 'mission' to their own ends and saw enormous social and economic opportunities in it, as well as integrating the morality associated with it in developing new ideas about status and respectability. It was an energetic intersection, embodied in returnee compatriots like Johnson.[41] In South Africa, the Khoisan, long marginalised and oppressed in the context of white colonial power, were similarly receptive to the protection and possibility offered by mission outposts and the concepts contained therein, reimagining their community and identity accordingly.[42] As we noted previously, among the Tshidi branch of the Tswana, women were early converts, at least in part in a quest to escape or mitigate socioeconomic subordination.[43] Meanwhile the Xhosa Tiyo Soga, becoming in 1856 the first African to be ordained in the territory, returned from Scotland to evangelise in the eastern Cape. Like Johnson and Crowther in West Africa, Soga and those who followed him formed a vital link between endogeneity and exogeneity, translating scripture into the Xhosa language and exhorting audiences to meld Christian faith with their own culture.[44] Other comparably positioned groups in South Africa would do likewise. Communities of *amakholwa*—isiZulu for 'believers'—acted as vital mediators between the internal and the external, and demonstrated the dexterity and vitality with which African Christians could reinterpret and adapt an Abrahamic faith in a rapidly shifting political, economic and cultural landscape to meet their own needs, and in ways that drew upon their own long-standing histories of reform and reimagination.[45] Ganda converts accepted painful death in the mid-1880s, as their Muslim compatriots had a decade earlier, in the face of royal persecution, and in so doing they were mobilising the well-established concept of *ekitiibwa*, honour and the dignity of personhood, and challenging overweening executive power—a recurrent problem with which the Ganda had long wrestled—as much as they were self-consciously following the example of Christ.[46] Conversion to Christianity on the part of particular communities, or elements within communities, was often the result of political breakdown and the perceived failure of older cosmologies; part of a longer-term embrace of new ideas or the reformation of old ones in an age of flux and uncertainty. And it could in broad terms have an emollient effect when it came to heightened levels of overtly *political* European intrusion. The presence of Anglicans in Buganda, or in Abeo-kuta, or the activism of a range of converts among the Fante, introduced a humectant dynamic to what would otherwise have been an altogether more jarring, ragged interaction between the local and the global.

However, such emollience would not endure. Christianity was quickly adapted to specifically local needs and concerns, while simultaneously being conceived in universal, liberationist terms, as we see a little later. It is also important to note that many of the figures involved would later be positioned as African patriots and proto-nationalists, and as forming the vanguard of Pan-Africanism, and at the time were seen to be vigorous champions of African political and cultural identity in the face of creeping European hegemony.[47] Crowther has been seen in these terms in the Nigerian context, for example.[48] James Africanus Horton was also a product of Sierra Leone, born there to Igbo parents who had been liberated and resettled, and was also an alumnus of Fourah Bay. But although initially headed for the clergy, he was selected for medical training instead, becoming one of the first African doctors trained in Britain and serving the British colonial army in the Gold Coast. He then became politically active, notably among the Fante, and was a prolific and prominent campaigner for constitutional government in the face of British recalcitrance. Horton had worked for and with the British; but he was, in the end, no kind of emollient—as his own writings make clear.[49] Again, it is critical to understand that these communities of intermediacy might work in the short to medium term to facilitate or host external influence, even outright political control: these were often paradoxical states in which communities, such as the Fante, might, in psychotherapeutic speak, hold apparently contradictory views at the same time (such as demanding British protection from the Asante, while also demanding greater political responsibility and autonomy *from* the British). But they were also manifestations of Africa's own revolutionary dynamics, and as such were not intrinsically well disposed to outside intrusion, but merely operated in pragmatic and opportunistic ways with it: in fact, in the longer term, they would frequently become implacably opposed to such impositions.

The Swahili and, often, Arabic-speaking commercial pioneers of east-ern and south-east Africa represent the community of intermediacy par excellence. The *wangwana* understood very well the risks and the oppor-tunities involved in navigating the interstitial landscape which they themselves had been at least partly responsible for creating. They helped forge the spindly but remarkably durable infrastructure which straddled the vast region between lakes Victoria and Malawi. Across a vast region, they influenced dress, speech, practices of healing and architecture; they married locally and—though not many were active proselytisers—inspired conversion to Islam.[50] Theirs was a rolling frontier of remarkable cultural and material transformation. It was in their wake that Europeans would follow, and their infrastructure which European colonial systems would seek to exploit. More broadly, Christianity and Islam generated new forms of social belonging and identification which were cultural and spiritual; but it is also no coincidence that these same communities were often commercial pioneers, people who were among the most vigorous par-ticipants in global trade and in the production, for example, of the cash crops discussed in chapter 4. Identification with global faith often also meant enthusiasm for global business, and so across the continent we see the emergence of effervescently liminal, intermediate communities em-bracing the things and behaviours of supposed modernity, and forming the adhesive which held these new empires together. Their presence, their energy, not only *shaped* empire, but made it *conceivable*; and they were not simply the creation of a distinctive late nineteenth-century global moment, but emblematic, and the latest iteration, of processes and dy-namics running through the long nineteenth century.

Into this extraordinarily eclectic mix came Europeans themselves, as liminal and multifarious as anyone else, in different capacities seeking to insert themselves into the spaces which might best generate some lever-age. No generalisation of these people is watertight: a heterogeneous group, they included those from almost every kind of social background and with an equally diverse range of hopes and ambitions, private and public. But they were all the consequence of Europe's own turbulent era, an outflux caused by rapid socioeconomic change and the pressures and stresses which resulted; by political persecution and marginalisation. In more than a few cases, they went because they could, and because the world seemed to open before them in the second half of the nineteenth century, offering more than they could possibly achieve or acquire at home. Squalid confinement might be replaced with exotic opportunity. Those who headed to Africa constituted a comparatively modest slice of the nineteenth-century migratory flows which amounted to a truly global phenomenon in this era.[51] But their impact was significant, because their peculiar brand of interstitial imperialism intersected with burgeoning communities of intermediacy, which settlers themselves would seek in time to manipulate. They, in time, added a new element, largely unknown before that point: namely, the use of their own revolution in print and knowledge production to frame the continent's 'condition' in brutally ra-cialised terms. Initially, however, they formed settler communities— vulnerable, at times hubristic, frequently prejudiced—creating compact zones of creole entrepreneurialism of their own, and, later, natural if not unproblematic points of entry and leverage for larger imperial projects. Such corridors of intrusion and reinvention dated back to the seventeenth and eighteenth centuries. The Portuguese in the Zambezi valley morphed into one of the most striking instances of creative liminality out of which grew a novel interethnic community: originating in the creation of grants of land (*prazos*) for Portuguese settlers, the latter evolved through local intermarriage into a vibrant, and violent, Luso-African community, at the apex of which were landowning warlords, the *prazeiros*, in control of slave armies (the Chikunda). The *prazeiros* increasingly asserted their independence from the metropole as they thrived on the regional slave and ivory trades.[52]

The Dutch at the Cape, and subsequently on the highveld, represent another such avenue of external intrusion, and proved remarkably robust as a community, with far-reaching consequences, becoming a crucial point of leverage both troublesome and fortuitous for later builders of empire and racially defined statehood in the region. The South African story is so well known as to require little more than a summary here. What began as a modest provisioning station for the Dutch East India Company at Table Bay in the middle of the seventeenth century became a territory characterised by aggressive colonial expansionism, as Dutch settlers

(*boeren*, or farmers) armed with guns and a brew of theological and racial conviction claimed ever more land from the autochthonous Khoisan.[53]
As they did so, they created frontiers of volatility and liminality within
which new communities emerged, including the mixed-race communities within Cape society which were the inevitable outcome of settler colonialism, and the Khoisan, compelled into a life of hunting, raiding and
trading at the northern edges of the territory.[54] A racial hierarchy had hardened by the early nineteenth century, reflected in the organisation of
labour, at the bottom stratum of which were African slaves, and the in-
dentured workers imported from Indonesia. They were situated below the
skilled and semi-skilled labour undertaken by mixed-race people known
as 'Cape Coloureds'. Meanwhile the exponential expansion of the trek-
boers into new areas of pasture was undergirded by a strengthening sense
of innate racial superiority and a God-given right to the land, resources
and labour of the benighted heathen.[55] To the east were the Xhosa, a society which represented more of an obstacle to colonial expansion, and
with whom relations were for much of the eighteenth century characterised as much by commerce and sexual congress as by conflict. But violence intensified when Boers began to encroach on the Zuurveld, an area
of crucial Xhosa pasture, in the late eighteenth century.[56] Cape colonial
society, therefore, had been a century and a half in the making by the
time the British showed up in the early nineteenth century, seizing
control of the Cape during Europe's Napoleonic wars, and complicating
the political positionality of a community which had long defined itself
against the 'Africa' of the interior. Trekboer independent-mindedness and
hostility toward colonial authority had already been expressed in brief
rebellions, in 1795 (against the Dutch East India Company itself) and 1799
(against the British). In the second half of the 1830s, following years of
liberalising reforms by the British administration culminating in the abolition of slavery, a multitude of Boer communities, usually extended family
groups, loaded up their wagons and crossed the Cape frontier 'into Africa'. Many of these 'Voortrekkers' operated at the level of subsistence, and
could not afford to pay for and protect labour formerly regarded as chattel, as required by the British authorities.[57] Moreover they resented the
refusal of the British to deploy armed force in expanding the Cape frontier

eastward. They now began to move gingerly across the veld to the north-east, edging their way along the corridors between African polities in search of space and sovereignty. This was the so-called 'Great Trek', as it was later styled in Afrikaner mythology.[58] As they did so, they both took advantage of and exacerbated the flux and mobility that had long characterised the region, and in particular the tensions between local polities, which at times in turn saw advantage in alliance with the well-armed newcomers. The Rolong assisted a contingent of Voortrekkers in fighting, and inflicting a major defeat on, the Ndebele in 1837, with the latter shifting north of the Limpopo as a consequence.[59] The Boers clashed, famously, with Dingane's Zulu in 1838—the 'battle of Blood River' saw a decisive defeat for the latter[60]—although for several decades thereafter they sought some form of cohabitation. They fashioned crude 'republics' in the uneasy zones between African political authority, including Natal on the fringes of the Zulu, and Orange Free State and Transvaal to the west and north respectively. As we have noted, the British briefly toyed with the idea of claiming these territories, and then abandoned it. But mounting conflict between the Orange Free State Boers and the Sotho kingdom led Moshoeshoe, in a diplomatic masterstroke, to request British protection, granted in 1868. It was not, for the Sotho, a surrender of sovereignty, but rather an explicit recognition of the perilous volatility of a region riven with fault lines.[61] In the process of establishing their 'republics' in the interior, the Boers became 'African' themselves, in the way of creole communities, as the ethnonym they later awarded themselves, 'Afrikaner', indicates. But they inhabited a striking cultural and political liminality; and in time, such settler populations often formed the very raw material of interstitial imperialism, even if inadvertently. By a curious enmeshing of episodic conflict and shared interest, 'white' South Africa was by the early years of the twentieth century created,[62] the outcome of an uneasy alliance of Anglo-metropolitan and Afrikaner culture—each representing a minority, but each turning their marginality, their numerical inferiority, into a reason for dominance; while in the process consigning the African majority to a brutal set of cultural, political and economic peripheries. But even on those peripheries, Africans continued to shape what South Africa *was*, in the most fundamental of ways.

For not entirely dissimilar reasons to the Sotho, the townspeople of coastal Algeria had seen at least some advantage in French control being imposed upon them in the 1830s, because they too were caught increasingly in a fault line created by weakened Ottoman authority and the opportunist predators of the hinterland mountains. But their positionality was quickly complicated by the expansion of the settler population in Algeria, just as settler colonialism was expanding in South Africa. Within twenty years of the French seizure of Algiers, there were some hundred thousand settlers, mostly congregated along the coastal strip with its considerable agricultural potential. By the 1890s, this had grown to around half a million—Spanish and Italian, as well as French—though the vast majority, as in southern Africa, were little more than subsistence farmers whose livelihoods were modest and at times perilous. Most French in Algeria later came to be known colloquially as *pied noirs*, 'black feet',[63] to distinguish them from the wealthier landowners, who were *colons*, or colonists—although Algeria would come to be regarded, not as a 'colony' or a 'protectorate', but as legally and constitutionally a part of France. In various ways that status would come to define the metropole as much as it did the 'periphery'.[64]

Later still, there were colonists in parts of east and central Africa, forming the basis of the overtly settler colonies of Southern Rhodesia and Kenya.[65] Africa was attractive for the marginalised, the adventurous, the avaricious, the desperate, the ambitious. In Kenya, from the early 1900s, settlers began to creep into the highlands through the lands of the Maasai, Luo and Kikuyu, gradually forming an eccentric, motley community. Most of them lived a fairly precarious existence, through hunting or smallholder farming, although in time they would be joined by a wealthier cohort of businessmen and aristocrats who staked out larger plantations, alienating land from African populations in the process.[66] Visions of riches would remain chimerical for most, as they would for those dreaming of gold who followed Cecil Rhodes and the agents of the British South Africa Company into the territory which became known as Southern Rhodesia (present-day Zimbabwe). They did mine some gold on a small scale, but most of it had already been successfully extracted by Africans themselves over the previous five centuries or more, and they made instead a modest living through farming and livestock.[67] As in Kenya, the most significant long-term impact on Africans themselves was in the expropriation of land, both violent and legalistic, and political marginalisation. Diverse though they were, and their origins discrete, the curious liminality of these white communities was markedly similar in form to many of the communities and landscapes within which they moved. Their intrusions were frequently forceful, and involved extreme violence. They formed some of the critical arteries of large-scale imperial expansion. But their lives were also invariably contingent on local circumstances, and were shaped by the environments into which they intruded. Equally inevitably, they depended on African insurgents, innovators and intermediaries, and those came in myriad forms, as they always had.

## The Leverage of Violence

AMONG THE MOST VISIBLE MANIFESTATIONS of African liminality and entrepreneurialism were the soldiers who comprised the bulk of European colonial armies, and without whom the myriad European interventions between the 1880s and 1900s would have been inconceivable. In some respects, the military phenomenon has its roots in the older practice of mercenary service, a long-standing one along the West African littoral, for example, where modestly sized but strategically pivotal commercial entities struggled to raise their own forces and so instead made extensive use of foreign mercenaries in war and in exercising influence across a wider area than would otherwise have been possible. Akwamu on the Gold Coast, for example, was noted for supplying mercenaries eastward to Ouidah and Allada by the early eighteenth century.[68] Many Yoruba military professionals were mercenaries during the nineteenth century, attaching themselves to war leaders who offered the best pay and largesse.[69] In an early iteration of 'martial race' thinking, to which we turn in more detail below, particular communities were often identified by their neighbours as being more 'warlike', rougher in their 'manners', and comparatively easily hired, as was the case around the northern end of Lake Tanganyika. Even Mirambo—regarded by most as being 'warlike'—appears to have made some use of Maasai soldiers who were almost certainly hired for the purpose of fighting the Ngoni. In the same neighbourhood, some of the less well-off coastal adventurers and traders made themselves guns for hire in local conflicts (which they may or may not have started in the first place) in exchange for slaves and ivory.[70] Early European traders in the Atlantic zone benefited from the practice, and in many ways the hiring of motley militias to protect commercial outposts along the West African coast represent the roots of later colonial armies. British merchants, for example, employed such militias along the Gold Coast, in Sierra Leone and Gambia, and in the Niger Delta, where the 'unit' was known as the Oil Rivers Irregulars (or the 'Forty Thieves').[71] They were a ragtag bunch of castaways, migrants and doubtless the occasional chancer, but in the later nineteenth century Europeans would seek to regulate and formalise these forces, modelling them according to a Western regimental 'tradition'.

In only a handful of cases were substantial bodies of European soldiers deployed on African soil: for example, the British in Sudan and, soon after, South Africa. More commonly, dozens of military engagements were carried out by armed units involving modest contingents of European officers, or armed representatives of chartered companies, at the head of rather larger numbers of local recruits, or recruits brought in from elsewhere in Africa (or, in a few instances, South Asia).[72] They were equipped with comparatively modern firearms, or at least more advanced military hardware than was available to most Africans, and, arguably more importantly, they were part of a system characterised by its sophisticated logistics. Decades of political and socioeconomic political flux and social insecurity had created a stratum of entrepreneurs of violence across the continent, professional men-at-arms able and willing to serve in particular causes in pursuit of political hegemony, socioeconomic status, adventure or simple pecuniary reward. They were often drawn from drifting, liminal populations, the refugees and migrants and displaced inhabiting the spaces created by political upheaval and economic transformation. Mercenaries, refugees, economic migrants and former slaves swelled the ranks of these new forces. These were the personnel, the product of a creative liminality, who formed the basis of most colonial armies and, ultimately, of colonial rule itself.

But Europeans sought to introduce some racial rigour into the process, and increasingly aimed at military recruitment from among peoples known for their 'martial' attributes. In essence, 'martial race' theory suggested that particular environments and contexts produced cultures, mentalities and bodies particularly suitable for military service—hardiness and manliness, stamina, a strong sense of loyalty and duty—whereas others did not. The idea took shape in mid-century British India, when it seemed that certain units had been more reliable and loyal during the Indian Rebellion than others.[73] In broad terms, lowlands and coastal areas were deemed to be unsuitable, producing 'races' and communities which were physically less healthy and likely to be morally weakened by their exposure to, indeed their immersion in, the vices of commerce and (semi-) civilisation. Instead, European officers looked to mountains and savannahs, which produced physically hardy and morally pure societies, and therefore produced men who could be relied upon to serve. But the idea of an intrinsically martial nature wasn't an exclusively European one. The local practice, already noted, of using mercenaries suggests as much. In Ethiopia, the Amhara deployed Oromo from the highlands—long seen as being especially formidable and skilled at warcraft—in their own imperial expansion into the southern lowlands in the 1890s, as part of a deliberate tactic of shock and awe.[74]

The relationship between the cumulative lived experience of particular ethnic and/or linguistic communities and the identities and characteristics attached to them by later colonial officials and ethnographers is often a nuanced, complex one.[75] Particular groups with long histories of involvement in violence in the course of the nineteenth century clearly did indeed exist: the Bambara, for example, who inhabited the Segu area around the banks of the upper Niger. The Bambara had had a turbulent time of it in the eighteenth and nineteenth centuries, forming the core of the Segu state closely tied to the slave trade, experiencing 'internal' political rifts and conflicts and buffeted by the rise of adjacent polities, notably forming part of Umar Tal's insurgent state in the mid-nineteenth century.[76] In the course of these events, the Bambara became practised soldiers, serving in a sequence of armies over several generations which were adept at the seizure of people and territory, while also themselves becoming the

victims of uncertain, turbulent times. Thus French officers in the late nineteenth century, having encountered the Bambara during their early encounters with the declining Tukolor state in the late 1870s and early 1880s,[77]
sought to recruit Bambara soldiers, identifying them as coming from a
'martial race'.[78] The Bambara, having long navigated insecurity, and with a
'tradition' of armed service, were able and willing: employment in French-
led armies was an extension of the violent entrepreneurialism which had
characterised much of their modern history. It was a dynamic which developed its own momentum. The Bambara were critical to the extension of
French control across the vast western Sahel region in the 1880s and 1890s.[79]
It was a situation which was replicated across the continent. The French,
again, recruited heavily among those who were both ravaged by war and
skilled practitioners of war themselves in seeking to impose control over
the equatorial region of present-day Gabon, Congo and Central African
Republic (known by its colonial moniker Ubangi-Shari). The most prominent French corps were the Tirailleurs sénégalais, founded in 1857 by Faidherbe and which had initially, as the name suggests, been recruited from
among Senegalese communities, including Wolof, who again had a long
history of armed servitude (as slave soldiers) and whose identity as slaves
was intimately intertwined with their specialism in violence, rooted in the
political and economic transformations across the western savannah in the
seventeenth and eighteenth centuries.[80] Later, recruits from across all
French African territories served in the Tirailleurs sénégalais, including
Bambara, and this multi-ethnic force—although it was the Bambara language that became the tongue of French colonial forces in Africa—was
again vital in the intermittent Franco–Tukolor wars across the upper
Niger.[81] The bulk of the French force that invaded Dahomey in 1892 were
also Tirailleurs sénégalais.[82]

Elsewhere, men were likewise propelled into colonial service as a result of commercial and political upheaval across their respective regions
over many decades, and colonial regiments were therefore in fact the direct outcome of Africa's own revolutions. Predictably, this was all framed
as an aspect of the civilising mission by later colonial architects and theo-
rists: Africa was a violently backward place, and therefore not only did
Europe have the right, nay, the responsibility, to intervene, but placing

some Africans in uniform would calm their savage inclinations (though not *too* much, which would somewhat defeat the purpose) and teach them discipline, structure, obedience.[83] Above all, of course, it was expedient and pragmatic: witness the French approach to their army in Algeria. The Armée d'Afrique was composed of several layers, of which the uppermost was the European infantry contingent, the *zouaves* (although even their uniforms, including their embellished tunics, drew on Berber style). Then there were the *spahis*, the Arab cavalry, and the *turcos*, the Turkish-Algerian infantry, each of them representing the French command's desire to harness the 'natural' fighting skills and certainly local knowledge of Algeria's various population groups.[84] It was a model which would be replicated widely in the decades ahead. In creating their West African units—for example the Royal West African Frontier Force—the British preferred the Hausa, whose tongue also became a military lingua franca, of the southern Sahel belt for their campaigns across what would become Nigeria. The Hausa, again, were identified as possessing distinctively martial characteristics. And, again, this was derived from Hausa lived experience, as an ethno-linguistic community which had experienced decades of violence, both religious (with several jihadist movements, including that leading to the creation of Sokoto, sweeping the region) and commercial (their long-standing involvement in the slave trade). The creation of Sokoto had led to the outmigration of many Hausa, especially toward the south, and in the later nineteenth century these communities were able and willing recruits into colonial forces. As a collective, Hausa agency, ambition and entrepreneurialism was critical in extending a particular form of 'British' imperialism across the Nigerian Middle Belt in what has been identified as a classic case of 'sub-imperialism'. Whether or not we accept the normative implications of that term, what is clear is that the Hausa used the entry of the British into the political landscape to assert dominance over the supposedly inferior, less developed populations of the Middle Belt.[85] In East Africa, the British had initially seconded contingents of their Indian army, with British officers commanding Punjabi and Sikh troops. But they came to rely heavily, again, on Ganda soldiers and specialist war leaders in seeking to realise territorial administration in the northern lacustrine region, and especially in their war against Bunyoro.[86] Longer-term, the Ganda were deemed too canny in political and commercial terms to be relied upon for military service, and so recruiters later turned increasingly to the people of the northern peripheries, for example Acholi, Langi or the communities of West Nile district in Uganda, or Kalenjin and Kamba in Kenya, for the requirements of what would became the King's African Rifles. Men from southern Sudan were preferred for the Sudan Defence Force, while efforts were made to tap into the military skills and knowledge of terrain in certain areas, hence the creation of the Somaliland Camel Corps.[87] German officers of the Schutztruppe relied on those they were able to recruit across the region in waging war against the Hehe and others in East Africa, the communities able and willing to fight after decades of upheaval and displacement in the areas to the south of Isike's road. And as we have noted, they depended heavily on local recruits in their campaigns along the road itself, culminating in Isike's own demise. Moving into the Eritrean highlands, the Italians were able to tap into the socioeconomic flux and anguish which was the corollary of the northern frontier zone, where communities had long been squeezed between the incursions and ambitions of Ethiopian empire-builders and various invaders from the direction of the coast. A process of reciprocal co-option led to the creation of a colonial army of *ascari*, who were deployed in the invasion of Ethiopia in 1896 and later in the Libyan campaigns, and whose armed service would form one of the foundations of a nascent national identity in Eritrea.[88] Perhaps the best, if also the most distressing, example of prolonged trauma producing ideal colonial warriors is in the Belgian Congo, where the ranks of the Force publique in the 1890s and 1900s were filled with the displaced and the rootless, able and willing to commit atrocities at the behest of European merchants interested only in extraction of resources, notably (and famously) rubber. A group known as 'Bangala', a composite of more than one ethno-linguistic community from across the central Congo basin, and later the Tetela, were favoured by recruiting officers.[89] Many of these, as elsewhere, were ex-slaves, the outcome of a half-century of socioeconomic transformation. The situation in the Congo demonstrates the extent to which Europe's supposed civilising mission— the result of its own restless instability—was enacted amidst the residue of a century of violence. And so too in Sudan, where the British relied heavily on those Sudanese troops from communities long displaced by religious and political upheaval, and able and willing to make their contribution to the 'British' triumph at Omdurman.[90] Moreover, collective identities rooted in the experience of military slavery across north-east Africa persisted into the twentieth century.[91]

With relatively modest numbers,[92] Europeans could achieve considerable leverage, inserting themselves in the fissures and applying pressure to the pivots as they moved through and between African states and societies. Yet in each of the cases outlined above, we can invert the statement: the Ganda, Hausa, Bambara, Acholi and others harnessed the British, the Germans, the French, in pursuit of at least short-term security, or seeking to advance either personal ambitions or collective strategies. Over time, some actively embraced the martial reputation which colonial service had attached to them, while the shared experience of service itself was often instrumental in forging new or consolidating extant identities. Across the continent, desperate people, people skilled in warcraft, with entrepreneurial (rather than strictly 'martial') proclivities, and often inhabiting insecure, liminal spaces within and between polities, espied opportunities in strange European projects, and were prepared to harness the latter for their own material and social gain, for all the risk and (frequently) humiliation involved. Critically, without this level of African input, and notwithstanding the relatively small numbers involved, there would have been no European 'Scramble for Africa', and certainly no European empire on the continent. In many respects, indeed, African colonial soldiers represented an extension of decades-long processes of insurgency, political reformation, socioeconomic transformation and demarcation of new spheres of influence. Unquestionably, an array of European actors—soldiers, government officials, commercial agents— had harnessed and repurposed those processes to their own ends: the suppression of insurgency, the patrolling of newly acquired borderlands and, rather more prosaically but also more importantly, the collection of tax. But they relied absolutely on African manpower, military skill, knowledge of terrain and tolerance of climate. And it was not merely a case of such manpower facilitating European imperial projects: Africans frequently actively shaped these, contributing to their tone and form, and often to their physical shape, helping to lay the foundations for the political and economic orders which were to follow. Still, it was a volatile arrangement, as forceful white recruiters or salaried chiefs tasked with expanding enlistment discovered in various places, including French West Africa and Nyasaland, during the First World War. Then, their aggressive overreach provoked the same response that other, more local, actors had encountered during the long nineteenth century: rebellion.

## Intrusions, Co-options and Insurgent Communities

LOCAL AGENCY AND WHAT IS OFTEN referred to as 'sub-imperialism' came in other forms, too, when particular political communities, often but not exclusively at the level of the state, undertook their own wars of conquest or expansion, harnessing and even working alongside European imperial projects as they did so. In some scenarios it is also important to acknowledge African input into the demarcation of territories on the ground. If we accept that around thirty per cent of Africa's colonial boundaries comprised the infamous straight lines which appear to have been drawn up irrespective of local exigencies, that leaves around seventy per cent of borders whose construction were almost certainly influenced, to a greater or lesser extent, by local actors, and certainly by local circumstances. European agents were continually compelled to take account of African dynamics at the micro level in drafting the boundaries for which they were responsible.[93] These were among the starkest instances of reciprocal co-option, so often a dynamic on which European empire in Africa was constructed; for Africans absorbed Europeans into their own political and economic and military contestations, and European 'men on the spot', whether representing governments or chartered companies, likewise harnessed Africa's volatile, entrepreneurial political culture and resultant liminality in pursuit of their own projects. How much one recognised what the other was up to doubtless varied from situation to situation. Perhaps on occasion the ignorance was wilful. But it is somehow fitting that modern European imperialism is the product, in large part, of various degrees of misunderstanding and miscommunication.

In some cases, the oft-used term 'sub-imperialism' does not do justice to what were in fact overt processes of *African* territorial or 'imperial' expansion, in which local actors either took advantage of partnerships with Europeans, or exploited local zones of instability to extend more formal control in a colonial or administrative sense. In the last decades of the century, no doubt the most dramatic instance of this was Ethiopia under Menelik. He had in fact already begun the process in the 1880s when *negus* (king) of Shewa, when Amhara armies pushed into the fertile farmlands to the south and west of the highland plateau, and into the Somali pasturelands to the south-east. In the 1890s, after Menelik had become emperor, the pace of expansion quickened, and highland settler-soldiers, predominantly Amhara, fanned out across a vast arc to the south, violently expropriating land and creating an empire in the empty spaces on the maps of Europeans still struggling with the concept of colonial rule in north-east Africa. Menelik's success was in part based on his accumulation, again, of a vast arsenal of weaponry over many years—the same cache which would serve him well at the battle of Adwa—but above all it was the culmination of the political and military transformation of Ethiopian statecraft over an even longer period. There was also a fair amount of political dexterity involved: for example, the strategic distribution of territorial governorships to a range of allies and also to those who needed to be watched; and in the wake of Adwa, Menelik was adroit at presenting Ethiopia to the world as the exception, not the rule. Within a few years, Addis Ababa, the new capital, was adorned with foreign embassies, a bank and a postal service, modern communications and a busy expatriate community keen to do business.[94] *Habesha* insurgency a few decades earlier had elicited sighs of despair from outside observers. Ethiopia the Solomonic empire was 'welcome' in the family of nations in the age of imperialism: not as an equal, for it remained only *semi-civilised*, but as a worthy enough associate.[95] In other contexts, the situation was a little more complex. British-led forces attacked and ultimately subdued the Sokoto Caliphate between 1900 and 1903. But after that point, much local authority was handed back to Muslim leaders in a paradigmatic enactment of 'indirect rule'.[96] It was a mutually beneficial arrangement: the British administration sought the stability of presumed legiti-

macy by restoring some degree of fiscal and judicial power—'native'
treasuries charged with the collection of revenue and local courts
with the dispensing of justice—to 'rightful' Muslim leaders, but at the
same time the latter, including a Fulani clerical and political elite, sought
to shore up their position through constitutional and legal machinery.[97]
They were still, after all, relative newcomers to political power themselves, and saw advantage in a working relationship with the British administration, especially, as we have noted, in the context of the Mahdist
challenge. A Mahdist revolt was suppressed in 1906, with the help of
the British. For much of their history, indeed, the Fulani had existed in
the interstices, migrating with their cattle on the edges of watchful sedentary states, and conversion to Islam had often been a markedly pragmatic decision: Islam offered a model of resistance and, in time, of government, with which they might navigate the liminal spaces into which
they had often been thrust. Adaptation to the new regime was, in that
context, no great leap. As Muslims, moreover, they could choose to 'submit' to the infidel ruler in body but not in mind. A similar scenario unfolded in Algeria, where, in spite of a substantial settler population, the
French authorities largely governed through extant coastal elites, much
as the Ottomans had done before them; and in Tunisia, through an educated professional class which was perceived as being, if not exactly
Francophile, then at least of a suitably modernising bent and even to
some extent *assimilé*.[98] This was not a question of 'who was co-opting
who', but rather of to what extent each was co-opting the other and who
gained most from the arrangement. In their different ways, European
colonial officials across the continent sought to co-opt Muslim elites in
order to legitimise and stabilise potentially insecure administrations. It
was sometimes a fragile arrangement: in Egypt, while the British largely
'governed' through the elite around Khedive Tawfiq in the 1880s, they
found that his son Abbas Hilmi in the 1890s and 1900s was less compli-
ant, and rather more sympathetic to the growing nationalist cause, which
necessitated the threat of armed force.[99] But there is no doubt that,
broadly speaking, 'indirect rule' was the outcome not only of resource-
bare European imperial systems whose agents sought a legitimating
creed with a bombast that scarcely concealed profound anxiety, but also

of Africa's longer-term internal transformation, creating energetic political (and religious) orders and cultures with which later intruders had no option but to work alongside.

One of the keys to successful foreign intrusion was the ability to mobilise armed support for interference in neighbours' internal affairs. Again, there was nothing inherently novel about this in African military and political culture, especially during the turbulent nineteenth century. Local intrusions and interventions in neighbours' internal conflicts and succession disputes were *de rigueur*, for obvious reasons: this was low-hanging fruit, in the pursuit of regional influence, though as a tactic it did come with some risk, especially if you happened to back the losing side; or if you backed the winning side but the victor quickly cooled on the relationship; or if your own military investment in a nearby civil war was substantial but your own forces took quite a beating in the course of it. There were long-term reputational as well as strategic hazards to be considered. But in the Great Lakes region of East Africa, notably, the risks were widely accepted and the practice was common. Rarely was 'internal' violence *purely* internal; civil wars were rarely hermetically sealed. The expanding scale of economic, military and political vision meant that the rewards for success could be great, and not usually to be eschewed in favour of a more conservative, safer approach. So Kabaka Suna's Buganda intervened in Karagwe's civil war in the mid-1850s, in large part because Karagwe itself now lay on a burgeoning trade route to the west of Lake Victoria connecting the region to the entrepôt of Unyanyembe and ultimately to the Indian Ocean world.[100] Suna's son Mutesa embarked on the same policy in Bunyoro's succession war in the late 1860s, supporting the eventual winner, Kabalega, who nonetheless would choose not to show his gratitude but would rather turn against his former backer with some vigour in the course of the 1870s.[101] Kabalega himself took advantage of Buganda's own civil war in 1889–90, and gave refuge to the ousted Muslim faction following Mwanga's restoration.[102] For that reason, indeed, the Ganda co-opted the British into their long-running struggle with the Nyoro—in which they had latterly been losing ground—in the course of the 1890s. A Ganda chiefly elite was also able to force through a form of constitutional monarchy via their partnership with the British, ultimately creating a careful balance of legislative and territorial power around the *kabaka* after 1900.[103] The British themselves, initially represented by Frederick Lugard and the Imperial British East Africa Company, had no compunction about doing some co-opting of their own at the same time, while a combination of military insecurity and a racialised view of the region led to them committing some of the worst atrocities of the era against the Nyoro. But at root this was a war that had nothing to do with them. While the little British expedition may have felt they were labouring heroically to impose order across what would eventually become the Uganda Protectorate, the reality was that they were being pulled into a network of local conflicts and harnessed by a range of groups in search of advantage in what had long been a tumultuous region. The Ganda genius—although a source of destabilisation within the future nation— was to engineer for themselves a privileged position within the 'colonial' order.[104] A Ganda elite identified itself as intrinsically superior and born to lead, and the British agreed, keen to work with hierarchical, preferably monarchical, systems undergirded by cultures which lauded privilege based on blood and which placed emphasis on deference. They looked, in other words, for systems much like their own. A similar dynamic was at work with respect to Tutsi elites in Rwanda and Burundi, which were identified by the Germans and then the Belgians as a racially superior caste in what was a massively simplified conceptualisation of sociopolitical structures and identities; but Tutsi elites were themselves heavily invested in the idea, depicting their hegemony over the Hutu as natural and perennial.[105]

Elsewhere, the dynamics of co-option were messier, or at least less linear. French policy in West Africa reflected a much greater degree of scepticism about the utility of extant inherited authority at the local level, and such elites—themselves the reflection, as we have noted, of internal fissures and power struggles—were somewhat marginalised by the appointment of *chefs de canton*, frequently members of a more autonomous, technocratic class of educated Africans who were seen as more reliable, efficient and pliant by the metropole. 'Indirect rule' in the Francophone territories thus took a rather different form, and offered opportunities to a different range of actors and agents at the local level.[106] Where there were no identifiably, usably 'organic' power structures, a combination of European leverage and African opportunism led to the creation of new forms of authority: in Sudan, in Tanganyika and in south-east Nigeria, where the legitimacy of such chieftainships would come to be challenged by Africans themselves.[107] Much has been made, correctly, of the clumsy, blundering nature of the colonial state in these scenarios; but equally this needs to be understood in terms of longer-term African entrepreneurialism and experimentation, reformism and recalcitrance. Lisbon may have imagined unambiguous blocs of Portuguese authority in Angola and Mozambique, but the reality was altogether more convoluted. In both territories, African wars and long-standing commercial and political competition were the main drivers of 'colonial' expansion, as the Portuguese found themselves drawn into the ongoing conflicts of the Yao and Ngoni, in Mozambique, and Ovimbundu and Chokwe and others across the forests and grasslands of Angola. On one level, Portuguese commercial agents and army officers were able to harness that violence in pursuit of their own ends, and certainly contributed to the violence in their own way; but on the other, it is a scenario which points to the largely illusory nature of 'colonial conquest', and suggests that in fact deep-rooted African dynamics of fission and fusion and armed entrepreneurialism constituted the basis on which the territories of Angola and Mozambique were created.[108] The Portuguese territories, moreover, illustrate the potency of creole culture in this context, for in both Mozambique and Angola there had emerged Luso-African communities whose various endeavours were critical to the establishment of a 'Portuguese' empire in Africa. In Mozambique, the *prazeiros* had long since come to dominate the Zambezi valley and were rough-hewn, often violent pioneers of the colonial project. In Angola, the *mestizo* or mixed-race community, along with the *assimilado* population, meaning those Africans who had become 'colonial citizens', were both the lifeblood and the professional backbone of the territory, especially along the coast, at least initially.[109]

Instances abound of African elites engaged in political work with *wazungu* which in hindsight seems profoundly inimical to their long-term interests. But this is teleology in its crudest form and, as with one-dimensional conceptualisations of how the external slave trade operated, diminishes the very idea of African agency. When the Tio chief Iloo I (the Makoko) signed his treaty with de Brazza in 1880, he didn't envision a surrender of sovereignty, no more than Moshoeshoe had a few years earlier in requesting British protection. He saw advantage in alliance, indeed partnership, vis-à-vis circling rivals and those who might do him harm both within and beyond his domain. He may not have fully grasped the implications of what de Brazza had proposed—many of which were in any case unknown at the time of signing, even to de Brazza himself—and lacked his French interlocutor's macro-level comprehension. But 'the Great Makoko', as the Teke paramount chief was styled, was no *ingénu*. He had long operated in a volatile, risky political landscape, one in which savvy commercial operators had effectively replaced older forms of inherited position as the true rulers of their communities. He was also operating from a position of relative domestic weakness, his own power being constrained by several senior chiefs. It was against their advice, indeed, that he correctly concluded, albeit with limited knowledge of the wider geopolitical context—as was the case with many Africans—that there were indeed advantages to be had in what the French were ostensibly offering; as did Ngalifourou, the deeply respected and authoritative figure who became 'queen mother' after her husband's death.[110] Other acceptances of 'protection' need similarly to be understood not as concessions of sovereignty, but as a reimagining of it, and as inventive ways of navigating turbulence, reflecting the political fluidity and creativity of the long nineteenth century. Other instances, noted elsewhere, include the Sotho and the Tswana; and the Lozi kingdom on the Barotse floodplain on the Zambezi. Here, the paramount ruler Lewanika—the 'unifier'—represented the insurgency which had overthrown minority Sotho rule in the mid-1860s, leading to the creation of a highly stratified, monarchical entity. He requested British crown protection and eventually had to settle for British South Africa Company protection, doing so, analogously to the rulers of Sokoto in the early 1900s, because he believed it would help him consolidate both his own position and that of the Lozi state after decades of internal instability.[111] Attempts to reposition oneself and shape the fluid political landscape didn't always work out, of course. Lewanika quickly became disenchanted with the arrangement when he understood how it was interpreted by the Company, and then by the British colonial admin-istration, and sought, unsuccessfully, a renegotiation. Others would come to similar realisations, only to find their room for manoeuvre re-stricted in unfamiliar ways, requiring new forms of creativity in coming to terms with the political and economic landscape. In a variation on the theme, when Tippu Tip initially accepted the governorship of the eastern reaches of the Belgian Congo Free State, it was a rational choice based on several decades of flux and flow, demonstrated cognisance of the much-reduced influence of Zanzibar across the region, and seemed to hold out the prospect of continued status—a status which Tippu Tip had long fought, both literally and figuratively, to establish. But the increasing vio-lence of the Belgian-run Force publique toward any form of resistance, real or perceived, restrictions on his and other prominent coastal merchants' ability to trade, and their lack of control over the new occidental centre of political and commercial gravity, eased the ageing entrepreneur toward retirement. He returned to settle in Zanzibar to enjoy the fruits of his, and countless others', labour.[112]

Internal upheaval, up to and including civil war, was often the outcome of foreign invasion, or in some cases facilitated foreign intrusion, allow-ing for maximum leverage with minimum risk or commitment. In almost all cases, these internal conflicts were the outcome of decades of height-ened militarism and armed political factionalism within polities and communities which were in different ways and in different contexts the products of creative volatility. The civil war which devastated the Zulu state between 1879 and 1884 was sparked by the British defeat of the army at Ulundi in July 1879. To be sure, the fissures and rivalries within the state had been deepening over several decades, but the civil war itself allowed the British to impose a new order on an exhausted and depleted polity.[113] They did so, moreover, with a violent ferocity not always recognised in accounts which tended to highlight supposed British heroism.[114] Internal conflagration in Buganda between 1888 and 1890 was ostensibly caused by politico-religious factions organised around imported faiths—Protestantism, Catholicism and Islam—which had deepened divisions within the kingdom since the 1870s.[115] The embrace by a number of Ganda of new faiths was indeed remarkable in the course of the 1880s. But such violent contestations had precedents in Ganda history, and the factionalism was also the outcome of a deep-rooted culture of competition and reformism at the kingdom's centre. Nonetheless, the 'religious wars' of the period, and the aftershocks which continued through the 1890s, offered an opportunity to the British to position themselves with a view to exercising leverage over both Buganda and the adjacent area.[116] The French took advantage of long-standing schisms within the boisterously unstable Dahomean sociopolitical elite to prise that kingdom open. These deeper patterns of rivalry and contestation became all the more visible, and were doubtless exacerbated, in the aftermath of the French conquest of the kingdom between 1892 and 1894, in not dissimilar fashion to the dynastic wrangling among the Zulu a few years earlier. The division of the central area of the old kingdom into separate districts led to local leaders, all members of the royal family, having themselves installed according to ceremonies previously reserved for the king himself, and arguing amongst themselves over who was in fact the rightful heir to the (now largely defunct) throne.[117] Even triumphant Ethiopia, having seen off the Italians at Adwa, was not immune from the turbulent discord of the era. As Menelik's army tramped homeward from Tigray, where they had inflicted a defeat with global resonance on a European army, it was attacked on its flanks by Tigrayans and the Azebo Oromo who had a very different perspective—a deeply hostile one—on Menelik's empire.[118] It was both a reflection of the region's troubled history, and a portent of things to come, although the Solomonic elite were able to contain these fissures for the time being.

The ebb and flow of African politics, in other words—the revolution in warcraft, the economic transformation, the resultant social and intellectual upheaval—opened up space for leverage both within and between polities, and often the key to European success was the identification of local allies amongst rival groups for whom the arrival of European armed expeditions was little more than the latest opportunity to secure advantage. Amidst this turbulent swirl, there emerged new pools and places of displaced, marginalised and dispossessed people along physical and social frontiers; communities which embraced the tradition of insurgency, utilising violence in the attempt to reshape the political and economic landscape. Rebellions took place among exploited farmers and pastoralists, and they occurred among political and religious elites whose polities and faiths had been decimated by invasion; in all cases, they involved people who had been placed in an intolerable liminality. At one time, these uprisings were framed in terms of nascent nationalism, the rebels posited as harbingers of a new era of political modernity, often joining together across cultural and linguistic frontiers to confront the colonial order.[119] For our purposes, they invariably represented not something intrinsically novel, but the continuation of a pattern of violent endeavour and reinvention, often driven by economic desperation, and by social and political aspiration, running through Africa's long nineteenth century. There was, now, an added dimension: namely, the creation of exploitative and oppressive colonial orders which demanded land, tax, labour and political obeisance unacceptable to many on the receiving end of invasion and co-option.[120]

Insurgent resistance movements appeared in a number of forms. African Muslims, like their co-religionists across Asia, were confronted with the advance of infidel power (both western European and Russian) throughout the nineteenth century. This was most tangibly manifest in the retreat of Ottoman power in the Mediterranean and in North Africa, beginning with the French intrusion into Algeria in the 1830s, and hastening in the period between the 1870s and the 1910s in Egypt, Libya and Tunisia. The looming threat infused the long-standing reformist Islamic tradition with new energy, up to and including violent insurrection; and sparked theological and intellectual debates about whether, and to what extent, selected putatively 'Western' ideas and concepts (territorial nationhood, secularism in public life, constitutional pluralism, the socioeconomics of mechanisation and industrialisation) might be adapted and repurposed in order to ward off the threat. For at least some across the Islamic world, it was a situation which imposed a sense of stressful transition—could one be 'modern' and Muslim at the same time, and if so in what ways?—and asked difficult questions about the ownership of 'modernity' and the identity of its agents, for the latter could be both European Christians and African Muslims.[121] In broad terms, in theory, Muslims, irrespective of locale, polity or *ethnie*, might unite under the banner of the faith to combat infidel invasion. In practice, differing visions of how to be Muslim in these altered circumstances, and the often bitter rivalry between particular sects and brotherhoods, meant that the unity proffered by membership of the *umma* was abstract at best, but mostly inconceivable.

Among the earliest instances of armed rejuvenation was in Algeria in the 1830s and 1840s, where Abd al-Qadir used the vision of reinvigorated Islam to co-opt a disparate collection of tribal horsemen into an anti-French, anti-infidel cause. The Qadiriyya persisted in the cause even after the capture and exile of their leader.[122] In Libya, in the wake of disorder in Tripoli following the death of its long-serving *pasha* Yusuf Karamanli in 1830, the Sanusiyya, founded by Sidi Muhammad ibn Ali al-Sanusi, were organised similarly around a need to renew the faith across the northern desert in order to resist infidel intrusions at the coast. The Sanusiyya created a remarkable network of alliances connecting the central Sahara with Cyrenaica and the Fezzan in the north and with Bornu and Wadai in the south, and remained the major power bloc in the Libyan interior deep into the twentieth century.[123] In Sudan, Egyptian encroachment involved the arrival of a class of foreign Muslim clerics, leading to the increasing popularity of Sufi brotherhoods which were at the forefront of anti-Egyptian reformist activism. One such was the Majdhubiyya; another was the Sammaniyya, whose presence pre-dated that of the Egyptians, and which expanded rapidly at the grassroots level where its criticism of local elites resonated.[124] It was from the ranks of the Sammaniyya that Muhammad Ahmad emerged to declare himself the Mahdi. In the 1880s, the Mahdists chose violent insurgency from the outset, as seemed appropriate given the perceived iniquities of aggressive, Turkish-speaking Egyptian rule and the millenarian vision of the movement.[125] In Egypt itself, a group of reformist army officers coalesced around the leadership of Colonel Ahmed Urabi in 1881–82, representing resistance to both foreign influence in Egypt and the corrupt, misguided regime of Khedive Tewfik. To a considerable extent the Urabist movement was the logical culmination of several decades of both Egyptian efforts at political and economic reformation and the European intrusion which accompanied it. In the middle of 1882, against a backdrop of rioting and disorder in Alexandria, the British first bombarded the city from the sea—the French fleet remained aloof from the rapidly evolving conflict—and then landed an army, defeating Urabi's forces at the battle of Tel-el-Kebir in September. Urabi was captured and exiled. But the particular political sentiment and ideology he apparently represented would only grow in the decades ahead.[126] To be sure, one of the arguments against the 'modernisation and emulation' model was that it seemed to lead inexorably to aggressive European influence, and did not, in fact, succeed in warding off the threat posed by European imperialism in the Mediterranean. This is precisely what had happened in Egypt; and in Tunisia, too, where between the 1830s and the 1860s the authorities chose cooperation with the British and French, with all the advantages it offered, and exhibited 'modernising' tendencies, including abolishing slavery, embracing 'free trade' and embarking on constitutional reform. Yet it still ended up with the French seizing Tunis in 1881, for reasons beyond Tunisia's immediate control.[127] The experiment had backfired. Urabists belonged to a cohort of nineteenth-century African reformers; but so too did the 'modernisers' of Tunis, who were not—as some would later brand them and their ilk—'collaborators' in the face of Western aggression but socioeconomic innovators and political entrepreneurs of a kind common across the continent throughout a century of change and challenge. The narrow focus on a particular outcome can lead us to neglect the intent behind the project.

Various forms of reform and renovation were also foremost in the minds of a host of other insurgents further south. There were uprisings among the Shona and Ndebele in 1896–97 against the British South Africa Company in Rhodesia, known as the Chimurenga; in German East Africa, the Maji Maji of 1905–7; the rising of the Nama and Herero in German South-West Africa in 1904; among the Zulu, the Bambatha rebellion of 1906–8. Often the insurgents' primary targets were other Africans, the headmen and functionaries and intermediaries and above all soldiers who had both co-opted and been co-opted by the colonial order. In many respects, for example, the Maji Maji uprising was as much a 'civil war', or an essentially local struggle over material and political resources, as an anticolonial insurrection focused on the new regime introduced by the Germans.[128] The Swahili uprising on the coast of German East Africa in 1888–89, it has likewise been suggested, was also a violent contest over access to the wealth and status linked to long-distance commerce into the

interior, a crisis several decades in the making.[129] The Ndebele-Shona uprising in Rhodesia in 1896 was in some ways remarkable in the way that
formerly disparate groups were apparently united—perhaps, some have
argued, under new forms of spiritual leadership—against the predations
of white settlers. Since the initial defeat of the Ndebele at the hands of the
British South Africa Company in 1893, many Ndebele and Shona had been
subjected to land alienation and forced labour. Yet sharp divisions were
very much in evidence, with a number of Ndebele military commanders
refusing to join the rebellion and seeing advantage in remaining allied to
the Company and the settler community. Some Shona groups likewise
remained unmoved, including those who were in subordinate, tributary
relationships with the Ndebele core, and these were fissures which were
clearly rooted in the earlier decades of the nineteenth century. In other
words, for many in the area, recent local political dynamics were as important as, if not more so than, any considerations around white settler intrusion into particular districts. Nonetheless, as with the Maji Maji in Tanzania,
twentieth-century nationalists would seek to frame the revolt as the opening salvo in a unified revolutionary struggle for freedom, as the Shona
term *chimurenga* implies.[130] The interpretation of these events is highly
political, and contingent, and the memory of them a matter of enormous
sensitivity. But it is important to emphasise continuity and culmination
at least as much as the rupture, the disjuncture, which such violence
has long been assumed to represent. It invariably contained novel elements, especially in terms of connectivity between the communities involved, the forms of leadership which emerged and the spiritual beliefs
and canvases that held rebellions together.[131] The gendered dimension to
this last sphere was significant. Women had long occupied prominent
religious roles, roles which were never more important in an age of social
and political turbulence, for they involved crucial relationships with ancestors and deities who might offer protection on multiple levels: in the
context of environment, harvest, rainfall, livestock.[132] The turbulence of
the late nineteenth and early twentieth centuries created space for new
forms of female agency. For example, in the early years of the twentieth
century, Muhumusa in northern Rwanda and Nyabingi in south-west
Uganda represented cults formed around the leadership provided by

female spirit mediumship. These constituted the cultural epicentres of reformist and salvationist insurgencies which were also often framed in anticolonial terms.[133] In Zimbabwe, the spirit medium Charwe was hanged for her supposedly seditious activities, but her spirit Nehanda endured, and became a focal point of anticolonial resistance.[134] At times violence had millenarian connotations, and the courage of fighters was reinforced by the introduction of protective, interventionist spiritual elements—such as the magical water during the Maji Maji uprising which, it was believed, would protect the rebels from German bullets. But for most people, in essence, such insurgencies didn't represent a new form of 'resistance', a term which is sometimes more problematic than it first appears.[135] They belonged to the revolutionary nineteenth century as much as to the twentieth, and probably more so, regardless of how they might later be used by history-hungry nationalists.[136] The increased volatility of the 1890s and 1900s doubtless often sharpened the conflict, and raised the stakes involved; but the violent events themselves were centrally concerned with long-standing, centrifugal contests over status, rights, obligations. Invariably, they represented the continuation by other means of earlier patterns of challenge, contest and reformism. In almost all cases, foreign colonial rule was only the latest element—albeit one associated with extraordinary brutality, in a number of different contexts—motivating violent, entrepreneurial reformism and self-assertion.

And so, too, with those converts to Christianity who turned that faith into something rather more disruptive than those who had introduced it could possibly have imagined. Within a few years of conversion, many Africans saw in the Christian Gospel, and indeed in the gloomier reaches of the Old Testament, messages and meanings which resonated with their times and their own circumstances, and over which, they understood instinctively, white missionaries had no monopoly. Christian faith swiftly constituted a new component in a deep history of reformism, contestation and insurgency. Christian ideas could also be the catalyst for crisis, as among the Xhosa, many of whom in 1857 slaughtered their own cattle— exhorted to do so by a young prophetess, Nongqawuse, who had absorbed radical Christian ideas—in the expectation that European power would be destroyed and society reborn imminently.[137] The immediate context is important: this was a moment of cattle disease as well as advancing political and military power from the direction of Cape Colony. But it was one of the more dramatic, and tragic, demonstrations of religious syncretism. The independent church movement (sometimes referred to as the 'Ethiopian' church movement, alluding to the biblical term for Africa itself) came in diverse forms, but the various churches themselves shared the notion of a revolutionary eschatology, especially poignant in a period of economic hardship, political uncertainty and social change. These were particularly prevalent in eastern and southern Africa in the early years of the twentieth century.[138] In some cases, reformed doctrine involved the rejection of monogamy, including by those African women converts who found the idea of monogamous marriage socially cloying and economically unfeasible. In other contexts, across Nyasaland and in Southern and Northern Rhodesia, the Jehovah's Witnesses' Watchtower movement reimagined the concept of salvation as proffering deliverance from the brutalities of life under colonial rule.[139] In Nyasaland in 1915, the revolt led by the charismatic preacher John Chilembwe, leader of his own church, was the consequence of outrage at the conditions under which Africans were living and dying under the tutelage of a British administration at war with the Germans. Chilembwe, killed by the British trying to escape, was of course the product of very current pressures and stresses in Nyasa society.[140] But he also belonged to a pantheon of illustrious revolutionaries and reformers stretching back into the nineteenth century: people who searched for new ideas about the nature of society and existence, identified obstacles to progress and sought to do better. The same can be said, a little later, of Simon Kimbangu in the Belgian Congo, who reconceptualised the Christian message as the promise of deliverance from colonial rule, but whose followers were quiet insurgents in the way that many had been in the region throughout the previous century. They withdrew their labour, their resources, their personhood, from a system they perceived as intrinsically illegitimate.[141] Decades of violent unsettlement in Congo had awarded the Christian message a particular power; but what these rebels were doing in the name of Kimbanguism would have been recognised by their insurgent predecessors, even if some of their methods and convictions might have been unfamiliar.

The age of global engagement intersected with the age of insurgent, reformist, confrontational political cultures, in other words. In this context, intermediacy could easily, and often did, morph into enmity, a mutation which reflected the searching turmoil of the long nineteenth century. The era of which the European 'Scramble' was a part was one in which Africa was being partitioned and repartitioned by a whole host of political, cultural, intellectual and economic actors: *African* actors, moreover, often inhabiting those liminal, transitional spaces which might sit between imagined blocs of solidity and stability, but whose experience was in fact, rather more commonly, one of instability and contestation. John Chilembwe and Samuel Ajayi Crowther might be framed as nationalists and patriots. The dangers here of presentism and teleology are clear enough. They were, however, products of a revolutionary nineteenth century. Likewise, an intellectual giant such as James Africanus Beale Horton might be claimed, not unreasonably and certainly understandably, by later generations of Pan-Africanists as one of their own. But he, too, was the corollary of the age of transition and transformation, in this case a transoceanic one too, one which saw him share a space with men like Edward Wilmot Blyden. It would come to be inhabited by people like W.E.B. Du Bois and later still Constance Cummings-John, who from their different vantage points across the Atlantic world would draw on the age of African revolution and creative volatility in seeking to shape and challenge the Eurocentric globality of which they were the outcome, and which in some cases they had even helped create. In the age of flux, nothing was ever safe, ever 'secure'; even as it transmuted, it produced new variants of liminality, of insurgency, and generated new points of leverage.

———

THE CULMINATION OF AFRICA'S TRANSFORMATIVE century involved convergence and co-option; but it was also chaotic. From a strictly military point of view, many African armies, met with superior firearms, attempted frontal assaults on the enemy's position, aiming to rapidly overwhelm those positions and bring variegated invasions to a shuddering halt. There were, in at least some societies, socio-cultural exigencies, too: ideas about heroism and courage, frequently, if not universally, expressed in terms of masculinity, required soldiers to attack the enemy in the open, and to be seen to be doing so. Occasionally, it worked—if only temporarily. But up against machine gun positions and breech-loaders, the infantry square or the extemporised *laager*, it was almost always doomed to failure. Other tactics had evolved during the course of the nineteenth century, however, including forms of what would later be understood as guerrilla warfare. In many ways this was an extension of methods employed by insurgent armies over several preceding decades. Comparatively centralised states might fall relatively swiftly in the context of the single decisive encounter; but in rugged or densely forested terrain, populated by small-scale, dispersed or decentralised polities, colonial armies fought for many years before European administrations could lay claim to functioning suzerainty over particular territories. The Portuguese were still fighting in Angola by the time the First World War broke out; in Côte d'Ivoire and the Niger Delta, the French and British respectively were compelled to conduct small-scale operations against defiant communities for many years. Elsewhere, Samori fought the French and their allies in the 1880s and 1890s using guerrilla tactics, striking suddenly at French columns and destroying the crops on which they depended. The Hehe fought the Germans in East Africa by launching surprise attacks on isolated outposts through the 1890s, and in the same period the Nyoro under Kabalega became adept at ambushing the invading Anglo-Ganda force.[142] In the wide open spaces of the northern Sahara, the Sanusiyya maintained highly mobile guerrilla warfare against the Italians deep into the twentieth century, and the Somali under Muhammad Abdille Hassan did the same against both Italians and British, and groups allied with them, from the end of the 1890s until 1920.[143] There was, again, nothing essentially novel about such tactics, which had been honed by revolutionary insurgents throughout the nineteenth century. The problem was that scorched earth tactics cut both ways, as Samori (captured in 1898) and Kabalega (in 1899) in particular discovered, and that the act of scorching the earth was in effect an act of self-harm. Colonial forces under German, French and British officers also proved brutally efficient in practising scorched earth tactics, and were, moreover, better able to bring in supplies from outside, as well as military reinforcements.

At the same time, of course, numerous African polities, some the product of nineteenth-century insurgencies, others more deeply-rooted, maintained a core unity in the face of the external threat which approached them across those liminal spaces. Unarguably the most 'successful' instance of this, by most standard criteria, was Ethiopia, which under Yohannes in the 1870s and 1880s had demonstrated an ability to strike hard and fast at encroaching dangers: against Egypt, Mahdist Sudan and, in an early portent, Italy.[144] The genius of the neo-Solomonic project was the appeal to a pan-Ethiopian unity and identity rooted in antiquity, enabling Yohannes and his successor Menelik to assemble large armies at moments of particular peril, armies drawn from a range of kingdoms and communities across the highlands which had spent much of the nineteenth century fighting one another. In this way, Menelik was able to face down yet another existential threat originating from the Eritrean frontier zone: this time an invading Italian force against which Menelik mustered somewhere in the region of a hundred thousand men at Adwa, in Tigray, in March 1896. The Italians were undone, too, by impatience, poor planning, blind hubris and their own domestic politics; but none of that detracts from the stunning speed of the Ethiopian victory, which was also made possible by large numbers of modern guns and sound tactics. This was the only instance of an African force decisively repelling an invading European or European-led army.[145] Still, where the Ethiopians succeeded, others drawing on centralised political cultures fared less well in seeking to face down an array of enemies, for they tended to fall relatively swiftly once a decisive battle had been lost. This is not how many of these states had previously fought their wars, which were generally waged at some distance from the core, and organised around attritional campaigns often lasting months or years. Thus Asante, Dahomey, Benin and the Zulu, for example, all fell fairly quickly.

Still, by the early 1890s, the biggest single handicap facing the African entrepreneurs whose predecessors had transformed the continent was the widening technological gap. European governments placed restrictions on the sale of firearms to Africans, which meant much diminished access to both guns and ammunition, which in turn meant a reliance on, and an ability to maintain, existing stocks. Some societies were already adept at repairing guns.[146] But commercial restrictions placed most people at a significant, and worsening, disadvantage. Firearms were one thing; but the technological gulf would have been apparent to most of the Dahomean soldiers trying—and failing—to inflict damage on the French gunboat *Topaz* on the Oueme River in 1892.[147] Machine guns positioned around European *laagers* decimated Ndebele insurgents in 1896, as they did the Zulu who threw themselves at the British during the Bambatha uprising a decade later.[148]

For millions of Africans, moreover, the ability to navigate the rapidly changing circumstances of the late nineteenth century was undermined by disease and environmental catastrophe. Inadvertently—though many Africans believed otherwise—intruding Europeans carried with them diseases which proved as devastating to communities as breech-loaders or Maxim guns. With Italian horses on the Red Sea coast came rinderpest, a deadly cattle epidemic which swept through north-east, east and southern Africa between the end of the 1880s and the middle of the 1890s.[149] The result, for many, was destitution. The cultural, economic and political basis of power in many societies—livestock—was destroyed, and with it the capacity to fight. This coincided with outbreaks of sleeping sickness, which affected both humans and animals, and which was the consequence in many areas of population decline or movement and the breakdown of mechanisms for ecological management.[150] Other diseases arrived with the European (and Asian) intruders, too: new strains of smallpox, jiggers, cholera, yellow fever, meningitis and sexually transmitted diseases such as syphilis and gonorrhoea.[151] They came with the traders and adventurers and soldiers, proving particularly devastating in communities which had had relatively limited interactions with foreign bodies previously. At the same time, across the Sahel belt and in north-east Africa, poor rainfall led to some of the worst famines in living memory: for example, in Sudan, Ethiopia and Kenya between the late 1880s and early 1900s.[152] Elsewhere, the arrival of new diseases was compounded by the food shortages and outright famines which were the result of wars and counterinsurgency campaigns involving scorched earth tactics in the 1890s and 1900s, and which had long-term impacts on health.[153] The catastrophic effects of a combination of food scarcity, disease and imperial warfare on equatorial Africans has been well documented.[154] Warfare of this kind had long been practised in Africa, by Africans themselves. But the European contribution was to increase the scale of it, and the consequent level of devastation. The African soldiers under their command knew what they were doing, because they had seen it before; in some cases, again, Africans, whether as individuals, or small groups, or state-level operatives, carried it out quite independently of, or in self-aware partnership with, the well-armed *wazungu*. But the level of human and material destruction is clear, and was the hallmark of European imperial ambition in Africa.[155] Many of the worst excesses were carried out by European officers themselves. The German response to the rebellion in what is today Namibia was to carry out genocide against the Nama and Herero.[156] In their East African territory, German reprisals against the Maji Maji insurgents involved mass destruction of villages, livestock and farmland, leading to a famine that killed perhaps a quarter of a million of Africans.[157] British officers laid waste to Bunyoro in the course of a bitter campaign of terror which was as much aimed at 'civilians' as at Kabalega's *barusura*,[158] and burnt and looted in Benin.[159] Across the continent, bodies swung from gallows, arable land smouldered, royal palaces lay in ruins. But if all this was the horrific working-out of Europeans' inner anxiety about the world, they would discover soon enough that these very acts of killing and destruction were themselves, by definition, exercises in liminality. Nothing definitive was happening here; even the dead would come to act again, taking their places amid ongoing exercises in insurgency and reformation.

Violence, ultimately, gave European actors the leverage required to create the thing we call 'empire' in these places. Africa's long nineteenth century was defined by violence; some of its greatest political and socioeconomic achievements were based on it. Africans' military skill, social aspiration, political fissiparity and capacity for co-option made others' empires possible. Europeans made their own distinctive contributions to the African revolution, and their own technologically and racially charged interventions were potent, even as these drew on African practices, knowledge and personnel. An array of European agents and representatives, themselves the product of insecurity, restlessness and expansionism, co-opted Africa's nineteenth-century revolution: at times deftly inserting themselves into political and military fissures, at other times blunderingly exploiting upheaval, and in both cases frequently relying on a dollop of good fortune. Ultimately, they harnessed volatility and transformation and repurposed it—and reframed it—in pursuit of their own projects of national renewal and reinvention.

# PART V

# Time and Place

# Act V

## Time on the Road

### I

MIRAMBO HAD A DREAM; a dream rooted in the past. As with all such visions, it was informed not just by a deep historical consciousness, but by both contemporary flux and ideas about what the future might hold. In this age of extraordinary turbulence, of political and economic and cultural transformation and contest, history *mattered*: it possessed new resonance, and emotive power.[1] It offered reassurance that there was a time when things had been 'better'—more prosperous, more stable, more glorious; and thus it provided much-needed points of reference in an uncertain era. It inspired insurrection, accordingly, and reformation, and offered guidance and models for the future. As Mirambo's spatial awareness and his territorial ambition increased, so too did his temporal imagination. Perhaps this had begun when he was a much younger man, travelling, like so many of his cohort, to the coast, seeing the ocean, working his 'passage' on the great caravan snaking across the region. No doubt his imagination was fired by material and political ambition, for his life to date had made him worldly and aspirational. But perhaps, too, he had begun to think about time itself: what the past meant, what relevance it had for his own epoch, what ideas it could offer about the future.

Mirambo believed, or came to believe, that his new state was, at least in part, the re-creation of a much older one, and that his violence—unfortunate but necessary—was above all about restoration, not destruction, nor even, in a sense, novelty.[2] He was, in essence, remaking an older state in the area named 'Usagali', which had been extensive, unifying all the peoples between lakes Tanganyika and Victoria, and incorporating Unyanyembe and current-day Urambo itself. That great kingdom's last ruler had been Mshimba: 'the lion'. He was wise, powerful, and was known for the large number of wives he kept in his various settlements, an indication of a teeming, urban population. Mshimba was Mirambo's moral and political compass. But other heroes, more ancient still, were also available, for Usagali itself had been the migrated version of an even older realm, 'Ukalaganza'. Ukalaganza, Mirambo asserted, was originally a sprawling empire in the east and north-east Congo basin, beyond both Burundi and Lake Tanganyika. Some of its people had migrated into present-day north-western Tanzania, and they formed the nucleus of Usagali. It is a story which in itself reminds us, as it doubtless did Mirambo, of the significance of fission and fusion, and these are the core elements in Mirambo's historical vision: people moving, like time itself, reconstituting and re-forming. Mirambo (or his transcriber Ebenezer Southon) was unclear about the reasons for that original migration; but he was presumably drawing on some long-established historical memories in the area, and other sources step in to (possibly) assist. Richard Burton, in the 1850s, had heard of Ukalaganza; and he claimed that upon the death of a particular ruler, "[h]is children and nobles divided and dismembered his dominations" with the old empire falling into the hands of "a rabble of petty chiefs". Burton's estimate was the beginning of the eighteenth century for these events.[3] Stanley also gathered some information on Ukalaganza, and proposed that the name of that last ruler was in fact 'Mwezi'—the "greatest king then known"—upon whose death the realm descended into chaos.[4] Mwezi, noted, according to Stanley, for his prowess in war and (again) his prudent governance, was also someone whom Mirambo could seek to emulate; a paragon and a template.[5]

But back to Mshimba, the last king of Usagali. He died, according to Southon (or, more appropriately, Mirambo himself), some "eight generations back";[6] which, depending on how we calculate it, might place it in the late seventeenth century; around the same time, or even earlier, that Burton proposed for the original collapse of Ukalaganza. But no matter: exact dates are neither here nor there; they certainly were not what mattered to Mirambo, and in any case European interlocutors likely got confused about chronology. To Mirambo, this was about the figurative, allusive, affective power of the past, or a particular ordering of it. His sentience about the significance of history, as well as being rooted, no doubt, in real events and actual collective memory, was sharpened by the age in which he lived: an age of insecurity, and danger, and anxiety, but also of possibility, aspiration and rejuvenation. In the midst of the turmoil, of which he was both cause and effect, Mirambo sought models of judicious, courageous governance; the success of his insurgency depended on it. We cannot know how much he talked of these things to his compatriots and lieutenants. At the local level, it may well be that he sought, almost certainly in continual discussion with those around him, to balance the assertion of a new political order, in which the chiefs of conquered districts were removed, against the careful placation of the ghostly ancestors of those same chiefs: a public disavowal of their history alongside a cautious respect for it. That is what we might deduce from the evidence supplied by a French trader, Philippe Broyon, a man who signed his name 'Broyon-Mirambo' because he claimed, in addition to being Mirambo's blood-brother, to have married one of his daughters.[7]

But Mirambo certainly had an interested audience in those outsiders with whom he conversed, Broyon included, and that may indeed be a key part of the story. Ebenezer Southon was convinced by these historical discourses, and impressed by them; Mirambo, Southon scribbled in his journal, was more than capable of surpassing the achievements of Mshimba of Usagali.[8] Perhaps Mirambo was making a deliberate point to the *mzungu*, whose very presence was indicative, albeit in a relatively lowly way, of the enormous shifts in space and time which Mirambo had seen unfolding in his own lifetime. He was almost certainly doing so to Jerome Becker, the International African Association agent to whom he asserted in 1882 that the 'problem', as he saw it, was that there were "too many chiefs" in the region; better to have power consolidated in a handful of large, visibly viable entities: his own state, naturally, plus Unyanyembe, Buganda, Zanzibar.[9] History backed him up (he *didn't* say, but may as well have done), for in the days of Mshimba and Mwezi, there was no such fragmentation, which meant weakness, and introversion. It was, of course, a markedly instinctive, or perhaps a very conscious, interpretation of the past: there was apparently no recognition of the need for fission, or the drivers of and indeed the opportunities presented by dissolution and disunity, of which Mirambo himself had taken full advantage. It was the paradox at the heart of Mirambo's vision of the past. Rather, history, for him, demonstrated the power of unity, and cohesion, and purpose. History was a living, pulsating, vibrant force through which to navigate liminality and upheaval, and there would have been no question in Mirambo's mind, or in the minds of anyone around him, that they were very much part of it.

## II

IT IS IRONIC, THEN, THAT OTHERS WERE MOVING through the neighbourhood with rather different interpretations of the past, and of the people on the road. Enter Captain Edward Hore—evangelist for the Church Missionary Society, master mariner and time traveller—who, along with Annie Hore, made his journey on the road between Bagamoyo and Ujiji in the late 1870s and early 1880s.[10] He discovered something remarkable: he found that moving westward along the road, one moved through time itself; almost, indeed, *backwards* in time.[11] Hore described, with unmistakeable contempt,

> a narrow margin on the sea-board of a doubtful oriental civilisation, and a broader margin of small native tribes mingled with the lowest of semi-civilised half-castes, and fast losing their distinctive nationalities. The outer band of civilisation has sucked the life-blood of these communities—quite paralysed the native germs of civilisation.

There is a lot going on here in Hore's head, emblematic of the hardening circles of thought about time and place—above all, about *race* and *culture*—in Europe in the second half of the nineteenth century. There is the scorn for coastal 'civilisation', a bastardised, degraded version of something; there is the idea that it has been sunk by venality and above all by miscegenation, which is regarded with horror here—"semi-civilised half-castes"—and the notion that this is the "outer band of civilisation", its polluted periphery, where the essences of true 'civilisation' become distorted and corrupted. And so, too, to time itself: for the filthy frontier consumes those innocent savages in its mire, poisoning and stunting their own development. A little further on, we come to those

> native tribes, of uneasy and apparently warlike aspect, too far from the coast to be completely overrun by the invading race, and therefore retaining, to some extent, the original native arts and customs: they seem in a chronic state of armed resistance to every one, and in most cases, as with the Wagogo, sufficiently powerful to demand a share in passing trade, in which, by their unsettled position, they are unable to take a legitimate share.

These were the communities caught up in the commercial turbulence, but too removed from the full flow of trade to be fully engaged in it; they are only damaged by it, and writhe in endless conflict as a result, seeking to extract something from the passing traffic but seemingly condemned to inhabit a violent purgatory; a civilisational gloaming.

Hore moved on. "Continuing west," he intoned to the learned folk of the Anthropological Institute of Great Britain and Ireland,

> we come to real Central African tribes, amongst whom only we can fairly look for real samples of the native African, and amongst whom we find evidence of capabilities which only require appropriate assistance to develop into civilisation—tribes indeed, which, isolated from the benefits of communication with the outer world, have also been, in many cases, isolated from the disturbing influences of such communication [. . .]. Hence in an observant journey into this region, instead of, as might be expected, going deeper into ignorance and barbarity, we regularly advance from the socially and physically degraded barbarian, settled often but a mile or two from the coast, to the real healthy active savage of the far interior, living in large orderly settlements, and pursuing the industries he has patiently acquired. It is not without substantial reason that extensive missionary organisations have sought a field of labour in the far interior.

Off-shoots of the doubtful civilisation referred to have penetrated even to the far interior, and settled, leech-like, upon some of these tribes, but except in certain isolated localities, and in the case of some small weak tribes, they have not taken possession. The slave trade, however, the original end and purpose of those distant representatives of civilisation, has left no part wholly untouched.[12]

The further west one follows the road, in other words, the purer and the more authentic the culture, and more admirable the society. This is the *real* Africa—a strikingly resilient concept, a mirage conjured by the white gaze, as familiar to the gap-year traveller and a certain type of journalist in our own era as it was to Hore's missionaries—which is in a sense beyond time, or the cloying, corroding version of it unravelling from the direction of the ocean. The true "native", the real "savage"— who is also, note, "healthy" and "active"—is isolated from this turbulent temporal current, even if hardly unaffected by the ubiquitous slave trade.

For Edward Hore, to move along the road was to pass through time itself and, ultimately, beyond it, whereupon one entered *African time*. He was by no means the only *mzungu* who framed temporality in particular ways in this neighbourhood, for increasingly Africa was conceptualised in terms of time as well as space; its geography a matter of relative progress and development as much as of topography and climate. If the 'Dark Continent' was a spatial construct, it was a historical one, too. This could manifest itself in different ways. Where Hore espied authenticity and purity, Burton sensed danger in the primordiality, threat in the howling places beyond the road which were the stuff of European nightmares. "[W]henever an advance beyond Unyanyembe had been made the theme of conversation," Burton recalled,

> Said bin Salim's countenance fell, and he dropped dark hints touching patience and the power of Allah to make things easy. Abdullah rendered the expression intelligible by asking me if I considered the caravan strong enough to dare the dangers of the road—which he grossly exaggerated—between Unyamwezi-land and Ujiji. I replied that I did, and that even if I did not, such bugbears should not cause delay. Abdullah smiled, but was too polite to tell me that he did not believe me.[13]

These spaces were deeply embedded in the European imagination, for Europeans imported to Africa ideas about the relationship between the landscape and time, between place and period.[14] Verney Lovett Cameron, moving through the area on behalf of the Royal Geographical Society in 1873–74, bore witness to the terrible devastation wrought by the slave trade, and presented the violent destruction as symptomatic of a distinctively timeless African condition in ways that would continue to echo in the decades to come. Cameron's road is a place of barbarity, and Africa the exemplar of pre-, possibly even anti-, modernity; this is a Hobbesian vision of poverty and violent savagery and lawlessness.[15] The violence is often systematic, and the awfulness appears to have its own grim internal logic. But it is also frequently random, and the destruction is wholesale. How poignant it must have been for Cameron, whose original mission had been to expedite the dispatch of Livingstone's body to the coast, and thence to Great Britain. With that accomplished, Cameron continued his explorations along and beyond the road, and as the good doctor's cadaver disappeared over the horizon toward the ocean, Cameron turned back to see the area seemingly consumed by tribulations on a biblical scale.

Livingstone's life and death had a profound influence on Victorian notions of global time. And then of course there was Stanley, striding out manfully to find the missing missionary, but, in reality, looking warily and perhaps even fearfully for himself. Stanley's journey is certainly an emotional one, and his Africa is framed in emotional ways:

> I am warned to prepare for a view of the Tanganika, for, from the top of a steep mountain the kirangozi says I can see it. I almost vent the feelings of my heart in cries. But wait, we must behold it first. And we press forward [. . .]. We are at last on the summit. Ah! not yet can it be seen. A little further on—just yonder, oh! there it is—[. . .] The Tanganika!—Hurrah! and the men respond to the exultant cry of the Anglo-Saxon with the lungs of Stentors, and the great forests and the hills seem to share in our triumph.[16]

Finding and meeting Livingstone was of ineffable importance to Stanley, and the turbulent emotion he feels as he approaches Lake Tanganyika and Ujiji will contrast with the infamously studied formality—ludicrous in context—with which he will soon greet Livingstone.[17]

Time swirled around Stanley; he brought it with him into the dark interior, in the same way as he brought rum and quinine and cloth and bullets. When he walked into the square in front of the old missionary's *tembe*, time actually seemed to stand still; but, of course, in this timeless continent, the meeting of the two white men at its very centre possessed a vivid sense of temporality and motion that no natives could possibly hope to match, with their endless, violent, pointless machinations and their obvious lack of any tangible achievement. It was a juxtaposition emphasised in the days ahead, when Stanley brought Livingstone up to speed on global current affairs—for the old man had no idea about the state of the world since he was last in touch with it. "Shortly I found myself enacting the part of an annual periodical to him", wrote Stanley. Luckily, but also with no sense of irony, given his hyperbolic inclinations,

[t]here was no need of exaggeration—of any penny-a-line news, or of any sensationalism. The world had witnessed and experienced much the last few years. The Pacific Railroad had been completed; Grant had been elected President of the United States; Egypt had been flooded with savans; the Cretan rebellion had terminated; a Spanish revolution had driven Isabella from the throne of Spain, and a Regent had been appointed; General Prim was assassinated; a Castelar had electrified Europe with his advanced ideas upon the liberty of worship; Prussia had humbled Denmark, and annexed Schleswig-Holstein, and her armies were now around Paris; the 'Man of Destiny' was a prisoner at Wilhelmshöhe; the Queen of Fashion and the Empress of the French was a fugitive; and the child born in the purple had lost for ever the Imperial crown destined for his head; the Napoleon dynasty was extinguished by the Prussians, Bismarck, and Von Moltke; and France, the proud empire, was humbled to the dust.[18]

It is a poignant scene indeed: events, sweeping ahead in the inexorable way they do in the civilised world, far away from here, in Ujiji. Time moves elsewhere: Stanley's arrival to find Livingstone is proof of that; but otherwise, not here. "What a budget of news it was to one who had emerged from the depths of the primeval forests of Manyuema!", mused Stanley, unable to conceal his delight at being the bearer of the budget. "The reflection of the dazzling light of civilisation was cast on him while Livingstone was thus listening in wonder to one of the most exciting pages of history ever repeated. How the puny deeds of barbarism paled before these!"[19]

And yet, in Stanley's excited subconscious, 'Africa' was a place where one could find one's own time, locate oneself, and be the best, most heroic, most able version of that self imaginable. In order for that to happen, 'Africa' needed to be preserved in a kind of aspic, which also involved sucking the time out of it, so it wouldn't spoil. It was a deliberate process of invention and juxtaposition. Thus, in the 1870s, if not earlier, we begin to espy the emergence of 'Africa' as a rather curious figment of the European imagination: a place to make Europeans look and feel good, especially in a world of tumult and stress and constant liminality, including (especially) that at home. Many have followed in Stanley's footsteps, gathering in village squares in the proverbial middle of nowhere, seemingly searching for Africa, but really looking for themselves.

Stanley was in fact quite interested in aspects of Africa's past. But 'Bula Matari', the breaker of rocks, also embodied the heightening racialism of the era, and represented the transition to a peculiarly ahistorical approach to the continent, an approach which undergirded the developmental Salvationism of which his hero Livingstone was the exemplar and in many ways the pioneer. When the two men met in the literal and conceptual heart of the continent, their encounter denoted a new form of energetic objectification. Civilisational history was to be denied to Africans. It would have been rather startling news to Mirambo. But what is clear is that, for all these characters, positionality and the perspectives it engendered were innately entwined with ideas about time itself; the perception of place and the conception of temporality were intimately entangled.

# 7

# Ways of Seeing, Being, and Remembering

## The Passion of Tewodros, and Other Histories

ON 13 APRIL 1868, EMPEROR TEWODROS—*negus negast*, king of kings, of Ethiopia—shot himself through the mouth using a handsome silver pistol which had been a present from Queen Victoria. The engraving read

*Presented*
*By*
*VICTORIA*
*Queen of Great Britain and Ireland*
*To*
*THEODORUS*
*Emperor of Abyssinia*
*As a slight token of her gratitude*
*For his kindness to her servant Plowden*
*1854.*[1]

"The King who had ruled from one frontier to the other", lamented one chronicle, "is so wretched that he swallows [pistol balls]. Over there, at Magdala, a cry echoed [. . . :] 'Have you seen the lion die there? He would have considered it a shame to be killed by the hand of a man.'"[2] In fact, according to at least one account, he had attempted the same thing the day before, but a shocked and loyal attendant had wrested the gun from

the hands of his despairing master. This time, there was no such intervention. "As soon as the storming party carried the outer gate," wrote ob-
server Captain Henry Hozier, "he exclaimed to those near him, 'Flee! I
release you from your allegiance. As for me, I shall never fall into the hands
of an enemy.'"[3] He died instantly. British soldiers were just metres away,
closing in on the last remnants of Tewodros's imperium, which now
amounted to little more than an area of the rocky outcrop known as Magdala, on the eastern escarpment of the Ethiopian highlands. The pistol
itself had presumably long been one of the emperor's favourite posses-
sions, and so it was only fitting that he used it to such definitive effect at
the end. He liked guns. He appreciated their power, but also what they
represented: namely, development, progress, and—had he been burdened
by the term—*modernity*. He had dedicated much of his adult life to getting hold of large numbers of them, of various shapes and sizes. Ironic, too,
then, that he had killed himself as he was hunted down by the British,
whose friendship he had long sought in pursuit of a righteous legacy
which he believed would be of mutual benefit: to Britain, that is, as well
as himself and his people.

The British government took a different view, on account of the
European hostages kept by Tewodros and the evident risk he posed to
their wellbeing and perhaps, too, the wider stability of the region. It was
one of the earliest examples in the modern era of armed European intervention in order to sever an African society from its savage past, and
proffer in return the opportunity for modernity—or at least an association with it. Unlike in the case of Lagos a few years earlier, however, the
British had no intention of remaining in the Ethiopian highlands. This
was a rescue operation, with clearly delimited objectives: the freeing of
the hostages, and the removal of the monstrous Tewodros, whose dispatch
provided semi-civilised Ethiopia with a shot at redemption: in short order,
the emperor had mutated from the courageous, manly, visionary pioneer
of Ethiopian quasi-modernity to the tragic and unstable and possibly psychopathic African despot, a trope which would prove resilient in the
decades ahead.[4] Notably, however, his progeny was deemed salvable. The
commander of the British expedition, Sir Robert Napier—an experienced
soldier, and the man who had stormed Peking and destroyed the Old

Summer Palace in 1860—took Tewodros's seven-year-old son Alemayu back to England, where he was sent to Rugby School. Perhaps the son could be refined, even civilised, even if the father could not; but the boy remained profoundly unhappy and died of pleurisy in 1879, his remains being interred at Windsor Castle.[5] The burden of his culture, and the British weather, had perhaps proven too much for Alemayu, and the curse of History could not be lifted.

Tewodros's act of self-destruction constitutes one of the most iconic and potent images from the era; but more importantly, it offers one of the best documented instances in the nineteenth century of a mobilisation of the past in pursuit of a particular political and cultural agenda. The insurgent Kassa Hailu believed himself to be the restorer of the ancient Solomonic state to its former glory, and envisaged a historical trajectory in which the highland empire had come under successive assaults from various directions, including from the Muslim polities which now surrounded Ethiopia on almost all sides, and the Oromo, framed as the invasive race of barbarians who had poisoned the body politic since the sixteenth century. He laid claim to the Holy Lands of Palestine, and to the Holy Places of Islam, as part of what he believed was Ethiopia's territorial and cultural inheritance.[6] Tewodros's reformist project was as much as anything else an intellectual one. The notion of Tewodros as a 'moderniser' has in many ways endured, cemented by work in the 1960s which commonly sought to identify such figures in the late 'precolonial' past.[7] There are indeed aspects of his material ambition and political vision which seem to bear out the epithet. And yet the mission he set himself was as much religio-historical, concerned with restoration and redemption, as it was concerned with 'modernity': the latter, indeed, amounted only to a set of tools by which to achieve the former. This was a Janus-like project, rooted equally in ancient religiosity and eschatology. Tewodros was propelled forward by the past, and by the idea, indeed the conviction, that the past could be melded with the present to meet contemporary (and looming) challenges. As the leader of an insurgency in a time of instability, Tewodros sought historical gravity. This wasn't quite the same thing as having possession of a vision of 'modernity', a notion imposed on him by subsequent chroniclers and a cohort of historians who came of age in the middle decades of the twentieth century. Nevertheless, Tewodros took his place in the Ethiopian pantheon of nation-builders, alongside Yohannes IV and Menelik II and numerous lieutenants, even if he was often deemed less successful than his successors, and the lasting image of him was his raging against the dying of the light on his rock at Magdala, consigning him to a curious historical gloaming.[8]

Ethiopian history in this period is often—usually, indeed—presented in exceptionalist terms. It seems, however, that an alternative perspective is worth proposing. Neo-Solomonism, as it came to be known, exemplifies a phenomenon unfolding across the continent in the course of the nineteenth century, even if it is rather better known than many similar kinds of movements. Tewodros is emblematic of something of an African historical revolution unfolding throughout the long nineteenth century, and especially intensively in its latter decades.[9] That transformation in the perceived power of historical thought was directly or indirectly the consequence of an era of heightened volatility, and of an expanded worldview in the age of global engagement and connectivity. While Europeans, as we see a little later in this chapter, were embarking on the production of racially infused interpretations of the African past, increasingly used to justify armed intervention, Africans were creating, or modifying, visions of that past in parallel with rapidly shifting political and economic circumstances and in many cases in response to the emergence of new political markets for historical knowledge. Millions of Africans sought new ways of investigating, resurrecting and contextualising the past. Temporal imaginaries and trajectories were critical in the creation of a new politics, and a range of political and economic actors, often framed as 'modernisers' seeking to design futures based on the glimpses they had of encroaching modernity, were in fact fixated by the past. In some cases, innovative political (and religious) forms inspired the quest for antiquity and genealogy; across the board, the past offered opportunities to articulate the legitimacy of, or infuse meaning into, the present. External interactions of a novel and intense nature gave rise to expanded notions of both time and space: there seems little doubt that prolonged interaction with traders, missionaries, explorers and, in time, colonial officials and army officers influenced thinking about the past and the epistemologies involved in defining it. As with other aspects of the transformative nineteenth century, the historical revolution was the product of both endogenous dynamics and exogenous impacts: shifts in the temporal imaginary were inspired by both political volatility and the advance of external frontiers on multiple levels. History had never mattered so much, nor was its framing a matter of such urgency. In the age of increasing global intrusion, in particular, the past became a crucial resource to be mobilised: witness the proliferation of historical writing across the continent in the 1900s and 1910s. But this cannot be separated from the decades of political reformism and material upheaval which preceded this 'literary moment'.

The production of historical narrative in the wake of insurgency was itself hardly unprecedented, of course: two of the finest blueprints date to the thirteenth century: in West Africa, with the emergence of the Epic of Sunjata following the great warrior-king's creation of the empire of Mali;[10] and in Ethiopia itself, where the putschist Amhara regime sponsored the production of the *Kebra Negast*, 'Chronicle of the Glory of the Kings', to assert its legitimacy through the creation of Solomonic mythology, at the core of which was the articulation of a direct link with God himself.[11] The latter, indeed, was the primary inspiration for Tewodros's own revolution; and Ethiopian historical culture flourished in the centuries that followed, through royal chronicles and political and religious testaments and treatises, as the highland polity refined a vision of itself, both temporally and spatially, in the face of challenges both internal and external.[12] Ethiopia and Mali offer two of the most dramatic exercises in historical imagination anywhere on the continent, and it is no coincidence that these rolling projects of temporal reinvention were the outcome of violent upheaval, and of a fundamental reordering of the political space. The *Kebra Negast* and the Sunjata Epic belong to an extraordinarily rich corpus of oral-historical literature in Africa, which has framed and narrated change, as well as positing continuity, across the continent's deeper temporal landscape. Other examples of the expression of historical thought in a similar period include that of the Swahili city-states, for which collections of traditions date to the early sixteenth century, and which were strongly influenced by Islamic styles of writing and content.[13]

Inevitably, our assessment of these developments in the long nineteenth century is, in some ways, speculative and intuitive—for the simple reason that our understanding of how historical thought was evolving in 'real time', as it were, is limited to a cluster of examples. But these cases are strongly suggestive of a rich and complex articulation of historical consciousness and memorialisation, and a process by which the past was energised in pursuit of state-building, in support of resistance, in the development of identity, in the creation of culture-heroes who were moral and political points of reference, in the idealisation of imagined homelands.[14] We can extrapolate from those scenarios a much broader pattern of temporal reform in an age of unprecedented volatility. History, and more specifically a sense of time, was critical to the evolution of statehood and the legitimisation of royal authority among the militarised monarchies of West Africa. By the beginning of the nineteenth century, Dahomean political structures and processes leaned heavily on the concept of temporal and indeed spiritual continuity—hugely important for a polity which had originated as an armed insurgency—and particular consequence was attached to the blessing bestowed by the dead upon the living. Hence the significance of the 'watering of the graves' of the ancestors, the annual ceremony at the centre of which were the deceased kings themselves. The relatively new state repurposed older forms of Fon material culture, and the conspicuous display of wealth and its celebration was a crucial pillar of state power: wealth derived from global trade, of course, but also refashioned local forms of artistic expression, as in the case of Dahomean appliqué cloth which was used to venerate ancestors and to emphasise political and military greatness, especially as it adorned public buildings and the tops of the umbrellas of senior chiefs and military commanders.[15] The dead—the past—had at least a hand in governance, and they did so through a direct relationship with the living, before the latter, too, joined them in the great plane of time.[16] Cutting through the obvious partisanship and titillation of contemporary European accounts, it is evident that the Dahomean state had a sharp sense of its own historical trajectory by the early nineteenth century.[17] The nineteenth century itself would see escalating debates over the direction of the kingdom, but those were based in essence around differing interpretations of that earlier history.

In Asante, too, origins—posited as 'tradition'—were crucial to the stability and continuity of state and society. Detailed understandings of provenance and elaborate job descriptions were on hand, by the eighteenth century, for every political office in the kingdom. The Golden Stool was the symbol of royal power, drawing on a deeper Akan tradition. Chiefs also had their own stools, although only the Asantehene had a new one made on the ascent to power. And ceremonial state swords were important, broadcasting military might, and embellished with ornaments and engravings which in metaphorical form emphasised moral might, too.[18] By the nineteenth century, senior state officials possessed staffs of office which emblematised the respect and dignity attached to office, the physical form of the elaborate descriptions which came with political authority.[19] The key purpose was to emphasise stasis and permanence, even, arguably, to the point of time being ahistorical, and of society being essentially unchanging.[20] Be that as it may, it was a vision of the past which undergirded royal authority, indeed was essential to it, and the royal court sought tightly to control these interpretations of time. Kingship was imbued with mythical attributes and values.[21] However, the interpretation of temporal stasis came increasingly under attack as the nineteenth century drew on, with the emergence of more radical groupings in Asante society expounding the idea of change over time, encompassing national military glory.[22] Dynamic visions of the past were expressed in orality, objects, offices and philosophical discourse, each of which were imbued with complex layers of meaning.[23]

Material culture, directly or indirectly representing historical thought, was essential equipment in the consolidation of emergent, insurgent statehood, and in the material manifestation and the projection of power. In some areas, insurgent culture-heroes moved across time and space, borrowed and adapted for current exigencies. This is demonstrable in central Africa, where Chokwe cultural production was the product of Luba and Lunda artistic, as well as physical, migration, and repurposed the fabled early seventeenth-century Luba leader Chibinda Ilunga as an icon of armed, entrepreneurial warriorhood. Chokwe craftsmen carved potent representations of Chibinda Ilunga in a period of great social and political flux, depicting him as determined and ferocious and equipped with a musket.[24] The development of an invigorated form of historical consciousness—contributing, ultimately, to a wider sense of belonging— is likewise evident among the Yoruba, emerging first in fractured fashion from the ashes of the collapsed Oyo state, and becoming consolidated by the 1890s. The limitations on our 'real time' perspective is an issue here, exemplifying a broader challenge: among the Yoruba, the weight of evidence for shifting African historical thought is concentrated at the end of the nineteenth century and in the early years of the twentieth.[25] Yet glimpses into historical consciousness in an earlier period are possible, not least in the emergence of orally transmitted histories and lineages linking the development of kingship (both in Oyo and across the wider cultural area) to the town of Ife.[26] At the same time, the centralisation of the Oyo state provided the kind of impetus to cultural expression which would lead in time to literary Yoruba, employed in the expression of historical vision.[27] Contemporary European accounts clearly refer to a distinct if rough-hewn nationhood in the area: the 'Youriba' of Clapperton's narrative, for example.[28] Hard political realities and skill in cultural and material production were met in the person of Ogun, god of both iron and war, and across the region an eclectic but intimately interconnected community of followers included wood-carvers, blacksmiths and professional soldiers.[29] Certainly, by century's end, a robust sense of historical group identity had come into being. Here, foreign influence was a powerful factor, in the form of missionary work and, more specifically, through the spread of Yoruba in translating the Bible into a local vernacular.[30] By the time Samuel Johnson produced his opus on the history of 'his people', completed in 1897, though only published for the first time in 1921, he felt able to frame 'the Yorubas' as a distinct community with shared cultural values, language and historical experience.[31] The violent turmoil of the nineteenth century could thus be interpreted, at least in hindsight, as a civil war; a turbulent aberration in the shared history of a formerly, and subsequently, united people. In the same period, Carl Christian Reindorf, a Ga cleric in the Gold Coast, sought to make sense of the turbulent era which had constituted his own lifetime by writing an interconnected history of the region, again drawing extensively on oral histories and, like Johnson, on his own experiences.[32] Johnson and Reindorf were both products and chroniclers of the West African variant of the nineteenth-century revolution, and the histories they wrote were very much part of that transformation.

History and its management were an intrinsic element of life itself in the lacustrine zone, too. In Buganda, it can be reasonably assumed that historical narratives and tropes, woven around mythical founder Kintu and other characters emblematic of long-term processes, were being busily developed in the course of the seventeenth and eighteenth centuries. Ideas about the significance of deeper temporality had been evolving over several centuries, and certainly since the era of the major northern migrations in the first half of the second millennium CE.[33] Kintu was the incarnation of several waves of such migration and was a temporal vehicle shared by a number of societies around the northern shore of Lake Victoria. There were others, too: Mukama, among the Soga chieftaincies, and in the west of Uganda, the burnishing of the mythology around the Chwezi, who morphed from short-lived political dynasty to deeply influential pantheon of deities, a spiritual network across a wide area.[34] Interpretations of these histories were critical in the formation of state and society in the region. In the course of the nineteenth century, control of the past was attended by a new urgency in the era of rapidly intensifying global exchange. Early nineteenth-century political and military reforms involved contestation over local histories, as locales and lineages competed over access to the centre as well as asserting themselves in the face of the centre.[35] In the 1860s and 1870s, there were apparently debates over lists of kings, in terms of both sequence and the relative importance of particular figures.[36] The story told to Stanley in 1875 about how an eighteenth-century *kabaka*, Mawanda, met with the ghostly vision of supposed founding father Kintu—who hadn't even appeared in the kinglist given to Speke in 1862—almost certainly reflected internal debates about the very provenance and nature of royal authority and the culture of violence which was by now seen to have infiltrated the polity.[37] The articulation of a rich cast of historical characters spoke to a sharpening sense of historical identity between the mid-nineteenth and early twentieth centuries, as the kingdom, and more specifically competing factions at its core, undergoing internal stresses and strains and confronted with a rapidly shifting external environment, experimented with particular visions of political authority and its historic role in the region. Taking advantage of this opportunity was Apolo Kagwa—Anglican convert, survivor of Buganda's political turmoil and civil war, and from 1890 chief minister of the kingdom—who worked closely with the small but energetic group of British administrators in the creation of the new political order in the 1890s and 1900s. As a core part of his political work, he wrote history: his *Basekabaka be Buganda*, 'The Kings of Buganda', which he first produced on his own printing press in 1901, was biblical in style and structure—a reflection of Kagwa's close reading of the main text in his life up to that point—and was aimed at the presentation of a particular version of the kingdom's past, drawing on oral histories. Buganda, in short, was the dominant power in the region, with a rich history of military glory (and some overcoming of disastrous defeats); its internal history offered much in the way of trial and tribulation, but wayward rulers might be held to account through the continual refinement of the kingdom's political systems and processes. Ultimately, Kagwa produced a rich resource, but more importantly for his purposes, this was an exercise in the assertion of authority against rivals and an attempt to create enduring biblical truth at the centre of a state in flux.[38]

Newly animated engagements with the past were clearly critical among longer-established polities, but they were no less important, and arguably even more so, in some ways, in insurgent and novel political and military orders. We have already noted the significance of a temporal imaginary to Mirambo. Elsewhere, insurgents and disrupters developed compelling historical visions, and swiftly created corpuses of performance art, poetry and oral literature to both reinforce and provide impetus to new political and cultural projects. A vivid process of historical thought is demonstrable among the Ngoni-speaking communities of southern Africa in the early nineteenth century, culminating in the rise of the Zulu state under Shaka. The Zulu revolution initiated, or certainly enhanced, existing patterns of historical poetic form and cultures of political remembrance: in the decades following Shaka's assassination, and especially as the external environment grew ever more menacing for the Zulu polity, history was crucial to the provision of moral and political ballast, and in the creation of tropes and exemplification of heroism for wider consumption.[39] In the midst of the Zulu revolution, moreover, women were critical—in more than one sense of the word—in the provision of sociopolitical commentary, and were among the most important producers of praise poetry and of the historical record.[40] In West Africa, in the case of the Hausa-Fulani political and religious order established in the wake of jihad, there was a concerted effort from the 1810s onward to reach into the deeper past to demonstrate a logical spiritual linear progression, culminating in the righteous struggle to re-establish true Islam in the region. The appearance of the Sokoto Caliphate followed jihadist violence, but this was an empire of scholarship as well as swords: the two, indeed, were scarcely divisible. What emerged was a new Islamic order built on literary histories which reached into the past for legitimacy and to reinforce a sense of inexorability.[41] Women were among the most prominent intellectuals, moreover, providing elegies on the virtues of departed leaders and offering critical moral and social commentaries for the consumption of the living.[42] On the other side of the continent, another polity which was in large part a reformist theocracy likewise sought consolidation through the mobilisation of the past: the Tigrayan emperor Yohannes IV, seeking to reconstruct the state in the wake of the insurgent Tewodros's implosion, sculpted neo-Solomonism out of material similar to that used by his predecessor, projecting the notion of an ancient imperium, as described in the *Kebra Negast*, beset by enemies, especially Muslim ones. He drove home the point in letters written to European monarchs; and, in search of internal stability, he reinstated Axum as the site of the royal coronation, self-consciously seeking to recreate the ancient empire of the fevered late nineteenth-century *habesha* imagination.[43]

The multi-faceted Christian mission across the continent represents an explicit process of global engagement being co-opted in the development of history, identity and culture. The translation of biblical text into the vernacular, and the work undertaken by missionaries to record oral histories and classify social behaviour and law, contributed to the solidification of collective identities and the adaptation of local epistemes and dynamics of belonging to evolving circumstances—as had happened throughout the nineteenth century. The literacy acquired through rudimentary mission education was an opportunity for cultural and political entrepreneurs and elites. In some ways paralleling similar developments in Europe itself,[44] historical identities were also forged explicitly through the local interpretation of newfound faith.[45] In these ways, the nineteenth century was reinterpreted and redesigned by elites and liminal communities alike, the moment of 'The Scramble' becoming the latest stage in a long sequence of reformations and opportunisms. Missionaries were, for the most part, inadvertent agents, though for sure they had their own local agendas and saw the advantage in seeking to bolster, even manipulate, central authority in the transmission of the Gospel. Africans were the primary cultural and spiritual agents in the process, however, supplying knowledge to white interlocutors and in the process recrafting their understanding of that information and repurposing it.[46] In some cases, more consolidated, corporate ethnic, cultural and linguistic communities resulted.[47] It was a vibrant, even chaotic exchange; an effect of nineteenth-century innovation as much as it was an outcome of the singular moment of European intrusion.

It was a dynamic which formed the basis, too, of indirect rule, forming a curious convergence of imagined and reinvented histories. If histories were being produced to meet the moment, the new political order involved the identification—and the self-identification—of historically robust groups capable of governing: Ganda, Yoruba, Fulani, Tutsi, to name but a handful. Europeans needed particular hierarchies, and in particular state-level elites, through whom to administrate. In their turn, particular African communities and their elites drew on nineteenth-century histories of reformism and entrepreneurship to position themselves to do so, another reciprocal co-option which led to the creation of Afro-European political and cultural orders. These combined some inventive uses of the past with a great deal of actual lived experience, and drew both on elements of existing, familiar political orders and on the creative adaptation of a newly presented range of alternatives.[48] Some groups were more successful than others, evidently. Ironically, given that in fact they were the latest incarnation of long-term African political flux and volatility, they sought above all to project legitimacy and permanence. Indirect rule reinforced the notion of tribal antiquity, awarded social meaning in bundles of 'traditions' and 'customs'; indeed, it was dependent on these.[49] Africans, it was argued, would be most content here, protected from the incomprehensible onslaught of modernity which would only serve to daze and confuse. The tribal order, rather, involved the preservation of history, and of the social order and control with which history was associated. It was now embellished with the fineries of European ceremonialism, an exercise in temporal landscape gardening, for elites would be honoured and titled and bemedaled, as and when appropriate.[50] This careful manicure led to some curious (and inaccurate) historical re-creations, as in the attempt in southern Nigeria in 1912 to remake the Oyo empire in its supposed eighteenth-century form, complete with *alafin* and royal court. Governor Lugard was keen on the initiative, as it would supposedly strengthen the indirect rule system in the area, but it was only possible through the eager involvement of a Yoruba elite who sensed an opportunity for an enhanced status rooted in past greatness, however counterfeit.[51] The Ganda understood their relationship with the British as a partnership, and set about extending their influence across a much wider area than had been the case in the nineteenth century, and particularly at the expense of long-time rival Bunyoro.[52] But this should be seen less in terms of its putative falsity and more in terms of its connection to the reformism and entrepreneurialism of the nineteenth century. The same holds for the other ethnic communities which the British made efforts to identify in other provinces in Uganda.[53] Sometimes, the racial dimensions to the exercise were overt. When the Germans (and later the Belgians) arrived in the area of Rwanda and Burundi, they encouraged a Tutsi elite to think of itself as an ancient aristocracy, with a monarch at the apex, superior in blood and culture to the Hutu farmers who comprised the bulk of the population. In the nineteenth century and earlier, these supposed 'ethnonyms' had largely denoted socioeconomic status. Now, they were infused with a racialised historicity: the Tutsi had arrived in the region from the north in the dim and distant past and brought with them skills in statecraft and warcraft, which they used to bring the Hutu to some kind of order. This was the essence of what would become known as the 'Hamitic myth.'[54] Importantly, the two groups were physically different—Tutsi were tall, Hutu were short, again emphasising the gulf in biological stock—

and Tutsi were cattle-keepers rather than farmers. But this was no one-way imposition; practicably, it could never have been that. The Tutsi had agency, and developed their own historical and physiological narratives, investing in the new order (and in the idea of a singular Tutsi monarchy, which hadn't existed in the nineteenth century), but in ways which made sense in the context of nineteenth-century political contestations and military expansionism.[55] Historical as well as political and religious work (these various categories in fact scarcely being divisible) in the late nineteenth and early twentieth centuries often involved an enlargement of scale, expressed through some of the authors highlighted earlier: Johnson for the Yoruba, for example, or Reindorf for the Akan—the latter a designation which wouldn't have made much sense to the people thus encompassed (Asante, Fante, Akim) in the mid-nineteenth century. In many respects, however, all of this represented the latest stage in an evolving process comprising the consolidation of collective identity, which was well under way in the course of the nineteenth century, and the exclusion and denigration of adjacent Others, equally deep-rooted.

Africans grasped the opportunities on offer, as they always had; Europeans sought bureaucratic and administrative exhibitions, manifesting a particular reading of 'tribal' history. It was an assumed stasis, moreover, which was reflected in the preservation and presentation of African material culture at home. Museum collections, booming in this period, portrayed a curious freeze-frame of the continent behind glass, a kind of taxidermy of humanity—at the very moment, ironically, of that continent's greatest flux.[56] Offering security to the colonial order, meanwhile, were African colonial soldiers, the direct corollary, as we have seen, of a revolutionary epoch. But while many European officers believed that an indigenous barbarism had propelled their *askari* into service, the latter would now be detached from that reprehensible history through their entry into civilised service and their acquisition of the dress, the conventions and the rituals of European military 'tradition'. These were warriors whose association with civilised modernity now permitted them to play a modest role in the grand pageant of European history. It was a stunning conceit that their own dynamic, explosive inheritance could be condemned and disavowed in this fashion: it would soon prove a fallacy.

In majority-Muslim territories, clerics and intellectuals endeavoured to draw on deep histories of reform to navigate the turbulent era of European expansion and to make sense of it as Muslims. This frequently involved a fusion of theology and history. The Salafiyya notably, were constructively atavistic insofar as they posited a vision of Islam which was rooted in the Qur'an and the Sunna, and in the righteous behaviour exhibited by eminent ancestors; but they also sought to engage with European ideas about the nation-state, for example, and eschewed blind adherence to 'tradition' at the expense of reason and science—which, in any case, were an intrinsic part of the Islamic heritage. Egypt was at the centre of these evolving debates in the late nineteenth and early twentieth centuries. For example, Jamal al-Din al-Afghani, a prominent member of the Egyptian Salafiyya, argued that it was perfectly possible to maintain the integrity of Islam and uphold the Faith as laid out by the Prophet while also embracing aspects of 'modernity': therein lay the future, he argued, for successful, independent Muslim states.[57] These deliberations intensified in the years following the defeat and exile of Urabi, and the assertion of British power in Egypt created a greater sense of urgency. Ethiopia, by apparent contrast, was triumphant after Adwa. Here, Menelik turned his back, at least partially, on the historic north—his Tigrayan predecessor's centre of gravity—and his and the Empress Taitu's establishment of a more southerly capital at Addis Ababa placed the seal on a new era of southern and eastern expansion as the new nation spread out into areas never historically part of Solomonic territory.[58] As the empire took shape, it attracted diplomatic endorsement and foreign investment; by the time Menelik died in 1913, electric light flickered gingerly across Addis Ababa. The Amhara fashioned an Ethiopian modernity in the early 1900s in keeping with a new national identity among the political class; a class which perceived, indeed which contributed to the creation of, a world in which they could assert the historicity of their political and cultural claims.[59] Nonetheless, the smoke of victorious battle had barely cleared before a new group of intellectuals and technocrats began to worry that the triumph at Adwa had been a lost opportunity, or even a curse; they fretted that Ethiopia remained rooted in some feudal past, and that the fruits of 'modernity' remained beyond their grasp. For some, at least, this compelled a very different interpretation of the turbulent nineteenth century: for what had those wars and contestations meant, after all? The wrangling over the past would only escalate in the decades ahead, a contest fought, broadly, between adherents of the 'Great Tradition'—a belief in the inexorability and superiority of Solomonic, *habesha* civilisation—and those with less faith in Ethiopia's assumed historic greatness, and its spiritual trajectory.[60]

The evidence, by the beginning of the early twentieth century, points toward variegated and multi-layered uses of time and the past in the formation of state and society, and in the meeting of new challenges, throughout the long nineteenth century. History attended political innovation and traumatic change, or was deployed to argue for the importance of stasis and continuity. History mattered, and time was critical, in the organisation of societal relations, in the legitimisation of political power and in the measurement of self-worth, both individual and collective.

## History and the *mzungu*

GEORG HEGEL SAID IT BEST, it seems. Africa, he declared in 1822, "is no historical part of the World; it has no movement or development to exhibit." Moreover, "Africa proper, as far as History goes back, has remained— for all purposes of connection with the rest of the World—shut up; it is [. . .] the land of childhood, which lying beyond the day of self-conscious history, is enveloped in the dark mantle of Night."[61] Exactly a century later, Frederick, Lord Lugard, offered a variation on the theme:

> As Roman imperialism laid the foundation of modern civilisation, and led the wild barbarians of these islands along the path of progress, so in Africa to-day we are repaying the debt and bringing to the dark places of the earth, the abode of barbarism and cruelty, the torch of culture and progress, while ministering to the material needs of our own civilisation.[62]

It was an act which fused self-interest and generosity of spirit. Above all it was the colonial-era articulation of the Hegelian vision: a continent hanging timeless and bloodied below Europe, beyond the normal ebb and flow of human endeavour. In fact, of course, quite a few European writers along the way had been very interested in Africa's past, in spite of its supposed sluggish historicity: from Archibald Dalzel's somewhat partisan 'reconstruction' of Dahomey's violent past (an elucidation of the importance of African agency if ever there was one), to James Bruce's grand and granular history of Ethiopia; from Speke's vision of the 'Hamitic' infusion in lacustrine East Africa, which supposedly created a semblance of civilisation, to Stanley's colourful romp through the history of Buganda.[63] To a degree, it was important for those gentlemen to present themselves as encountering momentous historical events and personalities, hitherto concealed from the world's gaze. In some ways, they represent the first drafts of European writing on African history; we foreign scholars come from ignominious stock. Still, by the end of the century, these histories had become markedly less important, and the continent's past had been excised from its new dawn; hence Lugard's channelling of the great German philosopher.

As Lugard explicitly indicated, moreover, much of this unfolded alongside an intensifying sense of Europe's own historical trajectory, and it is doubtless no coincidence that the establishment of History as a professional academic endeavour—a process of which Hegel himself was part, and rooted as it was in the rise of the nation-state[64]—had, in parallel, deleterious consequences for the histories of those 'dark places of the earth'. The developmental and presentist vision of Africa was intimately linked in the British context, for example, to the Victorian and Edwardian visions of Britain's own historical development. Lugard's vision was a triumphalist one; but triumphalism was not universal. The European search for historical meaning in the late nineteenth century was also intertwined with a creeping pessimism, anxieties about an increasingly threatening world, the fear of inevitable decline. Africa, enveloped in the dark mantle of Night, reassured Europeans of their own place in a dangerous world.[65] We can trace this history in literary output, from Shelley's 'Ozymandias', through Arnold's 'Dover Beach', to Kipling's 'Recessional': the latter produced during the peak of imperial pomp, and yet replete with inflections of grim temporality, of rise and inevitable fall.[66]

The re-historicising (and, in many cases, the de-historicising) of Africa took place in the context of the campaign against the slave trade, the first great global exercise in objectifying humanitarianism. The outcome of this was a hollowing out of the African past, and the imposition of various tropes and characteristics on African culture and society—the European invention of a kind of antithesis in an age of political and economic turbulence in Europe itself. Narratives were developed in Europe, representing the emergence of an epistemological dominance, which portrayed 'instability' as an abnormal, primitive, Hobbesian state of affairs;[67] and, more specifically, *African* instability as peculiarly dreadful. The anti-slave trade movement, led by people like Granville Sharp and William Wilberforce in Britain and Jacques Pierre Brissot in France, as well as prominent members of the African diaspora such as Olaudah Equiano, was unquestionably motivated by a sincere humanism, the corollary of Enlightenment thought.[68] But at the core of its vision was a benighted, beleaguered continent, whose only hope for salvation lay in benevolent intervention from outside. The stated aim of the African Association, indeed, was the delivery of this very salvation, based on a narrow, culturally specific interpretation of material wealth and associated 'progress'.[69] It was a vision which continues to define the relationship between Africa and the Global North to the present day. Above all, it was a process which involved the excision of Africa from civilised History. In parallel to this temporal marginalisation was the framing of the continent in terms of wild, undiscovered nature, revealed to the world by several generations of explorers. Its dramatic mountains, mighty rivers, and pounding waterfalls accentuated the ahistoricity of the people who lived amidst nature, and in the plethora of exploration literature they were often little more than murky accessories to the wildness. As a literary genre, this work was crucial to the flattening of the continent's past, even by those who, as we noted, were evidently quite interested in writing about the histories of the societies through which they passed, and in popularising certain ideas about the continent's brutal, bloody, licentious 'condition'. Time and place, again, were ineluctably enmeshed.

The development of a core set of ideas around the supposed African proclivity for mindless internecine violence, with both tragic victims and evil perpetrators, was a fundamental component of the European articulation of an African past. In particular, the notion took root that African polities and cultures were inherently flawed and rooted in a brutal disregard for human life. Hence the discourse constructed around Dahomey, for example—heavily influenced by missionary reportage—which was centred on the idea of the kingdom's savage bloodlust; likewise Asante, which was framed in terms of a destabilising barbarism, its history the singular story of self-aggrandising rapacity, and its ultimate destruction a matter of both necessity and salvation. Ritualistic and cyclic violence, lacking any of the grander motivations and aims of 'civilised' war in Europe, had long prevented any sense of meaningful 'development' or 'progress' in Africa.[70] Largely pointless internecine conflict ('civil war', in a more enlightened environment) was not an unfortunate exception, but the general rule. This alone justified armed intervention; but European writers also doubtless had an eye on their own national histories as they imposed temporal narratives on Africans, and thus imagined the latter as trapped at a particular moment in civilisational history. In some respects, then, the greatest sleight of hand on the part of European narrators, both at the time and subsequently, was the depiction of Africa as a vale of barbarity, a perennially brutalised and violently contorted set of cultures and societies, its internecine conflicts juxtaposed alongside, and thus justifying, the righteous violence of the civilising mission.[71] Alongside the notion of interminable and futile conflict was the vision of a diseased and famine-ridden environment, its inhabitants again crying out for intervention and salvation. European science was contrasted with the superstitious ignorance of Africans; the prevalence of smallpox, cholera, malaria and other diseases which had been brought under control in temperate Europe was seemingly evidence of the relationship between disease and development and suggested that Africans inhabited a strange medievality. Western medical knowledge could thus be applied to this vast tropical laboratory, objectifying Africans and controlling their bodies, rescuing them from their primordial physiological despond.[72] The frequency of famine, moreover—the result not only of native ignorance, but also of laziness—formed part of an oppressive backwardness which necessitated outside intervention. For Kipling, famously, the 'white man's burden' involved not only the waging of those "savage wars of peace"; it was also about the need to "Fill full the mouth of Famine / And bid the sickness cease."[73]

Racism was clearly critical to these lines of thought, for the deliberate diminution of Africans' humanity legitimated the killing and the destruction,[74] while also rendering the European intervention in Africa a matter of moral, humanitarian duty. The origins of European racism and its manifestation across the globe is the subject of a rich historiography, with some disagreement about when it started and why it developed in the ways it did—though there can be little doubt that blackness, for example, became synonymous with servitude with the escalation of the Atlantic slave trade.[75] In the course of the nineteenth century, racial thinking mutated but ultimately hardened into a corpus of thought about the personalities and cultures of black and brown people, and Africans were identified as possessing a particularly marked level of inferiority.[76] In the mid-eighteenth century, Jean-Jacques Rousseau, like Michel de Montaigne two centuries earlier, believed he discerned an admirably pristine state of innocence in supposedly 'savage' societies. He, famously, developed the notion of the 'noble savage' at one with Nature, a pure and dignified state disturbed only by the encroachment of so-called civilisation and, in particular, of ideas about wealth.[77] (We cannot know if our Captain Hore had read his Rousseau, but he was certainly channelling him on the road in the late nineteenth century.) Be that as it may, there was a marked if gradual shift from the notion of the African's capacity for redemption, encapsulated in the work and activism of everyone from Wilberforce and Brissot to Buxton and Faidherbe, to the conviction that no such improvement was possible, at least not without some vigorous intervention. The African character was flawed, and inclined toward depravity if left unsupervised.[78] There was a debate about whether this was by divine design or the result of environmental accident. According to the monogenetic position, which posited a common descent for all humans—and thus adhered to scriptural orthodoxy—differences between Europeans and Africans could be explained by environmental factors. The former were characterised by superior physical and mental capacity, and thus the products of elevated social and cultural environments, while the latter had been burdened by less favourable attributes and inhabited landscapes which fostered degeneracy; though their lot *might* be improved through careful nurture of their inherently debased natures. Polygenism, on the other hand, suggested that this failed to explain stark differences between the 'races' of the earth, which only made sense if various 'races' were understood as having evolved separately, with no common descent. It was therefore imperative that different races be kept apart: miscegenation was the root of genetic weakness.[79] Explicitly, Africa's lack of progress, indeed lack of meaningful *history*, was a matter of its racial composition; the absence of an elevated cultural production and civilisational achievement—as defined, of course, in Europe—reflected Africa's racial degradation. Again, ideas about place and time intersected. Africans were the children of humanity: at best, mere mimics of superior culture and behaviour, as Burton opined in a coastal West African context;[80] and Darwin's work was interpreted as demonstrating that some human communities were at a lower stage of evolutionary development than others. New science bolstered the hardening racism which was as much the product of social, religious and historical thought as it was of biology.[81] It was also the outcome of necessity: expanding empires and the social mobility open to a 'native' elite which was Christian, educated to a relatively advanced level, and in various ways 'Europeanised' necessitated rigidified racial boundaries in order to maintain social, cultural and political distance between governed and governing. In that sense 'race' was a deliberate construct, not simply an instinctive recoil at the sight of the Other, as had been suggested by Montaigne at the dawn of the Atlantic era. Whether confected or intuitive, however, notions about race fixed Africans firmly both in place and in time.

Race also, as we have observed, justified killing. There could be no negotiating with the barbarous; any improvement of Africans' position on the evolutionary spectrum required some rough treatment—unfortunate, perhaps, but necessary. The evident violence of empire-making produced a despairing backlash closer to home, for not everyone accepted the paradoxes and tensions embedded within the imperial imaginary. Do not sit comfortably at home, arch-imperialist Joseph Chamberlain berated his critics in a noted 1897 speech, and condemn the methods by which British civilisation has been carried to the heathen hordes; do not defend obvious tyrants just because they're black; do not whinge squeamishly about the fulfilment of Britain's imperial destiny.[82] French observers believed *les anglais* had been driven insane by ambition.[83] Critics of the new imperialism espied the projection of internal tensions outward, and the displacement of ideas about violent dysfunction onto the non-Western world. J. A. Hobson suggested as much in 1902; a number of Marxist writers followed suit, drawing on a novel corpus of political thought which was the outcome of Europe's own nineteenth-century trauma, and offering their own distinctive interpretation of the science of human history.[84] The depiction of the African past in a particularly gloomy hue, it was implied, was a feature of a capitalist order intent on ruthless extraction, but which contained the seeds of its own destruction. There were very few doubts that Africans were indeed primitive and somehow inferior, even among the more radical opponents of empire (though Hobson reserved most of his racist ire for the Jews); but they believed, fundamentally, that capitalism fed off the oppression of the European masses as much as it did hapless colonial subjects. Across the political spectrum, there were at least some who worried that vainglorious visions of a destiny rooted in a misreading of the past, pursued using reckless violence, risked the ruin of the very civilisation its advocates sought to promote.[85]

## The African Past and Its Malcontents

AS THE TWENTIETH CENTURY DREW ON, Africans in various realms of life wrestled with the meanings of the nineteenth century and with what the European 'Scramble' had represented. In the 1890s and 1900s, the experience of 'The Scramble' in real time was frequently indivisible from the turbulent, transformative events of recent decades. But in the course of that trauma, in the thickets of colonial experience, and above all in the nationalist imaginaries of the mid-twentieth century, the earlier period—the creativity and accomplishment as well as the violence—was often either misconstrued or became the subject of benign neglect.

Throughout the colonial period, of course, historical work continued to be produced with a focus on the pre-partition past, whether to preserve or cement local identities in a competitive (indeed threatening) political landscape, or in the attempt to ensure that such histories wouldn't be forgotten by younger generations.[86] Jacob Egharevba in Benin and John Nyakatura in Bunyoro are important examples from the 1930s and 1940s respectively.[87] In Buganda, history wars were fought in the 1920s and 1930s between clan historians eager to lay claim to Kintu, the kingdom's legendary founder, and to discredit the long-dominant Kagwa; history was also used by an older generation to lament the rapidly changing times, to portray an idealised vision of 'precolonial' life, and to criticise young people for their apparent desperation to dress and act like the *mzungu*.[88] The partition was the central pivot around which much of this history was written, explicitly or otherwise, and it became the temporal landmark, the supreme rupture, which increasingly impermeably demarcated the boundary between the old and the modern. A younger generation, meanwhile, grew increasingly sceptical about the indirect rule chiefs who seemed, often, to have more in common with European administrators than with their own people, and who came be to seen in many places as curious anachronisms, emblematic of a long-defunct past as well as of unsavoury deals with Europeans. Political activists and nationalists, by the 1930s and 1940s, had no qualms about mobilising nineteenth-century memories and identities at the local level in pursuit of grassroots political support; but they operated now within the parameters of colonial territories, the boundaries of future nations, and so, again, 'The Scramble' was, tacitly or overtly, the historic point of reference. As a consequence, the nineteenth century was by and large dispatched into a historical pre-dawn, with little utility beyond the evocation of a handful of heroic figures. Further afield, the diasporic activism of the Pan-African movement was rooted in the shared historical experiences of systemic racism, enslavement and European conquest, and again *resistance* to an oppressive global order was core to the achievement of collective as well as individual identity.[89] There were, of course, sound reasons for this—as there were for the philosophical meditations behind *négritude* in Francophone Africa, celebrating the essences of blackness and *Africanité*. It did come, however, at the expense of a more granular focus on the dynamics characterising Africa's own long nineteenth century and the agency involved therein.

For the late colonial and early postcolonial generation of writers, these were challenging issues, naturally enough. Achebe wrote about European conquest on the eve of Nigerian independence in terms of rupture, using Okonkwo's self-destruction in *Things Fall Apart* as the final act in a traumatic transition from one order—something precolonial—to another. There is a sense of loss and defeat in the climax. But in Ayi Kwei Armah's first few novels,[90] the pre-partition past is framed in rather more ambivalent terms. He discerned continuity between the deeper history of slaving chiefs and contemporary African elites, and suggested that Africa's present had been polluted by the lingering legacies of this nefarious past. In that landscape, the notion of a colonial rupture is rather less in evidence. In a slightly later novel, however, a more pristine conceptualisation of the 'precolonial' past appears in the form of 'Way', the essence of Africa's true self, representing the egalitarianism and communalism which have been betrayed by a sequence of corrupt and venal political local elites from the era of the slave trade to the postcolony.[91] In this context, temporal rupture is rather more prominent, though it is worth noting that Armah's time-frame is an elongated one. The seemingly irresolvable contest between the 'traditional'—a proxy for 'pre-partition' Africa—and the 'modern' was a theme explicitly explored in the work of Ugandan writer and scholar Okot p'Bitek, particularly in *Song of Lawino* (1966) and *Song of Ocol* (1967), extended poems which were written to be performed in the Luo language. In the first, Lawino, a wronged wife, berates her husband for rejecting his traditional culture and embracing *mzungu* dress, speech and mannerisms, and in particular for having gone off with a woman who is 'Westernised'. Ocol replies in the second 'song', disdaining both his wife and his culture for its cloying backwardness.[92] The Malian writer Yambo Ouologuem, however, had little time for romantic delusions about the deeper past. In one of his most celebrated novels, the fictional Sahelian kingdom of Nakem, violently and cruelly governed by the Saif dynasty over several centuries, is used to illustrate deep-rooted indigenous patterns of brutality and barbarity into which colonial administrators are co-opted. Narratively, 'The Scramble' and subsequent colonial 'moment' allows the book's horrendous protagonist Saif ben Isaac al-Heit to demonstrate his sanguinary Machiavellianism—and in that sense he serves as a rather unpleasant anticolonial antihero, manipulating (and occasionally murdering) colonial officials as much as he does his own people.[93]

In the same period, an Africanist historiographical resurgence in the 1950s and 1960s was largely focused on the 'precolonial', which was very much mainstream to the early professional Africanist academy. In some respects this was because the deeper past, and especially the nineteenth century, was seen as central to the nation-building exercises then under way; indeed the research undertaken by many historians in that generation, both African and expatriate, was overtly or implicitly linked to the emergence of new nations in the wake of decolonisation.[94] The endeavours of history departments across the continent amounted to the quest for a 'usable past'.[95] It's also worth remembering that colonial archives had not yet opened, the booming extractive industry which would develop around them still a thing of the future, and so African history *was* precolonial history. Some of the richest and most seminal work on the nineteenth century was done during this period; a lot of it has been cited in the earlier sections of this book. But it also reified the rupture represented by 'The Scramble', as the tendency in this particular genre of historical writing was to end 'c. 1900'. There was also a certain tension vis-à-vis the nation-building projects under the auspices of which much this scholarship was undertaken, for in searching for usable national heroes and meaningful processes of change it tended to breathe new life into *subnational* histories—giving rise to the spectre of 'tribalism', much-examined in this period;[96] and, as the Mozambican leader Samora Machel's famously pronounced, "For the nation to live, the tribe must die."[97]

Increasingly, Europe's supposedly brutally efficient, conquering violence in the late nineteenth and early twentieth centuries was placed in melancholic juxtaposition to Africa's violent contortions in the decades before that defining moment. The transformative nineteenth century had become somewhat indistinct, engulfed in fog, as an idea as well as a distinctive, seminal epoch: rather than the key actors being understood in their own right during an era of revolutionary change, they were increasingly seen as the exemplars of failed indigenous modernisation, or as emblematic of a violent instability which seemed to foreshadow the continent's turbulent present. African political leaders eyed the era with suspicion, and were at best selective about the putative purity of 'precolonial' culture, and at worst beheld it anxiously, seeing in it only tribalistic barbarity, or political machinations which were ill-suited to nationalist projects. For some, it was a time of darkness before the dawn of religious salvation. There was discomfort with the amount of violence which appeared to have preceded the 'colonial era', and a conviction that this could hardly be harnessed in the building of nations. In some striking respects, therefore, there was a curious convergence of modern African historical thought and the racialised histories which underpinned European imperialism in the first place, for the former too incorporated a version of Dark Continent mythology and associated imagery. In some respects, the historical academy—after its embrace of the deeper past in the period of decolonisation and early postcoloniality—was complicit in this, with scholarly work gravitating toward the twentieth century, with the nineteenth century becoming an anteroom, a prolonged moment of violent experimentalism infused with flashes of modernising energy which were ultimately subsumed within the global imperialism emanating from Europe.[98] This was ironic, given that, as we have noted, the long nineteenth century itself witnessed a remarkable transformation in historical consciousness about the deeper past. Nonetheless, developmental agendas, embraced by an array of African governments as well as their external partners, were underpinned by an ahistorical concept of 'modernisation', in which history was hollowed out and flattened. This led to the erosion of both capacity and confidence among professional historians within the continent, but also, simultaneously, the rise of emotional appeals to versions of the past at the local level. These appeals invariably involved the mobilisation of subnational identities which were hostile to developmental statehood.

The figure of Mirambo is illustrative. Some seventy years and more after his death, he had his moment in the sun in the 1950s and 1960s, when African history was 'rediscovered' in parallel with the emergence of nationalist movements and, ultimately, new nation-states. The Tanganyika Africa National Union adapted one of his war songs as a rallying anthem, and he had a street named after him in Dar es Salaam.[99] But he came to be regarded as an anachronism, a chilling echo of the tribalistic savagery beginning to thwart Africa's postcolonial ambition, and inimical to Nyerere's visions of national development—and certainly ill-suited to the bucolic environment described by Nyerere in his articulation of African socialism as a historical phenomenon.[100] There was little room in there for Mirambo, or indeed Msabila and his bush war. His grave was neglected and there was a marked a degree of local hostility to the memory of the man, who was, some said, "only a robber leader who attacked people on the roads and in the bush".[101] Still, at least Mirambo was only the victim of abandonment. In Uganda under Milton Obote, a rather bloodier project to defend the unitary nation from the anachronistic forces of nineteenth-century violence and division ended with the constitutional abolition of the major kingdoms, including Buganda, and the dispatch of the shell-shocked *kabaka* and his entourage into exile.[102]

For Africans in the second half of the twentieth century, violent instability in the nineteenth century was hugely problematic.[103] Some analysts might detect, in the 1970s, long-term continuities in the resurgence of a militarised African political culture;[104] but the nineteenth century itself was framed by an increasingly presentist vision of the continent which foreshortened the continent's historical trajectory, and within which much of the continent's past was conceived of as being largely irrelevant, or (somewhat paradoxically) downright dangerous. Valiant and dignified rebelliousness against foreign predation and invasion made for more efficacious political material than the messiness and turbulence of the nineteenth century; courage in the face of a simplified, monolithic, exogenous hegemony was the stuff from which modern nations might be carved. Thus 'agency'—a term often utilised, but only selectively so—was post-dated to the point of 'The Scramble', bolstering the narrative around abrupt conquest, and was in the main associated with 'resistance', which became the leitmotif of political (and much academic) discourse. In this way, Africa's globally engaged nineteenth-century transformation was lost in transition.[105] Nationalist movements, and the governments which frequently emerged from them, used, rather, the era of European conquest and 'The Scramble' as their historical benchmark, ossifying and indeed reifying that episode as a seismic temporal rupture. In some cases a more or less direct link was posited between modern nationalisms and anticolonial rebellions in the late nineteenth and early twentieth centuries.[106] The most dramatic manifestation of this was the decision by the Organisation of African Unity in 1963 to ratify the territorial demarcation which had taken place in the late nineteenth century, an explicit acceptance of the narrative that European reordering of the political landscape had created modern Africa, even at the moment of supposed decolonisation.[107] It was an act of diplomatic statecraft which in essence dispatched the revolutionary nineteenth century into a murky historical hinterland, consigning that remarkable era to, if not quite oblivion, then certainly a problematic temporality. It is difficult to criticise the decision on pragmatic grounds, in many respects: the alternative, it was argued, would be political chaos. Perhaps there is an interesting counterfactual debate to be had on that point. Either way, it was a concession of epic proportions, petrifying the notion that what had preceded 'The Scramble' was unusable; while also, ironically, perpetuating that era's more destructive aspects, with these now unfolding within the novel constraints of Western-style sovereign nationhood: the 'black man's burden', as one commentator famously had it.[108] Far from 1963 constituting some Westphalian moment, it represented a judgment on the part of Africa's new governing elites that the revolutionary momentum of Africa's global nineteenth century had had nothing to do with the European partition itself, or with 'modernity', and that its reformist, insurgent, innovative forces were ultimately inimical to Africa's 'development'.

For some, there is unease at the tendency to equate coloniality with modernity, and, in the context of now ubiquitous decolonising agendas, a concern that 'coloniality' itself is often somewhat simplistically conceived, and made so central to the debate.[109] But the reality is that the heroics involved in resisting nefarious global forces were easier to commemorate than anything more nuanced or complicated. It is striking that this should be so. Political instability was not the outcome of Africans' failure to embrace postcolonial modernity, but was rather emblematic of their embrace of global dynamics and of their efforts to reform polity, society and economy across a much longer timespan. Indeed those earlier endeavours might have offered models—illustrations of what succeeded and what failed—to nationalist elites in the era of decolonisation, who could have drawn more vigorously from the revolutionary nineteenth century for inspiration but who decided, ultimately, against such an exercise in historicisation.[110] The insurgent, unstable nature of those politics was soon regarded as unhelpful as new elites sought to consolidate the artifice of new nation-states, the harbingers of a supposed age of the de-/post-colonial. And it is indeed the case that the nuances and complexities of late nineteenth-century political turbulence at the local level were often genuinely inimical to nationalist projects.[111] A consequence of this has been that much twentieth-century African political thought, with some notable exceptions—for example, the idea of Afro-socialism, or Islamic thought—has flowed out of 'The Scramble', forming a new intellectual 'tradition' which generally eschews the deeper past and which has implicitly or otherwise positioned the partition as seminal, the key rupture in both space and time.[112]

And so, in 1989, President Yoweri Museveni, having only recently fought his way to power in Uganda after a bloody war at the head of the National Resistance Movement (NRM), could declare in a speech that "[b]efore colonial rule, we had backward tribal states here. If anyone tries to glamorise them, he is telling you a lie."[113] There was nothing to see in the nineteenth century except bloody mayhem and tribalism: 'The Scramble', by clear implication, was the beginning of Africa's mutation into something different, and to hanker after the past was only to champion backwardness and sectarianism. Many of Museveni's compatriots saw things rather differently, of course, and have come to mobilise ideas about the 'precolonial' past in order to subtly (and sometimes not so subtly) resist what is seen as an increasingly brutal, distant, putatively 'modernising' state.[114] At the same time, however, the era of European invasion itself did offer up some usable national heroes—which is why the NRM named two of its units after Kabalega and Mwanga, "noted Ugandan opponents of British imperialism".[115] How those two rulers sat in the context of Museveni's "backward tribal states" is a little less clear; but no matter. It was sufficient that they had been propelled, elevated, into the realm of heroic resistance on coming into contact with foreign invasion.[116]

Museveni and the NRM were part of a wave of reformist insurgencies between the 1960s and the 1990s, when armed liberation fronts saw themselves as instigators of revolutions which were motivated by ideas of social justice and political rebirth. In that sense, akin to the framing of upheavals in Europe and North America in the late eighteenth century, there was an implicit or explicit eschewal of the insurgencies and internal contestations of the deeper past as backward and pointlessly cyclical, contrasting these new 'modern' movements with those which had singularly failed in the 'precolonial' era.[117] No doubt, the latter had their inspirations to offer in this new ideological landscape. In South Africa, Shaka was episodically repurposed in the prolonged struggle to assert Black rights to land and sovereignty, and as a potent symbol of power in the face of one of the most brutal and overtly racial regimes on the planet. Particular ideas about 'Zuluness' or 'Zuluism' might only have truly crystallised in the early years of the twentieth century, but several cohorts of political activists, including Nelson Mandela and the ANC, subsequently drew on its nineteenth-century antecedents—and, for sure, there was plenty of usable material there—in crafting militant responses to the chronic material and political inequity enshrined in apartheid.[118] After the collapse of apartheid, there were also intense public debates about the Mfecane, and around the attendant issues of power, race and land, as scholars and politicians alike reached for a new national history based on a revised consensus.[119] Mobutu Sese Seko renamed Congo 'Zaire' and pursued what was rather sinisterly termed "a return to authenticity", which in many ways involved the restoration of 'precolonial' culture and political symbolism—although the regime took care to eschew ethnic identifications and sought to marginalise local 'traditional' rulers from the process.[120] The Sudan People's Liberation Movement made occasional forays into the nineteenth century to demonstrate a deeper history of foreign occupation and predation; Eritrean nationalists looked briefly to deeper histories of heroic struggle against Ethiopian aggression.[121] But fundamentally these were territories, and wars, which were framed as the corollaries of 'The Scramble' and the resultant colonial order, and rebels and activists designed their political manifestos accordingly. The nineteenth century offered slim pickings to revolutionary guerrillas in Eritrea. The legal and moral basis of Eritrean nationhood in particular was the fact that it had been an Italian colony, not that it had been a province of Ethiopia (albeit one that was the outcome of Italian failure at Adwa).[122] More broadly, there was a kind of reclamation of 'Dark Continent' mythology on the part of African actors, and a repurposing of the juxtaposition between past and present. Nineteenth-century violence had unfortunate associations, with seemingly endless internecine conflict, and with the notion that Africa was perennially 'troubled'; and although, as we have seen, rupture and rebirth were intrinsic to nineteenth-century African political culture, those insurrectionist endeavours were seen an unusable by a generation of rebels born in the middle decades of the twentieth century whose revolutionary causes could be more carefully, and more straightforwardly, defined in a colonial landscape.[123] When Thabo Mbeki, then deputy president of South Africa, spoke of an 'African renaissance' in the late 1990s, he was drawing on the ideas articulated half a century earlier by the eminent Senegalese scholar Cheikh Anta Diop.[124] The 'renaissance' concept drew inspiration from the idea of a shared past populated by heroes and characterised by the capacity to overcome seemingly insuperable challenges; but it leaned heavily toward the future, and at the core of its message was rupture, new beginnings, a more prosperous and self-confident future for Africa and Africans, even as the latter carried with them some perennial, existential, philosophical essences. The implication was that while history might offer some salutary reference points, it was the 'brighter future' that mattered, rooted in the consensus that the very 'condition' of the continent necessitated some kind of rebirth. Afro-pessimism was backward-looking, in other words; Afro-optimism was about the time to come.

Nationhood was conceptualised in terms of a very specific, twentieth-century—which is to say colonial (and postcolonial)—set of parameters. The deeper past occasionally made its way into public debates about the extent to which local and ethnic loyalties should be represented in celebrations of 'the nation', as in Ghana, where Asante identity was regarded by some as having been unfairly 'muted' in the course of festivities, and by others as something toxic and antithetical to the unity of the nation.[125] Many continued to take to heart Machel's enduring exhortation; but 'traditional' kings and cultural leaders, many, if not all, with their roots in the nineteenth century or earlier, continued to wield considerable influence in civil society and occasionally in the political sphere.[126] There were

also ongoing, and in some cases increasingly heated, debates about indigeneity and its implications for citizenship, in which particular interpretations of nineteenth-century (and earlier) history were central.[127] But the
broader tendency was toward foreshortening. In 2014 then-president
Goodluck Jonathan made a speech marking the centenary of the creation
of Nigeria in which he asserted that "[w]e are a nation of the future, not
of the past".[128] It was meant in more than one way, of course—including
what had become a fairly standard appeal to Nigerians to work positively
for a future that would be rather better than their recent past. But it was
also an implicit assertion about the historic inviolability of 'The Scramble' as the beginning of Nigeria's journey; little of use could be found in
the turbulent nineteenth century in that regard. It was an interpretation
replicated across the continent in the 2010s, when a number of African
nations celebrated landmark anniversaries and did so within the temporal parameters set by European conquest and colonialism, and with particular reference to postcolonial trajectories.[129] In a number of countries
in both Francophone and Anglophone Africa, governments sought, often
in the face of local opposition, to reclaim for the national story colonial-
era founders rather than supposedly more ambiguous and troublesome
African figures. One of the arguments made was that in a truly post-
imperial, post-racial world, Africans had every right to repurpose the
European architects of the 'Scramble' era, and of the territorial order, in
pursuit of viable national histories.[130] (Such projects were also, it was often
suggested, good for tourism.) A particularly noteworthy case was the Republic of the Congo, to where in 2006 the remains of Pierre Savorgnan
de Brazza were returned amid much pomp and formality, and reinterred
in the capital Brazzaville. Those bones were to form the centrepiece of a
new glass and marble mausoleum commemorating both de Brazza the
man (reconceived as an explorer rather than a 'colonialist') and the founding of the nation itself. Many Congolese boycotted the site—at first
because of its apparent celebration of colonial conquest (many people
didn't share the government's more sanguine view of this history), and
then, according to popular rumour, because of the negative spiritual energy emanating from the place and the 'black magic' which would strike
anyone entering it.[131] What was striking in Congo and elsewhere, however,

was the apparent newfound enthusiasm on the part of political elites for the rehabilitation of European characters from the era of 'The Scramble', and—the heated local debates this often provoked notwithstanding—in ways which complicated discussions around imperial memory at the centre of which, in South Africa and in Britain, was the question of public statues of Cecil Rhodes.[132]

In some cases, of course, there were very specific reasons for an aversion to certain bits of history. In Rwanda, European partition and colonial rule had meant the institutionalisation of an ethnic enmity, speciously projected backward into the primordial past, which it was argued led directly to the genocide of 1994. Over the past three decades, an increasingly authoritarian state has sought to simultaneously memorialise the genocide and carefully manage any discussion of the past—including banning ethnonyms.[133] Ethiopia's turbulent twentieth century, meanwhile, rendered history similarly problematic: on the occasion of welcoming in the country's new millennium (in 2007, following the Ethiopian calendar), the Tigrayan-led Ethiopian People's Revolutionary Democratic Front coalition government publicly declared its desire for an inclusive celebration of the national past, but in reality it was rather more selective than it was comprehensive. Part of the reason for this was the inability of the Tigrayan leadership to resist depicting several centuries of monarchical Amhara rule as anything other than bloody and awful. In this way, too—more relevant for our purposes—the Amhara emperor Menelik's victory at Adwa was problematic for many non-Amhara Ethiopians, including Tigrayans, and Prime Minister Meles Zenawi could never bring himself to stand, head bowed, at the feet of Menelik's statue on Adwa Day.[134]

## Stanley Must (Not) Fall

DURING THE SUMMER OF 2020, as Black Lives Matter protests swept the world, and as the Rhodes Must Fall movement escalated its campaign to have the statue of Cecil Rhodes removed from an Oxford college, the people of Denbigh in north Wales turned their attention to another statue: that of arguably their most famous son, Henry Morton Stanley. It wasn't the first time a monument to him had caused a stir in the town. A few years earlier, the bishop of St Asaph had led the criticism of a 'totem pole' which had been erected to commemorate the period Stanley spent in a local workhouse.[135] Now, it was the effigy of the man in the town centre which was at the centre of the dispute. Again, the bishop voiced his opinion that the Stanley was statue was inappropriate, given that he had "little respect for the natives of Africa", as the Right Revd. Gregory Cameron was quoted as saying.[136] A decade earlier, when the idea of the statue was first mooted, a letter of protest attracted some prominent signatories, including Jan Morris, Benjamin Zephaniah and Georges Nzongola-Ntalaja. Stanley, they asserted, was a murdering racist who had been complicit in the establishment of one of the most egregious colonial ventures on the continent. But the town council had forged ahead with the project regardless, citing an "extremely positive response" following a public consultation.[137] In June 2020, the bishop and other critics found themselves on the other side of the debate from folks such as local councillor Gwyneth Kensler, of the Welsh nationalist party Plaid Cymru, who opined that Stanley "loved Africans", was "not a racist", and had worked to improve Africans' lot by opposing the slave trade.[138] The council decided once again to gauge the sentiments of the Denbigh public by putting the removal of the statue to a vote. Six hundred people, from a population of a little over eight thousand, participated in the ballot the following year, and voted overwhelmingly (471 to 121) to retain the statue. The majority of the town's councillors likewise voted to keep the effigy in place.[139]

The Denbigh controversy was a micro-version of that taking place around Rhodes, which was itself emblematic of a much larger debate about the memory and experience of empire.[140] It is perhaps unfair to judge the good people of Denbigh for their decision to keep Stanley's likeness in the centre of their town, although inevitably the debate was characterised by emotion rather than actual historical knowledge—of Stanley himself, and certainly of the African context within which he operated. The outcome of the vote reflected, whether consciously or otherwise, a much deeper sense that 'The Scramble' and the colonialism which resulted from it had in fact been something worth celebrating and commemorating, emblematic of Britain as a force for good in the world, and that the conquest of Africa was a singular moment which, although of course there may been mistakes and missteps, had in fact been something overwhelmingly 'positive', probably for Africa (the public view on that one is a little hazy), but certainly for Britain.[141] For many others, colonial history was in desperate need of critical examination and exposure for the brutal, exploitative process that it really was. The subsequent 'culture wars'—bullishly and cynically confected by a dazed and confused Conservative government still reeling from the onset of the global pandemic—were centred on the role of statues across Britain which apparently glorified an imperial and racist past.[142] (One of Edward Colston, Bristolian slave trader, ended up in the river.)[143] But Africans themselves remained rather shadowy, one-dimensional characters in all this, and the chronological framework of the argument explicitly or implicitly positioned 'The Scramble' as an end, and a beginning; the fundamental cornerstone of modern African history. In Britain after Brexit, at least in part the dubious achievement of then-prime minister Boris Johnson, the populist right promoted—or re-energised—the idea that Britain had nothing to be ashamed of in any case.[144] But this was not solely about Brexit, however much Brexit encouraged a certain type of ahistorical myth-peddling and the reassertion of xenophobia. It has long been acceptable within the right-wing media to perpetuate old stereotypes and nasty tropes about Africa and Africans. Johnson himself, a singular and rather peculiar character in some ways but more broadly representative of a toxic, xenophobic English exceptionalism, illustrates the point. It was Johnson, after all, who some years earlier had famously chucked red meat at his readers when writing in the conservative *Daily Telegraph* about British prime minister Tony Blair's trip to the Democratic Republic of Congo: "No doubt the AK47s will fall silent, and the pangas will stop their hacking of human flesh, and the tribal warriors will all break out in watermelon smiles to see the big white chief touch down in his big white British taxpayer-funded bird." The word 'offensive' doesn't begin to do justice to this journalistic bilge (though 'imbecilic' might be appropriate); but on the writer went, suggesting that the Queen had come to love the Commonwealth in part because of its "cheering crowds of flag-waving piccaninnies".[145] And the same Johnson, the buffoonery disguising (or attempting to disguise) a vicious, narcissistic disregard for human life and the historical facts which shape it, who defended colonialism in Africa in another piece, asserting blithely, "The problem is not that we were once in charge, but that we are not in charge anymore." In an explicit nod toward the events of the late nineteenth century, he concluded, "The best fate for Africa would be if the old colonial powers, or their citizens, scrambled once again in her direction; on the understanding that this time they will not be asked to feel guilty."[146] Little wonder that later, when—somewhat improbably, and reflecting a deeper crisis in British political culture—Johnson ascended to the very heights of government, observers in Africa were utterly baffled, often dismayed, and regarded it as a symptom of Britain's sorry diminution.

The British did not have a monopoly on unapologetic histories of empire.[147] In France, as in Britain, the memorialisation and lionisation of the builders of empire began even at the moment of imperial expansion, and gained their own architectural (and infrastructural) momentum in the decades that followed.[148] In July 2007, in a notorious speech given in Dakar, Senegal, President Nicolas Sarkozy declared that "l'africain n'est pas pleinement entré dans l'histoire". France had done its best to assist the continent to join the great flow of human history and progress: empire had been fundamentally aimed at achieving just that, and of course colonialism may not have done everything it was supposed to; mistakes had been made. But what was, in the round, a noble and righteous endeavour had been wilfully misunderstood, including (presumably) by many in his own audience. But now Africans had to do more to help themselves.[149] There was plenty of backlash and public debate in the weeks and months following the speech;[150] but the fact that Sarkozy felt able to utter these words at all is in many respects remarkable. The encapsulation of the continent as emblematic of a particular kind of ahistoricity, and the freezing of the moment of 'The Scramble' as seminal—offering Africans an opportunity, since squandered, for improvement—reflects an attitude which is both of long standing and almost uniquely directed at this particular landmass. It reflected a relationship defined as much in terms of time as of space.

It seems unlikely that Boris Johnson has ever read Frantz Fanon, or at least fully understood him if he has (though Sarkozy might have); but the notion of 'Europe' itself as the outcome of the very overseas adventures that cynical dilettantes like Johnson saw in terms of *Boys' Own* japes seems never to have occurred to him. As Fanon put it, discussing the material plunder involved in empire, "Europe is literally the creation of the Third World."[151] One could extend this beyond plunder and into the realms of political discourse, national identity, or cultural output. Be that as it may, Africa continues to be subject to Scramblology: it is a place seemingly perennially ripe for adventure, plunder, exploration, extraction, humanitarian intervention, partition. Cold War demarcations of influence between the 1960s and the 1980s happened at the same time as economic collapse and apparent political vulnerability across the continent.[152] What followed were structural adjustment programmes and the rise of neoliberalism which in various ways led to dizzily high annual GDP growth rates, the 'Africa Rising' narrative, and reheated iterations of Scramblology.[153] With spiralling growth rates, economies which were booming, at least for the top few per cent of the population, and the apparent arrival of the continent as an economic powerhouse, there came the 'New Scramble' narrative. A new economic partition of the continent was under way, this time involving China, India and the Gulf States, in particular, while Russia has been expanding its influence over a number of years.[154] As ever, the continent was a place of massive opportunity. The demand for raw materials was driving African GDP rates upwards, while Chinese loans, offered without political conditions, enabled Beijing, as part of its 'belt and road' initiative, to elbow old colonial rivals out of the way in the desperate search for resources and influence. In the years following the global economic crash of 2008, creditors looked eagerly to Africa to offload cheap loans, although a debt crisis was soon mounting. But in the meantime, a new African elite benefited. It was a striking echo of an earlier epoch: carvings up, indebtedness, raw materials, influence. Presentist conceptualisations of African conditions and behaviours, which implicitly or otherwise held that much of the continent's putative 'pre-conquest' history was irrelevant, even dangerous, found their way into development discourse, with its roots in the late eighteenth and early nineteenth centuries, and its internal logic which had provided the legitimisation for the armed humanitarian intervention of the late nineteenth century.

One hardy perennial of Scramblology included the framing of the continent as a place in need of outside interventions to solve its manifold problems. In 2001, UK prime minister Tony Blair, channelling his inner David Livingstone and with his gaze fixed on a global legacy, declared that poverty in Africa was a "scar on the world's conscience".[155] Initiatives around famine and debt—no doubt well meaning, in the main—were launched in the years that followed. The crusading, interventionist humanitarianism of the Blair years later gave way to the 'doing business in Africa' agenda of the Cameron-led coalition.[156] As in the nineteenth century, Africa remained a place onto which to *project*: sometimes a landscape of sanguinary horror, sometimes a place of smiling resilience; always a place where outsiders could do good, save lives, improve the human condition.[157] Or, failing that, make money. Latterly, familiar images have been joined by the more terrifying—for some—prospect of Africans actually trying to *come to Europe* to escape their travails, or take advantage of supposedly generous welfare systems.

These notions made their way, too, into discourses on African violence, the savagery on display there, and novel elements were added to the military and security agendas in the age of global terrorism. The supposed 'new barbarism', as it was termed, was the portrait of a continent whose histories and futures were horrifically interlinked, and a savage and benighted world beyond the West (or, in one noted article from 1994, "outside the limousine") which was overpopulated and under-resourced, and seething with ancient tribal hatreds pursued with criminal intent.[158] Modernity had absolutely failed to take root: one only need look at Sierra Leone, or Liberia, or Somalia, or more recently Libya. There was, of course, acknowledgment of, though little acceptance of responsibility for, the devastations of the slave trade on the part of Global North actors. But more broadly the latter perpetuated a set of tropes and images about the continent which were rooted in the moment of partition and conquest. One of the most enduring of these was the Africa of crazed, irrational violence, generally seen, as we have noted, as the product of postcolonial dysfunction, which itself (depending on one's political viewpoint) was either rooted in the distortions engendered by the colonial moment, or reflected the fact that Africans had squandered the manifold advantages awarded them by colonialism. To seek the deeper roots and patterns of such contestation was to evoke the racial stereotypes of the late nineteenth century, which may have appealed to the populist political right across Europe, but which left many of a more responsible, putatively progressive bent rather more uncomfortable.

Popular cultural allusions and depictions of Africa sometimes seem to have shifted little in many decades, meanwhile. Change is happening—there is now likely to be a robust eschewal of 'white saviour' scenarios in television and film productions, for example—but glacially slowly; it is still common to have programmes made involving a celebrity undertaking journeys in the Dark Continent, as in the case of Griff Rhys-Jones and his *Slow Train through Africa*, in which the former TV comedian grins his way across the continent using hilariously inefficient railways.[159] All the while, there is a tinge of melancholy in the now-decrepit colonial infrastructure—*what efforts the colonials had made!*—which had temporarily tamed the African wilderness. The white man pulled out (Rhys-Jones doesn't actually say, but may as well have), and the wilderness reclaimed everything. In more serious productions, efforts to excavate the 'precolonial' past which are laudable in principle are often hampered by the enduring exoticism, or the strange romanticism, which is attached to African political culture.[160] In terms of film and TV production, an entire book might be devoted to the cinematic depiction of 'precolonial' Africa: suffice to say here that for much of the twentieth century such portrayals were bound up in tales of 'The Scramble'—such as seemingly endless retellings of the Zulu wars; or the British in Sudan; or, occasionally, of the slave trade.[161] Recent blockbusters such as those of the *Black Panther* franchise, or *The Woman King*, represent a considerable improvement in terms of the representation of Africa's nineteenth century.[162]

———

ALL OF THIS, albeit in a variety of ways, has tended to reinforce the great temporal divide between the modern period and something called the 'precolonial'. In the course of the twentieth century, Africa became divided up, nice and neat, into three big temporal blocs: precolonial, colonial, postcolonial.[163] In each of these, evidently, the colonial 'moment', lasting barely more than a couple of generations in most of the continent, was front and centre. 'The Scramble' formed the centrepiece, a profound and enduring rupture rather than a culmination involving long-term endogenous and exogenous processes which continue to resonate and mutate. The indeterminately long period preceding that moment came to be shorthanded as 'precolonial'.[164] 'The Scramble' apparently involved the conquest of time itself.[165] We don't need to be drawn into the great maze that constitutes discussions about the origins and meanings of 'modernity'— and it isn't something in which I am particularly interested—to observe that the onset of 'colonial invasion' supposedly involved the beginning of Africans' proper encounter with it.[166] The nineteenth century involved some warm-up, and even some efforts at modernising reform on a par with Qing China or Meiji Japan in the same period; but there was little comparable to the 'early modernity' proposed for other parts of the Global South,[167] and it was 'The Scramble' which announced, with the blare of a klaxon, Africa's arrival, albeit in a dishevelled and unready state, in global history.[168] The great rupture of the late nineteenth century was the critical point of departure, the temporal platform on which everyone stood to survey the unavailing carnage of the past, and to espy the opportunities to come. 'The Scramble' cast a long shadow; not just over what came after, but, more importantly for our purposes, over what went before.

# Epilogue

ISIKE WAS MURDERED BY THE GERMANS. He was also ultimately undone by the tempestuous dynamics which made his road, and which defined his era. But he had lived his life managing and harnessing those same dynamics, that same remarkable energy, to impressive effect. He had maintained his political position in the face of continual potential challenge, and governed Unyanyembe in an environment in which the polity was shaped by fissure and faction. He had channelled powerful commercial forces, which had unseated predecessors and episodically destabilised the state, to his own advantage, and to the advantage of those who attached their fortunes to his. The potency of those forces was never lost on him; he knew what he owed to them—personally, for he clearly did well from the business flowing between the Indian Ocean and the Congo basin, but also in terms of the position of his strategically positioned kingdom. But he also knew that those forces could destroy him, if he didn't keep the coastal community on-side, and consistently persuade its most powerful members that he was their best guarantee of continued prosperity. He lived his life surrounded by violence, running his own substantial army and being surrounded by a series of remarkable insurgencies, including, most importantly, that of Mirambo on the road to the west. It is a reasonable assumption, from the available evidence, that Isike and Mirambo never met. But they lived their lives in tumultuous symbiosis, in violent synergy. This region was a dangerous, vibrant neighbourhood, in which fortune might favour the brave but in which the brave often perished in pursuit of profit and reform, or indeed because of it. Isike used violence, while also seeking to mitigate its worst consequences. In the representatives of the German Empire, he was confronted by those who were both adept and lucky, and of course well armed, inserting themselves in the crevices which characterised the very entrepreneurial landscape of which Isike himself was a product, and which he had utilised so well since his youth. In the end, as Isike knew only too well, the revolutionary, global history of his road was a violent one. It was a scenario which was replicated across the continent throughout the long nineteenth century.

But Isike's death was not an end, brutal though it was—and it is shocking, still. Europeans perceived African violence, misinterpreted it, and inflicted a great deal of their own; though in doing so they were always less in control than they imagined. They relied on African personnel, and used methods which would not always have been unfamiliar to those on the receiving end, for Africans and Europeans had each honed their ability to practise violence, over several critical decades, and now they intersected to literally deadly effect. A combination of several decades of war, new diseases and hunger devastated swathes of sub-Saharan Africa.[1] Above all European imperialism was propelled by brutally racist, hubristic, anxious political and economic cultures. But the solidity of empire itself was an illusion, the corollary of liminality and insecurity, worked out in countless granular symbioses and co-options on the ground. The endeavours, and the processes, which shaped Isike's road, and which defined Africa's nineteenth century more broadly, continued to reverberate in the twentieth, and beyond. The periods neatly depicted as 'colonial' and 'postcolonial' cannot be comprehended without a deep knowledge of the nineteenth century. Understanding reformist insurgency, notably, as a nineteenth-century phenomenon allows us to pull backward in time those struggles for political rejuvenation and economic advancement normatively associated with the travails of the postcolony.

A history of the twentieth century within a framework which foregrounds the currents and subtleties of the nineteenth is illuminating. It reveals political cultures which were hugely adaptable, mobile, entrepreneurial and opportunist, and which were naturally given to reform and reinvention. It is suggestive of evolving collective and corporate identities which were both dynamic and flexible, while also being rooted in select, curated aspects of historical culture and memory. It is indicative of a capacity for economic adventurism and for opportunism, as well as for the innovation required to seize those opportunities. In that connection, social mobility and migratory patterns were the hallmarks of a transformative nineteenth century: people moved and followed prospects through their own volition, or they were compelled to do so. They often formed new ways of belonging and self-identifying in the process. These patterns persisted in the twentieth century, but they weren't the product of colonial modernity. Such a history is instructive in terms of the primacy of violence, too: millions of Africans lived with violence, and participated in it. Coercion and physical threat were core to much nineteenth-century reform and innovation; they were internalised and navigated, both among the enslaved and those who did the enslaving, and ideas about coercion and rights—both access to them and denial of them—continued to evolve in the twentieth century. The nineteenth-century military revolution, moreover, underscored the significance of arms and military service. This continued to mutate in the decades that followed, manifest in the colonial armies so fundamental to the functioning of the European imperial order, and then in the politicised national armies and the ostensibly novel forms of revolutionary insurgency from the middle decades of the twentieth century. There was no *pax colonica*;[2] it is as much a myth as the idea of unambiguous conquest. 'The Scramble' cannot be conceived of as some kind of complete process, neatly characterised by a beginning, a middle and an end. European empire in Africa was built in the interstices generated by African political and military energy; was absorbed into the social and economic infrastructure and entrepreneurialism which characterised the long nineteenth century; was made possible through the co-option and exploitation of African forces for change. Colonial officials governed much as nineteenth-century Africans had done, the areas under their nominal administrative control characterised by gradations of meaningful, practicable authority.[3] Colonial rule, to be sure, introduced new elements of instability and liminality into extant patterns; it could hardly have been otherwise when European imperialism was the product of profound turbulence and transformative volatility within Europe itself. But in essence it reflected deeper patterns of contest, violence and aspiration within Africa. Such a temporal repositioning frees us up to think about a much longer-term and much wider pattern of reform and innovation, which frequently, and with ever greater intensity, intersected with global forces.

These processes invariably generated new groupings of the marginalised, the exploited, the coerced, the dispossessed and the displaced, as well as those vibrantly hybrid communities which straddled multiple cultural and political systems and were well positioned to take advantage of them. Many others, positioned at the peripheries of state-building projects or buffeted by the collapse of political orders, sought to take advantage of new opportunities, offering—no doubt often with wary detachment—their services to putative new masters, or to causes to which they might profitably belong, all the while identifying ways and means of improving their lives.

In none of these spheres of endeavour is 'The Scramble' or the ensuing 'colonial period' adequate in explanatory power, denoting some form of rupture and intrinsic novelty. In each of them, it is the long nineteenth century—the *African* century—which is analytically and narratively potent. Colonial rule was in large part the product of the dynamics of that era, as well as being the corollary of Europe's own tumultuous expansionism. A long-established consensus suggests that, in the end, Africans achieved little in the nineteenth century which enabled them to exert meaningful influence on exogenous economic dynamics; that whatever political and military reforms they introduced were insufficient to ward off invasion and subordination, and that in any case escalating violence was ultimately devastatingly inimical to anything resembling 'development'. Arguments can certainly be made on each of these scores, and there can be no question that there was a great deal of trial and error on the part of political, economic and cultural entrepreneurs whose projects failed and caused considerable human misery in the process. But rather more critically, Africans' endeavours in the course of the nineteenth century influenced the very nature and form of external intrusion—up to, including, and beyond the putative 'Scramble for Africa'. In the late nineteenth and early twentieth centuries, the African political landscape was redrawn, with a series of boundary treaties over a number of years forming the basis of the majority of the continent's modern borders, and laying the territorial foundations for dozens of African nation-states. To be sure, this had far-reaching consequences, contributing to the creation of a novel set of challenges for the continent, and these problems have been thoroughly explored in a vast and diverse historiography. But the overwhelming focus on 'The Scramble' as a singular act of cartographic as well as political violence tends to marginalise Africans, and obscures the extent to which the European intervention was in many ways the latest stage in, and the culmination of, an African century of reformation, demarcation and innovation.

It is no doubt stating the obvious to assert that this did not end with Europe's intervention, even if the latter altered in important ways the circumstances and parameters within which ongoing projects of reform and renewal and aspiration took place. European intrusion, however, certainly did involve the calcification of a historical, or more appropriately ahistorical, narrative which posited 'instability' as a universally terrible proposition, symptomatic of chronic failure, and the cause of a disastrous material poverty with which Africans rapidly became associated.[4] 'Africa' as a concept, as a bundle of related images, was born, implicitly or explicitly juxtaposed with 'Western' achievement, or as the sad exception in an age of progressive modernity.[5] It is vital—especially given the need to complicate the 'decolonising' agendas now so prevalent across the discipline of history—to understand the degree to which partition and the political orders which followed it were the extension and outcome of Africa's global nineteenth century. Recognition of agency does not have to be conflated with attribution of some form of culpability. The historical reframing attempted in this book might help us to identify distinctive forms of change and vitality. The aim has certainly been to examine the nuance with respect to how people navigate, even at times embrace, instability; how they aspire and create within the liminal spaces such instability produces; and how they manage the leverage it facilitates. They do all these things in pursuit of better futures and usable pasts. Just like the authors, travelling on their own roads, who write books about them.

# NOTES

## Prologue

1. It is important to note for the record that it was never a 'single' track—however it appears on maps of the period—but instead an approximate route, and the 'road' itself regularly shifted a kilometre or two on either side owing to conflict or other blockages, or the presence (or absence) of reliable provisioning points for travelling merchants.

2. My apologies to Robin Law, who taught that course. Robin knows, I hope, the impact it had on me. Robin's colleague—Stirling University had *two* historians of Africa!—the late, and much beloved, John McCracken taught the follow-up course on Africa's twentieth century. Both offered superb courses with a more specialised focus later in the degree programme; I took them all.

3. Quoted in I. M. Lewis, 'History "Functionalised"', 3.

4. For example, Dalakoglu and Harvey, 'Roads and Anthropology'.

5. I'm thinking here of the wonderful Judt, *Ill Fares the Land*. Or, from a different time, place and certainly positionality, and more relevant for our purposes, the compelling Mphahlele, *African Image*.

## Act I

1. Gwassa, 'German Intervention', 111.

2. Iliffe, *Modern History of Tanganyika*, 104.

3. Lt. Tom von Prince, quoted in A. Roberts, 'The Nyamwezi', 142.

4. Lettow-Vorbeck, *My Reminiscences*, 45; Paice, *Tip and Run*, 57.

5. For example, Gildea, *Empires of the Mind*.

6. Still, Roberts has suggested that the fact that von Prince doesn't mention Isike's hanging in his own later account of these events might suggest a certain shame: A. Roberts, 'The Nyamwezi', 147 n. 13.

7. Achebe, *Things Fall Apart*, 147–48. The novel was first published in 1958. It drew its title from the W. B. Yeats's poem 'The Second Coming' (1919–20), written in the traumatic interstice between the First World War and the Irish war of independence.

8. A. Roberts, 'The Nyamwezi', 138; also Shorter, 'Nyungu-ya-Mawe'.

9. The vitality of the intra-African network is captured in a number of contributions to Gray and Birmingham, *Pre-colonial African Trade*. The identification of an Indian Ocean world, of which vast tracts of Africa were a vital part, has given rise to an energetic scholarship, neatly encapsulated in a special issue and special feature respectively of two leading Africanist journals. The first was concerned with 'Print Cultures, Nationalisms and Publics of the Indian Ocean', in *Africa* 81, no. 1 (2011); and the second was on 'Africa and the Indian Ocean', in *Journal of African History* 55, no. 2 (2014). See also Hall, *Empires of the Monsoon*.

10. Gleerup, 'Journey across Tanganyika', 138.

11. For example, R. Reid, *War in Pre-colonial Eastern Africa*, 115, 145, 170.

12. Emin Pasha was of German Jewish origin, a naturalist by academic training, and had spent much of the previous few years administering the sprawling Ottoman province on the Upper Nile before needing to be rescued following the rise of the Sudanese Mahdist state. He then entered the service of the German East Africa Company. See Schweitzer, *Emin Pasha*; H. M. Stanley, *In Darkest Africa*.

13. Gwassa, 'German Intervention', 111; W. O. Henderson, 'German East Africa', 131.

14. Raum, 'German East Africa', 180.

15. See for example Bertrand and Calafat, 'Global Microhistory'; and for a fascinating example in an African setting, D. Wright, *The World and a Very Small Place*.

# Chapter 1

1. A. Roberts, *Colonial Moment*. The essays in this volume first appeared in A. Roberts, *Cambridge History of Africa*, Vol. 7.

2. The sense is captured—at considerable length—in Lugard, *Dual Mandate*.

3. The vast majority of historians, of course, belong to 'Area Studies'. It's just that Europeanists, for example, are not widely regarded as such; only scholars of the Global South, which is itself a hangover from a decidedly colonial epistemology.

4. See also R. Reid, 'Past and Presentism'.

5. Much work has been done in recent years on the position of Africa in global history, and on the visibility and relevance of the continent in the burgeoning historiography on global history. The challenge has been—and continues to be—the seeming lack of proximity of Africa to the meaningful centres and flows of historical globality. The sub-field has encompassed an eclectic array of literary and scholarly work. See Afrocentric responses to cloying Eurocentrism—for example, Diop, *African Origin of Civilization*, or the idiosyncratic Van Sertima, *They Came Before Columbus*, or Asante, *History of Africa*—and a somewhat different tack in Bernal, *Black Athena*. Important critiques of these interpretations are offered by Lefkowitz, *Not Out of Africa*, and Howe, *Afrocentrism*. Rather more balanced, and certainly less polemical, interventions are offered by Bayart, 'Africa in the World'; by Cooper, *Africa in the World*; in the essays by Patrick Manning, Andrew Zimmerman and Isabel Hofmeyr ('Africa and World Historiography'; 'Africa in Imperial and Transnational History'; 'African History and Global Studies') in *JAH* Forum: 'Africa and Global History'; and by Simo, 'Writing World History in Africa'. An innovative analysis of Africans' role in the nineteenth-century global economic exchange is provided in Prestholdt, *Domesticating the World*. For local perspectives on a 'global past', see also R. Reid, 'Time and Distance'.

6. For this reason, indeed, I was rather taken aback by the 'stir' that a recent submission of my own to *The American Historical Review* made among one or two reviewers, when in fact I had anticipated rejection on the grounds of the piece not being especially original. The essay—a tugboat to the present slightly more cumbersome vessel—was, nonetheless, published as 'Africa's Revolutionary Nineteenth Century and the Idea of the "Scramble"'.

7. Keltie, *Partition of Africa*; Hobson, *Imperialism*; Lugard, *Dual Mandate*. Numerous others—including actors in the rapidly unfolding drama itself—penned their own literary monuments. A good example is British colonial administrator Harry Johnston, whose *History of the Colonization of Africa* did take a *longue durée* approach to various forms of invasion and conquest, but which ultimately focused on the singularly significant—and very recent—'moment' of the late nineteenth century. See also Oliver, *Sir Harry Johnston*.

8. A substantial, if in some ways disparate, body of scholarship on this subject has built up over many years. Walter, *Colonial Violence* is a good place to start; and see also an important

contribution from Wagner, 'Savage Warfare'. For useful overviews, see Vandervort, *Wars of Imperial Conquest*, and (on empire and war more broadly) Porch, *Wars of Empire*. For an example of place-specific research on the impact of colonial invasion, see Vansina, *Paths in the Rainforests*, 240–45.

9. Gildea, *Empires of the Mind*; D. Kennedy, *Imperial History Wars*.

10. And in any case, others have attempted the task already, albeit from the perspective of individual empires: see, for example, Flint, 'Britain and the Scramble for Africa'. Various other essays in the same volume of the *Oxford History of the British Empire* contain useful surveys. My own essay, 'Africa's Revolutionary Nineteenth Century and the Idea of the "Scramble"', offers some pointers, too.

11. Lonsdale, 'European Scramble'.

12. Pakenham, *Scramble for Africa*. For a more recent exemplar of the genre, albeit one which adopts a somewhat longer *durée*, see L. James, *Empires in the Sun*.

13. For example, Wesseling, *Divide and Rule*; M. E. Chamberlain, *Scramble for Africa*; Boahen, *UNESCO General History of Africa, Vol. 7*, and the Cambridge equivalent, Oliver and Sanderson, *Cambridge History of Africa, Vol. 6*; Robinson and Gallagher, *Africa and the Victorians*; C. Newbury, 'Great Britain and the Partition'; Vandervort, *Wars of Imperial Conquest*.

14. See the relevant chapters in, for example, Iliffe, *Africans*; Collins and Burns, *History of Sub-Saharan Africa*; Oliver and Atmore, *Africa since 1800*; R. Reid, *History of Modern Africa*.

15. An illustrative sample from a vast field might include: Burbank and Cooper, *Empires in World History*; S. Conrad, *German Colonialism*; Cain and Hopkins, *British Imperialism*; Kiernan, *European Empires*; J. Darwin, 'Imperialism and the Victorians'; J. Darwin, *After Tamerlane*; Cannadine, *Victorious Century*; Headrick, *Tools of Empire*; B. Porter, *Lion's Share*; Levine, *British Empire*; Hobsbawm, *Age of Empire*; Wesseling, *European Colonial Empires*; Hyam, *Britain's Imperial Century*.

16. Bayly's *Birth of the Modern World* set the pace; Osterhammel's *Transformation of the World* surpasses Bayly in terms of sheer weight of detail.

17. A couple of recent and partial exceptions to this are Gjersø, 'Scramble for East Africa'; and Press, *Rogue Empires*. However, this work is really more concerned with external rather than local protagonists and drivers. When John Parker and I were compiling a preliminary list of chapter topics for what eventually became *The Oxford Handbook of Modern African History* (Parker and Reid, *Oxford Handbook*) 'The Scramble' was very much present; but we couldn't find anyone to do it—one prominent colleague initially showed interest, but then stopped answering emails (this happened quite a lot)—and in the end we quietly dropped it.

18. Cain and Hopkins, *British Imperialism*; Burbank and Cooper, *Empires in World History*.

19. See for example McCaskie's superb essay, 'Cultural Encounters'.

20. There is a distinctive sub-field which has sought to explore imperial expansion in, say, Africa as it was experienced by metropolitan society, or as refracted through European culture, which is a conceptual nudge in the right direction: see A. Thompson, *Empire Strikes Back?*; Mackenzie, *Imperialism and Popular Culture*; Cannadine, *Ornamentalism*; Finaldi, *Italian National Identity*; J. Lewis, *Empire of Sentiment*; Sèbe, *Heroic Imperialists*.

21. For example: Vos, *Kongo in the Age of Empire*; McCaskie, *Asante Identities*; Doyle, *Crisis and Decline*; Leonardi, *Dealing with Government*; Leopold, *Inside West Nile*; Deutsch, *Emancipation without Abolition*.

22. A taste, at least, is provided in an early landmark collection, exhibiting how far the field had come in a few short years: Ranger, *Emerging Themes*. For a useful overview—along with a comprehensive bibliography—see Atieno-Odhiambo, 'From African Historiographies'. While much is made of the 'arrival' of Africanist historiography in the mid-twentieth century, African

history is of course rather older than that—several millennia older, indeed—as Alagoa reminds us in *The Practice of History in Africa*.

23. A *mea culpa* is in order: I did exactly the same in my first two books.

24. Uzoigwe, 'Pre-colonial Military Studies'; Uzoigwe, 'Warrior and the State'; Davidson, *Africa in Modern History*; Atmore, 'Africa on the Eve of Partition'; Boahen, *African Perspectives*; Coquery-Vidrovitch, *Africa and the Africans*; Táíwò, *How Colonialism Preempted Modernity*.

25. In fact, the question of African involvement in the process of partition has been around for several decades: see, for example, in the very first issue of the *Journal of African History*, Hargreaves, 'Towards a History'.

26. Touval, 'Treaties, Borders, and the Partition'; R. Robinson, 'Non-European Foundations'.

27. Sharman, 'Myths of Military Revolution'.

28. Fieldhouse, *Economics and Empire*.

29. Price, *Making Empire*; Low, *Fabrication of Empire*.

30. J. Darwin, 'Imperialism and the Victorians'.

31. A. Roberts, 'Sub-imperialism of the Baganda'; Ochonu, *Colonialism by Proxy*.

32. A good overview is offered in Law, *From Slave Trade to 'Legitimate' Commerce*. Specifically, see: A. G. Hopkins, 'Economic Imperialism', and also his seminal *Economic History of West Africa*, 165–66; Klein, 'Social and Economic Factors'; J. Reid, 'Warrior Aristocrats in Crisis'; Soumonni, 'Compatibility'; Austen, 'Abolition of the Overseas Slave Trade', and also his *African Economic History*, 101–2; Austin, 'Between Abolition and *jihad*'; Lynn, *Commerce and Economic Change*; Strickrodt, *Afro-European Trade*.

33. The proposition of insurgency as a category of historical analysis asks particular questions of the historian of modern Africa. In short, it is a phenomenon most readily associated with the second half of the twentieth century and the early decades of the twenty-first, the so-called 'postcolonial' era in which rebellion, civil war and the seemingly ubiquitous coup d'état proliferate. During this period, insurgency is the outcome of political instability which, it is commonly argued or at least strongly implied, is itself the product of a distinctively 'postcolonial' malaise: a botched decolonisation, indicative of something rotten at the very heart of the colonial entities that stumble into sovereign nationhood in the middle decades of the twentieth century. There is an enormous body of work which might be cited here—scholarship on the causes and nature of postcolonial conflict in Africa has thrived in the last quarter-century especially, much of it concerned with the resolution of such violence—but a sample of the some of the best writing should suffice: Clapham, *African Guerrillas*; Nhema and Zeleza, *Roots of African Conflicts*; Nhema and Zeleza, *Resolution of African Conflicts*; Kaarsholm, *Violence, Political Culture and Development*; P. D. Williams, *War and Conflict in Africa*; Chabal, Engel and Gentili, *Is Violence Inevitable*; Reno, *Warfare in Independent Africa*; Boas and Dunn, *African Guerrillas*; Decalo, *Coups and Army Rule*. Much of this work reflects the idea of the failure of modernity, or at least the breakdown of the political (and social) order and of the flimsy institutions supposedly created to facilitate modernity: for example, Richards, *Fighting for the Rain Forest*; Reno, *Warlord Politics*. Such political turmoil appeared, above all, to be rooted in the experience of colonialism itself.

34. In his work dealing with the armed and marginalised and insurgent groups that have characterised the modern age and indeed earlier epochs, Eric Hobsbawm drew a distinction between the bandit and the revolutionary: the former an outlaw, a criminal in the eyes of the establishment, but a champion of social justice and a hero in the eyes of the general populace; the latter an ideologically motivated manifestation of the turbulent politics of the twentieth century. In truth the distinction between the two groups is sometimes delicate. More importantly,

Hobsbawm's bandits and revolutionaries belonged to a particular category of social, political and economic malcontent, usually, if not exclusively, the product of Europe's turbulent modern age. The actors and the movements in our story can often be classified as bandits and revolutionaries in that fashion, although they are often other things, too. Still, as in many other areas, Hobsbawm has much to offer in thinking about categories for historical analysis. His two books are *Bandits*, first published in 1969, and *Revolutionaries*, which first appeared in 1973. A stimulating attempt to consider Hobsbawm, and the related work of eminent British social historian E. P. Thompson, in an African context is Crummey, *Banditry, Rebellion and Social Protest*.

35. Again, in our own era, violent volatility in the African context is framed in peculiarly negative ways, and has been understood in terms of the *failure*, the *absence*, of something, rather than recognising instability as both natural and creative. See, for example, the acclamation of 'stability' as facilitated by the evolution of institutions in Acemoglu and Robinson, *Why Nations Fail*; and Fukuyama, *Origins of Political Order*.

36. As we will see at later junctures, an important body of work has now emerged on this. See, for example, Echenberg, *Colonial Conscripts*; Moyd, *Violent Intermediaries*; Westwood, 'Military Culture in Senegambia'.

# Act II

1. A. Roberts, 'The Nyamwezi', 132; A. Roberts, 'Political Change', 72; Iliffe, *Modern History of Tanganyika*, 62.

2. For a relatively rare foray into this compelling 'moment' in regional history, see Gottberg, 'On the Historical Importance'. It is perhaps worth noting that a report on a Nyamwezi delegation, which supposedly contained an "heir apparent", at Zanzibar in 1839 suggested that "[t]he right of succession to the throne depends not on relationship [*viz.*, kinship or lineage] but on the strength and popularity of the aspirant": Burgess, 'Letters', 119.

3. Tippu Tip, *Maisha*, 15.

4. Ibid.

5. Ibid.

6. A. Roberts, 'The Nyamwezi', 131–32.

7. Tippu Tip, *Maisha*, 15, 17.

8. A. Roberts, 'The Nyamwezi', 131.

9. Burton, *Lake Regions*, 228–29.

10. Shorter, 'The Kimbu', 105, 107; A. Roberts, 'The Nyamwezi', 127.

11. The texts arising from Burton's and Speke's journey constitute our earliest contemporary reportage of Unyanyembe: see Burton, *Lake Regions*; Speke, *What Led to the Discovery*.

12. Speke, *Journal*, 113.

13. Ibid., 76–77.

14. Ibid., 77.

15. Ibid., 78.

16. Ibid.

17. Ibid., 79.

18. Burton, *Zanzibar*, 2:297.

19. Grant, *A Walk*, 54.

20. Ibid., 47.

21. Ibid., 52–53.

22. Speke, *Journal*, 88.

23. Ibid., 113.

24. Ibid., 87.

25. Ibid., 88.

26. Ibid., 91.

27. *Mzungu* literally means, in Kiswahili, 'one who wanders around'—originally connoting aimlessness and even insanity—and in the nineteenth century it came to refer to a white person across eastern and central Africa, as it does today. *Wazungu* (or *bazungu*) is the plural.

28. Speke, *Journal*, 95–96.

29. Ibid., 99.

30. H. M. Stanley, *How I Found Livingstone*, 544.

31. Speke, *Journal*, 110, 112.

32. Ibid., 137.

33. H. M. Stanley, *How I Found Livingstone*, 267; Tippu Tip, *Maisha*, 43.

34. The name means 'corpses'—as in one who 'makes corpses' through great military success.

35. Mirambo occupies a curious place in the historiographical firmament. He is, ostensibly, 'well known', or at least as celebrated as a nineteenth-century African figure can be. Yet his story and what it represents have become, curiously, rather taken for granted, duly acknowledged without apparently warranting much of a closer look. He was at the centre of a particular flurry of scholarly attention in the 1960s and 1970s, not least as the result of his positioning by the History Department at the University of Dar es Salaam as a figure of immense historical importance to the new nation of Tanzania. There hasn't been too much work on him subsequently, for reasons we'll come to in due course. Perhaps the starting point in terms of modern scholarship is R. J. Harvey, 'Mirambo'. To the best of my knowledge, only two substantial book-length publications have been dedicated to him. One is the now-classic N. R. Bennett, *Mirambo of Tanzania*; the other is Kabeya's richly detailed account based largely on local oral history, first published in Swahili as *Mtemi Mirambo*, and in English a decade later as *King Mirambo*. Otherwise, he occupied a prominent place in some of the foundational scholarship of the era: A. Roberts, *Tanzania before 1900*; Kimambo and Temu, *History of Tanzania*; Iliffe, *Modern History of Tanganyika*. In terms of my own work, see, for example, 'Mutesa and Mirambo' and *War in Pre-colonial Eastern Africa*, passim.

36. Iliffe, *Modern History of Tanganyika*, 11–12.

37. Kabeya, *King Mirambo*, 4; Broyon-Mirambo, 'Description of Unyamwesi', 32–33.

38. H. M. Stanley, *How I Found Livingstone*, 197.

39. Ibid., 196.

40. Broyon-Mirambo, 'Description of Unyamwesi', 33. Fundikira had been working as a porter in a caravan headed for the coast, perhaps in the early 1850s, when news reached him of his father Swetu's death, and his inheritance of Unyanyembe. According to Richard Burton, "he at once stacked his load and prepared to return home and rule. The rest of the gang, before allowing him to depart, taunted him severely, exclaiming, partly in jest, partly in earnest, 'Ah! now thou art still our comrade, but presently thou wilt torture and slay, fine and flog us'": Burton, *Lake Regions*, 300. Note the florid language which Burton uses to ventriloquise Fundikira's colleagues, who come across as a rumbustious crowd on some Shakespearean stage.

41. Tipp Tip, *Maisha*, 15.

42. H. M. Stanley, *How I Found Livingstone*, 196; Cameron, *Across Africa*, 1:77.

43. Cameron, *Across Africa*, 1:150–51.

44. Kirk to the Secretary to the Secretary of Government, 31 August 1869: *British Parliamentary Papers: Slave Trade*, 52:56–57.

45. Cameron, *Across Africa*, 1:150–51.

46. H. M. Stanley, *Through the Dark Continent*, 1:387.

47. H. M. Stanley, *How I Found Livingstone*, 479.

48. N. R. Bennett, *Stanley's Despatches*, 203.

49. Broyon, 'Description of Unyamwesi', 32–33. Broyon also suggests, however, that the co-optive approach involved a degree of spiritual precaution, and that Mirambo was reluctant to abolish local ruling lineages for fear of incurring the wrath of dead ancestors, commonly worshipped by the Nyamwezi: ibid., 34.

50. Ibid., 33.

51. Kabeya, *King Mirambo*, 19.

52. Quoted in A. Roberts, 'The Nyamwezi', 137.

53. Quoted in Kabeya, *King Mirambo*.

54. Quoted in R. Reid, *War in Pre-colonial Eastern Africa*, 212.

55. Quoted in A. Roberts, 'The Nyamwezi', 138.

56. Father Aylward Shorter is the doyen of work on Nyungu and the Kimbu in this period, his contributions including 'Nyungu-ya-Mawe'; 'The Kimbu'; *Nyungu-ya-Mawe*; and *Chiefship in Western Tanzania*.

57. H. M. Stanley, *Through the Dark Continent*, 1:387; also R. Reid, 'Mutesa and Mirambo', passim.

58. A. Roberts, 'The Nyamwezi', 132.

# Chapter 2

1. Robinson and Gallagher, *Africa and the Victorians*.

2. Iliffe, *Africans*, 1–2; and see also Lamphear, 'Sub-Saharan African Warfare', 171.

3. It begins, of course, with Frederick Jackson Turner's classic (though contested) interpretation of US history in the late nineteenth century: Turner, 'Significance of the Frontier'. See also Gerhard, 'Frontier'.

4. See also Brogan, *Penguin History of the United States*, 403; A. G. Hopkins, *American Empire*, 194.

5. Most importantly, Kopytoff, *African Frontier*, and in particular his own introductory essay, 'The Internal African Frontier'. There is also a useful overview essay by Kopytoff, 'Frontiers', in Middleton and Miller, *New Encyclopaedia*, 416–18. For insightful analysis of the role of boundaries and frontiers in colonial and postcolonial contexts, see also Herbst, *States and Power*; and I. M. Lewis, 'Frontier Fetishism'.

6. Kopytoff, 'Internal African Frontier', 12.

7. See also R. Reid, *Frontiers of Violence*.

8. See, for example, Innes et al., *Sunjata*; and Brooks, *Modern Translation*.

9. Seeking to compare sub-Saharan states with the feudal systems of western Europe and the monarchies of Asia, Jack Goody argued that the key distinction lay in technology, for, he wrote of African state systems, "both productivity and domination were of a limited kind": Goody, *Technology*, 47.

10. There was of course considerable diversity behind this generalisation. As Robin Law observed of West African states in the era of the slave trade, "the process of centralisation was not carried to a successful conclusion" in Oyo, compared with Asante, Benin and Dahomey: Law, *Oyo Empire*, 310.

11. As Law argued for one of Africa's ostensibly most 'successful' military states, Dahomey: Law, *Slave Coast*, 348ff.

12. Fisher, 'Eastern Maghrib'; Holt and Daly, *History of the Sudan*, chs 1 and 2.

13. Nurse and Philippson, *Bantu Languages*; Vansina, 'New Linguistic Evidence'; Ehret, 'Bantu Expansions'.

14. Inikori and Engerman, *Atlantic Slave Trade*; M'baye, 'Economic, Political and Social Impact'.

15. A sample would include Eric Williams's seminal work on the intimacy between capitalist economics and slavery: E. Williams, *Capitalism and Slavery*; Walter Rodney's pioneering, provocative thesis on the underdevelopment of Africa: Rodney, *How Europe Underdeveloped Africa*; and Joseph Inikori's incisive reassessment of the relationship between industrialisation in the Global North and an Atlantic economy based on the labour of enslaved Africans: Inikori, *Africans and the Industrial Revolution*. For a more conventionally Eurocentric analysis by comparison, see Davis, *Rise of the Atlantic Economies*.

16. Gilroy, *Black Atlantic*; Thornton, *Africa and Africans*; Sweet, *Recreating Africa*.

17. Law, *Oyo Empire*, ch. 3; R. S. Smith, *Kingdoms of the Yoruba*, chs 2 and 3.

18. Tilly, *Coercion*.

19. Ibid., 20ff.

20. There is a long-running debate, almost as old as the state itself, around the provenance and nature of Dahomey—in other words, over the extent to which Dahomey was the corollary of the slave trade, as well as one of its most vigorous practitioners. The consensus, it seems safe to suggest, is that the kingdom did indeed owe a great deal to the external commerce in enslaved people, in terms of roots, form and function. For a skilful navigation of the issues and the literature, see Law, 'Dahomey and the Slave Trade'.

21. Arhin, 'Asante Military Institutions'.

22. Searing, 'Aristocrats, Slaves and Peasants'; Klein, 'Impact of the Atlantic Slave Trade'.

23. Alpers, *Ivory and Slaves*, esp. 46–58; and McCracken, 'Nineteenth Century in Malawi', 97.

24. Thornton, *Kingdom of Kongo*; Thornton, 'Development of an African Catholic Church'.

25. D. Robinson, *Muslim Societies*, 114ff; a contemporary description is provided in 'Arab Faqīh, *Futūḥ al-Ḥabaša* (*The Conquest of Abyssinia*).

26. Beshah and Wolde Aregay, *Question of the Union*; Pennec and Toubkis, 'Reflections on the Notions'. See also contemporary Portuguese accounts of these events: Beckingham and Huntingford, *Some Records of Ethiopia*; Lockhart, 'Itinerário' of Jerónimo Lobo.

27. Crummey, *Land and Society*, ch. 3.

28. Marks and Gray, 'Southern Africa and Madagascar', 398ff.

# Chapter 3

1. I have argued this especially in R. Reid, *Warfare in African History*, specifically ch. 5.

2. S. Johnson, *History of the Yorubas*, 170.

3. Law, 'Constitutional Troubles of Oyo'; Law, *Oyo Empire*, 183–201.

4. S. Johnson, *History of the Yorubas*, 188.

5. Law, *Oyo Empire*, 261ff.

6. Connah, *African Civilizations*, 131.

7. Specifically, the Book of Judges: "In those days there was no king in Israel: every man did that which was right in his own eyes" (21:25, King James Bible).

8. The period has lain relatively neglected in recent decades, although see my own treatment of it in R. Reid, *Frontiers of Violence*, esp. ch. 3. Key analyses include Abir, *Ethiopia*; and Rubenson, 'Ethiopia and the Horn', and also Rubenson's detailed but ultimately somewhat teleological assessment in *Survival of Ethiopian Independence*. There are a number of contemporary or near-contemporary chronicles, including H. Weld Blundell's translated and edited *Royal Chronicle of Abyssinia*. James Bruce—the truculent and bombastic Scottish explorer whose seemingly fantastical accounts were initially disbelieved by many—witnessed the very beginnings of the Zemene Mesafint, by sheer chance, and offers a vital if tiresomely narcissistic account in his *Travels*.

9. Rubenson, 'Ethiopia and the Horn', 57ff.

10. Crummey, 'Banditry and Resistance'.

11. Quoted in R. Reid, *War in Pre-colonial Eastern Africa*, 93.

12. "O men", wrote one contemporary chronicler mournfully, "that time was as no time had been, for the Kingdom was split in two [...]. In the days of the Old Testament on account of the grievous sins of the people of Israel the Kingdom was divided among two tribes of Israel [...]. Today since God has kept his help away from us and has taken away the Lord who had been appointed King there have been made many rulers over Ethiopia [...]. There was no one to say, 'How is it that the kingdom has become contemptible to children and slaves? How is it that the Kingdom is a laughing stock to the uncircumcised?'": Pankhurst, *Ethiopian Royal Chronicles*, 140–42.

13. For example, Crummey, 'Tewodros as Reformer'.

14. Crummey, 'Violence of Tewodros'. The drama of the times is captured in an invaluable collection of contemporary letters penned by a range of Ethiopian protagonists: Rubenson, *Acta Aethiopica*.

15. Pankhurst, *Ethiopian Royal Chronicles*, 151; also Blanc, *Narrative of Captivity*, 333–35; R. Reid, *War in Pre-colonial Eastern Africa*, 95.

16. Crummey, 'Imperial Legitimacy'; Orlowska, 'Re-imagining Empire'.

17. Milkias and Metaferia, *Battle of Adwa*. For a contemporary assessment, bordering on the hagiographic in its admiration of the Ethiopian victory, see Berkeley, *Campaign of Adowa*.

18. Most notably, although he later revised the thesis, Ranger, 'Invention of Tradition'. The concept can just as readily be applied to various stages of Africa's transformative nineteenth century.

19. For a comprehensive and comparative survey, see Homewood, *Ecology*.

20. Insurrections and wars of expansion aimed at the proper application of the Faith in the Sahel belt date to the era of the Mali and Songhay states: for example, the Songhay ruler Muhammad Ture: see Hunwick, 'Religion and State'.

21. Fisher, 'Central Sahara'.

22. In a broader sense, it is worth observing that the Fulani were part of an eighteenth-century global phenomenon, with Islamist insurgencies in Arabia (the Wahhabi movement) and India (under Shah Wali Allah) erupting in the same period with the same revivalist objectives.

23. For example, D. Robinson, 'Islamic Revolution'.

24. For a recent assessment, see Lovejoy, *Jihad in West Africa*. Older, still hugely useful analyses include Murray Last's classic *The Sokoto Caliphate*; H.A.S. Johnston, *Fulani Empire*; and Smaldone's focus on the military side of things, *Warfare in the Sokoto Caliphate*.

25. Law, 'Making Sense of a Traditional Narrative'.

26. The term 'Sokoto Caliphate' itself was apparently coined in the mid-1960s by the foremost scholar of the region, Murray Last, with some assistance from his doctoral supervisor H.F.C. Smith—as he himself helpfully clarified in a recent book review: 'Text and Authority', 253.

27. See J. Wright, 'Turbulent Times', esp. 219–26.

28. The specifically military aspects of the Zulu revolution have been a source of fascination—and have drawn a particular kind of 'white gaze'—since Shaka himself first loomed into view. See, for example, Morris, *Washing of the Spears*; and Knight, *Anatomy of the Zulu Army*.

29. There has long been debate—often quite heated—about the causes and nature of the violent transformation summarised here: see, for example, Cobbing, 'Mfecane as Alibi'. In recent years, however, the controversies have cooled off somewhat and a consensus has emerged. For an excellent overview, see again J. Wright, 'Turbulent Times'. See also Hamilton, *Mfecane Aftermath*. For a contemporary European perspective, see, for example, Isaacs, *Travels and Adventures*.

30. Omer-Cooper, *Zulu Aftermath*.

31. As with many South African leaders, including Shaka himself, Mzilikazi and his polity have attracted a fair amount of more or less sensationalist assessment: see, for example, P. Becker, *Path of Blood*. See also Rasmussen, *Migrant Kingdom*. For a thoughtful, and critical, assessment of some of the issues arising from misappropriated histories of Mzilikazi and similarly 'martial' figures, see Ndlovu-Gatsheni, 'Who Ruled by the Spear?'.

32. For an excellent case study, see A. Roberts, *History of the Bemba*, for example 119–24.

33. Sanders, *Moshoeshoe*; L. M. Thompson, *Survival in Two Worlds*; Eldredge, *South African Kingdom*.

34. A vivid account—as rich in detail as it is outdated in its analytical tone—is provided in P. Becker, *Rule of Fear*. For an early attempt to rehabilitate a ruler who had been framed in unflattering terms for many years, see Okoye, 'Dingane: A Reappraisal'.

35. Ballard, 'John Dunn and Cetshwayo'.

36. Hanretta, 'Women, Marginality and the Zulu State'.

37. Guy, *Destruction of the Zulu Kingdom* remains superlative. For something approaching a classic account, Morris, *Washing of the Spears*, is still a great read, if somewhat dated in various respects; and Knight, *Anatomy of the Zulu Army* offers some useful detail on military operations and culture.

38. Dalzel, *History of Dahomy*, 218–19. See also Akinjogbin, 'Archibald Dalzel'.

39. Predictably enough, these have long been the focus of a particular kind of male gaze: for example, Duncan, *Travels in Western Africa*, 1:224–25, 227, and Richard Burton's descriptions of them in *Mission to Gelele*; and see Alpern, *Amazons of Black Sparta*. For a rather more nuanced, wide-ranging assessment, see Bay, *Wives of the Leopard*.

40. Forbes, *Dahomey and the Dahomans*, 2:89. In the late eighteenth century, Robert Norris described a civil war in which the rebellion of the *mehu* was crushed by the *agau*: Norris, *Memoirs*, 9.

41. Akinjogbin, *Dahomey and its Neighbours*, chs 5 and 6; Forbes, *Dahomey and the Dahomans*, 1:7.

42. Bay, 'Belief, Legitimacy and the Kpojito'; Bay, 'Servitude and Worldly Success'.

43. Awe, 'The Iyalode'.

44. Yoder, 'Fly and Elephant Parties'.

45. Brodie Cruickshank's 'Report of His Mission to the King of Dahomey', in 'Missions to the Kings of Ashanti & Dahomey: Dispatches from the Lieutenant-Governor of the Gold Coast': *British Parliamentary Papers: Slave Trade*, 50:17; see also C. Newbury, *Western Slave Coast*, 51.

46. Forbes, *Dahomey and the Dahomans*, 2:187–88.

47. Law, 'Politics of Commercial Transition'.

48. The evolution of these internal politics is dealt with at length in Ivor Wilks's landmark study, *Asante*; also McCaskie, *State and Society*.

49. Wilks, *Asante*, passim, but in particular chs 4–7; also, for specific case studies, Maier, 'The Dente Oracle', and Adu-Boahen, 'Pawn of Contesting Imperialists'.

50. Adjaye, *Diplomacy and Diplomats*.

51. Manu-Osafo, '"The days of their heedless power"'.

52. Aidoo, 'Asante Queen Mothers'.

53. David Lee Schoenbrun is one of the leading scholars of this early period: see *A Green Place, A Good Place*; and *The Names of the Python*.

54. For example, Nyakatura, *Anatomy*, 49. This text is a classic of Nyoro history writing which was first published as *Abakama ba Bunyoro-Kitara* in 1947. See also 'K.W.', 'Kings of Bunyoro-Kitara, Part 2', 80; and also Katoke, *Karagwe Kingdom*, 24.

55. Chrétien, *Great Lakes of Africa*, chs 2 and 3; Oliver, 'Discernible Developments'.

56. Kiwanuka, *History of Buganda*, 112ff.

57. Médard, *Le royaume du Buganda*, esp. chs 2 and 5; R. Reid, 'War and Militarism'; R. Reid, *Political Power*, ch. 9.

58. Reid and Médard, 'Merchants, Missions'; R. Reid, 'Warfare and Urbanisation', 56.

59. Kagwa, *Kings of Buganda*, first published as *Basekabaka ba Buganda* in 1901.

60. Southwold, 'Succession to the Throne'.

61. Musisi, 'Women, "Elite Polygyny", and Buganda'; Schiller, 'Royal Women'. In a pioneering study, Rhiannon Stephens explores this through the prism of motherhood in *A History of African Motherhood*, esp. ch. 5.

62. Twaddle, 'Emergence of Politico-Religious Groupings'; R. Reid, *Political Power*, 198ff.

63. Among the wealth of literature on Buganda's late nineteenth century experience, see Twaddle, 'Emergence of Politico-Religious Groupings'; Hanson, *Landed Obligation*; and, for an older, robustly narrative account, Low, 'Uganda'.

64. D. Newbury, 'Campaigns of Rwabugiri'.

65. Vansina, *Antecedents*, 164–73.

66. In addition to Vansina, *Antecedents*, see also Vansina, *L'Évolution du Royaume Rwanda*.

67. Uzoigwe, 'Succession and Civil War'.

68. There is an interesting comparison to be made here with the notion in Europe's classical antiquity of civil war as "a necessary and natural struggle": Armitage, *Civil Wars*, 78. In Rome, the distinction was made between short- and long-term interpretations of the phenomenon. "A short-term explanation", Armitage explains, "implied that civil war was accidental and unlikely to recur. The longer view would weave conflict into the very fabric of Roman history and imply deep-seated causes": ibid., 79.

69. Ford and Hall, 'History of Karagwe', 9; R. Reid, *War in Pre-colonial Eastern Africa*, 149.

70. Nyakatura, *Anatomy*, 100.

71. Doyle, *Crisis and Decline*, ch. 2; Beattie, *Nyoro State*, ch. 4. See also Nyakatura, *Anatomy*, 123ff.

72. Armitage, *Civil Wars*, passim.

73. E. A. Henderson, 'When States Implode'; Ali and Matthews, *Civil Wars in Africa*.

74. Cramer, *Civil War*.

75. Armitage, *Civil Wars*, 166.

76. A classic account is Verbeken, *Msiri, roi de Garenganze*. For a contemporary source related to the later life of the state, see Arnot, *Garenganze*. See also A. Roberts, 'The Nyamwezi', 134; A. Roberts, 'Nyamwezi Trade', 57, 67, 73; and St. John, 'Kazembe and the Tanganyika-Nyasa Corridor', 218.

77. For a good introduction, see Birmingham, *Trade and Conflict*; and more recently, see Linda Heywood's vivid study of the woman who was one of the most famous Imbangala leaders, *Njinga of Angola*.

78. R. L. Roberts, 'Production and Reproduction of Warrior States'; R. L. Roberts, *Warriors, Merchants, and Slaves*; Klein, 'Impact of the Atlantic Slave Trade'; Barry, *Senegambia* (first published in 1988 as *La Sénégambie du xvᵉ au xixᵉ siècle*), esp. Part 2; Westwood, 'Ceddo, Sofa, Tirailleur'. The drama of the era is beautifully, if imaginatively, recreated in Maryse Condé's famous novel *Segu*, first published (*Ségou: Les murailles de la terre*) in 1984.

79. Levtzion, 'North-West Africa', 176.

80. Thornton, *History of West Central Africa*.

81. Macola, *Kingdom of Kazembe*; and see also Macola, 'History of the Eastern Lunda Royal Capitals'. For an innovative and instructive analysis of historical memory in the area, see Gordon, 'History on the Luapula Retold'.

82. Alpers, *Ivory and Slaves*.

83. For a range of perspectives encompassing a lengthy timespan, see various essays in Spear and Waller, *Being Maasai*, in particular Galaty, 'Maasai Expansion', and Lamphear, 'Aspects of "Becoming Turkana"'. See also Lamphear, 'Brothers in Arms'.

84. Birmingham, 'Early African Trade'; J. C. Miller, 'Slaves, Slavers and Social Change'.

85. Isaacman and Isaacman, *Slavery and Beyond*; Isaacman and Peterson, 'Making the Chikunda'; Isaacman, 'Origin, Formation and Early History'.

86. 'Captain Jones's Report on the Egba Army in 1861', Appendix 1 in Ajayi and Smith, *Yoruba Warfare*, 132.

87. R. S. Smith, *Warfare and Diplomacy*, passim; R. Reid, 'Fragile Revolution', 400.

88. Freund, *African City*, 16.

89. Akintoye, *Revolution and Power Politics*; R. S. Smith, *Kingdoms of the Yoruba*; Lloyd, *Political Development*; Ajayi and Smith, *Yoruba Warfare*.

90. The story of Tewodros has been approached in various ways over time: see, for example, Rubenson, *King of Kings*; or Marsden, *Barefoot Emperor*. There is a wealth of contemporary reportage, too, which reflects shifting perceptions of him from broadly positive when he first emerged to almost wholly negative toward the end of his life: Plowden, *Travels in Abyssinia*, ch. 23; Stern, *Wanderings among the Falashas*; Rassam, *Narrative of the British Mission*.

91. Hassan, *Oromo of Ethiopia*; H. S. Lewis, *Jimma Abba Jifar*; Jalata, *Oromia and Ethiopia*, chs 1 and 3.

92. Brenner, *Shehus of Kukawa*; Hiribarren, *History of Borno*.

93. D. Robinson, *Holy War*.

94. Klein, 'Social and Economic Factors'.

95. The great resource is still Person's three-volume *Samori*.

96. Danziger, *Abd al-Qadir*.

97. E. E Evans-Pritchard's *The Sanusi of Cyrenaica* remains a rewarding read, allowing for its colonial-era context and provenance. See also Vandewalle, *History of Modern Libya*, chs 1 and 2.

98. Holt and Daly, *History of the Sudan*, Part 2; R. Gray, *History of the Southern Sudan*.

99. For a classic study, Holt, *Mahdist State*.

100. Al-Sayyid-Marsot, *Egypt in the Reign of Muhammad Ali*; Vatikiotis, *Modern History of Egypt*; Holt, 'Egypt', 22–33; Holt and Daly, *History of the Sudan*, chs 3–5.

101. The first consolidated effort to scrutinise the role of guns in a 'precolonial' context was a series of seminar papers presented at the University of London in 1968–69, which were later published as 'Papers on Firearms in Sub-Saharan Africa' 1 and 2, in the *Journal of African History* 12, nos 2 and 4 (1971). A sample of other work, chronologically organised, would include: Beachey, 'Arms Trade'; Legassick, 'Firearms, Horses'; A. Roberts, 'Firearms in North-Eastern Zambia'; Caulk, 'Firearms and Princely Power'; Law, 'Horses, Firearms and Political Power'; Inikori, 'Import of Firearms'; Wolde Aregay, 'Reappraisal of the Impact'; R. S. Smith, *Warfare and Diplomacy*; Thornton, *Warfare in Atlantic Africa*; R. Reid, *War in Pre-colonial Eastern Africa*; Macola, *Gun in Central Africa*.

# Act III

1. The earliest reference, for example, to contact between Nyamwezi country and the coast is in 1811, when it was reported that Nyamwezi slaves were being brought to Zanzibar for sale, and that the region had gained a reputation for wealth in ivory (and to a lesser extent gold): Burton, *Zanzibar*, 2:510. Burton further claims that the area was first visited in 1825 by two 'Arab' brothers, Musa and Sayyan, "preceding the Arab travellers, who in those days made their markets at Usanga and Usenga": Burton, *Lake Regions*, 423. 'Musa' was in fact Musa Mzuri, a wealthy Khoja who

financed much of the commercial activity emanating from Tabora. The central figure in an account by the geographer James MacQueen, Lief bin Said, would certainly have passed through various Nyamwezi districts in 1831: MacQueen, 'Visit of Lief ben Saied'. By the 1830s, as we have seen, commercial relations were firmly established between Zanzibari merchants and Unyanyembe, and between 1840 and 1850, coastal traders became permanently established at both Unyanyembe and Ujiji on the shore of Lake Tanganyika: for example, Burton, *Lake Regions*, 315.

2. Tippu Tip, *Maisha*, 99. It isn't an unproblematic story, however, and there may have been some hyperbole in this particular telling. See also N. R. Bennett, *Studies in East African History*, 84.

3. His significance—and his sense of his own importance—is reflected in the fact that he produced an autobiography: Tippu Tip, *Maisha*.

4. Iliffe, *Modern History of Tanganyika*, 46.

5. For a useful account, see Alison Smith, 'Southern Section of the Interior', esp. 288–95.

6. Hofmeyr, Kaarsholm and Frederiksen, 'Introduction', 1–4; Becker and Cabrita, 'Introduction', 161–64; Campbell, *Africa and the Indian Ocean World*.

7. Unomah and Webster, 'East Africa', remains a good point of entry.

8. One of the best analyses is still Sheriff, *Slaves, Spices and Ivory*; see also N. R. Bennett, *History of the Arab State*, and for a detailed, if somewhat skewed, contemporary account, the two volumes of Burton, *Zanzibar*.

9. Nurse and Spear, *Swahili*.

10. In truth the Swahili term *wangwana* is somewhat amorphous, often used to describe more than one social or ethnic category. It can indicate someone free of slave descent; a town dweller (as opposed to a 'savage' or 'barbarian'); and, relatedly, an educated, civilised person of personal integrity and dignity. The term is commonly used in the nineteenth century to describe leaders of coastal caravans. See, for example, Goyvaerts, 'Johannes Fabian', 483; Unomah and Webster, 'East Africa', 304–5.

11. For example, Sperling with Kagabo, 'Coastal Hinterland'.

12. Iliffe, *Modern History of Tanganyika*, 48; N. R. Bennett, 'Arab Impact', 229; and see also Bennett's later book-length study on the wider issues, *Arab versus European*.

13. For example, H. M. Stanley, *How I Found Livingstone*, 479.

14. Burton, *Lake Regions*, 321; E. C. Hore, 'On the Twelve Tribes', 10; R. Reid, *War in Pre-colonial Eastern Africa*, 143.

15. H. M. Stanley, *Through the Dark Continent*, 2:1–6.

16. E. C. Hore, 'On the Twelve Tribes', passim; R. Reid, *War in Pre-colonial Eastern Africa*, 116–19; N. R. Bennett, 'Arab Impact', 226–29. See also Gooding, *On the Frontiers*.

17. See the sketch map in H. M. Stanley, *How I Found Livingstone*, opposite 259; and also Pallaver, 'Triangle'.

18. Burton, *Lake Regions*, 229.

19. Cameron, *Across Africa*, 2:139–40.

20. H. Waller, *Last Journals*, 2:182.

21. Burton, *Lake Regions*, 229.

22. H. M. Stanley, *How I Found Livingstone*, 194.

23. H. Waller, *Last Journals*, 2:192.

24. This is the impression given in H. M. Stanley, *How I Found Livingstone*, 189ff; N. R. Bennett, *Stanley's Despatches*, 26; Burton, *Lake Regions*, 229–30.

25. Burton, *Lake Regions*, 232.

26. For example, Speke, *Journal*, 91.

27. Again, see N. R. Bennett, *Mirambo of Tanzania*; N. R. Bennett, *Arab versus European*; R. Reid, *War in Pre-colonial Eastern Africa*, esp. ch. 5.

28. N. R. Bennett, *Mirambo of Tanzania*, ch. 3. The nature of the struggle is examined at close proximity in H. M. Stanley, *How I Found Livingstone*, chs 8 and 9.

29. There is an extensive literature on this, some of which was cited in our earlier discussion of Mirambo. See, for example, A. Roberts, 'Nyamwezi Trade'; A. Roberts, 'The Nyamwezi'; Deutsch, 'Notes on the Rise of Slavery'; Rockel, *Carriers of Culture*; Greiner, *Human Porterage*.

30. Iliffe, *Africans*, 106, 110.

31. Burton, *Lake Regions*, 235.

32. As noted earlier, Nyamwezi slaves appear in Zanzibar in a report dated to 1811 (see n. 1 to this chapter), although we can't be sure how they got there—whether escorted by Nyamwezi or coastal merchants. At some point in the 1830s (Burton suggests "about one generation" before 1857) a Nyamwezi caravan passed through Gogo territory, remembered chiefly for the fact that the caravan leader ('Kafuke') was killed by the Gogo. This event apparently initiated ongoing hostility between Gogo and Nyamwezi, who "have never from that time crossed the country without fear and trembling": Burton, *Lake Regions*, 187, 214. The earliest reference to Nyamwezi traders and/or political leaders turning up in Zanzibar is in 1839, when a missionary, a Mr Burgess, met a group of them, one of whom "was the heir apparent to the throne". They were in Zanzibar, according to Burgess, to meet with the sultan to negotiate "a treaty for the safety and success of his subjects when on their trading expeditions": Burgess, 'Letters', 119. The author doesn't specify which chiefdom they came from, but it is fun to speculate that, if they hailed from Unyanyembe, the 'heir apparent' in question would probably have been Fundikira.

33. Mkasiwa himself told David Livingstone in 1872—by which time the *mtemi* was "about sixty years old, and partially paralytic"—that "he had gone as far as Katanga by the same Fipa route I now propose[d] to take, when a little boy following his father, who was a great trader": H. Waller, *Last Journals*, 2:180.

34. Deutsch, 'Notes on the Rise of Slavery'.

35. The intergenerational aspect of this transformation is clearly hugely significant, and while most work on 'youth' as a category of historical analysis tends to focus on the long twentieth century, there are a number of germane studies in Burton and Charton-Bigot, *Generations Past*; and see also R. Waller, 'Rebellious Youth', and for a useful conceptual overview, Argenti and Durham, 'Youth'.

36. Beachey, 'East African Ivory Trade'.

37. Roberts characterised Nyamwezi commercial endeavour as "progress towards an inevitable dead end": 'Nyamwezi Trade', 73.

38. The standard ethnographic work is Abrahams, *Peoples of Greater Unyamwezi*.

39. E. C. Hore, 'On the Twelve Tribes', 7; R. Reid, *War in Pre-colonial Eastern Africa*, 167–68.

40. These are mentioned in Burton, *Lake Regions*, 228, 269; Grant, 'Summary of Observations', 249; H. M. Stanley, *Through the Dark Continent*, 1:382, 383–84, 396.

41. Contemporary accounts commented on former settlements which had either been abandoned or deliberately destroyed along the road between 1850s and 1870s: Cameron, *Across Africa*, 1:152; H. M. Stanley, *How I Found Livingstone*, 211–12, 219.

42. See for example a pioneering study of the region, Kjekshus, *Ecology Control*.

# Chapter 4

1. African economic history has enjoyed something of a revival in recent years, as an array of scholars, relative newcomers and senior alike (though these days the distinction seems quickly to blur), have reinvigorated the field, often through macro-level, *longue durée*-approach

interpretations of African development. Anything like a comprehensive sweep of the literature would be impossible here, but a sense of the field, at least of the last few years, is provided in surveys by A. G. Hopkins, 'New Economic History', and Jerven, 'Economic Growth'; and in a collection of essays in Akyeampong et al., *Africa's Development in Historical Perspective*. For a stimulating earlier intervention, see Cooper, 'Africa and the World Economy'. It is with some trepidation that one contemplates entering that particular auditorium, so I won't. I have reservations about some of the arguments put forward in recent years—whether 'reversal of fortune'-type blockbusters, or grand schemata based on sketchy demographic data—but I admire the chutzpah underpinning them, and in general they are presented by people who seem to know what they're talking about. I am determined that what follows will emphatically not be a 'new contribution' to *economic* history, which would be vain and delusional, but rather a survey of *socio*economic developments, integrating material and commercial innovation and aspiration as well as social change.

2. A long-term perspective of this dynamic is offered in Inikori, 'Africa and the Globalization Process'.

3. Law, *Slave Coast*, 276–77; also Law, 'Ideologies of Royal Power'.

4. McCaskie, 'Accumulation, Wealth and Belief'.

5. This has been revealed by archaeological work: for example, Ogundiran, 'Material Life and Domestic Economy'; Norman, 'Hueda (Whydah) Country and Town'.

6. Several essays in the special issue *Slavery & Abolition* 9, no. 3 (1988) have made important contributions to our understanding of these dynamics: Austen, '19th Century Islamic Slave Trade'; Ewald, 'Nile Valley System'; Ahmad, 'Ethiopian Slave Exports'; and Fernyhough, 'Slavery and the Slave Trade in Southern Ethiopia'. See also Abir, 'Southern Ethiopia'; Pankhurst, *Economic History of Ethiopia*, ch. 3; Moore-Harell, 'Economic and Social Aspects'.

7. Arrowsmith-Brown, *Prutky's Travels*, 25, 152, 179; Gobat, *Journal of Three Years' Residence*, 39; Plowden, *Travels in Abyssinia*, 20; Parkyns, *Life in Abyssinia*, 177.

8. Caulk, 'Firearms and Princely Power'; and the encyclopaedic account of commerce in Pankhurst, *Economic History of Ethiopia*, ch. 9.

9. Crummey, 'Violence of Tewodros', 71–72, 75; Blanc, *Narrative of Captivity*, 8–9, 50, 90–91. See also various contemporary letters which detail Tewodros's travails in the north: Birru Petros to Antoine d'Abbadie, 26 November 1858, Aregawi Subagadis to Theodore Gilbert, 30 December 1860, Asseggahen to Antoine d'Abbadie, 14 January 1866, and Asseggahen to Antoine d'Abbadie, 15 April 1867, in Rubenson, *Acta Aethiopica*. Again, this has sometimes been couched in terms of efforts at 'modernisation', which is ultimately unhelpfully prescriptive.

10. This is detailed in Marcus, *Life and Times of Menelik II*, esp. ch. 3. For an account of an unusual participant in this trade, the French surrealist pioneer and poet Arthur Rimbaud, see Nicholl, *Somebody Else*.

11. For a thoughtful historical perspective, see Donham, 'Old Abyssinia'. There are a number of contemporary sources attesting first hand to these developments: among the most detailed is by the Russian military attaché Alexander Bulatovich, *Ethiopia through Russian Eyes*.

12. In some rather crude respects, perhaps, a series of polities along the Atlantic seaboard began life in much the same way, in Tilly's provocative interpretation, as many European states: namely, as criminal rackets which became very good at generating the wealth needed to finance violence: Tilly, *Coercion*.

13. The brother of the ruler of Allada apparently paid Agaja, then king of Dahomey, for an armed intervention to assist him in his struggle for the throne, suggesting, prima facie, a rather more basic pecuniary motivation: Law, *Slave Coast*, 278–87. Law's major study of Ouidah itself begins with the Dahomean conquest: Law, *Ouidah*.

14. Wilks, *Asante*, passim; R. L. Roberts, 'Production and Reproduction of Warrior States'; R. L. Roberts, *Warriors, Merchants, and Slaves*, passim; Law, *Oyo Empire*, esp. ch. 10.

15. Musisi, 'Women, "Elite Polygyny", and Buganda'; R. Reid, 'Human Booty in Buganda'; Kiwanuka, *History of Buganda*, 99–100; Wrigley, *Kingship and State*, ch. 10; Hanson, *Landed Obligation*, ch. 3.

16. Kagwa, *Kings of Buganda*, 99–101.

17. J. M. Gray, 'Ahmed bin Ibrahim'. There was a brief period in the late 1850s when the merchants were denied entry to the kingdom, probably because the transition from the reign of Suna to that of Mutesa was a politically sensitive moment: R. Reid, *History of Modern Uganda*, 204.

18. Hartwig, 'Victoria Nyanza'; R. Reid, 'Ganda on Lake Victoria'.

19. Quoted in *Missions catholiques* 14 (1882), 89–90.

20. Quoted in R. Reid, *Political Power*, 169.

21. Speke, *Journal*, 284, 288.

22. Burton, *Lake Regions*, 396–97, 424; H. M. Stanley, *Through the Dark Continent*, 1:356–57. A few years later, in the mid-1880s, it was reported by the missionary-cum-gunrunner Charles Stokes that the Karagwe political elite had "tired of the Arab tyrannical rule" and driven the merchants out: quoted in R. Reid, *War in Pre-colonial Eastern Africa*, 114.

23. Schmidt, *Peasants, Traders, and Wives*.

24. Lovejoy, *Transformations in Slavery*, 192–94; Atmore, 'Africa on the Eve of Partition', 54, 56; Isichei, *History of West Africa*, 184–85; Person, 'Western Africa', 238ff.

25. O'Fahey, *Darfur Sultanate*.

26. Lovejoy, *Salt of the Desert Sun*; Lovejoy, 'Concubinage'; Klein, 'Women in Slavery'.

27. A range of contexts and specificities is explored in Coles and Mack, *Hausa Women*.

28. R. L. Roberts, 'Women's Work'; Olivier de Sardan, 'Songhay-Zarma Female Slave'.

29. Lovejoy, 'Plantations in the Economy'.

30. J. Wright, 'Control of Women's Labour'. For a comprehensive overview, see, for example, Birmingham and Marks, 'Southern Africa'.

31. Guy, 'Ecological Factors', 112–18. For a somewhat dated assessment but one which is still of interest in terms of conceptualisation, see Gluckman, 'Kingdom of the Zulu', esp. 28–34.

32. J. Wright, 'Turbulent Times', 230ff.

33. Al-Sayyid-Marsot, *Egypt in the Reign of Muhammad Ali*, passim; also Rivlin, *Agricultural Policy*.

34. For example, Ewald, 'The Nile Valley System'.

35. Mansfield, *Nasser's Egypt*, 20.

36. Robinson and Gallagher, *Africa and the Victorians*, chs 4 and 5; and for a useful overview, Holt, 'Egypt', 33–50.

37. There is a growing focus, long overdue, on these links. See, for example, Draper, 'City of London and Slavery'.

38. There is a vast literature on this, but the various contributions in Law, *From Slave Trade to "Legitimate" Commerce* is a good place to start. See also A. G. Hopkins, *Economic History*, ch. 4; Austen, *African Economic History*, ch. 5; Lynn, *Commerce and Economic Change*; Law, Schwartz and Strickrodt, *Commercial Agriculture*; and Strickrodt, *Afro-European Trade*, ch. 6.

39. Work by Law is essential reading on this: see for example Law, *Ouidah*, ch. 5; Law, 'Politics of Commercial Transition'; and Law, 'Evolution of the Brazilian Community'.

40. Lovejoy, 'Yoruba Factor'; R. S. Smith, *Warfare and Diplomacy*, 31–32.

41. Ajayi and Smith, *Yoruba Warfare*, 37–39; Akintoye, *Revolution and Power Politics*, 34.

42. Afonja, 'Changing Modes of Production'; Denzer, 'Yoruba Women'.

43. Ajayi and Smith, *Yoruba Warfare*; Mba, *Nigerian Women Mobilised*. Women also supplied provisions to slaving expeditions in the early nineteenth-century Kongo region: Broadhead, 'Slave Wives, Free Sisters'.

44. R. S. Smith, *Warfare and Diplomacy*, 106, 110–11, 115, 131.

45. A. G. Hopkins, 'Economic Imperialism'; and A. G. Hopkins, *Economic History*, 165–66. Also, Lovejoy and Richardson, 'Initial "Crisis of Adaptation"', and Lynn, 'West African Palm Oil Trade'.

46. Klein, 'Social and Economic Factors'; Barry, *Senegambia*, Parts 3 and 4.

47. For example, see Eltis, *Economic Growth*, 62–77.

48. For example, Wilks, *Asante*, 683ff.

49. Austin, 'Between Abolition and *jihad*'.

50. Soumonni, 'Compatibility'; J. Reid, 'Warrior Aristocrats'.

51. Law, 'Royal Monopoly and Private Enterprise'.

52. E. F. White, *Sierra Leone's Settler Women Traders*.

53. For example, Mann, *Marrying Well*.

54. Broadhead, 'Slave Wives, Free Sisters'.

55. A. G. Hopkins, *Economic History*, 192–95, 197–98, 220.

56. Suret-Canale, *French Colonialism*, 199–204 and passim.

57. Bassett, 'Development of Cotton'.

58. Hill, *Migrant Cocoa Farmers*; Austin, 'Emergence of Capitalist Relations'; Austin, *Land, Labour and Capital*.

59. Ogutu, 'Cultivation of Coffee'.

60. Engdahl, *Exchange of Cotton*; also, Ehrlich, 'Uganda Economy', esp. 395–422.

61. S. Conrad, *German Colonialism*, 94; Manning, *Francophone Sub-Saharan Africa*, 45, 49; Suret-Canale, *French Colonialism*, 132–33.

62. Tignor, *Egypt*, ch. 10.

63. Barnett, *Gezira Scheme*.

64. For contemporary assessments of the supposed transformation engendered by colonial rule, see Lugard, *Dual Mandate*; and McPhee, *Economic Revolution*. See also Hogendorn, 'Economic Initiative'; Tosh, 'Cash Crop Revolution'; Austen, *African Economic History*, 124–29.

65. S. Martin, *Palm Oil and Protest*, esp. ch. 2; and see also Martin's essay, 'Slaves, Igbo Women and Palm Oil'.

66. See, for example, Guyer, 'Wealth in People'.

67. Wrigley, 'Changing Economic Structure', 17–27; R. Reid, *Political Power*, 160ff.

68. For a brief summation, see Thornton, *Warfare in Atlantic Africa*, 116–17.

69. It is worth noting that the very first doctoral project on African history, using sources (including oral) then regarded as unconventional, was concerned with these very place, time and phenomena: namely, Kenneth O. Dike's study of the region while at King's College London, published as *Trade and Politics in the Niger Delta*. Seventy years on, it remains remarkably fresh and inspirational. See also Jones, *Trading States of the Oil Rivers*; and Northrup, *Trade without Rulers*.

70. The classic account is Cookey, *King Jaja of the Niger Delta*; also Ofonagoro, 'Notes on the Ancestry of Mbanaso Okwaraozurumba'. And see also Ofonagoro's thoughtful review of Cookey and others in his 'Commercial Revolution'.

71. Ekejiuba, 'Omu Okwei'.

72. Vansina, *Tio Kingdom*; also Harms, *River of Wealth*.

73. Nair, *Politics and Society*; Latham, *Old Calabar*.

74. The East African slave trade (including the Red Sea and Persian Gulf as well as the Indian Ocean) awaits the kind of comprehensive analysis which the Atlantic world has long

attracted. No doubt there are methodological and indeed linguistic challenges, compared to studying the commerce in the Western hemisphere; but some major advances have been made, including, as noted earlier, a collection of essays in a special issue of *Slavery & Abolition* (vol. 9, no. 3 [1988]), edited by William Gervase Clarence-Smith: *The Economics of the Indian Ocean Slave Trade in the Nineteenth Century*. Important groundwork was also laid by Harris, *African Presence in Asia*, and Beachey, *Slave Trade of Eastern Africa*; and vital insights have been provided by studies of specific areas, including Alpers, *Ivory and Slaves*; Deutsch, *Emancipation without Abolition*; Médard and Doyle, *Slavery in the Great Lakes Region*; and Miran, *Red Sea Citizens*.

75. Relatedly, and more broadly, for an interesting reflection on the kingdom's putative relationship with the forces of 'modernisation', see Twaddle, 'Ganda Receptivity'.

76. Alpers, *Ivory and Slaves*.

77. Ambler, *Kenyan Communities*.

78. H. M. Stanley, *Through the Dark Continent*, 1:294; R. Reid, *War in Pre-colonial Eastern Africa*, 153.

79. Isaacman and Isaacman, *Slavery and Beyond*.

80. See for example Birmingham, *Short History of Modern Angola*, esp. chs 3–5; and see also an older account, focusing more on Portuguese imperialism, Clarence-Smith, *Slaves, Peasants and Capitalists*.

81. Birmingham, *Trade and Conflict*.

82. J. C. Miller, 'Cokwe Trade and Conquest'.

83. Galaty, 'Maasai Expansion', 77–83; Lamphear, 'Brothers in Arms', 86–94. For a slightly later, early colonial iteration of some of these developments, see also R. Waller, 'Bad Boys in the Bush?'.

84. A. G. Hopkins, *Economic History*, 223–24.

85. Mann, *Slavery and the Birth*; Watson, 'Civil Disorder'; Mabogunje, *Urbanization in Nigeria*; Freund, *African City*, 51ff.

86. Eckert, 'Urbanization in Colonial and Post-colonial West Africa', 209. On Ouidah itself, see Law, *Ouidah*.

87. R. S. Smith, *Warfare and Diplomacy*, ch. 6.

88. R. Reid, *War in Pre-colonial Eastern Africa*, 161–70; R. Reid, 'Warfare and Urbanisation'.

89. See for example Allina-Pisano, 'Resistance'.

90. Kjekshus, *Ecology Control*; Lyons, *Colonial Disease*; Worboys, 'Comparative History of Sleeping Sickness'; Webel, *Politics of Disease Control*.

91. For example, Hourani, *History of the Arab Peoples*, 302ff; and see also Ryzova, *Age of the Efendiyya*.

92. John Lonsdale memorably suggested that "modern tribes were often born on the way to work" in an early colonial context: Lonsdale, 'European Scramble', 758; and this is no doubt as accurate as it is pithy. But the process unquestionably pre-dates the early twentieth century.

93. A fixation with 'ethnicity' in African history is no longer—thankfully, in many ways—as potent as it was in the 1980s and 1990s, which was a time (bearing in mind events in Rwanda and South Africa, and African political and global developments more broadly) when the concept seemed particularly pertinent. As a category of analysis, albeit a contested one, it shouldn't be any less significant now, but the heat, perhaps, has gone out of the scholarly argument a little. Suffice to say here that the centre of intellectual gravity leaned toward the notion that 'tribalism'—or 'ethnicity'—was essentially, in the colonial or 'modern' context, a matter of instrumentalism, of deliberate and self-conscious construction: for example, Hobsbawm and Ranger, *Invention of Tradition*, in which the most pertinent essay is Ranger's on Africa, 'Inven-

tion of Tradition in Colonial Africa'; Young, *African Colonial State*, 232ff. Useful overviews can be found in R. Waller, 'Ethnicity and Identity', and Spear, 'Introduction'; and Lentz, 'Ethnicity' provides a helpful summary. Others, and I have myself long been drawn to this interpretation, have eschewed the modernist position and pointed to the deeper roots of particular collective, corporate, cultural identities: Chrétien and Prunier, *Les Ethnies ont une histoire*; Chabal and Daloz, *Africa Works*, 57; Spear, 'Neo-traditionalism', 16ff. Ranger himself went on to critique his own original argument as oversimplifying complex processes in 'Invention of Tradition Revisited'. For specific studies of the precolonial roots of 'ethnic' identity see, for example, Cassanelli, *Shaping of Somali Society*; Nurse and Spear, *Swahili*; Atkinson, *Roots of Ethnicity*. I also accept—in a way that perhaps I didn't a few years ago—that these identities could be markedly fluent and mobile, and contingent, though I refuse to accept that this precludes elements of a primordialist argument. See, for example, Armstrong, *Nations before Nationalism*; A. D. Smith, *Myths and Memories*; and a collection of essays drawing upon, and critiquing, the thesis that 'nations' and *ethnies* have pre-modern roots: Guibernau and Hutchinson, *History and National Destiny*. An illuminating set of analyses is also found in Spickard, *Race and Nation*.

94. A key point of reference here is the analysis, which remains incisive and relevant, in Barth, *Ethnic Groups and Boundaries*.

95. Peel, *Religious Encounter*; Chimhundu, 'Early Missionaries'.

96. For an astute assessment of the 'colonial moment' in this context, see Spear, 'Neo-traditionalism'.

97. Twaddle, 'Muslim Revolution'; Wrigley, 'Christian Revolution'.

98. For a characteristically thoughtful consideration of some relevant themes, see Peel, 'Conversion and Tradition'.

99. Comaroff, *Body of Power*.

100. Comaroff and Comaroff, *Of Revelation and Revolution*; Houle, *Making African Christianity*.

101. That said, of course, some hugely important work has already been done to retrieve and preserve lived experiences and perspectives. See, for example, Bellagamba, Greene and Klein, *African Voices on Slavery*; and Wright, *Strategies of Slaves*.

102. Curtin, *Atlantic Slave Trade*, ch. 8; Lovejoy, *Transformations in Slavery*, ch. 7.

103. Lydon, *On Trans-Saharan Trails*.

104. Hanson, 'Stolen People', and R. Reid, 'Human Booty in Buganda'.

105. See, for example, Mbilinyi, 'Wife, Slave and Subject'.

106. In addition to Wright, *Strategies of Slaves*, see also Alpers, 'Story of Swema'.

107. Alpers, 'State, Merchant Capital, and Gender Relations'.

108. Oboler, *Women, Power, and Economic Change*; Robertson, *Trouble Showed the Way*; Clark, 'Land and Food'.

109. Lovejoy, *Transformations in Slavery*, chs 9 and 10. And see also a superb range of case studies in two landmark volumes: Miers and Kopytoff, *Slavery in Africa*, and Miers and Roberts, *End of Slavery*.

110. Roberts and Miers, 'Introduction', esp. 19ff.

111. It's true that this perspective contrasts somewhat with what are often altogether gloomier diagnoses of African economic performance in the 'postcolonial' age. See also Gareth Austin's superb long view of innovation in the face of numerous challenges: Austin, 'Resources, Techniques, and Strategies'.

112. Inikori and Engerman, *Atlantic Slave Trade*; M'baye, 'Economic, Political and Social Impact'; Nunn, 'Historical Lgacies'; and Nunn, 'Long-Term Effects'. See also Acemoglu, Johnson and Robinson, 'Reversal of Fortune', and a constructive critique of the long-term approach taken in that essay, in Austin, 'The "Reversal of Fortune" Thesis'.

113. Pomeranz, *Great Divergence*. I'm certainly not the first to point out the degree to which this Alpha Debate in global history circles in effect re-marginalises Africa: see Cooper, *Africa in the World*, 11–14.

114. A. G. Hopkins, 'Economic Imperialism', essentially argues for African weakness in the face of such pressure; on the other side of the argument, see Austen, 'Abolition of the Overseas Slave Trade'; Austen, *African Economic History*, 101–2; and Austin, 'Between Abolition and *jihad*'.

## Act IV

1. Stanley's account of the Ethiopia campaign, and of the British war against Asante in 1873 on which he also reported, are contained in his *Coomassie and Magdala*.

2. The full account, of course, is in H. M. Stanley, *How I Found Livingstone*.

3. For example, Bierman, *Dark Safari*, 26–29.

4. For a stimulating point of reference, see Maya Jasanoff's superb reconceptualisation of the life and times of Joseph Conrad, *The Dawn Watch*. Stanley himself is the subject of a number of biographical or semi-biographical studies, but see in particular Bierman, *Dark Safari*; Gallop, *Mr Stanley, I Presume?*; Jeal, *Stanley*. He told his own life story, though some of the supposed factual accuracy might be disputed, in a work edited by his widow and published posthumously: H. M. Stanley, *Autobiography*.

5. H. M. Stanley, *Through the Dark Continent*.

6. See for example ibid., vol. 1, ch. 14. He was also smitten by Kabaka Mutesa of Buganda—it isn't entirely clear if the feeling was mutual—leading him to write a letter to the *Daily Telegraph*, exhorting missionaries to come to the kingdom: Ingrams, *Uganda*, 7–10.

7. Buxton, *African Slave Trade*; 'David Livingstone's Cambridge Lectures', in Harlow and Carter, *Archives of Empire*.

8. Among the innumerable biographies of the man, Jeal, *Livingstone* is superior. See also Pachai, *Livingstone, Man of Africa*; Mackenzie and Skipwith, *David Livingstone*; and J. Lewis, *Empire of Sentiment*.

9. Franey, *Victorian Travel Writing*; Youngs, *Travellers in Africa*. See also H. M. Stanley's later works on Congo and the Emin Pasha expedition: *The Congo and the Founding of Its Free State*, and *In Darkest Africa*.

10. See for example the list Stanley provides of a crew of men handpicked for the final push to Ujiji in 1871 in H. M. Stanley, *How I Found Livingstone*, 311–13.

11. Perras, *Carl Peters*.

12. S. Conrad, *German Colonialism*, 25–26, 32, 50, 146; W. O. Henderson, 'German East Africa', 124–28; Burrow, *Crisis of Reason*, 125, 132–36; Perraudin and Zimmerer, *German Colonialism*. See also Peters's own idiosyncratic musings about his earlier travels, including in Buganda, in Peters, *New Light on Dark Africa*.

13. The military force had originally been known as the 'Wissmanntruppe', named after the noted African explorer Captain Hermann Wissmann, now Reich commissioner for the territory. It was designated the Imperial Protectorate Force for German East Africa in 1889: W. O. Henderson, 'German East Africa', 129; Moyd, *Violent Intermediaries*, 6.

14. For a useful summary, see Gwassa, 'German Intervention', 111–12. For an overview of the larger regional and imperial context, see S. Conrad, *German Colonialism*, 50–54.

15. Lettow-Vorbeck, *My Reminiscences*, 4. Von Prince, of course, produced his own account, *Gegen Araber und Wahehe* (Against Arabs and Wahehe).

16. A.J.P. Taylor, *Germany's First Bid*, is a landmark study.

17. Von Prince belongs to the generation which is at the centre of Isabel Hull's provocative study of German imperial violence, *Absolute Destruction*.

18. N. R. Bennett, *Mirambo of Tanzania*, 157–59.

19. W. O. Henderson, 'German East Africa', 129.

20. Moyd, *Violent Intermediaries*, 37; R. Reid, *History of Modern Uganda*, 295–96.

21. Moyd, *Violent Intermediaries*, 37; J. Wright, 'Turbulent Times', 227–28; Davenport, *South Africa*, 60–61.

22. Moyd, *Violent Intermediaries*, 37.

23. W. O. Henderson, German East Africa', 133.

24. Moyd, *Violent Intermediaries*, 37–38. The Manyema fulfilled the role of a number of late nineteenth-century stereotypes in the European—and, it seems, the local—imagination. Stanley wrote, "One really does not know whether to pity or to despise the natives of Manyema. Many are amiable enough to deserve good and kind treatment, but others are hardly human [. . .]. They are humble and liberal to the strong-armed Arab, savage and murderous and cannibalistic to small bands, and every slain man provides a banquet of meat for the forest-natives of Manyema": H. M. Stanley, *Through the Dark Continent*, 2:67–68.

25. Iliffe, *Modern History of Tanganyika*, 117.

26. A. Roberts, 'The Nyamwezi', 138–39.

## Chapter 5

1. There is a growing body of scholarship on the African presence in Europe itself: in many ways the pioneer was Ivan Van Sertima, whose work included, as editor, *African Presence in Early Europe*, and the field has since developed in sophisticated directions. See for example Northrup, *Africa's Discovery of Europe*; Earle and Lowe, *Black Africans in Renaissance Europe*; Otele, *African Europeans*.

2. For example, Robinson and Gallagher, *Africa and the Victorians*.

3. Dyson, *In Pursuit of Ancient Pasts*, 20ff.

4. Said, *Orientalism*, 80–88; see also Mitchell, *Colonising Egypt*.

5. This was one of the arguments in Adam Smith's *An Inquiry into the Nature and Causes of the Wealth of Nations*. Smith proposed that enslaved labour was always going to be more expensive and less efficient than the alternative, because enslaved workers had no incentive to increase their productivity.

6. Ward, 'British West Indies', 425.

7. A recent study explores this, and other, dynamics: Richardson, *Principles and Agents*.

8. There is a huge body of literature on Toussaint Louverture and the Haitian revolution. Fine recent studies include Hazareesingh, *Black Spartacus*, and Girard, *Toussaint Louverture*. The classic account, of course, is C.L.R. James, *Black Jacobins*. In London in the same period, the abolitionist charge was led, among others, by Olaudah Equiano: see his *Interesting Narrative*.

9. This was long a source of horrified fascination to the British themselves, who were thus able to construct an entire world existing alongside, but distinct from, civilisation: of bloody barbarity, and gruesome ritualism. See, for example, Frazer, *Golden Bough*, 497.

10. Adjaye, *Diplomacy and Diplomats*, 104–5.

11. Algerian corsairs, named after the French term for privateers, had been known to raid for slaves as far away as the southern shores of Cornwall from the early seventeenth century: Colley, *Captives*, 49, 85.

12. McDougall, *History of Algeria*, chs 1 and 2.

13. In the context of post-revolutionary political turmoil in France, Bugeaud was the product of a very particular environment; but in the decades to come, many would wrestle with—and would come to separate—the idea of growing democratic enfranchisement at home and the intrinsically undemocratic nature of 'empire'.

14. See, for example, Sullivan, *Thomas-Robert Bugeaud*. For an indication of Bugeaud's influence on the thinking around colonial warfare in the later nineteenth century, see Callwell, *Small Wars*, 128–29.

15. Vandervort, *Wars of Imperial Conquest*, 69; Hourani, *History of the Arab Peoples*, 269–70.

16. Holt, 'Egypt', 22–33.

17. Mostert, *Frontiers*; Price, *Making Empire*.

18. Legassick and Ross, 'From Slave Economy to Settler Capitalism', 280.

19. Kiewiet, 'British Colonial Policy'.

20. Price, *Making Empire*; Legassick and Ross, 'From Slave Economy to Settler Capitalism'; Bundy, *Rise and Fall*.

21. Palmerston's adage is quoted in Flournoy, *British Policy towards Morocco*, 69–70.

22. Buxton, *African Slave Trade*.

23. See, for example, Bovill, *Niger Explored*; Isichei, *History of West Africa*, 161.

24. Mann, *Slavery and the Birth*, 89ff.

25. Manning, *Francophone Sub-Saharan Africa*, 12–14; on Napoleon III, see W.H.C. Smith, *Second Empire and Commune*, and, for an informative overview, Aldrich, *Greater France*.

26. Echenberg, *Colonial Conscripts*.

27. Lawrence, *Imperial Rule*, 108–9.

28. These events have attracted a fair amount of literary attention, as they offer plenty in the way of tragedy, heroism and Victorian derring-do: see, for example, D. Bates, *Abyssinian Difficulty*; Myatt, *March to Magdala*; and Marsden, *Barefoot Emperor*. For contemporary descriptions, see H. M. Stanley, *Coomassie and Magdala*; Markham, *History of the Abyssinian Expedition*; and, from a rather more succinct Ethiopian perspective, Asseggahen to Antoine d'Abbadie, 26 November 1868, doc. no. 248 in Rubenson, *Acta Aethiopica*.

29. This view of Tewodros—in stark contrast to earlier, more admiring assessments of him—pervades contemporary European sources, including Blanc, *Narrative of Captivity*; Rassam, *Narrative of the British Mission*.

30. Lynn, 'British Policy'.

31. B. Porter, *Absent-Minded Imperialists*, 165–67.

32. For example, Saul, *The Myth of the Great Depression*; Cameron and Neal, *Concise Economic History*, 234–35, 241, 280. For a clear and measured assessment, Matthias, *First Industrial Nation*, 361–69.

33. Austen, *African Economic History*, 123–25; and see a brace of articles by Munro, 'Monopolists and Speculators', and 'British Rubber Companies'. See also Munro, *Maritime Enterprise and Empire*.

34. There is now an extensive literature on Belgium and the Congo, from older studies such as Ascherson, *King Incorporated*, and Slade, *King Leopold's Congo*, to more recent (and generally more excoriating) analyses: notably Hochschild, *King Leopold's Ghost*; Vanthemsche, *Belgium and the Congo*; Van Reybrouck, *Congo*, ch. 2. See also H. M. Stanley's own account in *The Congo and the Founding of Its Free State*.

35. The context is brilliantly, and famously, captured in Joseph Conrad's novella *Heart of Darkness*. See also Hochschild, *King Leopold's Ghost*; Louis, 'Roger Casement and the Congo'.

36. For example, Alexander, 'E. D. Morel'.

37. Hargreaves, *Prelude to the Partition*, ch. 3.

38. For example, Stafford, 'Scientific Exploration'.

39. This is explored in granular detail in Hargreaves, *West Africa Partitioned*.

40. One of the best studies, despite its age, remains Kanya-Forstner, *Conquest of the Western Sudan*.

41. The outstanding study is Vansina, *Tio Kingdom*.

42. Manning, *Francophone Sub-Saharan Africa*, 15–16; Petringa, *Brazza*; and, for decent narrative detail but framed in a somewhat anachronistic manner, Berenson, *Heroes of Empire*, ch. 2.

43. For domestic political context, Andrew and Kanya-Forstner, 'French "Colonial Party"'.

44. Pearson, 'Economic Imperialism'.

45. A. G. Hopkins, 'Economic Imperialism', passim. For Benin, Docherty, *Blood and Bronze* is a fine recent study.

46. Muffett, *Concerning Brave Captains*.

47. S. Conrad, *German Colonialism*, 42–50, for a succinct overview; also Austen and Derrick, *Middlemen of the Cameroons Rivers*.

48. Turrell, *Capital and Labour*.

49. The 1879 Anglo–Zulu war has long attracted attention, and has generated writing which belongs to a particular genre of colonial military history. See David, *Zulu*; Bartlett, *Zulu*; Snook, *How Can Man Die Better*; Snook, *Like Wolves on the Fold*; Knight, *Zulu Rising*.

50. Etherington, Harries and Mbenga, 'From Colonial Hegemonies', 384.

51. Laband, *Transvaal Rebellion*.

52. Trapido, 'Imperialism, Settler Identities, and Colonial Capitalism'.

53. Nasson, *South African War*; Pakenham, *Boer War*. This much-studied conflict can no longer accurately be regarded, as it was for many decades, as a 'white man's war' (reflected in the older nomenclature 'Boer War'). See, for example, Nasson, *Abraham Esau's War*.

54. Marks, 'War and Union'.

55. Some of the finest work in the Africanist historical canon has been done on this particular subject. An illustrative sample might include: Jones and Müller, *South African Economy*; Jeeves, *Migrant Labour*; Van Onselen, *Chibaro*; Johnstone, *Class, Race and Gold*; F. Wilson, *Labour in the South African Gold Mines*.

56. Marks, 'Southern Africa, 1867–1886', 360–61; Marks, 'Southern and Central Africa, 1886–1910', 423; Etherington, Harries and Mbenga, 'From Colonial Hegemonies'; Tallie, *Queering Colonial Natal*.

57. Holt, 'Egypt', 33–50.

58. Schölch, '"Men on the Spot"'. For an interesting contemporary analysis of the crisis and its aftermath, see Colvin, *Making of Modern Egypt*.

59. M. D. Lewis, *Divided Rule*, ch. 1.

60. The account in Lytton Strachey's celebrated if idiosyncratic volume *Eminent Victorians* is worth reading for a sense of the place Gordon occupied in the British imagination. See also Pollock, *Gordon*.

61. Spiers, 'Reconquest of the Sudan'; Holt, *Mahdist State*, ch. 12; and for a Sudanese perspective, Zilfu, *Karari*. For something of a classic eye-witness account, see Churchill, *River War*.

62. P. Wright, *Conflict on the Nile*; Sanderson, *England, Europe, and the Upper Nile*; Moorehead, *White Nile*, 338–45.

63. For an innovative analysis of Fashoda, the issues it elucidates and the wider context, see D. L. Lewis, *Race to Fashoda*.

64. Sheriff, *Slaves, Spices and Ivory*, 235–38.

65. Whitehouse, 'Building of the Kenya and Uganda Railway'.

66. This is one of the core ideas pursued in my *History of Modern Uganda*.

67. One of the earliest studies, for the Royal Empire Society, is Crowe, *Berlin West Africa Conference*; and arguably the best collection of essays on the subject is Förster, Mommsen and Robinson, *Bismarck, Europe and Africa*. A lively account can be found in Pakenham, *Scramble for Africa*, ch. 14. For a long-term perspective, see Adebajo, *Curse of Berlin*.

68. See for example the contemporary assessment in Keltie, *Partition of Africa*, ch. 14.

69. For the actual agreement arising from the meeting, see 'General Act of the Conference of Berlin', in Harlow and Carter, *Archives of Empire*, 28–42. Later agreements—notably that signed in Brussels in 1890—added to or modified the framework established at Berlin.

70. Duggan, *Force of Destiny*, esp. Part Five. One of the great works in Italian is of course Del Boca, *Gli italiani in Africa orientale*. A particularly incisive analysis of the relationship between Italian nation-building and empire can be found in Finaldi, *Italian National Identity*.

71. Axelson, *Portugal and the Scramble for Africa*; Newitt, *Short History of Mozambique*, esp. chs 3–5.

72. Sheer volume of material prevents anything pretending to be a historiographical summary. There is no better narrative overview than that provided by J. M. Roberts, *Penguin History of Europe*, 341–467. Roberts, predictably, characterises the era as 'The European Age'. For a less overtly Eurocentric and more nuanced analysis, see Bayly, *Birth of the Modern World*.

73. For example, see A. D. Smith, *Myths and Memories*, 6, 8, 30. It is also worth noting that one of the core criticisms of imperialism, beginning in the late nineteenth century, was that it was incompatible with democracy and the rights associated with citizenship, supposedly pillars of the modern nation-state: Hobson, *Imperialism*, 113ff; also Koebner and Schmidt, *Imperialism*, passim; B. Porter, *Critics of Empire*, ch. 3.

74. Gellner, *Nations and Nationalism*; Hobsbawm, *Nations and Nationalism*; Gat with Yakobson, *Nations*, 246–59.

75. Bridge and Bullen, *Great Powers*, esp. 227–33.

76. J. Darwin, 'Empire and Ethnicity', esp. 155–64.

77. Joll, *Europe Since 1870*, ch. 4. Older scholarship posited this interpretation—a self-evidently Eurocentric one, which unwittingly or otherwise largely erased Africans as meaningful agents—as the only plausible one for what transpired in the late nineteenth century: see, for example, A.J.P. Taylor, *Struggle for Mastery*; and, a more updated version of the basic thesis, Bridge and Bullen, *Great Powers*.

78. A. D. Smith, *Ethnic Origins of Nations*.

79. Howard, *War in European History*, chs 5 and 6; P. H. Wilson, 'European Warfare'; P. Kennedy, *Rise and Fall of the Great Powers*, ch. 4; Collins, *War and Empire*; Lee, *Waging War*, chs 9–11.

80. For a helpful summary, see Parker, 'Introduction'.

81. Murray, 'Industrialization of War'; McNeill, *Pursuit of Power*, chs 6–8; Bond, *War and Society in Europe*, ch. 2.

82. N. Ferguson, *Civilization*, is fairly typical of the 'European exceptionalism' school; see also Landes, 'Why Europe and the West?'. For a somewhat more balanced, nuanced view, see Inikori, *Africans and the Industrial Revolution*; and Pomeranz, *Great Divergence*, esp. chs 4 and 6.

83. Kemp, *Industrialization*; Cameron and Neal, *Concise Economic History*, chs 8 and 9; Evans, *Forging of the Modern State*, esp. Part 2; and, of course, Cain and Hopkins, *British Imperialism*.

84. Hastings, *Construction of Nationhood*; Samson, *Race and Empire*; Kiernan, *Lords of Human Kind*; Stocking, *Victorian Anthropology*. One of the most incisive studies in an African context, if now several decades old, is Curtin, *Image of Africa*.

85. McCulloch, *History of Christianity*, 750. It is important to note that in the British context much of this domestic missionary work was undertaken by nonconformists, especially various groupings of Methodists, rather than by the Church of England, which was seen as increasingly out of touch and which was losing ground in many urban centres: Cannadine, *Victorious Century*, 126–29.

86. A. Porter, *Religion versus Empire*; A. Porter, 'Religion, Missionary Enthusiasm, and Empire'; B. Stanley, *Bible and the Flag*; McCulloch, *History of Christianity*, chs 21–23. For perspectives on particular areas, see, for example, Ajayi, *Christian Missions*; Oliver, *Missionary Factor*; and Elbourne, *Blood Ground*.

87. The White Fathers were founded by the archbishop of Algiers, Charles-Martial Allemand-Lavigerie, on whom see, for example, the richly detailed if at times hagiographic contemporary assessment in R. F. Clarke, *Cardinal Lavigerie*.

88. In many respects, Christopher Fyfe's great opus, *A History of Sierra Leone*, remains unsurpassed.

89. Maxwell, 'Christianity', 265–67.

90. Jeal, *Livingstone*, 7–8.

91. Faupel, *African Holocaust*.

92. These events are mournfully narrated in Mackay, *Pioneer Missionary*, 262, 265, 267–68.

93. Tudesco, 'Missionaries and French Imperialism'.

94. Oliver, *Missionary Factor*, 94–96.

95. Robinson and Gallagher, *Africa and the Victorians*, 307–11, 314–23, 326–30, is rich in narrative detail.

96. Hargreaves, *Prelude to the Partition*, 54; see also Pallinder-Law, 'Aborted Modernization in West Africa?'; and Táíwò, *How Colonialism Preempted Modernity*, 225ff. Richard Burton was more dismissive of the supposed advances made by Christian missionaries: Burton, *Abeokuta*, 1:171, 244–48.

97. Omer-Cooper, *History of Southern Africa*, 131–32.

98. Volz, 'Written On Our Hearts'; Comaroff and Comaroff, 'Christianity and Colonialism'; and Comaroff and Comaroff, *Of Revelation and Revolution*.

99. The late John McCracken's insightful and sensitive mastery of Malawian history is well known: see both his *Politics and Christianity in Malawi*, and *History of Malawi*, esp. ch. 2. See also A. Roberts, *History of Zambia*, 162–70.

100. For Boahen, this was absolutely the deciding factor in the great struggle between Europeans and Africans: Boahen, *African Perspectives*, 56–57. And also, of course, Headrick, *Tools of Empire*.

101. P. Kennedy, *Rise and Fall of British Naval Mastery*, chs 6 and 7.

102. This well-worn couplet is in Belloc, *Modern Traveller*.

103. Dupuy and Dupuy, *Collins Encyclopaedia of Military History*, 900–902; Strachan, *European Armies*, chs 6–8.

104. Curtin, *Disease and Empire*.

105. Hallett, 'European Approach'; Hallett, *Penetration of Africa*; Rotberg, *Africa and Its Explorers*; Hibbert, *Africa Explored*; Sattin, *Gates of Africa*.

106. Stafford, 'Scientific Exploration'; Stafford, *Scientist of Empire*.

107. For example, R. Porter, *Enlightenment*, 147–49.

108. Sattin, *Gates of Africa*.

109. Stafford, *Scientist of Empire*.

110. Kiernan, *Lords of Human Kind*, remains useful; also Daunton and Halpern, *Empire and Others*.

111. The British Niger expeditions of 1841 and 1854 are again worth noting here: see Bovill, *Niger Explored*.

112. Bruce, *Travels*; Park, *Travels*; Clapperton, *Journal*; Livingstone and Livingstone, *Narrative of an Expedition*; H. Waller, *Last Journals*; Speke, *Journal*; Burton, *Lake Regions*; Cameron, *Across Africa*; H. M. Stanley, *Through the Dark Continent*. For some source analysis,

see, for example, Heintze and Jones, *European Sources*; Thornton, 'European Documents'; Jennings, 'They Called Themselves Iloikop'; R. Reid, 'Violence and Its Sources'.

113. See, for example, Kuper, *Reinvention of Primitive Society*, chs 1 and 2.

114. Tilley and Gordon, *Ordering Africa*.

## Chapter 6

1. Again, anyone who contemplates these issues owes an enormous debt to Igor Kopytoff. See, for example, his essay 'The Internal African Frontier', in Kopytoff, *African Frontier*.

2. Law, 'Slave-Raiders and Middlemen', 53–54.

3. See Wilks, *Asante*, 60ff for an overview of the operation of what he termed 'Greater Asante'.

4. Lewin, *Asante before the British*; Wilks, *Asante*, passim; and for a rich primary source, compiled on the instructions of the exiled Asantehene Prempeh I in the Seychelles in the early 1900s, see Boahen et al., 'History of Ashanti Kings'. Internal instability in outlying tributary provinces could also be profoundly destabilising, of course, for Asante itself as well as local polities. A vivid account of such a set of circumstances in the northern kingdom of Gonja is provided in Braimah, *Two Isanwurfos*.

5. Ajayi and Smith, *Yoruba Warfare*, 37–39, 116–17.

6. These perspectives were shared by—and may have influenced—the British government's representative in the region in the early 1860s, who was none other than Richard Francis Burton, fresh from his punctuated procession through central East Africa. See, for example, his accounts in *Wanderings in West Africa* and *Mission to Gelele*.

7. S. Johnson, *History of the Yorubas*, esp. chs 33–35; Akintoye, *Revolution and Power Politics*, ch. 7; A. G. Hopkins, 'Economic Imperialism'.

8. Peel, *Religious Encounter*, chs 1 and 2.

9. R. Reid, *Political Power*, ch. 4.

10. For example, Crummey, *Land and Society*, 111, 198. James Bruce had a particular 'take' on the preeminence of the 'Galla', as the Oromo were previously (and pejoratively) known, in the late eighteenth century: Bruce, *Travels*, 2:680, 696. See also Plowden, *Travels in Abyssinia*, notably chs 3 and 4.

11. Omer-Cooper, *History of Southern Africa*, 65–66; Phiri, 'Political change among the Chewa and Yao', 62–63.

12. Vansina, *Antecedents*; D. Newbury, 'Bunyabungo'; Katoke, *Karagwe Kingdom*; Karugire, *History of the Kingdom of Nkore*; Steinhart, 'Emergence of Bunyoro'.

13. Hargreaves, 'Western Africa', 257–58, 276.

14. I survey this tendency from a historiographical perspective in R. Reid, 'Challenge of the Past'.

15. The ambiguity of the area can be understood through Haggai Erlich's rich biography of Ethiopia's chief sentinel in the north, Ras Alula: *Ras Alula and the Scramble for Africa*.

16. Caulk, 'Yohannes IV'.

17. For an adept examination within a Marxian framework of the limitations on, and fragmentary nature of, political power in Ethiopia, see Crummey, 'Abyssinian Feudalism'.

18. S. G. Miller, *History of Modern Morocco*, chs 1–3; and see also Pennell, *Morocco since 1830*.

19. Pennell, *Country with a Government*; and by the same author, 'Ideology and Practical Politics'.

20. Person, 'Western Africa', 247; Hargreaves, 'Western Africa', 258–59, 275.

21. Person, 'Samori and Resistance'.

22. A. G. Hopkins, *Economic History*, 155.

23. Austen, *African Economic History*, 122–96; A. G. Hopkins, *Economic History*, 167–86; Fieldhouse, *West and the Third World*, 127–222.

24. Ikime, *Merchant Prince of the Niger Delta*.

25. A full and sympathetic account is offered in Cookey, *King Jaja of the Niger Delta*.

26. Some fine work has been done on the subject of links and mediators in the twentieth-century colonial context, though rather less in the context of Africa's global nineteenth century. See, for example, Lawrance, Osborn and Roberts, *Intermediaries, Interpreters and Clerks*.

27. Work by Suzanne Schwarz is particularly important here, including, for example, 'Reconstructing the Life Histories of Liberated Africans'; and see also Schwarz and Lovejoy, *Slavery, Abolition and the Transition*.

28. Gilroy, *Black Atlantic*; Thornton, *Africa and Africans*.

29. Huberich, *Political and Legislative History of Liberia*; Staudenras, *African Colonization Movement*; and, though it hasn't aged so well in its depictions of indigenous African populations, J. W. Smith, *Sojourners*.

30. For example, Akpan, 'Black Imperialism'.

31. McCaskie, 'Cultural Encounters', 671–72, 676, 677.

32. For a contemporary account, H. M. Stanley, *Coomassie and Magdala*, Part 2; for a summary, Vandervort, *Wars of Imperial Conquest*, 84–101; Farwell, *Queen Victoria's Little Wars*, ch. 17.

33. Táíwò, *How Colonialism Preempted Modernity*, esp. ch. 6.

34. Again, see Lawrance, Osborn and Roberts, *Intermediaries, Interpreters and Clerks*, for both context and case studies.

35. For example, Brown, *Tunisia of Ahmad Bey*.

36. Thornton, 'Afro-Christian Syncretism' offers a useful examination of the processes involved in a central African context, where a Portuguese Catholic presence had been established for some time.

37. R. Horton, 'African Conversion'; R. Horton, 'On the Rationality of Conversion'; Peel, 'Conversion and Tradition'.

38. See, for example, Carretta and Reese, *Life and Letters of Philip Quaque*.

39. Ajayi, *Christian Missions*; Ayandele, *Missionary Impact*; Sanneh, 'The CMS and the African Transformation'.

40. Falola, *Pioneer, Patriot and Patriarch*.

41. Two still important studies from the 1960s demonstrate this with admirable clarity: Ajayi, *Christian Missions*; and Ayandele, *Missionary Impact*.

42. Elbourne, *Blood Ground*.

43. Comaroff, *Body of Power*.

44. D. Williams, *Journal and Selected Writings*; D. Williams, *Umfundisi*; Nxasana, 'Journey of the African'.

45. Houle, *Making African Christianity*.

46. Iliffe, *Honour in African History*, 168–80, offers a particularly engaging account of this. Ganda Christian martyrdom has long received more attention than that of their Muslim compatriots in the mid-1870s, described by Kagwa in *Kings of Buganda*, 171–72, for reasons of cultural discrimination that continue to resonate in Uganda today: R. Reid, *History of Modern Uganda*, 175.

47. See the useful collection of biographies in Adi and Sherwood, *Pan-African History*.

48. Ajayi, *Patriot to the Core*.

49. J.A.B. Horton, *West African Countries and Peoples*; and see George Shepperson's 'Introduction' to a 1969 Edinburgh University Press edition of this work. Also, Fyfe, *Africanus Horton*.

50. See Sperling with Kagabo, 'Coastal Hinterland'.

51. For example, McKeown, 'Global Migration'; Belich, *Replenishing the Earth*; Thompson and Magee, *Empire and Globalisation*.

52. Newitt, *History of Mozambique*, esp. ch. 6.

53. The early period of Dutch settlement is detailed in Riebeeck, *Journal*.

54. Ross, 'Khoesan and Immigrants'.

55. The evolution of these ideas can be surveyed in du Toit and Giliomee, *Afrikaner Political Thought*, and vividly explored with a literary intensity in Rian Malan's superb *My Traitor's Heart*. See also Legassick and Ross, 'From Slave Economy to Settler Capitalism'.

56. Crais, *White Supremacy and Black Resistance*.

57. Legassick and Ross, 'From Slave Economy to Settler Capitalism', 285ff.

58. See for example the classic Walker, *Great Trek*; also Meintjes, *Voortrekker*.

59. Omer-Cooper, *History of Southern Africa*, 77.

60. See the lucid account in P. Becker, *Rule of Fear*, esp. Part 3.

61. Eldredge, *South African Kingdom*; Sanders, *Moshoeshoe*.

62. For a long view of how these identities were created, see again Trapido, 'Imperialism, Settler Identities, and Colonial Capitalism'.

63. The origin of the term remains obscure, with explanations ranging from military footwear in the 1830s to the skin colourisation involved in wine-making. Either way, French Algerians came to claim the term as their own. See Stora, '"Southern" World of the *Pieds Noirs*'.

64. McDougall, *History and the Culture of Nationalism*, ch. 2; Lawrence, *Imperial Rule*, 73–90. For broader histories of the territory, see, again, McDougall, *History of Algeria*; Ageron, *Modern Algeria*; Ruedy, *Modern Algeria*.

65. Mosley, *Settler Economies*.

66. Shadle, *Souls of White Folk*; Lonsdale and Berman, 'Coping with the Contradictions'.

67. Palmer, *Land and Racial Domination in Rhodesia*; Phimister, *Economic and Social History of Zimbabwe*.

68. Bosman, *New and Accurate Description*, 395–96; Law, *Further Correspondence of the Royal African Company*, 55–56, items 69, 70 and 71.

69. For example, R. S. Smith, *Warfare and Diplomacy*, 57–58.

70. R. Reid, *War in Pre-colonial Eastern Africa*, 90, 112.

71. Lunt, *Imperial Sunset*, 174–75.

72. There is now a rich literature on the significance of local forces in the European 'Scramble', and indeed in European imperialism more globally, reflecting a shift in the scholarly consensus over the past two or three decades. See, for example, Vandervort, 'War and Imperial Expansion'; Lahti and Moyd, 'In Service of Empires'; Killingray, 'Colonial Warfare in West Africa'.

73. Streets, *Martial Races*.

74. Bulatovich, *Ethiopia through Russian Eyes*, 66. The notion of the Oromo as a fearsomely bloodthirsty, 'martial' people in the Amhara imagination dates to the sixteenth century, as attested to in a 1593 manuscript, 'History of the Galla', by a monk named Bahrey: see Beckingham and Huntingford, *Some Records of Ethiopia*. As noted earlier, 'Galla' is an older, pejorative term for the Oromo. The practice of co-opting Oromo into the army (who thereby increased their own leverage over the highland polity from within) began in the course of the seventeenth century, and seems to have intensified in the second half of the nineteenth. Ironically, the depiction of certain groups of Oromo (who were by no means a united bloc) as warlike and savage also justified extreme violence toward them in the same period.

75. For an enormously important contribution to our understanding of these issues, see Osborne, *Making Martial Races*. This volume came out too late for me to make full use of it here, but the book will remain the standard work on the subject for some time to come.

76. R. L. Roberts, 'Production and Reproduction of Warrior States'; D. Robinson, *Holy War*; R. L. Roberts, *Warriors, Merchants, and Slaves*.

77. Hargreaves, *Prelude to the Partition*, 122–24, 257–58, 262–64.

78. Hargreaves, 'Western Africa', 267; and see the official perspective in Ditte, *Observations sur la guerre dans les colonies*, 52–53.

79. Kanya-Forstner, *Conquest of the Western Sudan*.

80. Echenberg, *Colonial Conscripts*, ch. 2; Westwood, 'Military Culture in Senegambia'; Westwood, 'Ceddo, Sofa, Tirailleur'.

81. Manning, *Francophone Sub-Saharan Africa*, 63.

82. Ibid.

83. For example, Lugard, *Dual Mandate*, 17, 574ff.

84. Perkins, *Qaids, Captains, and Colons*.

85. Ochonu, *Colonialism by Proxy*.

86. Steinhart, *Conflict and Collaboration*, esp. ch. 3; Low, *Fabrication of Empire*, esp. ch. 5.

87. For example, see Osborne, *Ethnicity and Empire in Kenya*; Omara-Otunnu, *Politics and the Military in Uganda*; Parsons, *African Rank-and-File*. See also Killingray and Omissi, *Guardians of Empire*; and Lunt, *Imperial Sunset*.

88. Negash, *Italian Colonialism in Eritrea*; Chelati Dirar, 'Colonialism and the Construction of National Identities'. For an interpretation of Eritrea as a 'frontier nation', see R. Reid, *Frontiers of Violence*.

89. Manning, *Francophone Sub-Saharan Africa*, 63.

90. Lamothe, *Slaves of Fortune*.

91. D. H. Johnson, 'Structure of a Legacy'.

92. Before the First World War, most regional colonial armies were modest in size—two or three thousand men—although the Congolese Force publique was about twenty thousand-strong in the 1900s. See also Lunt, *Imperial Sunset*, Part 2; and for a broader survey, Clayton and Killingray, *Khaki and Blue*.

93. See for example Touval, 'Treaties, Borders, and the Partition', 291.

94. For an interesting contemporary snapshot, see Wylde, *Modern Abyssinia*; and some insights into early Addis Ababa society are provided in Garretson, *Victorian Gentleman*.

95. A generation later, the Italian Fascist government would campaign tirelessly to project Ethiopian 'civilisation' as a façade, and an affront which could only be addressed through armed intervention in the late nineteenth-century sense.

96. There is of course an enormous body of literature on indirect rule, but there is no better place to start than with Lugard himself in *Dual Mandate*.

97. Tibenderana, 'Role of the British Administration'.

98. Perkins, *History of Modern Tunisia*, ch. 2.

99. Al-Sayyid-Marsot, 'British Occupation of Egypt'.

100. Burton, *Lake Regions*, 396–97, 424.

101. Kagwa, *Kings of Buganda*, 159; Beattie, *Nyoro State*, 68ff.

102. R. Reid, *History of Modern Uganda*, 156.

103. This was one of the core elements enshrined in the Uganda Agreement of 1900, a keystone piece of colonial legislation: see, for example, Low, 'Making and Implementation'.

104. In addition to work cited above, see A. Roberts, 'Sub-imperialism of the Baganda'. A close reading of Lugard's own account of the period reveals more local agency than he perhaps would have knowingly conceded. See for example his *Rise of Our East African Empire*; and Perham, *Lugard*, Part 3.

105. Lemarchand, *Dynamics of Violence*, ch. 3; Prunier, *Rwanda Crisis*, 23ff.

106. Crowder, 'Indirect Rule'. In terms of data on the respective systems in operation in the early decades of the twentieth century, Hailey, *African Survey* (first published in 1938, and substantially revised and expanded in 1957), remains an extraordinary resource.

107. See for example Afigbo, *Warrant Chiefs*.

108. Newitt, *Short History of Mozambique*, chs 3–5; also, Axelson, *Portugal and the Scramble for Africa*.

109. These social categories are explored in Birmingham, *Short History of Modern Angola*.

110. The most lucid account of these events, as well as the wider political and social contexts within which they can be understood, is in Vansina, *Tio Kingdom*. For a neat summary, see Manning, *Francophone Sub-Saharan Africa*, 15–16.

111. A. Roberts, *History of Zambia*, 133–35, 159ff; also, Mainga, *Bulozi under the Luyana Kings*.

112. N. R. Bennett, *Arab versus European*.

113. Guy, *Destruction of the Zulu Kingdom*; Laband, *Kingdom in Crisis*.

114. Lieven, '"Butchering the brutes"'.

115. These events have received a fair amount of scholarly attention over the years: see Twaddle, 'Muslim Revolution'; Twaddle, 'Emergence of Politico-Religious Groupings'; Michael Wright, *Buganda in the Heroic Age*; Rowe, 'Purge of Christians'; Wrigley, 'Christian Revolution'; Kasozi, *Spread of Islam*. For contemporary perspectives, see Mackay, *Pioneer Missionary*; Ashe, *Chronicles of Uganda*; and Kagwa, *Kings of Buganda*, 166–67.

116. This comes through in the many detailed treatments of the region's turbulent 1890s that have appeared over the years. See, for example, the work of Tony Low, who enjoyed remarkable scholarly longevity, from 'Uganda: The Establishment of the Protectorate' to *Fabrication of Empire*.

117. Law, 'Politics of Commercial Transition', 230ff; Manning, *Francophone Sub-Saharan Africa*, 68, 72–73; Law, *Ouidah*, 271–76.

118. Wylde, *Modern Abyssinia*, 56, 214–15.

119. Famously, Ranger, 'Connexions, Part 1' and 'Connexions, Part 2', respectively.

120. Among the first scholars to seriously re-examine the utility of the generic term 'African resistance' were Allen Isaacman and Barbara Isaacman, in an essay which remains relevant: 'Resistance and Collaboration'. More broadly, see also Abbink, de Bruijn and van Walraven, *Rethinking Resistance*.

121. For an overview of the nature of the debates within nineteenth-century Islam, see Lapidus, *History of Islamic Societies*, 453–68, and Esposito, *Islam*, ch. 4.

122. Danziger, *Abd al-Qadir*.

123. Vandewalle, *History of Modern Libya*, chs 1 and 2; for good surveys, see also J. Wright, *History of Libya*, which has been revised and reissued several times, and Ahmida, *Making of Modern Libya*, esp. ch. 3.

124. Holt and Daly, *History of the Sudan*, Part 2; R. Gray, *History of the Southern Sudan*.

125. Holt, *Mahdist State*, esp. chs 1 and 2.

126. Al-Sayyid-Marsot, 'British Occupation of Egypt', 653–54. Urabi himself has been subjected to various rounds of revision, and has been positioned on a spectrum from illegitimate putschist to leader of a genuine sociopolitical revolution: see Mayer, *Changing Past*. For a couple of interesting snapshots in the age of Nasserist nationalism, see Little, *Modern Egypt*, 43–45 and ch. 5; and Mansfield, *Nasser's Egypt*, 22.

127. Perkins, *History of Modern Tunisia*, ch. 1.

128. Various angles and interpretations are covered in Giblin and Monson, *Maji Maji*. In addition, see Iliffe, 'Organisation of the Maji-Maji Rebellion'; Iliffe, *Tanganyika under German Rule*; Gwassa, 'African Methods of Warfare'; Gwassa, 'Kinjikitile and the Ideology'; Redmond, 'Maji Maji in Ungoni'; Ranger, 'Religious Movements and Politics'; Marcia Wright, 'Maji Maji';

Monson, 'Relocating Maji Maji'; Sunseri, 'Reinterpreting a Colonial Rebellion'; F. Becker, 'Traders, "Big Men" and Prophets'. Contemporary experiences can be glimpsed in Gwassa and Iliffe, *Records of the Maji Maji Rising*.

129. Glassman, *Feasts and Riot*.

130. Beach, 'Chimurenga'; Ranger, *Revolt in Southern Rhodesia*; Cobbing, 'Absent Priesthood'; Palmer, 'War and Land in Rhodesia'. Selous, *Sunshine and Storm*, by the noted hunter and writer, is a useful—if inevitably skewed—contemporary account.

131. Isaacman and Isaacman, 'Resistance and Collaboration'.

132. For example, see Mandala, *Work and Control in a Peasant Economy*.

133. I. Berger, 'Rebels or Status-Seekers?'; Des Forges, '"The drum is greater"'; Freedman, *Nyabingi*; and E. Hopkins, 'Nyabingi Cult'.

134. For details on this particular case study, as well as a superb elucidation of the broader context, see Lan, *Guns and Rain*.

135. Giblin, *History of the Excluded*, esp. ch. 1.

136. Ranger, 'Connexions', Parts 1 and 2.

137. Peires, *The Dead Will Arise*; and an earlier essay by the same author, 'Central Beliefs of the Xhosa Cattle-Killing'.

138. Maxwell, 'Historicising Christian Independency'; Cabrita, *Text and Authority*; Welbourn, *East African Rebels*.

139. For example, in the Nyasa context, see McCracken, *History of Malawi*, 12, 123–24.

140. For an invaluable collection of primary sources on the rebellion, gathered as part of an official inquiry into the events themselves, see McCracken, *Voices from the Chilembwe Rising*; and see also Shepperson and Price, *Independent African*.

141. M.-L. Martin, *Kimbangu*.

142. For a detailed and accessible account of particular campaigns, see Vandervort, *Wars of Imperial Conquest*, ch. 4.

143. I. M. Lewis, *Modern History of the Somali*, ch. 4. Italy only secured anything approaching full control of Libya in 1934, following a programme of violent brutality against the civilian population. Even then, the Sanusiyya revived their active hostility to the Fascist administration during the Second World War, making a vital contribution to the British military campaign in North Africa in the early 1940s. See a classic anthropological study, Evans-Pritchard, *Sanusi of Cyrenaica*.

144. Rubenson, *Survival of Ethiopian Independence*, 288ff.

145. There is, of course, a vast literature on the Ethiopian triumph at Adwa, from the awed contemporary accounts—such as Wylde, *Modern Abyssinia*, or Berkeley, *Campaign of Adowa*—to various scholarly interpretations. See for example Dunn, '"For God, Emperor, and Country!"'; Marcus, *Life and Times of Menelik II*, ch. 6; Milkias and Metaferia, *Battle of Adwa*; Rubenson, 'Adwa 1896'. We need to be careful, though, not to reify Adwa in the way that many do, especially in a European context, owing to the enduring cult of the 'decisive battle'. As I hope I have indicated throughout, this tendency toward 'footballisation' neglects the much subtler ways in which the Afro-European encounter unfolded during this period. The Italians, of course, returned in 1935, this time with a little more success—though it was short-lived.

146. For example, Legassick, 'Firearms, Horses'.

147. Porch, *Wars of Empire*, 116–17.

148. For example, in the Rhodesian context, see Selous, *Sunshine and Storm*, 44, 45.

149. For example, Van Onselen, 'Reactions to Rinderpest'.

150. The classic analysis is Ford, *Role of the Trypanosomiases*.

151. See, for example, various contributions to Azevedo, Hartwig and Patterson, *Disease in African History*; and various contributions to *JAH* Forum: 'Health and Illness in African

History'. In terms of area-specific studies, see Doyle, *Before HIV*; and Tuck, 'Syphilis, Sexuality and Social Control'.

152. Pankhurst and Johnson, 'Great Drought'.

153. One of the clearest examples of this is the deleterious impact on female fertility of the famine which followed the suppression of the Maji Maji revolt by the Germans: Culwick and Culwick, 'Study of Population in Ulanga'.

154. Vansina, *Paths in the Rainforests*, 240–45; see also an examination of both social disruption and material violence in Vos, *Kongo in the Age of Empire*.

155. See Walter, *Colonial Violence* for a penetrating analysis, and Vandervort, *Wars of Imperial Conquest*, for a useful narrative survey. Cocker, *Rivers of Blood*, offers a more global perspective on the subject through a series of case studies. In some ways this aspect of the European imperial project forms part of the 'culture wars' largely manufactured by the political right in Britain. Whether one sees it as important to highlight the violence inherent in imperialism, or is rather of the belief that such a focus distracts from the intrinsic benevolence of empire, has come to be regarded as a pretty clear indication of political leaning.

156. Some have identified the roots of Nazism—or at least certain elements of Nazi ideology—in the Second Reich's violence in what is today Namibia. See Olusoga and Erichsen, *The Kaiser's Holocaust*. Also Gewald, *Herero Heroes*; Zimmerer and Zeller, *Genocide in German South-West Africa*. Germany is also the only European nation, at the time of writing, to have formally and publicly apologised for the violence of its colonial project, as opposed to the more commonplace expressions of 'regret' that unfortunate things happened: see Meldrum, 'German Minister Says Sorry' (report in *The Guardian*, 16 August 2004).

157. See Iliffe, drawing on G.C.K. Gwassa's doctoral thesis, in *Modern History of Tanganyika*, 200.

158. Beattie, *Nyoro State*, 73–75; Steinhart, *Conflict and Collaboration*, 58–97. For a typically cold-blooded first-hand account, see Colvile, *Land of the Nile Springs*. These wars set Bunyoro on a spiral of decline and underdevelopment from which the region has yet to fully recover: see, for example, Doyle, *Crisis and Decline*.

159. Hicks, *Brutish Museums*.

## Act V

1. This was not, according to one eminent historian, particularly unusual in times of stress and turmoil: Plumb, *Death of the Past*, 33–34.

2. Much of this is derived from conversations which Mirambo had with a London Missionary Society missionary, Ebenezer Southon, between 1878 and 1880, which the latter assiduously committed to paper. Southon died soon after, before he could publish any of his own material, but a transcription of his history of the region—a great deal of which was again seemingly gleaned from talking to Mirambo—has been published in N. R. Bennett, *Studies in East African History*. See also R. Reid, *War in Pre-colonial Eastern Africa*, 34–37.

3. Burton, *Lake Regions*, 284.

4. H. M. Stanley, *How I Found Livingstone*, 517–18.

5. I used the admittedly hazy figure of Mwezi as the titular hook and opening gambit in R. Reid, '"None could stand before him"', 19.

6. R. Reid, *War in Pre-colonial Eastern Africa*, 36.

7. Broyon-Mirambo, 'Description of Unyamwezi', 33–34; and see also N. R. Bennett, 'Philippe Broyon'.

8. R. Reid, *War in Pre-colonial Eastern Africa*, 36.

9. Quoted in A. Roberts, 'The Nyamwezi', 137.

10. They both published books on their travels and sojourns: A. B. Hore, *To Lake Tanganyika*; E. C. Hore, *Tanganyika*.

11. E. C. Hore, 'On the Twelve Tribes'.

12. Ibid., 3–4.

13. Burton, *Lake Regions*, 222.

14. This is an idea which has been eloquently explored in Schama, *Landscape and Memory*.

15. Cameron, *Across Africa*, esp. vol. 1.

16. H. M. Stanley, *How I Found Livingstone*, 406.

17. That greeting—"Dr Livingstone, I presume?"—would torment Stanley for the rest of his days, attracting the kind of derision he had dreaded throughout his life. He claimed, in later life, that he couldn't think of anything else to say: Bierman, *Dark Safari*, 111–14. Thus, ironically, was arguably the greatest moment in Stanley's life to become frozen in time, in the most unwelcome of ways. It is worth contrasting the assumed formality of the greeting as it appears in print with Spencer Tracey's portrayal of Stanley in the 1939 film *Stanley and Livingstone*, directed by Henry King and Otto Brower: in the relevant scene, Tracey's fever-ravaged explorer cuts a raddled figure alongside Richard Greene's apparently quite fit and well Livingstone, and he delivers the line with a moving and exhausted diffidence, a pregnant pause inserted before 'I presume?'. The scene is intercut with a shot of a crowd of curious, awed African extras who appear to have been filmed separately (cinematic technology at the time possibly precluding doing otherwise)—thus emphasising the dramatic bubble within which the two protagonists are operating.

18. H. M. Stanley, *How I Found Livingstone*, 415.

19. Ibid., 415–16.

## Chapter 7

1. H. M. Stanley, *Coomassie and Magdala*, 449. The main title of this chapter is in part inspired by John Berger's *Ways of Seeing*, to which scholars of all fields, and not just of visual culture, owe much.

2. Pankhurst, *Ethiopian Royal Chronicles*, 157–58.

3. Hozier, *British Expedition*, 237.

4. In 1855, Walter Plowden described Tewodros admiringly thus: "The King Theodorus is young in years, vigorous in all manly exercises, of a striking countenance, peculiarly polite and engaging when pleased, and mostly displaying great tact and delicacy [. . . . He is] of untiring energy, both mental and bodily, [and] his personal and moral daring are boundless" (Plowden, *Travels in Abyssinia*, 455). A little over a decade later, Clements Markham's assessment was a touch more qualified: "His misdeeds had been numerous, his cruelties horrible", although "he was not without great and noble qualities" (Markham, *History of the Abyssinian Expedition*, 354). The crucial context was Europeans' own deep-rooted fascination with the idea of Ethiopia itself, a place which had long inspired a particular awe as the ancient, Christian 'kingdom of Prester John' in the medieval imagination, and which was awarded its own particular temporality accordingly: see for example Sorenson, *Imagining Ethiopia*, 21ff, and Carnochan, *Golden Legends*.

5. Greenfield, *Ethiopia*, 83–84; and see BBC news reports: Blunt, 'Ethiopia Seeks Prince's Remains' (3 June 2007); and Tamirat and Macaulay, 'Ethiopia's Prince Alemayehu' (22 May 2023).

6. Dufton, *Narrative of a Journey*, 118.

7. For example, Crummey, 'Tewodros as Reformer'.

8. See for example Assefaw, 'Tewodros in Ethiopian Historical Fiction'.

9. With due recognition of the core idea underpinning F. Smith Fussner's study of the flourishing of historical writing in late Elizabethan and early Stuart England, *The Historical Revolution*.

10. Sunjata, a warrior of humble origin who overcame seemingly insuperable odds thanks to powerful female characters, was the focus of an epic narrative performed by *griots* (bards) in the centuries which followed his leadership of the Mande insurrection against the Soninke state of Ghana. In many ways it became the historical centrepiece of political culture in the region long after the Mali empire itself disintegrated in the course of the sixteenth century. The Sunjata Epic was interpreted and performed in different ways over time, but at the core of its performance was generally the conviction that one day Mali would rise again to dominate the savannah region. Its continual retelling reflected the ineffable significance of the glorious past in the reinforcement of identity, and the past's importance in informing the present and offering some guidance—and hope—for the future. See, for example, Innes et al., *Sunjata*, and also Okpewho, 'African Oral Epics'; and Okpewho, *Epic in Africa*.

11. Yekuno Amlak's coup d'état in 1270 against the Zagwe dynasty—depicted by subsequent chroniclers as a bunch of grasping usurpers—was later reframed as the restoration of an ancient regime, with Menelik I, portrayed as the son of King Solomon and Queen Makeda of Saba/Sheba, at its core. By the early fourteenth century, the *Kebra Negast* had been redacted from various sources (rabbinic traditions, Judaic, Christian and Islamic texts, and well-established stories and tropes from across the Red Sea world) to present the narrative of a biblical nation, one blessed by God as the New Zion with a divine covenant represented by possession the Tabernacle (the Ark of the Covenant) as evidence of its sanctity. As tales of rupture and rebirth went, it was pretty potent, one of the greatest exercises in political propaganda in African history, and surely one of the most impressive anywhere in the world. See Brooks, *Modern Translation*.

12. The chronicles produced during the reign of Amda Tsion in the first half of the fourteenth century are among the finest examples of textual achievement in the region's early history: see Huntingford, *Glorious Victories of 'Āmda Ṣeyon*. In the following century, Emperor Zara Yaqob was responsible for some of the foundational texts of the state's spatial, cultural and historical memory, either as author or as patron. These included works—most notably *Mashafa Birhan* (The book of light)—which were implicitly or overtly works of historical thought, though of course in many ways, focused as they were on God and Ethiopians' place in the firmament, a recurrent motif was Ethiopia as *beyond* time. For a useful summary, see Ullendorff, *Ethiopians*, 141ff. A powerful sense of historical trajectory was developed in the seventeenth and eighteenth centuries, sponsored by the Gondarine state: Crummey, *Land and Society*, chs 3–5. With the collapse of the centralised state at the end of the eighteenth century, chroniclers lamented in explicitly historical terms the death of Ethiopia and the destruction of the imperial and spiritual ideal at its core: the term 'Zemene Mesafint' (The age of the princes) was a self-consciously Old Testament allusion and compared Ethiopia's travails with those of biblical Israel: see for example Blundell, *Royal Chronicle*. It was this period, as we have seen, into which Tewodros himself was born, and the bloody chaos of which he would seek to end.

13. A. M. Mazrui, 'Swahili Literary Tradition', 201. As with other cases noted below, the bulk of recorded Swahili historical tradition dates to the late nineteenth and early twentieth centuries: see Nurse and Spear, *Swahili*, 29–31 and 118 n. 3—but the emergence of historical culture along the coast can be discerned much earlier.

14. See the patchy but informative Alagoa, *Practice of History in Africa*; or Atieno-Odhiambo, 'From African Historiographies'.

15. Herskovits, *Dahomey*, 2:315; Adams, 'Fon Appliquéd Cloths'; Skertchly, *Dahomey*, 193–94.

16. For example, Snelgrave, *New Account*, 12, 31.

17. For example, Dalzel, *History of Dahomy*; also, Law, 'Dahomey and the Slave Trade'.

18. Rattray, *Religion and Art*; Cole and Ross, *Arts of Ghana*.

19. Wilks, *Asante*, 470–74.

20. Ibid., 668, 669.

21. Ibid., 669–70.

22. Ibid., 671–72.

23. Some of the most remarkable work in this realm has been done by Tom McCaskie: see for example 'Komfo Anokye of Asante'.

24. Bastin, *Statuettes tshokwe*, 287; Bastin, *Sculpture tshokwe*, 31ff; Gillon, *Short History of African Art*, 296–97.

25. Law, *Oyo Empire*, 12–13.

26. Ibid., 26–27.

27. Izevbaye, 'West African Literature', 489.

28. Clapperton, *Journal of a Second Expedition*, ch. 2.

29. Gillon, *Short History of African Art*, 247.

30. Peel, *Religious Encounter*, chs 1 and 2.

31. S. Johnson, *History of the Yorubas*. See also Law, 'Early Yoruba Historiography'; and Barber, 'I. B. Akinyele'.

32. Reindorf, *History of the Gold Coast and Asante*. See also Omosini, 'Carl Christian Reindorf'.

33. For example, Wrigley, *Kingship and State*; Kodesh, *Beyond the Royal Gaze*, esp. ch. 2.

34. Cohen, *Historical Tradition of Busoga*; Nyakatura, *Anatomy*, 50ff.

35. Hanson, *Landed Obligation*, chs 2 and 3; Schoenbrun, *Names of the Python*, chs 4 and 5.

36. Speke, *Journal*, 252; H. M. Stanley, *Through the Dark Continent*, 1:298; and see Henige, '"Disease of Writing"'.

37. H. M. Stanley, *Through the Dark Continent*, 1:275–81; and see Yoder, 'Quest for Kintu'. For innovative work on the historical imaginary in the deeper past, see Kodesh, *Beyond the Royal Gaze*, and also Kodesh, 'History from the Healer's Shrine'.

38. For a widely used English translation, under the editorship of Semakula Kiwanuka, see Kagwa, *Kings of Buganda*, cited often in the course of this book. Kagwa himself went on to write other work on the clans and customs of the kingdom. He also worked closely with a CMS missionary, John Roscoe, who used a great deal of Kagwa's material in his own writings. For analysis of epistemology and context, see Rowe, 'Myth, Memoir and Moral Admonition'; Wrigley, *Kingship and State*; and R. Reid, 'Ghosts in the Academy'.

39. Mphande, 'Heroic and Praise Poetry'; and see L. White, 'Power and the Praise Poem', and Vail and White, *Power and the Praise Poem*.

40. Gunner, 'Songs of Innocence and Experience'. In eastern Africa, too, in apparent defiance of their socioeconomic vulnerability women composed songs and chants to both exhort men to greater deeds and lambast those who had fallen short: R. Reid, *War in Pre-colonial Eastern Africa*, 155, 215.

41. Last, *Sokoto Caliphate*, 207ff; and, a fine recent study, Naylor, *From Rebels to Rulers*.

42. Boyd, 'Fulani Women Poets'.

43. See the letter Yohannes wrote in 1872 to Queen Victoria along these lines, quoted in R. Reid, *War in Pre-colonial Eastern Africa*, 28–29; also, Portal, *My Mission to Abyssinia*, 5–6. For analysis and context, see Orlowska, 'Re-imagining Empire'; Gabre-Selassie, *Yohannes IV of Ethiopia*.

44. See for example J. Bennett, *God and Progress*.

45. For example, see Wild-Wood, 'Bible Translation'. This is also a powerful thread running through Earle, *Colonial Buganda*.

46. See the various contributions to Tilley and Gordon, *Ordering Africa*.

47. Peel, *Religious Encounter*; Chimhundu, 'Early Missionaries'.

48. There was no doubt some 'inventing' going on: of 'traditions', of precedent, of political custom and language. But this has tended to be exaggerated in some of the scholarship, and in any case rather misses the critical point that cultures of ongoing (re)invention had deep roots, in the nineteenth century and earlier. For a perspective on the debate regarding the impact of colonial rule, see Spear, 'Neo-traditionalism'; for a landmark contribution, Ranger, 'Invention of Tradition in Colonial Africa', and of course Ranger's own revision of his original argument, 'Invention of Tradition Revisited'.

49. Iliffe, Modern History of Tanganyika, 323.

50. Cannadine, Ornamentalism.

51. Atanda, New Oyo Empire.

52. Oliver, Sir Harry Johnston, 332–33. In one of the starkest examples of the period's enduring legacy, Bunyoro remained underdeveloped for decades. "Our spirit is dead," the Nyoro prime minister told an anthropologist in 1953: Beattie, Nyoro State, 32.

53. Young, African Colonial State, 232–34.

54. The concept is expounded in Seligman, Races of Africa.

55. Chrétien, Great Lakes of Africa, esp. ch. 4.

56. Coombes, Reinventing Africa.

57. For a useful summary, see Lapidus, History of Islamic Societies, 516–18.

58. Prouty, Empress Taytu and Menilek II.

59. Zewde, Pioneers of Change in Ethiopia.

60. Work by Sara Marzagora is especially important here: see, for example, her 'Alterity, Coloniality and Modernity'; and 'History in Twentieth-Century Ethiopia'.

61. Hegel, 'Africa', 21, 28: extracts from Hegel, Philosophy of History. In fact, Hegel was himself echoing, whether knowingly or serendipitously, Edward Gibbon's beautifully rendered but eccentrically curated ruminations on Ethiopia—a representation, in some respects, of Africa as a whole. Of the Ethiopians, he famously wrote, they "slept near a thousand years, forgetful of the world, by whom they were forgotten", having been isolated by the rise of Islam, and were only "awoken" by the Portuguese: Gibbon, History of the Decline and Fall, 6:81.

62. Lugard, Dual Mandate, 618.

63. Dalzel, History of Dahomy; Bruce, Travels; Speke, Journal, esp. ch. 9; H. M. Stanley, Through the Dark Continent, vol. 1, esp. ch. 14.

64. Burrow, History of Histories, esp. ch. 25; Woolf, Global History of History, ch. 7.

65. English history, for example, developed in new directions and with renewed vigour in the nineteenth century following the Romantic movement's discovery of a classical inheritance—a reinvention which was in many ways the outcome of the Napoleonic Wars, when Europe was closed off to the Grand Tour. This led to a generation of aesthetes staying at home and rediscovering England: on this see, for example, Colls, Identity of England, 61, 250, 260.

66. At the close of the nineteenth century, a level of anxiety about the world (sometimes emblematised by stories about forces beyond it) is also manifest in Bram Stoker's Dracula, or H. G. Wells's War of the Worlds, or indeed Conrad's Heart of Darkness. On this see also Brantlinger, Rule of Darkness. For a near-contemporary chronicle of this distinctive 'moment', see Jackson, Eighteen Nineties.

67. In the mid-seventeenth century, Thomas Hobbes proposed that war itself was indicative of lawless primitivity, emblematic of the absence of social order and governance: Hobbes, Leviathan, 109, 110, 128. He knew of what he wrote, producing his great work in the shadow of the English Civil War.

68. Quinney, 'Decisions on Slavery'; Oldfield, Popular Politics and British Anti-Slavery; Richardson, Principles and Agents. For some revealing primary source material, see Révolution française et l'abolition, and Wilberforce, 'William Wilberforce, in the House of Commons'.

69. In 1839 Thomas Fowell Buxton provided a neat summary of this position: "Legitimate commerce would put down the slave trade, by demonstrating the superior value of man as a labourer on the soil, to man as an object of merchandise; and if conducted on wise and equitable principles, might be the precursor, or rather the attendant, of civilization, peace and Christianity, to the unenlightened, warlike and heathen tribes who now so fearfully prey on each other, to supply the slave markets of the New World. In this view of the subject, the merchant, the philanthropist, the patriot, and the Christian, may unite": Buxton, *African Slave Trade*, 306. Little progress was made in the decades that followed: toward the end of his life, Livingstone famously exhorted all right-minded foreigners to "help heal this open sore of the world", although he was specifically referring to eastern and central Africa; quoted in Oliver, *Missionary Factor*, 34. The resilience of the nefarious commerce reinforced the notion of a kind of timeless savagery, whose destruction could only be effected by robust external intervention.

70. A modern genealogy of this line of thought can be traced to the great Prussian thinker on war, Carl von Clausewitz, who declared in his hugely influential tome that "[s]avage peoples are ruled by passion, civilized peoples by the mind", and that European rationality and reason rendered their organisation of warcraft superior to those who were limited to "the crude expression of instinct": Clausewitz, *On War*, 84–85. The theme was developed in Callwell, *Small Wars*, and further elaborated in Harry Holbert Turney-High's major work, *Primitive War*.

71. Lugard was explicit on the point: *Dual Mandate*, 17.

72. For example, Arnold, *Imperial Medicine and Indigenous Societies*.

73. Kipling, 'White Man's Burden', 273.

74. It was necessary, in the words of Mr Kurtz in Conrad's *Heart of Darkness*, to "exterminate all the brutes". See Sven Lindqvist's provocative and eloquent *"Exterminate All the Brutes"*.

75. Bethencourt, *Racisms*; Fredrickson, *Racism*; Sweet, 'Iberian Roots'; Glassman, 'Slower than a Massacre'; Samson, *Race and Empire*. See also J. Harvey, *Story of Black*, ch. 7.

76. Stocking, *Victorian Anthropology*; Lorimer, *Colour, Class and the Victorians*.

77. Rousseau, *Discourse on the Origin of Inequality*, 24, 37. Rousseau was writing in 1754. Montaigne had written admiringly of the Tupinamba of Brazil in the 1570s, especially their "noble and disinterested" way of war. "[W]e all call barbarous", he admonished his readers, "anything that is contrary to our own habits": Montaigne, 'On Cannibals', 108, 114–15.

78. For an eloquent and informative account of British thinking, for example, see McCaskie, 'Cultural Encounters'.

79. See for example Malik, *Meaning of Race*.

80. By Burton, see *Wanderings in West Africa*, *Abeokuta and the Camaroons Mountains* and *Mission to Gelele*.

81. The seminal text, of course, was Charles Darwin's *On the Origin of Species*.

82. J. Chamberlain, 'True Conception of Empire', 213–14. It isn't difficult to imagine what he would have had to say about 'remoaners' and 'snowflakes' in our own era.

83. Koebner and Schmidt, *Imperialism*, 244.

84. Hobson, *Imperialism*; and, closely following much of Hobson's argument, Lenin, *Imperialism*. For an accessible survey of Marxist writing—more accessible, usually, than the original work itself—including that of Rudolf Hilferding, Rosa Luxemburg, Karl Kautsky and Nikolai Bukharin, see Brewer, *Marxist Theories of Imperialism*; and Mommsen, *Theories of Imperialism*, ch. 2.

85. See for example Webb, *Our Partnership*, 194–95; and more broadly, B. Porter, *Critics of Empire*.

86. See the illuminating contributions to Peterson and Macola, *Recasting the Past*.

87. Jacob Egharevba's *A Short History of Benin* was first published in English in Lagos in 1934, and several more editions followed: see Usuanlele and Falola, 'Comparison of Jacob Eghareva's "Ekhere Vb Itan Edo"'. In Bunyoro, John Nyakatura produced his *Abakama ba Bunyoro-Kitara* (The kings of Bunyoro-Kitara) in 1947; for an accessible and annotated English translation, cited above, see *Anatomy*, under the editorship of Godfrey Uzoigwe. Nyakatura was by no means the first to write up the kingdom's history: in the mid-1930s, for example, the Mukama of Bunyoro himself had produced a series of illuminating articles under a pseudonym. See 'K.W.', 'Kings of Bunyoro-Kitara', Parts 1, 2 and 3. However, one of the core and explicit purposes behind Nyakatura's literary efforts was to remind his readers of the kingdom's former greatness, and of its destruction at the hands of rapacious invaders, from both near (the Ganda) and far (the British).

88. R. Reid, 'Ghosts in the Academy', 358–60; Rowe, 'Myth, Memoir and Moral Admonition', passim. For an example, see the Kabaka of Buganda's 1935 pamphlet 'Education, Civilisation and Foreignisation in Buganda'.

89. Adi, *Pan-Africanism*; J. H. Clarke, *Marcus Garvey*. Rastafarianism, with its roots in the Caribbean, was organised around the deification of the Ethiopian emperor, but the actual historicity underpinning the movement's ideology might be described as idiosyncratic at best: see, for example, P. B. Clarke, *Black Paradise*.

90. *The Beautyful Ones Are Not Yet Born* (1968); *Fragments* (1970); *Why Are We So Blest?* (1972).

91. *Two Thousand Seasons* (1973).

92. p'Bitek, *Song of Lawino; Song of Ocol*.

93. Ouologuem's *Bound to Violence* (1971) was first published as *Le Devoir de violence* (1968), with the violence of the title conceptualised as something intrinsic to African state and society.

94. The essence is captured in Ranger, *Emerging Themes*. See also Falola, *Nationalism and African Intellectuals*, 223–60; Falola and Aderinto, *Nigeria, Nationalism, and Writing History*; Vansina, *Living with Africa*, 111–36; Oliver, *In the Realms of Gold*.

95. Ranger, 'Towards a Usable African Past'.

96. For example, Gulliver, *Tradition and Transition in East Africa*.

97. Quoted in Mamdani, *Citizen and Subject*, 135.

98. Dipesh Chakrabarty refers to the millions existing beyond European time as being in the "waiting room of history": Chakrabarty, *Provincializing Europe*, 7.

99. Kabeya, *King Mirambo*, ix–xi.

100. Nyerere, *'Ujamaa'*.

101. Kabeya, *King Mirambo*, x–xi.

102. Low, *Buganda in Modern History*, 245–46; Kabaka of Buganda, *Desecration of My Kingdom*. The kingdoms were only restored in 1993 under the strict condition that they would be apolitical and purely 'cultural'.

103. See also R. Reid, 'Remembering and Forgetting Mirambo'.

104. Most notably, A. A. Mazrui, 'Resurrection of the Warrior Tradition'.

105. It is pervasive. After I gave a seminar presentation (to an African university audience) dealing with the reframing of partition in the context of Africa's revolutionary nineteenth century, there was not a single question in the Q&A on the nineteenth century, which had formed the bulk of the paper: pretty much every question was on 'The Scramble' itself, on the imposition of borders, on the political implications of European conquest, on who was to blame for it all. This reflects the hegemony of the 'colonial' experience in scholarly circles on the continent and even a certain degree of lack of interest in 'the precolonial'.

106. Ranger, 'Connexions', Parts 1 and 2.

107. The OAU Charter was signed at Addis Ababa on 25 May 1963 (and can be viewed at https://au.int/sites/default/files/treaties/7759-file-oau_charter_1963.pdf). The essential tenets were reiterated on 11 July 2000 at Lomé, when the Constitutive Act of the African Union (available at https://au.int/sites/default/files/pages/34873-file-constitutiveact_en.pdf) was signed.

108. Davidson, *Black Man's Burden*.

109. Táíwò, *Against Decolonisation*.

110. The point was made at the time by Hodgkin, 'Relevance of "Western" Ideas', 66.

111. For instance, oral historical research undertaken in southern Mali revealed a much greater degree of ambivalence, indeed hostility, toward putative 'national hero' Samori: memories which were of little use to those who would posit him as something of a founding figure: Peterson, 'History, Memory and the Legacy of Samori'.

112. See, for example, a useful survey in G. Martin, *African Political Thought*.

113. Museveni, *What is Africa's Problem?*, 163.

114. R. Reid, 'Time and Distance'.

115. Museveni, *Sowing the Mustard Seed*, 137.

116. In 2009 Kabalega was officially declared a 'national hero'. No such honour came the way of Mwanga, however, whose homosexuality was problematic in Museveni's Uganda.

117. For a broader analysis of the idea, see Armitage, *Civil Wars*, ch. 4.

118. Hallencreutz, 'Thomas Mofolo and Nelson Mandela'; Mandela, *Long Walk to Freedom*, 274–75. By the 1980s, Zulu nationalists sought to monopolise these histories, which they regarded as exclusively theirs, not all of South Africa's: Hamilton, *Terrific Majesty*, 202–3. In addition, more broadly, see Wylie, *Myth of Iron*; and Carton, Laband and Sithole, *Zulu Identities*.

119. J. Wright, 'Mfecane Debates'; Hamilton, *Mfecane Aftermath*; I. R. Smith, 'New Lessons in South Africa's History'. That consensus is reflected in Hamilton, Mbenga and Ross, *Cambridge History of South Africa, Vol. 1*: see in particular their 'Editors' Introduction', 13–14.

120. Young and Turner, *Rise and Decline*.

121. D. H. Johnson, 'New History'; Haile, 'Historical Background', 11–17, and Tseggai, 'History of the Eritrean Struggle', 67–70. In the case of both South Sudan and Eritrea, of course, it was also perfectly reasonable for broadly 'sympathetic' scholars to outline the deeper historical dynamics which created the conditions for later armed struggle: for example, D. H. Johnson, *Root Causes*, ch. 1; Thomas, *South Sudan*, ch. 2; Davidson, 'Historical Note'; Greenfield, 'Precolonial and Colonial History', esp. 16–24.

122. See Eritrean People's Liberation Front, 'National Democratic Programme'.

123. For an incisive analysis of categories of 'rebel' in twentieth-century Africa, see Reno, *Warfare in Independent Africa*, esp. chs 2–4.

124. Mbeki, 'African Renaissance' (speech at the United Nations University, 9 April 1998); see too Bongmba, 'Reflections on Thabo Mbeki's African Renaissance'. For the original inspiration, see Diop, *Towards the African Renaissance*. There was also much talk in the 1990s concerning Africa's 'new breed' of leaders, characterised as pragmatic, intelligent, ready to address the failings of the recent past. The group supposedly included Meles Zenawi (Ethiopia), Olusegun Obasanjo (Nigeria), Paul Kagame (Rwanda), Yoweri Museveni (Uganda) and Isaias Afeworki (Eritrea). See Clapham, 'Discerning the New Africa'.

125. Lentz, '"Ghana@50"'.

126. Kantai et al., 'Kings: Adapt or Die!'; and 'Kings without Kingdoms' in Bichach, *Uganda 1986–2011*.

127. For example, Prestholdt, 'Politics of the Soil'; Glassman, 'Creole Nationalists'.

128. 'President Jonathan's Centenary Address'.

129. R. Reid, 'States of Anxiety', 244–46.

130. Sèbe, 'From Post-colonialism'. More broadly, see Geppert and Müller, *Sites of Imperial Memory*.

131. Bernault, 'Colonial Bones'.

132. Sèbe, 'From Post-colonialism', 947ff.

133. See, for example, a thoughtful exploration of the uses of history in Jessee, *Negotiating Genocide in Rwanda*; also, Mathys, 'Bringing History Back In'.

134. Orlowska, 'Forging a Nation'; R. Reid, 'States of Anxiety', 258–59. More recently, the tables have turned once more, the EPRDF regime has been dismantled, and Tigray has been devastated by a terrible conflict in which historical memory has played a significant role.

135. BBC News, 10 June 2011: 'Bishop of St Asaph "disappointed" by HM Stanley Statue'.

136. BBC News, 12 June 2020: 'Bishop of St Asaph Wants Henry Morton Stanley Statues Removed'.

137. BBC News, 26 August 2010: 'More than 50 Prominent Names Oppose Stanley Statue'.

138. BBC News, 15 June 2020: 'Henry Morton Stanley Statue Row: Explorer "not racist"'.

139. BBC News, 27 October 2021: 'Africa Explorer HM Stanley Statue to Stay in Denbigh'.

140. Beinart, 'Rhodes Must Fall'.

141. This is an extension of the enduring fixation in Britain with the nineteenth century, and in particular with the Victorian era: a time (according to the normative and popular interpretation) of national self-confidence and world-beating accomplishment: see the wonderfully meditative Samuel, *Theatres of Memory*; and for an example of a particular genre, Paxman, *Victorians*.

142. In fact these debates had been bubbling away for some time with regard to the secondary school history curriculum. For many on the political right in the early years of the twenty-first century, there needed to be a shift back toward the unabashed celebration of 'national heroes', with a view to rejuvenating a sense of English national identity. History teachers had long been on the front line in this respect. See Cannadine, Keating and Sheldon, *Right Kind of History*.

143. Farrer, 'Who Was Edward Colston?' (report in *The Guardian*, 8 June 2020).

144. Gildea, *Empires of the Mind*; also Dorling and Tomlinson, *Rule Britannia*.

145. B. Johnson, 'If Blair's So Good at Running the Congo'.

146. B. Johnson, 'Africa is a Mess'. The same dismissive, generalising, patronising framing of Africa permeates British political discourse, especially—if not exclusively—on the Conservative Right. Note, for example, then-defence secretary Michael Fallon's repeated reference to the enduring problem of "these countries"—he was specifically talking about South Sudan and Somalia—as a generic allusion to troubled, tribal Africa: interview on the BBC *Today* programme, 8 September 2016.

147. History wars were by no means confined to Britain. In an Australian context, see for example Brantlinger, '"Black Armband" versus "White Blindfold" History'; and for a global survey, Black, *Contesting History*.

148. Sèbe, *Heroic Imperialists*.

149. Ba, 'Africans Still Seething' (*Reuters* report, 5 September 2007).

150. See for example Mbembe, 'L'Afrique de Nicolas Sarkozy'.

151. Fanon, *Wretched of the Earth*, 81.

152. Southern Africa and the Horn were especially enmeshed in Cold War dynamics: for useful snapshots, see Carter and O'Meara, *Southern Africa*, and Legum and Lee, *Horn of Africa*; Brind, 'Soviet Policy'; Gavshon, *Crisis in Africa*. It should go without saying, of course, that Africans—or more specifically their putative representatives—were not uniformly 'victims' in this context, but co-opted global ideological dynamics, as they always had, with a view to achieving more local objectives: see Westad, *Global Cold War*, esp. chs 6 and 7.

153. I. Taylor, *Africa Rising?*.

154. Carmody, *New Scramble*; Alden, *China in Africa*; I. Taylor, 'India's Rise in Africa'; I. Taylor, *China and Africa*; Alden, Large and de Oliveira, *China Returns to Africa*; Rotberg, *China into Africa*; Norbrook and Van Halen, 'Africa's Emerging Partners'; Ramani, *Russia in Africa*.

155. BBC News, 2 October 2001: 'Blair Promises to Stand By Africa'; McGreal, 'Blair Confronts "Scar on the World's Conscience"' (*The Guardian*, 7 February 2002).

156. Cargill, *More with Less*. Both positions were redolent of late nineteenth- and early-twentieth century strategies, but Foreign Office officials nevertheless bemoaned to me the fact that there was no continuity or consistency in British engagement with Africa, and remarkably little sense of a historically rooted relationship with the continent. In reality, many African governments don't care much either way, and are more likely to be attracted to China's 'strings-free' advances. The ambivalence felt toward the British was exposed in 2018, when beleaguered UK prime minister Theresa May visited Kenya in search of post-Brexit trade opportunities, only to be pointedly reminded by Uhuru Kenyatta—whose father had been detained during the Mau Mau insurgency in the 1950s—that no British premier had visited the country in thirty years. May compounded the sadness of the expedition by dancing awkwardly with some students. As ever, Boris Johnson—May's erstwhile foreign minister—had laid the groundwork for the trip's difficulty a couple of years earlier, when he made yet another of his racist contributions by suggesting that US president Barack Obama had an "ancestral dislike" for the UK on account of his being part-Kenyan: 'Boris Johnson Criticised for "Racist" Obama Comments' (*Aljazeera*, 23 April 2016).

157. Pinkney, *NGOs, Africa and the Global Order*; and see also a stimulating intervention by J. Ferguson, *Global Shadows*.

158. Richards, *Fighting for the Rain Forest*; Kaplan, 'Coming Anarchy'.

159. *Slow Train through Africa*, documentary miniseries, ITV, 2015.

160. I was an advisor on the BBC's *Lost Kingdoms of Africa*, and urged the producers in vain to reconsider the title of the series. Fronted by the superb Gus Casely-Hayford, the tone was nonetheless one of astonishment that the 'lost kingdoms' themselves still existed in some shape or form, rather than being living, breathing historical entities with a very real significance in people's lives. See *The Lost Kingdoms of Africa*, documentary TV series (two series), BBC, 2010; 2012.

161. For example, there have been numerous versions of *The Four Feathers*, a 1902 novel by A.E.W. Mason about a man who is shunned and disgraced when he quits his regiment in the British Army on the eve of the campaign to Sudan in the 1880s, but who later finds redemption through extraordinary courage when he makes his own way to Sudan in disguise. There were several silent versions, but the most notable productions were in 1939, 1955 (entitled *Storm over the Nile*), and 1978. By the time we get to the 2002 iteration, with Kate Hudson and Heath Ledger, the protagonist, notably, questions the very legitimacy of empire, while a more prominent role is given to his African companion. The trope of the wise and courageous African character has already begun to take shape by this time: for example, Morgan Freeman alongside Kevin Costner's *Robin Hood* (1991), and Djimon Hounsou as the loyal support to Russell Crowe's *Gladiator* (2000). The most famous Zulu movies are *Zulu* (1964) and *Zulu Dawn* (1979), both directed by Cy Endfield. Werner Herzog's *Cobra Verde* (1987), set in nineteenth-century Dahomey and based on the Bruce Chatwin novel *The Viceroy of Ouidah*, saw Klaus Kinski as the simmering, psychopathic slave trader surrounded by bloody barbarity and bare breasts. Also worth noting here is J. Elder Wills's *Song of Freedom* (1936), starring the great black performer and activist Paul Robeson, about a British dockworker with an extraordinary singing voice who discovers he is the rightful heir to the throne of the fictional West African kingdom of Casanga—with seemingly some similarities to Dahomey, prominent in the Western

imagination—and who ultimately wins it back. Casanga is chronically undeveloped, though, and the Robeson character's ability to straddle two worlds means he can bring technology and medicine from the West to the benighted kingdom. The nod to the power of the civilising mission notwithstanding, this was apparently Robeson's attempt to make amends for his appearance in Zoltán Korda's *Sanders of the River* (1935), criticised by many in the African diaspora, in which he acted out every available racial and cultural stereotype in his depiction of an African colonial subject interacting with his white superiors.

162. The *Black Panther* films (2018–) are obviously part of the Marvel Cinematic Universe and involve superhero characters with access to incredible technology. Gina Prince-Bythewood's *The Woman King* (2022), starring the extraordinary Viola Davis and set in 1820s Dahomey, is notable in that its action takes place in a (more or less) historically accurate context, and considerable efforts were evidently made to reconstruct the history of Dahomey, both its internal workings and its external relations. As noted above, it is by no means the first representation of Dahomey on screen, but it is the first—if we exclude *Song of Freedom*, with its obvious allusions to the kingdom—in which the main characters are black, and female.

163. The periodisation of African history is ripe for redefinition. In a characteristically eloquent essay, for example, Stephen Ellis interrogated the notion of 'contemporary Africa' and wondered whether a more evolved, nuanced interpretation of temporality and periodisation wasn't possible—indeed necessary—for Africa, given our expanded understanding of both developments within the continent and the relationship of those developments with the wider world: Ellis, 'Writing Histories'. For a broader set of ruminations on the nature of time, chronology and historical memory, see Jewsiewicki and Mudimbe, 'Africans' Memories'.

164. Even the term 'precolonial' itself is apparently open to definition. An eminent scholar, known for their work on the 'precolonial' past, once told me that they considered me 'only just' a historian of 'precolonial' history, as I worked on the nineteenth century—a period evidently perilously close to being tainted by contact with the colonial period. The term 'decolonisation', as currently defined in a broader epistemological sense, is also open to scrutiny in this respect: it throws into shade everything that came before. What does 'decolonising' mean in the context of the 'precolonial'?

165. It was part of a larger process by which the West came to dominate the very meaning and measurement of time itself, creating a system by which everyone else was expected to measure themselves: see, for example, Goody, *Theft of History*.

166. Mitchell, 'Stage of Modernity'; Chakrabarty, *Provincializing Europe*, esp. ch. 1; Chakrabarty, 'Muddle of Modernity'. For an example of an Africanist engagement with the concept, see Deutsch, Probst and Schmidt, *African Modernities*.

167. For example, Woodside, *Lost Modernities*.

168. This seems to me to be the case despite the partial exceptions, noted earlier, of work done on the Atlantic and Indian Ocean worlds for the period between the sixteenth and the nineteenth centuries, which has certainly contributed to the repositioning of African societies within a transnational/global frame.

## Epilogue

1. Hard data are notoriously hard to come by for the late nineteenth and early twentieth centuries, but estimates for central and equatorial Africa, for example, suggest net population loss between the 1890s and the 1920s: Fetter, *Demography from Scanty Evidence*.

2. R. Reid, *Warfare in African History*, 141–42, 145.

3. For example, Herbst, *States and Power*, 94–95, 262.

4. This is a strand of scholarly thought which appears in work which tends to laud particular forms of human achievement, including 'robust institutions', usually if not exclusively associated with 'The West'. See for example Fukuyama, *Origins of Political Order*, and Acemoglu and Robinson, *Why Nations Fail*.

5. There seemed to be a spate of this kind of work in the years after '9/11'. See, for example, N. Ferguson, *Civilization*; Pinker, *Better Angels of Our Nature*. As samples of gloomy analyses of the 'state' of what used to be called 'The Third World', see Harrison, *Inside the Third World*, or Kaplan, 'Coming Anarchy'. R. H. Bates, *When Things Fell Apart*, offers a more scientific assessment. For the confection of distinctive narratives around Africa, the work of Mudimbe is crucial: in particular, *The Invention of Africa*, and *The Idea of Africa*. See too my own ruminations on some of these issues in R. Reid, 'Horror, Hubris and Humanity'.

# BIBLIOGRAPHY

Abbink, Jon, Mirjam de Bruijn and Klaas van Walraven, eds. *Rethinking Resistance: Revolt and Violence in African History*. Leiden: Brill, 2003.

Abir, Mordechai. *Ethiopia: The Era of the Princes*. London: Longmans, 1968.

Abir, Mordechai. 'Southern Ethiopia'. In *Pre-colonial African Trade: Essays on Trade in Central and Eastern Africa before 1900*, edited by Richard Gray and David Birmingham, 119–37. London: Oxford University Press, 1970.

Abrahams, R. G. *The Peoples of Greater Unyamwezi, Tanzania*. London: International African Institute, 1967.

Acemoglu, Daron, Simon Johnson and James A. Robinson. 'Reversal of Fortune: Geography and Institutions in the Making of the Modern World Income Distribution'. *Quarterly Journal of Economics* 117, no. 4 (2002): 1231–94.

Acemoglu, Daron and James A. Robinson. *Why Nations Fail: The Origins of Power, Prosperity and Poverty*. London: Profile Books, 2012.

Achebe, Chinua. *Things Fall Apart*. Oxford: Heinemann, 1986 [1958].

Adams, Moni. 'Fon Appliquéd Cloths'. *African Arts* 13, no. 2 (1980): 28–41.

Adebajo, Adekeye. *The Curse of Berlin: Africa after the Cold War*. London: Hurst, 2010.

Adi, Hakim. *Pan-Africanism: A History*. London: Bloomsbury, 2018.

Adi, Hakim and Marika Sherwood. *Pan-African History: Political Figures from Africa and the Diaspora since 1787*. London: Routledge, 2003.

Adjaye, Joseph K. *Diplomacy and Diplomats in 19th Century Asante*. Trenton, NJ: Africa World Press, 1996 [1984].

Adu-Boahen, Kwabena. 'Pawn of Contesting Imperialists: Nkoransa in the Anglo-Asante Rivalry in Northwest Ghana, 1874–1900'. *Journal of Philosophy and Culture* 3, no. 2 (2006): 55–85.

Afigbo, A. E. *The Warrant Chiefs: Indirect Rule in Southeastern Nigeria, 1891–1929*. London: Longman, 1972.

Afonja, Simi. 'Changing Modes of Production and the Sexual Division of Labour among the Yoruba'. *Signs* 7, no. 2 (1981): 299–313.

'Africa and the Indian Ocean'. Special feature, *Journal of African History* 55, no. 2 (2014): 161ff.

Ageron, Charles-Robert. *Modern Algeria: A History from 1830 to the Present*. London: Hurst, 1991.

Ahmad, Abdussamad H. 'Ethiopian Slave Exports at Matamma, Massawa and Tajura, c. 1830–1885'. *Slavery & Abolition* 9, no. 3 (1988): 93–102.

Ahmida, Ali Abdullatif. *The Making of Modern Libya: State Formation, Colonization, and Resistance*. Albany, NY: State University of New York Press, 1994.

Aidoo, Agnes Akosua. 'Asante Queen Mothers in Government and Politics in the Nineteenth Century'. *Journal of the Historical Society of Nigeria* 9, no. 1 (1977): 1–13.

Ajayi, J. F. Ade. *Christian Missions in Nigeria, 1841–1891: The Making of a New Elite*. London: Longmans, 1965.

Ajayi, J. F. Ade. *A Patriot to the Core: Bishop Ajayi Crowther*. Ibadan: Spectrum Books, 2001.

Ajayi, J. F. Ade and Robert S. Smith. *Yoruba Warfare in the Nineteenth Century*. Ibadan and Cambridge: Ibadan University Press/Cambridge University Press, 1964.

Akinjogbin, I. A. 'Archibald Dalzel: Slave Trader and Historian of Dahomey'. *Journal of African History* 7, no. 1 (1966): 67–78.

Akinjogbin, I. A. *Dahomey and its Neighbours, 1708–1818*. Cambridge: Cambridge University Press, 1967.

Akintoye, S. A. *Revolution and Power Politics in Yorubaland, 1840–1893: Ibadan Expansion and the Rise of Ekitiparapo*. London: Longman, 1971.

Akpan, Monday B. 'Black Imperialism: Americo-Liberian Rule over the African Peoples of Liberia, 1841–1964'. *Canadian Journal of African Studies* 7, no. 2 (1973): 217–36.

Akyeampong, Emmanuel, Robert H. Bates, Nathan Nunn and James A. Robinson, eds. *Africa's Development in Historical Perspective*. Cambridge: Cambridge University Press, 2014.

Alagoa, Ebiegberi Joe. *The Practice of History in Africa: A History of African Historiography*. Port Harcourt: Onyoma Research Publications, 2006.

Alden, Chris. *China in Africa*. New York: Zed Books, 2007.

Alden, Chris, Daniel Large and Ricardo Soares de Oliveira, eds. *China Returns to Africa: A Rising Power and a Continent Embrace*. London: Hurst, 2008.

Aldrich, Robert. *Greater France: A History of French Overseas Expansion*. Basingstoke: Macmillan, 1996.

Alexander, Nathan G. 'E. D. Morel (1873–1924), the Congo Reform Association, and the History of Human Rights'. *Britain and the World* 9, no. 2 (2016): 213–35.

Ali, Taisier M. and Robert O. Matthews, eds. *Civil Wars in Africa: Roots and Resolution*. Montreal and Kingston: McGill-Queen's University Press, 1999.

Allina-Pisano, Eric. 'Resistance and the Social History of Africa'. *Journal of Social History* 37, no. 1 (2003): 187–98.

Alpern, Stanley B. *Amazons of Black Sparta: The Women Warriors of Dahomey*. New York: New York University Press, 2011.

Alpers, Edward A. *Ivory and Slaves in East Central Africa: Changing Patterns of International Trade to the Later Nineteenth Century*. London: Heinemann, 1975.

Alpers, Edward A. 'State, Merchant Capital, and Gender Relations in Southern Mozambique to the End of the Nineteenth Century: Some Tentative Hypotheses'. *African Economic History* 13 (1984): 23–55.

Alpers, Edward A. 'The Story of Swema: Female Vulnerability in Nineteenth-Century East Africa'. In *Women and Slavery in Africa*, edited by Claire Robertson and Martin A. Klein, 85–219. Madison, WI: University of Wisconsin Press, 1983.

Al-Sayyid-Marsot, Afaf Lutfi. 'The British Occupation of Egypt from 1882'. In *The Oxford History of the British Empire, Volume 3: The Nineteenth Century*, edited by Andrew Porter, 651–64. Oxford: Oxford University Press, 1999.

Al-Sayyid-Marsot, Afaf Lutfi. *Egypt in the Reign of Muhammad Ali*. Cambridge: Cambridge University Press, 1984.

Ambler, Charles H. *Kenyan Communities in the Age of Imperialism*. New Haven, CT: Yale University Press, 1988.

Andrew, C. M. and A. S. Kanya-Forstner. 'The French "Colonial Party": Its Composition, Aims and Influence, 1885–1914'. *The Historical Journal* 14, no. 1 (1971): 99–128.

'Arab Faqīh (Šihāb ad-Din Aḥmad bin 'Abd al-Qāder bin Sālem bin 'Utmān). *Futūḥ al-Ḥabaša: The Conquest of Abyssinia*, translated by Paul Lester Stenhouse, with annotations by Richard Pankhurst. Hollywood, CA: Tsehai, 2003.

Argenti, Nicolas and Deborah Durham. 'Youth'. In *The Oxford Handbook of Modern African History*, edited by John Parker and Richard Reid, 396–413. Oxford: Oxford University Press, 2013.

Arhin, Kwame. 'Asante Military Institutions'. *Journal of African Studies* 7, no. 1 (1980): 22–30.

Armah, Ayi Kwei. *The Beautyful Ones Are Not Yet Born*. London: Heinemann, 1968.

Armah, Ayi Kwei. *Fragments*. London: Heinemann, 1970.

Armah, Ayi Kwei. *Two Thousand Seasons*. London: Heinemann, 1973.

Armah, Ayi Kwei. *Why Are We So Blest?* London: Heinemann, 1972.

Armitage, David. *Civil Wars: A History in Ideas*. New Haven, CT: Yale University Press, 2017.

Armstrong, John A. *Nations before Nationalism*. Chapel Hill, NC: University of North Carolina Press, 1982.

Arnold, David, ed. *Imperial Medicine and Indigenous Societies*. Manchester: Manchester University Press, 1988.

Arnot, Frederick Stanley. *Garenganze; or, Seven Years' Pioneer Mission Work in Central Africa*. London: J. E. Hawkins, 1889.

Arrowsmith-Brown, J. H., trans. and ed. *Prutky's Travels in Ethiopia and Other Countries*. London: Hakluyt Society, 1991.

Asante, Molefi Kete. *The History of Africa: The Quest for Eternal Harmony*. New York: Routledge, 2019 [2007].

Ascherson, Neal. *The King Incorporated: Leopold II in the Age of Trusts*. London: Allen & Unwin, 1963.

Ashe, Robert Pickering. *Chronicles of Uganda*. London: Hodder & Stoughton, 1894.

Assefaw, Taye. 'Tewodros in Ethiopian Historical Fiction'. *Journal of Ethiopian Studies* 16 (1983): 115–28.

Atanda, J. A. *The New Oyo Empire: Indirect Rule and Change in Western Nigeria, 1894–1934*. London: Longman, 1973.

Atieno-Odhiambo, E. S. 'From African Historiographies to an African Philosophy of History'. In *Africanizing Knowledge: African Studies Across the Disciplines*, edited by Toyin Falola and Christian Jennings, 13–63. New Brunswick, NJ: Transaction Publishers, 2002.

Atkinson, Ronald R. *The Roots of Ethnicity: The Origins of the Acholi of Uganda before 1800*. Philadelphia: University of Pennsylvania Press, 1994.

Atmore, A. E. 'Africa on the Eve of Partition'. In *The Cambridge History of Africa, Volume 6: 1870–1905*, edited by Roland Oliver and G. N. Sanderson, 10–95. Cambridge: Cambridge University Press, 1985.

Austen, Ralph. 'The 19th Century Islamic Slave Trade from East Africa (Swahili and Red Sea Coasts): A Tentative Census'. *Slavery & Abolition* 9, no. 3 (1988): 21–44.

Austen, Ralph. 'The Abolition of the Overseas Slave Trade: A Distorted Theme in West African History'. *Journal of the Historical Society of Nigeria* 5, no. 2 (1970): 257–74.

Austen, Ralph. *African Economic History: Internal Development and External Dependency*. London: James Currey, 1987.

Austen, Ralph and Jonathan Derrick. *Middlemen of the Cameroons Rivers: The Duala and Their Hinterland, c. 1600–c. 1900*. Cambridge: Cambridge University Press, 1999.

Austin, Gareth. 'Between Abolition and *jihad*: The Asante Response to the Ending of the Atlantic Slave Trade, 1807–1896'. In *From Slave Trade to 'Legitimate' Commerce: Commercial*

*Transition in Nineteenth-Century West Africa*, edited by Robin Law, 93–118. Cambridge: Cambridge University Press, 1995.

Austin, Gareth. 'The Emergence of Capitalist Relations in South Asante Cocoa-Farming, c. 1916–1933'. *Journal of African History* 28, no. 2 (1987): 259–79.

Austin, Gareth. *Land, Labour and Capital in Ghana: From Slavery to Free Labour in Asante, 1807–1956*. Rochester, NY: University of Rochester Press, 2005.

Austin, Gareth. 'Resources, Techniques, and Strategies South of the Sahara: Revising the Factor Endowments Perspective on African Economic Development, 1500–2000'. *Economic History Review* 61, no. 3 (2008): 587–624.

Austin, Gareth. 'The "Reversal of Fortune" Thesis and the Compression of History: Perspectives from African and Comparative History'. *Journal of International Development* 20, no. 8 (2008): 996–1027.

Awe, Bolanle. 'The Iyalode in the Traditional Yoruba Political System'. In *Sexual Stratification: A Cross-cultural View*, edited by Alice Schlegel, 144–60. New York: Columbia University Press, 1977.

Axelson, E. V. *Portugal and the Scramble for Africa*. Johannesburg: Witwatersrand University Press, 1967.

Ayandele, E. A. *The Missionary Impact on Modern Nigeria, 1842–1914*. London: Longman, 1966.

Azevedo, Mario Joaquim, Gerald W. Hartwig and K. David Patterson, eds. *Disease in African History: An Introductory Survey and Case Studies*. Durham, NC: Duke University Press, 1978.

Ba, Diadie. 'Africans Still Seething over Sarkozy Speech'. *Reuters*, 5 September 2007. Available at https://www.reuters.com/article/idUSL05130346/ (accessed 15 March 2024).

Ballard, Charles C. 'John Dunn and Cetshwayo: The Material Foundations of Political Power in the Zulu Kingdom, 1857–1878'. *Journal of African History* 21, no. 1 (1980): 75–91.

Barber, Karin. 'I. B. Akinyele and Early Yoruba Print Culture'. In *Recasting the Past: History Writing and Political Work in Modern Africa*, edited by Derek R. Peterson and Giacomo Macola, 31–49. Athens, OH: Ohio University Press, 2009.

Barnett, Tony. *The Gezira Scheme: An Illusion of Development*. London: Cass, 1977.

Barry, Boubacar. *Senegambia and the Atlantic Slave Trade*, translated by Ayi Kwei Armah. Cambridge: Cambridge University Press, 1998 [Fr. 1988].

Barth, Fredrik, ed. *Ethnic Groups and Boundaries: The Social Organization of Culture Difference*. London: Allen & Unwin, 1969.

Bartlett, W. B. *Zulu: Queen Victoria's Most Famous Little War*. Stroud: The History Press, 2010.

Bassett, Thomas J. 'The Development of Cotton in Northern Ivory Coast, 1910–1965'. *Journal of African History* 29, no. 2 (1988): 267–84.

Bastin, Marie-Louise. *La Sculpture tshokwe*. Meudon: A. & F. Chaffin, 1982.

Bastin, Marie-Louise. *Statuettes tshokwe du héros civilisateur Tshibinda Ilunga*. Arnouville: Collection Arts d'Afrique noire, 1978.

Bates, D. *The Abyssinian Difficulty: The Emperor Theodorus and the Magdala Campaign, 1867–68*. Oxford: Oxford University Press, 1979.

Bates, Robert H. *When Things Fell Apart: State Failure in Late-Century Africa*. Cambridge: Cambridge University Press, 2008.

Bay, Edna G. 'Belief, Legitimacy and the Kpojito: An Institutional History of the Queen Mother in Precolonial Dahomey'. *Journal of African History* 36, no. 1 (1995): 1–27.

Bay, Edna G. 'Servitude and Worldly Success in the Palace of Dahomey'. In *Women and Slavery in Africa*, edited by Claire Robertson and Martin A. Klein, 340–67. Madison, WI: University of Wisconsin Press, 1983.

Bay, Edna G. *Wives of the Leopard: Gender, Politics, and Culture in the Kingdom of Dahomey.* Charlottesville, VA: University of Virginia Press, 1998.

Bayart, Jean-François. 'Africa in the World: A History of Extraversion'. *African Affairs* 99, no. 395 (2000): 217–67.

Bayly, C. A. *The Birth of the Modern World, 1780–1914: Global Connections and Comparisons.* Malden, MA: Blackwell, 2004.

BBC News, 2 October 2001. 'Blair Promises to Stand By Africa'. Available at http://news.bbc.co.uk/1/hi/world/africa/1575428.stm (accessed 15 March 2024).

BBC News, 10 June 2011. 'Bishop of St Asaph "disappointed" by HM Stanley Statue'. Available at https://www.bbc.co.uk/news/uk-wales-north-east-wales-13710941 (accessed 15 March 2024).

BBC News, 26 August 2010. 'More than 50 Prominent Names Oppose Stanley Statue'. Available at https://www.bbc.co.uk/news/uk-wales-north-east-wales-11101125 (accessed 15 March 2024).

BBC News, 12 June 2020. 'Bishop of St Asaph Wants Henry Morton Stanley Statues Removed'. Available at https://www.bbc.co.uk/news/uk-wales-53029390 (accessed 15 March 2024).

BBC News, 15 June 2020. 'Henry Morton Stanley Statue Row: Explorer "not racist"'. Available at https://www.bbc.co.uk/news/uk-wales-53056739 (accessed 15 March 2024).

BBC News, 27 October 2021. 'Africa Explorer HM Stanley Statue to Stay in Denbigh'. Available at https://www.bbc.co.uk/news/uk-wales-59069612 (accessed 15 March 2024).

Beach, D. N. 'Chimurenga: The Shona Risings of 1896–97'. *Journal of African History* 20, no. 3 (1979): 395–420.

Beachey, R. W. 'The Arms Trade in East Africa in the Late Nineteenth Century'. *Journal of African History* 3, no. 3 (1962): 451–67.

Beachey, R. W. 'The East African Ivory Trade in the Nineteenth Century'. *Journal of African History* 8, no. 2 (1967): 269–90.

Beachey, R. W. *The Slave Trade of Eastern Africa.* London: Collings, 1976.

Beattie, John. *The Nyoro State.* Oxford: Clarendon Press, 1971.

Becker, Felicitas. 'Traders, "Big Men", and Prophets: Political Continuity and Crisis in the Maji Maji Rebellion in Southeast Tanzania'. *Journal of African History* 45, no. 1 (2004): 1–22.

Becker, Felicitas and Joel Cabrita. 'Introduction: Performing Citizenship and Enacting Exclusion on Africa's Indian Ocean Littoral'. *Journal of African History* 55, no. 2 (2014): 161–71.

Becker, Peter. *Path of Blood: The Rise and Conquests of Mzilikazi, Founder of the Matabele Tribe of Southern Africa.* London: Longmans, 1962.

Becker, Peter. *Rule of Fear: The Life and Times of Dingane, King of the Zulu.* London: Allen Lane, 1964.

Beckingham, C. F. and G.W.B. Huntingford, trans. and eds. *Some Records of Ethiopia 1593–1646: Being Extracts from 'The History of High Ethiopia or Abassia', by Manoel de Almeida.* London: Hakluyt Society, 1954.

Beinart, William. 'Rhodes Must Fall: The Uses of Historical Evidence in the Statue Debate in Oxford, 2015–16'. Paper presented at the 'Conference on Racialisation and Publicness in Africa and the African Diaspora', African Studies Centre, Oxford, June 2019.

Belich, James. *Replenishing the Earth: The Settler Revolution and the Rise of the Anglo-World, 1783–1939.* Oxford: Oxford University Press, 2009.

Bellagamba, Alice, Sandra E. Greene and Martin A. Klein, eds. *African Voices on Slavery and the Slave Trade.* Cambridge: Cambridge University Press, 2013.

Belloc, Hilaire. *The Modern Traveller.* London: Edward Arnold, 1898.

Bennett, Joshua. *God and Progress: Religion and History in British Intellectual Culture, 1845–1914.* Oxford: Oxford University Press, 2019.

Bennett, Norman R. 'The Arab Impact'. In *Zamani: A Survey of East African History*, edited by B. A. Ogot and J. A. Kieran, 216–37. Nairobi: East African Publishing House, 1968.

Bennett, Norman R. *Arab versus European: Diplomacy and War in Nineteenth-Century East Central Africa*. New York: Africana Publishing Company, 1986.

Bennett, Norman R. *A History of the Arab State of Zanzibar*. London: Methuen, 1978.

Bennett, Norman R. *Mirambo of Tanzania, ca. 1840–1884*. New York: Oxford University Press, 1971.

Bennett, Norman R. 'Philippe Broyon: Pioneer Trader in East Africa'. *African Affairs* 62, no. 247 (1963): 156–64.

Bennett, Norman R., ed. *Stanley's Despatches to 'The New York Herald', 1871–1872, 1874–1877*. Boston, MA: Boston University Press, 1970.

Bennett, Norman R. *Studies in East African History*. Boston, MA: Boston University Press, 1963.

Berenson, Edward. *Heroes of Empire: Five Charismatic Men and the Conquest of Africa*. Berkeley, CA: University of California Press, 2011.

Berger, Iris. 'Rebels or Status-Seekers? Women as Spirit-Mediums in East Africa'. In *Women in Africa: Studies in Social and Economic Change*, edited by Nancy Hafkin and Edna Bay, 157–81. Stanford, CA: Stanford University Press, 1976.

Berger, John. *Ways of Seeing*. London: Penguin/BBC, 1972.

Berkeley, G. F.-H. *The Campaign of Adowa and the Rise of Menelik*. New York: Negro Universities Press, 1969 [1902].

Bernal, Martin. *Black Athena: The Afroasiatic Roots of Classical Civilization, Volume 1: The Fabrication of Ancient Greece*. New Brunswick, NJ: Rutgers University Press, 1987.

Bernault, Florence. 'Colonial Bones: The 2006 Burial of Savorgnan de Brazza in the Congo'. *African Affairs* 109, no. 436 (2010): 367–90.

Bertrand, Romain and Guillaume Calafat. 'Global Microhistory: A Case to Follow'. *Annales* 73, no. 1 (2018): 3–17.

Beshah, Girmah and Merid Wolde Aregay. *The Question of the Union of the Churches in Luso-Ethiopian Relations, 1500–1632*. Lisbon: Junta de Investigações do Ultramar and Centro de Estudos Históricos Ultramarinos, 1964.

Bethencourt, Francisco. *Racisms: From the Crusades to the Twentieth Century*. Princeton, NJ: Princeton University Press, 2014.

Bichachi, Charles Odoobo, ed. *Uganda 1986–2011: NRM 25 Years. Politics, Policies, and Personalities*. Kampala: Tourguide Publications, 2011.

Bierman, John. *Dark Safari: The Life behind the Legend of Henry Morton Stanley*. Austin, TX: University of Texas Press, 1993.

Birmingham, David. 'Early African Trade in Angola and Its Hinterland'. In *Pre-colonial African Trade: Essays on Trade in Central and Eastern Africa before 1900*, edited by Richard Gray and David Birmingham, 163–73. London: Oxford University Press, 1970.

Birmingham, David. *A Short History of Modern Angola*. London: Hurst, 2015.

Birmingham, David. *Trade and Conflict in Angola: The Mbundu and Their Neighbours under the Influence of the Portuguese, 1483–1790*. Oxford: Clarendon Press, 1966.

Birmingham, David and Shula Marks. 'Southern Africa'. In *The Cambridge History of Africa, Volume 3: c. 1050–c. 1600*, edited by Roland Oliver, 567–620. Cambridge: Cambridge University Press, 1977.

Black, Jeremy. *Contesting History: Narratives of Public History*. London: Bloomsbury, 2014.

Blanc, Henry. *A Narrative of Captivity in Abyssinia*. London: Frank Cass, 1970 [1868].

Blundell, H. Weld, trans. and ed. *The Royal Chronicle of Abyssinia, 1769–1840*. Cambridge: Cambridge University Press, 1922.

Blunt, Elizabeth. 'Ethiopia Seeks Prince's Remains'. BBC News, 3 June 2007. Available at http://news.bbc.co.uk/1/hi/world/africa/6716921.stm (accessed 15 March 2024).

Boahen, A. Adu. *African Perspectives on Colonialism*. Baltimore: Johns Hopkins University Press, 1987.

Boahen, A. Adu, ed. *UNESCO General History of Africa, Volume 7: Africa under Colonial Domination, 1880–1935*. London: James Currey, 1990.

Boahen, A. Adu, Emmanuel Akyeampong, Nancy Lawler, T. C. McCaskie and Ivor Wilks, eds. *'The History of Ashanti Kings and the Whole Country Itself' and Other Writings, by Otumfuo, Nana Agyeman Prempeh I*. Oxford: Oxford University Press, 2003.

Boas, Marten and Kevin C. Dunn, eds. *African Guerrillas: Raging against the Machine*. Boulder, CO: Lynne Rienner, 2007.

Bond, Brian. *War and Society in Europe, 1870–1970*. London: Sutton Publishing, 1984.

Bongmba, Elias K. 'Reflections on Thabo Mbeki's African Renaissance'. *Journal of Southern African Studies* 30, no. 2 (2004): 291–316.

'Boris Johnson Criticised for "Racist" Obama Comments'. *Aljazeera*, 23 April 2016. Available at https://www.aljazeera.com/news/2016/4/23/boris-johnson-criticised-for-racist-obama-comments (accessed 15 March 2024).

Bosman, William. *A New and Accurate Description of the Coast of Guinea*. London: James Knapton & Daniel Midwinter, 1705.

Bovill, E. W. *The Niger Explored*. London: Oxford University Press, 1968.

Boyd, Jean. 'The Fulani Women Poets'. In *Pastoralists of the West African Savannah*, edited by M. Adamu and A.H.M. Kirk-Greene, 127–42. Manchester: Manchester University Press, 1986.

Braimah, J. A. *The Two Isanwurfos*. London: Longmans, 1967.

Brantlinger, Patrick. '"Black Armband" versus "White Blindfold" History in Australia'. *Victorian Studies* 46, no. 4 (2004): 655–74.

Brantlinger, Patrick. *Rule of Darkness: British Literature and Imperialism, 1830–1914*. Ithaca, NY: Cornell University Press, 1988.

Brenner, Louis. *The Shehus of Kukawa: A History of the al-Kenemi Dynasty of Bornu*. Oxford: Clarendon Press, 1973.

Brewer, Anthony. *Marxist Theories of Imperialism: A Critical Survey*. London: Routledge & Kegan Paul, 1980.

Bridge, F. R. and Roger Bullen. *The Great Powers and the European States System, 1814–1914*. Harlow: Pearson, 2005.

Brind, Harry. 'Soviet Policy in the Horn of Africa'. *International Affairs* 60, no. 1 (1983–84): 75–95.

*British Parliamentary Papers: Slave Trade*, 90 vols. Shannon: Irish University Press, 1968–.

Broadhead, Susan Herlin. 'Slave Wives, Free Sisters: Bakongo Women and Slavery, c. 1700–1850'. In *Women and Slavery in Africa*, edited by Claire Robertson and Martin A. Klein, 160–78. Madison, WI: University of Wisconsin Press, 1983.

Brogan, Hugh. *The Penguin History of the United States of America*. London: Penguin, 1985.

Brooks, Miguel F., ed. and trans. *A Modern Translation of the 'Kebra Nagast' (The Glory of the Kings)*. Lawrenceville, NJ: Red Sea Press, 1995.

Brown, L. Carl *The Tunisia of Ahmad Bey, 1837–1855*. Princeton, NJ: Princeton University Press, 1974.

Broyon-Mirambo, Philippe. 'Description of Unyamwesi, the Territory of King Mirambo, and the Best Route Thither from the East Coast'. *Proceedings of the Royal Geographical Society* 22 (1877): 28–36.

Bruce, James. *Travels to Discover the Source of the Nile, in the Years 1768, 1769, 1770, 1771, 1772, and 1773*, 5 vols. London: G.G.J. & J. Robinson, 1790.

Bulatovich, Alexander. *Ethiopia through Russian Eyes: Country in Transition, 1896–1898*, edited and translated by Richard Seltzer. Lawrenceville, NJ: Red Sea Press, 2000.

Bundy, Colin. *The Rise and Fall of the South African Peasantry*. London and Cape Town: James Currey/David Philip, 1988 [1979].

Burbank, Jane and Frederick Cooper. *Empires in World History: Power and the Politics of Difference*. Princeton, NJ: Princeton University Press, 2010.

Burgess, E. 'Letters from Mr Burgess dated 11 September 1839'. *Missionary Herald* 87 (1840): 118–21.

Burrow, John W. *The Crisis of Reason: European Thought, 1848–1914*. New Haven, CT: Yale University Press, 2000.

Burrow, John W. *A History of Histories: Epics, Chronicles, Romances and Inquiries from Herodotus and Thucydides to the Twentieth Century*. London: Penguin, 2009.

Burton, Andrew and Hélène Charton-Bigot, eds. *Generations Past: Youth in East African History*. Athens, OH: Ohio University Press, 2010.

Burton, Richard F. *Abeokuta and the Camaroons Mountains*, 2 vols. London: Tinsley Brothers, 1863.

Burton, Richard F. *The Lake Regions of Central Africa*. New York: Dover Publications, 1995 [1860].

Burton, Richard F. *A Mission to Gelele, King of Dahome*, 2 vols. London: Tinsley Brothers, 1864.

Burton, Richard F. *Wanderings in West Africa: From Liverpool to Fernando Po*, 2 vols. London: Tinsley Brothers, 1863.

Burton, Richard F. *Zanzibar: City, Island and Coast*, 2 vols. London: Tinsley Brothers, 1872.

Buxton, Thomas Fowell. *The African Slave Trade*. London: John Murray, 1839.

Cabrita, Joel. *Text and Authority in the South African Nazaretha Church*. Cambridge: Cambridge University Press, 2014.

Cain, P. J. and A. G. Hopkins. *British Imperialism, 1688–2000*. London: Longman, 2002 [1993].

Callwell, C. E. *Small Wars: Their Principles and Practice*. London: His Majesty's Stationery Office, 1906 [1896].

Cameron, Verney Lovett *Across Africa*, 2 vols. London: Daldy, Isbister, 1877.

Cameron, Rondo and Larry Neal, *A Concise Economic History of the World: From Palaeolithic Times to the Present*. New York: Oxford University Press, 2003.

Campbell, Gwyn. *Africa and the Indian Ocean World from Early Times to circa 1900*. Cambridge: Cambridge University Press, 2019.

Cannadine, David. *Ornamentalism: How the British Saw Their Empire*. London: Penguin, 2001.

Cannadine, David. *Victorious Century: The United Kingdom, 1800–1906*. London: Penguin, 2018.

Cannadine, David, Jenny Keating and Nicola Sheldon. *The Right Kind of History: Teaching the Past in Twentieth-Century England*. Basingstoke: Palgrave Macmillan, 2011.

Cargill, Tom. *More with Less: Trends in UK Diplomatic Engagement in Sub-Saharan Africa*. London: Chatham House Africa Programme Paper, 2011.

Carmody, Padraig. *The New Scramble for Africa*. Cambridge: Polity, 2016.

Carnochan, W. B. *Golden Legends: Images of Abyssinia, Samuel Johnson to Bob Marley*. Stanford, CA: Stanford University Press, 2008.

Carretta, Vincent and Ty M. Reese, eds. *The Life and Letters of Philip Quaque: The First African Anglican Missionary*. Athens, GA: University of Georgia Press, 2010.

Carter, Gwendolen M. and Patrick O'Meara, eds. *Southern Africa: The Continuing Crisis*. Bloomington, IN: Indiana University Press, 1979.

Carton, Benedict, John Laband and Jabulani Sithole, eds. *Zulu Identities: Being Zulu, Past and Present*. Scottsville: University of KwaZulu-Natal Press, 2008.

Cassanelli, Lee V. *The Shaping of Somali Society: Reconstructing the History of a Pastoral People, 1600–1900*. Philadelphia: University of Pennsylvania Press, 1982.

Caulk, Richard. 'Firearms and Princely Power in Ethiopia in the Nineteenth Century'. *Journal of African History* 13, no. 4 (1972): 609–30.

Caulk, Richard. 'Yohannes IV, the Mahdists and the Partition of North East Africa'. *Transafrican Journal of History* 1, no. 2 (1971): 22–42.

Chabal, Patrick and Jean-Pascal Daloz. *Africa Works: Disorder as Political Instrument*. Oxford: James Currey, 1999.

Chabal, Patrick, Ulf Engel and Anna-Maria Gentili, eds. *Is Violence Inevitable in Africa? Theories of Conflict and Approaches to Conflict Prevention*. Leiden: Brill, 2005.

Chakrabarty, Dipesh. 'The Muddle of Modernity'. *American Historical Review* 116, no. 3 (2011): 663–75.

Chakrabarty, Dipesh. *Provincializing Europe: Postcolonial Thought and Historical Difference*. Princeton, NJ: Princeton University Press, 2000.

Chamberlain, Joseph. 'The True Conception of Empire'. In *Empire Writing: An Anthology of Colonial Literature 1870–1918*, edited by Elleke Boehmer, 212–15. Oxford: Oxford University Press, 1998.

Chamberlain, Muriel E. *The Scramble for Africa*. London: Pearson, 2010. [1974].

Chelati Dirar, Uoldelul. 'Colonialism and the Construction of National Identities: The Case of Eritrea'. *Journal of Eastern African Studies* 1, no. 2 (2007): 256–76.

Chimhundu, Herbert. 'Early Missionaries and the Ethnolinguistic Factor during the "Invention of Tribalism" in Zimbabwe'. *Journal of African History* 33, no. 1 (1992): 87–109.

Chrétien, Jean-Pierre. *The Great Lakes of Africa: Two Thousand Years of History*, translated by Scott Straus. New York: Zone Books, 2003.

Chrétien, Jean-Pierre and Gérard Prunier, eds. *Les Ethnies ont une histoire*. Paris: Karthala, 1989.

Churchill, Winston Spencer. *The River War: An Historical Account of the Reconquest of the Soudan*. London: Longmans, Green & Co., 1902 [1899].

Clapham, Christopher, ed. *African Guerrillas*. Oxford: James Currey, 1998.

Clapham, Christopher. 'Discerning the New Africa'. *International Affairs* 74, no. 2 (1998): 263–69.

Clapperton, Hugh. *Journal of a Second Expedition into the Interior of Africa, from the Bight of Benin to Soccatoo*. London: John Murray, 1829.

Clarence-Smith, William Gervase, ed. *The Economics of the Indian Ocean Slave Trade in the Nineteenth Century*. Special issue of *Slavery & Abolition* (vol. 9, no. 3 [1988]).

Clarence-Smith, William Gervase. *Slaves, Peasants and Capitalists in Southern Angola, 1840–1926*. Cambridge: Cambridge University Press, 1979.

Clark, Carolyn M. 'Land and Food, Women and Power, in Nineteenth-Century Kikuyu'. *Africa* 50, no. 4 (1980): 357–70.

Clarke, John Henrik. *Marcus Garvey and the Vision of Africa*. New York: Vintage, 1974.

Clarke, Peter B. *Black Paradise: The Rastafarian Movement*. Wellingborough: The Aquarian Press, 1986.

Clarke, Richard F., ed. *Cardinal Lavigerie and the African Slave Trade*. London: Longmans, Green & Co., 1889.

Clausewitz, Carl von. *On War*, translated and edited by Michael Howard and Peter Paret. London: Everyman's Library, 1993 [Ger. 1832].

Clayton, Anthony and David Killingray. *Khaki and Blue: Military and Police in British Colonial Africa*. Athens, OH: Ohio University Press, 1989.

Cobbing, Julian. 'The Absent Priesthood: Another Look at the Rhodesian Risings of 1896–97'. *Journal of African History* 18, no. 1 (1977): 61–84.

Cobbing, Julian. 'The Mfecane as Alibi: Thoughts on Dithkong and Mbolompo'. *Journal of African History* 29, no. 3 (1988): 487–519.

Cocker, Mark. *Rivers of Blood, Rivers of Gold: Europe's Conflict with Tribal Peoples*. London: Pimlico, 1999.

Cohen, D. W. *The Historical Tradition of Busoga: Mukama and Kintu*. Oxford: Clarendon Press, 1972.

Cole, Herbert M. and Doran H. Ross. *The Arts of Ghana*. Los Angeles: Museum of Cultural History, University of California, 1977.

Coles, Catherine and Beverly Mack, eds. *Hausa Women in the Twentieth Century*. Madison, WI: University of Wisconsin Press, 1991.

Colley, Linda. *Captives: Britain, Empire and the World, 1600–1850*. London: Jonathan Cape, 2002.

Collins, Bruce. *War and Empire: The Expansion of Britain, 1790–1830*. Harlow: Pearson, 2010.

Collins, Robert O. and James M. Burns. *A History of Sub-Saharan Africa*. Cambridge: Cambridge University Press, 2007.

Colls, Robert. *Identity of England*. Oxford: Oxford University Press, 2002.

Colvile, Henry. *The Land of the Nile Springs; Being Chiefly an Account of How We Fought Kabarega*. London: Edward Arnold, 1895.

Colvin, Auckland. *The Making of Modern Egypt*. London: Thomas Nelson & Sons, 1906.

Comaroff, Jean. *Body of Power, Spirit of Resistance: The Culture and History of a South African People*. Chicago: University of Chicago Press, 1985.

Comaroff, Jean and John Comaroff. 'Christianity and Colonialism in South Africa'. *American Ethnologist* 13 (1986): 1–22.

Comaroff, Jean and John Comaroff. *Of Revelation and Revolution, Volume 1: Christianity, Colonialism, and Consciousness in South Africa*. Chicago: University of Chicago Press, 1991.

Condé, Maryse. *Segu*, translated by Barbara Bray. London: Penguin, 2017 [Fr. 1983].

Connah, Graham. *African Civilizations: Precolonial Cities and States in Tropical Africa: An Archaeological Perspective*. Cambridge: Cambridge University Press, 1987.

Conrad, Joseph. *Heart of Darkness*. London: The Folio Society, 1997 [1899].

Conrad, Sebastian. *German Colonialism: A Short History*. Cambridge: Cambridge University Press, 2012.

'Constitutive Act of the African Union'. Available at https://au.int/sites/default/files/pages/34873 -file-constitutiveact_en.pdf (accessed 15 March 2024).

Cookey, S.J.S. *King Jaja of the Niger Delta: His Life and Times, 1821–1891*. New York: NOK, 1974.

Coombes, Annie. *Reinventing Africa: Museums, Material Culture, and Popular Imagination in Late Victorian and Edwardian England*. New Haven, CT: Yale University Press, 1994.

Cooper, Frederick. 'Africa and the World Economy'. *African Studies Review* 24, nos 2–3 (1981): 1–86.

Cooper, Frederick. *Africa in the World: Capitalism, Empire, Nation-State*. Cambridge, MA: Harvard University Press, 2014.

Coquery-Vidrovitch, Catherine. *Africa and the Africans in the Nineteenth Century: A Turbulent History*, translated by Mary Baker. Armonk, NY: M. E. Sharpe, 2009 [Fr. 1999].

Crais, Clifton C. *White Supremacy and Black Resistance in Pre-Industrial South Africa: The Making of the Colonial Order in the Eastern Cape, 1770–1865*. Cambridge: Cambridge University Press, 1992.

Cramer, Christopher. *Civil War Is Not a Stupid Thing: Accounting for Violence in Developing Countries*. London: Hurst, 2006.

Crowder, Michael. 'Indirect Rule: French and British Style'. *Africa* 34, no. 3 (1964): 197–205.

Crowe, S. E. *The Berlin West Africa Conference, 1884–1885*. London: Longmans, Green & Co., 1942.

Crummey, Donald. 'Abyssinian Feudalism'. *Past and Present* 89 (1980): 115–38.

Crummey, Donald. 'Banditry and Resistance: Noble and Peasant in Nineteenth-Century Ethiopia'. In *Banditry, Rebellion and Social Protest in Africa*, edited by Donald Crummey, 133–49. London: James Currey, 1986.

Crummey, Donald, ed. *Banditry, Rebellion and Social Protest in Africa*. London: James Currey, 1986.

Crummey, Donald. 'Imperial Legitimacy and the Creation of Neo-Solomonic Ideology in 19th-Century Ethiopia'. *Cahiers d'études africaines* 28, no. 109 (1988): 13–43.

Crummey, Donald. *Land and Society in the Christian Kingdom of Ethiopia: From the Thirteenth to the Twentieth Century*. Oxford: James Currey, 2000.

Crummey, Donald. 'Tewodros as Reformer and Moderniser'. *Journal of African History* 10, no. 3 (1969): 457–69.

Crummey, Donald. 'The Violence of Tewodros'. In *War and Society in Africa*, edited by B. A. Ogot, 65–84. London: Frank Cass, 1972.

Culwick, A. T. and G. M. Culwick. 'A Study of Population in Ulanga, Tanganyika Territory'. *Sociological Review* 30 (1938): 365–79; (continued in) *Sociological Review* 31 (1939): 25–43.

Curtin, Philip D. *The Atlantic Slave Trade: A Census*. Madison, WI: University of Wisconsin Press, 1969.

Curtin, Philip D. *Disease and Empire: The Health of European Troops in the Conquest of Africa*. Cambridge: Cambridge University Press, 1998.

Curtin, Philip D. *The Image of Africa: British Ideas and Action, 1780–1850*, 2 vols. Madison, WI: University of Wisconsin Press, 1964.

Dalakoglu, Dimitris and Penny Harvey. 'Roads and Anthropology: Ethnographic Perspectives on Space, Time and (Im)mobility'. *Mobilities* 7, no. 4 (2012): 459–65.

Dalzel, Archibald. *The History of Dahomy, an Inland Kingdom of Africa*. London: Cass, 1967 [1793].

Danziger, Raphael *Abd al-Qadir and the Algerians*. New York: Homes & Maier, 1977.

Darwin, Charles. *On the Origin of Species*. London: John Murray, 1859.

Darwin, John. *After Tamerlane: The Rise and Fall of Global Empires, 1400–2000*. London: Penguin, 2007.

Darwin, John. 'Empire and Ethnicity'. In *Nationalism and War*, edited by John A. Hall and Sinisa Malesevic, 147–71. Cambridge: Cambridge University Press, 2013.

Darwin, John. 'Imperialism and the Victorians: The Dynamics of Territorial Expansion'. *The English Historical Review* 112, no. 447 (1997): 614–42.

Daunton, Martin and Rick Halpern, eds. *Empire and Others: British Encounters with Indigenous Peoples, 1600–1850*. London: UCL Press, 1999.

Davenport, T.R.H. *South Africa: A Modern History*. London: Macmillan, 1991.

David, Saul. *Zulu: The Heroism and Tragedy of the Zulu War of 1879*. London: Viking, 2004.

Davidson, Basil. *Africa in Modern History: The Search for a New Society*. London: Penguin, 1978.

Davidson, Basil. *The Black Man's Burden: Africa and the Curse of the Nation-State*. London: James Currey, 1992.

Davidson, Basil. 'An Historical Note'. In *Behind the War in Eritrea*, edited by Basil Davidson, Lionel Cliffe and Bereket Habte Selassie, 11–15. Nottingham: Spokesman, 1980.

Davis, Ralph. *The Rise of the Atlantic Economies*. London: Weidenfeld & Nicolson, 1973.

Decalo, Samuel. *Coups and Army Rule in Africa*. New Haven, CT: Yale University Press, 1990.

Del Boca, Angelo. *Gli italiani in Africa orientale, 1: Dall'Unità alla marcia su Roma*. Rome: Laterza, 1976.

Denzer, LaRay. 'Yoruba Women: A Historiographical Study'. *International Journal of African Historical Studies* 27, no. 1 (1994): 1–39.

Des Forges, Alison. '"The drum is greater than the shout": The 1912 Rebellion in Northern Rwanda'. In *Banditry, Rebellion and Social Protest in Africa*, edited by Donald Crummey, 311–31. London: James Currey, 1986.

Deutsch, Jan-Georg. *Emancipation without Abolition in German East Africa, c. 1884–1914*. Oxford: James Currey, 2006.

Deutsch, Jan-Georg. 'Notes on the Rise of Slavery and Social Change in Unyamwezi, c. 1860–1900'. In *Slavery in the Great Lakes Region of East Africa*, edited by Henri Médard and Shane Doyle, 76–110. Oxford: James Currey, 2007.

Deutsch, Jan-Georg, Peter Probst and Heike Schmidt, eds. *African Modernities: Entangled Meanings in Current Debate*. Oxford: James Currey, 2002.

Dike, Kenneth O. *Trade and Politics in the Niger Delta, 1830–1885*. Oxford: Clarendon Press, 1956.

Diop, Cheikh Anta. *The African Origin of Civilization: Myth or Reality*, edited and translated by Mercer Cook. New York: Lawrence Hill, 1974.

Diop, Cheikh Anta. *Towards the African Renaissance: Essays in African Culture and Development, 1946–1960*, translated by Egbuna P. Modum. London: Karnak House, 1996.

Ditte, Albert. *Observations sur la guerre dans les colonies: Organisation, exécution ; Conférences faites à l'École supérieure de guerre*. Paris: H. Charles-Lavauzelle, 1905.

Docherty, Paddy. *Blood and Bronze: The British Empire and the Sack of Benin*. London: Hurst, 2021.

Donham, Donald. 'Old Abyssinia and the New Ethiopian Empire: Themes in Social History'. In *The Southern Marches of Imperial Ethiopia: Essays in History and Social Anthropology*, edited by Donald L. Donham and Wendy James, 3–48. Oxford: James Currey, 2002 [1986].

Dorling, Danny and Sally Tomlinson. *Rule Britannia: Brexit and the End of Empire*. London: Biteback Publishing, 2019.

Doyle, Shane. *Before HIV: Sexuality, Infertility and Mortality in East Africa, 1900–1980*. Oxford: Oxford University Press, 2013.

Doyle, Shane. *Crisis and Decline in Bunyoro: Population and Environment in Western Uganda, 1860–1955*. Oxford: James Currey, 2006.

Draper, Nick. 'The City of London and Slavery: Evidence from the First Dock Companies, 1795–1800'. *Economic History Review* 61, no. 2 (2008): 432–66.

Dufton, Henry. *Narrative of a Journey through Abyssinia in 1862–3*. London: Chapman & Hall, 1867.

Duggan, Christopher. *The Force of Destiny: A History of Italy since 1796*. London: Penguin, 2008.

Duncan, John. *Travels in Western Africa, in 1845 and 1846*, 2 vols. London: Richard Bentley, 1847.

Dunn, John. '"For God, Emperor, and Country!" The Evolution of Ethiopia's Nineteenth-Century Army'. *War in History* 1, no. 3 (1994): 278–99.

Dupuy, R. Ernest and Trevor N. Dupuy. *The Collins Encyclopaedia of Military History: From 3500 BC to the Present*. London: BCA/HarperCollins, 1993.

Du Toit, André and Hermann Giliomee, eds. *Afrikaner Political Thought: Analysis and Documents, Volume 1: 1780–1850*. Cape Town: David Philip, 1983.

Dyson, Stephen L. *In Pursuit of Ancient Pasts: A History of Classical Archaeology in the Nineteenth and Twentieth Centuries*. New Haven, CT: Yale University Press, 2006.

Earle, Jonathon L. *Colonial Buganda and the End of Empire: Political Thought and Historical Imagination in Africa.* Cambridge: Cambridge University Press, 2017.

Earle, T. F. and K.J.P. Lowe, eds. *Black Africans in Renaissance Europe.* Cambridge: Cambridge University Press, 2005.

Echenberg, Myron. *Colonial Conscripts: The Tirailleurs Sénégalais in French West Africa, 1857–1960.* Portsmouth, NH: Heinemann, 1991.

Eckert, Andreas. 'Urbanization in Colonial and Post-colonial West Africa.' In *Themes in West Africa's History*, edited by Emmanuel Kwaku Akyeampong, 208–23. Athens, OH: Ohio University Press, 2006.

Egharevba, Jacob. *A Short History of Benin.* Lagos: CMS Bookshop, 1934.

Ehret, Christopher. 'Bantu Expansions: Re-envisioning a Central Problem of Early African History.' *International Journal of African Historical Studies* 34, no. 1 (2001): 5–42.

Ehrlich, Cyril. 'The Uganda Economy, 1903–1945.' In *History of East Africa, Volume 2*, edited by Vincent Harlow and E. M. Chilver, 395–475. Oxford: Oxford University Press, 1965.

Ekejiuba, Felicia. 'Omu Okwei, the Merchant Queen of Ossomari: A Biographical Sketch.' *Journal of the Historical Society of Nigeria* 3, no. 4 (1967): 633–46.

Elbourne, Elizabeth. *Blood Ground: Colonialism, Missions, and the Contest for Christianity in Cape Colony and Britain, 1799–1853.* Montreal and Kingston: McGill-Queen's University Press, 2002.

Eldredge, Elizabeth A. *A South African Kingdom: The Pursuit of Security in Nineteenth-Century Lesotho.* Cambridge: Cambridge University Press, 1993.

Ellis, Stephen. 'Writing Histories of Contemporary Africa.' *Journal of African History* 43, no. 1 (2002): 1–26.

Eltis, David. *Economic Growth and the Ending of the Transatlantic Slave Trade.* Oxford: Oxford University Press, 1987.

Engdahl, Torbjorn. *The Exchange of Cotton: Ugandan Peasants, Colonial Market Regulations, and the Organisation of the International Cotton Trade, 1904–1918.* Uppsala: Acta Universitatis Upsaliensis, 1999.

Equiano, Olaudah. *The Interesting Narrative and Other Writings*, edited by Vincent Carretta. London: Penguin, 1995 [1789].

Eritrean People's Liberation Front. 'National Democratic Programme, Eritrean People's Liberation Front, March 1987.' In *The Long Struggle of Eritrea for Independence and Constructive Peace*, edited by Lionel Cliffe and Basil Davidson, 205–13. Trenton, NJ: Red Sea Press, 1988.

Erlich, Haggai. *Ras Alula and the Scramble for Africa: A Political Biography; Ethiopia and Eritrea, 1875–1897.* Lawrenceville, NJ: Red Sea Press, 1996.

Esposito, John L. *Islam: The Straight Path*: Oxford: Oxford University Press, 2005.

Etherington, Norman, Patrick Harries and Bernard K. Mbenga. 'From Colonial Hegemonies to Imperial Conquest, 1840–1880.' In *The Cambridge History of South Africa, Volume 1: From Early Times to 1885*, edited by Carolyn Hamilton, Bernard K. Mbenga and Robert Ross, 319–91. Cambridge: Cambridge University Press, 2010.

Evans, Eric J. *The Forging of the Modern State: Early Industrial Britain, 1783–1870.* London: Longman, 1983.

Evans-Pritchard, E. E. *The Sanusi of Cyrenaica.* Oxford: Clarendon Press, 1949.

Ewald, Janet J. 'The Nile Valley System and the Red Sea Slave Trade, 1820–1880.' *Slavery & Abolition* 9, no. 3 (1988): 71–92.

Falola, Toyin. *Nationalism and African Intellectuals.* Rochester, NY: University of Rochester Press, 2001.

Falola, Toyin, ed. *Pioneer, Patriot and Patriarch: Samuel Johnson and the Yoruba People*. Madison, WI: University of Wisconsin Press, 1993.

Falola, Toyin and Saheed Aderinto. *Nigeria, Nationalism, and Writing History*. Rochester, NY: University of Rochester Press, 2010.

Fanon, Frantz. *The Wretched of the Earth*, translated by Constance Farrington. London: Penguin, 1990 [Fr. 1961].

Farrer, Martin. 'Who Was Edward Colston and Why Was His Bristol Statue Toppled?' *The Guardian*, 8 June 2020. Available at https://www.theguardian.com/uk-news/2020/jun/08 /who-was-edward-colston-and-why-was-his-bristol-statue-toppled-slave-trader-black -lives-matter-protests (accessed 15 March 2024).

Farwell, Byron. *Queen Victoria's Little Wars*. London: Allen Lane, 1973.

Faupel, John F. *African Holocaust: The Story of the Uganda Martyrs*. London: Geoffrey Chapman, 1965.

Ferguson, James. *Global Shadows: Africa in the Neoliberal World Order*. Durham, NC: Duke University Press, 2006.

Ferguson, Niall. *Civilization: The West and the Rest*. London: Allen Lane, 2011.

Fernyhough, Timothy. 'Slavery and the Slave Trade in Southern Ethiopia in the 19th Century'. *Slavery & Abolition* 9, no. 3 (1988): 103–30.

Fetter, Bruce, ed. *Demography from Scanty Evidence: Central Africa in the Colonial Era*. Boulder, CO: Lynne Rienner, 1990.

Fieldhouse, David K. *Economics and Empire, 1830–1914*. London: Weidenfeld & Nicolson, 1973.

Fieldhouse, David K. *The West and the Third World*. Oxford: Blackwell, 1999.

Finaldi, Giuseppe Maria. *Italian National Identity in the Scramble for Africa: Italy's African Wars in the Era of Nation-Building, 1870–1900*. Bern: Peter Lang, 2009.

Fisher, Humphrey. 'The Central Sahara and Sudan'. In *The Cambridge History of Africa, Volume 4: c. 1600–c. 1790*, edited by Richard Gray, 58–141. Cambridge: Cambridge University Press, 1975.

Fisher, Humphrey. 'The Eastern Maghrib and the Central Sudan'. In *The Cambridge History of Africa, Volume 3: c. 1050–c. 1600*, edited by Roland Oliver, 232–330. Cambridge: Cambridge University Press, 1977.

Flint, John E. 'Britain and the Scramble for Africa'. In *The Oxford History of the British Empire, Volume 5: Historiography*, edited by Robin W. Winks, 450-62. Oxford: Oxford University Press, 1999.

Flournoy, F. R. *British Policy towards Morocco in the Age of Palmerston (1830–1856)*. London: P. S. King, 1935.

Forbes, Frederick E. *Dahomey and the Dahomans*, 2 vols. London: Longman, Brown, Green, and Longmans, 1851.

Ford, John. *The Role of the Trypanosomiases in African Ecology: A Study of the Tsetse Fly Problem*. Oxford: Clarendon Press, 1971.

Ford, J. and R. de Z. Hall. 'The History of Karagwe (Bukoba District)'. *Tanganyika Notes and Records* 24 (December 1947): 3–27.

Förster, Stig, Wolfgang J. Mommsen and Ronald Robinson, eds. *Bismarck, Europe and Africa: The Berlin Africa Conference 1884–1885 and the Onset of Partition*. Oxford: Oxford University Press, 1988.

Franey, Laura E. *Victorian Travel Writing and Imperial Violence: British Writing on Africa, 1855–1902*. Basingstoke: Palgrave Macmillan, 2003.

Frazer, James George. *The Golden Bough: A Study in Magic and Religion*. Ware: Wordsworth Reference, 1993 [author's abridged version, first published 1922; original full text in two volumes published 1890].

Fredrickson, George M. *Racism: A Short History*. Princeton, NJ: Princeton University Press, 2015.

Freedman, Jim. *Nyabingi: The Social History of an African Divinity*. Tervuren: Musée royal de l'Afrique centrale, 1984.

Freund, Bill. *The African City: A History*. Cambridge: Cambridge University Press, 2007.

Fukuyama, Francis. *The Origins of Political Order: From Prehuman Times to the French Revolution*. London: Profile Books, 2011.

Fussner, F. Smith. *The Historical Revolution: English Historical Writing and Thought, 1580–1640*. London: Routledge & Kegan Paul, 1962.

Fyfe, Christopher. *Africanus Horton, 1835–1883: West African Scientist and Patriot*. New York: Oxford University Press, 1972.

Fyfe, Christopher. *A History of Sierra Leone*. London: Oxford University Press, 1962.

Gabre-Selassie, Zewde. *Yohannes IV of Ethiopia: A Political Biography*. Oxford: Clarendon Press, 1975.

Galaty, John G. 'Maasai Expansion and the New East African Pastoralism'. In *Being Maasai: Ethnicity and Identity in East Africa*, edited by Thomas Spear and Richard Waller, 61–86. Oxford: James Currey, 1993.

Gallop, Alan. *Mr Stanley, I Presume? The Life and Explorations of Henry Morton Stanley*. Stroud: Sutton, 2004.

Garretson, Peter P. *A Victorian Gentleman and Ethiopian Nationalist: The Life and Times of Hakim Warqenah, Dr Charles Martin*. Woodbridge: James Currey, 2012.

Gat, Azar, with Alexander Yakobson. *Nations: The Long History and Deep Roots of Political Ethnicity and Nationalism*. Cambridge: Cambridge University Press, 2013.

Gavshon, Arthur L. *Crisis in Africa: Battleground of East and West*. Harmondsworth: Penguin, 1981.

Gellner, Ernest. *Nations and Nationalism*. Malden, MA: Blackwell, 1983.

Geppert, Dominik and Frank Lorenz Müller, eds. *Sites of Imperial Memory: Commemorating Colonial Rule in the Nineteenth and Twentieth Centuries*. Manchester: Manchester University Press, 2015.

Gerhard, Dietrich. 'The Frontier in Comparative View'. *Comparative Studies in Society and History* 1, no. 3 (1959): 205–29.

Gewald, Jan-Bart. *Herero Heroes: A Socio-political History of the Herero of Namibia, 1890–1923*. Oxford: James Currey, 1998.

Gibbon, Edward. *The History of the Decline and Fall of the Roman Empire, Volume 6: Mohammed and the Rise of the Arabs*. London: Folio, 1988 [1789].

Giblin, James L. *A History of the Excluded: Making Family a Refuge from State in Twentieth-Century Tanzania*. Oxford: James Currey, 2005.

Giblin, James and Jamie Monson, eds. *Maji Maji: Lifting the Fog of War*. Leiden: Brill, 2010.

Gildea, Robert. *Empires of the Mind: The Colonial Past and the Politics of the Present*. Cambridge: Cambridge University Press, 2019.

Gillon, Werner. *A Short History of African Art*. London: Penguin, 1991.

Gilroy, Paul. *The Black Atlantic: Modernity and Double Consciousness*. Cambridge, MA: Harvard University Press, 1993.

Girard, Philippe R. *Toussaint Louverture: A Revolutionary Life*. New York: Basic Books, 2016.

Gjersø, Jonas Fossli. 'The Scramble for East Africa: British Motives Reconsidered, 1884–95'. *Journal of Imperial and Commonwealth History* 43, no. 5 (2015): 831–60.

Glassman, Jonathon. 'Creole Nationalists and the Search for Nativist Authenticity in Twentieth-Century Zanzibar: The Limits of Cosmopolitanism'. *Journal of African History* 55, no. 2 (2014). 229–47.

Glassman, Jonathon. *Feasts and Riot: Revelry, Rebellion and Popular Consciousness on the Swahili Coast, 1856–88*. Portsmouth, NH: Heinemann, 1995.

Glassman, Jonathon. 'Slower than a Massacre: The Multiple Sources of Racial Thought in Colonial Africa'. *The American Historical Review* 109, no. 3 (2004): 720–54.

Gleerup, Edvard. 'A Journey across Tanganyika in 1886', translated by Per Hassing and edited by Norman R. Bennett. *Tanganyika Notes and Records* 58/59 (1962): 129–47.

Gluckman, Max. 'The Kingdom of the Zulu of South Africa'. In *African Political Systems*, edited by M. Fortes and E. E. Evans-Pritchard, 25–55. London: Oxford University Press, 1940.

Gobat, S. *Journal of Three Years' Residence in Abyssinia*. New York: Negro Universities Press, 1969 [1851].

Gooding, Philip. *On the Frontiers of the Indian Ocean World: A History of Lake Tanganyika, c .1830–1890*. Cambridge: Cambridge University Press, 2022.

Goody, Jack. *Technology, Tradition and the State in Africa*. London: Oxford University Press, 1971.

Goody, Jack. *The Theft of History*. Cambridge: Cambridge University Press, 2006.

Gordon, David. 'History on the Luapula Retold: Landscape, Memory and Identity in the Kazembe Kingdom'. *Journal of African History* 47, no. 1 (2006): 21–42.

Gottberg, A. 'On the Historical Importance of the Crisis of the Fundikira Empire'. In *Afrika-Studien*, edited by W. Markov, 63–83. Leipzig: Karl-Marx-Universität, 1967.

Goyvaerts, Didier. 'Johannes Fabian, *Language and Colonial Power*' (review article). *Journal of Linguistics* 23, no. 2 (1987). 481–86.

Grant, James A. 'Summary of Observations on the Geography, Climate, and Natural History of the Lake Region of Equatorial Africa'. *Journal of the Royal Geographical Society* 42 (1872): 243–342.

Grant, James A. *A Walk across Africa*. Edinburgh: William Blackwood & Sons, 1864.

Gray, J. M. 'Ahmed bin Ibrahim: The First Arab to Reach Buganda'. *Uganda Journal* 11, no. 2 (1947): 80–97.

Gray, Richard. *A History of the Southern Sudan, 1839–1889*. London: Oxford University Press, 1961.

Gray, Richard and David Birmingham, eds. *Pre-colonial African Trade: Essays on Trade in Central and Eastern Africa before 1900*. London: Oxford University Press, 1970.

Greenfield, Richard. *Ethiopia: A New Political History*. London: Pall Mall Press, 1965.

Greenfield, Richard. 'Pre-colonial and Colonial History'. In *Behind the War in Eritrea*, edited by Basil Davidson, Lionel Cliffe and Bereket Habte Selassie, 16–31. Nottingham: Spokesman, 1980.

Greiner, Andreas. *Human Porterage and Colonial State Formation in German East Africa, 1880s–1914: Tensions of Transport*. Basingstoke: Palgrave Macmillan, 2022.

Guibernau, Montserrat and John Hutchinson, eds. *History and National Destiny: Ethnosymbolism and Its Critics*. Oxford: Blackwell, 2004.

Gulliver, P. H., ed. *Tradition and Transition in East Africa: Studies in the Tribal Element in the Modern Era*. London: Routledge & Kegan Paul, 1969.

Gunner, Elizabeth. 'Songs of Innocence and Experience: Women as Composers and Performers of *Izibongo*, Zulu Praise Poetry'. *Research in African Literatures* 10, no. 2 (1979): 239–67.

Guy, Jeff. *The Destruction of the Zulu Kingdom: The Civil War in Zululand, 1879–1884*. Pietermaritzburg: University of Natal Press, 1994.

Guy, Jeff. 'Ecological Factors in the Rise of Shaka and the Zulu Kingdom'. In *Economy and Society in Pre-Industrial South Africa*, edited by Shula Marks and Anthony Atmore, 102–19. London: Longman, 1980.

Guyer, Jane I. 'Wealth in People, Wealth in Things—Introduction'. *Journal of African History* 36, no. 1 (1995): 83–90.

Gwassa, G.C.K. 'African Methods of Warfare during the Maji Maji War of 1905–7'. In *War and Society in Africa*, edited by B. A. Ogot, 123–48. London: Frank Cass, 1972.

Gwassa, G.C.K. 'The German Intervention and African Resistance in Tanzania'. In *A History of Tanzania*, edited by I. N. Kimambo and A. J. Temu, 85–122. Nairobi: East African Publishing House, 1969.

Gwassa, G.C.K. 'Kinjikitile and the Ideology of Maji Maji'. In *The Historical Study of African Religion, with Special Reference to East and Central Africa*, edited by T. O. Ranger and I. N. Kimambo, 202–17. London: Heinemann, 1972.

Gwassa, G.C.K. and J. Iliffe, eds. *Records of the Maji Maji Rising, Part One*. Nairobi: East African Publishing House, 1967.

Haile, Semere. 'Historical Background to the Ethiopia–Eritrea Conflict'. In *The Long Struggle of Eritrea for Independence and Constructive Peace*, edited by Lionel Cliffe and Basil Davidson, 11–31. Trenton, NJ: Red Sea Press, 1988.

Hailey, William Malcolm. *An African Survey: A Study of Problems Arising in Africa South of the Sahara*. London: Oxford University Press, 1938.

Hailey, William Malcolm. *An African Survey: A Study of Problems Arising in Africa South of the Sahara* (revised, expanded edition). London: Oxford University Press, 1957.

Hall, Richard. *Empires of the Monsoon: A History of the Indian Ocean and Its Invaders*. London: HarperCollins, 1996.

Hallencreutz, Carl F. 'Thomas Mofolo and Nelson Mandela on King Shaka and Dingane'. In *Culture in Africa: An Appeal for Pluralism*, edited by Raoul Granqvist, 185–194. Uppsala: Nordiska Afrikainstitutet, 1993.

Hallett, Robin. 'The European Approach to the Interior of Africa in the Eighteenth Century'. *Journal of African History* 4, no. 2 (1963): 191–206.

Hallett, Robin. *The Penetration of Africa: European Enterprise and Exploration, Principally in Northern and Western Africa up to 1830*. London: Routledge & Kegan Paul, 1965.

Hamilton, Carolyn, ed. *The Mfecane Aftermath: Reconstructive Debates in Southern African History*. Johannesburg and Pietermaritzburg: Witwatersrand University Press/University of Natal Press, 1995.

Hamilton, Carolyn. *Terrific Majesty: The Powers of Shaka Zulu and the Limits of Historical Invention*. Cape Town: David Philip, 1998.

Hamilton, Carolyn, Bernard K. Mbenga and Robert Ross. 'Editors' Introduction'. In *The Cambridge History of South Africa, Volume 1: From Early Times to 1885*, edited by Carolyn Hamilton, Bernard K. Mbenga and Robert Ross, xi–xviii. Cambridge: Cambridge University Press, 2010.

Hanretta, Sean. 'Women, Marginality and the Zulu State: Women's Institutions and Power in the Early Nineteenth Century'. *Journal of African History* 39 no. 3 (1998): 389–415.

Hanson, Holly. *Landed Obligation: The Practice of Power in Buganda*. Portsmouth, NH: Heinemann, 2003.

Hanson, Holly. 'Stolen People and Autonomous Chiefs in Nineteenth-Century Buganda: The Social Consequences of Non-free Followers'. In *Slavery in the Great Lakes Region of East Africa*, edited by Henri Médard and Shane Doyle, 161–73. Oxford: James Currey, 2007.

Hargreaves, John D. *Prelude to the Partition of West Africa*. London: Macmillan, 1966.

Hargreaves, John D. 'Towards a History of the Partition of Africa', *Journal of African History* 1, no. 1 (1960): 97–109.

Hargreaves, John D. *West Africa Partitioned*, 2 vols. London: Macmillan, 1974.

Hargreaves, John D. 'Western Africa, 1886–1905'. In *The Cambridge History of Africa, Volume 6: 1870–1905*, edited by Roland Oliver and G. N. Sanderson, 257–97. Cambridge: Cambridge University Press, 1985.

Harlow, Barbara and Mia Carter, eds. *Archives of Empire, Volume 2: The Scramble for Africa*. Durham, NC: Duke University Press, 2003.

Harms, Robert W. *River of Wealth, River of Sorrow: The Central Zaire Basin in the Era of the Slave and Ivory Trade, 1500–1891*. New Haven, CT: Yale University Press, 1981.

Harris, Joseph E. *The African Presence in Asia: Consequences of the East African Slave Trade*. Evanston, IL: Northwestern University Press, 1971.

Harrison, Paul. *Inside the Third World: The Anatomy of Poverty*. London: Penguin, 1979.

Hartwig, G. W. 'The Victoria Nyanza as a Trade Route in the Nineteenth Century'. *Journal of African History* 11, no. 4 (1970): 535–52.

Harvey, John. *The Story of Black*. London: Reaktion Books, 2013.

Harvey, Ronald J. 'Mirambo, the "Napoleon of Central Africa"'. *Tanganyika Notes and Records* 28 (1950): 10–28.

Hassan, Mohammed. *The Oromo of Ethiopia: A History, 1570–1860*. Cambridge: Cambridge University Press, 1990.

Hastings, Adrian. *The Construction of Nationhood: Ethnicity, Religion, and Nationalism*. Cambridge: Cambridge University Press, 1997.

Hazareesingh, Sudhir. *Black Spartacus: The Epic Life of Toussaint Louverture*. London: Allen Lane, 2020.

Headrick, Daniel. *The Tools of Empire: Technology and European Imperialism in the Nineteenth Century*. New York: Oxford University Press, 1981.

Hegel, G.W.F. 'Africa'. In *Archives of Empire, Volume 2: The Scramble for Africa*, edited by Barbara Harlow and Mia Carter, 21–28. Durham, NC: Duke University Press, 2003.

Hegel, G.W.F. *The Philosophy of History*, translated by J. Sibree. New York: Dover, 1956 [Ger. 1837].

Heintze, Beatrix and Adam Jones, eds. *European Sources for Sub-Saharan Africa before 1900: Use and Abuse*. Special edition of *Paideuma* 33 (1987).

Henderson, Errol A. 'When States Implode: Africa's Civil Wars, 1950–1992'. In *The Roots of African Conflicts: The Causes and Costs*, edited by Alfred Nhema and Paul Tiyambe-Zeleza, 51–70. Oxford: James Currey, 2008.

Henderson, W. O. 'German East Africa, 1884–1918'. In *History of East Africa, Volume 2*, edited by Vincent Harlow and E. M. Chilver, 123–62. Oxford: Oxford University Press, 1965.

Henige, David. '"The Disease of Writing": Ganda and Nyoro Kinglists in a Newly Literate World'. In *The African Past Speaks: Essays on Oral Tradition and History*, edited by Joseph C. Miller, 240–61. Folkestone and Hamden, CT: William Dawson/Archon Books, 1980.

Herbst, Jeffrey. *States and Power in Africa: Comparative Lessons in Authority and Control*. Princeton, NJ: Princeton University Press, 2000.

Herskovits, Melville. *Dahomey, an Ancient West African Kingdom*, 2 vols. New York: J. J. Augustin, 1938.

Heywood, Linda. *Njinga of Angola: Africa's Warrior Queen*. Cambridge, MA: Harvard University Press, 2017.

Hibbert, Christopher. *Africa Explored: Europeans in the Dark Continent, 1769–1889*. Harmondsworth: Penguin, 1984.

Hicks, Dan. *The Brutish Museums: The Benin Bronzes, Colonial Violence and Cultural Restitution*. London: Pluto Press, 2020.

Hill, Polly. *The Migrant Cocoa Farmers of Southern Ghana: A Study in Rural Capitalism*. Cambridge: Cambridge University Press, 1963.

Hiribarren, Vincent. *A History of Borno: Trans-Saharan African Empire to Failing Nigerian State*. London: Hurst, 2017.

Hobbes, Thomas. *Leviathan, or the Matter, Forme and Power of a Common-Wealth, Ecclesiasticall and Civill*. London: Printed for Andrew Crooke by William Wilson, 1651.

Hobsbawm, Eric. *The Age of Empire, 1875–1914*. London: Abacus, 1994.

Hobsbawm, Eric. *Bandits*. London: Abacus, 2001 [1969].

Hobsbawm, Eric. *Nations and Nationalism since 1780: Programme, Myth, Reality*. Cambridge: Cambridge University Press, 1990.

Hobsbawm, Eric. *Revolutionaries*. London: Abacus, 2007 [1973].

Hobsbawm, Eric and Terence Ranger, eds. *The Invention of Tradition*. Cambridge University Press, 1983.

Hobson, J. A. *Imperialism: A Study*. London: Unwin Hyman, 1938 [1902].

Hochschild, Adam. *King Leopold's Ghost: A Story of Greed, Terror, and Heroism in Colonial Africa*. Boston, MA: Houghton Mifflin, 1998.

Hodgkin, Thomas. 'The Relevance of "Western" Ideas for the New African States'. In *Self-Government in Modernizing Nations*, edited by J. Roland Pennock, 50–80. Englewood Cliffs, NJ: Prentice-Hall, 1964.

Hofmeyr, Isabel. 'African History and Global Studies: A View from South Africa'. *Journal of African History* 54, no. 3 (2013): 341–49.

Hofmeyr, Isabel, Preben Kaarsholm and Bodil Folke Frederiksen. 'Introduction: Print Cultures, Nationalisms and Publics of the Indian Ocean'. *Africa* 81, no. 1 (2011): 1–22.

Hogendorn, Jan S. 'Economic Initiative and African Cash Farming: Pre-colonial Origins and Early Colonial Developments'. In *Colonialism in Africa 1870–1960, Volume 4: The Economics of Colonialism*, edited by Peter Duignan and L. H. Gann, 283–328. Cambridge: Cambridge University Press, 1975.

Holt, P. M. 'Egypt and the Nile Valley'. In *The Cambridge History of Africa, Volume 5: c. 1790–c .1870*, edited by J. E. Flint, 13–50. Cambridge: Cambridge University Press, 1976.

Holt, P. M. *The Mahdist State in the Sudan, 1881–1898: A Study of Its Origins, Development and Overthrow*. Oxford: Clarendon Press, 1958.

Holt, P. M. and M. W. Daly. *A History of the Sudan: From the Coming of Islam to the Present Day*. London: Longman, 2000.

Homewood, Katherine. *Ecology of African Pastoralist Societies*. Oxford: James Currey, 2008.

Hopkins, A. G. *American Empire: A Global History*. Princeton, NJ: Princeton University Press, 2018.

Hopkins, A. G. *An Economic History of West Africa*. London: Longman, 1973.

Hopkins, A. G. 'Economic Imperialism in West Africa: Lagos, 1880–1892'. *Economic History Review* 21, no. 3 (1968): 580–600.

Hopkins, A. G. 'The New Economic History of Africa'. *Journal of African History* 50, no. 2 (2009): 155–77.

Hopkins, Elizabeth. 'The Nyabingi Cult of Southwestern Uganda'. In *Protest and Power in Black Africa*, edited by Robert I. Rotberg and Ali A. Mazrui, 258–336. New York: Oxford University Press, 1970.

Hore, Annie B. *To Lake Tanganyika in a Bath Chair*. London: S. Low, Marston, Searle & Rivington, 1889.

Hore, Edward C. 'On the Twelve Tribes of Tanganyika'. *Journal of the Anthropological Institute* 12 (1883): 2–21.

Hore, Edward C. *Tanganyika: Eleven Years in Central Africa*. London: Edward Stanford, 1892.

Horton, James Africanus Beale. *West African Countries and Peoples, British and Native, and a Vindication of the African Race*. London: W. J. Johnson, 1868.

Horton, Robin. 'African Conversion'. *Africa* 41, no. 2 (1971): 85–108.

Horton, Robin. 'On the Rationality of Conversion. Part 2'. *Africa* 45, no. 4 (1975): 373–99.

Houle, Robert J. *Making African Christianity: Africans Reimagining Their Faith in Colonial Southern Africa*. Bethlehem, PA: Lehigh University Press, 2011.

Hourani, Albert. *A History of the Arab Peoples*. New York: Warner Books, 1992.

Howard, Michael. *War in European History*. Oxford: Oxford University Press, 2009 [1976].

Howe, Stephen. *Afrocentrism: Mythical Pasts and Imagined Homes*. London: Verso, 1998.

Hozier, Henry M. *The British Expedition to Abyssinia*. London: Macmillan & Co., 1869.

Huberich, Charles. *The Political and Legislative History of Liberia*. New York: Central Book Co., 1947.

Hull, Isabel. *Absolute Destruction: Military Culture and the Practices of War in Imperial Germany*. Ithaca, NY: Cornell University Press, 2005.

Huntingford, G.W.B., ed. and trans. *The Glorious Victories of ʿĀmda Ṣeyon, King of Ethiopia*. London: Oxford University Press, 1965.

Hunwick, J. O. 'Religion and State in the Songhay Empire, 1464–1591'. In *Islam in Tropical Africa*, edited by I. M. Lewis, 296–315. London: Oxford University Press, 1966.

Hyam, Ronald. *Britain's Imperial Century, 1815–1914: A Study of Empire and Expansion*. Basingstoke: Palgrave Macmillan, 2002 [1976].

Ikime, Obaro. *Merchant Prince of the Niger Delta: The Rise and Fall of Nana Olomu, Last Governor of the Benin River*. London: Heinemann, 1968.

Iliffe, John. *Africans: The History of a Continent*. Cambridge: Cambridge University Press, 2007 [1995].

Iliffe, John. *Honour in African History*. Cambridge: Cambridge University Press, 2005.

Iliffe, John. *A Modern History of Tanganyika*. Cambridge: Cambridge University Press, 1979.

Iliffe, John. 'The Organisation of the Maji-Maji Rebellion'. *Journal of African History* 8, no. 3 (1967): 495–512.

Iliffe, John. *Tanganyika under German Rule, 1905–1912*. Cambridge: Cambridge University Press, 1969.

Ingrams, Harold. *Uganda: A Crisis of Nationhood*. London: Her Majesty's Stationery Office, 1960.

Inikori, Joseph E. 'Africa and the Globalization Process: Western Africa, 1450–1850'. *Journal of Global History* 2, no. 1 (2007): 63–86.

Inikori, Joseph E. *Africans and the Industrial Revolution in England: A Study in International Trade and Economic Development*. Cambridge: Cambridge University Press, 2002.

Inikori, Joseph E. 'The Import of Firearms into West Africa, 1750–1807: A Quantitative Analysis'. *Journal of African History* 18, no. 3 (1977): 339–68.

Inikori, Joseph and Stanley Engerman, eds. *The Atlantic Slave Trade: Effects on Economies, Societies, and Peoples in Africa, the Americas, and Europe*. Durham, NC: Duke University Press, 1992.

Innes, Gordon, Bakari Sidibe, Lucy Duran and Graham Furniss, trans. and eds. *Sunjata: Gambian Versions of the Mande Epic by Bamba Suso and Banna Kanute*. London: Penguin, 1999.

Isaacman, Allen. 'The Origin, Formation and Early History of the Chikunda of South Central Africa'. *Journal of African History* 13, no. 3 (1972): 443–61.

Isaacman, Allen F. and Barbara S. Isaacman. 'Resistance and Collaboration in Southern and Central Africa, c. 1850–1920'. *International Journal of African Historical Studies* 10, no. 1 (1977): 31–62.

Isaacman, Allen F. and Barbara S. Isaacman. *Slavery and Beyond: The Making of Men and Chikunda Ethnic Identities in the Unstable World of South-Central Africa, 1750–1920*. Portsmouth, NH: Heinemann, 2004.

Isaacman, Allen and Derek Peterson. 'Making the Chikunda: Military Slavery and Ethnicity in Southern Africa, 1750–1900'. *International Journal of African Historical Studies* 36, no. 2 (2003): 257–81.

Isaacs, Nathaniel. *Travels and Adventures in Eastern Africa, Descriptive of the Zoolus, Their Manners, Customs, etc. etc., with a Sketch of Natal*, 2 vols. London: E. Churton, 1836.

Isichei, Elizabeth. *History of West Africa since 1800*. London: Macmillan, 1977.

Izevbaye, Dan S. 'West African Literature in English: Beginnings to the Mid-seventies'. In *The Cambridge History of African and Caribbean Literature, Volume 2*, edited by F. Abiola Irele and Simon Gikandi, 472–503. Cambridge: Cambridge University Press, 2004.

Jackson, Holbrook. *The Eighteen Nineties: A Review of Art and Ideas at the Close of the Nineteenth Century*. Harmondsworth: Penguin, 1950 [1913].

*JAH* Forum: 'Africa and Global History'. *Journal of African History* 54, no. 3 (2013).

*JAH* Forum: 'Health and Illness in African History'. *Journal of African History* 54, no. 1 (2013).

Jalata, Asafa. *Oromia and Ethiopia: State Formation and Ethnonational Conflict, 1868–2004*. Trenton, NJ: Red Sea Press, 2005.

James, C.L.R. *The Black Jacobins: Toussaint L'Ouverture and the San Domingo Revolution*. New York: Secker & Warburg, 1938.

James, Lawrence. *Empires in the Sun: The Struggle for the Mastery of Africa, 1830–1990*. London: Weidenfeld & Nicolson, 2016.

Jasanoff, Maya. *The Dawn Watch: Joseph Conrad in a Global World*. London: William Collins, 2017.

Jeal, Tim. *Livingstone*. New Haven, CT: Yale University Press, 2013 [1973].

Jeal, Tim. *Stanley: The Impossible Life of Africa's Greatest Explorer*. London: Faber, 2007.

Jeeves, Alan. *Migrant Labour in South Africa's Mining Economy: The Struggle for the Gold Mines' Labour Supply, 1890–1920*. Montreal and Kingston: McGill-Queen's University Press, 1985.

Jennings, Christian. 'They Called Themselves Iloikop: Rethinking Pastoralist History in Nineteenth-Century East Africa'. In *Sources and Methods in African History: Spoken, Written, Unearthed*, edited by Toyin Falola and Christian Jennings, 173–94. Rochester, NY: University of Rochester Press, 2003.

Jerven, Morten. 'Economic Growth'. In *The Oxford Handbook of Modern African History*, edited by John Parker and Richard Reid, 414–33. Oxford: Oxford University Press, 2013.

Jessee, Erin. *Negotiating Genocide in Rwanda: The Politics of History*. Cham: Springer, 2017.

Jewsiewicki, B. and V. Y. Mudimbe. 'Africans' Memories and Contemporary History of Africa'. *History and Theory* 32, no. 4 (1993): 1–11.

Johnson, Boris. 'Africa is a Mess, but We Can't Blame Colonialism'. *The Spectator*, 2 February 2002.

Johnson, Boris. 'If Blair's So Good at Running the Congo, Let Him Stay There'. *The Daily Telegraph*, 10 January 2002. Available at https://www.telegraph.co.uk/politics/0/blairs-good-running-congo-let-stay/ (accessed 15 March 2024).

Johnson, Douglas H. 'A New History for a New Nation: The Search for South Sudan's Usable Past'. Keynote address at the 9th International South Sudan and Sudan Studies Conference, Bonn, 23–25 July 2012.

Johnson, Douglas H. *The Root Causes of Sudan's Civil Wars*. Oxford: James Currey, 2003.

Johnson, Douglas H. 'The Structure of a Legacy: Military Slavery in Northeast Africa'. *Ethnohistory* 36, no. 1 (1989): 72–88.

Johnson, Samuel. *The History of the Yorubas: From the Earliest Times to the Beginning of the British Protectorate.* London: Routledge & Sons, 1921.

Johnston, Harry. *A History of the Colonization of Africa by Alien Races.* Cambridge: Cambridge University Press, 1913 [1899].

Johnston, H.A.S. *The Fulani Empire of Sokoto.* London: Oxford University Press, 1967.

Johnstone, Frederick A. *Class, Race and Gold: A Study of Class Relations and Racial Discrimination in South Africa.* London: Routledge & Kegan Paul, 1976.

Joll, James. *Europe since 1870: An International History.* London: Penguin, 1973.

Jones, G. I. *The Trading States of the Oil Rivers: A Study of Political Development in Eastern Nigeria.* London: Oxford University Press, 1963.

Jones, Stuart and André Müller. *The South African Economy, 1910–1990.* Basingstoke: Macmillan, 1992.

Judt, Tony. *Ill Fares the Land: A Treatise on Our Present Discontents.* London: Penguin, 2010.

Kaarsholm, Preben, ed. *Violence, Political Culture and Development in Africa.* Oxford: James Currey, 2006.

Kabaka of Buganda, The. 'Education, Civilisation and Foreignisation in Buganda' (1935). In *The Mind of Buganda: Documents in the Modern History of a Kingdom*, edited by D. A. Low, 104–8. London: Heinemann, 1971.

Kabaka of Buganda, The. *Desecration of My Kingdom.* London: Constable, 1967.

Kabeya, John B. *King Mirambo: One of the Heroes of Tanzania.* Nairobi: East African Literature Bureau, 1976.

Kabeya, John B. *Mtemi Mirambo: Mtawala shujaa wa Kinyamwezi.* Nairobi: East African Literature Bureau, 1966.

Kagwa, Apolo. *The Kings of Buganda*, translated and edited by M.S.M. Kiwanuka. Nairobi: East African Publishing House, 1971.

Kanya-Forstner, A. S. *The Conquest of the Western Sudan: A Study of French Military Imperialism.* Cambridge: Cambridge University Press, 1969.

Kaplan, Robert D. 'The Coming Anarchy'. *The Atlantic Monthly*, February 1994, 44–76.

Karugire, Samwiri. *A History of the Kingdom of Nkore in Western Uganda to 1896.* Oxford: Clarendon Press, 1971.

Kasozi, Abdu B. K. *The Spread of Islam in Uganda.* Nairobi: Oxford University Press, 1986.

Katoke, I. K. *The Karagwe Kingdom.* Nairobi: East African Publishing House, 1975.

Keltie, J. Scott. *The Partition of Africa.* London: Edward Stanford, 1895 [1893].

Kemp, Tom. *Industrialization in Nineteenth-Century Europe.* London: Longman, 1969.

Kennedy, Dane. *The Imperial History Wars: Debating the British Empire.* London: Bloomsbury, 2018.

Kennedy, Paul. *The Rise and Fall of British Naval Mastery.* London: Penguin, 2004 [1976].

Kennedy, Paul. *The Rise and Fall of the Great Powers: Economic Change and Military Conflict from 1500 to 2000.* London: Fontana Press, 1988.

Kiernan, V. G. *European Empires from Conquest to Collapse, 1815–1960.* Leicester: Leicester University Press, 1982.

Kiernan, V. G. *The Lords of Human Kind: European Attitudes to the Outside World in the Imperial Age.* London: Pelican, 1969.

Kiewiet, C. W. de. 'British Colonial Policy and the South African Republics, 1848–1872'. London: Longmans, Green & Co., 1929.

Killingray, David. 'Colonial Warfare in West Africa, 1870–1914'. In *Imperialism and War: Essays on Colonial Wars in Asia and Africa*, edited by J. A. de Moor and H. L. Wesseling, 146–167. Leiden: Brill, 1989.

Killingray, David and David Omissi, eds. *Guardians of Empire: The Armed Forces of the Colonial Powers, c. 1700–1964*. Manchester: Manchester University Press, 1999.

Kimambo, I. N. and A. J. Temu, eds. *A History of Tanzania*. Nairobi: East African Publishing House, 1969.

Kantai, Parselelo, Greg Mthembu-Salter, Patrick Smith, Prince Ofori-Atta and Marshall Van Valen. 'Kings: Adapt or Die!' *The Africa Report*, no. 54, October 2013.

Kipling, Rudyard. 'The White Man's Burden' (1899). In *Empire Writing: An Anthology of Colonial Literature, 1870–1918*, edited by Elleke Boehmer, 273–74. Oxford: Oxford University Press, 1998.

Kiwanuka, M.S.M. *A History of Buganda: From the Foundation of the Kingdom to 1900*. London: Longman, 1971.

Kjekshus, Helge. *Ecology Control and Economic Development in East African History: the case of Tanganyika, 1850–1950*. London: James Currey, 1996 [1977].

Klein, Martin. 'The Impact of the Atlantic Slave Trade on the Societies of the Western Sudan'. *Social Science History* 14 (1990): 231–53.

Klein, Martin. 'Social and Economic Factors in the Muslim Revolution in Senegambia'. *Journal of African History* 13, no. 3 (1972): 419–41.

Klein, Martin. 'Women in Slavery in the Western Sudan'. In *Women and Slavery in Africa*, edited by Claire Robertson and Martin A. Klein, 67–92. Madison, WI: University of Wisconsin Press, 1983.

Knight, Ian. *The Anatomy of the Zulu Army: From Shaka to Cetshwayo, 1818–1879*. London: Wrens Park, 1999.

Knight, Ian. *Zulu Rising: The Epic Story of Isandlwana and Rorke's Drift*. London: Macmillan, 2010.

Kodesh, Neil. *Beyond the Royal Gaze: Clanship and Public Healing in Buganda*. Charlottesville, VA: University of Virginia Press, 2010.

Kodesh, Neil. 'History from the Healer's Shrine: Genre, Historical Imagination and Early Ganda History'. *Comparative Studies in Society and History* 49, no. 3 (2007): 527–52.

Koebner, R. and Helmut Dan Schmidt. *Imperialism: The Story and Significance of a Political Word, 1840–1960*. Cambridge: Cambridge University Press, 1964.

Kopytoff, Igor, ed. *The African Frontier: The Reproduction of Traditional African Societies*. Bloomington, IN: Indiana University Press, 1987.

Kopytoff, Igor. 'Frontiers'. In *New Encyclopedia of Africa, Volume 2*, edited by J. Middleton and J. C. Miller, 416–18. Detroit: Thomson Gale, 2008.

Kopytoff, Igor. 'The Internal African Frontier: The Making of African Political Culture'. In *The African Frontier: The Reproduction of Traditional African Societies*, edited by Igor Kopytoff, 3–84. Bloomington, IN: Indiana University Press, 1987.

Kuper, Adam. *The Reinvention of Primitive Society: Transformations of a Myth*. Abingdon: Routledge, 2005.

'K.W.' 'The Kings of Bunyoro-Kitara, Part 1'. *Uganda Journal* 3, no. 2 (1935): 155–60.

'K.W.' 'The Kings of Bunyoro-Kitara, Part 2'. *Uganda Journal* 4, no. 1 (1936): 75–83.

'K.W.' 'The Kings of Bunyoro-Kitara, Part 3'. *Uganda Journal* 5, no. 2 (1937): 53–68.

Laband, John. *Kingdom in Crisis: The Zulu Response to the British Invasion of 1879*. Manchester: Manchester University Press, 1992.

Laband, John. *The Transvaal Rebellion: The First Boer War, 1880–1881*. Abingdon: Routledge, 2014.

Lahti, Janne and Michelle R. Moyd. 'In Service of Empires: Apaches and Askaris as Colonial Soldiers'. In *German and United States Colonialism in a Connected World: Entangled Empires*, edited by Janne Lahti, 253–76. Basingstoke: Palgrave Macmillan, 2020.

Lamothe, Ronald M. *Slaves of Fortune: Sudanese Soldiers and the River War, 1896–1898*. Woodbridge: James Currey, 2011.

Lamphear, John. 'Aspects of "Becoming Turkana": Interactions and Assimilation Between Maa- and Ateker-Speakers'. In *Being Maasai: Ethnicity and Identity in East Africa*, edited by Thomas Spear and Richard Waller, 87–104. Oxford: James Currey, 1993.

Lamphear, John. 'Brothers in Arms: Military Aspects of East African Age-Class Systems in Historical Perspective'. In *Conflict, Age and Power in North East Africa: Age Systems in Transition*, edited by Eisei Kurimoto and Simon Simonse, 79–97. Oxford: James Currey, 1998.

Lamphear, John. 'Sub-Saharan African Warfare'. In *War in the Modern World Since 1815*, edited by Jeremy Black, 169–91. London: Routledge, 2003.

Lan, David. *Guns and Rain: Guerrillas and Spirit Mediums in Zimbabwe*. Berkeley, CA: University of California Press, 1985.

Landes, David S. 'Why Europe and the West? Why Not China?' *Journal of Economic Perspectives* 20, no. 2 (2006): 3–22.

Lapidus, Ira M. *A History of Islamic Societies*. Cambridge: Cambridge University Press, 2002.

Last, Murray. *The Sokoto Caliphate*. London: Longmans, 1967.

Last, Murray. 'Text and Authority in Nineteenth Century Nigeria'. *Journal of African History* 63, no. 2 (2022): 252–53.

Latham, A.J.H. *Old Calabar, 1600–1891: The Impact of the International Economy upon a Traditional Society*. Oxford: Clarendon Press, 1973.

Law, Robin. 'The Constitutional Troubles of Oyo in the Eighteenth Century'. *Journal of African History* 12, no. 1 (1971): 25–44.

Law, Robin. 'Dahomey and the Slave Trade: Reflections on the Historiography of the Rise of Dahomey'. *Journal of African History* 27, no. 2 (1986): 237–67.

Law, Robin. 'Early Yoruba Historiography'. *History in Africa* 3 (1976): 69–89.

Law, Robin. 'The Evolution of the Brazilian Community in Ouidah'. *Slavery & Abolition* 22, no. 1 (2001): 22–41.

Law, Robin, ed. *From Slave Trade to 'Legitimate' Commerce: Commercial Transition in Nineteenth-Century West Africa*. Cambridge: Cambridge University Press, 1995.

Law, Robin, ed. *Further Correspondence of the Royal African Company of England Relating to the 'Slave Coast', 1681–1699*. Madison, WI: University of Wisconsin Press, 1992.

Law, Robin. 'Horses, Firearms and Political Power in Pre-colonial West Africa'. *Past and Present* 72, no. 1 (1976): 112–32.

Law, Robin. 'Ideologies of Royal Power: The Dissolution and Reconstruction of Political Authority on the "Slave Coast", 1680–1750'. *Africa* 57, no. 3 (1987): 321–44.

Law, Robin. 'Making Sense of a Traditional Narrative: Political Disintegration in the Kingdom of Oyo'. *Cahiers d'études africaines* 22, nos 87–88 (1982): 387–401.

Law, Robin. *Ouidah: The Social History of a West African Slaving 'Port', 1727–1892*. Athens, OH: Ohio University Press, 2004.

Law, Robin. *The Oyo Empire c. 1600–c. 1836: A West African Imperialism in the Era of the Atlantic Slave Trade*. Oxford: Clarendon Press, 1977.

Law, Robin. 'The Politics of Commercial Transition: Factional Conflict in Dahomey in the Context of the Ending of the Atlantic Slave Trade'. *Journal of African History* 38, no. 2 (1997): 213–33.

Law, Robin. 'Royal Monopoly and Private Enterprise in the Atlantic Trade: The Case of Dahomey'. *Journal of African History* 18, no. 4 (1977): 555–77.

Law, Robin. *The Slave Coast of West Africa, 1550–1750: The Impact of the Atlantic Slave Trade on an African Society*. Oxford: Clarendon Press, 1991.

Law, Robin. 'Slave-Raiders and Middlemen, Monopolists and Free-Traders: The Supply of Slaves for the Atlantic Trade in Dahomey, c. 1715–1850.' *Journal of African History* 30, no. 1 (1989): 45–68.

Law, Robin, Suzanne Schwartz and Silke Strickrodt, eds. *Commercial Agriculture, the Slave Trade and Slavery in Atlantic Africa.* Woodbridge: James Currey, 2013.

Lawrance, Benjamin N., Emily Lynn Osborn and Richard L. Roberts, eds. *Intermediaries, Interpreters and Clerks: African Employees in the Making of Colonial Africa.* Madison, WI: University of Wisconsin Press, 2006.

Lawrence, Adria K. *Imperial Rule and the Politics of Nationalism: Anti-Colonial Protest in the French Empire.* Cambridge: Cambridge University Press, 2013.

Lee, Wayne E. *Waging War: Conflict, Culture, and Innovation in World History.* Oxford: Oxford University Press, 2016.

Lefkowitz, Mary. *Not Out of Africa: How Afrocentrism Became an Excuse to Teach Myth as History.* New York: Basic Books, 1996.

Legassick, Martin. 'Firearms, Horses and Samorian Army Organisation, 1870–1898.' *Journal of African History* 7, no. 1 (1966): 95–115.

Legassick, Martin and Robert Ross. 'From Slave Economy to Settler Capitalism: The Cape Colony and Its Extension, 1800–1854.' In *The Cambridge History of South Africa, Volume 1: From Early Times to 1885,* edited by Carolyn Hamilton, Bernard K. Mbenga and Robert Ross, 253–318. Cambridge: Cambridge University Press, 2010.

Legum, Colin and Bill Lee. *The Horn of Africa in Continuing Crisis.* New York: Africana Publishing Co., 1979.

Lemarchand, René. *The Dynamics of Violence in Central Africa.* Philadelphia: University of Pennsylvania Press, 2009.

Lenin, V. I. *Imperialism, the Highest Stage of Capitalism: A Popular Outline.* New York: International Publishers, 1939 [Rus., 1917].

Lentz, Carola. 'Ethnicity'. In *New Encyclopedia of Africa, Volume 2,* edited by J. Middleton and J. C. Miller, 313–19. Detroit: Thomson Gale, 2008.

Lentz, Carola. '"Ghana@50": Celebrating the Nation—Debating the Nation'. *Johannes Gutenberg-Universität, Department of Anthropology and African Studies, Working Papers* 120 (2010).

Leonardi, Cherry. *Dealing with Government in South Sudan: Histories of Chiefship, Community, and State.* Woodbridge: James Currey, 2013.

Leopold, Mark. *Inside West Nile: Violence, History, and Representation on an African Frontier.* Oxford: James Currey, 2005.

Lettow-Vorbeck, Paul Emil von. *My Reminiscences of East Africa.* London: Hurst & Blackett, 1920 [Ger. 1920]

Levine, Philippa. *The British Empire: Sunrise to Sunset.* London: Longman, 2007.

Levtzion, Nehemia. 'North-West Africa: From the Maghrib to the Fringes of the Forest'. In *The Cambridge History of Africa, Volume 4: c. 1600–c. 1790,* edited by Richard Gray, 142–222. Cambridge Cambridge University Press, 1975.

Lewin, Thomas J. *Asante before the British: The Prempean Years, 1875–1900.* Lawrence, KS: Regents Press of Kansas, 1975.

Lewis, David Levering. *The Race to Fashoda: European Colonialism and African Resistance in the Scramble for Africa.* London: Bloomsbury, 1988.

Lewis, Herbert S. *Jimma Abba Jifar, an Oromo Monarchy: Ethiopia 1830–1932.* Lawrenceville, NJ: Red Sea Press, 2001 [1965].

Lewis, Ioan M. 'Frontier Fetishism and the "Ethiopianisation" of Africa'. In *Arguments with Ethnography: Comparative Approaches to History, Politics and Religion,* edited by Ioan M. Lewis, 58–68. London: The Athlone Press, 1999.

Lewis, Ioan M. 'History "Functionalised"'. In *Arguments with Ethnography: Comparative Approaches to History, Politics and Religion*, edited by Ioan M. Lewis, 1–11. London: The Athlone Press, 1999.

Lewis, Ioan M. *A Modern History of the Somali*. Oxford: James Currey, 2002 [1965].

Lewis, Joanna. *Empire of Sentiment: The Death of Livingstone and the Myth of Victorian Imperialism*. Cambridge: Cambridge University Press, 2018.

Lewis, Mary Dewhurst. *Divided Rule: Sovereignty and Empire in French Tunisia, 1881–1938*. Berkeley, CA: University of California Press, 2014.

Lieven, Michael. '"Butchering the brutes all over the place": Total War and Massacre in Zululand, 1879'. *History* 84, no. 276 (1999): 614–32.

Lindqvist, Sven. *"Exterminate All the Brutes": One Man's Odyssey into the Heart of Darkness and the Origins of European Genocide*. London: Granta, 1997.

Little, Tom. *Modern Egypt*. London: Ernest Benn, 1967.

Livingstone, David and Charles Livingstone. *Narrative of an Expedition to the Zambesi and its Tributaries*. Stroud: Nonsuch, 2005 [1865].

Lloyd, Peter C. *The Political Development of Yoruba Kingdoms in the Eighteenth and Nineteenth Centuries*. London: Royal Anthropological Institute, 1971.

Lockhart, Donald M., trans. *The 'Itinerário' of Jerónimo Lobo*. London: Hakluyt Society, 1984.

Lonsdale, John. 'The European Scramble and Conquest in African History'. In *The Cambridge History of Africa, Volume 6: 1870–1905*, edited by Roland Oliver and G. N. Sanderson, 680–766. Cambridge: Cambridge University Press, 1985.

Lonsdale, John and Bruce Berman. 'Coping with the Contradictions: The Development of the Colonial State in Kenya, 1895–1914'. *Journal of African History* 20, no. 4 (1979): 487–505.

Lorimer, Douglas A. *Colour, Class and the Victorians: English Attitudes to the Negro in the Mid-nineteenth Century*. Leicester: Leicester University Press, 1978.

Louis, William Roger. 'Roger Casement and the Congo'. *Journal of African History* 5, no. 1 (1964): 99–120.

Lovejoy, Paul E. 'Concubinage and the Status of Women Slaves in Early Colonial Nigeria'. *Journal of African History* 29, no. 2 (1988): 245–66.

Lovejoy, Paul E. *Jihad in West Africa during the Age of Revolutions*. Athens, OH: University of Ohio Press, 2016.

Lovejoy, Paul E. 'Plantations in the Economy of the Sokoto Caliphate'. *Journal of African History* 19, no. 3 (1978): 341–68.

Lovejoy, Paul E. *Salt of the Desert Sun: A History of Salt Production and Trade in the Central Sudan*. Cambridge: Cambridge University Press, 1986.

Lovejoy, Paul E. *Transformations in Slavery: A History of Slavery in Africa*. Cambridge: Cambridge University Press, 1983.

Lovejoy, Paul E. 'The Yoruba Factor in the Trans-Atlantic Slave Trade'. In *The Yoruba Diaspora in the Atlantic World*, edited by Toyin Falola and Matt D. Childs, 40–55. Bloomington, IN: Indiana University Press, 2004.

Lovejoy, Paul E. and David Richardson. 'The Initial "Crisis of Adaptation": The Impact of British Abolition on the Atlantic Slave Trade in West Africa, 1808–1820'. In *From Slave Trade to 'Legitimate' Commerce: Commercial Transition in Nineteenth-Century West Africa*, edited by Robin Law, 32–56. Cambridge: Cambridge University Press, 1995.

Low, D. A. *Buganda in Modern History*. London: Weidenfeld & Nicolson, 1971.

Low, D. A. *Fabrication of Empire: The British and the Uganda Kingdoms, 1890–1902*. Cambridge: Cambridge University Press, 2009.

Low, D. A. 'The Making and Implementation of the Uganda Agreement of 1900'. In D. A. Low and R. C. Pratt, *Buganda and British Overrule, 1900–1955: Two Studies*, 1–159. London: Oxford University Press, 1960.

Low, D. A. 'Uganda: The Establishment of the Protectorate, 1894–1919'. In *History of East Africa, Volume 2*, edited by V. Harlow and E. M. Chilver, 57–120. Oxford: Clarendon Press, 1965.

Lugard, Frederick D. *The Dual Mandate in British Tropical Africa*. Edinburgh: William Blackwood & Sons, 1923 [1922].

Lugard, Frederick D. *The Rise of Our East African Empire*, 2 vols. Edinburgh: William Blackwood & Sons, 1893.

Lunt, James. *Imperial Sunset: Frontier Soldiering in the 20th Century*. London: Macdonald Futura Publishers, 1981.

Lydon, Ghislaine. *On Trans-Saharan Trails: Islamic Law, Trade Networks and Cross-Cultural Exchange in Nineteenth-Century Western Africa*. Cambridge: Cambridge University Press, 2009.

Lynn, Martin. 'British Policy, Trade, and Informal Empire in the Mid-nineteenth Century'. In *The Oxford History of the British Empire, Volume 3: The Nineteenth Century*, edited by Andrew Porter, 101–21. Oxford: Oxford University Press, 1999.

Lynn, Martin. *Commerce and Economic Change in West Africa: The Palm Oil Trade in the Nineteenth Century*. Cambridge: Cambridge University Press, 1997.

Lynn, Martin. 'The West African Palm Oil Trade in the Nineteenth Century and the "Crisis of Adaptation"'. In *From Slave Trade to 'Legitimate' Commerce: Commercial Transition in Nineteenth-Century West Africa*, edited by Robin Law, 57–77. Cambridge: Cambridge University Press, 1995.

Lyons, Maryinez. *The Colonial Disease: A Social History of Sleeping Sickness in Northern Zaire, 1900–1940*. Cambridge: Cambridge University Press, 1992.

M'baye, Babacar. 'The Economic, Political and Social Impact of the Atlantic Slave Trade on Africa'. *The European Legacy* 11, no. 6 (2006): 607–22.

Mabogunje, A. L. *Urbanization in Nigeria*. London: University of London Press, 1968.

Mackay, Alexander. *A. M. Mackay, Pioneer Missionary of the Church Missionary Society to Uganda*, edited by [his sister] Alexina Harrison. London: Hodder & Stoughton, 1890.

Mackenzie, John, ed. *Imperialism and Popular Culture*. Manchester: Manchester University Press, 1986.

Mackenzie, John and Joanna Skipwith, eds. *David Livingstone and the Victorian Encounter with Africa*. London: National Portrait Gallery, 1996.

Macola, Giacomo. *The Gun in Central Africa: A History of Technology and Politics*. Athens, OH: Ohio University Press, 2016.

Macola, Giacomo. 'The History of the Eastern Lunda Royal Capitals to 1900'. In *The Urban Experience in Eastern Africa, c. 1750–2000* (*Azania* special volume 36–37), edited by Andrew Burton, 31–45. Nairobi: British Institute in Eastern Africa, 2002.

Macola, Giacomo. *The Kingdom of Kazembe: History and Politics in North-Eastern Zambia and Katanga to 1950*. Hamburg: Lit Verlag, 2002.

MacQueen, James. 'The Visit of Lief ben Saied to the Great African Lakes'. *Journal of the Royal Geographical Society* 15 (1845): 371–76.

Maier, D.J.E. 'The Dente Oracle, the Bron Confederation, and Asante: Religion and the Politics of Secession'. *Journal of African History* 22, no. 2 (1981): 229–43.

Mainga, Mutumba. *Bulozi under the Luyana Kings: Political Evolution and State Formation in Pre-colonial Zambia*. London: Longmans, 1973.

Malan, Rian. *My Traitor's Heart: Blood and Bad Dreams; A South African Explores the Madness in His Country, His Tribe and Himself*. London: Vintage, 1990.

Malik, Kenan. *The Meaning of Race: Race, History and Culture in Western Society*. Basingstoke: Macmillan, 1996.

Mamdani, Mahmood. *Citizen and Subject: Contemporary Africa and the Legacy of Late Colonialism*. Princeton, NJ: Princeton University Press, 1996.

Mandala, Elias C. *Work and Control in a Peasant Economy: A History of the Lower Tchiri Valley in Malawi, 1859–1960*. Madison, WI: University of Wisconsin Press, 1990.

Mandela, Nelson. *Long Walk to Freedom*. London: BCA, 1995.

Mann, Kristin. *Marrying Well: Marriage, Status and Social Change among the Educated Elite in Colonial Lagos*. Cambridge: Cambridge University Press, 1985.

Mann, Kristin. *Slavery and the Birth of an African City: Lagos, 1760–1900*. Bloomington, IN: Indiana University Press, 2007.

Manning, Patrick. 'African and World Historiography'. *Journal of African History* 54, no. 3 (2013): 319–30.

Manning, Patrick. *Francophone Sub-Saharan Africa, 1880–1995*. Cambridge: Cambridge University Press, 1998.

Mansfield, Peter. *Nasser's Egypt*. London: Penguin, 1969.

Manu-Osafo, Manuel J. '"The days of their heedless power were over and done": Dynamics of Power in the Military Structures of the Precolonial Asante State, 1874–1900'. *Journal of African History* 62, no. 2 (2021): 254–70.

Marcus, Harold. *The Life and Times of Menelik II: Ethiopia 1844–1913*. Oxford: Clarendon Press, 1975.

Markham, Clements. *A History of the Abyssinian Expedition*. London: Macmillan & Co., 1869.

Marks, Shula. 'Southern Africa, 1867–1886'. In *The Cambridge History of Africa: Volume 6: 1870–1905*, edited by Roland Oliver and G. N. Sanderson, 359–421. Cambridge: Cambridge University Press, 1985.

Marks, Shula. 'Southern and Central Africa, 1886–1910'. In *The Cambridge History of Africa: Volume 6: 1870–1905*, edited by Roland Oliver and G. N. Sanderson, 422–92. Cambridge: Cambridge University Press, 1985.

Marks, Shula. 'War and Union, 1899–1910'. In *The Cambridge History of South Africa, Volume 2: 1885–1994*, edited by Robert Ross, Anne Kelk Mager and Bill Nasson, 157–210. Cambridge: Cambridge University Press, 2011.

Marks, Shula and Richard Gray. 'Southern Africa and Madagascar'. In *The Cambridge History of Africa, Volume 4: c. 1600–c. 1790*, edited byRichard Gray, 384–468. Cambridge: Cambridge University Press, 1975.

Marsden, Philip. *The Barefoot Emperor: An Ethiopian Tragedy*. London: Harper, 2007.

Martin, Guy. *African Political Thought*. New York: Palgrave Macmillan, 2012.

Martin, Marie-Louise. *Kimbangu: An African Prophet and His Church*. Oxford: Blackwell, 1975.

Martin, Susan. *Palm Oil and Protest: An Economic History of the Ngwa Region, South-Eastern Nigeria, 1800–1980*. Cambridge: Cambridge University Press, 1988.

Martin, Susan. 'Slaves, Igbo Women and Palm Oil in the Nineteenth Century'. In *From Slave Trade to 'Legitimate' Commerce: Commercial Transition in Nineteenth-Century West Africa*, edited by Robin Law, 172–94. Cambridge: Cambridge University Press, 1995.

Marzagora, Sara. 'Alterity, Coloniality and Modernity in Ethiopian Political Thought: The First Three Generations of 20th Century Amharic-Language Intellectuals'. PhD thesis, SOAS, University of London, 2015.

Marzagora, Sara. 'History in Twentieth-Century Ethiopia: The "Great Tradition" and the Counter-Histories of National Failure'. *Journal of African History* 58, no. 3 (2017): 425–44.

Mathys, Gillian. 'Bringing History Back In: Past, Present and Conflict in Rwanda and the Eastern Democratic Republic of Congo'. *Journal of African History* 58, no. 3 (2017): 465–87.

Matthias, Peter. *The First Industrial Nation: An Economic History of Britain, 1700–1914*. London: Routledge, 1989 [1969].

Maxwell, David. 'Christianity'. In *The Oxford Handbook of Modern African History*, edited by John Parker and Richard Reid, 263–80. Oxford: Oxford University Press, 2013.

Maxwell, David. 'Historicising Christian Independency: The Southern African Pentecostal Movement, c. 1908–1960'. *Journal of African History* 40, no. 2 (1999): 243–64.

Mayer, Thomas. *The Changing Past: Egyptian Historiography of the Urabi Revolt, 1882–1983*. Gainesville, FL: University of Florida Press, 1988.

Mazrui, Alamin M. 'The Swahili Literary Tradition: An Intercultural Heritage'. In *The Cambridge History of African and Caribbean Literature, Volume 1*, edited by F. Abiola Irele and Simon Gikandi, 199–226. Cambridge: Cambridge University Press, 2004.

Mazrui, Ali A. 'The Resurrection of the Warrior Tradition in African Political Culture'. *Journal of Modern African Studies* 13, no. 1 (1975): 67–84.

Mba, Nina Emma. *Nigerian Women Mobilised: Women's Political Activity in Southern Nigeria, 1900–1965*. Berkeley, CA: Institute of International Studies, 1982.

Mbeki, Thabo. 'The African Renaissance, South Africa and the World'. Speech at the United Nations University, 9 April 1998. Available at https://archive.unu.edu/unupress/mbeki.html (accessed 15 March 2024).

Mbembe, Achille. 'L'Afrique de Nicolas Sarkozy'. *Mouvements* 4, no. 52 (2007) : 65–73.

Mbilinyi, Marjorie. 'Wife, Slave and Subject of the King: The Oppression of Women in the Shambala Kingdom'. *Tanzania Notes and Records* 88/89 (1981): 1–13.

McCaskie, Tom. 'Accumulation, Wealth and Belief in Asante History, 1: To the Close of the Nineteenth Century'. *Africa* 53, no. 1 (1983): 23–43.

McCaskie, Tom. *Asante Identities: History and Modernity in an African Village, 1850–1950*. Edinburgh: Edinburgh University Press, 2000.

McCaskie, Tom. 'Cultural Encounters: Britain and Africa in the Nineteenth Century'. In *The Oxford History of the British Empire, Volume 3: The Nineteenth Century*, edited by Andrew Porter, 665–89. Oxford: Oxford University Press, 1999.

McCaskie, Tom. 'Komfo Anokye of Asante: Meaning, History and Philosophy in an African Society'. *Journal of African History* 27, no. 2 (1986): 315–39.

McCaskie, Tom. *State and Society in Pre-colonial Asante*. Cambridge: Cambridge University Press, 1995.

McCracken, John. *A History of Malawi, 1859–1966*. Woodbridge: James Currey, 2012.

McCracken, John. 'The Nineteenth Century in Malawi'. In *Aspects of Central African History*, edited by T. O. Ranger, 97–111. London: Heinemann, 1968.

McCracken, John. *Politics and Christianity in Malawi, 1875–1940: The Impact of the Livingstonia Mission in the Northern Province*. Cambridge: Cambridge University Press, 1977.

McCracken, John, ed. *Voices from the Chilembwe Rising: Witness Testimonies Made to the Nyasaland Rising Commission of Inquiry, 1915*. Oxford: Oxford University Press, 2015.

McCulloch, Diarmaid. *A History of Christianity*. London: Allen Lane, 2009.

McDougall, James. *History and the Culture of Nationalism in Algeria*. Cambridge: Cambridge University Press, 2006.

McDougall, James. *A History of Algeria*. Cambridge: Cambridge University Press, 2017.

McGreal, Chris. 'Blair Confronts "Scar on the World's Conscience"'. *The Guardian*, 7 February 2002. Available at https://www.theguardian.com/world/2002/feb/07/politics.development (accessed 15 March 2024).

McKeown, Adam. 'Global Migration, 1846–1940'. *Journal of World History* 15, no. 2 (2004): 155–89.

McNeill, William H. *The Pursuit of Power: Technology, Armed Force and Society since AD 1000*. Chicago: University of Chicago Press, 1982.

McPhee, Allan. *The Economic Revolution in British West Africa*. London: George Routledge & Sons, 1926.

Médard, Henri. *Le Royaume du Buganda au xix^e siècle: Mutations politiques et religieuses d'un ancient état d'Afrique de l'Est*. Paris: Karthala, 2007.

Médard, Henri and Shane Doyle, eds. *Slavery in the Great Lakes Region of East Africa*. Oxford: James Currey, 2007.

Meintjes, Johannes. *The Voortrekkers: The Story of the Great Trek and the Making of South Africa*. London: Cassell, 1973.

Meldrum, Andrew. 'German Minister Says Sorry for Genocide in Namibia'. *The Guardian*, 16 August 2004. Available at https://www.theguardian.com/world/2004/aug/16/germany.andrewmeldrum (accessed 15 March 2024).

Miers, Suzanne and Igor Kopytoff, eds. *Slavery in Africa: Historical and Anthropological Perspectives*. Madison, WI: University of Wisconsin Press, 1977.

Miers, Suzanne and Richard Roberts, eds. *The End of Slavery in Africa*. Madison, WI: University of Wisconsin Press, 1988.

Milkias, Paulos and Getachew Metaferia, eds. *The Battle of Adwa: Reflections on Ethiopia's Historic Victory against European Colonialism*. New York: Algora Publishing, 2005.

Miller, Joseph C. 'Cokwe Trade and Conquest in the Nineteenth Century'. In *Pre-colonial African Trade: Essays on Trade in Central and Eastern Africa before 1900*, edited by Richard Gray and David Birmingham, 175–201. London: Oxford University Press, 1970.

Miller, Joseph C. 'Slaves, Slavers and Social Change in Nineteenth-Century Kasanje'. In *Social Change in Angola*, edited by Franz-Wilhelm Heimer, 9–29. Munich: Weltforum Verlag, 1973.

Miller, Susan Gilson. *A History of Modern Morocco*. Cambridge: Cambridge University Press, 2013.

Miran, Jonathan. *Red Sea Citizens: Cosmopolitan Society and Cultural Change in Massawa*. Bloomington, IN: Indiana University Press, 2009.

*Missions catholiques, Les*, 14 (1882).

Mitchell, Timothy. *Colonising Egypt*. Berkeley, CA: University of California Press, 1988.

Mitchell, Timothy. 'The Stage of Modernity'. In *Questions of Modernity*, edited by Timothy Mitchell, 1–34. Minneapolis: University of Minnesota Press, 2000.

Mommsen, Wolfgang J. *Theories of Imperialism*. London: Weidenfeld & Nicolson, 1981.

Monson, Jamie. 'Relocating Maji Maji: The Politics of Alliance and Authority in the Southern Highlands of Tanganyika, 1870–1918'. *Journal of African History* 39 (1998): 95–120.

Montaigne, Michel de. 'On Cannibals'. In Michel de Montaigne, *Essays*, translated by J. M. Cohen, 105–19. London: Penguin, 1993 [Fr. c. 1580].

Moore-Harell, Alice. 'Economic and Social Aspects of the Slave Trade in Ethiopia and the Sudan in the Second Half of the Nineteenth Century'. *International Journal of African Historical Studies* 23, nos 2–3 (1999): 407–21.

Moorehead, Alan. *The White Nile*. London: Penguin, 1963.

Morris, Donald R. *The Washing of the Spears: The Rise and Fall of the Zulu Nation*. London: Pimlico, 1994 [1965].

Mosley, Paul. *The Settler Economies: Studies in the Economic History of Kenya and Southern Rhodesia*. Cambridge: Cambridge University Press, 1983.

Mostert, Noel. *Frontiers: The Epic of South Africa's Creation and the Tragedy of the Xhosa People*. London: Jonathan Cape, 1992.

Moyd, Michelle. *Violent Intermediaries: African Soldiers, Conquest, and Everyday Colonialism in German East Africa*. Athens, OH: Ohio University Press, 2014.

Mphahlele, Ezekiel. *The African Image*. London: Faber & Faber, 1962.

Mphande, Lupenga. 'Heroic and Praise Poetry in South Africa'. In *The Cambridge History of African and Caribbean Literature, Volume 1*, edited by F. Abiola Irele and Simon Gikandi, 71–97. Cambridge: Cambridge University Press, 2004.

Mudimbe, V. Y. *The Idea of Africa*. Bloomington, IN: Indiana University Press, 1994.

Mudimbe, V. Y. *The Invention of Africa: Gnosis, Philosophy, and the Order of Knowledge*. Bloomington, IN: Indiana University Press, 1988.

Muffett, D.J.M. *Concerning Brave Captains: Being a History of the British Occupation of Kano and Sokoto and of the Last Stand of the Fulani Forces*. London: André Deutsch, 1964.

Munro, J. Forbes. 'British Rubber Companies in East Africa before the First World War'. *Journal of African History* 24, no. 3 (1983): 369–79.

Munro, J. Forbes. *Maritime Enterprise and Empire: Sir William Mackinnon and His Business Network, 1823–93*. Woodbridge: Boydell Press, 2003.

Munro, J. Forbes. 'Monopolists and Speculators: British Investment in West African Rubber, 1905–1914'. *Journal of African History* 22, no. 2 (1981): 263–78.

Murray, Williamson A. 'The Industrialization of War, 1815–1871'. In *The Cambridge History of Warfare*, edited by Geoffrey Parker, 219–48. Cambridge: Cambridge University Press, 2005.

Museveni, Yoweri K. *Sowing the Mustard Seed: The Struggle for Freedom and Democracy in Uganda*. Oxford: Macmillan, 1997.

Museveni, Yoweri K. *What is Africa's Problem?* Minneapolis: University of Minnesota Press, 2000.

Musisi, Nakanyike B. 'Women, "Elite Polygyny", and Buganda State Formation'. *Signs* 16, no. 4 (1991): 757–86.

Myatt, Frederick. *The March to Magdala: The Abyssinian War of 1868*. London: Leo Cooper, 1970.

Nair, Kannan K. *Politics and Society in South Eastern Nigeria, 1841–1906: A Study of Power, Diplomacy and Commerce in Old Calabar*. London: Frank Cass, 1972.

Nasson, Bill. *Abraham Esau's War: A Black South African War in the Cape, 1899–1902*. Cambridge: Cambridge University Press, 1991.

Nasson, Bill. *The South African War, 1899–1902*. London: Hodder Arnold, 1999.

Naylor, Paul. *From Rebels to Rulers: Writing Legitimacy in the Early Sokoto State*. Woodbridge: James Currey, 2021.

Ndlovu-Gatsheni, Sabelo J. 'Who Ruled by the Spear? Rethinking the Form of Governance in the Ndebele State'. *African Studies Quarterly* 10, nos 2–3 (2008): 71–94.

Negash, Tekeste. *Italian Colonialism in Eritrea, 1882–1941: Policies, Praxis and Impact*. Uppsala: University of Uppsala, 1987.

Newbury, Colin. 'Great Britain and the Partition of Africa, 1870–1914'. In *The Oxford History of the British Empire, Volume 3: The Nineteenth Century*, edited by Andrew Porter, 624–50. Oxford: Oxford University Press, 1999.

Newbury, Colin. *The Western Slave Coast and Its Rulers*. Oxford: Clarendon Press, 1961.

Newbury, David. 'Bunyabungo: The Western Frontier in Rwanda, ca. 1750–1850'. In David Newbury, *The Land Beyond the Mists: Essays on Identity and Authority in Precolonial Congo and Rwanda*, 204–28. Athens, OH: Ohio University Press, 2009.

Newbury, David. 'The Campaigns of Rwabugiri'. In David Newbury, *The Land Beyond the Mists: Essays on Identity and Authority in Precolonial Congo and Rwanda*, 129–141. Athens, OH: Ohio University Press, 2009.

Newitt, Malyn. *A History of Mozambique*. London: Hurst, 1995.

Newitt, Malyn. *A Short History of Mozambique*. London: Hurst, 2017.

Nhema, Alfred and Paul Tiyambe Zeleza, eds. *The Resolution of African Conflicts: The Management of Conflict Resolution and Post-conflict Reconstruction*. Oxford: James Currey, 2008.

Nhema, Alfred and Paul Tiyambe Zeleza, eds. *The Roots of African Conflicts: The Causes and Costs*. Oxford: James Currey, 2008.

Nicholl, Charles. *Somebody Else: Arthur Rimbaud in Africa, 1880–1891*. London: Vintage, 1998.

Norbrook, Nicholas and Marshall Van Halen. 'Africa's Emerging Partners: Friend or Foe?' *The Africa Report*, June 2011.

Norman, Neil L. 'Hueda (Whydah) Country and Town: Archaeological Perspectives on the Rise and Collapse of an African Atlantic Kingdom'. *International Journal of African Historical Studies* 42, no. 3 (2009): 387–410.

Norris, Robert. *Memoirs of the Reign of Bossa Ahadee, King of Dahomy*. London: W. Lowndes, 1789.

Northrup, David. *Africa's Discovery of Europe, 1450–1850*. Oxford: Oxford University Press, 2002.

Northrup, David. *Trade without Rulers: Precolonial Economic Development in South-Eastern Nigeria*. Oxford: Clarendon Press, 1978.

Nunn, Nathan. 'Historical Legacies: A Model Linking Africa's Past to its Current Underdevelopment'. *Journal of Development Economics* 83, no. 1 (2007): 157–75.

Nunn, Nathan. 'The Long-Term Effects of Africa's Slave Trades'. *Quarterly Journal of Economics* 123, no. 1 (2008): 139–76.

Nurse, Derek and Gerard Philippson, eds. *The Bantu Languages*. New York: Routledge, 2003.

Nurse, Derek and Thomas Spear. *The Swahili: Reconstructing the History and Language of an African Society, 800–1500*. Philadelphia: University of Pennsylvania Press, 1985.

Nxasana, Thulani. 'The Journey of the African as Missionary: The Journal and Selected Writings of the Reverend Tiyo Soga'. *English in Africa* 38, no. 2 (2011): 61–76.

Nyakatura, John. *Anatomy of an African Kingdom: A History of Bunyoro-Kitara*, edited by G. N. Uzoigwe. Garden City, NY: Anchor Press/Doubleday, 1973.

Nyerere, Julius K. '*Ujamaa': The Basis of African Socialism*. Dar es Salaam: Tanganyika Standard, 1962.

'OAU Charter'. Available at https://au.int/sites/default/files/treaties/7759-file-oau_charter_1963.pdf (accessed 15 March 2024).

Oboler, Regina Smith. *Women, Power, and Economic Change: The Nandi of Kenya*. Stanford, CA: Stanford University Press, 1985.

Ochonu, Moses. *Colonialism by Proxy: Hausa Imperial Agents and Middle Belt Consciousness in Nigeria*. Bloomington, IN: Indiana University Press, 2014.

O'Fahey, R. S. *The Darfur Sultanate: A History*. London: Hurst, 2008.

Ofonagoro, Walter I. 'Commercial Revolution in Southern Nigeria'. *Journal of Modern African Studies* 15, no. 1 (1977): 169–74.

Ofonagoro, Walter I. 'Notes on the Ancestry of Mbanaso Okwaraozurumba, Otherwise Known as King Jaja of Opobo, 1821–1891'. *Journal of the Historical Society of Nigeria* 9, no. 3 (1978): 145–56.

Ogundiran, Akinwumi. 'Material Life and Domestic Economy in a Frontier of the Oyo Empire during the Mid-Atlantic Age'. *International Journal of African Historical Studies* 42, no. 3 (2009): 351–85.

Ogutu, M. A. 'The Cultivation of Coffee among the Chagga of Tanzania, 1919–1939', *Agricultural History* 46, no. 2 (1972): 279–90.

Okoye, Felix N. C. 'Dingane: A Reappraisal'. *Journal of African History* 10, no. 2 (1969): 221–35.

Okpewho, Isidore. 'African Oral Epics'. In *The Cambridge History of African and Caribbean Literature, Volume 1*, edited by F. Abiola Irele and Simon Gikandi, 98–116. Cambridge: Cambridge University Press, 2004.

Okpewho, Isidore. *The Epic in Africa: Toward a Petics of the Oral Performance*. New York: Columbia University Press, 1979.

Oldfield, J. R. *Popular Politics and British Anti-Slavery: The Mobilization of Public Opinion against the Slave Trade, 1783–1807*. Manchester: Manchester University Press, 1995.

Oliver, Roland. 'Discernible Developments in the Interior, c. 1500–1840', in *History of East Africa, Volume 1*, edited by Roland Oliver and Gervase Mathew, 169–211. Oxford: Clarendon Press, 1963.

Oliver, Roland. *In the Realms of Gold: Pioneering in African History*. Madison, WI: University of Wisconsin Press, 1997.

Oliver, Roland. *The Missionary Factor in East Africa*. London: Longman, 1965.

Oliver, Roland. *Sir Harry Johnston and the Scramble for Africa*. London: Chatto & Windus, 1957.

Oliver, Roland and Anthony Atmore. *Africa since 1800*. Cambridge: Cambridge University Press, 2005 [1967].

Oliver, Roland and G. N. Sanderson, eds. *The Cambridge History of Africa, Volume 6: 1870–1905*. Cambridge: Cambridge University Press, 1985.

Olivier de Sardan, Jean-Pierre. 'The Songhay-Zarma Female Slave: Relations of Production and Ideological Status'. In *Women and Slavery in Africa*, edited by Claire Robertson and Martin A. Klein, 130–43. Madison, WI: University of Wisconsin Press, 1983.

Olusoga, David and Casper W. Erichsen. *The Kaiser's Holocaust: Germany's Forgotten Genocide and the Colonial Roots of Nazism*. London: Faber & Faber, 2010.

Omara-Otunnu, Amii *Politics and the Military in Uganda, 1890–1985*. Basingstoke: Macmillan, 1987.

Omer-Cooper, J. D. *History of Southern Africa*. London: James Currey/Heinemann, 1987.

Omer-Cooper, J. D. *The Zulu Aftermath: A Nineteenth-Century Revolution in Bantu Africa*. London: Longmans, 1966.

Omosini, Olufemi. 'Carl Christian Reindorf: His Contributions to and Place in the Development of Modern West African Historiography'. *Journal of the Historical Society of Nigeria* 10, no. 2 (1980): 71–86.

Orlowska, Izabela. 'Forging a Nation: The Ethiopian Millennium Celebration and the Multi-Ethnic State'. *Nations and Nationalism* 19, no. 2 (2013): 296–316.

Orlowska, Izabela. 'Re-imagining Empire: Ethiopian Political Culture under Yohannis IV (1872–89)'. PhD thesis, University of London, 2006.

Osborne, Myles. *Ethnicity and Empire in Kenya: Loyalty and Martial Race Among the Kamba, c.1800 to the Present*. Cambridge: Cambridge University Press, 2014.

Osborne, Myles, ed. *Making Martial Races: Gender, Society, and Warfare in Africa*. Athens, OH: Ohio University Press, 2024.

Osterhammel, Jurgen. *The Transformation of the World: A Global History of the Nineteenth Century*. Princeton, NJ: Princeton University Press, 2014.

Otele, Olivette. *African Europeans: An Untold Story*. London: Hurst, 2020.

Ouologuem, Yambo. *Bound to Violence*, translated by Ralph Manheim. London: Heinemann, 1971 [Fr. 1968].

Pachai, Bridglal, ed. *Livingstone, Man of Africa: Memorial Essays, 1873–1973*. London: Longman, 1973.

Paice, Edward. *Tip and Run: The Untold Tragedy of the Great War in Africa*. London: Phoenix, 2008.

Pakenham, Thomas. *The Boer War*. London: Weidenfeld & Nicolson, 1979.

Pakenham, Thomas. *The Scramble for Africa, 1876–1912*. London: Weidenfeld & Nicolson, 1991.

Pallaver, Karin. 'A Triangle: Spatial Processes of Urbanization and Political Power in 19th-Century Tabora, Tanzania'. *Afriques: débats, méthodes et terrains d'histoire* 11 (2020): 1–28.

Pallinder-Law, Agneta. 'Aborted Modernization in West Africa? The Case of Abeokuta'. *Journal of African History* 15, no. 1 (1974): 65–82.

Palmer, Robin H. *Land and Racial Domination in Rhodesia*. London: Heinemann, 1977.

Palmer, Robin H. 'War and Land in Rhodesia in the 1890s'. In *War and Society in Africa*, edited by Bethwell A. Ogot, 85–107. London: Frank Cass, 1972.

Pankhurst, Richard. *Economic History of Ethiopia, 1800–1935*. Addis Ababa: Haile Sellassie I University Press, 1968.

Pankhurst, Richard, ed. *The Ethiopian Royal Chronicles*. Addis Ababa: Oxford University Press, 1967.

Pankhurst, Richard and Douglas Johnson. 'The Great Drought and Famine of 1888–92 in Northeast Africa'. In *The Ecology of Survival: Case Studies from Northeast African History*, edited by Douglas Johnson and David Anderson, 47–70. London: Lester Crook, 1988.

'Papers on Firearms in Sub-Saharan Africa, 1'. Special feature, *Journal of African History* 12, no. 2 (1971): 172ff.

'Papers on Firearms in Sub-Saharan Africa, 2'. Special feature, *Journal of African History* 12, no. 4 (1971): 517ff.

Park, Mungo. *Travels in the Interior Districts of Africa*. London: W. Bulmer & Co., 1799.

Parker, Geoffrey. 'Introduction: The Western Way of War'. In *The Cambridge History of Warfare*, edited by Geoffrey Parker, 1–11. Cambridge: Cambridge University Press, 2005.

Parker, John and Richard Reid, eds. *The Oxford Handbook of Modern African History*. Oxford: Oxford University Press, 2013.

Parkyns, Mansfield. *Life in Abyssinia: Being Notes Collected During Three Years' Residence and Travels in that Country*. London: Frank Cass, 1966 [1853].

Parsons, Timothy H. *The African Rank-and-File: Social Implications of Colonial Military Service in the King's African Rifles, 1902–1964*. Portsmouth, NH: Heinemann, 1999.

Paxman, Jeremy. *The Victorians: Britain through the Paintings of the Age*. London: BBC, 2009.

p'Bitek, Okot. *Song of Lawino; Song of Ocol*. Johannesburg: Heinemann, 1984 [1966; 1967].

Pearson, Scott R. 'The Economic Imperialism of the Royal Niger Company'. *Food Research Institute Studies* 10 (1971): 69–88.

Peel, J.D.Y. 'Conversion and Tradition in Two African Societies: Ijebu and Buganda'. *Past and Present* 77, no. 1 (1977): 108–41.

Peel, J.D.Y. *Religious Encounter and the Making of the Yoruba*. Bloomington, IN: Indiana University Press, 2000.

Peires, Jeff B. 'The Central Beliefs of the Xhosa Cattle-Killing'. *Journal of African History* 28, no. 1 (1987): 43–63.

Peires, Jeff B. *The Dead Will Arise: Nongqawuse and the Great Xhosa Cattle-Killing Movement of 1856–57*. Johannesburg and London: Ravan Press/James Currey, 1989.

Pennec, Hervé and Dimitri Toubkis. 'Reflections on the Notions of "Empire" and "Kingdom" in Seventeenth-Century Ethiopia: Royal Power and Local Power'. *Journal of Early Modern History* 8, nos 3–4 (2004): 229–58.

Pennell, C. R. *A Country with a Government and a Flag: The Rif War in Morocco, 1921–1926*. Boulder, CO: Outwell, Wisbech, 1986.

Pennell, C. R. 'Ideology and Practical Politics: A Case Study of the Rif War in Morocco, 1921–1926'. *International Journal of Middle East Studies* 14, no. 1 (1982): 19–33.

Pennell, C. R. *Morocco since 1830: A History*. London: Hurst, 2000.

Perham, Margery. *Lugard: The Years of Adventure, 1858–1898; A Maker of Modern Africa*. London: Collins, 1956.

Perkins, Kenneth J. *A History of Modern Tunisia*. Cambridge: Cambridge University Press, 2014 [2005].

Perkins, Kenneth J. *Qaids, Captains, and Colons: French Military Administration in the Colonial Maghrib, 1844–1934*. New York: Africana Publishing Co., 1981.

Perras, Arne. *Carl Peters and German Imperialism, 1856–1918: A Political Bography.* Oxford: Clarendon Press, 2004.

Perraudin, Michael and Jürgen Zimmerer, eds. *German Colonialism and National Identity.* New York: Routledge, 2011.

Person, Yves. 'Samori and Resistance to the French'. In *Protest and Power in Black Africa*, edited by Robert I. Rotberg and Ali A. Mazrui, 80–112. New York: Oxford University Press, 1970.

Person, Yves. *Samori, une révolution Dyula*, 3 vols. Dakar: IFAN, 1968–75.

Person, Yves. 'Western Africa, 1870–1886'. In *The Cambridge History of Africa, Volume 6: 1870–1905*, edited by Roland Oliver and G. N. Sanderson, 208–256. Cambridge: Cambridge University Press, 1985.

Peters, Carl. *New Light on Dark Africa: Being the Narrative of the German Emin Pash Expedition, [...]*, translated by H. W. Dulcken. London: Ward, Lock & Co., 1891 [Ger. 1891].

Peterson, Brian J. 'History, Memory and the Legacy of Samori in Southern Mali, c. 1880–1898'. *Journal of African History* 49, no. 2 (2008): 261–79.

Peterson, Derek R. and Giacomo Macola, eds. *Recasting the Past: History Writing and Political Work in Modern Africa.* Athens, OH: Ohio University Press, 2009.

Petringa, Maria. *Brazza, a Life for Africa.* Bloomington, IN: AuthorHouse, 2006.

Phimister, Ian. *An Economic and Social History of Zimbabwe, 1890–1948: Capital Accumulation and Class Struggle.* London: Longman, 1987.

Phiri, Kings M. 'Political Change among the Chewa and Yao of the Lake Malawi Region, c. 1750–1900'. In *State Formation in Eastern Africa*, edited by Ahmed Idha Salim, 53–69. Nairobi: Heinemann, 1984.

Pinker, Steven. *The Better Angels of Our Nature: A History of Violence and Humanity.* London: Penguin, 2011.

Pinkney, Robert. *NGOs, Africa and the Global Order.* Basingstoke: Palgrave Macmillan, 2009.

Plowden, Walter Chichele. *Travels in Abyssinia and the Galla Country*, edited by Trevor Chichele Plowden. London: Longmans, Green, 1868.

Plumb, J. H. *The Death of the Past.* London: Pelican, 1973.

Pollock, John. *Gordon: The Man behind the Legend.* London: Constable, 1993.

Pomeranz, Kenneth. *The Great Divergence: China, Europe, and the Making of the Modern World Economy.* Princeton, NJ: Princeton University Press, 2000.

Porch, Douglas. *Wars of Empire.* London: Cassell, 2000.

Portal, Gerald. *My Mission to Abyssinia.* London: Edward Arnold, 1892.

Porter, Andrew. 'Religion, Missionary Enthusiasm, and Empire'. In *The Oxford History of the British Empire, Volume 3: The Nineteenth Century*, edited by Andrew Porter, 222–46. Oxford: Oxford University Press, 1999.

Porter, Andrew. *Religion versus Empire: British Protestant Missionaries and Overseas Expansion, 1700–1914.* Manchester: Manchester University Press, 2004.

Porter, Bernard. *The Absent-Minded Imperialists: What the British Really Thought about Empire.* Oxford: Oxford University Press, 2004.

Porter, Bernard. *Critics of Empire: British Radicals and the Imperial Challenge.* London: I. B. Tauris, 2008.

Porter, Bernard. *The Lion's Share: A Short History of British Imperialism, 1850–2004.* London: Longman, 2004 [1976].

Porter, Roy. *Enlightenment: Britain and the Creation of the Modern World.* London: Penguin, 2001.

'President Jonathan's Centenary Address to the Nation'. *Nigeria Bulletin*, 27 February 2014.

Press, Steven. *Rogue Empires: Contracts and Conmen in Europe's Scramble for Africa.* Cambridge, MA: Harvard University Press, 2017.

Prestholdt, Jeremy. *Domesticating the World: African Consumerism and the Genealogies of Globalization.* Berkeley, CA: University of California Press, 2008.

Prestholdt, Jeremy. 'Politics of the Soil: Separatism, Autochthony, and Decolonisation at the Kenyan Coast'. *Journal of African History* 55, no. 2 (2014): 249–70.

Price, Richard. *Making Empire: Colonial Encounters and the Creation of Imperial Rule in Nineteenth-Century Africa.* Cambridge: Cambridge University Press, 2008.

Prince, Tom von. *Gegen Araber und Wahehe.* Berlin: Ernst Siegfried Mittler und Sohn, 1914.

'Print Cultures, Nationalisms and Publics in the Indian Ocean'. Special issue, *Africa* 81, no. 1 (2011).

Prouty, Chris. *Empress Taytu and Menilek II: Ethiopia 1883–1910.* Trenton, NJ: Red Sea Press, 1986.

Prunier, Gérard. *The Rwanda Crisis: History of a Genocide.* London: Hurst, 1995.

Quinney, Valerie. 'Decisions on Slavery, the Slave Trade, and Civil Rights for Negroes in the Early French Revolution'. *Journal of Negro History* 55, no. 2 (1970): 117–30.

Ramani, Samuel. *Russia in Africa: Resurgent Great Power or Bellicose Pretender?* London: Hurst, 2023.

Ranger, Terence O. 'Connexions between "Primary Resistance" Movements and Modern Mass Nationalism in East and Central Africa, Part 1'. *Journal of African History* 9, no. 3 (1968): 437–53.

Ranger, Terence O. 'Connexions between "Primary Resistance" Movements and Modern Mass Nationalism in East and Central Africa, Part 2'. *Journal of African History* 9, no. 4 (1968): 631–41.

Ranger, Terence O., ed. *Emerging Themes of African History: Proceedings of the International Congress of African Historians, Dar es Salaam, October 1965.* Nairobi: Heinemann, 1968.

Ranger, Terence O. 'The Invention of Tradition in Colonial Africa'. In *The Invention of Tradition*, edited by Eric Hobsbawm and Terence Ranger, 211–62. Cambridge University Press, 1983.

Ranger, Terence O. 'The Invention of Tradition Revisited: The Case of Africa'. In *Legitimacy and the State in Twentieth-Century Africa*, edited by Terence Ranger and Olufemi Vaughan, 62–111. London: Palgrave Macmillan, 1993.

Ranger, Terence O. 'Religious Movements and Politics in Sub-Saharan Africa'. *African Studies Review* 29, no. 2 (1986): 1–69.

Ranger, Terence O. *Revolt in Southern Rhodesia, 1896–97.* London: Heinemann, 1967.

Ranger, Terence O. 'Towards a Usable African Past'. In *African Studies Since 1945: A Tribute to Basil Davidson*, edited by Christopher Fyfe, 17–30. London: Longman, 1976.

Rasmussen, R. Kent. *Migrant Kingdom: Mzilikazi's Ndebele in South Africa.* London and Cape Town: Rex Collings/David Philip, 1978.

Rassam, Hormuzd. *Narrative of the British Mission to Theodore, King of Abyssinia*, 2 vols. London: John Murray, 1869.

Rattray, R. S. *Religion and Art in Ashanti.* London: Clarendon Press, 1927.

Raum, O. F. 'German East Africa: Changes in African Tribal Life under German Administration, 1892–1914'. In *History of East Africa, Volume 2*, edited by Vincent Harlow and E. M. Chilver, 163–207. Oxford: Oxford University Press, 1965.

Redmond, Patrick M. 'Maji Maji in Ungoni: A Reappraisal of Existing Historiography'. *International Journal of African Historical Studies* 8, no. 3 (1975): 407–24.

Reid, John. 'Warrior Aristocrats in Crisis: The Political Effects of the Transition from the Slave Trade to Palm Oil Commerce in the Nineteenth Century Kingdom of Dahomey'. PhD thesis, University of Stirling, 1986.

Reid, Richard. 'Africa's Revolutionary Nineteenth Century and the Idea of the "Scramble"'. *The American Historical Review* 26, no. 4 (2021): 1424–47.

Reid, Richard. 'The Challenge of the Past: The Struggle for Historical Legitimacy in Independent Eritrea'. *History in Africa* 28 (2001): 239–72.

Reid, Richard. 'The Fragile Revolution: Rethinking War and Development in Africa's Violent Nineteenth Century'. In *Africa's Development in Historical Perspective*, edited by Emmanuel Akyeampong, Robert H. Bates, Nathan Nunn and James A. Robinson, 393–423. Cambridge: Cambridge University Press, 2014.

Reid, Richard. *Frontiers of Violence in Northeast Africa: Genealogies of Conflict since c. 1800.* Oxford: Oxford University Press, 2011.

Reid, Richard. 'The Ganda on Lake Victoria: A Nineteenth-Century East African Imperialism'. *Journal of African History* 39, no. 3 (1998): 349–63.

Reid, Richard. 'Ghosts in the Academy: Historians and Historical Consciousness in the Making of Modern Uganda'. *Comparative Studies in Society and History* 56, no. 2 (2014): 351–380.

Reid, Richard. *A History of Modern Africa, 1800 to the Present.* Hoboken, NJ: Wiley, 2020 [2008].

Reid, Richard. *A History of Modern Uganda.* Cambridge: Cambridge University Press, 2017.

Reid, Richard. 'Horror, Hubris and Humanity: The International Engagement with Africa, 1914–2014'. *International Affairs* 90, no. 1 (2014): 143–65

Reid, Richard. 'Human Booty in Buganda: Some Observations on the Seizure of People in War, c. 1700–1890'. In *Slavery in the Great Lakes Region of East Africa*, edited by Henri Médard and Shane Doyle, 145–60. Oxford: James Currey, 2007.

Reid, Richard. 'Mutesa and Mirambo: Thoughts on East African Warfare and Diplomacy in the Nineteenth Century'. *International Journal of African Historical Studies* 31, no. 1 (1998): 73–89.

Reid, Richard. '"None could stand before him in the battle, none ever reigned so wisely as he": The Expansion and Significance of Violence in Early Modern Africa'. In *A Global History of Early Modern Violence*, edited by Erica Charters, Marie Houllemare and Peter H. Wilson, 19–36. Manchester: Manchester University Press, 2020.

Reid, Richard. 'Past and Presentism: The "Precolonial" and the Foreshortening of African History'. *Journal of African History* 52, no. 2 (2011): 135–55.

Reid, Richard. *Political Power in Pre-colonial Buganda: Economy, Society and Warfare in the Nineteenth Century.* Oxford: James Currey, 2002.

Reid, Richard. 'Remembering and Forgetting Mirambo: Histories of War in Modern Africa'. *Small Wars & Insurgencies* 30, nos 4–5 (2019): 1040–69.

Reid, Richard. 'States of Anxiety: History and Nation in Modern Africa'. *Past and Present* 229 (2015): 239–69.

Reid, Richard. 'Time and Distance: Reflections on Local and Global History from East Africa'. *Transactions of the Royal Historical Society* 29 (2019): 253–72.

Reid, Richard. 'Violence and Its Sources: European Witnesses to the Military Revolution in Nineteenth-Century Eastern Africa'. In *The Power of Doubt: Essays in Honor of David Henige*, edited by Paul Landau, 41–59. Madison, WI: Parallel Press, 2011

Reid, Richard. 'War and Militarism in Pre-colonial Buganda'. *Azania* 34 (1999): 45–60.

Reid, Richard. 'Warfare and Urbanisation: The Relationship between Town and Conflict in Pre-colonial Eastern Africa'. In *The Urban Experience in Eastern Africa, c. 1750–2000 (Azania* special volume 36–37), edited by Andrew Burton, 46–62. Nairobi: British Institute in Eastern Africa, 2002.

Reid, Richard. *Warfare in African History.* Cambridge: Cambridge University Press, 2012.

Reid, Richard. *War in Pre-colonial Eastern Africa: The Patterns and Meanings of State-Level Conflict in the Nineteenth Century.* Oxford: James Currey, 2007.

Reid, Richard and Henri Médard. 'Merchants, Missions and the Remaking of the Urban Environment in Buganda, c. 1840–c. 1890'. In *Africa's Urban Past*, edited by David M. Anderson and Richard Rathbone, 98–108. Oxford: James Currey, 2000.

Reindorf, Carl Christian. *The History of the Gold Coast and Asante, Based on Traditions and Historical Facts Comprising a Period of More Than Three Centuries from about 1500 to 1860*. Accra: Ghana Universities Press, 1966 [1895].

Reno, William. *Warfare in Independent Africa*. New York: Cambridge University Press, 2011.

Reno, William. *Warlord Politics and African States*. Boulder, CO: Lynne Rienner, 1999.

*Révolution française et l'abolition de l'esclavage, La*, 12 vols. Paris: Éditions d'histoire sociale, 1968.

Richards, Paul. *Fighting for the Rain Forest: War, Youth and Resources in Sierra Leone*. Portsmouth, NH: Heinemann, 1996.

Richardson, David. *Principles and Agents: The British Slave Trade and Its Abolition*. New Haven, CT: Yale University Press, 2022.

Riebeeck, Jan van. *The Journal of Jan Van Riebeeck*, edited by H. B. Thom, translated by J. Smuts, 3 vols. Cape Town: Van Riebeeck Society, 1952–58.

Rivlin, Helen Anne B. *The Agricultural Policy of Muhammad Ali in Egypt*. Cambridge, MA: Harvard University Press, 1961.

Roberts, Andrew, ed. *The Cambridge History of Africa, Volume 7: 1905–1940*. Cambridge: Cambridge University Press, 1986.

Roberts, Andrew. *The Colonial Moment in Africa: Essays on the Movement of Minds and Materials, 1900–1940*. Cambridge: Cambridge University Press, 1990.

Roberts, Andrew. 'Firearms in North-Eastern Zambia before 1900'. *Transafrican Journal of History* 1, no. 2 (1971): 3–21.

Roberts, Andrew. *A History of the Bemba: Political Growth and Change in North-Eastern Zambia before 1900*. London: Longman, 1973.

Roberts, Andrew. *A History of Zambia*. New York: Africana Publishing Company, 1976.

Roberts, Andrew. 'The Nyamwezi'. In *Tanzania before 1900*, edited by Andrew Roberts, 117–50. Nairobi: East African Publishing House, 1968.

Roberts, Andrew. 'Nyamwezi Trade'. In *Pre-colonial African Trade: Essays on Trade in Central and Eastern Africa before 1900*, edited by Richard Gray and David Birmingham, 39–74. London: Oxford University Press, 1970.

Roberts, Andrew. 'Political Change in the Nineteenth Century'. In *A History of Tanzania*, edited by I. N. Kimambo and A. J. Temu, 57–84. Nairobi: East African Publishing House, 1969.

Roberts, Andrew. 'The Sub-imperialism of the Baganda'. *Journal of African History* 3, no. 3 (1962): 435–50.

Roberts, Andrew, ed. *Tanzania before 1900*. Nairobi: East African Publishing House, 1968.

Roberts, J. M. *The Penguin History of Europe*. London: Penguin, 1997.

Roberts, Richard L. 'Production and Reproduction of Warrior States: Segu Bambara and Segu Tokolor, c. 1712–1890'. *International Journal of African Historical Studies* 13, no. 3 (1980): 389–419.

Roberts, Richard L. *Warriors, Merchants, and Slaves: The State and the Economy in the Middle Niger Valley, 1700–1914*. Stanford, CA: Stanford University Press, 1987.

Roberts, Richard L. 'Women's Work and Women's Property: Household Social Relations in the Maraka Textile Industry of the Nineteenth Century'. *Comparative Studies in Society and History* 26, no. 2 (1984): 229–50.

Roberts, Richard and Suzanne Miers. 'Introduction: The End of Slavery in Africa'. In *The End of Slavery in Africa*, edited by Suzanne Miers and Richard Roberts, 3–68. Madison, WI: University of Wisconsin Press, 1988.

Robertson, Claire. *Trouble Showed the Way: Women, Men, and Trade in the Nairobi Area, 1890–1990*. Bloomington, IN: Indiana University Press, 1997.

Robinson, David. *The Holy War of Umar Tal*. Oxford: Clarendon Press, 1985.

Robinson, David. 'The Islamic Revolution of Futa Toro'. *International Journal of African Historical Studies* 8, no. 2 (1975): 185–221.

Robinson, David. *Muslim Societies in African History*. Cambridge: Cambridge University Press, 2004.

Robinson, Ronald. 'Non-European Foundations of European Imperialism: Sketch for a Theory of Collaboration'. In *Studies in the Theory of Imperialism*, edited by Roger Owen and Bob Sutcliffe, 117–42. London: Longman, 1972.

Robinson, Ronald and John Gallagher. *Africa and the Victorians: The Official Mind of Imperialism*. London: Macmillan, 1981 [1961].

Rockel, Stephen. *Carriers of Culture: Labor on the Road in Nineteenth-Century East Africa*. Portsmouth, NH: Heinemann, 2006.

Rodney, Walter. *How Europe Underdeveloped Africa*. London: Bogle-L'Ouverture Publications, 1972.

Ross, Robert. 'Khoesan and Immigrants: The Emergence of Colonial Society in the Cape, 1500–1800'. In *The Cambridge History of South Africa, Volume 1: From Early Times to 1885*, edited by Carolyn Hamilton, Bernard K. Mbenga and Robert Ross, 168–210. Cambridge: Cambridge University Press, 2010.

Rotberg, Robert I. *Africa and Its Explorers: Motives, Methods, and Impact*. Cambridge, MA: Harvard University Press, 1970.

Rotberg, Robert I., ed. *China into Africa: Trade, Aid and Influence*. Washington, DC: Brookings Institution Press, 2008.

Rousseau, Jean-Jacques. *Discourse on the Origin of Inequality*, translated by Elizabeth S. Haldane and edited by Greg Boroson. New York: Dover, 2004 [Fr. 1754].

Rowe, John. 'Myth, Memoir and Moral Admonition: Luganda Historical Writing, 1893–1969'. *Uganda Journal* 33, no. 1 (1969): 17–40; with an addendum in *Uganda Journal* 34, no. 1 (1970): 217–19.

Rowe, John. 'The Purge of Christians at Mwanga's Court'. *Journal of African History* 5, no. 1 (1964): 55–72.

Rubenson, Sven, ed. *Acta Aethiopica, Volume 2: Tewodros and His Contemporaries, 1855–1868*. Addis Ababa: Addis Ababa University Press/Lund University Press, 1994.

Rubenson, Sven. 'Adwa 1896: The Resounding Protest'. In *Protest and Power in Black Africa*, edited by Robert I. Rotberg and Ali A. Mazrui, 113–44. New York: Oxford University Press, 1970.

Rubenson, Sven. 'Ethiopia and the Horn'. In *The Cambridge History of Africa, Volume 5: c. 1790–c. 1870*, edited by J. E. Flint, 51–98. Cambridge: Cambridge University Press, 1976.

Rubenson, Sven. *King of Kings: Tewodros of Ethiopia*. Addis Ababa: Oxford University Press, 1966.

Rubenson, Sven. *The Survival of Ethiopian Independence*. London: Heinemann, 1976.

Ruedy, John *Modern Algeria: The Origins and Development of a Nation*. Bloomington, IN: Indiana University Press, 1992.

Ryzova, Lucie. *The Age of the Efendiyya: Passages to Modernity in National-Colonial Egypt*. Oxford: Oxford University Press, 2014.

Said, Edward W. *Orientalism*. London: Penguin, 2003 [1978].

Samson, Jane. *Race and Empire*. Harlow: Pearson Longman, 2005.

Samuel, Raphael. *Theatres of Memory: Past and Present in Contemporary Culture*. London: Verso, 2012 [1994].

Sanders, Peter. *Moshoeshoe: Chief of the Sotho*. London: Heinemann, 1975.

Sanderson, G. N. *England, Europe, and the Upper Nile, 1882–1899: A Study of the Partition of Africa*. Edinburgh: Edinburgh University Press, 1965.

Sanneh, Lamin. 'The CMS and the African Transformation: Samuel Ajayi Crowther and the Opening of Nigeria'. In *The Church Missionary Society and World Christianity, 1799–1999*, edited by Kevin Ward and Brian Stanley, 173–97. Grand Rapids, MI: William B. Eerdmans Publishing Co., 2000.

Sattin, Anthony. *The Gates of Africa: Death, Discovery and the Search for Timbuktu*. London: HarperCollins, 2003.

Saul, S. B. *The Myth of the Great Depression, 1873–1896*. London: Macmillan, 1969.

Schama, Simon. *Landscape and Memory*. London: Fontana Press, 1995.

Schiller, L. 'The Royal Women of Buganda'. *International Journal of African Historical Studies* 23, no. 3 (1990): 455–73.

Schmidt, Elizabeth. *Peasants, Traders, and Wives: Shona Women in the History of Zimbabwe, 1870–1939*. Portsmouth, NH: Heinemann, 1992.

Schoenbrun, David Lee. *A Green Place, A Good Place: Agrarian Change, Gender, and Social Identity in the Great Lakes Region to the 15th Century*. Portsmouth, NH: Heinemann, 1998.

Schoenbrun, David Lee. *The Names of the Python: Belonging in East Africa, 900–1300*. Madison, WI: University of Wisconsin Press, 2021.

Schölch, Alexander. 'The "Men on the Spot" and the English Occupation of Egypt in 1882'. *The Historical Journal* 19, no. 3 (1976): 773–85.

Schwarz, Suzanne. 'Reconstructing the Life Histories of Liberated Africans: Sierra Leone in the Early Nineteenth Century'. *History in Africa* 39 (2012): 175–207.

Schwarz, Suzanne and Paul E. Lovejoy, eds. *Slavery, Abolition and the Transition to Colonialism in Sierra Leone*. Trenton, NJ: Africa World Press, 2015.

Schweitzer, G. *Emin Pasha: His Life and Work*, 2 vols. London: Constable, 1898.

Searing, James F. 'Aristocrats, Slaves and Peasants: Power and Dependency in the Wolof States, 1700–1850'. *International Journal of African Historical Studies* 21, no. 3 (1988): 475–503.

Sèbe, Berny. 'From Post-colonialism to Cosmopolitan Nation-Building? British and French Imperial Heroes in Twenty-First-Century Africa'. *Journal of Imperial and Commonwealth History* 42, no. 5 (2014): 936–68.

Sèbe, Berny. *Heroic Imperialists in Africa: The Promotion of British and French Colonial Heroes, 1870–1939*. Manchester: Manchester University Press, 2013.

Seligman, C. G. *The Races of Africa*. London: Thornton Butterworth, 1930.

Selous, Frederick Courtenay. *Sunshine and Storm in Rhodesia*. London: Rowland Ward, 1896.

Shadle, Brett. *The Souls of White Folk: White Settlers in Kenya, 1900s–1920s*. Manchester: Manchester University Press, 2015.

Sharman, J. C. 'Myths of Military Revolution: European Expansionism and Eurocentrism'. *European Journal of International Relations* 24, no. 3 (2018): 491–513.

Shepperson, George. 'Introduction' to James Africanus Beale Horton, *West African Countries and Peoples* (repr.). Edinburgh: Edinburgh University Press, 1969.

Shepperson, George and Thomas Price. *Independent African: John Chilembwe and the Nyasaland Native Rising*. Edinburgh: Edinburgh University Press, 1958.

Sheriff, Abdul. *Slaves, Spices and Ivory in Zanzibar: Integration of an East African Commercial Empire into the World Economy, 1770–1873*. London: James Currey, 1987.

Shorter, Aylward. *Chiefship in Western Tanzania: A Political History of the Kimbu*. Oxford: Clarendon Press, 1972.

Shorter, Aylward. 'The Kimbu'. In *Tanzania before 1900*, edited by Andrew Roberts, 96–116. Nairobi: East African Publishing House, 1968.

Shorter, Aylward. 'Nyungu-ya-Mawe and the Empire of the Ruga-Ruga'. *Journal of African History* 9, no. 2 (1968): 235–59.

Shorter, Aylward. *Nyungu-ya-Mawe: Leadership in Nineteenth-Century Tanzania*. Nairobi: East African Publishing House, 1969.

Simo, David. 'Writing World History in Africa: Opportunities, Constraints and Challenges'. In *Global History, Globally: Research and Practice Around the World*, edited by Sven Beckert and Dominic Sachsenmaier, 235–50. London: Bloomsbury, 2018.

Skertchly, J. Alfred. *Dahomey As It Is*. London: Chapman & Hall, 1874.

Slade, Ruth. *King Leopold's Congo*. London: Oxford University Press, 1962.

Smaldone, Joseph P. *Warfare in the Sokoto Caliphate: Historical and Sociological Perspectives*. Cambridge: Cambridge University Press, 1977.

Smith, Adam. *An Inquiry into the Nature and Causes of the Wealth of Nations*. Edinburgh: Thomas Nelson, 1840 [1776].

Smith, Alison. 'The Southern Section of the Interior, 1840–1884'. In *History of East Africa, Volume 1*, edited by Roland Oliver and Gervase Mathew, 253–96. Oxford: Clarendon Press, 1963.

Smith, Anthony D. *The Ethnic Origins of Nations*. Malden, MA: Blackwell, 1986.

Smith, Anthony D. *Myths and Memories of the Nation*. Oxford: Oxford University Press, 1999.

Smith, Iain R. 'New Lessons in South Africa's History'. *History Today*, July 1993.

Smith, James Wesley. *Sojourners in Search of Freedom: The Settlement of Liberia by Black Americans*. Lanham, MD: University Press of America, 1987.

Smith, Robert S. *Kingdoms of the Yoruba*. Madison, WI: University of Wisconsin Press, 1988 [1969].

Smith, Robert S. *Warfare and Diplomacy in Pre-colonial West Africa*. London: James Currey, 1989 [1976].

Smith, W.H.C. *Second Empire and Commune: France 1848–1871*. London: Longman, 1985.

Snelgrave, William. *A New Account of Some Parts of Guinea and the Slave Trade*. London: James, John & Paul Knapton, 1734.

Snook, Mike. *How Can Man Die Better: The Secrets of Isandlwana Revealed*. London: Greenhill Books, 2005.

Snook, Mike. *Like Wolves on the Fold: The Defence of Rorke's Drift*. London: Greenhill Books, 2006.

Sorenson, John. *Imagining Ethiopia: Struggles for History and Identity in the Horn of Africa*. New Brunswick, NJ: Rutgers University Press, 1993.

Soumonni, Elisée. 'The Compatibility of the Slave and Palm Oil Trades in Dahomey, 1818–1858'. In *From Slave Trade to 'Legitimate' Commerce: Commercial Transition in Nineteenth-Century West Africa*, edited by Robin Law, 78–92. Cambridge: Cambridge University Press, 1995.

Southwold, Martin. 'Succession to the Throne in Buganda'. In *Succession to High Office*, edited by Jack Goody, 82–126. Cambridge: Cambridge University Press, 1966.

Spear, Thomas. 'Introduction'. In *Being Maasai: Ethnicity and Identity in East Africa*, edited by Thomas Spear and Richard Waller, 1–18. Oxford: James Currey, 1993.

Spear, Thomas. 'Neo-traditionalism and the Limits of Invention in British Colonial Africa'. *Journal of African History* 44, no. 1 (2003): 3–27.

Spear, Thomas and Richard Waller, eds. *Being Maasai: Ethnicity and Identity in East Africa*. Oxford: James Currey, 1993.

Speke, John Hanning. *Journal of the Discovery of the Source of the Nile*. Edinburgh: William Blackwood & Sons, 1863.

Speke, John Hanning. *What Led to the Discovery of the Source of the Nile*. Edinburgh: William Blackwood & Sons, 1864.

Sperling, David C., with additional material by Jose H. Kagabo. 'The Coastal Hinterland and Interior of East Africa'. In *The History of Islam in Africa*, edited by Nehemia Levtzion and Randall L. Pouwels, 273–302. Athens, OH: Ohio University Press, 2000.

Spickard, Paul, ed. *Race and Nation: Ethnic Systems in the Modern World*. New York: Routledge, 2005.

Spiers, Edward M. 'Reconquest of the Sudan, 1896–1898'. In *Queen Victoria's Wars: British Military Campaigns, 1857–1902*, edited by Stephen M. Miller, 260–80. Cambridge: Cambridge University Press, 2021.

Stafford, Robert A. 'Scientific Exploration and Empire'. In *The Oxford History of the British Empire, Volume 3: The Nineteenth Century*, edited by Andrew Porter, 294–319. Oxford: Oxford University Press, 1999.

Stafford, Robert A. *Scientist of Empire: Sir Roderick Murchison, Scientific Exploration and Victorian Imperialism*. Cambridge: Cambridge University Press, 1989.

Stanley, Brian. *The Bible and the Flag: Protestant Missions and British Imperialism in the Nineteenth and Twentieth Centuries*. Leicester: Apollos, 1990.

Stanley, Henry Morton. *The Autobiography of Henry Morton Stanley*, edited by Dorothy Stanley. London: Sampson Low, Marston, 1909.

Stanley, Henry Morton. *The Congo and the Founding of Its Free State*, 2 vols. London: Sampson Low, Marston, Searle & Rivington, 1885.

Stanley, Henry Morton. *Coomassie and Magdala: The Story of Two British Campaigns in Africa*. New York: Harper & Brothers, 1874.

Stanley, Henry Morton. *How I Found Livingstone*. London: Sampson Low, Marston, Low & Searle, 1872.

Stanley, Henry Morton. *In Darkest Africa*, 2 vols. London: Sampson Low, Marston, Searle & Rivington, 1890.

Stanley, Henry Morton. *Through the Dark Continent*, 2 vols. London: George Newnes, 1899 [1878].

Staudenras, P. J. *The African Colonization Movement 1816–1865*. New York: Columbia University Press, 1961.

Steinhart, Edward I. *Conflict and Collaboration: The Kingdoms of Western Uganda, 1890–1907*. Princeton, NJ: Princeton University Press, 1977.

Steinhart, Edward. I. 'The Emergence of Bunyoro: The Tributary Mode of Productionand the Formation of the State, 1400–1900'. In *State Formation in Eastern Africa*, edited by Ahmed Idha Salim, 70–90. Nairobi: Heinemann, 1984.

Stephens, Rhiannon. *A History of African Motherhood: The Case of Uganda, 700–1900*. Cambridge: Cambridge University Press, 2013.

Stern, Henry. *Wanderings among the Falashas in Abyssinia*. London: Cass, 1968 [1862].

St. John, Christopher. 'Kazembe and the Tanganyika-Nyasa Corridor, 1800–1890', including 'A Note by Dr Aylward Shorter'. In *Pre-colonial African Trade: Essays on Trade in Central and Eastern Africa before 1900*, edited by Richard Gray and David Birmingham, 202–30. London: Oxford University Press, 1970.,

Stocking, George W. *Victorian Anthropology*. New York: The Free Press, 1987.

Stora, Benjamin. 'The "Southern" World of the *Pieds Noirs*: References to and Representations of Europeans in Colonial Algeria'. In *Settler Colonialism in the Twentieth Century: Projects, Practices, Lgacies*, edited by Caroline Elkins and Susan Pedersen, 225–41. New York: Routledge, 2005.

Strachan, Hew. *European Armies and the Conduct of War*. London: Allen & Unwin, 1983.

Strachey, Lytton. *Eminent Victorians*. Oxford: Oxford University Press, 2003 [1918].

Streets, Heather. *Martial Races: The Military, Race and Masculinity in British Imperial Culture, 1857–1914*. Manchester: Manchester University Press, 2004.

Strickrodt, Silke. *Afro-European Trade in the Atlantic World: The Western Slave Coast, c. 1550–c. 1885*. Woodbridge: James Currey, 2015.

Sullivan, Antony T. *Thomas-Robert Bugeaud, France and Algeria, 1784–1849: Politics, Power and the Good Society*. Hamden, CT: Archon Books, 1983.

Sunseri, Thaddeus. 'Reinterpreting a Colonial Rebellion: Forestry and Social Control in German East Africa, 1874–1915'. *Environmental History* 8, no. 3 (2003): 430–51.

Suret-Canale, Jean. *French Colonialism in Tropical Africa, 1900–1945*, translated by Till Gottheiner. London: C. Hurst, 1971 [Fr. 1964].

Sweet, James H. 'The Iberian Roots of American Racist Thought'. *William and Mary Quarterly* 54, no. 1 (1997): 143–66.

Sweet, James H. *Recreating Africa: Culture, Kinship, and Religion in the African-Portuguese World, 1441–1770*. Chapel Hill, NC: University of North Carolina Press, 2003.

Táíwò, Olúfẹ́mi. *Against Decolonisation: Taking African Agency Seriously*. London: Hurst, 2022.

Táíwò, Olúfẹ́mi. *How Colonialism Preempted Modernity in Africa*. Bloomington, IN: Indiana University Press, 2010.

Tallie, T. J. *Queering Colonial Natal: Indigeneity and the Violence of Belonging in Southern Africa*. Minneapolis: University of Minnesota Press, 2019.

Tamirat, Jibat and Cecilia Macaulay. 'Ethiopia's Prince Alemayeju: Buckingham Palace Rejects Calls to Return Royal's Body'. BBC News, 22 May 2023. Available at https://www.bbc.co.uk/news/world-africa-65588663 (accessed 15 March 2024).

Taylor, A.J.P. *Germany's First Bid for Colonies, 1884–1885: A Move in Bismarck's European Policy*. London: Macmillan & Co., 1938.

Taylor, A.J.P. *The Struggle for Mastery in Europe, 1848–1918*. Oxford: Clarendon Press, 1954.

Taylor, Ian. *Africa Rising? BRICS—Diversifying Dependency*. Woodbridge: James Currey, 2014.

Taylor, Ian. *China and Africa: Engagement and Compromise*. London: Routledge, 2006.

Taylor, Ian. 'India's Rise in Africa'. *International Affairs* 88, no. 4 (2012): 779–98.

Thomas, Edward. *South Sudan: A Slow Liberation*. London: Zed Books, 2015.

Thompson, Andrew. *The Empire Strikes Back? The Impact of Imperialism on Britain from the Mid-nineteenth Century*. London: Longman, 2005.

Thompson, Andrew and Gary Magee. *Empire and Globalisation: Networks of People, Goods and Capital in the British World, c. 1850–1914*. Cambridge: Cambridge University Press, 2010.

Thompson, Leonard M. *Survival in Two Worlds: Moshoeshoe of Lesotho, 1786–1870*. Oxford: Clarendon Press, 1975.

Thornton, John K. *Africa and Africans in the Making of the Atlantic World, 1400–1800*. Cambridge: Cambridge University Press, 1998.

Thornton, John K. 'Afro-Christian Syncretism in the Kingdom of Kongo'. *Journal of African History*, 54, no. 1 (2013): 53–77.

Thornton, John K. 'The Development of an African Catholic Church in the Kingdom of the Kongo, 1491–1750'. *Journal of African History* 25, no. 2 (1984): 147–67.

Thornton, John K. 'European Documents and African History'. In *Writing African History*, edited by John Edward Philips, 254–65. Rochester, NY: University of Rochester Press, 2005.

Thornton, John K. *A History of West Central Africa to 1850*. Cambridge: Cambridge University Press, 2020.

Thornton, John K. *The Kingdom of Kongo: Civil War and Transition, 1641–1718*. Madison, WI: University of Wisconsin Press, 1983.

Thornton, John K. *Warfare in Atlantic Africa, 1500–1800*. London: UCL Press, 1999.

Tibenderana, P. K. 'The Role of the British Administration in the Appointment of the Emirs of Northern Nigeria, 1903–1931: The Case of Sokoto Province'. *Journal of African History* 28, no. 2 (1987): 231–57.

Tignor, Robert L. *Egypt: A Short History*. Princeton, NJ: Princeton University Press, 2011.

Tilley, Helen with Robert Gordon, eds. *Ordering Africa: Anthropology, European Imperialism, and the Politics of Knowledge*. Manchester: Manchester University Press, 2007.

Tilly, Charles. *Coercion, Capital, and European States, AD 990–1992*. Cambridge, MA: Blackwell, 1992.

Tippu Tip. *Maisha ya Hamed bin Muhammed el Murjebi yaani Tippu Tip*, translated by W. H. Whitely. Nairobi: East African Literature Bureau, 1966.

Tosh, John. 'The Cash Crop Revolution in Tropical Africa: An Agricultural Reappraisal'. *African Affairs* 79 (1980): 79–94.

Touval, Saadia. 'Treaties, Borders and the Partition of Africa'. *Journal of African History* 7, no. 2 (1966): 279–92.

Trapido, Stanley. 'Imperialism, Settler Identities, and Colonial Capitalism: The Hundred-Year Origins of the 1899 South African War'. In *The Cambridge History of South Africa, Volume 2: 1885–1994*, edited by Robert Ross, Anne Kelk Mager and Bill Nasson, 66–101. Cambridge: Cambridge University Press, 2011.

Tseggai, Araya. 'The History of the Eritrean Struggle'. In *The Long Struggle of Eritrea for Independence and Constructive Peace*, edited by Lionel Cliffe and Basil Davidson, 67–84. Trenton, NJ: Red Sea Press, 1988.

Tuck, Michael. 'Syphilis, Sexuality and Social Control: A History of Venereal Disease in Colonial Uganda'. PhD dissertation, Northwestern University, 1997.

Tudesco, James Patrick. 'Missionaries and French Imperialism: The Role of Catholic Missionaries in French Colonial Expansion, 1880–1905'. PhD dissertation, University of Connecticut, 1980.

Turner, Frederick Jackson. 'The Significance of the Frontier in American History'. In *Frontier and Section: Selected Essays*, edited by R. A. Billington, 28–36. Englewood Cliffs, NJ: Prentice-Hall, 1961.

Turney-High, Harry Holbert. *Primitive War: Its Practice and Concepts*. Columbia, SC: University of South Carolina Press, 1949.

Turrell, Robert Vicat. *Capital and Labour on the Kimberley Diamond Fields, 1871–1890*. Cambridge: Cambridge University Press, 1987.

Twaddle, Michael. 'The Emergence of Politico-Religious Groupings in Late Nineteenth-Century Buganda'. *Journal of African History* 29, no. 1 (1988): 81–92.

Twaddle, Michael. 'Ganda Receptivity to Change'. *Journal of African History* 15, no. 2 (1974): 303–15.

Twaddle, Michael. 'The Muslim Revolution in Buganda'. *African Affairs* 71, no. 282 (1972): 54–72.

Ullendorff, Edward. *The Ethiopians: An Introduction to Country and People*. London: Oxford University Press, 1973.

Unomah, A. C. and J. B. Webster. 'East Africa: The Expansion of Commerce'. In *The Cambridge History of Africa, Volume 5: c. 1790–c. 1870*, edited by J. E. Flint, 270–318. Cambridge: Cambridge University Press, 1976.

Usuanlele, Uyilawa and Toyin Falola. 'A Comparison of Jacob Eghareva's "Ekhere Vb Itan Edo" and the Four Editions of its English Translation, "A Short History of Benin"'. *History in Africa* 25 (1998): 361–86.

Uzoigwe, Godfrey N. 'Pre-colonial Military Studies in Africa'. *Journal of Modern African Studies* 13, no. 3 (1975): 469–81.

Uzoigwe, Godfrey N. 'Succession and Civil War in Bunyoro-Kitara'. *International Journal of African Historical Studies* 6, no. 1 (1973): 49–71.

Uzoigwe, Godfrey N. 'The Warrior and the State in Pre-colonial Africa: Comparative Perspectives'. In *The Warrior Tradition in Modern Africa*, edited by Ali A. Mazrui, 20–47. Leiden: Brill, 1977.

Vail, Leroy and Landeg White, *Power and the Praise Poem: Southern African Voices in History*. London: James Currey, 1991.

Van Onselen, Charles. *Chibaro: African Mine Labour in Southern Rhodesia, 1900–1933*. London: Pluto Press, 1976.

Van Onselen, Charles. 'Reactions to Rinderpest in Southern Africa, 1896–97'. *Journal of African History* 13, no. 3 (1972): 473–88.

Van Reybrouck, David. *Congo: The Epic History of a People*. London: Fourth Estate, 2015.

Van Sertima, Ivan, ed. *African Presence in Early Europe*. New Brunswick, NJ: Transaction Books, 1985.

Van Sertima, Ivan. *They Came Before Columbus: The African Presence in Ancient America*. New York: Random House, 2003 [1976].

Vandervort, Bruce. *Wars of Imperial Conquest in Africa, 1830–1914*. Bloomington, IN: Indiana University Press, 1998.

Vandervort, Bruce. 'War and Imperial Expansion'. In *The Cambridge History of War, Volume 4: War and the Modern World*, edited by Roger Chickering, Dennis Showalter and Hans van de Ven, 69–93. Cambridge: Cambridge University Press, 2012.

Vandewalle, Dirk. *A History of Modern Libya*. Cambridge: Cambridge University Press, 2014.

Vansina, Jan. *Antecedents to Modern Rwanda: The Nyiginya kingdom*. Madison, WI: University of Wisconsin Press, 2004.

Vansina, Jan. *L'Évolution du Royaume Rwanda des origines à 1900*. Brussels: Académie royale des sciences d'outre-mer, 1962.

Vansina, Jan. *Living with Africa*. Madison, WI: University of Wisconsin Press, 1994.

Vansina, Jan. 'New Linguistic Evidence and "the Bantu Expansion"'. *Journal of African History* 36, no. 2 (1995): 173–95.

Vansina, Jan. *Paths in the Rainforests: Toward a History of Political Tradition in Equatorial Africa*. London: James Currey, 1990.

Vansina, Jan. *The Tio Kingdom of the Middle Congo, 1880–1892*. London: Oxford University Press, 1973.

Vanthemsche, Guy. *Belgium and the Congo, 1885–1980*. Cambridge: Cambridge University Press, 2012.

Vatikiotis, P. J. *The Modern History of Egypt*. London: Weidenfeld & Nicolson, 1969.

Verbeken, Auguste. *Msiri, roi de Garenganze*. Brussels: Louis Cuypers, 1956.

Volz, Stephen. 'Written On Our Hearts: Tswana Christians and the "Word of God" in the Mid-nineteenth Century'. *Journal of Religion in Africa* 38 (2008): 112–40.

Vos, Jelmer. *Kongo in the Age of Empire, 1860–1913: The Breakdown of a Moral Order*. Madison, WI: University of Wisconsin Press, 2015.

Wagner, Kim. 'Savage Warfare: Violence and the Rule of Colonial Difference in Early British Counterinsurgency'. *History Workshop Journal* 85 (2018): 217–37.

Walker, Eric. *The Great Trek*. London: Adam and Charles Black, 1934.

Waller, Horace, ed. *The Last Journals of David Livingstone in Central Africa*, 2 vols. London: John Murray, 1874.

Waller, Richard. 'Bad Boys in the Bush? Disciplining Murran in Colonial Maasailand'. In *Generations Past: Youth in East African History*, edited by Andrew Burton and Hélène Charton-Bigot, 135–74. Athens, OH: Ohio University Press, 2010.

Waller, Richard. 'Ethnicity and Identity'. In *The Oxford Handbook of Modern African History*, edited by John Parker and Richard Reid, 94–113. Oxford: Oxford University Press, 2013.

Waller, Richard. 'Rebellious Youth in Colonial Africa'. *Journal of African History* 47, no. 1 (2006): 77–92.

Walter, Dierk. *Colonial Violence: European Empires and the Use of Force*. London: Hurst, 2017.

Ward, J. R. 'The British West Indies in the Age of Abolition, 1748–1815'. In *The Oxford History of the British Empire, Volume 2: The Eighteenth Century*, edited by P. J. Marshall, 415–39. Oxford: Oxford University Press, 1998.

Watson, Ruth. *'Civil Disorder is the Disease of Ibadan': Chieftaincy and Civil Culture in a Yoruba City*. Athens, OH: Ohio University Press, 2003.

Webb, Beatrice. *Our Partnership*, edited by Barbara Drake and Margaret I. Cole. London: Longmans, 1948.

Webel, Mari K. *The Politics of Disease Control: Sleeping Sickness in Eastern Africa, 1890–1920*. Athens, OH: Ohio University Press, 2019.

Welbourn, F. B. *East African Rebels: A Study of Some Independent Churches*. London: SCM Press, 1961.

Wesseling, H. L. *Divide and Rule: The Partition of Africa, 1880–1914*. Westport, CT: Praeger, 1996.

Wesseling, H. L. *The European Colonial Empires, 1815–1919*. London: Longman, 2004.

Westad, Odd Arne. *The Global Cold War: Third World Interventions and the Making of Our Times*. Cambridge: Cambridge University Press, 2007.

Westwood, Sarah Davis. '*Ceddo, Sofa, Tirailleur*: Slave Status and Military Identity in Nineteenth-Century Senegambia'. *Slavery & Abolition* 39, no. 3 (2018): 518–39.

Westwood, Sarah Davis. 'Military Culture in Senegambia and the Origins of the *Tirailleurs Sénégalais* Army, 1750–1910'. PhD dissertation, Boston University, 2018.

White, E. Frances. *Sierra Leone's Settler Women Traders: Women on the Afro-European Frontier*. Ann Arbor, MI: University of Michigan Press, 1987.

White, Landeg. 'Power and the Praise Poem'. *Journal of Southern African Studies* 9, no. 1 (1982): 8–32.

Whitehouse, G. C. 'The Building of the Kenya and Uganda Railway'. *Uganda Journal* 12, no. 1 (1948): 1–15.

Wilberforce, William. 'William Wilberforce, in the House of Commons, Pictures the Slave Trade in All Its Horror [12 May 1789]'. In *Archives of Empire, Volume 2: The Scramble for Africa*, edited by Barbara Harlow and Mia Carter, 93–100. Durham, NC: Duke University Press, 2003.

Wild-Wood, Emma. 'Bible Translation and the Formation of Corporate Identity in Uganda and Congo, 1900–40'. *Journal of African History* 58, no. 3 (2017): 489–507.

Wilks, Ivor. *Asante in the Nineteenth Century: The Structure and Evolution of a Political Order*. Cambridge: Cambridge University Press, 1975.

Williams, Donovan, ed. *The Journal and Selected Writings of the Reverend Tiyo Soga*. Cape Town: A. A. Balkema, 1983.

Williams, Donovan. *Umfundisi: A Biography of Tiyo Soga, 1829–1871*. Lovedale: Lovedale Press, 1978.

Williams, Eric. *Capitalism and Slavery*. New York: Capricorn Books, 1966 [1944].

Williams, Paul D. *War and Conflict in Africa*. Cambridge: Polity, 2016 [2011.]

Wilson, Francis. *Labour in the South African Gold Mines, 1911–1969*. Cambridge: Cambridge University Press, 1972.

Wilson, Peter H. 'European Warfare, 1815–2000'. In *War in the Modern World Since 1815*, edited by Jeremy Black, 192–216. London: Routledge, 2003.

Wolde Aregay, Merid. 'A Reappraisal of the Impact of Firearms in the History of Warfare in Ethiopia (c. 1500–1800)'. *Journal of Ethiopian Studies* 14 (1980): 98–121.

Woodside, Alexander. *Lost Modernities: China, Vietnam, Korea, and the Hazards of World History*. Cambridge, MA: Harvard University Press, 2006.

Woolf, Daniel. *A Global History of History*. Cambridge: Cambridge University Press, 2011.

Worboys, Michael. 'The Comparative History of Sleeping Sickness in East and Central Africa, 1900–1914'. *History of Science* 32, no. 1 (1994): 89–102.

Wright, Donald R. *The World and a Very Small Place in Africa: A History of Globalization in Niumi, The Gambia.* New York: Sharpe, 1997.

Wright, John. 'Control of Women's Labour in the Zulu Kingdom'. In *Before and After Shaka: Papers in Nguni History*, edited by Jeff Peires, 82–99. Grahamstown: Institute of Social and Economic Research, 1981.

Wright, John. *A History of Libya.* London: Hurst, 2012.

Wright, John. 'Mfecane Debates'. *The Southern African Review of Books* 39–40, September/October and November/December 1995 (double issue): 18–19.

Wright, John. 'Turbulent Times: Political Transformations in the North and East, 1760s–1830s'. In *The Cambridge History of South Africa, Volume 1: From Early Times to 1885*, edited by Carolyn Hamilton, Bernard K. Mbenga and Robert Ross, 211–52. Cambridge: Cambridge University Press, 2010.

Wright, Marcia. 'Maji Maji: Prophecy and Historiography'. In *Revealing Prophets: Prophecy in Eastern African History*, edited by David M. Anderson and Douglas H. Johnson, 124–42. London: James Currey, 1995.

Wright, Marcia, ed. *Strategies of Slaves and Women: Life Stories from East and Central Africa.* New York: Lilian Barber Press, 1993.

Wright, Michael. *Buganda in the Heroic Age.* London: Oxford University Press, 1971.

Wright, Patricia. *Conflict on the Nile: The Fashoda Incident of 1898.* London: Heinemann, 1972.

Wrigley, Christopher C. 'The Changing Economic Structure of Buganda'. In *The King's Men: Leadership and Status in Buganda on the Eve of Independence*, edited by L. A. Fallers, 16–63. London: Oxford University Press, 1964.

Wrigley, Christopher C. 'The Christian Revolution in Buganda'. *Comparative Studies in Society and History* 2, no. 1 (1959): 33–48.

Wrigley, Christopher C. *Kingship and State: The Buganda Dynasty.* Cambridge: Cambridge University Press, 1996.

Wylde, Augustus. *Modern Abyssinia.* London: Methuen & Co., 1901.

Wylie, Dan. *Myth of Iron: Shaka in History.* Scottsville: University of KwaZulu-Natal Press, 2006.

Yoder, John C. 'Fly and Elephant Parties: Political Polarization in Dahomey, 1840–1870'. *Journal of African History* 15, no. 3 (1974): 417–32.

Yoder, John C. 'The Quest for Kintu and the Search for Peace: Mythology and Morality in Nineteenth-Century Buganda'. *History in Africa* 15 (1988): 363–76.

Young, Crawford. *The African Colonial State in Comparative Perspective.* New Haven, CT: Yale University Press, 1994.

Young, Crawford and Thomas Turner. *The Rise and Decline of the Zairian State.* Madison, WI: University of Wisconsin Press, 1985.

Youngs, Tim. *Travellers in Africa: British Travelogues, 1850–1900.* Manchester: Manchester University Press, 1994.

Zewde, Bahru. *Pioneers of Change in Ethiopia: The Reformist Intellectuals of the Early Twentieth Century.* Oxford: James Currey, 2002.

Zilfu, Ismat Hasan. *Karari: The Sudanese Account of the Battle of Omdurman.* London: F. Warne, 1980.

Zimmerer, Jurgen and Joachim Zeller, eds. *Genocide in German South-West Africa: The Colonial War of 1904–1908 and Its Aftermath.* Pontypool: Merlin Press, 2008.

Zimmerman, Andrew. 'Africa in Imperial and Transnational History: Multi-sited Historiography and the Necessity of Theory'. *Journal of African History* 54, no. 3 (2013): 331–40.

# INDEX

Abbas Hilmi, 235
Abdallah, Muhammad 'Ahmad ibn (the Mahdi), 96, 97, 243. *See also* Mahdists
Abdallahi, 97
Abdullah, Khamis bin, 38, 262
Abdullahi, 68
Abeokuta, 78, 91, 128, 129, 131, 140, 196, 208, 209, 220
Achebe, Chinua, 5–6, 289
Acholi, 231, 232
Addis Ababa, 234, 280, 339n94
Adwa, battle of, 65, 189, 212, 234, 241, 250, 280, 296, 298, 341n145
al-Afghani, Jamal al-Din, 280
Afonja, 60, 61
Afrikaners, 184, 224. *See also* Boers
Afrocentrism, 312n5
Ahmadu Seku, 94, 213
Akan, 54, 272, 279
Algeria, 96, 172–73, 176, 177, 178, 212, 217, 225, 230, 235, 242, 243, 331n11, 338n63
*amakholwa*, 145, 219
Amhara, 49, 120, 138, 228, 234, 270, 280, 298, 338n74. *See also* Ethiopia; *habesha*
Amir, Snay bin, 31, 33, 35
Angola, 90, 148, 168, 190, 238, 249
anti-slave trade movement, abolitionists, 75, 147, 170–71, 193, 215, 283, 331n8
Armah, Ayi Kwei, 289
Asante, 54, 77, 78–80, 117, 120, 130, 171–72, 177, 178, 181, 183, 208, 216, 220, 250, 272, 279, 284, 296, 336n4

Bagamoyo, 7, 10, 158, 260
Bambara, 88–89, 94, 228–29, 232
Bambatha rebellion, 244, 251
Bangala, 231
al-Bashir, Ahmad al-Tayyib ibn, 96

Belgium, 15, 141, 149, 162, 179, 180, 189, 190, 194, 231, 237, 240, 247, 278. *See also* Congo Free State; Leopold II
Bemba, 71, 197
Benin, 183, 250, 252, 288, 348n87
Berlin Conference, 188–89, 214, 334n69
Bismarck, Otto von, 162, 163, 164, 183, 188–89
Blair, Tony, 300, 303
Blyden, Edward Wilmot, 248
Boers, 73, 74, 170, 174, 183, 184, 197, 222–24. *See also* Afrikaners
Bonny, 135–36
Bornu, 93–94, 243
Brazil, Brazilians, 23, 77, 128, 137
Brissot, Jacques Pierre, 283, 285
Britain: civilising mission, 171, 175, 187, 194, 263, 283, 334n85; domestic politics, 174–75, 178, 350n146, 351n156; historical culture and memory, 282, 298, 299–301, 342n155, 350n141; imperialism, colonial rule, 15, 17, 53, 73, 74, 79, 83, 98, 127, 132, 133, 162, 165, 166, 169, 170, 173–88, 189, 190, 196–97, 202, 203, 209, 211, 213, 214, 215, 216–17, 223–24, 225, 227, 231–32, 234–35, 236–37, 240, 241, 243, 244, 247, 249–50, 252, 266–68, 275, 278, 286–87, 312n7, 333n60, 336n6; relations with African states, 77, 78, 131, 135, 168, 171–72, 175, 178, 187, 209, 214, 216–17, 220, 236–37, 239, 244, 266, 267; socioeconomic change, 158, 334n85
British South Africa Company, 179, 197, 225, 239, 244, 245
Bruce, James, 200, 282, 318n8, 336n10
Buganda, 44, 81–83, 84, 86, 117, 121–23, 133, 134, 137, 138, 142, 144, 146, 195, 196, 210, 219, 220, 230–31, 232, 236–37, 240–41, 249, 259, 274–75, 277, 278, 282, 288, 292, 326n17, 330n6, 337n46, 339n104, 345n38, 349n116